2003

Technology and Exceptional
Individuals

Technology and Exceptional Individuals

꒜ Third Edition ꒜

Edited by Jimmy D. Lindsey

8700 Shoal Creek Boulevard
Austin, Texas 78757-6897
800/897-3202   Fax 800/397-7633
Order online at http://www.proedinc.com

© 2000, 1993, 1987 by PRO-ED, Inc.
8700 Shoal Creek Boulevard
Austin, Texas 78757-6897
800/897-3202   Fax 800/397-7633
Order online at http://www.proedinc.com

Library of Congress Cataloging-in-Publication Data

Technology and exceptional individuals / edited by Jimmy D. Lindsey. —
    3rd ed.
        p.   cm.
    Rev. ed. of: Computers and exceptional individuals. 2nd ed. 1993.
    Includes bibliographical references and indexes.
    ISBN 0-89079-790-0 (alk. paper)
    1. Handicapped children—Education—United States—Data
processing.   2. Special education—United States—Data processing.
3. Computer-assisted instruction—United States.   I. Lindsey, Jimmy
D.   II. Computers and exceptional individuals.
LC4024.C64   1999
371.9`0973—dc21   98-44790
                                                           CIP

This book is designed in Goudy.

Production Director: Alan Grimes
Production Coordinator: Dolly Fisk Jackson
Managing Editor: Chris Olson
Art Director: Thomas Barkley
Designer: Jason Crosier
Print Buyer: Alicia Woods
Preproduction Coordinator: Chris Anne Worsham
Project Editor: Debra Berman
Staff Copyeditor: Martin Wilson
Publishing Assistant: Jason Morris

Printed in the United States of America

3   4   5   6   7   8   9   10   03   02   01

*I dedicate this third edition to those members of the PRO-ED family
who made it possible: Publisher Donald D. Hammill;
Executive Editor James R. Patton; Assistant Editor Robin A. Spencer;
production staff Alan Grimes, Dolly Fisk Jackson, Chris Olson,
Thomas Barkley, Jason Crosier, Alicia Woods,
Chris Anne Worsham, Debra Berman, and John Means Cooper;
and Administrative Assistant Loretta Scott.*

Contents

6

Software Evaluation and Development ✒ 133
Florence M. Taber-Brown

7

The Use of Technology To Enhance Personal Productivity ✒ 161
Dave L. Edyburn and J. Emmett Gardner

8

Integrating Technology To Support Effective Instruction ✒ 191
J. Emmett Gardner and Dave L. Edyburn

Section III: Specific Inclusive and Categorical Applications ᔓ *241*

9
Technology for Individuals with Mild Disabilities ᔓ *243*
Cynthia M. Okolo

10
Technology for Individuals with Speech and Language Disorders ᔓ *303*
Paula S. Cochran

11
Technology for Individuals with Severe and Physical Disabilities ᔓ *327*
John Langone

Preface

The purpose of the third edition of *Technology and Exceptional Individuals* (previously titled *Computers and Exceptional Individuals*) is to again provide a practical discussion of current technology for individuals with disabilities, gifts, and talents. It delineates general and specific technologies that are being used (or will be used in the near future) with and by exceptional individuals in inclusive and categorical settings. Technology and special education jargons have been minimized. Practicality is stressed in the suggested technology descriptions, activities, and resources included in the chapters and appendixes.

Intended for a varied audience, this book can be used by undergraduate and graduate students taking an introductory or methods course on technology and exceptional individuals. General and special educators, other professionals (e.g., speech–language clinicians, physical and occupational therapists, psychologists), and paraprofessionals can use it in inservice activities designed to advance competencies in technology and special education. Technology theorists and manufacturers can significantly increase their insight into technology concepts related to exceptionalities by reading this book. Finally, individuals with disabilities, gifts, and talents interested in learning about specific hardware and software can develop a foundation for this knowledge by reading this book.

The third edition of *Technology and Exceptional Individuals* has four sections composed of 14 chapters. In Section I, Foundation, three chapters introduce exceptional individuals and technology. Chapter 1 provides a foundation for technology and exceptional individuals and presents a functional approach to service delivery—no technology to high technology. Chapter 2 introduces general and specific hardware concepts (e.g., central processing units, input devices, networks), and Chapter 3 introduces software concepts and describes different categories for software (e.g., operating systems, application, educational).

Section II, The Technology Program, Access, and Productivity, includes five chapters that provide general multidisciplinary and practical considerations relative to understanding and meeting the technology needs of exceptional individuals in inclusive and other settings. Chapter 4, a new chapter to this book, addresses issues relative to implementing technology programs in inclusive settings. Chapter 5, a second new chapter to this book, addressees issues relative to ensuring that exceptional individuals have access to technology by removing barriers (hardware, environmental), provides general recommendation for making hardware accessible (e.g., desktops, portables, networks), and continues the discussion of the importance of evaluation to identify technology needs. Chapter 6 outlines principles and procedures for evaluating software and for developing software for personal and instructional productivity. Chapters 7 and 8 were developed by revising and expanding Chapter 13 from the second edition of this book. Chapter 7 presents the concept of technology-enhanced professional productivity and describes an "electronic toolbox" professionals can develop to increase their productivity. Chapter 8 discusses concepts to enhance instructional productivity in inclusive and segregated settings.

Section III, Specific Inclusive and Categorical Applications, has five chapters. Chapters 9 through 13 define exceptional individuals, provide a brief review of the literature related to technology and these individuals, and delineate general and specific technology applications for inclusive and segregated settings. Section IV, Technology Evaluation and Research Concepts, includes Chapter 14, which provides principles and procedures for evaluating the technology program and conducting research studies to add to the developing literature on technology and exceptional individuals. Finally, nine appendixes and two indexes are included to enhance chapter content, to promote reading economy, or to facilitate research purposes.

I believe readers will find the third edition of this book a welcome addition to the increasing number of works on technology and exceptional individuals because of its practical approach to hardware and software issues, recommended activities and resources, and inclusive and categorical concepts. As in previous editions, the chapter authors and I have done everything we can to ensure that the content is current. However, as we have repeatedly noted, technology continues to advance so rapidly that what is currently being read or experienced is, as Steinhoff, Jordan, and Babbitt state in Chapter 2, "only a portent of what is to come." Almost daily, this technological advancement is made evident in newspapers, in magazines and journals, on television, and on the Internet and World Wide Web: complete six-generation or Pentium computer systems for $500? Palm-size computer with the power of a desktop? 1000 MHz CPUs? Windows 98—is 2000 next? Internet 2? This reporting can only serve to advance technology concepts for exceptional individuals and those persons who work with them. It goes without saying that the reader of this book should use current publications to supplement the information we provide.

Acknowledgments

I am indebted to a number of people for helping me develop this third edition. I want to again thank Donald D. Hammill, PRO-ED publisher, for making the continuing editions of *Technology and Exceptional Individuals* possible. I want to thank James R. "Jim" Patton, PRO-ED executive editor, for his patience, continuous support, and insightful suggestions as this edition evolved. You are the "Real Deal," Jimbo! I am indebted to the contributing authors, who did everything I asked of them to ensure that their chapters and appendixes reflect the current state of the art. An editor could not have worked with a more competent and willing cadre of writers. I am also indebted to three Southern University–Baton Rouge graduate students—David P. Fuller (graduated), Monica P. Morris, and Jeanne B. Roane—for their clerical, proofreading, or research-related support. I also thank David for the Herculean effort put forth to secure needed resource information (Appendix I).

I also want to thank those persons who, in addition to the authors, provided the photographs used throughout this book. These individuals included Robin D. Thibodeaux (Hattiesburg, MS), Carolyn F. Woods (Gulfport, MS), Tim Barcus (Kirksville, MO), Larry Gigax (Prenkte Romich Company), WBGB TV (Joan Avallone, Boston, MA) and the National Technical Institute for the Deaf (Rochester, NY), Judy Seiler (Humanware, Loomis, CA), and Ed Washington (Lafayette, LA). I also want to thank present or former colleagues (Cora Blanks and Henry E. Teller, Jr.), friends (Rodney W. Woods, Neil Gowdy, and G&G Microsystems), family members (Jonathan, Camille, and Hank), and the staff and patrons of the de l'Epee Deaf Center (Gulfport, MS) for giving me permission to include their photographs in this book. I am especially indebted to Carolyn F. Woods, who coordinated the overall photograph efforts for this edition. Thank you very much, Carolyn, and I am of the opinion that only your artistic talents and kindness exceed your photograph acumen.

And, as always, I must recognize a number of individuals who made the first and second editions of this book a reality or contributed to their success: good friends Drs. Greg H. Frith and Earl H. Cheek, Jr.; Southern University–Baton Rouge administrators Augustus C. Blanks and Oscar Mitchell; and chapter authors Philip Archer, Glen L. Bull, Philippa H. Campbell, Lou Esposito, Alonzo E. Hannaford, Alan Hofmeister, Jeffrey W. Hummell, James E. Johnson, Carole M. Lick, Timothy H. Little, Tom Lough, Gary E. Rushakoff, and Ron Thorkildsen. Sadly, I must express recognition in memoriam to Drs. Blanks and Rushakoff.

The editor expresses his sincere thanks to the following individuals for their assistance in developing the name and subject indexes: Nicki Anselmo-Skelton, Cindy Bozeman, Nicole Casidy, David Fuller, Janice Hartner, Marolie Hayes, Meagan Holeman, Camille and Reneé Lindsey, and Joseph Persac. Special thanks are also extended to selected students enrolled in my courses and speech pathology and psychology majors enrolled in Professors Regina Patterson's, Barabara Guillory's and Reginald Rackley's courses.

Finally, for the past 12 months or so I told anyone who would listen that a number of interesting experiences with this edition proved that the third time was not necessarily a charm. I must now retract these words. This book was blessed when PRO-ED asked Debra Berman to be our copyeditor, and she accepted. Debra, I thank you for everything you did to improve the readability and other attributes of this edition. The chapter and appendix authors and I know that the effort you put forth was above and beyond what was expected, and you have added more than charm to our scholarly endeavor. You should also know that I have put you on my December holiday list through the third millennium—Y3K.

Section I

❧   ❧   ❧

Foundation

This section introduces technology and exceptional individuals, the hardware domain, and the software domain.

Technology tools can be found in all segments of society. (Photograph by Jimmy D. Lindsey)

Chapter 1

৵ ৵ ৵

Technology and Exceptionality Foundations

A. Edward Blackhurst
University of Kentucky, Lexington

Elizabeth A. Lahm
University of Kentucky, Lexington

In the following story, a young man named Kevin Burberry speaks about his experience with technology.[1]

The best way for you to know what a life with cerebral palsy is like is to imagine yourself as a marionette. And also imagine trying to get a glass of water to drink. You see the glass, you reach for the glass with your arm, and, just when you are about to grasp it with your hand, somebody pulls the string on your arm causing your limb to suddenly jerk, toppling the glass. The water spills, and you do not get a drink. This lack of coordination is something which I have to live with every day, and it can be very frustrating if I allow it to be.

The type of cerebral palsy which I have affects only my muscle coordination. I cannot walk, hold a pencil, or verbalize—you have to remember that the tongue is a muscle and therefore it is affected. About the only aspect of my being that is not touched by the cerebral palsy is my intelligence, although some people I know would differ with that point. Early in my life my parents recognized that I

had the capacity to learn and began to teach me whatever you teach a 1-year-old.

A question: How do you teach your child with a severe disability to count? The answer is found in a rocking chair. What my mother did was count while she rocked me. For example, every time she would complete a rocking motion with the chair she would say the number in sequence; 1, 2, 3, all the way to 10. Mom would repeat the task several times during the night.

Then one night my mother decided to leave out a number; 1, 2, 4. Suddenly, I would get mad and hit her on the chest. She would ask me, "Did I leave out a number?" I would grunt indicating "yes." Then Mom would go through every number until the correct one was called, I would hit her letting her know that she said the right digit. Rocking is how I learned to count.

As with every child there came the time when my parents did all that they could to educate me at home. At the age of 4 I was enrolled in a preschool where we lived. There I met a lady by the name of Mrs. Ross who taught me how to read. Why did I need to know how to read? Because once I knew how to read I could begin to spell what I wanted. I could begin to communicate.

This point in the story yields itself to the first piece of assistive technology that ever benefited me. What Mrs. Ross had done was to staple the letters of the alphabet onto a set of three wooden boards, and have me spell out my responses by pointing to the letters

Preparation of this manuscript was supported, in part, by Grant #H180U50025, Examination of the Effectiveness of a Functional Approach to the Delivery of Assistive Technology Services in Schools, from the Division of Innovation and Development, Office of Special Education Programs, U.S. Department of Education. The perspectives presented herein do not necessarily reflect the official position of the U.S. Department of Education.

[1]This story is quoted with permission from Kevin Burberry.

with my hand. Now, there was a problem with this method of communication. You need to remember that I do not have fine motor control, and therefore I had a hard time pointing to the individual letters—for example, I might look at the letter 'q' and hit 'l'. And, let's face it, hitting a staple with a flailing hand does not feel good.

Fortunately, my father recognized this problem and said, "His eyes get to the letter long before his hand does; why don't we start following where he is looking to find out what he is saying." The result of Dad's discovery was this simple Plexiglas alphabet board which I used to talk with my eyes. Can you imagine going through 12 years of public education by spelling everything you had to say with your eyes? That is what I did. And, it takes a strong individual to stay by my side each day to find out what I want to communicate. Turnover among my aides at school was high—about one person every 2 years.

Then in 1982 we found the Prentke Romich Company which specializes in electronic equipment for people with severe disabilities. At the time Prentke Romich made a product called the Express 3 which was similar to the Liberator—the computer that I am using today—except very simplistic. I had to spell every word, letter by letter. It was very slow. While I used the Express 3 to write papers in high school and my first 5 years of college, I could not communicate with it well because of this limitation. The computer was too awkward. The board was still the fastest method for me to talk.

In October of 1993, with the help of the State Department of Vocational Rehabilitation, I received the Liberator—also made by the same company—along with several other pieces of equipment. The Liberator is quite a computer. It is fast because, unlike the Express 3, this system uses icons (or pictures) to facilitate my communication needs. Rather than having to spell my sentences one letter at a time (as I did with the Express), I connect several icons together in a sequence to form sentences. For instance, suppose that I want to ask somebody, "May I have a drink please?" I would activate the squares display-ing the challis icon and the question mark icon in succession with my infrared pointer mounted on the side of my glasses to retrieve the question from the Liberator's memory. Although what I have just described does not do justice to the Liberator, it gives you an idea of my rapid typing rate.

In addition to the Liberator, Vocational Rehabilitation purchased an entire Macintosh computer including a flat-bed scanner which serves as a copy machine for the computer, a CD-ROM to read and/or listen to material stored on compact disc, and a fax modem to send papers to my professors and letters to my friends. Also, the fact that the Liberator connects to the Macintosh by a wireless remote means that I can go into my room, do work on the computer, and leave without dealing with any wires.

Together these two computer packages— the Liberator and the Macintosh system— have opened some major avenues of communication for me. For example, one day I found myself giving an interview by e-mail to a lady out in California. Not even in my wildest dreams did I imagine that I would be doing such things.

At the other end, the Liberator has made it possible for me not to be tethered to somebody every minute of every day. As my mother can tell you, all she has to do is give me my meals, assist me with the bathroom, turn a page of the book that I am reading, and give me an occasional drink. When we are at home she can be anywhere in the house doing anything she wants without worrying about me.

Not only is this freedom felt by my parents, but my aides have one less function to perform. Before the Liberator came, my assistants had to take my notes while figuring out what I was saying with the board. Now I can raise questions in class while they type away on the laptop computer.

Doing various activities by myself not only frees other people to do their own business, but it makes me feel like I do not have to impose on them as much. One of the unfortunate aspects about being totally disabled is the knowledge that you have to depend upon everybody to sacrifice what they are doing to tend to you. For example, when you come over to my house to watch television with me I do not want you to be distracted from the program because you have to find out what I have to say on the board. I would like for you to enjoy yourself. And the Liberator makes that situation possible. This computer lives up to its name. I truly feel liberated after 25 years of total dependence.

Kevin Burberry delivered his story to a class of university students preparing to be special education teachers. He entered his story into the Liberator communication aid, which he then used to "speak" his presentation to the class. Later, he sent the text of his story to us via electronic mail. Kevin's story provides a dramatic illustration of the use of technology and the tremendous potential that it can have for enabling a person with disabilities to function in society. Many more examples of technology applications for people who exhibit a wide range of exceptionalities are presented in this book.

The purpose of this chapter is to provide information about basic terms and concepts that can serve as a foundation for the understanding of information contained in the remaining chapters of this book. An overview of five different types of technology is provided and the differences among the types explained. Because the book focuses on individuals with exceptionalities, the meaning of such terminology is explained, accompanied by descriptions of the various types of exceptionalities that will be addressed. Legal mandates associated with the provision of technology services to individuals with exceptionalities are examined, followed by an explanation of the technology continuum.

As applications of technology for individuals with exceptionalities have evolved, there has been a tendency for decisions to be made on the basis of the nature of the exceptionality or the availability of a specific device (e.g., "Billy can't speak; therefore, I would recommend an electronic communication aid"). Unfortunately, such approaches often have led to the acquisition of expensive devices that have been inappropriate for the given circumstances. This chapter presents an alternative to this way of making technology decisions. The importance of the use of theory to guide decision making is described, followed by a description of a unifying functional model that places technology in its proper perspective and identifies the variables and their interrelationships that should be considered when making decisions about the types of technology to use in the delivery of services to individuals with exceptionalities.

Areas of function that can be facilitated through the use of various technologies are described and examples provided to illustrate the concepts presented. Resources to support the use of technology also are identified. The chapter closes with a summary of concepts you should keep in mind as you read the other chapters in this book.

Types of Technology

To many people, the term *technology* triggers images of complex devices such as computers, robots, communication satellites, rockets and spaceships, video games, advanced military equipment, the Internet, and similar highly sophisticated machines. Such perceptions have been acquired and reinforced through exposure to televised reports of fascinating devices and news articles about them, science fiction books and movies, and use of equipment such as automobiles, telephones, computers, and automatic teller machines.

Like the general population, educators have seen the use of technology grow. Since Pressey developed the first teaching machine in 1926 (Nazzaro, 1977), technology applications in schools have tended to focus on the acquisition and use of equipment, such as film projectors, audio and video tape recorders, overhead projectors, and computers.

Since the early 1960s, however, a trend has emerged that is changing the way technology in education is perceived. At that time, educators began considering the concept of *instructional technology*. Subsequently, after considerable deliberation, a congressional Commission on

Instructional Technology (1970) concluded that technology involved more than just hardware. The commission concluded that, in addition to the use of devices and equipment, instructional technology also involves a systematic way of designing and delivering instruction. At about the same time, Haring (1970) reached a similar conclusion when he examined the use of instructional technology in special education.

These distinctions were further defined in a comprehensive review that concluded that there were two types of technology applications in special education: media technology and systems technology (Blackhurst & Hofmeister, 1980). The former focused on the use of various devices, whereas the latter focused primarily on systematic approaches to instruction.

With the rapid development of microcomputer technology, increased research on instructional procedures, and the invention of new devices and equipment to aid those with health problems, physical disabilities, and sensory impairments, the years since the 1980 review have witnessed a very dramatic evolution (Blackhurst & Cross, 1993). The current perspective is a broad one in which six types of technology are recognized: the technology of teaching, instructional technology, assistive technology, medical technology, technology productivity tools, and information technology (Blackhurst, 1997).

Technology use is increasing and user age is decreasing. (Photograph by Jimmy D. Lindsey)

Technology of Teaching

The technology of teaching refers to instructional approaches that are systematically designed and applied in precise ways. Such approaches typically include the use of well-defined objectives, precise instructional procedures based on the tasks that students are required to learn, small units of instruction that are carefully sequenced, a high degree of teacher activity, high levels of student involvement, liberal use of reinforcement, and careful monitoring of student performance. Instructional procedures that embody many of these principles include direct instruction (Carnine, Silbert, & Kameenui, 1990), applied behavior analysis (Alberto & Troutman, 1995; Wolery, Bailey, & Sugai, 1988), competency-

based instruction (Blackhurst, 1977), learning strategies (Deshler & Schumaker, 1986), and response prompting (Wolery, Ault, & Doyle, 1992). Most often, machines and equipment are not involved when implementing various technologies of teaching; however, they can be, as discussed later.

Instructional Technology

Although there are differing opinions about the nature of instructional technology, the Commission on Instructional Technology (1970) provided the following definition:

> Instructional technology is a systematic way of designing, carrying out, and evaluating the total process of learning and teaching in terms of specific objectives, based on research in human learning and communication, and employing a combination of human and non-human resources to bring about more effective instruction. (p. 199)

Typical applications of instructional technology may use conventional media such as videotapes, computer-assisted instruction, or more complex systems, such as hypermedia programs in which computers are used to control the display of audio and visual images stored on videodisc (Blackhurst & Morse, 1996). The use of telecommunication systems, particularly the Internet (Williams, 1995) and its World Wide Web component (Williams,

1996), has great promise for use in classrooms and for distance education. Computer software systems are now available that can be used to manage the delivery of instruction via the Web. Such systems have been used successfully to deliver instruction on topics related to special education (Blackhurst, Hales, & Lahm, in press).

It is important to note the various components of the Commission on Instructional Technology's (1970) definition and to realize that technology is really a tool for the delivery of instruction. In this conceptualization, technological devices are considered as means to an end and not an end in and of themselves. Use of technology cannot compensate for instruction that is poorly designed or implemented.

Assistive Technology

Assistive technology employs the use of various types of services and devices designed to help people with disabilities function within the environment (King, 1999). Assistive technologies include mechanical, electronic, and microprocessor-based equipment; nonmechanical and nonelectronic aids; and specialized instructional materials, services, and strategies. People with disabilities can use this technology to (a) assist them in learning, (b) make the environment more accessible, (c) enable them to compete in the workplace, (d) enhance their independence, and (e) otherwise improve their quality of life. These may include commercially available or homemade devices that are specially designed to meet the idiosyncratic needs of a particular individual (Melichar & Blackhurst, 1993). Examples include communication aids, alternative computer keyboards, adaptive switches, and services such as those provided by speech–language pathologists.

Medical Technology

Advances constantly are being made in medical technology. In addition to seemingly miraculous surgical procedures that are technology based, many individuals are dependent upon medical technology to stay alive or to function outside of hospitals and other medical settings.

It is not uncommon to see people in home and community settings who use medical technology. This also is the case with some students in schools. For example, some devices provide respiratory assistance through oxygen supplementation and mechanical ventilation. Others, such as cardiorespiratory monitors and pulse oximeters, are used as surveillance devices that alert an attendant to a potential vitality problem. Nutritive assistive devices can assist in tube feeding or elimination through ostomies. Intravenous therapy can be provided through medication infusion and kidney function can be assumed by kidney dialysis machines (Batshaw & Perret, 1992). In addition to keeping people alive, technologies such as these can enable people to fully participate in school, community, and work activities.

Technology Productivity Tools

As the name implies, technology productivity tools are computer software, hardware, and related systems that enable people to work more effectively and efficiently. For example, computer software such as database programs can be used to store and rapidly retrieve information; word processing programs can be used to easily edit text material; fax machines can facilitate the transmission of written documents over long distances; expert system computer programs can aid in decision making, such as weather forecasting; and video conferencing facilities can reduce the need for travel.

Information Technology

Information technologies can provide access to knowledge and resources that can facilitate the use and application of each of the prior types of technology. Notable among the various resources for professionals is the Educational Resources Information Center (ERIC) database, which enables people to search much of the world's literature related to education. The Council for Exceptional Children maintains a large database of information related specifically to people with disabilities and those who are gifted. The most predominant of the information technologies is the Internet, particularly its World Wide Web (Web) component. Not only can the Internet provide information to professionals who provide special education services, but Web sites can be used by people with disabilities to facilitate learning, productivity, personal enrichment, and the use of leisure time. (Addresses and useful Web sites are provided in Appendixes H and I.)

Each of the types of technology discussed has significant implications for the delivery of special education services. It is important to remember, however, that these also may be used in combination. For example, students with breathing difficulties who also are unable to use their hands to operate a computer keyboard may benefit from the use of a respirator (medical technology) and a voice-operated computer (assistive technology). This type of computer delivers instruction from a software program that was designed to deliver spelling instruction (instructional technology) using a constant time delay response prompt fading instructional procedure (technology of teaching). The teacher can then store student progress reports in an electronic gradebook program and use a word processing program to prepare a report for the student's parents (technology productivity tool). The teacher may also access the Web to search for additional information that would be useful in providing instruction (information technology).

Although this example may be somewhat extreme, it serves to place the various types of technology into perspective. In reality, it is more likely that only one or two types of technology would be used simultaneously. Other chapters in this book will provide additional elaboration of the different types of technologies and the variations that are possible within each type.

Exceptionality Terms and Concepts

Although many of the technology concepts presented in this book have universal applications,

the primary focus is on applications that have particular relevance to exceptional individuals. This term encompasses individuals with unique gifts and talents, as well as those with disabilities.

Exceptional individuals are those who have physical, mental, behavioral, communication, or sensory characteristics that differ from the majority of people in society to the extent that they require special accommodations to enable them to develop and perform to their maximum capacity. Such accommodations may take the form of services such as special education, speech and language therapy, psychotherapy, physical therapy, occupational therapy, and vocational rehabilitation. Accommodations in the environment may be reflected in such things as curb cuts, braille markings on elevator buttons, ramps, automatic door openers, and wheelchair lifts in buses. Technology accommodations, such as captioned television, machines that can translate written text to speech, adapted switches that can be used to control equipment, and computers that can recognize spoken commands, also may be required for large segments of this population.

Children and adults who are included in the category of exceptional individuals include those with communication problems, hearing losses, physical disabilities, visual impairments, mental retardation, learning disabilities, emotional and behavioral disorders, multiple disabilities, high intelligence, and unique talents. Estimates of the number of exceptional children range from 10% to 15% of the school-aged population (Blackhurst & Berdine, 1993). When one takes into consideration adults who have acquired disabilities as a result of accidents and illnesses and the portion of society affected by the diseases of aging, the percentage is considerably higher.

Following are brief descriptions of the different categories of exceptional individuals for which technology applications are described in this book. The concepts presented in the first two sections of the book have broad implications across all categories of exceptionality, whereas the third section addresses applications that have particular relevance to specific categories. For additional information about characteristics of exceptional individuals, the reader is referred to the book edited by Blackhurst and Berdine (1993).

Individuals with Mild Disabilities

By far, the largest group of exceptional individuals consists of those who have mild disabilities. Included in this category are those who have learning disabilities, mild forms of mental retardation, or emotional and behavioral disorders. These apparently heterogeneous categories are grouped together because research and practice have shown that specific technologies of teaching and instructional technologies appear to be equally effective, regardless of the diagnostic categories in which an individual has been placed. Note, however, that we are referring to those with *mild* disabilities. As the severity of learning disability, mental retardation, or behavioral disorder increases, there is greater discrepancy in functional abilities across those groups, which necessitate differing educational and treatment procedures.

With respect to educational and treatment programs for people with mild disabilities, it has been found that such individuals are more like those without disabilities than they are different. With appropriate special education, rehabilitation, and related services, they are able to function in society. Such individuals are capable of holding jobs, maintaining families, participating in recreational activities, and otherwise making contributions to the community.

The trend in school programs for those with mild disabilities is to include them, to the greatest extent possible, in general classrooms with students who do not have disabilities. In such cases, special education is often provided directly within the general education classroom through collaborative efforts between the general education teacher and the special education teacher. In other cases, students visit a resource teacher for specific assistance that cannot be efficiently provided within the general education class.

Systematic methods of instruction, instructional technology, and the use of technology productivity tools can be very effective in facilitating learning of students with mild disabilities and enhancing their ability to function in a variety of school and work environments. Chapter 9 provides specific examples of the use of technology with this population.

Individuals with Speech and Language Disorders

A basic concept underlying communication is the fact that speech and language are not synonymous. The differentiation between the two has important implications for teaching and also for the type of treatment or therapy a person with a communication problem might receive. *Language* is an arbitrary system of symbols used to convey meaning about things and events in the environment. The symbols typically used to convey this meaning are words and word combinations. Language has a receptive component and an expressive component. It can be expressed visually (as in sign language) or tactilely (as in braille). *Speech,* on the other hand, is the oral production of the sounds of language.

It is possible for a person to have good language skills (understanding) and poor speech. Similarly, it is possible for a person to be able to articulate various speech sounds but have poor language skills. If a person has poor speech, it is important that listeners should not infer that the person also has poor language skills. This is often one of the mistaken assumptions made by people when they first encounter individuals, such as Kevin, who have cerebral palsy.

Language problems are far more severe than speech problems. Although others are more aware of a person's speech problems because they are typically more noticeable, language problems create greater difficulty in school because people depend upon language for virtually all of learning. Can you imagine what it might be like to try to learn how to read if you could not understand the teacher's instructions? It is critical for teachers and parents to be particularly alert for potential language problems and identify them before their effects become so serious that the children are hopelessly behind in their education.

Creative engineers, software designers, and computer programmers have developed numerous ingenious ways to use technology to assist those with speech and language disabilities. Information about such applications is provided in Chapter 10.

Individuals with Severe and Physical Disabilities

Individuals with severe and physical disabilities may have one or more problems. Included may be problems of ambulation, problems associated with health, severe mental retardation, or multiple disabilities.

Many individuals with ambulation problems have had spinal cord injuries incurred in accidents, others have contracted diseases that have attacked the nervous system, and others were born with conditions that affect their ability to move about. A number of these people may be able to locomote with the assistance of wheelchairs, braces, crutches, or canes.

Health problems may range from mild to severe. In fact, some conditions may actually be life threatening. People who fall into this latter category are referred to as "medically fragile" and require the use of life support systems. Although many medically fragile individuals require home or hospital care, others may function fairly well in society. It may be necessary for some children to be away from school or for some adults to be away from work on a regular basis during which they require medical care, such as kidney dialysis.

Some individuals have convulsive disorders, such as epilepsy. In addition to knowing about ways to treat various types of seizures, those providing technology services need to know that photic stimulation, such as sunlight glittering through venetian blinds, flickering television and computer monitors, and fluorescent lighting, may precipitate seizures in some individuals who have convulsive disorders.

Some individuals with physical disabilities also have severe mental retardation. Such people are often said to have severe developmental disabilities. This is a heterogeneous population. Some may be blind, some may be deaf, some may be deaf–blind. Some engage in appropriate social interactions, whereas others engage in self-stimulatory behavior. All require extensive supports for many of their life activities, such as communication, mobility, self-care, and learning. In the past, many people with severe developmental disabilities were placed in residential institutions. The current trend is to provide education and services that will enable such individuals to remain at home or in community-based assisted living facilities and supported work environments.

Numerous assistive technologies have been developed to assist the functioning of those with severe and physical disabilities. Chapter 11 provides information about the range of disabilities within this group and specific technology applications that are available.

Individuals with Sensory Impairments

People with sensory impairments are those who have difficulty hearing or seeing or both. People with hearing impairments fall into one of two classifications: deaf or hard of hearing. A person who is deaf has a hearing impairment so severe that he or she cannot understand information presented orally with or without a hearing aid. A person who is hard of hearing has residual hearing that is sufficient to enable the processing and understanding of information that is presented orally. Usually, people who are hard of hearing require the use of hearing aids or other audio amplification to hear such information.

Many individuals who are hard of hearing function quite adequately in society with the assistance of hearing aids. A large number of people who are deaf also can function very well, although their ability to do so is greatly enhanced if they learn to read lips (speechread), have the services of interpreters who can translate speech into sign language, or use technology such as captioned television and special communication devices that enable them to transmit typed communication over commercial telephone lines.

Individuals who have visual impairments typically fall into two categories: those who are blind and those who have partial sight. Although the legal definitions of blindness and partial sightedness focus on the extent of the visual acuity and visual field of an individual, such measures do not indicate much about a person's ability to function in society. Functionally, the major factor that differentiates these two conditions is the ability to use printed information. That is, people with partial sight can use materials that convey conventional text and other visual aids, such as pictures, whereas those who are blind must rely upon braille and auditory and tactile materials to gain information. Most partially seeing individuals can function satisfactorily in society with the use of large-size printed materials and devices that can help them use their remaining vision. Many individuals who are blind also can function very well; however, they may require additional supports, such as braille materials, auditory tapes, guide dogs, and human assistance, in order to maximize their abilities.

The smallest group of exceptional individuals comprises those who are both deaf and blind. Most people, when posed with the hypothetical question of which would be worse, blindness or deafness, choose blindness. However, Helen Keller, who was both deaf and blind, often stated that deafness was the more serious disability. The reason for this is that deafness impairs the ability to communicate. Not only is it difficult to hear what others are saying, but the development of both speech and language skills is hindered.

A number of fascinating technological applications have been developed for those who have hearing losses and visual impairments. Chapter 12 provides information about such applications.

Individuals with Unique Gifts and Talents

People with unique gifts and talents also are included among those considered to be exceptional individuals. Those who are considered to be gifted or talented exhibit extremely high capabilities in intellectual, creative, academic, psychomotor, visual and performing arts, or leadership pursuits. Comprising about 3% of the population, such people are our leading artists, scientists, dancers, teachers, authors, physicians, all-American athletes, and business and industry executives, to name a few.

Giftedness is not limited only to people with very high intelligence, although students with this characteristic are the ones that most people think about when this subject is raised. In addition, contrary to what many people think, those

who are gifted and talented are not the eccentric, maladjusted "bookworms" that often are depicted in the mass media. Research has shown that gifted children, for example, are generally better adjusted, brighter, and healthier than other students. Similarly, most gifted students enjoy school and do not create difficulties in school.

Some students who are gifted exhibit problems that can interfere with their education, however. Students who are able to function at grade levels higher than the one in which they are placed may become bored with school. They may have little tolerance for activities of their classmates that they believe to be juvenile or inappropriate. Some may appear eager to dominate classroom discussions because of their superior fund of knowledge and curiosity about the nature of things. Others, who have talents in the creative and performing arts, may become dissatisfied with school programs because the curriculum does not provide opportunities for them to pursue their interests. Not all gifted students are like this, of course, but those who are have interpersonal problems that may interfere with their happiness and learning. It is important that special education services, advanced placement opportunities, and access to technology applications be made available to such individuals in order for them to maximize their great potential.

Specific technology applications for individuals with unique gifts and talents are described in Chapter 13.

Technology Legal Mandates

Over the years, the federal government has played a pivotal role in stimulating technology applications in special education and rehabilitation. This stimulation has been in the form of federal laws and regulations that have included technology mandates and funding to support a wide variety of technology research and development, training, and service activities.

Legislated support for technology can be traced back to Public Law (P.L.) 45-186 in 1879, which awarded $10,000 to the American Printing

House for the Blind to produce braille materials. Numerous other laws have been established to support services to people with disabilities (see Nazzaro, 1977). Several of those laws represent legal mandates that relate to the provision of services to people with disabilities. (No such legislation exists for those who have unique gifts or talents. Consequently, the term *disabilities* is used in place of *exceptionality* in this section.) Such mandates exist in both state and federal legislation. Space limitations preclude the listing of state mandates; however, it should be noted that many state laws and regulations mirror the federal requirements. Of the many federal laws that have implications for providing services to people with disabilities, the four described in this section have the greatest impact on the provision of technology services.

The Vocational Rehabilitation Amendments

Section 504 of the Rehabilitation Act of 1973 (P.L. 93-112) is perhaps the most important piece of legislation ever enacted for people with disabilities. The language in Section 504 is almost identical to that of the Civil Rights Act of 1964, which applied to racial discrimination, and that of Title IX of the Education Amendments of 1972, which addressed discrimination in education on the basis of gender. The enactment of Section 504 reflects the realization that those with disabilities, too, had been subjected to discrimination for many years.

In 1986, P.L. 99-506 amended the Rehabilitation Act of 1973 by adding Section 508 to that act. Section 508 ensures access to computers and other electronic office equipment in places of federal employment. The guidelines ensure that users with disabilities can access and use the same computer databases and applications programs as other users. Users with disabilities also must be able to manipulate data and related information sources to attain the same results as other users, and will have the necessary adaptations needed to communicate with others on their system.

The Individuals with Disabilities Education Act

Special education and related services for students are mandated by federal laws that have their roots in the Education for All Handicapped Children Act of 1975 (P.L. 94-142). That law was amended in 1991 (P.L. 101-476) and again in 1997 (P.L. 105-17). It is now known as the Individuals with Disabilities Education Act (IDEA). IDEA guarantees the right of all children with disabilities to a free and appropriate education in the least restrictive environment (see Box 1.1).

The legal guarantees for an Individualized Education Program (IEP), originally spelled out in P.L. 94-142, have since been extended to preschool programs for students who are entitled to an Individualized Family Services Plan (IFSP) and to those who are eligible for rehabilitation services through the development of an Individualized Written Rehabilitation Plan (IWRP). As part of such planning processes, parents, teachers, rehabilitation counselors, related personnel, administrators, and the individual with disabilities are required to consider the technologies that may be useful in helping a child meet the objectives in the IEP, IFSP, or IWRP.

The Technology-Related Assistance for People with Disabilities Act

The Technology-Related Assistance for Individuals with Disabilities Act (P.L. 100-407) was signed into law in 1988. Under the auspices of the Tech Act, as it is called, all states are developing systems for providing a variety of technology assistance to children and adults with disabilities and their parents and guardians. The purpose of the Tech Act is to provide financial assistance to the states to enable them to conduct needs assessments, identify technology resources, provide assistive technology services, and conduct public awareness programs, among other beneficial activities.

The potential of assistive technology was recognized through the enactment of the Tech Act.

Box 1.1. IEP Guarantees

When school personnel make decisions about the most appropriate educational program for students with disabilities, IDEA mandates that they must adhere to the following:

- Students' parents must be notified in writing when they are to be tested for possible special education placement. The parents are assigned *due process rights* that ensure procedural safeguards in all matters related to their child's evaluation and educational placement.

- Each student is entitled to an education in the *least restrictive environment*. This means that, to the extent possible, they should receive education in settings designed for students without disabilities.

- Any diagnostic tests must be administered to students in ways that do not discriminate against them. For example, if English is not their native language, *nondiscriminatory assessment* procedures would need to be initiated.

- Students are entitled to an *Individualized Education Program* (IEP) that specifies their strengths and weaknesses, educational goals, objectives, those who are responsible for their education, and dates for reassessment and revision of the IEP. Their parents must be involved in planning for the IEP, as should the student, to the extent possible.

- All students eligible for special education services must be *considered for assistive technology devices and services* when their IEPs are developed or reviewed.

- Students' families should expect *confidentiality* and *right to privacy* concerning records regarding them, their school placement, and related activities.

- If students' parents are unable to be involved in their education planning, they are entitled to the services of a *parent surrogate*.

- Students enrolled in special education are entitled to *free and appropriate education* services until they are 21 years old.

The definition of assistive technology that was included in the act was modified slightly in the federal regulations for IDEA to make the definition more applicable to children with disabilities:

> Assistive technology means any item, piece of equipment or product system, whether acquired commercially off the shelf, modified, or customized, that is used to increase, maintain, or improve the functional capabilities of children with disabilities. (*Federal Register*, August 19, 1991, p. 41272)

The federal regulations went on to state that an array of services also is included when considering applications of assistive technology. Such services include evaluation of a person's needs for assistive technology devices, purchasing or leasing assistive technology devices for people, de-

signing and fabricating devices, coordinating services offered by those who provide assistive technology services, providing training or technical assistance to a person who uses assistive technology, and training and technical assistance to those who work with people who use assistive technology devices, such as teachers or employers.

The Americans with Disabilities Act

Signed into law in 1990, the Americans with Disabilities Act (P.L. 101-336) has broadened the definition of those who are considered to have disabilities. It also broadens the types of agencies and employers covered by Section 508 requirements and mandates additional protections, such as accessible public transportation systems, communication systems that enable people who are deaf to communicate over telephone lines, and access to public buildings for people with physical disabilities and sensory impairments. These requirements are opening many avenues of employment for people with disabilities who were previously excluded from office work because of inaccessible equipment.

The Technology Continuum

When considering technology applications for individuals with disabilities, a useful perspective is to view various types of technology as tools that can be used in helping individuals overcome problems they have in responding to demands placed on them from the environment. The environmental demands may come from the home, the school, or the community. In that vein, it is helpful to think about a continuum that ranges from "high-tech" to "no-tech" solutions to problems. For example, high-tech solutions are those that involve the use of sophisticated devices, such as computers and interactive multimedia systems. Medium-tech solutions include the use of less complicated electronic or mechanical devices, such as videocassette players and wheelchairs. Low-tech solutions are less sophisticated and can include things such as adapted spoon handles, Velcro fasteners, or raised desks that can accommodate a wheelchair. No-tech solutions are those that do not require devices or equipment. These might involve the use of systematic teaching procedures or the services of related services personnel such as physical therapists, occupational therapists, or speech–language pathologists.

In making decisions about the type of technology tools or supports a particular person might require, a good approach is to start with the no-tech solutions and then work up the continuum as needed. For example, in teaching home economics to a student with one arm, it might be better to teach the student how to wedge a mixing bowl into a drawer and hold it with a hip while stirring than to purchase an expensive medium-tech electric mixer that is equipped to stabilize the mixing bowl while it is being operated.

Too often, when making technology decisions, there is a tendency to start at the upper end of the technology continuum when, in fact, it is better to start at a lower point. For example, when making IEP decisions about students whose handwriting is difficult to recognize, it is not uncommon to hear recommendations that the student should be provided with a laptop computer to take from class to class (cost: $1,500 to $3,000). In reality, an electronic keyboard with memory that can be downloaded into a desktop computer later in the day may be more appropriate (cost: about $300). Although the student in this example may eventually require a laptop computer, the electronic keyboard may be a better place to start.

The Importance of Theory

In teaching students of any age, regardless of whether they have been identified as exceptional, an important perspective is to use theories about teaching and learning to guide instructional practices. Here is an example of how theory can be used to guide the selection of instructional software: One of the major criticisms of computer-assisted instruction (CAI) is that its use is too frequently restricted to routine drill-and-practice software. Unfortunately, such criticism is often justified, not because drill-and-practice software is bad, but because it is used inappropriately. A theoretical perspective about *stages of learning* (Haring, Lovitt, Eaton, & Hansen, 1978) can help to guide appropriate use.

Selection of the appropriate type of computer software should be based on each student's stage of learning for the content under consideration. For example, students just beginning to learn addition facts are in the *acquisition stage* of learning. Teachers should use *tutorial* or *discovery* software for those students. When they master their addition facts, they move into the *proficiency stage* of learning (sometimes called the *fluency stage*).

At that point, the teacher should switch to drill-and-practice software to teach the students to respond quickly and accurately as the addition facts are presented.

It is important for students to be able to use information that they have learned in other contexts. This is called the *generalization stage* of learning. In this stage, the teacher should select a software program other than the one being used, but of the same general type, in order to determine whether the students can transfer the information learned in one program to another. The teacher also should provide activities away from the computer to determine whether the students can transfer their learnings to different contexts.

It is important for students to remember their addition facts. This is referred to as the *maintenance stage* of learning. A period of time after the students have mastered the addition facts, the teacher again uses drill-and-practice software, sometimes couched in an educational game format, to determine whether the students have remembered their facts. If not, tutorial software again may be used as a remedial tool.

The final stage of learning is the *application stage*. In this stage the teacher might use *simulation* or *problem-solving* software to determine whether the students can apply their mastery of the addition facts to other situations, such as word problems. Tutorial software programs may be used to actually teach the students how to apply the facts that they have mastered.

This example illustrates how important it is for professionals to know about stages of learning and the different types of educational software appropriate for each. Without such knowledge, it is easy to make one of the most frequent errors in instructional applications of computers: namely, inappropriate selection and use of computer software. Too often, students are assigned the use of a software program that is not suitable for their stage of learning, such as drill-and-practice software instead of tutorial software during the acquisition stage of learning.

Theories are useful not only for guiding the selection and use of computer-assisted instruction,

Technology tools promote exceptional individuals' independence. (Photograph by Carolyn F. Woods)

but also for developing computer-based teaching materials. For example, theories about situated cognition (Cognition and Technology Group at Vanderbilt Learning Technology Center, 1993) have led to the development of hypermedia programs that include video examples that serve as conceptual anchors for learners. Research has shown that such programs are effective in teaching children (Bottge & Hasselbring, 1993; Hasselbring, Goin, & Wissick, 1989) and in providing preservice and inservice training for professionals (Blackhurst & Morse, 1996). Theories about near-errorless teaching procedures, such as the constant time delay response prompting procedure, have led to the development of computer software for teaching spelling to students with learning disabilities (Edwards, Blackhurst, & Koorland, 1995; Stevens, Blackhurst, & Slaton, 1991).

Sometimes, theories are used to generate conceptual models, which are often represented as graphic figures that display variables and their interrelationships. Conceptual models have many practical implications for practitioners. Among these are the following:

- Models can serve as the conceptual underpinning for a given set of activities.

- They provide a graphic representation of the variables associated with the topic of interest and their interrelationships.

- They are useful in helping to define needed policies, procedures, and activities and for assigning job responsibilities.

- They facilitate communication among staff who use them and are helpful in communicating information about the topic of interest to others.

- Some planning models can be used to define activities, events, constraints, sequences, and timelines that can then be used for project planning and monitoring.

- They can be used to identify elements of an activity that require evaluation.

Later in this chapter, a conceptual model about the delivery of special education and other services and the use of technology in supporting these services is described. When examining that model, reflect on the listed points to see how they relate to the application of the concepts represented in the model.

Model building is consistent with the earlier conceptualization about the use of systematic approaches for the design of instruction. The literature contains a number of useful theoretical models that have implications for special educators. See, for example, models for diagnostic teaching (Cartwright & Cartwright, 1972), designing special education personnel preparation programs (Blackhurst, 1977), using progressive time delay with students who have severe developmental disabilities (Gast & Schuster, 1993), and designing programs for special education continuing professional development (Blackhurst, 1993).

With respect to the value of theory, one thing seems clear: The most effective teachers are those who have a thorough grounding in theories of learning and instruction and use them to guide their instructional activities. They are able to articulate a rationale for their teaching procedures; they exhibit self-confidence in their abilities; they are comfortable and secure in discharging their professional responsibilities; and, most important, their students learn. The next section

presents a theoretical perspective that can be quite useful in planning and delivering special education, rehabilitation, and related services for exceptional individuals, with an emphasis on those that relate to the use of technology.

A Functional Approach to Service Delivery

When decisions are being made about the provision of services for individuals with disabilities, the real issue is the problem the person has in functioning within his or her environment. For example, a preschooler with cerebral palsy may lack the fine muscle control that will permit him or her to fasten buttons so that he or she can dress independently. An elementary student with a visual impairment may be unable to use printed material that is being used for instruction in a language arts class. A high school student, due to an unknown cause, may be unable to solve math problems. Similarly, an adult who has been in an automobile accident may have had a severe head injury that has impaired his or her ability to speak clearly.

In each of these cases, an environmental demand has been placed on the person to perform some function that will be difficult to execute because of a set of unique circumstances or a restriction in functional capability caused by the lack of personal resources. For example, the people lack the physical or mental capability to button, read, calculate, or speak.

Everybody faces environmental demands daily. The goal of professionals is to understand the processes and relate them to the lives of exceptional individuals who face more complex and restrictive situations. There is the need to know many things, such as the nature of the demands that are being placed on the individual from the environment and how those demands create the requirements to perform different human functions, such as learning, walking, talking, seeing, and hearing. It is important to know how such requirements are—or are not—being met by the person and how factors such as the person's perceptions and the availability of personal resources such as intelligence, sight, hearing, and mobility can affect the responses that can be made. In addition, it is important to understand how availability of external supports, such as special education, different types of therapy, and technology, can affect the individual's ability to produce functional responses to the environmental demands.

Although each exceptional individual is unique, the common challenge is to identify and apply the best possible array of educational, rehabilitation, technology, and related services that will provide support, adjustment, or compensation for the person's functional needs or deficits. A variety of responses may be appropriate. For example, Velcro fasteners may be used to replace buttons on garments for the child having difficulty with buttoning. Braille or audio materials may be provided for the child who cannot read conventional print. The student who has difficulty calculating may require specialized, intense direct math instruction, whereas a computerized device that produces speech may enable the adult who cannot talk to communicate.

A Unifying Functional Model

The unifying functional model displayed in Figure 1.1 has been developed to illustrate the different elements of life associated with a functional approach to special education, rehabilitation, and related services, including the provision of medical, instructional, and assistive technologies. The items in each box of the figure are meant to be illustrative and not all-inclusive.

To illustrate the elements of the model, their interrelationships, and application of the model to special education and the use of assistive technology, let us consider a hypothetical fifth grader, named Joe, who was born with a partially formed right hand. His left hand is fully functional. He also has a mild learning disability. He receives most of his education in a regular class with support services from a resource teacher and occupational therapist. He has just entered a middle school in which all entering students are expected to enroll in a keyboarding class.

Let us begin with the box at the bottom of the model, labeled *environment and context*. The environment we are dealing with is the computer laboratory. The context is that Joe's teacher wants to teach Joe keyboarding skills so that he can use the computers available in the school. The environment and context place *functional demands* on everybody. The demand placed on Joe is to participate in the class and learn how to operate the computer keyboard.

In preparing to make responses to environmental demands, people *explore options* available that will enable them to respond in a constructive fashion to the demand. In school programs, options typically include assessments, experimentation with different options, and making adaptations. In Joe's case, he and the teacher might explore options such as assessing Joe's abilities to locate and use the keys with one hand, software solutions such as one-handed typing programs, and various types of alternate keyboards.

One's *personal perceptions* play a big part in exploring response options and making a decision about which one to accept. For example, some people may, or may not, perceive that a need exists or that they have a problem. People also have perceptions about the psychological, physical, and monetary costs of different alternatives and their consequences.

A second factor in making decisions about response strategies relates to the *personal resources* that people have available to them. These relate to their abilities in areas such as physical functioning, cognitive ability, intelligence, motivation, speech, and other personal dimensions that can be used in producing actions.

A third factor influencing decisions relates to the *external supports* a person has available. Supports are resources available to assist individuals in responding to environmental demands. For example, family members can provide both emotional and physical support. Social service agencies can provide supportive services, such as instruction about ways to cope with environmental pressures. Health insurance agencies can sometimes provide financial support for the purchase of assistive and adaptive devices. Special

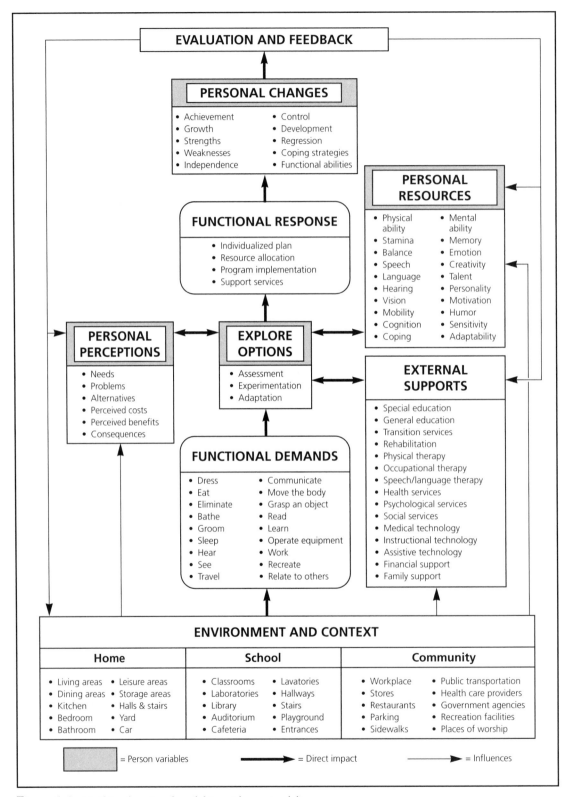

Figure 1.1. Unifying functional model to guide service delivery.

education is another major form of external support, as are the use of technology devices and the delivery of various technology services.

Let us consider how all of these areas impact on Joe. In the area of perception, Joe realizes that he has a problem in using a conventional keyboard, yet he wants to find a way to participate in the class. In surveying his personal resources, Joe and his teacher conclude that he has the cognitive abilities to understand the keyboard and to meet the intellectual requirements of the course. In addition, he has a fierce desire to do things for himself.

In further exploration of options, he decides against using an alternative keyboard because he thinks it will "make him look different." In the area of external supports, his teacher suggests that he start by using a software option that can be used in conjunction with standard instruction about the location of the keys.

The *functional response* is the result of the assessment, experimentation, and decision making that was just described. In Joe's case, this will be the use of special software that enables a person to do one-handed keyboarding. Consequently, this approach is written into his IEP, the special software is located, instruction is implemented, and the services of an occupational therapist are procured to assist in teaching Joe how to use one hand to operate the keyboard and access the special software.

As a result of the functional response to the environmental demand, *personal changes* occur. Such changes may be dramatic or subtle, depending upon the nature of the environmental demand, the decision making that was done, and the nature of the resources that were expended and the supports provided.

Through subsequent evaluation, the hypothetical Joe has improved his ability to function in his environment by using specialized software to participate in the keyboarding class. Feedback (as represented by the arrows emanating from the *evaluation and feedback* element of the model) also may lead to the selection of additional technologies. For example, word prediction software and the use of macro programs that automatically type frequently used words and phrases may be added to his repertoire. As Joe matures and gains confidence in his abilities, he might eventually elect to try an adaptive keyboard that will enable him to improve his keyboarding speed.

Thus, the process represented in the functional model becomes a dynamic one, in which demands constantly change, as do personal perceptions, personal supports, external supports, and examination of alternative solutions. The result is changing functional responses to the environmental demands that lead to personal changes, which, in turn, have the potential for changing all of the other factors illustrated in the model.

Note that the model, as presented in this two-dimensional format, represents a "snapshot" of a person's situation at a single moment in time. As such, it does not reflect the fact that changes are constantly occurring in each component and that these changes have the potential for impacting on the other components and subsequently on the functional responses made by the child.

The final feature to note in the model is the shaded areas. These represent personal variables. As noted, the model, as presented, is two-dimensional. However, the central focus is the individual and the decisions that are involved in assisting that individual in responding to environmental demands. That process is certainly complex and more than a two-dimensional one.

Implications of the Functional Model

Several implications can be drawn from the unifying functional model in Figure 1.1. It places the various types of technology devices and services into proper perspective—namely, as external supports. It helps in understanding how a person functions, what factors are important in making decisions, and how the decisions that are made can impact on that person. It also identifies many of the factors that should be taken into consideration when making decisions about the nature of services that are provided to a given individual. Also, it illustrates interrelationships of component factors and their potential for influencing each other. Although the model does not define cause–effect relationships, it does help people realize that many factors are involved and that they interact in complex ways.

The model provides direction for those making referrals of individuals for technology and other services. Those who make referrals should be aware of the model and its components. Furthermore, they should be encouraged to obtain as much information as possible about the various factors and provide data about them as part of the referral process. For example, the model can guide prereferral activities, assessment, and instructional planning activities. By attending to the factors in the model, and others that may be identified, those performing assessments of children who have been referred for technology services can use the model to identify variables that should be evaluated for their potential impact on a child. Assessments of those variables should generate data that can aid in making decisions about the types of technology and related services that could help children respond successfully to environmental demands. Such decisions should result in the incorporation of technology services in the IEPs for children enrolled in special education programs.

Finally, although the functional model was originally developed to guide the delivery of assistive technology services (Melichar & Blackhurst, 1993), the perspective that has emerged since the model was conceptualized is that it can be used to guide the delivery of *all* special education, rehabilitation, and related services. Examples of ways in which an earlier version of the model can be applied in virtually every area of special education are provided in an introductory special education textbook (Blackhurst & Berdine, 1993).

Keep this model in mind while reading the other chapters in this book. It should help in recalling the many variables that are involved in making decisions about the use of technology and some of the complex interrelationships that exist among those variables. Of primary importance is the concept that technology decisions should be based on the functions that individuals must perform in response to the demands placed on them from the environment. Decisions should *not* be based solely on the type of disability an individual has or the existence of a piece of technology equipment.

Technology Applications

Unfortunately, many decisions about applications of technology for exceptional individuals are "device driven." As new devices appear on the market, it is not uncommon to find that consumers, parents, vendors, and professionals advocate strongly for their acquisition and use with different students, often with less than satisfactory results. Instead of getting caught up in the allure of new products with intriguing features, a more appropriate perspective is to make decisions about the use of technology based on functions that the prospective users must perform in response to demands that are placed upon them from the environment. This approach also facilitates the federal requirements, noted earlier, which require that technologies are used to improve the individual's ability to function.

Following are descriptions of seven functional areas and how technology applications and services may be applied in each. Examples, in the form of vignettes, are provided to illustrate concepts presented earlier in this chapter, with particular emphasis on how the functional model facilitates an analysis of the circumstances surrounding the vignette and decision making about the use of technology and its impact. Embedded in the vignettes is information about the use of technology with exceptional individuals and resources that can be used to support technology decision making. Several technology productivity tools also are illustrated.

Existence

Functions associated with existence are those responses that are needed to sustain life. These functions include eating, elimination, bathing, dressing, grooming, and sleeping. Special education services, particularly those for preschool children and those with severe disabilities, may focus on teaching children to perform such functions. Those who have temporary disabilities due to surgery and those who may have been injured in accidents also may require assistive technologies to aid them in performing functions associated with existence that they were able to do independently prior to their surgeries or accidents. Special devices, such as button hooks, weighted eating utensils, bathtub lifts and seats, and combs with long handles, may be provided to assist people in performing those functions. Assistance in using such devices also may be provided by occupational therapists.

The following vignette about Randy illustrates the area of existence and the application of technology to assist in achieving an environmental demand. It also illustrates the use of two computer programs to locate assistive technologies.

Existence Vignette: Locating Assistive Devices

Randy is a 15-year-old male who recently had surgical treatment for severe scoliosis, or curvature of the spine. The surgery included implantation of a metal rod along his spinal column and a full-body cast. Randy can walk, but he requires assistance to move from the bed to an upright position. He spends large amounts of time lying in bed, where he is unable to sit up. When he drinks liquids, he must use a straw and position the container to his side. This is awkward and results in frequent spills.

Randy's parents would like to find a way to assist him to drink liquids independently while lying in a prone position. They contact Randy's occupational therapist, who uses two computer programs to locate information about drinking cups that could be purchased for Randy's use. The therapist recommends a vacuum cup and shows catalogs to Randy's parents so they can place an order for one that Randy can use.

Functional Analysis

Environment and Context:	At home in bed, desiring a drink
Functional Demand:	Drinking while lying down
Explore Options:	Change positions; Request assistance from parents; Locate a cup that can be used lying down
Personal Perceptions:	An adapted cup is more independent; Changing positions requires assistance; Request may be inconvenient for parents
Personal Resources:	Physical ability to reach the cup when in a prone position
External Supports:	Occupational therapist to locate an appropriate cup
Functional Response:	Use of a vacuum cup to allow drinking from a prone position
Personal Changes:	Randy can independently drink liquids while lying down.
Evaluation and Feedback:	Randy enjoys his independence and the ability to get a drink when he needs one.

Randy's vignette illustrates one of the functions performed by occupational therapists. Not only do they provide direct assistance to individuals with disabilities in the activities of daily living, they also are important sources of information about assistive technologies.

The computer programs alluded to in the vignette are *CO-NET* (Trace Center, 1996) and the *Adaptive Device Locator System* (ADLS) (Academic Software, 1996). These programs can be used to locate literally thousands of devices that can be used to meet a wide array of functional needs. Both programs have versions that can be used on either Macintosh or IBM (and compatible) computers, although CO-NET requires a CD-ROM drive. The ABLEDATA database can be searched on the World Wide Web [http://www.trace.wisc.edu/tcel/abledata/index.html or at http://www.abledata.com/database.htm], and an on-line version of the ADLS was being developed when this book went to press [http://www.acsw.com].

Although the use of either program results in the identification of assistive devices, they use different approaches to arrive at their recommendations. The ADLS uses a search strategy that reflects the functional approach described in this chapter. Users do not have to know about the names of devices or the device vendors in order

to conduct a search; rather, they focus on the functions that an individual needs to perform.

Here is an example of how the occupational therapist (OT) located information for Randy's parents: When the ADLS program was loaded into the computer, the OT saw an opening screen that displayed seven functional areas, as illustrated in Figure 1.2A. A definition of an area is provided at the bottom of the screen when a mouse click selects one of the areas. Because Randy's needs relate to existence, the OT selected that category by double-clicking the mouse. New options were presented in the window in the upper right of the screen. With each double-click, the selected option was moved to the upper left window and a new series of options was presented. For example, after the option *feeding* was

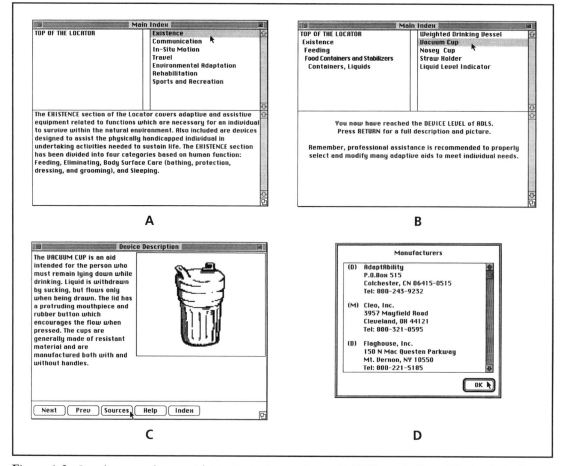

Figure 1.2. Sample screens from an *Adaptive Device Locator System* (ADLS) search. From *Adaptive Device Locator System,* by Academic Software, 1996, Lexington, KY: Author.

selected, these items were displayed in the option window: *food containers and stabilizers, grasp and manipulation of food,* and *transport of food to mouth.* The OT clicked on *food containers and stabilizers* and the search continued. At the completion of the search, five different types of containers for liquids were displayed as on the right side of Figure 1.2B. The OT then selected the *vacuum cup* option, and the information illustrated in Figure 1.2C appeared, showing a line drawing and information describing the features of vacuum cups. The OT then clicked on *Sources,* and a list of distributors and manufacturers of vacuum cups appeared in a scrolling window, as illustrated in Figure 1.2D. The OT could then elect to automatically print letters to the vendors requesting copies of their catalogs. A list of 19 companies that manufactured or distributed vacuum cups was retrieved as a result of this search.

The OT then turned to the CO-NET program to search for additional information. The CO-NET CD-ROM disc holds several different resources. One of these is a database of information about more than 20,000 assistive devices. The Macintosh version of the program is called *Hyper-ABLEDATA* and the IBM-compatible version is called *DOS-ABLEDATA.*

Here is how the OT used Hyper-ABLEDATA: After the program was loaded into the computer, the Main Menu appeared, as illustrated in Figure 1.3A. Unlike ADLS, there are four different ways to search for assistive devices. The OT could search by type of product, product name, or company name. A Boolean word search, which looks for terms that are connected by words such as *and, or,* or *not* also can be performed to broaden or narrow searches. In our example, the OT elects to search by product name. Because a vacuum cup was identified as a result of the use of ADLS, the words *vacuum cup* were entered into the dialog box that requested the name of a product. In response to that request, the screen in Figure 1.3B notified the OT that four products that contained the name vacuum cup were located. When the OT clicked on the second term, information about a specific vacuum cup was displayed, as in Figure 1.3C. This screen displays a description of a specific vacuum cup and information about its

manufacturer, including the cost of the item at the time it was entered in the database.

Note the other options that are available at this screen. The envelope can be clicked to write a letter to the company requesting a catalog; the information can be printed by clicking the print button; a picture of the vacuum cup can be obtained; and information about prior and next vacuum cups can be obtained. A user that has partial sight can click on the magnifying glass icon to obtain the information in larger type. The owl icon can be clicked to produce spoken prompts for those who are blind. By clicking on the paperclip icon, the information can be filed on disk for future reference.

Note that in Figure 1.3C the generic name assigned to vacuum cups by Hyper-ABLEDATA is *CUP WITH SPOUT.* The OT can return to the Main Menu and then conduct a search by type of product. If that is done, screens displaying the nested contents of types of devices contained in Hyper-ABLEDATA are displayed. The OT first clicked on *PERSONAL CARE,* and a new list

Computers have many uses in the home. (Photograph by Carolyn F. Woods)

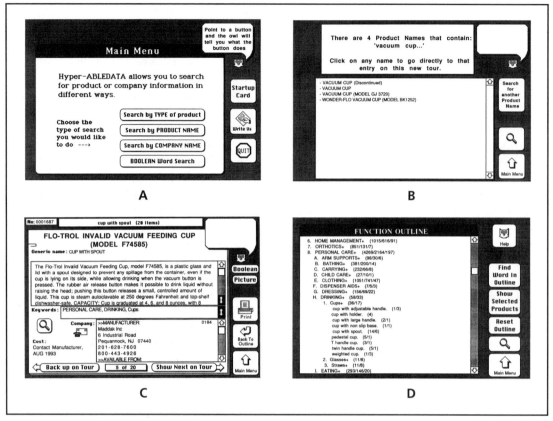

Figure 1.3. Sample screens from a *Hyper-ABLEDATA* search. From *Hyper-ABLEDATA*, by Trace Center, 1996, Madison: University of Wisconsin, Trace Center.

appeared. *DRINKING* was then clicked followed by *Cups*. As can be seen from the information in Figure 1.3D, *cup with spout* is one of the options. The numbers in parentheses indicate the number of items listed in the database. The second number refers to the number of items included in the database that have been discontinued.

Clearly, technology productivity tools such as ADLS and Hyper-ABLEDATA can provide valuable resources for those interested in assistive technology applications for individuals with disabilities (see Box 1.2). For those who do not have access to computers, a number of useful print resources also are available that provide information about assistive technologies and their vendors. Some of those resources are highlighted later in this chapter.

Communication

The reception, internalization, and expression of information are functions included in the category of communication. Communication aids, speech synthesizers, telephone amplifiers, hearing aids, and the services of speech–language pathologists and audiologists might be appropriate to support communication functions.

Most people think about problems related to speaking and hearing when they think about the function of communication. However, communication also can involve the production and reception of nonverbal information, as illustrated in the following vignette about Sonya, which describes alternate ways to input information into a computer.

Box 1.2. Differences Between ADLS and Hyper-ABLEDATA

Note the differences between the ways that ADLS and Hyper-ABLEDATA perform searches for devices. ADLS searches according to functions that *people* need to perform, whereas the function outline used in Hyper-ABLEDATA refers to the functions that *devices* perform. Furthermore, ADLS locates generic categories of devices, whereas Hyper-ABLEDATA locates information about specific devices. Hyper-ABLEDATA also provides alternative methods for conducting searches and provides some photos of specific devices, whereas ADLS, which retrieves categories of devices, provides a sketch that is representative of the category. Hyper-ABLEDATA also provides sound samples to illustrate the output from devices that produce synthetic speech.

It is interesting to note that the results of searches using these computer programs sometimes differ. For example, in the searches conducted for Randy's vignette, ADLS identified 19 vendors that could supply vacuum cups, whereas Hyper-ABLEDATA identified 8 vendors. Of those, only 5 were identified by both programs. Thus, both programs identified vendors that were not included in the other's databases.

The major conclusion that can be drawn from this analysis is that both ADLS and Hyper-ABLEDATA should be used in tandem when searching for assistive technologies. If a user does not know the name of a particular device or its vendor, ADLS should be used first. Hyper-ABLEDATA can then be searched using the generic name as the product type to identify specific devices. The other search options provided by Hyper-ABLEDATA can then be used to further define the search. In many cases, searches of both systems may enhance the likelihood of generating the most comprehensive list of vendors for various devices.

It also should be noted that the CO-NET CD-ROM contains a variety of other resources that are useful for those interested in technology. Users can access directories of agencies that provide services and programs related to technology and disabilities, lists of information resources such as documents and videotapes, and a library of the full text of related documents such as legislation, position papers, manuals, and handbooks.

Communication Vignette: Continuum of Technology Options

Sonya is a certified public accountant with an accounting firm. She is an invaluable employee who specializes in conducting financial audits for large companies. Sonya spends much of her workday using electronic spreadsheets and specialized accounting software on her computer.

In recent months Sonya found that she was having increasing difficulty typing letters with her left hand. She attributed her problems to carpal tunnel syndrome, a repetitive strain injury caused by continual typing. When she consulted her doctor, however, tests revealed that she had a rare disease, similar to muscular dystrophy, in which the voluntary muscles progressively weaken and degenerate until they can no longer function.

A representative from human resources at her office contacted representatives from the company's health maintenance organization to provide information about ways to modify Sonya's work station to enable her to continue with her job. A variety of options, ranging from modified computer software, to alternate keyboards, to a voice-operated computer were considered. Because Sonya could type very well with her right hand, the decision was made to acquire a computer software program that enabled the keyboard to be reconfigured so that Sonya could type with one hand. Because Sonya's physicians predicted that her condition would gradually worsen, a plan was developed for implementation of different options, as needed.

Functional Analysis

Environment and Context:	At work, using a computer
Functional Demand:	Typing when having the use of only one hand
Explore Options:	Providing an assistant; Sticky-key computer access program; One-handed keyboarding software program; Modified keyboards; Voice-activated computer
Personal Perceptions:	Prefers to work independently, not with an assistant; Wants to continue working as an auditor
Personal Resources:	Able to operate the keys on the keyboard with right hand
External Supports:	Supportive employer; Access to resources to purchase software and hardware; Specialist advice about modifications
Functional Response:	Use a one-handed keyboarding software program
Personal Changes:	Sonya can continue to work independently; Satisfaction with the knowledge that accommodations can be made to enable her to function in her job
Evaluation and Feedback:	Other options are implemented as Sonya's medical condition warrants.

Reference was made earlier in this chapter to the technology continuum. The example provided at that time was a continuum that ranged from no-tech to high-tech solutions. Sonya's vignette indicates how the concept of a continuum also can be applied *within* a particular level of technology, from the least intrusive to most instrusive intervention.

In this vignette, for example, several options were considered, all of which are of a high-tech nature. The simplest of these options is a computer software program, referred to as "sticky keys," which enables a user to activate keys on a computer keyboard that require simultaneous key presses, as in the use of the shift key with a letter key to produce capital letters. This option would be best for a person who might require the use of a single finger, hand or mouth stick, or head wand to operate the keyboard. This enables an individual to use a hunt-and-peck system of typing.

Further up the continuum is the use of a software program that reconfigures the computer keyboard to make the most commonly used letters more accessible when one hand is placed on the home row keys of the keyboard. Key caps can be purchased to rename the computer keys with the new configuration. Figure 1.4A shows an example of a keyboard reconfigured for a one-

handed typing program. As with the sticky keys option, the computer can be set to activate such programs when it is turned on. With training, users can achieve typing speeds of 60% to 90% of their original two-handed rate. This is the option that was initially selected for Sonya.

As Sonya's ability to make the muscle movements necessary for a conventional keyboard decreases, an alternative keyboard may become necessary. Figure 1.4B shows a mini-keyboard that can be activated with minimal movements of the fingers. In Sonya's case, if it becomes necessary for her to use a wheelchair, the mini-keyboard can be attached to an extension on the arm of her wheelchair or be placed on the wheelchair table.

Still further up the technology continuum, Sonya may require the use of a chording keyboard, as illustrated in Figure 1.4C. This type of keyboard activates the computer through simultaneous pressing of combinations of the seven keys, rather than through the use of the full complement of keys, as in the mini-keyboard.

If Sonya's condition reaches the point where she can no longer use her hands to type, a voice-activated computer system could be obtained to enable her to enter information by speaking. Evans (1997) pointed out that voice-activated

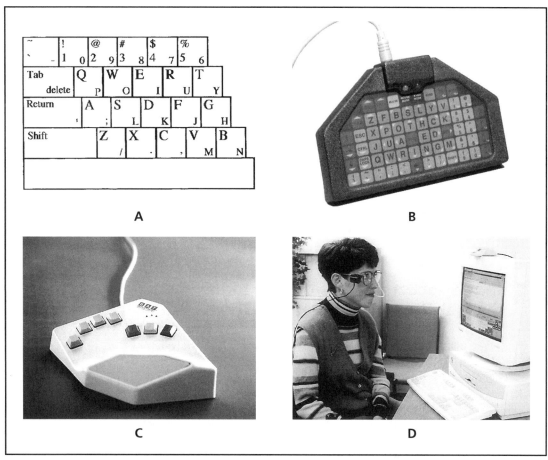

Figure 1.4. Examples of different computer input systems: (A) keyboard reconfigured for one-handed typing (Half-QWERTY Keyboard, made by Matias Corporation); (B) mini-keyboard (TASH Mini-Keyboard, made by TASH International, Inc.); (C) chording keyboard (BAT Personal Keyboard, made by Infogrip, Inc.); and (D) puff-activated system (Head Master Plus, made by Prentke Romich Co.).

computer systems are becoming more and more sophisticated. Speech-recognition software programs with 22,000-word vocabularies costing less than $100 are now available for conventional computers. Users can dictate up to 50 words per minute, but it is necessary to pause between words. This-is-called-discrete-speech,-and-you-must-talk-like-this. The newest generation of speech recognition technology is referred to as continuous, or natural, speech. Such systems boast more than 230,000-word vocabularies with 30,000 being active at any one time. In these more expensive systems, there is no need to pause between words. Undoubtedly, speech-recognition capabilities will increase and prices will decrease over time.

In the event that Sonya's condition becomes such that she cannot speak, she may be able to continue to operate her computer via a system that enables her to control a computer mouse via head movements and activate the mouse by puffing or blowing on a pneumatic switch, shaped like a straw, that she can hold in her mouth. Such a system is illustrated in Figure 1.4D.

Sonya's vignette illustrates several important concepts related to the use of technology. First, it underscores the importance of considering options along a continuum of technological sophistication. Second, it illustrates the concept of selecting a solution that is best suited for the individual's functional abilities. Third, it shows that the least intrusive, and lower tech, solution should be selected, if at all possible. Fourth, it illustrates the value of planning and the designation of alternatives for future contingencies. Finally, it highlights the role that evaluation and feedback play in making technology decisions. Thus, as functional abilities change, appropriate modifications can be implemented.

Body Support, Alignment, and Positioning

Some children need assistance to maintain a stable position or to support portions of their body. Braces, support harnesses, slings, and body pro-

tectors are useful devices in this functional category, as are the services of a physical therapist (PT). Other medical and allied health personnel also may provide supporting services with functions in this category. For example, an orthotist may assist in fitting and fabricating braces (orthoses) and a prosthetist may be involved in selecting and fitting artificial limbs (prostheses). The following vignette about Mary Lou illustrates the selection of a specialized device for a student with a physical disability and how a PT might assist a special education teacher in implementing a solution to a child's functional problem requiring body support.

Body Support and Positioning Vignette: Physical Therapy Services

Mary Lou is an 8-year-old with cerebral palsy. She is described as being persistently hypotonic, meaning that her muscles are floppy and her joints are excessively loose. The condition affects her entire body, including her ability to balance herself with her trunk muscles, but her lower body is especially "low tone."

Mary Lou is in an integrated nongraded primary class in school. Students engage in a variety of activities that require that they be standing or moving from activity center to activity center at various parts of the day. Although Mary Lou uses a wheelchair, her teacher observes that she is left out of many of the face-to-face interactions with other students as they engage in the activities in which they are standing.

The teacher consults with a physical therapist who works with students with physical disabilities in the school. The physical therapist is very supportive of providing opportunities for Mary Lou to be in a vertical position for periods of time during the day since this will help to promote the development of her muscles and bones.

The physical therapist recommends a standing table with wheels for Mary Lou. After it is obtained, she instructs the teacher on how to transfer Mary Lou from her wheelchair to the standing table and provides additional information about safety tips in moving the table from place to place.

Functional Analysis

Environment and Context:	At school while participating in group activities
Functional Demands:	Standing during a group activity and being able to interact socially
Explore Options:	Standing table that is easy to move around the room; Special wheelchair that can be used to elevate the user into a vertical position
Personal Perceptions:	Enjoys engaging in all group activities
Personal Resources:	Mary Lou can tolerate standing for 15-minute periods if properly positioned
External Supports:	Physical therapy services are available; The local Lions Club would like to sponsor Mary Lou this year.
Functional Response:	Mary Lou's teacher is able to assist her in using the standing table; Mary Lou is able to participate in group activities in different locations in the classroom.

Personal Changes:	Mary Lou participates in more student interactions and develops more needed strength in her lower limbs.	develops additional academic skills and better interpersonal interaction skills as a result of being able to engage in more face-to-face interactions with classmates.
Evaluation and Feedback:	Mary Lou can tolerate longer and more frequent standing sessions during the day; She	

Mary Lou's vignette illustrates several important concepts with respect to assistive technology. First, notice that the cheaper, low-tech option was selected for Mary Lou. Although power wheelchairs that enable users to automatically lift themselves to a vertical position (see Figure 1.5A) are quite remarkable and contribute to independence, they also are very expensive. The standing table (Figure 1.5B) is a good alternative and costs considerably less. This is particularly appropriate at this time, because Mary Lou is still growing and will require new wheelchairs until she has reached maturity. At that time, it may be appropriate to expend the resources needed to acquire a high-tech wheelchair that will enable Mary Lou to raise herself to a vertical position independently.

Second, it is very important to make sure that appropriate specialists are involved in making decisions about the selection and use of assistive

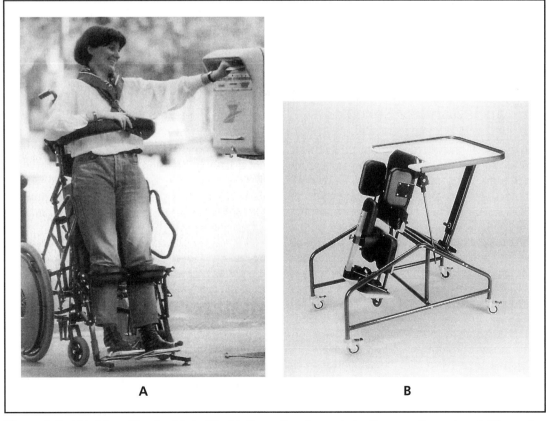

A   **B**

Figure 1.5. (A) Adjustable wheelchair (Tumble Forms Stander, made by Sammons Preston); and (B) standing table (Lifestand, made by Independence Providers, Inc.).

technologies. In Mary Lou's case, the PT was able to make decisions about the length of time that it was appropriate for Mary Lou to be in a standing position, the type of device that was most appropriate for her, and when to increase the time that Mary Lou used her standing device. In addition, the PT was able to provide the appropriate training on how to transfer Mary Lou from her wheelchair to the standing table and back. Lifting and transferring can be tricky with some students who have disabilities. There are correct and incorrect ways to accomplish this that minimize the risk of injury to both the student and the person doing the lifting and transferring.

The use of external resources to support the purchase of various devices also should be noted. Often, school budgets are such that it is difficult to locate funds to purchase specialized devices such as Mary Lou's standing table. Service agencies that operate in the community are frequently good sources for this type of financial aid when school resources are not available. Remember, however, that it is the school's responsibility to provide equipment that is written into the stu-dent's IEP. External resources should be viewed as supplemental and should not abrogate the school's responsibility for supplying appropriate supplies and equipment needed for the delivery of education for exceptional children.

Travel and Mobility

Functions in the travel and mobility category include the ability to move horizontally, vertically, or laterally. Wheelchairs, special lifts, canes, walkers, specially adapted tricycles, and crutches can be used to support these functions. Specialists, such as physicians, occupational therapists, and physical therapists, frequently are involved in making decisions about assistive technologies for individuals who have difficulty with functions related to travel. Those who provide mobility training for children who are blind also may be called upon to provide services associated with this category, as in the following vignette about Martha.

 ## Travel and Mobility Vignette: Orientation and Mobility Services

Martha is a 16-year-old high school student who is blind. She has above average intellectual ability and is in the college preparatory track in school. Her family just moved to a new community and Martha will be attending a new high school in the fall.

She currently uses a sonar cane and functions quite well in familiar environments. She is somewhat apprehensive about being in a new school and is concerned about the amount of time it will take her to learn directions between classes and that classrooms may change each semester. She would like some assistance in learning the school's layout so she does not start off poorly.

Martha's parents contact the director of special education in the new school district and request that an IEP be developed for Martha. During the IEP meeting, an agreement is reached to provide the services of an itinerant resource teacher who will provide support services to Martha. The itinerant teacher will assist in obtaining either braille or audiotaped versions of Martha's books and will work with Martha's teachers to provide alternate forms of tests and assignments that may be necessary.

An orientation and mobility specialist is retained by the school district to help Martha learn about the physical layout of her new school and how to locate rooms that she will use. Arrangements are made to provide training to Martha late in the summer, prior to the opening of school, and to provide follow-up services once school is in session.

Functional Analysis

Environment and Context:	In school, locating different rooms

Functional Demands:	Navigating in a new school environment	External Supports:	Orientation and mobility specialist
Explore Options:	Full-time personal attendant to guide her between classes; A student buddy to walk with her; Use of a guide dog; Specific orientation and mobility training with her sonic cane	Functional Response:	Training is provided to teach Martha how to travel between classes independently and within the allowed time; She has several companions who usually walk with her of their own free choice.
Personal Perceptions:	Martha does not want a full-time attendant because she is capable of traveling independently when the surroundings are familiar; She doesn't want to be assigned a buddy and be a burden on anyone; She is confident that with practice and time she can learn the school's layout and function independently.	Personal Changes:	Martha does not hesitate to go anywhere within the building or on the school's campus; Now she wants to learn the immediate neighborhood and eventually take the public bus to school.
Personal Resources:	Martha has previously learned to navigate school environments with the help of a trainer; She is good at using her laser cane; She is motivated to be independent.	Evaluation and Feedback:	The orientation and mobility specialist periodically observes Martha and provides her with feedback on her progress and tips to enhance her navigation skills.

Although technology (e.g., the sonar cane) is mentioned in Martha's vignette, the important thing to notice is the role of the orientation and mobility specialist. As with the prior vignettes that highlighted the contributions of OTs and PTs, specialists provide important services in the application of technologies as well as no-tech solutions to problems that individuals have in functioning within their environment. Such solutions reflect the intent of including *services* in the definitions of technology that were described earlier in this chapter.

Environmental Adaptation

The environment can be adapted for the person or the person can adapt to the environment. This category of technology applications includes functions associated with such adaptations as seen in the performance of many of the activities of daily living, both indoors and outdoors. Examples of functions include driving an automobile, food preparation, operation of appliances, and alteration of the living space.

It may be necessary to make a number of modifications to school facilities to accommodate functions in this category. For example, enlarged door knobs, special switches for controlling computers, grabbers to reach items on high shelves, raised chalkboards and desks so that a student in a wheelchair can use them, and ramps to accommodate wheelchairs may be required. Often, assistive technology specialists and rehabilitation engineers are called upon to provide help with environmental adaptations, In addition, consumer support groups also may provide assistance, as in the following vignette about Michael.

Environmental Adaptation Vignette: Consumer Resources

Michael is a gifted 10-year-old who was injured during spring vacation in a bike accident. He is permanently paralyzed from the neck down. He is recuperating at home and will miss the remainder of the school year.

His parents are interested in making modifications to their home to enable Michael to function as independently as possible. They contact the local Alliance for Technology Access (ATA) Center for advice about how to proceed. A meeting is arranged with an assistive technology specialist who works at the center.

The assistive technology specialist has arranged a demonstration of a variety of devices that can be operated with switches that Michael could control by various head movements, muscle movements, or voice activation. The assistive technology specialist discusses Michael's interests and finds that he likes to read, listen to compact discs (CDs), watch television, play computer games, and talk to friends on the phone. He also needs to be able to turn the lights in his room on and off and activate a signaling device to alert his parents for his need for assistance when they are in different parts of the house.

A visit is arranged to the home of an adult who also is paralyzed and uses a number of environmental adaptations in his home. The home has been equipped with a number of devices that can be operated by different switches and others that have been fabricated by a rehabilitation engineer who is a part-time volunteer with the ATA. The rehabilitation engineer has developed remote-controlled door openers, a voice-activated telephone system, and special switches that can be used to operate various appliances. The visit helps Michael's parents see some of the options that are available to enable him to function independently.

The assistive technology specialist and rehabilitation engineer then visit Michael's home to conduct an evaluation of the devices that need to be operated and to conduct an assessment of Michael's needs, the voluntary responses he can make, and his range of motion. They find that he can make very slight head movements, can blink his eyes, and has good control of his chin, mouth, breathing, and speech.

Discussions with medical personnel indicate that Michael should be able to use an electric wheel-chair when he fully recuperates from his injuries. There is some possibility that he may regain partial use of one of his hands, but that will not be known until after he begins physical therapy.

The assistive technology specialist borrows a number of different switches from the ATA Center and connects them to Michael's CD player and television set. An automatic page turner is connected to a switch that Michael can activate with a slight nod of his head. Different switches are tried to determine which are most easily used and which ones Michael prefers. After a tryout period, decisions are made about the switches that appear to be most functional, and Michael's parents purchase them for him.

The rehabilitation engineer fabricates an electronic transmitter that enables Michael to activate the telephone with a speaker phone and automatic dialing system. He also assists in designing a ramp and automatic door openers for use when Michael is able to use a wheelchair. He provides specifications for making adaptations to sinks, toilets, and tables that will accommodate a wheelchair user. He also explains options for different lifts that can be used to transfer Michael into a bathtub.

Because of the expense involved, decisions about computer access are deferred until the extent of Michael's use of his hands can be determined. Options are defined, however, ranging from the use of an alternate keyboard to the use of a computer equipped with a mouth-activated pneumatic switch system.

It is anticipated that Michael will be able to return to school in the fall when he is able to use his electric wheelchair. The assistive technology specialist and rehabilitation engineer provide information to Michael's parents that will assist them in working with school officials over the summer to ensure that accommodations necessary for Michael are in place when he returns to school.

Functional Analysis

Environment and Context:	In bedroom at home; Recuperating from serious accident
Functional Demands:	Need to operate various pieces of equipment

Explore Options:	Full-time attendant to tend to Michael's needs; Switches to operate devices; Purchase of high-end devices	Functional Response:	Switch systems are put in place to enable Michael to control equipment in his room; Home adaptations are designed in preparation for his use of a wheelchair.
Personal Perceptions:	Michael wants to be able to operate equipment on his own time schedule; He does not want a personal attendant at all times; He wants to be as independent as possible; He wants to be able to communicate with his friends.	Personal Changes:	Michael is able to operate devices that enable him to continue the pursuit of his various interests; He is optimistic that he will be able to continue in school and maintain his friendships with his peers.
Personal Resources:	Michael can control the movement of his head, chin, mouth, and eyeblinks; He can breathe normally and speak; He has a good sense of humor.	Evaluation and Feedback:	As Michael gains ability to use the various switches and other environmental adaptations, his parents will acquire more sophisticated devices, such as computer systems, to enhance his ability to function.
External Supports:	Alliance for Technology Access Center; Assistive technology specialist; Rehabilitation engineer; Family resources to purchase devices		

Michael's vignette illustrates three important concepts. First is the role that various switches can play in making adaptations that can enable people to function in the environment. Switches can be used to operate appliances, turn equipment on and off, and activate different electronic devices. Although such applications appear obvious, the types of switches that are available and the ways some can be activated are amazing. Some switches, as illustrated in Figure 1.6A, resemble buttons that can be activated by a finger press, a foot press, or a press by any part of the body that can be moved. Others are plate switches that can be attached to a wheelchair and activated by head movements, as illustrated in Figure 1.6B. More sophisticated switches, as illustrated in Figure 1.6C, can be operated by any muscle such as an eye blink that is under voluntary control, whereas others can be placed in the mouth and activated by pressure of the tongue and teeth, as illustrated in Figure 1.6D. Pneumatic switches that respond to sipping and blowing air also can be used, as can scanning devices that highlight different options that can be activated by a

switch. Ingenious switches and their applications will continue to be developed to enable people to control the operation of equipment in their environments.

A second concept in Michael's vignette is the services that can be provided by assistive technology specialists and rehabilitation engineers. These are relatively new professional roles that have evolved parallel to the developments in assistive technology.

The final point to note in this vignette is the role that the Alliance for Technology Access (ATA) Center performs. Numerous agencies are evolving throughout the nation to provide services to technology consumers and their families. Some of these centers are part of the ATA network. Others were developed as a result of stimulation of activities under the auspices of the Tech Act, which was described earlier in this chapter. In some cases, the ATA Centers are affiliated with those that were developed through the Tech Act. At the time this chapter was written, every state had a coordinating office for Tech Act activities. Contact information for the state

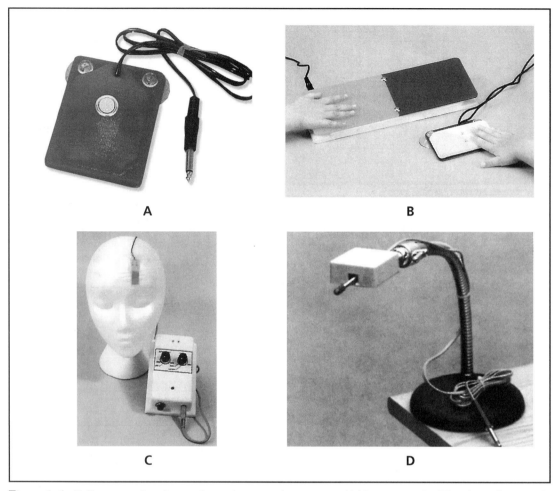

Figure 1.6. Different switches that can be used to control equipment: (A) button switch, (B) rocking plate switch, (C) twitch switch, and (D) tongue switch (all from Enabling Devices).

coordinating office in each state can be obtained by contacting Rehabilitation Engineering and Assistive Technology Society of North America (RESNA), an organization that provides technical assistance and coordinating services to the projects funded under the Tech Act. Locations of the ATA Centers can be obtained from the ATA central office, whose address and World Wide Web site can be found later in this chapter.

Learning, Education, and Rehabilitation

Functions in the learning, education, and rehabilitation category include those associated with

school activities and various types of therapies and rehabilitation processes. Special and general education teachers, speech–language pathologists, rehabilitation counselors, psychologists, and others may be involved in providing direct services to exceptional individuals. In addition, numerous technologies may be used within the context of schools. Included may be computer-assisted instruction, instructional audiotapes, print magnifiers, book holders, and other materials and equipment that can facilitate learning. Many of these devices are integrated into systematic instructional programs that reflect the technology of teaching.

Following are two vignettes that demonstrate different approaches to the use of technology in teaching. Teachers in both cases use technology productivity tools to assist them in making decisions to guide their instructional practices. The first teacher uses the information to design instructional strategies for preschool students with disabilities, whereas the second conducts a research project to determine the type of technology to use to teach several students with learning disabilities.

Education and Learning Vignette: Technology of Teaching

Danny is a 5-year-old male with moderate cognitive delays. He attends a preschool program at a neighborhood school that provides services to students with and without disabilities in an integrated setting. Danny has difficulty remembering the letters of the alphabet when participating in class activities.

His special education teacher has tried various instructional techniques, such as error correction, use of peer tutors, and drill-and-practice flashcards, with little consistent success. She has heard about a teaching strategy, called constant time delay, that is used to deliver instruction in such a fashion that minimizes the errors that students make during learning. She wonders whether this procedure is appropriate for Danny.

She uses the Internet to access the Educational Resources Information Center (ERIC) database to locate articles about time delay. She finds several research studies that report the effectiveness of this approach with preschool students who have disabilities. She also finds information about how to implement the procedure in naturalistic settings.

She designs a systematic program of instruction for her students, including Danny, and implements it when the students are in three of the learning centers in her classroom. She finds that all are able to master letter identification. Subsequently, she uses the time delay procedure to teach other skills that involve memorization.

Functional Analysis

Environment and Context:	Preschool classroom instruction on letter recognition; Instruction is embedded in naturalistic settings while students are engaged in learning center activities; Students with and without developmental delays are integrated into the classroom
Functional Demands:	Name letters of the alphabet when presented visually to student
Explore Options:	Use teacher prompting during instructional activities; Use an error correction instructional procedure; Use a peer buddy to help Danny; Provide daily flashcard drills; Use a near-errorless learning procedure
Personal Perceptions:	Danny does not perceive a problem. He is happy to be in school and enjoys being with his friends. Some frustration is becoming evident as he makes errors in letter identification activities.
Personal Resources:	Danny is a compliant and happy child; He has good

Exceptional persons must be prepared to use technology in all segments of society. (Photograph by Carolyn F. Woods)

	expressive skills; He can recognize colors and shapes, follows directions, knows what it means to wait.		cedure that is embedded into activities conducted in learning centers; Instruction is targeted at all students in the instructional groups.
External Supports:	Special education teacher; Access to the Internet; Availability of 3 learning centers: book, writing, and fine motor; Access to materials for use in learning centers	Personal Changes:	Danny is enjoying more success while learning letters; His accuracy has improved.
Functional Response:	Teacher develops a constant time delay instructional pro-	Evaluation and Feedback:	On the annual IEP review, Danny achieved his objectives for letter recognition.

The principal of Danny's school placed a computer in the teacher's lounge and connected it via modem to an Internet service provider so that teachers could access the many resources that are on the Internet telecommunication network and send and receive electronic mail. Users of the Internet can access the ERIC database, which contains abstracts of published articles and other documents about a host of educational topics. Many universities provide public access to their ERIC databases.

Danny's teacher logged onto the ERIC database at a local university and initiated a search for information about the time delay instructional procedure and its applications for preschoolers. Examples of her ERIC search are provided in Figure 1.7. She initiated a Boolean search strategy, as illustrated in Figure 1.7A. At the *NEXT COMMAND:* prompt, she typed *k=(time delay) and preschool.* She put the words in parentheses to tell the computer system to find only those articles in which the words *time* and *delay* appeared next to each other. She then used the Boolean operator *and* to include preschool. After she pressed the return key, the computer searched the thousands of abstracts contained in the ERIC system and located only those that contained the descriptors *time delay* and *preschool.* As can be seen from Figure 1.7B, abstracts of 28 articles were identified that might have relevance for her search.

She then decided to narrow her search to the topic of reading, and added that descriptor to the

search specifications, as illustrated in Figure 1.7B. Consequently, the search was narrowed to two articles, as illustrated in Figure 1.7C. She then examined each of the abstracts by typing the abstract number at the *NEXT COMMAND:* prompt and retrieved information such as that in Figure 1.7D, which she printed for reference purposes. She added additional descriptors related to applying time delay in naturalistic environments and located several articles related to that topic that had relevance for her needs. She printed copies of the relevant abstracts and took them to the university library to obtain copies of the entire article.

Most research libraries have access to the ERIC system, either in print form or via computer. It also is possible to pose questions to ERIC via the World Wide Web and receive a response via electronic mail within a few days (access this service via http://ericir.sunsite.syr.edu). Although many articles about individuals with disabilities are included in the ERIC system, it is important to note that a more complete resource is available through *Exceptional Child Education Resources,* which is published by the ERIC Clearinghouse on Disabilities and Gifted Education, operated by the Council for Exceptional Children in Reston, Virginia.

Danny's teacher examined the information she obtained and then designed a system for using time delay to teach letters while students were in three of the learning centers in the classroom. In using time delay, she would present the letters

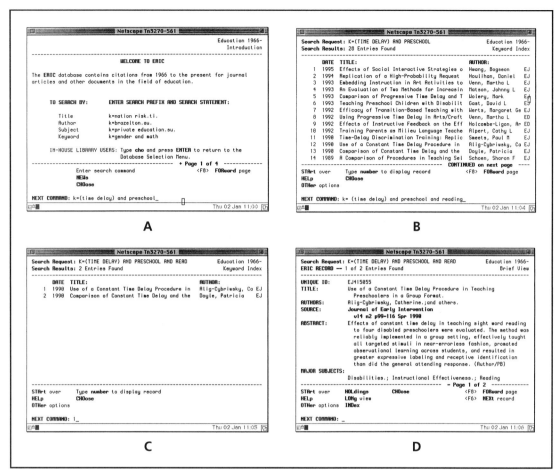

Figure 1.7. Sample screens from an Educational Resources Information Center (ERIC) search.

in sets of two in various contexts (e.g., felt letters in the book center, letters on blocks in the fine motor center, and letters on the dry-erase board in the writing center). When presenting a letter, she would say, "Look! What letter?" and then wait 3 seconds for a response. Students were instructed to wait if they did not know the answer. If they did not know the answer, the teacher would name the letter after the 3-second delay. If they answered incorrectly, they were told, "No. Wait if you don't know." As the students got used to the procedure, they learned to wait. As a result of repetitions, they would gradually associate the name of the letter with its shape and would be able to name it correctly before the 3-second delay was up.

Constant time delay has been shown to be a powerful technology of teaching anything that needs to be memorized. Examples of research that has shown it to be effective in situations similar to Danny's can be examined in the work of Alig-Cybriwsky, Wolery, and Gast (1990), Blackhurst (1997), and Doyle, Wolery, Gast, Ault, and Wiley (1990). Additional applications of near-errorless teaching procedures are provided by Wolery et al. (1992).

The following vignette illustrates the role that a special education resource teacher can play in the application of instructional technology in a school program.

Education and Learning Vignette: Instructional Technology

Mr. Meanor is a fourth-grade teacher who has five students with learning disabilities integrated into his classroom for most of the day. He is teaching multiplication and division facts to the students. A corner of his classroom contains four computers that his students use on a regular basis in several subject areas. He has located a computer program that can be used with students at the acquisition level to assist in teaching multiplication facts, and the students are regularly assigned time to use the computer program for this math activity.

Although students who use the program appear to learn their facts fairly quickly, he notices that three of the five students with learning disabilities are not progressing as rapidly as the other students, yet they seem to be able to master other mathematical concepts. Consequently, he seeks the advice of Ms. Champion, the special education resource teacher, to solicit suggestions about what may be creating the difficulties for the three students.

Ms. Champion observes the students while they are working on the computer and notices that the students who are successful seem to be able to operate the computer with no difficulty, whereas the three students with learning disabilities seem to be having difficulty locating the number keys. Although the computer program only requires the students to type the number keys and the return key, the students who are having difficulty often appear to be searching for the appropriate keys and sometimes press function keys, which have numbers on them, instead of the numeric keys.

She speculates that the students appear to be distracted by the complex array of function keys, numeric keypad, and the other keys and wonders whether the use of an alternate keyboard, with fewer keys, may be less distracting to those students. She decides to conduct an action research project to determine whether an alternate keyboard may be more appropriate for those students than the conventional keyboard.

Ms. Champion returns to her room and performs a consultation with an expert computer system, called *The Single Subject Research Advisor* (SSRA) (Blackhurst, Schuster, Ault, & Doyle, 1996). This program presents questions to her about her problem. Based on her answers to the questions, the SSRA recommends that she conduct a study that uses an adapted alternating treatment research design to determine whether there are any differences in acquisition of multiplication facts based on the type of keyboard that is used.

She obtains an IntelliKeys membrane keyboard with an overlay that displays only numbers and a backspace and return key on it and proceeds to conduct a study that compares the academic achievement of students using the different keyboards. She finds that the students who were having difficulty learned their multiplication facts faster when they used the alternate keyboard. Consequently, Mr. Meanor uses the alternate keyboard when the three students with learning disabilities use the multiplication program, with good results.

Functional Analysis

Environment and Context:	Fourth-grade integrated classroom during mathematics instruction for students with learning disabilities
Functional Demands:	Learn multiplication facts using the computer
Explore Options:	Use of regular keyboard; Use of alternate keyboard
Personal Perceptions:	The students like using the computer; They are frustrated that they are not learning as fast as some of their peers.
Personal Resources:	The students have the cognitive ability to master multiplication facts; Those having difficulty appear to be distracted by the keyboard.
External Supports:	Special education resource teacher; *The Single Subject Research Advisor* expert system; IntelliKeys keyboard; Supportive teacher who will permit research in the classroom

Functional Response:	Students use the alternate keyboard with the math facts software program.	Evaluation and Feedback:	Use of the alternate keyboard is successful; Exploration of devising other keyboards for other applications
Personal Changes:	Students master the multiplication tables.		

This vignette about Mr. Meanor illustrates the importance of making empirical decisions about technology options that might be available. Although it is not always possible to do so, every effort should be made to make instructional decisions—not only those related to technology—on the basis of data. In many cases, simply collecting performance data through classroom observations can be sufficient. In other cases, it is helpful to conduct classroom research projects to obtain the necessary data.

The vignette also illustrates the use of the SSRA (Blackhurst et al., 1996), which is a technology productivity tool. This software program is known as an expert system because it was designed to simulate the behavior of a human expert. For example, a human expert on single-subject research designs would ask a person interested in conducting a study a series of questions, such as those in Figure 1.8A and 1.8B. In Figure 1.8A, for example, the SSRA asks about the purpose of the research and provides a decision

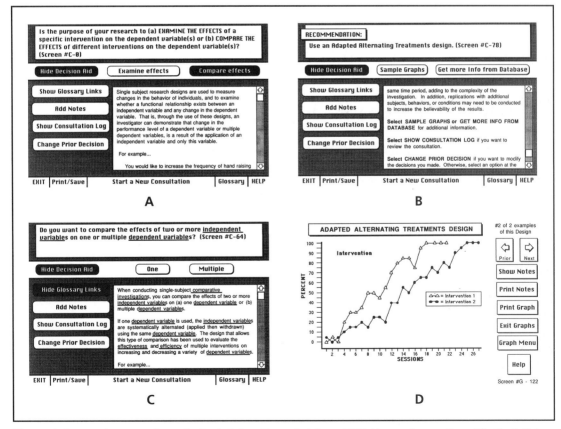

Figure 1.8. Sample screens from *The Single Subject Research Advisor* (SSRA) consultation. From *The Single Subject Research Advisor,* by A. E. Blackhurst, J. W. Schuster, M. J. Ault, and P. M. Doyle, 1996, Lexington, KY: Department of Special Education and Rehabilitation Counseling, University of Kentucky.

aid, displayed in the lower right of the screen, to help the person answer the question. In this case, Ms. Champion wanted to compare effects of the two different keyboards, so she clicked on the "Compare effects" button, subsequently highlighted as displayed in Figure 1.8A. Other questions were asked, such as the one in Figure 1.8B. Human experts can define terms. If Ms. Champion clicked on any of the underlined terms, she could obtain a definition of that term. Eventually, the SSRA would have enough information to make a recommendation, such as that illustrated in Figure 1.8C. Additional options are available to help her decide how to conduct her study. A good consultant can provide recommendations about how to analyze the data obtained from the study. The SSRA provides illustrations of how Ms. Champion might graph the data for her study, as illustrated in Figure 1.8D. In this example, the graph with the open triangles represents the use of the alternate keyboard, thus indicating that the students learned faster when they used that option. Readers can expect to see more expert systems developed to assist in providing various services related to exceptional individuals.

Sports, Leisure, and Recreation

Functions associated with group and individual sports and productive use of leisure time are included in this category. The services of a person trained in adapted physical education may provide a valuable resource in this area. In addition, a wide array of equipment and devices can facilitate functions in this category, including balls that emit audible beeps so that children who are blind can hear them, specially designed skis for skiers with one leg, braille playing cards, and wheelchairs for basketball players who cannot walk or run.

Many leisure and recreation activities require adaptations of current equipment or not highly specialized new equipment. Some do not require any adaptations at all, as in the following vignette about Max.

Leisure and Recreation Vignette: Telecommunications

Max has been retired for 4 years. He has used a hearing aid for about 10 years, but his hearing has continued to deteriorate and he is almost completely deaf. He always enjoyed listening to music, watching television, and talking long distance to his son and daughter and five grandchildren. He purchased a new television that enabled him to read captions to compensate for his inability to hear the sound on the programs. Even with the use of an amplified telephone, however, he is now unable to hear conversations on the telephone.

He also enjoyed playing golf. However, his loss of hearing made him feel uncomfortable with his golfing partners, and his arthritis made it increasingly difficult to swing. Consequently, Max gave up playing golf.

During a family vacation gathering, his oldest granddaughter suggested that he purchase a computer and modem so that he could send electronic mail to family members and explore information on the World Wide Web. Max now spends several hours each day at his computer. He sends e-mail to his family, subscribes to newsgroups on topics of interest, "surfs the Web," and plays computer golf. Although the latter is no substitute for actual golf, he enjoys the game and regularly beats his old golfing buddies who stop by to visit.

Functional Analysis

Environment and Context:	At home; Unable to communicate via phone; No longer able to engage in his favorite sport
Functional Demands:	Communicate with family members; Engage in leisure activities to remain occupied
Explore Options:	Use of a telephone device for people who are deaf; Connect a computer to the Internet
Personal Perceptions:	Wants to be able to communicate with family; Willing to

		Personal Changes:	Max is pleased that he is able to communicate; Keeps occupied; Improves his happiness with his retirement
	explore technology options; Accepts the fact that he cannot play golf any longer		
Personal Resources:	Has the ability to operate a computer	Evaluation and Feedback:	Max is successful in his use of the computer; As he becomes more knowledgeable and skilled in its use, he contributes actively in the Internet community.
External Supports:	Financial resources to purchase a computer; Family members who also have computer access; Supportive friends		
Functional Response:	Connect a computer to the Internet; Obtain software programs		

Many more examples of technology services and devices could be provided, but these should be sufficient to illustrate the importance of attending to human functions when planning and implementing technology applications in special education, rehabilitation, and related services. Also note, with this perspective, that it is more relevant to focus on the functions that a person can perform and those in which difficulty is experienced than to focus on a diagnostic label or disability category when planning special education services. Such an orientation enables teachers and those providing related services to more directly address a person's needs.

Concluding Concepts

The information provided in this chapter has been designed to provide a foundation and context for analyzing and understanding the information that is presented in subsequent chapters. In addition to using the functional model to help organize your thinking about technology, as you read the following chapters, keep in mind the following points:

- Assistive technology devices and services must be considered for every student with an IEP. It is the responsibility of the IEP team to be knowledgeable about assistive technology devices and services in order to make good decisions about their selection and use.

- Technology decisions should be made on the basis of the demands that are placed on people from the environment and the functions that must be performed in order to respond to those demands, not on the basis of a person's exceptionality or the availability of a piece of equipment.

- Technology applications involve more than just the use of devices and equipment. Services provided by a variety of professional personnel are a critical factor in the successful use of technology.

- Decisions about the use of technology for individuals are best made by teams of people, including, whenever possible, the person who will be using the technology.

- It helps to view technology solutions across a continuum of possibilities, ranging from no-tech to high-tech and least intrusive to most intrusive. Initial consideration should be given first to lower tech and less intrusive solutions rather than those at the higher end of the technology continuum.

- Because of the newness of the field, technology decision makers are forced to rely heavily on hunches and professional judgment in the absence of research evidence. There is a considerable need for additional research in all areas related to technology applications.

- The lack of technology knowledge and skills is one of the major barriers to greater implementation of technology. It is incumbent upon professionals to engage in professional development programs that will enhance their abilities to use technology.

Finally, remember that technology is not a panacea. Technology devices and services are external supports—tools that can have dramatic effects on individuals with exceptionalities, as illustrated by Kevin's story at the beginning of this chapter and by the vignettes, all of which are based on actual cases. Although the vignettes portray successes, some technology applications may not result in such satisfactory solutions. As discussed, many variables can affect technology selection and use. The challenge is to take those variables into consideration in order to make the wisest possible decisions about the selection of technology for each individual. Proper training and supports also must be provided for technology users and for those who interact with them. Additionally, as technology use is implemented, performance must be closely monitored and appropriate modifications made in response to evaluative feedback. Only if such activities are approached in a thoughtful and systematic manner can technology help exceptional individuals reach their full potential.

Resources

Numerous print resources are available to provide additional information about technology applications in special education. Those published since 1992 that are particularly helpful include the work of the Alliance for Technology Access (1996) and books by Bain and Leger (1997), Beukelman and Mirenda (1992), Chambers (1997), Church and Glennen (1992), Cook and Hussey (1995), Flippo, Inge, and Barcus (1995), Galvin and Sherer (1996), Glennen and DeCoste (1997), Lewis (1993), Light and Binger (1998), Male (1994), Ray and Warden (1995), Scherer (1993), and Silverman (1995). Also, the first and second editions of this book (Lindsey, 1987, 1993) provide unique and comparative information about technology and exceptional individuals.

Several agencies provide useful information in the form of journals, newsletters, special reports, conferences, and training sessions.

Organizations

Alliance for Technology Access
2175 East Francisco Boulevard, Suite L
San Rafael, CA 94901
Voice: 415/455-4575

American Occupational Therapy Association (AOTA)
P.O. Box 31220
4720 Montgomery Lane
Bethesda, MD 20824-1220
Voice: 800/377-8555

American Speech-Language-Hearing Association (ASHA)
10801 Rockville Pike
Rockville, MD 20852
Voice: 301/897-5700 or 800/638-8355

Center for Applied Special Technology (CAST)
39 Cross Street
Peabody, MA 01960
Voice: 508/531-8555

Closing the Gap
P.O. Box 68
Henderson, MN 56044
email:ctgap@aol.com
Voice: 507/248-3294
Fax: 507/248-3810

Council for Exceptional Children (CEC)
Technology and Media Division (TAM)
1920 Association Drive
Reston, VA 20191-1589
Voice: 703/620-3660 or 800/845-6232

National Lekotek Center
2100 Rige Avenue
Evanston, IL 60201-2796
Voice: 847/328-0001
Fax: 847/328-5514

National Rehabilitation Information Center (NARIC)
8455 Colesville Road
Suite 935
Silver Springs, MD 20910
Voice: 800/346-2742

Rehabilitation Engineering and Assistive Technology Society of North America (RESNA)
1700 N. Moore Street
Suite 200
Arlington, VA 22209-1903
Voice: 703/524-6686

Trace Research and Development Center
Waisman Center
University of Wisconsin–Madison
1500 Highland Avenue
Madison, WI 53705
Voice: 608/262-6966

On-line Resources

The World Wide Web (Web) contains numerous sites devoted to exceptionalities. Many of those sites also provide information about technology applications. Sponsors of several of the sites that provide particularly useful information are listed here with their Web addresses. Note that the Web is an ever-expanding resource. By the time this book is published, there will be many additional sites, and some of the listed sites may have been discontinued or have different addresses. Learn how to use Web search engines to locate new resources as they become available.

ABLEDATA
Web: http://www.abledata.com/index.htm

Adaptive Computing Technology Center
Web: http://www.missouri.edu:80/~ccact/

Alliance for Technology Access
Web: http://www.ataccess.org

Apple Computer's Disability Connection
Web: http://www2.apple.com/disability/welcome.html

AT-ONLINE
Web: http://www.asel.udel.edu/at-online/assistive.html

Council for Exceptional Children
Web: http:/www.cec.sped.org

DREAMMS for Kids
Web: http://www.dreamms.org/

Equal Access to Software and Information (EASI)
Web: http://www.rit.edu/~easi/index.html

Hood College Special Education Resources on the Internet
Web: http://www.hood.edu/seri/

IBM Special Needs Solutions
Web: http://www.austin.ibm.com/sns/index.html

Internet Resources for Special Children
Web: http://www.irsc.org

Jim Lubin's disABILITY Information and Resources
Web: http://www.eskimo.com/~jlubin/disabled.html

National Rehabilitation Information Center
Web: http://www.cais.com/naric/

Rehabilitation Engineering and Assistive Technology Society of North America (RESNA)
Web: http://www.resna.org/resna/reshome.htm

Special Needs Education Network
Web: http://www.schoolnet.ca/sne/

Trace Research and Development Center
Web: http://www.trace.wisc.edu

University of Kentucky Special Education and Rehabilitation Internet Resources
Web: http://serc.gws.uky.edu/www/resources/resmenu.html

Yahoo! Education: Special Education
Web: http://www.yahoo.com/Education/Special_Education/

References

Academic Software. (1996). *Adaptive device locator system* [Computer program]. Lexington, KY: Author.

Alberto, P. A., & Troutman, A. C. (1995). *Applied behavior analysis for teachers* (4th ed.). Columbus, OH: Merrill.

Alig-Cybriwsky, C., Wolery, M., & Gast, D. L. (1990). Use of a constant time delay procedure in teaching preschoolers in a group format. *Journal of Early Intervention, 14*(2), 99–116.

Alliance for Technology Access. (1996). *Computer resources for people with disabilities: A guide to exploring today's assistive technology.* San Rafael, CA: Author.

Americans with Disabilities Act of 1990, 42 U.S.C. § 12101 *et seq.*

Bain, B. K., & Leger, D. (Eds.). (1997). *Assistive technology: An interdisciplinary approach.* New York: Churchill Livingston.

Batshaw, M. L., & Perret, Y. M. (1992). *Children with disabilities: A medical primer.* Baltimore: Brookes.

Beukelman, D. R., & Mirenda, P. (1992). *Augmentative and alternate communication: Management of severe communication disorders in children and adults.* Baltimore: Brookes.

Blackhurst, A. E. (1977). Competency-based special education personnel preparation. In R. D. Kneedler & S. G. Tarver (Eds.), *Changing perspectives in special education* (pp. 156–182). Columbus, OH: Merrill.

Blackhurst, A. E. (1993). Continuing professional development. In A. E. Blackhurst & W. H. Berdine (Eds.), *An introduction to special education* (3rd ed., pp. 218–233). New York: HarperCollins.

Blackhurst, A. E. (1997). Perspectives on technology in special education. *Teaching Exceptional Children, 29*(5), 41–48.

Blackhurst, A. E., & Berdine, W. H. (Eds.). (1993). *An introduction to special education* (3rd ed.). New York: HarperCollins.

Blackhurst, A. E., & Cross, D. P. (1993). Technology in special education. In A. E. Blackhurst & W. H. Berdine (Eds.), *An introduction to special education* (3rd ed., pp. 77–103). New York: HarperCollins.

Blackhurst, A. E., Hales, R. M., & Lahm, E. A. (in press). Using an education server software system to deliver special education coursework via the World Wide Web. *Journal of Special Education Technology.*

Blackhurst, A. E., & Hofmeister, A. M. (1980). Technology in special education. In L. Mann & D. Sabatino (Eds.), *Fourth review of special education* (pp. 199–228). New York: Grune & Stratton.

Blackhurst, A. E., & Morse, T. E. (1996). Using anchored instruction to teach about assistive technology. *Focus on Autism and Other Developmental Disabilities, 11,* 131–141.

Blackhurst, A. E., Schuster, J. W., Ault, M. J., & Doyle, P. M. (1996). *The single subject research advisor* [Computer program]. Lexington: Department of Special Education and Rehabilitation Counseling, University of Kentucky.

Bottge, B. A., & Hasselbring, T. S. (1993). A comparison of two approaches for teaching complex, authentic mathematics problems to adolescents in remedial math classes. *Exceptional Children, 59,* 556–566.

Carnine, D. W., Silbert, J., & Kameenui, E. J. (1990). *Direct instruction reading* (2nd ed.). Columbus, OH: Merrill.

Cartwright, G. P., & Cartwright, C. A. (1972). Gilding the lily: Comments on the training-based model. *Exceptional Children, 39*(3), 231–234.

Chambers, A. C. (1997). *Has technology been considered? A guide for IEP teams.* Albuquerque, NM: Council of Administrators of Special Education.

Church, G., & Glennen, S. (1992). *The handbook of assistive technology.* San Diego: Singular.

Cognition and Technology Group at Vanderbilt Learning Technology Center. (1993). Anchored instruction and situated cognition revisited. *Educational Technology, 33*(3), 52–70.

Commission on Instructional Technology. (1970). *To improve learning: A report to the President and the Congress of the United States.* Washington, DC: U.S. Government Printing Office.

Cook, A. M., & Hussey, S. M. (1995). *Assistive technologies: Principles and practice.* St. Louis, MO: Mosby.

Deshler, D. D., & Schumaker, J. B. (1986). Learning strategies: An instructional alternative for low-achieving adolescents. *Exceptional Children, 52*(6), 583–590.

Doyle, P. M., Wolery, M., Gast, D. L., Ault, M. J., & Wiley, K. (1990). Comparison of constant time delay and the system of least prompts in teaching preschoolers with developmental delays. *Research in Developmental Disabilities, 11,* 1–22.

Education for All Handicapped Children Act of 1975, 20 U.S.C. § 1400 *et seq.*

Edwards, B. J., Blackhurst, A. E., & Koorland, M. A. (1995). Computer-assisted constant time delay prompting to teach abbreviation spelling to adolescents with mild learning disabilities. *Journal of Special Education Technology, 12,* 301–311.

Evans, D. (1997, January 5). Speech-translating software may get more use in 1997. *Herald-Leader Newspaper* (Lexington, KY).

Flippo, K. F., Inge, K. J., & Barcus, J. M. (Eds.). (1995). *Assistive technology: A resource for school, work, and community.* Baltimore: Brookes.

Galvin, J. C., & Scherer, M. J. (1996). *Evaluating, selecting, and using appropriate assistive technology.* Gaithersburg, MD: Aspen.

Gast, D. L., & Schuster, J. W. (1993). Students with severe developmental disabilities. In A. E. Blackhurst & W. H. Berdine (Eds.), *An introduction to special education* (3rd ed., pp. 454–491). New York: HarperCollins.

Glennen, S. L., & DeCoste, D. C. (1997). *Handbook of augmentative and alternative communication.* San Diego: Singular.

Haring, N. G. (1970). The new curriculum design in special education. *Educational Technology, 10,* 24–31.

Haring, N. G., Lovitt, T. C., Eaton, M. D., & Hansen, C. L. (1978). *The fourth R: Research in the classroom.* Columbus, OH: Merrill.

Hasselbring, T. S., Goin, L. I., & Wissick, C. (1989). Making knowledge meaningful: Applications of hypermedia. *Journal of Special Education Technology, 10,* 62–72.

Individuals with Disabilities Education Act of 1990, 20 U.S.C. § 1400 *et seq.*

King, T. W. (1999). *Assistive technology: Essential human factors.* Needham Heights, MA: Allyn & Bacon.

Lewis, R. B. (1993). *Special education technology.* Pacific Grove, CA: Brooke Cole.

Light, J. C., & Binger, C. (1998). *Building communicative competence with individuals who use augmentative and alternative communication.* Baltimore: Brookes.

Lindsey, J. D. (Ed.). (1987). *Computers and exceptional individuals.* Columbus, OH: Merrill.

Lindsey, J. D. (Ed.). (1993). *Computers and exceptional individuals* (2nd ed.). Austin, TX: PRO-ED.

Male, M. (1994). *Technology for inclusion: Meeting the special needs of all students* (2nd ed.). Needham Heights, MA: Allyn & Bacon.

Melichar, J. F., & Blackhurst, A. E. (1993). *Introduction to a functional approach to assistive technology* [Training Module]. Department of Special Education and Rehabilitation Counseling, University of Kentucky, Lexington.

Nazzaro, J. N. (1977). *Exceptional timetables: Historic events affecting the handicapped and gifted.* Reston, VA: Council for Exceptional Children.

Ray, J. R., & Warden, M. K. (1995). *Technology, computers, and the special needs learner.* Albany, NY: Delmar.

Rehabilitation Act of 1973, 29 U.S.C. § 701 *et seq.*

Scherer, M. J. (1993). *Living in the state of stuck: How technology impacts the lives of people with disabilities.* Cambridge, MA: Brookline.

Silverman, F. H. (1995). *Communication for the speechless* (3rd ed.). Needham Heights, MA: Allyn & Bacon.

Stevens, K. B., Blackhurst, A. E., & Slaton, D. B. (1991). Teaching memorized spelling with a microcomputer: Time delay and computer-assisted instruction. *Journal of Applied Behavior Analysis, 24,* 153–160.

Technology-Related Assistance for Individuals with Disabilities Act of 1988, 29 U.S.C. § 2201 *et seq.*

Trace Center. (1996). *CO-NET* [CD-ROM program]. Madison: University of Wisconsin, Author.

Williams, B. (1995). *The Internet for teachers.* Foster City, CA: IDG Books Worldwide.

Williams, B. (1996). *The World Wide Web for teachers.* Foster City, CA: IDG Books Worldwide.

Wolery, M., Ault, M. J., & Doyle, P. M. (1992). *Teaching students with moderate and severe disabilities: Use of response prompting procedures.* White Plains, NY: Longman.

Wolery, M., Bailey, D. B., & Sugai, G. M. (1988). *Effective teaching: Principles of applied behavior analysis with exceptional students.* Boston: Allyn & Bacon.

Chapter 2

⤳　　　⤳　　　⤳

The Hardware Domain

Carl R. Steinhoff
University of Nevada, Las Vegas

Teresa L. Jordan
University of Nevada, Las Vegas

Beatrice C. Babbitt
University of Nevada, Las Vegas

In this chapter, we address how computers (i.e., hardware) function, with an emphasis on the practical use of computers with and by persons with special needs. For these individuals, technology—particularly the development of portable, light, powerful, and user-friendly devices (e.g., laptops, notebooks, and Personal Digital Assistants)—has and will continue to affect their abilities to perform in educational settings (see Chapters 5 and 7), as well as in home and community environments (see Howard, 1998).

As defined in Appendix A of this book, hardware is "the physical equipment that makes up a computer system." In this chapter, we take a generic approach, supplemented by discussions of specific equipment presently available, to delineate and describe pertinent computer components and peripherals. Because of the exponential rate of development of both hardware and software technology (see Desmond, 1999; Landau, 1999), the content and illustrations in this chapter and in the appendixes (see Appendixes B, C, D, F, and H) should be viewed as only a portent of what is to come. Although the Wright brothers could not have foreseen the development of the jet airplane within such a short time span after their first flight, the pace of innovation in computer technology far outstrips the growth of technology in the field of aviation.

The computer is simply a device that multiplies users' capacity to perform certain kinds of tasks. Much in the same way that machinery enhanced the productivity of farmers and factory workers during the Industrial Revolution, the computer now enables individuals to engage in a variety of activities at a level of effectiveness previously thought unattainable. See Chapter 1 and later chapters in this book for listings of printed resources concerning technology and its use by and with exceptional individuals (also see Lewis, 1993; Lindsey, 1987, 1993).

The Computer

The concept of the computer is not new (e.g., the Chinese invented the abacus about 4000 B.C.). In the early 19th century, the first computer-like device was devised by Charles Babbage, assisted by Ada, the Countess of Lovelace and daughter of Lord Byron. Babbage invented a machine he called an analytical engine, which was designed to calculate tables of mathematical functions. In 1889 Herman Hollerith invented a method of

A computer hardware system has numerous components. (Photograph by Carolyn F. Woods)

storing data that included a type of punched card as well as equipment for processing the information stored. The U.S. Census Bureau first used it in 1890.

During the 1930s and 1940s, computing machinery progressed from electromechanical to electronic devices. The Electronic Numerical Integrator and Calculator (ENIAC), the world's first all-electronic computer, was completed in 1946. The device had about 19,000 tubes, weighed 60,000 pounds, and could perform 300 calculations per second. However, the real breakthrough in computer design came, also in 1946, when John von Neumann operationalized his concept of the stored program. Previously, programs (i.e., the sequence of operations of the machine) were determined by the manual setting of plugs or switches or were directed by punched cards or punched paper tape. All modern computers use von Neumann's basic idea of storing a program within the computer's own memory.

Continuing evolution and revolution in the field of electronics have led to the development of the microprocessor, which is an entire computer circuit printed on an area no larger than a fingernail. This so-called fifth-generation technology allows computer processing at speeds of millions of instructions per second. These amazing chips also provide the means to use sophisticated input/output devices driven by complicated programs with large memory requirements. Over the years, the trend in computer hardware has been toward increased miniaturization, increased capability, and decreasing cost. Complete sixth- and seventh-generation systems can be purchased for less than $1,500. However, the Internet or Network Computer, which has limited power and memory but downloads software programs (e.g., word processing, spreadsheets) as needed, is one of the developing hardware systems at variance with the "smaller and more powerful" trend and is an interesting technology to consider (Cook, 1998). Appendix B has an overview of the development of computer principles and theories. Also, Campbell-Kelly and Aspray (1996) and Shurkin (1996) have published interesting histories of computer evolution.

The Computer System

A computer system is an interrelated set of components working together as a unit (Shelly & Cashman, 1990). In its simplest form, a computer system consists of these components:

1. An input device that enables the user to input data to the computer

2. A processing unit that includes the central processing unit (CPU)

3. Disk drives for storage and access of data

4. Main memory

5. Output devices, such as the monitor (also known as a cathode ray tube [CRT]) and various printing and/or plotting devices that produce hard copies of processed input

A diagram of a fully configured system is shown in Figure 2.1.

Modern computer systems vary in speed, size, and complexity. The CPU of a microcomputer is called a processor or microprocessor, and the latest CPU designs (see http://www.ugeek.com) employ processor chips from such companies as Intel Corporation (e.g., Pentium I, II, III), Digital Equipment Corporation (e.g., Alpha), Advanced Micro Devices (e.g., K5, K6, K6-2, K6-3, K7), National Semiconductor (e.g., Cyrix 6x86, MII, MIII), and Apple, Inc. (e.g., PowerPC 601, 603, 604, G3, G4). Today, most PCs—IBMs and compatibles (e.g., Compaq, Dell, Gateway)—are powered by Intel's Pentium I, II, and III processors that operate from 75 to 450/550 MHz (Heid & Snyder, 1998; Howard, 1998), but 600- to 800-MHz chips are being developed by Intel and other companies (AMD K7, Cyrix MIII) and should be in computers as you read this book. Also, IBM has described a 1,000-MHz chip (http:// www.ibm.com/News/1998/02/Is980204. html); Intel's P7 Willamette will process at 1,000 MHz; and Sun Microsystems' UltraSparc V will have 1,500-MHz microprocessor capability.

For the Macintosh line of desktop computers, the PowerPC 600 family of microprocessors (e.g., 601, 603, 604) powers most machines and cur-

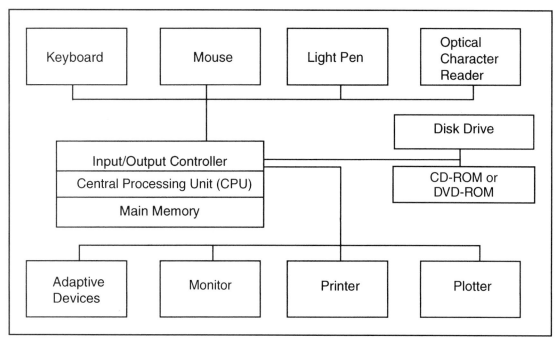

Figure 2.1. An extended microcomputer system.

rently operates at 150 MHz to 200/300/400 MHz. However, Apple's new PowerPC G family of processor (G3 and G4) is now powering the next "wave" of Macintosh iMac and desktop computers, and these microprocessors have "Pentium and above" 200- to 450/550-MHz speed (http:// www. apple.com/powermac/technologies/g3.html). Like their PC counterparts, the G chips are fully integrated and provide the interconnectivity power to access the Internet and to run full-motion video.

Computers with more powerful CPUs, complex peripherals, and the ability to provide many time-sharing users are called workstations and mini-computers. Although the distinctions between desktop microcomputers, workstations, and mini-computers have blurred, workstations lie between desktop microcomputers and minicomputers in power and resources. They are used as stand-alone systems, or linked together to form Local Area Networks (LANs), have dual processor capabilities and extensive storage, and support applications requiring moderate to intensive computing power or graphics (e.g., engineer-

ing or desktop publishing—see http://webopedia. internet.com/TERM/w/workstation.html). Popular workstations used today are Sun Micro-systems' UltraSPARC series, IBM's Intellistation series, and Silicon Graphic's Visual Workstation series.

The minicomputer, a term that is not heard very much today, lies between the workstation and mainframe computer (http://webopedia.internet. com/TERM/m/minicomputer.html). Small and medium companies purchased the IBM System/ 36 and other minicomputers as an alternative to the limiting capabilities of a desktop microcom-puter and the expensive mainframe system. The minicomputer offered multiprocessing systems, supported 4 to 200 users at the same time, and had extensive memory (e.g., 20 gigabytes of RAM and approximately one terabyte of stor-age). "In recent years, the minicomputer has evolved into the 'mid range server' and is part of a network"—IBM's AS/400e system (see http:// whatis.com/minicomp.htm).

Larger, faster, and with greater storage capacity than minicomputers, the most complex computer systems are called mainframes. These machines are characterized by great processing speed, enormous memory, many complicated input/output devices, and the capability for a very large number of simultaneous users supported by a number of linked CPUs that control the system. Mainframe computers also support a host of communications networks that allow users from distant locations to do their computing.

Finally, recent advances in electronic miniaturization have revolutionized the hardware domain and led to the development of innovative and powerful portable technology. For example, laptop and notebook computers measuring 8½ × 11 inches, weighing 2 to 13 pounds, and possessing the capabilities of desktop computers (e.g., Pentium or PowerPC processor, Super Video Graphics Array or SVGA display, extensive random access memory [RAM], large hard drive, fast CD-ROM or DVD drive, 56K modem) are now relatively inexpensive (less than $1,000) and are being used by children, youths, and adults (e.g., IBM's ThinkPad and Apple's PowerBook and iBook). Even more exciting is the continuing development of the Personal Digital Assistant (PDA) technology that is producing palm- or hand-held devices for use in the home, school, and community (e.g., Newton, Hewlett-Packard Color Palmtop PC, Sharp HC Handheld PC, and 3Com's PalmPilot). Depending on the manufacturer and cost, these hand-held devices may have color displays and extensive RAM, measure 4 × 8 inches, weigh less than 1 pound, are powered by AA or AAA batteries, come with extensive software (e.g., Windows CE applications—word processing, database, spreadsheet, and presentation), have printing and Internet capabilities, and can be connected to desktop computers for synchronization purposes. Meanwhile, pen-based personal computing technology with its gridpad or tablet-like input capabilities and built-in handwriting recognition and application software (e.g., spreadsheet) continues to evolve and be used by nonexceptional and exceptional individuals (see Glitman, 1992; Johnson, 1991a, 1991b). Chapters 5 and 7 also provide information about portable technology and its use by and with exceptional individuals.

The Central Processing Unit

The central processing unit (CPU) is the device that controls the operation of the computer. It has the ability to receive data, decode it, and execute the instructions contained within that data. A CPU acts through a set of specific functions designed into its circuitry. These native functions are enabled through a set of commands known as an operating system, frequently called a disk operating system (see Chapter 2 and http://whatis.com/), because they are stored on the hard disk in many microsystems (e.g., PC-DOS, MS-DOS, Windows 3.X/95/98/NT, Linux).

For example, the DOS command **save** would instruct the CPU to turn on a disk drive, read a file stored in memory, transport the data to that drive, save it, and provide it with a user-selected name. The CPU contains an arithmetic section that enables it to perform calculations and a logic and decision-making section that allows it to perform Boolean functions (i.e., to determine if data are equal to, unequal to, greater than, or less than a reference datum).

A diagram of the device in a microcomputer that performs the functions of a CPU, a microprocessor, appears in Figure 2.2. The input/output (I/O) controller, the electronic link between the microprocessor and the external environment, makes it possible for data provided by various input devices to be read, stored in memory, and hence directed to the arithmetic logic unit (ALU). Additionally, the I/O controller directs data to appropriate output devices, such as disk drives or printers. The I/O controller provides timing and control for the microprocessor system.

Intel's Pentium, Advanced Micro Devices' K, National Semiconductor's Cyrix, and Apple's PowerPC G families of chips are examples of the powerful microprocessors that power current desktop and portable computers (again 75 to 450/550 MHz, with 600- to 1,000-MHz chips available or soon to be installed). These processors have millions of transistors (e.g., Pentium II 7.5 million, PowerPC G4 10.5 million, Advanced Micro Devices K7 22 million), can address bil-

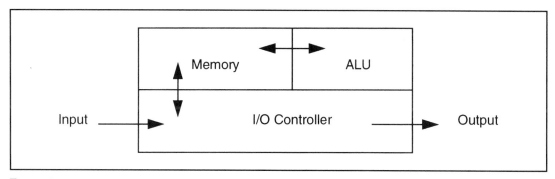

Figure 2.2. A simple microprocessor. ALU = arithmetic logic unit; I/O = input/output.

lions of bytes (gigabytes) of RAM, and have a virtual memory address capacity in the trillions of bytes (e.g., Pentium II Processor addresses 64 terabytes). A comparison of some of the recent popular hardware configurations using the above microprocessors can be secured by visiting local computer stores or accessing the Web sites of major hardware and retail companies (e.g., Apple, IBM, Compaq, Dell, Gateway, Hewlett-Packard, CompUSA). As stated above, specifications for available and developing microprocessors can be found at http://www.ugeek.com/.

The memory section of the microprocessor system stores both programs and raw data. Processed data are also stored in memory in its altered form. Microcomputers generally use two kinds of memory systems. Working or primary memory is generally described as random access memory (RAM). RAM is individually addressable, which means each character or byte of information has its own address and can be located directly. Think of a bank of mailboxes in a post office and you will have a fair idea of what RAM is. Each box has its own address and can be accessed without disturbing any other box. In the case of RAM, each location contains a single piece of information. RAM is volatile, which means that data can be stored only as long as electrical power is applied to the memory circuit; if power is not maintained, the data stored in RAM are lost.

Read-only memory (ROM) permanently stores program data. Information needed over and over again, such as an operating system or an application program (e.g., word processing) can be permanently stored in ROM in the latest microcomputers; ROM memory cannot be erased or overwritten. Some ROM chips can be individually programmed, and they are called programmable read-only memory (PROM). A form of ROM that can be used many times is called erasable programmable read-only memory (EPROM).

Input/Output Devices

Input/output (I/O) devices are the components of the computer system that allow a user to command and control the processing of data. Input devices provide the means for the CPU or microprocessor to read data for processing, whereas output devices provide the end product, or outcome of processing, in a form specified by the user. These devices are controlled by the I/O controller described previously, which in turn is under the control of the operating system, which in turn is under the control of an application program loaded in memory. Although some devices function as either input or output mechanisms, some can function in both roles. Shelly and Cashman (1990) provided excellent discussions of the technical aspects and utility of these devices. Monthly technology magazines (e.g., *PC World* and *Macworld*) also have articles describing and evaluating these devices.

Keyboards

The device most frequently used to enter data is the keyboard, and the device most frequently

Assistive devices facilitate input. (Photograph by Carolyn F. Woods)

used to display information is the monitor or cathode ray tube (CRT). If a child were to push the 'A' key on the keyboard, the encoder chip within the keyboard circuit would transmit the binary coded decimal (BCD) representation of that letter in ASCII (American Standard Code for Information Interchange), or 01000001, to the CPU, where it is stored. The output section of the CPU would "instruct" the monitor or CRT to display a pattern of dots that the child would recognize as the letter that was typed. The letter would be placed next to the cursor, a visible symbol that indicates where on the monitor screen characters are to be displayed. In its simplest form, a keyboard is a typewriter-like device containing a set of keys for letters, numbers, and special characters. Some keyboards contain a 10-key numeric pad for fast data entry. Additionally, some keyboards contain function keys that can be programmed for special use when used with the appropriate software.

Many variations of the standard computer keyboard have been developed to meet the needs of individuals of different ages, abilities, and disabilities. *Large keyboards with a reduced number of input areas* work well for young children, and children who are mentally or physically challenged. They are particularly useful for programs that can be operated with only a few keys (see Chapters 1, 5, and 11). *Mini-keyboards,* which are versions of the standard keyboard compressed into a small unit, work well for individuals with a small range of motion or who operate a computer with one hand. *Ergonomically designed keyboards* are used to reduce keyboarding stress and fatigue (e.g., Microsoft's Natural Keyboard and PC Concepts' Mac Wave Keyboard).

Light Pens

Light pens are input devices used with specialized software to draw images in color directly on the display screen of the CRT. They can also be used by educators and exceptional individuals who have problems using the keyboard to run programs by pointing the light at objects or instructions on the monitor screen. For example, pointing the light at a picture of a trash basket will clear the screen and create a new file.

Graphics Tablets, Touchpads or Gridpads, and Touch Screens

Touch-sensitive controllers allow a user to (a) select shapes or specialized images from a palette using a stylus-like device, thus eliminating the need for the tedious and painstaking programming of shapes, or (b) move the cursor across the screen. The Koala Pad, by Koala Technologies, has been a very popular graphic device used with and by exceptional individuals to call up and run software programs. WACOM's Artpad II with its Ultra Pen is another such device for inputting information. Graphics tablets, like light pens, eliminate the need for using the keyboard to input data. Also, a number of external touchpads or gridpads, such as Crique's Easy Cat and Smart Cat Touchpads, can be used instead of a mouse to access and run programs. These devices are also being found in increasing numbers "bundled" on keyboards (e.g., PC Accessories' Ergo 107-Key Windows 95 Keyboard with Touchpad).

An interesting variation of the graphics tablet is the TouchWindow by Edmark Corporation. It is a transparent plastic screen that attaches to a computer monitor. Touching the screen with a finger will direct input to the computer. A variety of software has been written to be compatible with the TouchWindow. Command spots, such as answer selection or forward and back, must be visible on the monitor. When the person touches the screen, the command is executed. The Touch-Window is especially useful for young children who tend to look at their pointing finger while typing rather than at the screen and hence do not see the action performed. The TouchWindow allows them to look and see the result.

Optical Character Readers and Scanners

Optical character readers (OCRs) and scanners are input devices that can read hand-printed or typewritten characters directly into the memory of a computer. For example, a video camera at the end of the OCR translates letters into electrical impulses, which are then converted to an ASCII text file. These data can then be edited by most standard word processing programs. Sophisticated OCRs, such as the Reading Edge by Xerox Imaging Systems, Inc., recognize letters and numbers and have the ability to read the text back to the user in a synthesized voice. Different languages can be recognized when different memory cards are inserted into the device. Scanned documents can be transferred to a computer through a serial port, saved in memory, and edited. An OCR, which incorporates speech output, acts as a reading machine, thus expanding the access of students with disabilities (e.g., those who are blind) to a wide range of print materials not readily available on audiotape.

Flatbed and hand-held scanners, ranging in cost from $50 to $500, are also being used in increasing numbers to convert printed text and images as detailed as photographs to digital data (e.g., Mustek, Epson, and Hewlett Packard). The "lower end" devices use charge-coupled device (CCD) technology, whereas the expensive or "higher end" scanners use photomultiplier tube (PMT) technology (e.g., Optronics ColorGetters is a PMT desktop model; see http://www.com/mem/shop/fyiScanTechTech.html). In general, the factors that are considered when buying a scanner are cost, software included, paper size, scanning speed, resolution, and paper handling

(e.g., automatic document feeder). Scanners that permit the user to scan a variety of documents (e.g., color and black-and-white), that automatically enhance scanned images (e.g., eliminating jagged lines), and that retain the original formats of scanned documents in an application program (e.g., word processing) can promote personal and instructional productivity (e.g., Hewlett Packard ScanJet series—5100, 6100).

The Mouse

The mouse, invented by Xerox and popularized by Apple, has revolutionized the control and manipulation of text and graphics. The device is a ball held against a set of sensors, which convert relative motion into signals that control the screen position. A useful mouse adaptation, which is found on FastTRAP by Microspeed, Inc., uses a trackball in a box. The user moves the ball to emulate the mouse. Either the left or right button can be used to perform the "click" function. An important addition is the center button which toggles the "drag lock" feature, which eliminates having to hold down a key and move the trackball simultaneously. Altra's Felix is a variation of the trackball in that its base does not move but a "handle" moves within a 1-inch square to navigate the entire screen. Joysticks are another familiar input device that may more closely match the physical capabilities for some individuals.

The Single Switch

An important input device for many individuals with physical challenges and for young children is the single switch. A single switch usually works in concert with an onscreen keyboard and scanning software. The scanning software highlights the onscreen keyboard row by row. The user activates the switch when the desired row is reached. Then the computer scans the letters and symbols in that row one by one. The user activates the single switch when the desired letter or symbol is highlighted. If the user is operating a word processor, the letter is added to the text in the word processor window.

Single switches may take the form of large round buttons, various shaped toggle switches, squeeze switches, sip and puff switches, and eye gaze switches. Because the variety of single switches is almost endless, the ability to run a computer using a single switch has opened the world of computing to almost anyone who has control of a single muscle or muscle group. Chapters 5 and 11 provide additional information about switches.

The Monitor or CRT

The most common output device is the monitor, also known as the CRT. The CRT is a television-like device that can display upper- and lowercase letters and complex graphic displays, as well as special characters. Screen types include monochrome, color, plasma, and liquid crystal displays (LCD). Plasma and LCD are sometimes called flat panel display screens and are most often used as output devices for notebook-size computers because of their small size.

Whereas early screens displayed white characters on a black background, today's screen displays feature full video graphics array (VGA) color capable of displaying 256 colors and more. Modern systems use a memory- (bit-) mapped display that allows each pixel or dot on the monitor screen to have its own address in the computer's memory. Eight-bit color displays of 256 colors on screens using 640 × 480 pixel resolution are common, and 16-bit color for display of up to 32,768 colors can be obtained on monitors using 640 × 480 pixel resolution. With super video graphics array (SVGA) capability and an accelerated graphics card installed (24-bit at 1,280 × 1,024 pixels), the monitor (CRT) can display up to 16.7 million colors on Apple color monitors of up to 17 inches. IBM and compatible computers offer monitors that range in size from 14 inches to 21 inches, and large televisions are being used with some technology functions (e.g., Web TV).

The most advanced systems feature touch input, inverse video, flexible sizing of characters, boldfacing, scrolling, split screen images, paging, and the graphical user interface (GUI). The latest GUIs go beyond bit-mapped images to PostScript for image generation. The Power Macintosh Series and Performa Series using the Macintosh Operating System version 7.5 and above can use PostScript for image generation. Several new display technologies feature virtual image where the action moves from display to display in a multiple-screen setup.

Screen magnification programs, designed for individuals who are blind or have low vision have as their primary purpose the magnification of images on the standard computer screen (CRT). CloseView from Apple Computer, Inc., enlarges the screen image on a Macintosh from 2 to 16 times. Zoomtext from AI Squared provides similar magnification for DOS and Microsoft Windows environments. These screen magnification programs generally work with most application programs and enlarge all screen items, including text, command icons, and graphics.

The Printer

Another common output device is the printer. One type of printer, the *dot matrix,* uses a series of wires that, when pressed against a ribbon, cause small dots to be printed on a sheet of paper or acetate. The pattern of dots forms the desired letter or character. Operating under the control of appropriate software commands (a printer driver) embedded within an applications program, a dot matrix printer reproduces dots in the same fashion as the CRT. Initially thought to be good only for drafts, the modern dot matrix printer, using up to 24 wires in its print head, now provides low-cost, high-speed, high-quality output. Additional types of printers include the following:

1. *Ink jet printers* spray ink onto a page, producing a dense, high-quality image. Ink jet printers can also produce high-quality color graphics on acetate to create overhead transparencies.

2. *Laser printers* continue to be the latest innovation in microcomputer printer technology (Kehoe, 1992). Laser light is used to create high-quality images that rival those produced by conventional printing technologies. These

are by far the most used type of printers, not only in business applications, but also with personal and at-home printing needs.

3. *Plotters* use pens of different colors to create high-quality graphics output. Plotters are generally used in the production of business graphics.

Disk Drives

Computers need to access data as well as store it. Data may be in the form of a program needed to drive the computer, or in the form of information, such as in a small database needed by an application program already resident in memory. Processed data, likewise, need to be stored accurately and in a manner that facilitates rapid retrieval. The input/output device that performs this function is called the disk drive.

Disk drives made for personal computers are generally of two types. The most common uses a 3.5-inch "microfloppy" diskette that has a storage capacity of at least 1.4 million bytes (megabytes, or MB). Also available today is the external SuperDisk that can read and write to the 3.5-inch diskette as well as a 120-MB diskette. Greater storage capacity is achieved by use of a Winchester or hard disk system. Hard disks are sealed units that operate at a higher speed than do floppy drives and have a storage capacity of billions of bytes (gigabytes, or GB) of storage (e.g., Western Digital's 6.4-GB and larger hard drives). In addition to their vastly increased storage capacity, hard disks access data at significantly higher speeds than floppies, making them popular for users who need speed and large storage capacity. A number of different kinds of hard disk drives have been developed. The more recent designs feature removable disk cartridges and "streaming tape" devices whose purpose is to provide an inexpensive method of copying and storing large files for archival purposes.

Optical Disk Systems

The continuing innovations in hardware input and output devices and storage systems feature the use of optical disks similar in nature to those produced for the home video and audio markets. These include the videodisc, Compact Disc Read-Only Memory (CD-ROM), and the most recent innovation Digital Video (or Versatile) Disk (DVD). The advantages of optical disk systems include multimedia capabilities, speed of access, and storage capacity.

As described by Hofmeister and Thorkildsen (1993, pp. 87–89), the standard laser videodisc looks like a long-playing (LP) record and is shiny, white, and metallic in appearance. In "the laser reflective format, the player directs a low-power laser beam onto the disc surface, where it strikes either a tiny pit or the more reflective surface between the billions of pits etched in the surface" (p. 87). The videodisc stores the same type of information as videotape, but the user can access in one or two seconds any of the 54,000 individual, high-quality frames on one side of the disc. There are five levels or classifications for individual videodisc formats (Hofmeister & Thorkildsen, 1993):

- Level 0—These systems are linear players, have limited interactive capabilities, and function like videotape players and movie projectors.

- Level I—These systems have "quick frame access, still frame, and fast visual-scanning functions; two user-selectable audio channels; and chapter and picture stops" (p. 88).

- Level II—These systems "add the intelligence of an internal computer to the Level 1 functions. . . . Complex combinations of functions can then be conducted automatically or triggered by input through the player's control panel" (p. 88).

- Level III—These systems "consist of a videodisc player linked to a computer . . . [to allow] the simultaneous display of both computer- and videodisc-generated material. At Level III, the read, write, and storage functions of the computer are added" (p. 88).

- Level IV—These systems are distinguished "from a Level III system by the additional power of the computer software. If some type of artificial intelligence software is used, it is usually classified as Level IV, although there is considerable disagreement about the functions and components of a Level IV system" (pp. 88–89).

The introduction of compact disk optical-laser technology a few years ago—CD-ROM, WORM (Write Once, Read Many), and CD-R (Recordable)—has revolutionized computing. The 4.5-inch, shiny metallic CD discs use "microscopic pits on an aluminized layer of a polycarbonate disc" to store 650 MB of media (ROM text, graphics, sound, etc.) or the equivalent of 500 high-density 3.5-inch diskettes or 333,000 pages of text (see www.graycat.net/cdrom/Default.htm). The first-generation CD disk drive transfer speed was 150,000 bytes per second (150 KB), and this speed was subsequently doubled and then quadrupled so that CD drives can now be purchased that provide 6X to 50X access or transfer rate speed (e.g., 150 KB X 32 = 4,800 KB). These CD-ROM systems make it possible to store large programs (e.g., integrated programs such as Microsoft Office, Lotus SmartSuite, Corel Office, ClarisWorks) and libraries of data (e.g., an entire encyclopedia on one disc) and are radically changing the way information is delivered in many types of community and educational settings. The recent introduction of CD systems that both "read and write" (CD-R) also demonstrates the potential this technology holds for individuals with special needs and the merest glimpse of things to come (e.g., Hewlett Packard's external and internal SureStor CD-Writer Plus).

Currently, while computer users are just getting accustomed to CD-ROM or CD-R systems or have just upgraded to a faster CD drive (e.g., 32X), this technology is being replaced by digital video or versatile disc systems (DVD-Video for television and DVD-ROM, DVD-RAM, or DVD+RW for computers; DVD+RW is being "championed" by Hewlett-Packard and Sony among other companies—see Andrews, 1999). This optical disc system also uses microscopic pits and laser-beam technology—digital zeros and ones—to store media by arranging data in a spiral pattern from the outer edge to the inner edge of the DVD disc. Using two layers of data, one imposed on another, and changing the focus of the laser to read both levels, DVD-ROM discs will hold 4.7 to 17 GB whereas DVD-RAM, with its record and erase capability, will hold between 2.6 and 4 GB. As the cost for the evolving generations of DVD drive is dropping considerably to less than $400, new PC computer systems are being offered in retail stores and over the Internet/World Wide Web with these digital-optical drives (e.g., Compaq's Presario 4850, Micron's Millennia XKU), and higher end Macintosh computers (e.g., 600s, G3) can take advantage of available DVD systems (e.g., Elecede Technologies' CoolDVD DVD-ROM upgrade kit).

Modem

Another useful I/O device, the modem, translates digital information (i.e., ASCII data) into electrical waveforms that can be transmitted over telephone lines or broadcast over the air, and changes this analog data back into its original digital format at a remote receiving site. Modems transmit data at specific baud rates (bits per second); thus, a 28.8- or 33.6-baud modem (the current modems of most users engaging in telecommunications) allows communication at approximately 28,800 or 33,600 bits per second (Kpbs). Recent advances in technology have resulted in the development of modems for personal computers that transmit and receive data at approximately 56 K or Kpbs, and even faster modems and systems (e.g., 400 Kpbs Hughes' DirecPC) will be available as new technologies are developed (e.g., fiber-optic wiring, digital cable, the "Second Internet," satellite linkage).

Transmission of information to individuals with disabilities via modem is often preferred if the individual's workstation is equipped with the necessary input and output devices. It saves the steps of translating from text on paper to an accessible format, as well as the problems with platform incompatibility when exchanging disks. Similarly, for some individuals with disabilities, it is easier to send an electronic version of a document than to physically handle and mail printed text. Importantly, modems are the gateway to the information highway as well.

Speech Recognition and Synthesis

Perhaps the most fascinating development in I/O device technology has been in the area of speech recognition. Spoken words are actually used to direct the operation of the computer. It works as follows:

1. First, the spoken words are translated into digital components that are stored by the computer.

2. Next, using the appropriate software, these patterns of digitized speech are linked to particular program or operating system commands.

3. Finally, a system vocabulary is developed (up to several hundred words) that allows the user to command and control the computer and its peripheral devices.

The computer can also be used to transform words stored in memory into sound patterns that resemble human speech. The device that accomplishes this is called a speech synthesizer. This device works in the following manner:

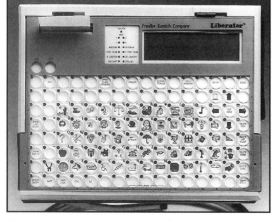

Computer systems can use symbols to represent words, sentences, or phrases. (Photograph courtesy of Prentke Romich Co. of Wooster, OH)

1. A program reads words stored in memory and translates combinations of letters into phonemes, which are then combined into sound.

2. Sophisticated software is used to make these sounds mirror human speech.

3. Application software lets each letter be sounded out individually or in combination with other letters to make words.

The capabilities of speech recognition systems have expanded dramatically. Early speech recognition systems allowed the user to give voice commands to operate the computer. Today's systems allow text and data to be entered using voice as well. Chapters 5 and 11 provide additional information concerning speech recognition and synthesis as they relate to exceptional individuals.

Assistive and Adaptive Technology

For individuals with specific disabilities or challenges, the growing availability of adaptive computer technology provides the opportunity for a quantum improvement in their quality of life (King, 1999). Adaptive devices are commonly grouped into three major categories: assistive devices, input devices, and output devices. As defined by the Center for Special Education Technology, assistive devices permit the user to complete specific tasks by modifying or bypassing the conventional method with an alternative method. Input devices provide modified or alternative methods of data entry into a computer or other microprocessor-based device. Output devices provide modified or alternative methods of receiving information from a computer or other microprocessor-based device. Assistive devices include the following:

1. Environmental control systems that transmit computer information over distance without wires. These devices permit persons with physical disabilities to control lamps,

appliances, telephones, door openers, and call systems. These systems are often used at home or work, but their potential for use in classrooms has not been explored to any great degree.

2. Electronic communication and writing aids that allow people who cannot speak clearly to communicate by inputting messages into a computer or recording device, which then plays the message on command, converts the message into synthesized speech, or displays the message as text. These devices are usually portable so the person can use them at home, in school, and in the community.

Adaptive input devices include the following:

1. Among others, sip-and-puff switches, eye movement and eye gaze systems, head movement systems, manual switches, light-sensitive systems, movement- or voice-activated systems, and pressure-sensitive systems.

2. Modifications to adjust command sequences so that typical two- or three-key simultaneous commands can be entered sequentially. These programs also allow the user to turn off or adjust the timing on the repeat key feature to avoid the repetition of a single key if it is held too long. Many of these adaptations are "bundled" with new computers to support or provide access as required by accessibility requirements of federal and state legislation (e.g., the Americans with Disabilities Act of 1990).

3. Keyboard emulating interfaces (KEIs) to enable a communication board or alternate keyboard to communicate effectively with a computer. When the device is designed to operate with an industry standard protocol, it can be plugged into a standard KEI, which is then plugged into a computer much like a standard keyboard. A useful feature in an educational environment is the ability to daisy chain input devices so that the standard keyboard and mouse as well as the adaptive input device are functional at the same time. This allows teacher and student or two students with differing input needs to work cooperatively at the computer.

4. Voice-input devices to permit the user to issue verbal commands and input text and data by voice rather than manually inputting the commands.

Adaptive output devices include the following:

1. Screen magnification software and hardware products to magnify the image on a standard computer screen. Magnification software such as CloseView from Apple Computer magnifies the screen from 2 to 16 times. Transparent magnifying screens can be attached to the face of the computer monitor to magnify text.

2. Voice-output screen readers to translate standard software screens to speech. This technology is beneficial for those who are blind or visually impaired. Many students with learning disabilities benefit as well by having the text read aloud.

3. Reading machines combine to translate the printed word through an optical recognition system (OCR) into a synthesized voice. Sophisticated systems can save this translation on tape for later listening. This system has been effectively used to translate required classroom readings into a form that can be studied and reviewed immediately or at a later time. OCR translations can also be transmitted to a computer, where they can be accessed via a standard word processor.

4. Telecommunications devices for the deaf (TDDs) to permit individuals who are deaf to communicate over the telephone. A TDD consists of three components: a typewriter-like keyboard, a telephone modem, and a readout display that shows the messages. In the past, a TDD was required by both parties attempting to communicate by phone. Telephone companies now provide operators who translate TDD messages to voice messages and vice versa when only one party possesses a TDD. This service allows educators to more easily communicate with parents who are deaf.

5. Computerized embosser printers to produce hard braille copies for the blind. The refreshable braille display is the newest innovation

in this area. Usually a rectangular device, the refreshable braille display has small pins that raise and lower electronically to form braille characters. The user moves a hand along the characters to read them. Then the next line of text is created, hence the term refreshable braille.

The devices described represent the beginning of an exciting period of growth in the field. As understanding of the human body increases and computer technology advances, the marriage between the human body and sophisticated computer-like devices will evolve (e.g., bionic limbs, artificial eyes). The last few years have witnessed explosive growth in the development of assistive devices and adaptive input and output devices.

Advances in processing speed and memory capabilities have promoted this explosive growth. Advances revolve around the integration of various input/output (I/O) and functional capabilities. For example, voice-input devices combined with word-prediction software capabilities allow the user to speak a single letter, view a numbered list of words that begin with that letter, choose the needed word by speaking a number, and have the word inserted in text on the word processor. This capability can expand the vocabulary recognized by the voice recognition systems and make it accessible to some individuals whose speech was too unreliable for such systems in the past.

Portability and durability are also important features of assistive technology, particularly when it is used to support communication. Devices are becoming smaller, lighter weight, and more durable. These are important features in educational environments with children. As understanding of the functional needs of children in educational environments increases and computer technology advances, the marriage between learning needs and sophisticated assistive technologies will evolve.

Assistive technology concepts are discussed in Chapters 5, 10, 11, and 12. Additional information concerning these devices can also be found in the printed resources and on the Internet and World Wide Web sites identified in this book (e.g., access http://www.aces.k12ct.us/~crocker/ats/index.htm). Needs First is also an excellent

interactive database program to determine available augmentative communication systems (http://www.coexpectional.com/needsffirst.html).

Computer Networking

When one combines elements of two or more computer systems (e.g., personal computers, workstations, minicomputers, mainframe computers), communications devices, and specialized storage and output devices, the resultant system is called a network. Basically three types of networks have been used in recent years:

1. The *star network* generally consists of a host CPU (generally a minicomputer) to which several terminals or personal computers are connected (see Figure 2.3).

2. A *ring network* consists of three or more computers arranged in a circular configuration (see Figure 2.4). Ring networks are useful in situations where it is necessary for each unit in an organization to do its own data processing yet desirable for these departments to update each other's files through direct computer-to-computer communication.

3. The *bus network* consists of two or more computers or peripherals that share a common line of communication (see Figure 2.5). Bus networks are most commonly used in local area networks (LANs).

Star networks are generally used in schools to provide a low-cost, time-sharing environment. In such a system, students use dedicated terminals to access computer-assisted instruction (CAI) modules or to learn computer programming. The advantages of these systems include the ability to share files, programs, secondary storage, and complex peripherals such as high-speed printers and plotters. A number of school systems have computerized school libraries, thus providing the means to conduct automated bibliographic searches.

The linking of minicomputers and mainframe computers in ring networks has been of great benefit to school administrators, who as a result have the power of distributed data processing. This

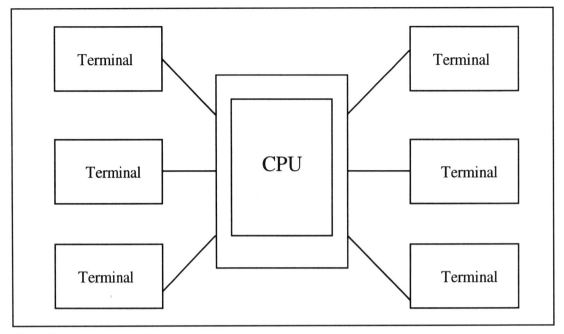

Figure 2.3. A star network.

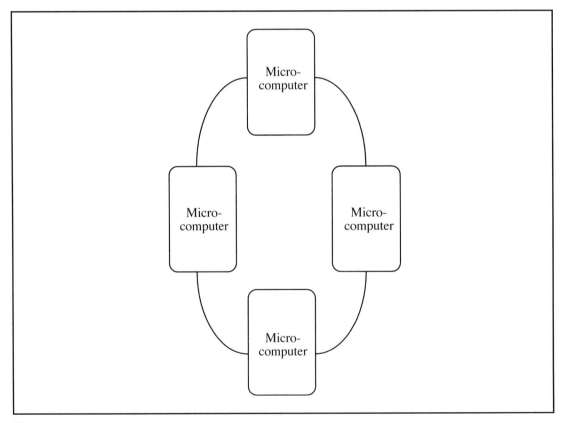

Figure 2.4. A ring network.

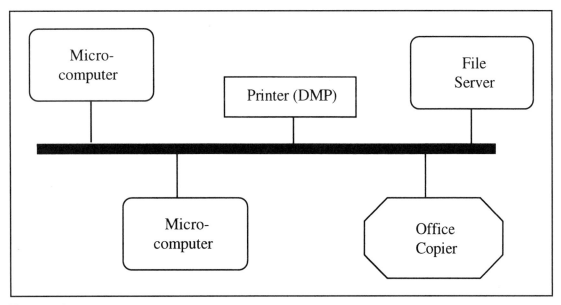

Figure 2.5. A bus network.

kind of networking provides more computing power than could be provided by a single unit. Systems of this kind are used for the processing and storage of student records, database management, and electronic mail. Some state education departments have developed extensive systems for sending to and receiving from local educational units important information electronically. The actual processing of data occurs in steps at each distribution level, making the power of the system greater than that of any single computer.

Microcomputers can be linked together to share expensive peripherals, such as plotters, printers, and modems. The bus network or communications system that makes this possible is the local area network (LAN). An example of a modern LAN is the Ethernet system, which allows microcomputers to communicate directly with each other and with peripherals, mainframes, other LANs, and "intelligent" office equipment. Ethernet is only a hardware transport technology, as are token bus, token ring, and PCnet. As a matter of fact, Novell Netware, a popular LAN software, is available for each of the above transport technologies.

A number of companies (e.g., Apple, IBM, and 3M) currently produce LANs for microcomputers. Computer networks provide the means to share information electronically. With a personal computer and a modem, a user can communicate with agencies that provide information about the latest technology and career opportunities through an electronic bulletin board. The electronic bulletin board also provides the means for people with disabilities to communicate among themselves and with others.

Consumer Hardware Information

The growth of microcomputer applications for individuals with special needs has been spectacular, and the end is nowhere in sight. Those responsible for the selection and purchase of these devices need to choose wisely and to expend scarce funds only after all alternatives have been carefully weighed. The following steps should be considered in the selection and purchase of computer equipment:

1. *Define need.* Try to assess what your mission is and what computer resources are actually needed to accomplish it. What do you intend to do with the equipment you purchase? Because

people tend to support what they create, involve a broad spectrum of parents, students (whenever possible), and professionals in the needs assessment process.

2. *Assess performance.* After specifying the features of the system you require, secure demonstration units from competing vendors, and test each system thoroughly before committing your school district to an expensive purchase. Determine the availability of specialized software and consider system expansion. Can the system grow with your needs? Choose carefully; you and your students may have to live with your choice for some time.

3. *Provide maintenance.* The more complicated the device, the more apt it will be to experience a malfunction. Your school system must have the in-house capability of making timely repairs. The increased emphasis on interoperability and connectivity to accomplish educational goals, coupled with more sophisticated systems and more reliance on software solutions, means that dramatic new strains are placed on support systems, particularly in-house support systems. If your school system does not have the resources to support its hardware, the vendor you choose must be able to assure timely repairs. Additionally, the vendor should be available (and able) to answer questions regarding the operation of the equipment purchased. The selection of a vendor is at least as important as the selection of the equipment itself. Remember, the most advanced device is useless if it cannot be supported in the field. You should also be keenly aware of the fact that software support requires considerably more education and training than does hardware support.

4. *Provide feedback.* Because of the rapid developments taking place in this field, professionals are in the unique position of being able to effect change. Make every effort to provide vendors with assessments of how their equipment performs and what changes you deem desirable. They do listen.

Maximizing the effective performance of computer systems involves taking into account who will be using the equipment and the circumstances under which it will be operated. The following suggestions in the design, selection, and evaluation of hardware systems may be helpful:

1. *Purchase quality.* Because students are hard on equipment, it pays to buy industrial- or commercial-grade equipment. Although it might be politically expedient to purchase more units of a lower quality brand, the long-term cost of expensive maintenance (not to mention downtime) will negate the initial allure of a low purchase price. Quality is cheaper in the long run.

2. *Try before you buy.* Purchase plug-compatible equipment. Because of the special needs of your clientele, many unique configurations of equipment will be engineered by imaginative professionals. Care should be taken to ensure that specialized keyboards, CRTs, CPUs, and voice units adhere to the same I/O standards. What will work with an Apple or IBM may not work with a look-alike clone. Try before you buy.

3. *Prepare the user.* Take steps to provide a receptive professional environment for the introduction of these new devices. Because new technology often requires realignments and adjustments in professional role relationships, the intelligent consumer will create an administrative climate that supports innovation and change.

Notebook computers can have speech synthesis capabilities. (Photograph courtesy of Humanware)

4. *Provide education and training.* Professionals, students, and parents need education about the purposes of various technologies and they need ongoing training in their use. Without this education and training, devices will be underused or quickly discarded when frustrations arise.

5. *Get a second opinion.* Get objective opinions from outside experts when evaluating the purchase of complicated and expensive systems. Although the local staff usually has the experience and expertise to make a reasoned decision, there is merit in seeking the advice of a disinterested third party.

6. *Check out the manufacturer.* Make every attempt to purchase equipment from manufacturers who have the financial resources to support the equipment they sell. A number of school districts and agencies throughout the United States made unwise short-term decisions and now possess inventories of equipment that must be cannibalized for maintenance.

Intelligent consumers are an asset to any school district or agency fortunate enough to have them on their staff. The ability to delineate hardware strengths and weaknesses, design and conduct hardware needs assessment, and purchase and maintain essential equipment are important professional skills that modern educators must possess. Hardware consumer issues relating to exceptional individuals are discussed throughout the remaining chapters.

Summary

In this chapter we have provided an overview of the concepts necessary to appreciate and understand how a computer functions and have described frequently used devices. We presented some practical suggestions to aid users in the selection of computer systems. Because the computer hardware field is constantly changing, studying the latest journals, attending the appropriate conferences, and reading the news every day are important. General and special educators, other professionals, and exceptional individuals who are willing to master the general concepts of computer technology will be able to communi-

cate their operational needs to hardware designers. The synergy developed from such a partnership will lead to a dazzling array of devices that will magnify the human potential of children, youths, and adults who have disabilities or are gifted and talented.

Resources

Organizations

ABLEDATA
National Rehabilitation Information Center
4407 Eighth Street NE
Catholic University
Washington, DC 20017
Web: http://www.abledata.com/index.htm

Apple Special Education Division
Apple Computer
20525 South 36M
Cupertino, CA 95014
Web: http://www.apple.com/disability/welcome.html

Association for Special Education Technology (ASET)
P.O. Box 152
Allen, TX 75002-0152
(No internet address available)

Council for Exceptional Children/Information Center for Special Education Technology
1290 Association Drive
Reston, VA 22091-1589
Web: http://www.cec.sped.org

IBM National Support Center for Persons with Disabilities
P.O. Box 2150
Atlanta, GA 30055
Web: http://www.ibm.com

IBM/Special Needs Exchange
c/o LINC Resources
P.O. Box 434
Pawtucket, RI 02862
Web: http://www.link.org

National Center to Improve Practice in Special Education Through Technology, Media and Materials (NCIP)

Education Development Center, Inc.
55 Chapel Street
Newton, MA 02158-1060
Web: http://www.edc.org/FSC/NCIP

Journals

Bulletin of Science and Technology for the Handicapped. This quarterly newsletter describes recent computer advances for handicapped persons. *Contact:* American Association for the Advancement of Science, 1776 Massachusetts Avenue, Washington, DC 20036.

Catalyst. This bimonthly newsletter covers a variety of special education computer topics such as software, hardware, and pertinent regulations. *Contact:* Western Center for Microcomputers in Special Education, Suite 275, 1259 El Camino Real, Menlo Park, CA 94025.

Closing the Gap. This compact bimonthly newspaper provides information about microcomputer programs and devices that help handicapped individuals close the gap between themselves and the rest of society. The organization that publishes it, also named Closing the Gap, has a database of in-depth information on software producers, products, practices, and procedures; a comprehensive text on practices and procedures is also available. One issue of the newsletter is a directory covering producers, products, practices, and procedures related to technology and individuals with disabilities. *Contact:* Closing the Gap, P.O. Box 68, Henderson, MN 56044.

Journal of Special Education Technology. The purpose of this journal is to provide a vehicle for the proliferation of information, research, and reports of innovative practices regarding the application of educational technology toward the development and education of exceptional children. The journal is published four times a year and is sponsored by the Technology and Media Division of the Council for Exceptional Children.

Books

Barta, B., Telem, M., & Gev, Y., (Eds.). (1995). *Information technology in educational management.* New York: Chapman and Hall.

Baschman, E. (Ed.). (1995). *The electronic classroom: A handbook for education in the electronic environment.* Medford, NJ: Information Today.

Beynon, J., & Mackay, H. H. (1993). *Computers into classrooms: More questions than answers.* Washington, DC: Falmer Press.

Bollough, R. V. (1991). *Classroom applications of microcomputers* (2nd ed.). New York: Merrill.

Brierley, B., & Kemble, I. (1991). *Computers as a tool in language teaching.* New York: E. Horwood.

Brownell, G. (1992). *Computers and teaching* (2nd ed.). St. Paul, MN: West Publishing.

DeCorte, E. (1992). *Computer-based learning environments and problem solving.* New York: Springer Verlag.

Finch, C. R. (1993). *Curriculum development in vocational and technical education: Planning, content, and implementation.* Needham Heights, MA: Allyn & Bacon.

Hoschka, P. (Ed.). (1996). *Computers as assistants: A new generation of support systems.* Mahwah, NJ: Erlbaum.

Jonassen, D. H. (1996). *Computers in the classroom: Mindtools for critical thinking.* Englewood Cliffs, NJ: Merrill.

Lindsey, J. D. (1993). *Computers and exceptional individuals* (2nd ed.). Austin, TX: PRO-ED.

Male, M. (1994). *Teaching for inclusion: Meeting the special needs of all students* (2nd ed.). Needham Heights, MA: Allyn & Bacon.

Perkins, D. N. (Ed.). (1995). *Software goes to school: Teaching for understanding with new technologies.* New York: Oxford University Press.

Rawlins, G. (1996). *Moths to the flame: The seductions of computer technology.* Cambridge, MA: MIT Press.

Shofield, J. W. (1995). *Computers and classroom culture.* New York: Cambridge University Press.

Sewell, D. (1990). *New tools for new minds: A cognitive perspective on the use of computers with young children.* New York: St. Martin's Press.

Assistive or Adaptive Devices

Information about assistive and adaptive devices can be secured following the procedures recommended in Chapter 1 or by contacting companies identified in this book. This information can also be found by using a search directory or engine to issue the following subject in the search field: *Hardware + Assistive* or *Hardware (Assistive)*.

Other information can be obtained through the following World Wide Web addresses:

Adaptive/Assistive Technology Resources
Web: http://www.nchrtm.okstate.edu

ATEN Manufacturer's List
Web: http://www.aten.com

Needs First
Web: http://www.coexceptinal.com/needsfirst.html

Prentke Romich Company
Web: http://www.prentrom.com

Special Education Resources on the Internet
Web: http://www.hood.edu/seri/me.htm

Zygo Industries
Web: http://www.zygo-usa.com

Laboratory–Practicum Activities

▶ 1. List three goals you will achieve in the next 3 months to enhance your technology hardware knowledge. Use technology to develop your goals, to describe how you will achieve these goals, and to manage the achievement of the goals.

▶ 2. Contact the computer manufacturers listed in Appendix I and ask to be placed on their mailing lists. At the end of this course, provide your instructor and peers with a report of the responses you received from your contacts.

▶ 3. Access the Web site for one of the computer vendors listed above and one of the on-line computer stores (e.g., http://www.pcmall.com or http://www.comp usa.com). Describe the advantages and disadvantages these Web sites offer for securing information about the computer systems offered.

▶ 4. Compare and contrast the use of word processing on a desktop computer and on a Personal Digital Assistant (PDA). If called upon, what would you recommend to professionals who are thinking about having their students or clients use a PDA for word processing?

▶ 5. Compare and contrast a computer network at your university or college and in a local school or agency. Use technology to record and provide your findings to your course instructor and peers.

▶ 6. Engage in word processing activities on an older and a newer PC (e.g., 8086 or 8088 vs. Pentium II 333+ MHz) and on an Apple IIe (or c or gs) and a Macintosh PowerPC (604e or G3). Describe the "speeds" of the older and newer systems.

▶ 7. Write to the manufacturers of computer-assisted devices and ask to be placed on their mailing lists. Use the information they send you and the descriptions in this text to create your own file of adaptive devices.

▶ 8. Visit a special education classroom or setting that uses computers and computer-assisted devices. Interview the teacher and (if possible) the students concerning the utility and effectiveness of these devices. Prepare a brief oral report of your findings.

▶ 9. Visit a school or agency that has different hardware systems and compatible adaptive devices. Have someone temporarily disable you (e.g., bind your arms, blindfold you, place a gag over your mouth) and then try to learn to use some of these devices.

References

Americans with Disabilities Act of 1990, 42 U.S.C. § 12101 *et seq.*

Andrews, D. (1999, February). Fast, vast, and rewritable DVD-RAM finally arrive. *PC World*, pp. 62–64.

Campbell-Kelly, M., & Aspray, W. (1996). *Computer: A history of the information machine.* New York: Basic Books.

Cook, W. J. (1998, February 16). Men in blue. *U.S. News and World Report*, pp. 45–49.

Desmond, M. (1999, February). Your PC in the new millennium. *PC World*, pp. 104–116.

Glitman, R. (1992). Pen PCs: Mission—critical note takers that return to basics. *PC World, 10*(1), 89–90.

Heid, J., & Snyder, B. (1998, January). Processors leap ahead. *PC World*, pp. 58–62.

Hofmeister, A., & Thorkildsen, R. (1993). Interactive videodisc and exceptional individuals. In J. D. Lindsey (Ed.), *Computers and exceptional individuals* (2nd ed., pp. 87–107). Austin, TX: PRO-ED.

Howard, B. (1998). High-end notebooks. *PC Magazine, 17*(2), 100–151.

Johnson, L. B. (199la). Computing with a pen. *PC Today, 5*(10), 8–10.

Johnson, L. B. (1991b). Taking the computer industry by the hand: Options in hand held computing. *PC Today, 5*(9), 8–13.

Kehoe, D. M. (1992). A laser on every desk. *PC World, 10*(4), 118–133.

King, T. W. (1999). *Assistive technology: Essential human factors*. Needham Heights, MA: Allyn & Bacon.

Landau, T. (1999, March). Sherlock powering searching. *Macworld*, pp. 89–91.

Lewis, R. B. (1993). *Special education technology: Classroom applications*. Pacific Grove, CA: Brooks/Cole.

Lindsey, J. D. (Ed.). (1987). *Computers and exceptional individuals*. Columbus, OH: Merrill.

Lindsey, J. D. (Ed.). (1993). *Computers and exceptional individuals* (2nd ed.). Austin, TX: PRO-ED.

New chip introduced. (1998, March 5). Business briefs by the Associated Press. *The Advocate*, p. 2D.

Shelly, G., & Cashman, T. J. (1990). *Computer fundamentals for an information age*. Brea, CA: Anaheun.

Shurkin, J. N. (1996). *Engines of the mind: The evolution of the computer from mainframes to microprocessors*. New York: Norton Press.

Chapter 3

The Software Domain

James H. Wiebe
California State University, Los Angeles

If hardware consists of the physical components of the computer—the plastic, metal, wire, and silicon parts and peripherals discussed in Chapter 2—then what is software? The term *software* may conjure up images of the less durable products used with computers, such as paper or floppy diskettes. Software actually is a set of instructions (programs) written in BASIC, C++, Pascal, machine language, or some other code that a computer can understand and execute, and is sold in a package. A software package typically consists of a box containing a set of 3.5-inch program diskettes or a CD-ROM (Compact Disk Read-Only Memory) or a DVD-ROM (Digitial Video [or Versatile] Disc Read-Only Memory), a reference manual, and often a tutorial manual and/or programs. In this chapter I discuss the spectrum of software available for use by professionals and exceptional persons. Except where noted, all software titles discussed are available in both Windows and Macintosh versions. While thinking about or taking steps to secure the latest computer or peripherals (e.g., second, third, or later generation DVD drives), potential buyers should keep in mind that "hardware remains a step ahead of software" (Andrews, 1998, p. 208) so the specific program desired for state-of-the-art hardware may not yet be available.

Software is soft because it is nonpermanent—it is stored in RAM, the nonpermanent portion of a computer memory. A set of instructions placed in the computer's random access memory (RAM) may be deleted simply by turning the computer off, by loading another program into memory, or by using a computer command to clear memory.

A computer without software is like an artist's empty canvas. The artist can turn the blank canvas into anything from a line drawing to a colorful abstract or an impressionistic landscape. Likewise, software can turn the computer into an accounting tool, a machine for teaching French, an arcade game, or a machine that keeps track of a student's progress through a set of objectives. Software allows a computer to recognize and act upon spoken commands, monitor brain signals to activate artificial limbs, or read text from a book and print the braille equivalent. The possibilities are endless.

A Historical Perspective

Software programs stored on 3.5-inch diskettes, CD-ROMs, and DVD-ROMs are relatively new additions to computer technology. When the first

Software availability and libraries are increasing. (Photograph by Carolyn F. Woods)

computer was invented (see Appendix B), instructions were given by changing the wiring on what looked like a telephone operator's switchboard. Later, instructions were given to computers by cards with holes punched in them. The holes in the cards represented a language the computer could understand—binary code. Programming a computer in binary code was an extremely difficult and tedious task. Eventually, someone realized that programming could be made simpler by developing an intermediate language between English (or German, French, etc.) and the computer's machine language (i.e., the language built into a computer by the manufacturer). The first types of software were programs that translated between high-level (English-like) programming commands and machine language. Appendix C presents descriptions and examples of computer languages.

Early computers had to be specifically programmed by the user for each task that users wanted to accomplish. The applications programs of today, such as word processing, statistical packages, and spreadsheets, had not yet been invented. A person who wanted a software program to keep track of company sales or inventory wrote, or hired someone to write, a COBOL (Common Business Oriented Language) program to accomplish the task. In the 1950s and 1960s, companies such as IBM produced and sold applications programs for their computers so the users would not have to write their own programs. In the late 1950s and early 1960s, third-party software developers, such as Computer Science Corporation, began to create programs for computers sold by other companies, and a new industry was born (*Software*, 1985).

Now tens of thousands of programs and software packages are available for almost every imaginable use. These programs range from essential, nonglamorous tools such as operating systems, to general-purpose tools such as word processors, to highly specific programs such as educational games or programs that allow professionals to generate Individualized Education Plans (IEPs). The publishers of these programs range from Fortune 500 companies (e.g., Microsoft Corporation, IBM) to large educational software corporations

(e.g., Sunburst) to professionals who produce and sell a single product out of their home.

System Software

Before microcomputers came upon the scene more than 20 years ago, a person who wanted to run a computer program or analyze a set of data wrote out lines of code on paper, took them to a keypunch machine and prepared cards, and then carried the cards to the person who operated the computer. The operator stacked the cards into a card reader and punched a series of buttons on the control monitor that caused the cards to be fed into the card reader. The holes on the cards were translated into electrical impulses that the computer could understand, and the computer program was executed.

Operating Systems

Now computers come complete with software that serves the function of the computer operator—the operating system (e.g., Mac OS; see Pogue, 1999). Operating systems, a series of housekeeping programs provided by the computer manufacturer, allow the computer to function. The operating system allows the user to move a mouse to make choices on the screen, receive and process input from the keyboard, load and run programs, save programs, activate a printer, copy disks, rename programs, and perform many more functions. For example, when the user points to an icon representing a program and double-clicks with a mouse, it is the operating system that recognizes this command, retrieves the program from the disk, and gets it going.

In the early days of personal computers, 1977 to 1982, each manufacturer developed its own operating system. The problem was that programs written for an Apple computer would not run on a Commodore, Radio Shack, or Atari, and vice versa. Control Program for Microcomputers (CP/M) was the first successful operating system developed to be used on a variety of computers. Then IBM entered the market with the IBM PC, and other computer makers started using IBM's operating system. As a result, the IBM operating system, PC-DOS (called MS-DOS on other systems, now just called DOS), became the industry standard for the majority of computers sold in the 1980s and early 1990s. Currently, major operating systems are Windows 95 or higher, Windows NT, UNIX, Linux, and the Macintosh Operating System (OS). However, by the time you read this book, the next version of Windows—2000—and the higher level and more powerful version of Macintosh OS—Rhapsody—could be on the shelf and installed on new computers.

Operating systems are a major factor in determining whether a given piece of software will run on a given computer. Even when computers are somewhat different internally, such as Dell and Compaq computers, they will be able to run the same software if and when they share a common operating system. Even Intel, AMD, and Cyrix processor-based computers (computers that run the Windows operating system) and Macintoshes

can be made to run the same programs if they share (or simulate) the same operating system. For example, SoftWindows and SoftWindows 95 (Insignia Solutions) is software that allows Macintosh computers to run Windows software, and SoftWindows 95 is Internet ready with Microsoft's Web browser Internet Explorer.

Graphical User Interfaces

An important part of modern operating systems is the graphical user interface (GUI), which allows computer users to use pull-down menus, scroll bars, icons, buttons, dialog boxes, and so on, to interact with the computer (see Figure 3.1). Prior to the GUI, computer users had to learn to use a variety of arcane commands, such as "copy a:*.* c:\wp50\group5" to use computers. Before GUIs, it was generally accepted that only technically sophisticated or experienced computer users (e.g., technologists, scientists, business professionals)

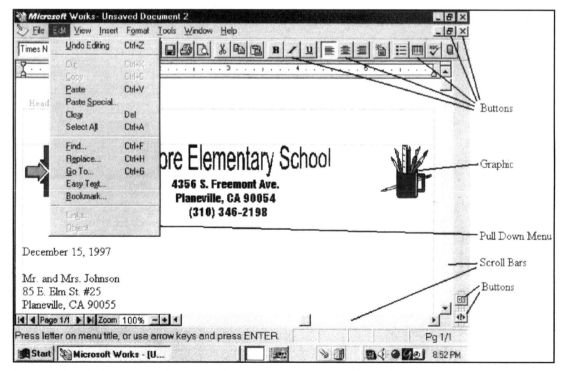

Figure 3.1. Word processing edit commands for Microsoft Works 4.0 for Windows 95.

could use computers. Since GUIs, it is generally accepted that anyone can use computers.

The GUI was invented by the Xerox Palo Alto Research Center (Xerox PARC) in the late 1970s. It was first implemented on microcomputers by Apple Corporation with the Lisa Computer in 1983. It finally became widely accepted and used when Apple came out with the Macintosh computer a year later. It took longer for the GUI to become standard in the IBM-compatible world. After a couple of attempts to add GUI capabilities to DOS, Microsoft was finally successful with the widespread acceptance of Windows 3.0 in the late 1980s. Shortly after its introduction, Windows became the standard operating system for the vast majority of computers sold worldwide. Windows NT is another version of Windows that is used in business and educational settings to run networks and World Wide Web sites, and to run high-end business applications.

One of the most important benefits of Windows, as with the Macintosh operating system, is that different programs have a similar set of commands and techniques for accomplishing particular tasks (e.g., getting a printout). Thus, the learning curve is significantly reduced when a person needs to learn to use a new kind of program, because the strategies learned with one application will be similar on another. Also, because all GUIs are similar, moving from one platform (e.g., a Macintosh) to another (e.g., a Windows machine) is easy.

Programming Languages

The language computers understand is binary code (e.g., 00111110, 0011010). To complicate matters further, each major class of computer has its own, unique machine language. A program written for an Apple II computer in its machine language will not work on a Gateway computer because they have different types of machine languages. Higher level programming languages were developed in part to solve this problem. FORTRAN, for example, is virtually the same on all machines. To run a program in FORTRAN, the computer user simply uses a specific interpreter or compiler to translate FORTRAN into the machine language a particular computer understands.

Higher level programming languages were also designed to allow a human to give instructions to computers in commands that more closely resemble human language than binary code. They consist of statements like *print, repeat,* and *call.* Typically, the instructions for translating these high-level, English-like commands into machine language are contained on disk and are loaded into the computer just like any other program. Thus, programming languages like PC LOGO, Visual BASIC, or C++ are sold as packages by software vendors, much like other software packages. Programming languages are used by professional software developers to create other software packages—word processors, communications packages, and computer-based instruction.

Before the widespread existence of software packages, programming languages were extensively taught in schools. Seymour Papert (1980), among other proponents of teaching programming to students, argued that learning to program gives students ultimate power over the capabilities of computers, allowing them to use computers as tools to explore mathematics and other subjects. Papert and his colleagues at the Artificial Intelligence Laboratory at the Massachusetts Institute of Technology developed the programming language, LOGO, specifically for children. LOGO has been used widely in Grades K through 8 and in special education (e.g., Jones, 1996), and the first edition of this book had a chapter on LOGO (see Bull, Lough, & Cochran, 1989). BASIC is a widely available language that is often taught to students in middle and high school computer literacy courses. A form of BASIC is also used to program calculators frequently used in high school mathematics classes. Pascal and C++ are the programming languages taught in computer science classes at the high school and college levels. With the huge increase in the number and variety of software packages available for classroom use, the teaching of computer programming has declined substantially in recent years in relation to other uses of computers, especially in Grades K through 8. Also, the educational benefits of learning to program have been strongly questioned by some educators (e.g., Wiburg & Carter, 1994).

Application Software

The largest segment of the software market at present comprises programs designed to organize or manage functions at work, in the home, or at school. These software programs turn computers into smart typewriters, calculators, filing systems, or communication devices and have changed the way people do business. They are also making an impact on the way students are taught, particularly individuals with disabilities, gifts, and talents; the way subject matter is presented; and the way classrooms are managed. The seven categories of applications software that can be used by educators and exceptional individuals include word processors, desktop publishers, spreadsheets, database managers, communications programs, graphics, integrated software packages, and multimedia development tools.

Word Processors

Word processing software turns a computer into a smart typewriter, allowing educators and exceptional persons to enter text, format it, and make editorial or format changes. The user may cut and paste, moving parts of text from one paragraph to another location, or search for and replace sequences of letters or words. Most important, text produced can be saved on disk and recalled at any time to make additions or changes.

The possibilities for using word processors in education with or by exceptional individuals are endless. Professionals may use them to correspond, plan lessons, develop examinations, generate IEPs, or produce student worksheets. Combined with database managers, spreadsheets, and/or graphics programs, word processing software also can be used to prepare evaluation reports that include data about class projects and students' achievements. Exceptional students and adults can gather data and write up the results of a scientific experiment or write a short story with a word processor. Students tend to be more enthusiastic about rewriting and editing their work when using word processors for writing assignments than when they write using pencil and paper, although the overall quality of students' writing does not appear to change when students use a word processor (Daiute, 1985).

Many word processing packages are available for every type of computer, ranging from inexpensive programs with few features to powerful programs with many features. Standard features most users expect in a modern word processor include the ability to insert or overwrite text, move text around within the document, insert footers and headers, number pages, find and replace words or other sequences of characters, underline, center, change margins, change spacing in the text, check spelling, and use a built-in thesaurus. Word processors created for Windows and Macintosh computers will have the ability to insert pictures, use a large variety of type styles and sizes, put borders around and shade blocks of text for emphasis, divide pages into columns, and so on. For a detailed discussion of the features of a particular word processor, consult the documentation or advertising brochures for the package and the reviews that appear in computer journals when the package is released.

The list of word processors and their features is far too long and complex to discuss here. Among the more important word processors for business use and serious writers are WordPerfect (Corel), Microsoft Word (Microsoft), and Word Pro (Lotus). For general classroom and home use, the most important word processors are the word processing subprograms of such integrated programs as Microsoft Works and Office (Microsoft), SmartSuite and Corel Suite (Corel), and ClarisWorks (Claris). It should be noted that these integrated programs also contain spreadsheets; database managers; and graphic, presentation, and/or communications components.

A number of "older" and new-generation versions of stand-alone word processors can be used by and with exceptional children and youths. These user-friendly processors include Bank Street Writer (Scholastic), HomeWord Plus (Sierra

On-Line), Dr. Peet's Talk/Writer (Hartley), and Snoopy Writer (American School Publishers). These programs are being replaced by word processors that are somewhat powerful (e.g., The Learning Company's The Student Writing Center has a 100,000-word spell checker and 660,000-word thesaurus; Hartley's Write This Way has a 50,000-word dictionary), have some desktop publishing features (e.g., Brøderbund's The Amazing Writing Machine), and offer multisensory experiences (e.g., Hartley's Write This Way; The Learning Company's Read, Write, and Type!). Degnan and Hummel (1985) and Thormann (1995) have published excellent articles on using word processing programs with exceptional students.

Earlier stand-alone word processors had limited if any capabilities in checking the grammar and style of the text produced. When using these programs, users may be able to locate spell and grammar checkers (e.g., WordPerfect's Grammatik, WordStar's Correct Grammar, and Rightsoft/Que's RightWriter).

Desktop Publishers

Desktop publishing programs are specialized word processors that allow the user to design newsletters, posters, banners, fliers, greeting cards, or other documents. Typically they allow the user to create page layouts, use a variety of colors, print text in columns, use a variety of text styles and sizes, create pictures using drawing tools, use premade graphics ("clip art"), create fancy text ("word art"), highlight sections of text with borders or shading, and import graphics created with other programs. Two of the more popular higher level desktop publishing packages are Microsoft Publisher (Microsoft) and PageMaker (Adobe), whereas younger "publishers" will enjoy using The Children's Writing & Publishing Center (The Learning Company) and Creative Writer (Microsoft). Furthermore, many modern word processors, especially those that run on Macintosh or Windows computers, have most features of the better desktop publishers. Microsoft Word, Corel WordPerfect, and ClarisWorks Word Processing are examples of word processors that have desktop publishing features.

Professionals and students will find desktop publishers to be among the most useful of software packages. These products can be used to print documents in bold text for the visually challenged, create motivating and eye-catching text and graphics, enliven creative professional-looking reports, and so on.

Electronic Spreadsheets

Spreadsheet programs, originally developed to computerize accountants' planning sheets, have extended far beyond their original use and have become standard in the home and classroom. A spreadsheet consists of an empty work area of rows and columns. Into this work area, the user may place labels (e.g., months of the year or students' names), numerical data (e.g., students' test scores), or formulas. For example, in a spreadsheet used to keep track of student grades, column 1 could contain students' names, column 2 their identification numbers, and columns 3 to 15 their scores on various assignments and tests. Column 16 could contain a formula for calculating the final grade for each student. Most spreadsheet programs are capable of holding thousands of rows and hundreds of columns of information.

Figure 3.2 presents a spreadsheet screen of student grades created with Microsoft Works. The screen shows only a portion of the spreadsheet. To move the "window" (the computer screen) to

Desktop publishing tools allow the user to design newsletters and posters. (Photograph by Carolyn F. Woods)

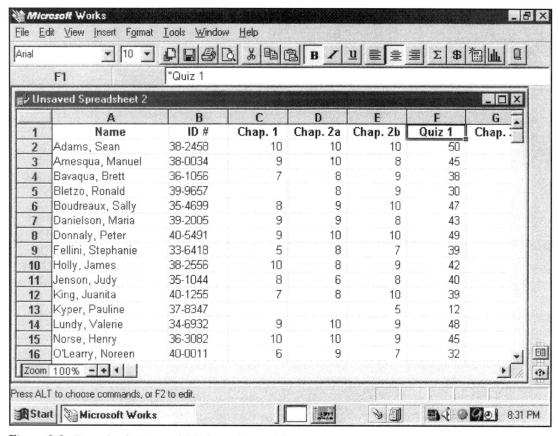

Figure 3.2. Example of a Microsoft Works grade spreadsheet.

other parts of the spreadsheet, the arrow keys or the mouse is used.

One of the major reasons why spreadsheets are so popular is that they allow "what if" speculations. For example, if a school's enrollment drops by 78 exceptional pupils next year, special education staff salaries increase 5%, and utility costs increase 3%, what will the operating budget for the year be? On the other hand, what if utility costs for instructional settings increase only 1%? Spreadsheets are designed to make this type of speculation very simple. If Juanita King's score for Quiz 1 in the spreadsheet in Figure 3.2 were changed to 45, the computer would automatically compute and print her average as soon as the score was entered.

Spreadsheet programs may be used to keep track of student grades, pupil cash accounts, or school budgets. They can also be used by exceptional individuals in such activities as household management, science and business, data management and evaluation, and mathematical problem solving. When combined with word processing programs, they may be used to print results of computations in documents and reports. For example, if the user is running a federal project, he or she could use the spreadsheet program to keep track of the budget and then incorporate that information into the yearly reports (e.g., by using a word processor and spreadsheet that are compatible). Exceptional adults could use spreadsheets to monitor income and expenses and to generate budgets.

Some of the more important spreadsheet packages that may be purchased as stand-alone or found as subprograms in integrated programs are Excel (Microsoft), Lotus 1-2-3 (Lotus), and Quattro Pro (Corel). Microsoft Works and ClarisWorks have excellent spreadsheet subprograms. All of these will create a large variety of types of graphs and charts (e.g., bar, line, scatter, pie) using the data in a spreadsheet. This feature can greatly enhance grant proposals or reports on projects involving special individuals.

Database Managers

Database managers are designed as computerized filing cabinets. These programs enable users to keep records on individuals and inventories of materials, and to recall and manipulate stored data in a variety of ways. A *database record*, equivalent to a file folder in a standard file system, can be designed by the user to fit the application (e.g., for 16 students in a class, 16 records must be created, one for each student). Locations in a record capable of holding one item of data (e.g., a person's last name or social security number) are called *fields*. A database design, complete with all its fields, labels, and so on, but no data, is called a *template*. For example, a template for students in a federally funded project for exceptional children might include fields for each student's name, address, birth date, zip code, disabilities or gifts, test scores, and so on. Once the data have been entered and stored using this template, the user can select and print out information on all students living in a certain zip code, all those with a certain disability, and those with a specific challenge who scored below a certain test score. Database managers can also arrange information in alphabetical or numerical order for any categories of information contained. Most database managers even do arithmetical computations, such as finding the average reading score of all pupils who are blind and in the sixth grade or totaling incomes from several sources for exceptional adults.

Professional-level databases that may be purchased as stand-alone or found as subprograms in integrated programs include Access (Microsoft), Approach (Lotus), and dBase (Boreland). Integrated packages such as Microsoft Works and Office, SmartSuite, Corel WordPerfect Suite, and ClarisWorks allow for powerful integration of database managers with word processors, for example, to create form letters or mailing labels from the information in a database. For example,

addresses in a database could be used with a word processing program to print mailing addresses on letters to parents of students in a particular program. These programs may also be used by exceptional individuals themselves to access and manipulate information. At one level, students may manipulate databases created by others. For example, Who Was Born on Your Birthday? (MicroMedia Publishing) is a database for Microsoft Works containing the birth dates, ages, occupations, and nationalities of over 10,000 famous people. At another level, the professional may design and enter a database template, then have the students gather data, enter them into the database, and investigate the information in the database. Finally, students may design their own database, gather the appropriate data, and then enter and manipulate the data.

Communications Software

Communications software packages are programs designed to help computers communicate with other computers. Modems, which allow computers to communicate over telephone lines, were discussed in Chapter 2. Modems by themselves cannot transmit data across the wires. They require software to tell them what to do and to orchestrate the communication between computers. Communications software does such things as store and dial the telephone numbers of the on-line resources that the user wants to access, display the data being sent from another computer on the user's screen, send the information the user types on the keyboard to the modem so that the modem can send it over the telephone line, translate the data the modem receives (the data the modem receives is comprised exclusively of 1s and 0s) into English or whatever language is being used, find a word-processed file on disk and attach it to a message being sent, and so on. Stand-alone programs that are used today for communication include Procomm Plus (Quarterdeck) and BetterTelnet (Sassy Communications), whereas some communication programs come bundled with the computer (e.g., Windows HyperTerminal).

Communications software permits individuals to communicate with people at different locations through keyboards or other input devices, computer screens, modems, and telephone lines. It also allows word processing files or database records to be transmitted from one location to another. For example, if a user had a federal project in Tempe, Arizona, with remote sites on several Indian reservations in northern Arizona, the remote site directors could transmit reports over telephone lines, and the project coordinator could save them on diskette and compile them later into a larger report. These programs also allow students to access computerized databases; to access on-line resources provided by their school, school district, or state department of education; or to use commercial on-line services such as America Online (AOL).[1]

Communications software ranges from the least sophisticated programs, which turn the computer into a "dumb" terminal whose keyboard and screen act only as input and output devices for the other computer; to sophisticated general-purpose programs, which allow the user to send files back and forth, to print text from another computer, and to send and receive electronic mail; to special-purpose programs, such as those that allow the user to use commercial on-line services such as America Online. A variety of public domain and commercial programs are available for each type of computer. In addition, the integrated packages Microsoft Works and ClarisWorks, among others, include communications subprograms. A local computer software store can help the user determine which package is appropriate for a specific system.

Internet Browsers

The development of the Internet and World Wide Web (WWW) has resulted in the newest and most exciting and powerful types of communication—"surfing" or browsing (see Appendix H). Software programs that permit users to surf are called *Web browsers*, and the two primary browsers being used today are Netscape's Navigator/Communicator and Microsoft's Internet Explorer. These programs have different functions and capabilities (see "Make Your Browser Sing," 1998), but they allow users to access the vast resources of the Web and other resources on the Internet ("Internet Explorer Gets Back to Basics," 1999). The Internet is a worldwide network that connects local networks—those on college campuses, school districts, governmental agencies, and businesses and industry. Because of the Internet, a student at California Institute of Technology, for example, can send electronic mail (e-mail) simultaneously to his mother who is a librarian in Germany and to family and friends in other parts of the world, or a graduate student at Indiana University can log into the computer at the Library of Congress in Washington, D.C., to find a particular book. The Web makes a variety of *multimedia* resources (in addition to text, multimedia includes sound, graphics, and motion video) available through the Internet. Individuals can access the Web from their home, school, or business computers using a Web browser and a modem. School computers that are directly connected to a network (and the Internet) need only a Web browser, not a modem. To access the Web from home, the user probably needs to subscribe to a Web service provider (college students are usually provided with access to the Internet by their campus for free or for a minimal charge). People who subscribe to commercial on-line services such as America Online, CompuServe, or Microsoft Network will be able to use the communications software provided by their service to access the Internet and the Web. Those who subscribe to a local, regional, or national Internet provider (e.g., EATEL, Bell-South, or AT&T) may also receive needed communications software. Figure 3.3 presents the Web browser, Netscape, and a Web site that may be of interest to professionals.

The World Wide Web offers a huge array of resources to professionals and exceptional

---

[1]To access commercial on-line services such as America Online, Compuserve, or Microsoft Network, the user must install the communications software provided by the company—general-purpose communications software such as those that come with Microsoft Works and ClarisWorks will not allow the user to access these services.

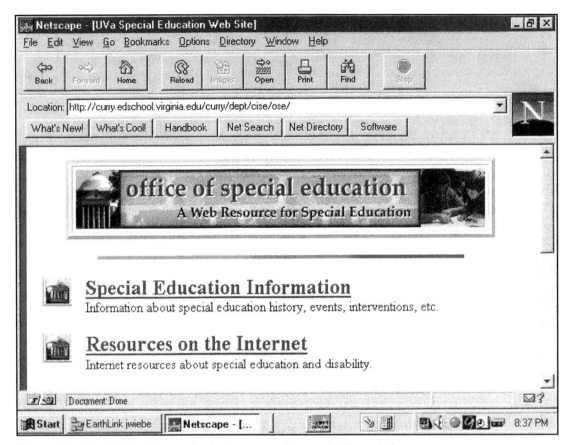

Figure 3.3. World Wide Web page for the University of Virginia College of Education.

individuals. Virtually all universities offer many Web services, including information about their campus, class schedules, the latest information about various classes and degree programs, and information about coming campus events. Many universities are starting to teach courses over the World Wide Web. Research reports of all kinds—many of interest to professionals or students with gifts and talents—are available via the Web. A huge number of companies provide information about their products on-line, including those who provide adaptive devices and other resources for individuals with challenges. Students can obtain information for school projects, ranging from information about national parks to weather information. Much of the information available on the Internet is much more recent and up to date than what is available through traditional print resources. However, because this new medium does not have many of the restric-

tions of more traditional media—editors, review boards, Federal Communications Commission requirements, and so on—caution is urged. Some of the information that is accessible on the Web is inaccurate, inflammatory, sexually explicit, or otherwise problematical.

Search Directories and Engines

In addition to promoting the evolution of very powerful and user-friendly Web browsers, the Internet and World Wide Web have also provided the impetus for the development of search directories or engines. As poignantly stated by the Kansas City Public Library in its "Introduction to Search Engines" Web page (http://www.kcpl.lib.mo.us/search/srchengines.htm),

The Internet has tens of millions of sites at this time [information verified and updated

9/97]; growth is exponential and bibliographic control does not exist. To find the proverbial needle in the immense haystack (or tiny fly in the Web), you use two basic approaches: a search engine or a subject guide [directory] such as Yahoo or Magellan. Subject guides are fine for browsing general topics, but for specific information use a search engine.

According to Sullivan (http://searchenginewatch. internet.com/facts/major.html), search engines—also called "spiders" or "crawlers"—run automatically and constantly visit Web sites to catalog information on Web pages. Directories, on the other hand, are created by humans who receive Web site information and assign these data to appropriate categories. Search engines tend to find more information than directories, but directories can provide better search results. Feldman (see http://www.infoday.com/searcher/may/story3. htm) reported that there are approximately 1,800 search engines accessing 50 million Web sites, and the more popular search engines are associated with browser Search menu functions—Infoseek, Excite, AltaVista, HotBot, Open Text, and Lycos.

A number of Web sites provide ready access to the major search engines or descriptions of these engines—BeauCoup, All-in-One Search Page, and Search Engine Watch. One of the more interesting Web sites is The Front Page's Collection of Search Engines (http://thefrontpage.com/search/search.html). From this site, users can read about and access 68 engines:

25 "Search the WWW"—WebCrawler, AltaVista, Infoseek, Lycos, etc.

4 "Search for People & Businesses—Four11, BigFoot, WhoWhere, etc.

1 "Search NewsGroups"—"DejaNews" tracks 10,000+ b groups

3 "Search the Private Club"—The Whole Internet Catalog (AOL), CompuServe, and Prodigy

3 "Search Reference Desks"—Reference Desk, Virtual Library, and ILTNetVirtual Reference Desk

32 "Specific Items, Pursuits & Categories"—College Net, Educational Resources, Postal Services, Zoo Links and Animal Pages, etc.

Some professionals and exceptional individuals may be interested in creating their own Web resources (sometimes called Web pages or Web sites—sites really have more than one page or link) to provide information for others. For example, a professional might want to create a Web site to share with others resources he or she has developed for working with adults who have a specific disability. Or, students with disabilities, challenges, gifts, or talents could create Web sites to share their creative or academic work with the world. Many schools and school districts around the world have created Web sites to share information about their schools and the outstanding work of their pupils. One way to create Web sites is to use raw HyperText Markup Language (HTML), a set of instructions for creating Internet-based multimedia (similar to a programming language) that is recognized by Web browsers. Many word processors (e.g., Microsoft Word) and desktop publishers (e.g., Microsoft Publisher) allow users to create documents, and then translate the document into HTML format so that it can be transmitted over the World Wide Web. To create a Web site, the user needs a powerful computer (exclusively dedicated to running the Web site), called a Web server, which is connected to the Internet and software (e.g., Microsoft's Front Page) to manage the site. Many articles and books are dedicated to the subject of creating a Web site (e.g., Bull, Bull, & Sigmon, 1995; Cafolla & Knee, 1996, 1996–1997; Castro, 1996; Groves, 1996).

Finally, the Internet and World Wide Web offer a storehouse of information on software—companies, titles, costs, and evaluations. In addition to using a browser or search engine to find and explore these resources, users often include specific Web sites in their Bookmarks. The Software Sharing Resource Library offers a World Catalog of Software that lists 400,000 entries by such areas as Children and Internet (http://www.ssrl.rtp.com443/Harvest/brokers/reuse/query.html). Educational Software Institute's Web site at http://www.edsoft.com provides information on

8,000 educational programs and 350 companies (e.g., hardware and software characteristics, program strengths and weaknesses, costs, purchasing). Other interesting software Web sites include Edutainment Catalog, Cyberian Outpost, Creative Computer, and MicroWarehouse.

Graphics

Graphics packages provide the basic tools to create charts, graphs, illustrations, and pictures on the computer. Further, most provide a large number of precreated pictures (called clip art) and photographs that can be inserted into documents. Most of these packages often make use of the mouse to create pictures, but high-end packages can also use a graphics tablet (a stylus is used on a flat, touch-sensitive surface to create pictures). To create pictures, the stylus or mouse is moved across a surface, and these motions are recorded on the computer screen. These packages allow the individual to choose the type of shape to be drawn, as well as its color, size, and location. Squares, rectangles, circles, and other shapes can be created with a couple of clicks of the mouse button. Some graphics packages also allow defined shapes to be animated. The best computer-assisted instruction (CAI) programs make extensive use of graphics and animation. For example, a program designed to teach about the human digestive system would be incomplete without pictures of the system. Even better would be animated pictures showing food moving down the esophagus and into the stomach and through the rest of the body. Both Microsoft Works and ClarisWorks contain graphics subprograms. CorelDraw! (Corel) and Harvard Graphics (Software Publishing) are popular, high-end graphics packages. Another graphics program that is being used in a growing number of settings is Kai's Power Tools (Metatools).

Integrated Software Packages

Increasing numbers of "superprograms" are available that combine and integrate many or all of the above applications categories (e.g., Microsoft Office; see Arar, 1999). These integrated packages may contain programs for word processing, databases, spreadsheets, graphics, and communications. Although the tasks may be possible with separate programs, integrated programs have the advantage of compatibility. Data created in one application can easily be used in another. This is not likely to be true of stand-alone programs, such as CorelDraw! and Lotus 1-2-3, especially when mixing programs produced by different publishers. Integrated packages can be used with and by exceptional individuals for business, home, or school purposes to create a file with one type of application and use it in another. For example, Microsoft Works has a word processor that allows the professional to write a letter to students' parents and a database program that can keep information about the class. Because it is an integrated package, only the Microsoft Works program needs to be put in the computer to accomplish both functions. It will also merge the letter and information about the class. ClarisWorks (Claris), Microsoft Works and Office (Microsoft), Corel WordPerfect Suite (Corel), and SmartSuite (Lotus) are the major integrated software packages used in home, school, and community settings.

Multimedia Development Tools and Authoring Systems

In 1988, Apple developed a new type of computer tool, called HyperCard (Claris), for the Macintosh. This tool is essentially an enhanced database manager that stores information on "cards" (records) in "stacks" (databases). In addition to storing text and numbers like traditional database managers, however, it can be used to store graphics, sounds, and video clips. For example, a card could contain a picture of an American robin and text describing its habitat and diet. In addition, the card could be set up so that if the user points to and clicks on the bird's beak the computer would play its song. Another feature is that the user can add *buttons*—"hot spots" on the screen that cause something to happen (like displaying another card on the screen or showing an animated sequence)—to cards and program them to do what the user wants. Hyper-Card spawned the development of a number of similar tools. One of the most popular for use in the classroom is HyperStudio (Roger Wagner). Others include Digital Chisel (Pierian Spring Software), LinkWay (IBM), and Director Multimedia Studio (Macromedia).

Because of their many capabilities, multimedia development tools like HyperStudio and Director Multimedia Studio are used extensively by educators to create computer-based lessons for their students. They are much easier to learn and much cheaper than their high-end cousins, the authoring systems (discussed later). Professionals use tools similar to graphics packages and desktop publishers to put text, graphics, buttons, and so forth, on the screen and to link screens together. Cards (screens) may contain text, sound, pictures, video clips, or even links to the World Wide Web, designed to teach or practice various concepts. Multimedia development tools, especially HyperStudio and Digital Chisel, are simple enough that they can be used by students as young as third and fourth graders to create multimedia reports and screen-based presentations (Sharp, 1996).

A group of programs that are similar in many ways to multimedia development tools, but much more expensive and powerful, are *authoring systems*. These programs are used by serious educational software developers to create professional-level computer-based instruction packages. These packages allow users not only to put text, graphics, animation, buttons, and video clips on the screen, but also to create a variety of interactions with students. For example, they can be used to create multiple-choice questions and evaluate student answers or can be programmed to determine if a student has pointed to and clicked on a specific area of the screen. They also have built-in capabilities for storing a record of student answers, time on task, and so on, in a disk file. Authorware (Macromedia) is an excellent authoring system for professionals who want to create commercially viable computer-based lessons for their students and clients.

CD-ROM and DVD-ROM Software

CD-ROM and DVD-ROM technologies were introduced in Chapter 2. These software media really are not a separate category from other types of software. The same kinds of programs that can be stored and distributed on floppy diskettes are being distributed on CD-ROMs and, in the upcoming months, on DVD-ROMs. However, many, if not most, large software packages today are distributed on CD-ROM disks (DVD-ROM disks will be used for some programs) because a single CD-ROM disk holds the same amount of information as several hundred 3.5-inch floppy diskettes. A modern fully featured word processor, for example, might take up 20 or 30 floppy diskettes, and a modern instructional software package with lots of sound, graphics, and motion video might fill 50 or more floppy diskettes. Significant time and effort would be required to copy a program from all those diskettes onto a hard drive. With each new generation, software programs are becoming more powerful, offering more features and help systems, and requiring more disk space (e.g., 100s of megabytes).

Another advantage of computer-based instruction packages (programs designed to teach something) on CD-ROMs is that the user needs to

Database tools permit the user to organize, manipulate, and store textual and numerical information. (Photograph by Carolyn F. Woods)

copy only a small part of the contents of the CD-ROM onto the hard drive—the rest of the program remains on the CD-ROM and is loaded into the computer's memory as needed while the program is running. Of course, when using programs like this, the CD-ROM must be in the CD-ROM drive while the program is running. If the user were required to copy the entire contents of a CD-ROM onto the hard drive in order to be able to use the program, the hard drive of older computers could be filled immediately by one or two programs.

Software publishers prefer to distribute software on CD-ROM because it is difficult to illegally copy CD-ROM disks. Also, if several students in a school setting will be using the software concurrently, the school must buy one CD-ROM for each computer station where the software is being used. Teachers like CD-ROMs because they are small and compact and are more durable than floppy diskettes.

Those writing grant proposals or looking for published articles about research findings or specific teaching techniques will find the Educational Resources Information Center (ERIC) CD-ROM resource to be valuable. With an appropriate CD-ROM drive and the ERIC CD-ROM, professionals may customize their literature searches and print article titles or abstracts on their printers.

A number of excellent Web sites and printed resources offer information about CD-ROM and DVD-ROM media. The Web sites can be accessed using a search engine (e.g., HotBot or Excite) and the typed subject *CD-ROM* or *DVD-ROM*. Tangley (1998) addressed important concerns about the use of CD-ROM technology (e.g., some CD-ROM disks become unreliable after 5 years), whereas Leemon's (1997) and Andrews's (1998) articles should answer most questions about DVD technology.

Educational Software

The applications software discussed previously is not designed for any specific setting and may be used in business, home applications, or educational settings. However, there is a category of software that is used more in schools than anywhere else—educational or instructional software. This section introduces educational software and describes its use. Subsequent chapters describe specific examples of software that can be used with particular exceptional individuals.

Historical Perspective

Before the advent of the personal computer, a number of attempts were made to use the computer as an instructional tool. The PLATO project, started at the University of Illinois in 1959 under support of the National Science Foundation, was funded to develop computer programs to teach many traditional school subjects. The project achieved many of its goals and built up a large library of courses widely used in colleges, high schools, businesses, and the military.

During the first days of PLATO and other similar projects, a number of pioneers predicted a major revolution in education. According to Suppes (1966), "One can predict that in a few more years millions of school children will have access to . . . the personal services of a tutor as well-informed and responsive as Aristotle (computer-assisted instruction [CAI])" (p. 207). Despite predictions like these, 30 years later the impact of computerized instruction is just beginning to be felt in schools. In fact, with few exceptions, learning is still delivered by teachers and textbooks. Computers, television, and other media account for only a small fraction of school instruction. This is changing, however, in schools with non-traditional settings designed for exceptional students, at-risk students, adult learners, and business training.

The reason it has taken so long for computers and related technology to contribute to children's education in traditional classrooms has to do with the allocation of resources. Before microcomputers, schools—especially elementary schools—had little access to computers, and when they did, the computers were used for administrative rather than instructional purposes. Furthermore, schools had little money to spend for software. Software developers, rather than developing top-quality, inexpensive products for schools, put their efforts into business-oriented products.

During the past few years, there has been a dramatic change. Although a typical educational professional today is lucky to have more than a couple of computers in the classroom or to have limited, shared access in a computer laboratory, the installed base of computers is increasing substantially each year. There is also a move toward more powerful computing systems, such as Macintosh's Power PC and Intel-type Pentium computers. Major companies such as IBM, Microsoft, Disney Corporation, and Reader's Digest have also become involved in publishing educational software. The result is a new generation of well-designed software products for schools.

Software Categories

Many thousands of software packages and programs are designed for educational use. They range from free software that may be copied and used at will (see the "Public Domain Software and Freeware" section later in this chapter) to published packages costing thousands of dollars. They are available for all types of computing hardware and operating systems, and they are designed to accomplish a wide variety of educational goals from providing a few minutes of exciting practice on multiplication facts to programs that help students write poetry.

There are several major categories of educational software: tutorial, simulation, demonstration–information–reference, drill-and-practice, games, student utilities, tests, and teacher utilities. Even though many software packages do not fit neatly into a single category, it is useful to be acquainted with these categories so that a particular package may be matched with the professional's educational objectives. For example, and as described in Chapter 1, it would be inappropriate to expect a package to provide initial instruction on the meaning of addition and subtraction of whole numbers if it was designed instead to provide *practice* on addition and subtraction skills (with the assumption that appropriate meanings and computational strategies had already been introduced by the professional).

Tutorial

Tutorial programs present information to the learner, usually by setting up a dialogue with the student. For example, one screen in a program on volcanoes might print a few sentences of text, contain buttons the student could click on to hear a voice saying the text, have a button to see an animated illustration of what happens when a volcano explodes, and so on. To go to the next screen, the learner would be presented with one or more questions and, based on the input, the program would go to new material, repeat the previous information, or branch to another part of the program (e.g., less difficult material). Tour of the Macintosh (Apple), for example, teaches users how to use the mouse to accomplish basic operations on the Macintosh computer.

A tutorial depends heavily on the ability of the instructional designer to develop an appropriate and effective level of interaction between the learner and the program. Tutorials must be more than electronic page-turners and should anticipate the types of errors users will make. If a student does not understand the concept, a tutorial should provide feedback that leads to improved understanding. This can occur only if the software developer is able to foresee the more common types of mistakes students will make. The ability to catch these kinds of mistakes and provide appropriate feedback is called instructional error trapping.

Simulation

Simulation programs give the learner some aspect of a real-life experience. For example, a program written for a high school family life course might simulate household budgeting for new families. A popular simulation is SimCity 2000 (Maxis), SimTown for younger users, which allows the user to create and manage a new city or one of several existing cities in the world. The program includes graphics, sound, on-line help, and budget advisors.

A subcategory of simulations is the adventure game. In some ways, these programs are similar to arcade-type games—the player must overcome various obstacles to achieve an objective. However, arcade games are designed merely to entertain, whereas adventure games are designed to teach. One of the best known adventure games is Oregon Trail (MECC). In this program, students relive the experience of crossing the western United States in a covered wagon. If they make the right decisions, they will eventually reach their destination. In the process of playing the game, students learn about life in frontier America. Another popular set of adventure games is the Carmen Sandiego (Brøderbund) series, including Where in the World Is Carmen Sandiego? Where in the U.S.A. Is Carmen Sandiego? and Where in Europe Is Carmen Sandiego? In these games, students play the part of a detective and gather clues in the attempt to solve crimes. To play the games, students must read, problem solve, apply map skills, use reference skills to discover geographic locations and other facts, and record data in a miniature database.

Demonstration–Information–Reference

Some programs are designed to present information to a user. Typically, demonstration programs are designed to be used as part of a lesson presented through a different format or medium and do not make use of interactive instruction.

Demonstration programs can be used the way a film or filmstrip would be used. For example, a high school chemistry class might make use of a program that shows, through graphics, what happens when certain dangerous chemicals are mixed together. The program could be interactive to the extent of asking which chemicals and quantities to mix, but would not query users about the demonstration. Its purpose would be to enhance a lecture or discussion about chemicals.

Informational or resource programs are designed to be a resource, similar to a reference book, dictionary, or encyclopedia. Many of the best informational programs are in the area of social studies. Encarta Encyclopedia Deluxe (Microsoft) and Grolier Multimedia Encyclopedia Deluxe (Electronic Publishing) are examples of encyclopedias on CD-ROM. Along with traditional text and pictures, these resources contain sound and video clips and even motivational activities. For example, Encarta users can see and hear a video clip of Martin Luther King's "I have a dream . . ." speech. In addition, students can combine keywords to do the kind of complex searches that are impossible in a traditional, print-based encyclopedia. PC Globe, Mac Globe, PC USA, and Mac USA (Brøderbund) are computer-based atlases with outstanding maps of various sorts (health statistics, elevations, etc.), databases of information about countries or states, and the ability to create bar charts comparing the countries or states.

Drill-and-Practice

Drill-and-practice programs have been, and probably will continue to be, the primary software used by professionals working with exceptional individuals (Baby, 1992). In this type of program, no new material is presented. Instead, the user practices on material already presented by responding to questions or other appropriate stimuli about facts, ideas, or relationships. The program will then tell the user whether the response is right or wrong, perhaps giving a hint and another try, before going to the next question.

Drill-and-practice programs vary greatly in sophistication, ranging from the unimaginative electronic "ditto sheet" to elaborate and exciting video games. A low-end example is a program that simply places math exercises (e.g., "$55.00 - 51.12 = ?$") on the screen, to which the student responds by typing the answers. At the upper end are programs that embed the problems in arcade-type games or simulations. For example, in "classic" Alien Addition (SRA/DLM), students must match the answer on the laser cannon with an addition problem on an invading alien spaceship in order to blast the space ship. Math Blasters Plus (Davidson) is also an exciting arcade-type program. In Green Globs and Graphing Equations (Sunburst), students get points by entering algebraic equations to hit green globs appearing on a graph. In most cases the more sophisticated the equation, the more points scored (e.g., the equation for a circle located in the proper place may hit more green clubs than the equation for a straight line).

Games and Problem Solving

Games have long been a part of general and special education. Many teachers have found ways to meet instructional objectives with board games, bingo-type games, and athletic games. The computer has added a new dimension to game playing. Before the computer, games required two or more people. With the computer, it is now possible for an individual to play a game against the computer. Since most children, adolescents, and adults find games to be extremely motivating, computerized educational games may be used to motivate even the most reluctant learner to learn new concepts, practice previously learned skills, or take tests. Word Man (SRA/DLM) was one of the earlier excellent games with its multilevels (e.g., 1 to 4, increasing in difficulty) and multispeeds (e.g., 1 to 9, decreasing user reaction time), requiring the user to match homonyms, synonyms, and antonyms. Today's commercial and educational software catalogues continue to offer a variety of these types of programs (e.g., Hartley, Edmark, Special Times). Tetris (Spectrim Holobyte) is a spatial game that involves moving or rotating shapes descending on the screen to fill rows on the screen. Although there is no specific educational objective involved in games like Tetris, one might argue that it develops spatial skills, which in turn are correlated with mathematical achievement.

Some educational games do not form a separate category of educational software but provide drill-and-practice, instruction, a simulated experience, or a combination of these. Other games have no instructional goal but are intended solely for entertainment. However, some of these games also have educational merit because they teach problem solving and logical thinking, develop motor skills, and/or develop spatial visualization capabilities. Games like Tetris can also be used as a reward for student time on task or other positive behaviors.

Student Utilities

Another group of educational software programs does not fit into any of the previous categories. These programs help students accomplish different kinds of tasks in the classroom. Examples of these software programs include The Children's Writing & Publishing Center and Writing Center (The Learning Company), Storybook Maker Deluxe (Hartley), and KidWorks (Davidson). These programs combine powerful features in word processing, picture selection, and page design to help children produce illustrated reports, letters, stories, and newsletters. Thormann (1995) discussed the use of Kid Pix (Brøderbund) and other student utilities with children who have language-learning disabilities and other physical challenges.

Tests

Computerized testing offers some hope of relief from the drudgery of test taking in schools, especially for students who are challenged or low achieving. By nature, standardized, normed pencil-and-paper tests are time-consuming and require that students face numerous questions, many of which they cannot answer. The computer promises to reduce test-taking time and anxiety considerably by quickly determining the student's level of achievement and presenting questions only at that level. Other exciting possibilities offered by computerized testing are embedding tests in game formats and collecting much more meaningful and accurate information about students. Computer software programs also assist general and special educators in generating, administering, scoring, and assessing tests. For example, MicroTest III (Chariot Software) allows educators to develop tests containing multiple-choice, true–false, matching, and free format types of questions. Educators can create a large bank of test questions, then select a subset of the questions to include on a particular test (e.g., those questions from a particular chapter). MicroTest III also enables the user to create computer-based exams. Report Writer: WISCIII/

WISC-R/WPPSI-R (Psychological Assessment) can be used to provide a four- to five-page report interpreting the student's demographic information and Wechsler test results among other data. Other chapters in this text delineate and describe test programs that can be used with exceptional individuals.

Teacher Utilities

Somewhere between general applications programs and software that teaches or helps students accomplish some task are programs specifically designed to help teachers manage their classrooms. For example, a number of companies produce grade-book programs (e.g., Jackson Software's GradeQuick and Misty City Software's Grade Machine), and some produce programs for generating teaching–learning materials (e.g., Hartley's Friday Afternoon). Chalkware Education Solution (101 Norwalk Court, Vacaville, CA 95687) has a popular program for writing IEPs and keeping track of educational objectives. Teachers can get a demonstration copy of this IEP program from Chalkware's Web site (http://www.iepwae.com). The Minnesota Educational Computing Consortium (MECC) has developed several programs to produce a variety of educational puzzles and worksheets. Other chapters in

Technology utility tools permit professionals to manage classroom assignments and activities. (Photograph by Carolyn F. Woods)

this book provide specific details about pertinent teacher utility programs for personal and instructional productivity.

Videodisc Software

Videodisc software comes in two formats. One is constant linear velocity (CLV), which is capable of holding 2 hours of motion video and is used primarily for continuous viewing, as with a movie. The other format is constant angular velocity (CAV), which is capable of holding 100,000 still frames, 1 hour of motion video, or a combination of still and motion video. Both formats produce high-resolution pictures and high-quality stereo sound. Although many popular motion pictures and educational films (e.g., episodes of the Nova series) have been recorded in the CLV format, it is the CAV format that has outstanding potential in education.

Videodiscs recorded in the CAV format may be used in a variety of ways in the classroom. One way to use them is in the stand-alone mode. The professional or students may use a hand-held controller to view frames or video sequences on educational videodiscs. For example, students may take a guided tour through the National Gallery of Art or view individual paintings or details from the paintings on the National Gallery of Art videodisc.

At another level, a computer may be used to control the videodisc player (see Chapter 2). HyperCard (Apple Computer), HyperStudio (Roger Wagner Publishing), and ToolBook (Asymetrix) may be used to control videodisc players. These packages may be programmed to show specific still frames, play video sequences, or print text on the video screen. It is also possible to purchase premade HyperCard or HyperStudio stacks or other programs that control specific videodiscs. For example, National Gallery of Art Laserguide (Videodisc Publishing) is a HyperCard stack that may be used to select works on the disc according to the artist, the artist's nationality, the period of the painting, its style, its medium, and so forth. In the future, companies will offer more packages providing instruction by combining the interactive capabilities of the computer and the outstanding graphics and sound capabilities of videodisc (Sales, 1989).

Obtaining Software

General-purpose and educational software packages are available from a variety of sources. Stores that sell computer systems often sell software too. Many major retailers, such as Wal Mart and Sam's, Office Depot, Office Max, and Sears, sell software. Computer discount houses, such as Comp USA, often sell software at substantially reduced prices. Certain companies, such as Microsoft Corporation, sell software directly to professionals at even greater discounts or may provide their programs free to educators (e.g., Netscape's Navigator/ Communicator).

Certain types of educational software are readily available at retail computer hardware and software stores. Examples are Math Blaster, Where in the U.S.A. Is Carmen Sandiego? and Print Shop. Other educational software titles, such as the problem-solving software from Hartley and Sunburst Corporation, are not typically sold in software stores. Most major metropolitan areas, however, have professional supply or educational software stores that have a large range of software titles. Another option is mail order companies that specialize in educational software, for example, Scholastic Corporation (P.O. Box 7502, Jefferson City, MO 65402), Educational Resources (1550 Executive Drive, Elgin, IL 60123), Edmark (P.O. Box 97021, Redmond, WA 98073), and Educational Software Institute (4213 South 94th Street, Omaha, NE 68127). More obscure titles will be available only by dealing directly with the publisher. One of the more exciting avenues for finding software is using the Internet/World Wide Web and a search engine (e.g., AltaVista)—Search: Software (Reading).

Public Domain Software and Freeware

Sometimes software programs developed by individuals or businesses for fun or for specific purposes are not copyrighted or the copyright has expired. This software usually becomes available to the general public and is called *public domain software* or *freeware*. These programs include games, educational applications, business routines, and useful utilities. Computer hobbyists have long used and appreciated public domain programs.

Public domain software and freeware are not always free unless friends or coworkers share copies. Computer user groups often maintain libraries of public domain software and freeware and offer their libraries to members for a nominal charge. In addition, some of these programs are available through the Internet and the World Wide Web.

Software Needs Assessment

The process of software evaluation focuses on the value of a particular piece of software (see Chapter 6 and Appendix D), and the ways to secure this information continue to evolve (e.g., visit the Educational Software Institute Web Site: http:///www.edsoft.com). Needs assessment, on the other hand, examines a given educational setting to determine what materials can result in maximum learning. The result of a needs assessment will usually be a category of software that can form the foundation for a more detailed search for appropriate packages. Needs assessment is often done on a district- or program-wide basis in order to standardize hardware and software purchases. An added benefit is that educators may be able to get multiple-copy discounts on the software purchased.

Even if an educator has a budget and the equipment, the process of software selection is never done in a vacuum. There is often a need to coordinate software usage with that of other classrooms, schools, projects, or sites. If one teacher plans to use a computer to write reports about a project, for example, and there are other projects in the school that do similar types of tasks, it would be wise for the teacher to consider the software already in use. That way, if one computer or the software fails, a backup is available.

Nothing is more frustrating than to have a file containing text or data that cannot be used until a computer is repaired or until the publisher sends a replacement copy of the software. In general, it is often best to make some kind of district or project decision about software purchases based on needs assessments.

Summary

The real computer revolution is taking place in the area of software as people think up new tasks for computers to do and better ways to accomplish them. For example, the Internet "software revolution" has just begun, and efforts to "wed or interface" Web browsers, operating systems, and application programs promise struggles, pitfalls, and technology benefits (see Heltzel, 1998). The most exciting revolution is in software that can help individuals learn and overcome disabilities and challenges. The chapters that follow provide additional information about software programs or tools that can be used by professionals and individuals with disabilities, gifts, and talents in school, home, and community settings.

Resources

Organizations

The International Technology Education Association
Web: http://www.itea.org

Technology for All American Project
Web: http://scholar.lib.vt.edu/TAA/TAA.html

Software Sharing Resource Library
Web: http://www.ssrl.rtp.com443/Harvest/brokers/reuse/query.html

Educational Software Institute
Web: http://www.edsoft.com prov

Journals

Electronic Learning. This journal is published eight times a year and provides general and specific information about software, computer literacy, instructional applications, and broad issues about computers in education. *Contact:* Scholastic Inc., 555 Broadway, New York City, NY 10012.

Learning and Leading with Technology (formerly The Computing Teacher). This journal, published monthly, addresses elementary and secondary computer issues for beginners, experienced computer users, and technology and other educational leaders. It is published nine times a year. *Contact:* International Society for Technology in Education, 1787 Agate Street, Eugene, OR 97403-1923.

Technology and Learning. This journal, published 8 times a year, is written for educators in K–12 schools. It reviews hardware and software products, gives suggestions for integrating technology into the classroom, and discusses issues relating to technology in education. *Contact:* Peter Li, Inc., P.O. Box 49727, Dayton, OH 45449-0727.

T.H.E. Journal: Technological Horizons in Education. Eleven issues of this journal are published a year. The journal provides information about new hardware and software products of interest to teachers of Grades K–12 and higher education. Articles cover the use of technology in education. *Contact:* T.H.E. Journal L.L.C., 150 El Camino Real, Suite 112, Tustin, CA 92780-3670.

Laboratory–Practicum Activities

▶ 1. List three goals you will achieve in the next 3 months to enhance your technology software knowledge. Use technology to develop your goals, to describe how you will achieve these goals, and to manage the achievement of the goals.

▶ 2. Find a recent journal article reviewing a tutorial, simulation, or drill-and-practice software package in your interest area (e.g., math, science, social studies). What are the hardware requirements for this piece of software? What are the instructional objectives of the program? What features of the program set it apart from other programs in the same area? Would you consider purchasing it for your classroom? Why or why not?

▶ 3. Access the Web site of a company that sells educational software and for which you have a copy of their most recent catalogue. Compare and contrast how the software information is presented.

▶ 4. Interview three or four people who use computers for word processing, spreadsheets, and databases on a regular basis. Which programs do they use now and have they used in the past? If the programs are different, why did they change? What are the reported strengths and weaknesses of the new programs they are using?

▶ 5. Interview two professionals who use utility programs for personal and instructional productivity. What are the programs they use, and how do they use them? What recommendations would they make for improving these programs?

▶ 6. Access the Educational Software Institute's Web site (http://www.edsoft.com) and secure evaluation information on two of your favorite software programs (e.g., on reading comprehension). How do the Web site evaluations compare with your facts about and opinions of the programs? How do they compare with evaluations from other sources? How is the information at this Web site different from what is presented at The Software Sharing Resource Library's World Catalog of Software (http://www.ssrl.rtp.com 443/Harvest/brokers/reuse/query.html)?

▶ 7. Find a piece of instructional software covering an area that you normally teach (or will teach) in your classroom. Have one of your students use the program while you observe. What was the student's reaction to the program? What is the instructional objective of the program, and how useful was the program in achieving that objective? Compare the approach and success of the program in meeting its goal with your own classroom approach to meeting the same goal. What advantages and disadvantages does the software have compared to your regular classroom instruction?

▶ 8. Use Microsoft Word on a Macintosh and then on an IBM or compatible PC. Pre-

sent to your course instructor and peers a summary of the word processing similarities and differences you found.

▶ 9. Collaborate with your peers to create a database listing the hardware and software products named in this chapter. This information can be secured from catalogs or Web sites. Include each vendor's address, telephone and fax numbers, Uniform Resource Locator (URL) or Web site, e-mail address, product platforms (e.g., DOS, Windows, Macintosh), site license information, and cost.

▶ 10. A recent visit to the Internet and Word Wide Web and a search using the search engines AltaVista and HotBot and the search field words *Software + company* produced 5,456,894 and 1,731,226 hits/sites/pages, respectively. Hypothesize the number of hits/sites/pages you would find today using the same search engines and words and conduct the searches to confirm or negate your hypotheses. Where any of the top 20 AltaVista and HotBot hits/sites/pages similar? If it took 3 minutes to access and view each AltaVista hit/site/page, how many total hours would you need to view all of the AltaVista hits/sites/pages?

References

Andrews, D. (1998, January). DVD finally. *PC World*, pp. 195–208.

Arar, Y. (1999, February). Microsoft Office 2000 offers new apps and Web tools. *PC World*, pp. 51–54.

Baby, J. (1992). Curriculum applications in special education computing. *Journal of Computer-Based Instruction, 19*(1), 1–5.

Bull, G., Bull, G., & Sigmon, T. (1995). Mining the Internet: Preparing for the Internet revolution. *Learning and Leading with Technology, 23*(1), 59–62.

Bull, G., Lough, T., & Cochran, P. (1989). LOGO and exceptional individuals. In J. D. Lindsey (Ed.), *Computers and exceptional individuals* (pp. 169–187). Columbus, OH: Merrill.

Cafolla, R., & Knee, R. (1996). Creating World Wide Web sites. *Learning and Leading with Technology, 24*(3), 6–9.

Cafolla, R., & Knee, R. (1996–1997). Creating World Wide Web sites: Part 2. Implementing your site. *Learning and Leading with Technology, 24*(4), 36–39.

Castro, E. (1996). *HTML for the World Wide Web*. Berkeley, CA: Peachpit Press.

Daiute, C. (1985). *Writing and computers*. Reading, MA: Addison-Wesley.

Degnan, S. C., & Hummel, J. W. (1985). Word processing for special students: Worth the effort. *T.H.E. Journal, 12*(6), 80–82.

Groves, D. (1996). *The Web page workbook*. Wilsonville, OR: Franklin, Beedle & Associates.

Heltzel, P. (1998, January). Netscape ups ante on managing files from your browser. *PC World*, pp. 63–64.

Internet Explorer gets back to basics. (1999, March). *Macworld*, pp. 27, 30.

Jones, S. J. (1996). Logo in special education. *Learning and Leading with Technology, 23*(7), 22–24.

Leemon, S. (1997, November). Is it DVD time? *FamilyPC*, pp. 133–138.

Make your browser sing. (1998, February). *FamilyPC*, pp. 44–46.

Papert, S. (1980). *Mindstorms: Children, computers, and powerful ideas*. New York: Basic Books.

Pogue, D. (1999, March). On the trail of Mac OS 8.5. *Macworld*, pp. 82–86.

Sales, G. C. (1989). Videodisc technology: Function and formats. *Computing Teacher, 16*(5), 34–35, 56.

Sharp, V. (1996). *Computer education for teachers*. Madison, WI: Brown & Benchmark.

Software. (1985). Alexandria, VA: Time-Life Books.

Suppes, D. (1966). The use of computers in education. *Scientific American, 215*(3), 202–220.

Tangley, L. (1998, February 16). Whoops, there goes another CD-ROM. *U.S. News & World Report*, pp. 67–68.

Thormann, J. (1995). Special children, special challenges. *Learning and Leading with Technology, 23*(3), 56–59.

Wiburg, K., & Carter, B. (1994). Thinking with computers. *The Computing Teacher, 22*(1), 7–10.

Section II

୬   ୬   ୬

The Technology Program, Access, and Productivity

Section II provides general and specific considerations relative to providing technology to exceptional individuals in inclusive and other settings. The issues addressed are implementing and managing the program, ensuring access by removing barriers, software evaluation and development, and personal and instructional productivity.

Computer labs provide exceptional individuals with valuable technology-related experiences. (Photograph by Carolyn F. Woods)

Chapter 4

৵   ৵   ৵

Planning and Implementing Technology Programs in Inclusive Settings

Ted S. Hasselbring
Peabody College at Vanderbilt University,
Nashville, Tennessee

Brian A. Bottge
University of Wisconsin–Madison

For many educators the recent infusion of computer technology into schools has been both troubling and exciting (Walczak, 1999)—troubling because many teachers have not been shown how to appropriately use technology in their teaching, and exciting because of the possibilities that the information age brings to teaching and learning. According to the U.S. Congressional Office of Technology Assessment (OTA) (1995), K–12 schools expanded their inventory of computers from 2.4 million units to 3.5 million units from 1989 to 1992, almost a 50% increase. In 1996 it was estimated that schools had one computer for every nine students, or about 5.8 million computers in all (U.S. Department of Education, 1996).

Much of this rapid growth in computer availability has been fueled by the promise that technology will improve education (Kavanaugh-Brown, 1999). This optimism is shared by politicians (e.g., Goals 2000: Educate America Act of 1994), national teacher groups (e.g., National Council of Teachers of Mathematics), and local boards of education across the country. The current beliefs in the power of computer technology to improve education are similar to those held a decade ago when the percentage of schools with one or more computers rose from 18% to 95% during the years spanning 1981 to 1987 (U.S. Congressional OTA, 1988). At that time many educators and advocates of technology predicted that the motivating characteristics and almost limitless potential of computers would lead to important gains in student achievement. However, meta-analyses comparing computer-assisted instruction (CAI) to conventional instructional methods revealed only limited benefits of CAI (Clark & Salomon, 1986).

The renewed confidence in technology in the 1990s comes when many more options for applying technology to learning are available than during the 1980s, a decade dominated by drill-and-practice programs. As districts scramble to wire buildings for networking and Internet access, cognitive science is uncovering newer instructional applications for technology. For example, the constructivist philosophy encourages students to take more responsibility for their learning and, thus, expects students to attach more importance and meaning to what they learn. In this teaching and learning model, the teacher's role is to help students find resources that will enable them to reach their learning objectives. The potential for students to use technology to meet these objectives is greatly enhanced by the rapid development of the Internet and the information resources of the World Wide Web. Students now have vast stores of knowledge and information available to them at their fingertips. Thus, newer technological applications seem closely aligned to current theories of learning.

At a time when more integrative technologies are helping teachers to explore student-centered approaches to learning, special educators are engaged in a debate about the most appropriate educational placement of students with disabilities.

The discussion centers on strategies for including students with disabilities in the mainstream classrooms and the factors that promote and hinder such practices. The primary issue in these discussions involves how students with disabilities can receive an appropriate education in general education settings. On one side of the discussion are advocates of a full inclusion model who see no need for segregating students based on somewhat arbitrary labels and descriptions (e.g., Lipsky & Gartner, 1992). On the other side are those who hold a more traditional point of view and suggest that children with disabilities can profit from special instruction services by specially trained professionals in more restricted settings (e.g., Lieberman, 1992).

Our purpose for writing this chapter is not to promote a theory of learning, a specific use of technology, or an instructional setting. Rather, we hope to provide teachers and administrators with practical ways of deriving from technology the best possible classroom applications given the available resources. First, we identify the substantive issues in each of the trends that we touched on above, a prerequisite for understanding the effective use of technology in inclusive settings. Next, we discuss several purposes for using technology and the resources necessary for accomplishing these purposes. Some of these concepts have been addressed in previous editions of this book, and in other chapters of this book (e.g., Chapters 1, 3, 7, 8, and 9). Finally, we provide a practical way of developing a technology plan that can be implemented at the school or district level. We believe that a workable technology plan will enable schools and districts to make use of the potential that technology has to offer learners with special needs.

In our attempts to explain the issues, we have tried to keep things simple. In doing so we may have fallen victim to the saying, "To every complex problem there is a simple solution, and it is almost always wrong." However, we have taken this position because we know that highly theoretical, abstract explanations almost never find their way into busy classrooms. Whenever possible, we have provided classroom examples that we have used or have seen other teachers use, hoping that readers can make relevant connections between their situations and our descriptions.

The Inclusive Classroom

The movement to include students with identified disabilities in general education environments continues to grow. Predicated on the least restrictive environment clause of the Education for All Handicapped Children Act of 1975, and reaffirmed by subsequent amendments to that act known as the Individuals with Disabilities Education Act of 1990 (IDEA) and the 1997 Amendments, the law advocates education for students with disabilities in general education settings. The term *inclusion* means that all students, to the extent possible, should be educated in general education classrooms. Stainback, Stainback, and Jackson (1992) outlined what is meant by full inclusion: All children must be included in both the educational and social life of their schools and classrooms. The basic goal is to not leave anyone out of school and classroom communities from the very beginning (thus, integration can be abandoned since no one has to go back to the

Technology can be used to include exceptional students in the educational and social aspects of schools and classrooms. (Photograph by Carolyn F. Woods)

mainstream). The focus shall be on the support needs of all students and personnel.

Whereas few would argue with the goal of educating students with disabilities in general education classrooms, successful reintegration of students with special needs into general education classrooms has proven far more difficult in practice than had been expected. Some of the difficulty has come from confusion over the expectations and roles of general education and special education teachers who find themselves working closely together as students with disabilities return to mainstream classrooms. The process of making accommodations and assigning teaching responsibilities will center on the goal of organizing instruction around individual differences, regardless of whether students have identified disabilities (Stainback, Stainback, East, & Sapon-Shevin, 1994). This will involve large amounts of staff development to help teachers make classroom adaptations for students with special needs (Baker & Zigmond, 1990; Ysseldyke, Thurlow, Wotruba, & Nanaia, 1990).

Heightened Expectations for All Students

At the same time that students with special needs are returning to general education classrooms, there are added pressures on classroom teachers to raise the achievement of all students. Since the release of the1985 Carnegie Foundation report titled *A Nation at Risk* (National Commission on Excellence in Education, 1983), national, state, and local movements have modified requirements for graduation, heightened expectations for student learning, and promoted learning outcomes that are more in sync with employer expectations.

Most of the curricular changes resulted in higher standards in areas such as reading, writing, speaking, listening, and math. These expectations are not new and have always been goals of education in one form or another; however, in addition to learning the basic skills, students are now also expected to solve challenging problems of the kind found in everyday life and employment settings. For example, Pollak (cited in

National Council of Teachers of Mathematics, 1989, p. 4) summarized the following expectations in mathematics:

1. The ability to set up problems with appropriate operations

2. Knowledge of a variety of techniques to approach and work on problems

3. Understanding of the underlying mathematical features of a problem

4. The ability to work with others on problems

5. The ability to see the applicability of mathematical ideas to common and complex problems

6. Preparation for open problem situations, since most real problems are not well formulated

7. Belief in the utility and value of mathematics

The changes in expectations have caused educators to rethink how instruction should be delivered. Not unlike discovery learning approaches advocated by Bruner (1960) decades ago, teachers are now urged to figure out ways in which learners can take on more responsibility for their own learning. This does not mean that teachers stand by as students fend for themselves. Rather, the goal of the teacher in a constructivist environment is to devise situations that enable students to build on what they already know by actively seeking new information. This information can be gained by inquiry methods that often involve collaboration with classmates and topic experts. Dwyer (1996) provided a useful summary of these changes, as shown in Table 4.1.

Creating Technology Environments that Support Meaningful Learning

Embedded in the spirit of modified standards and changing pedagogy is a rekindled expectation that technology will finally realize its full potential. The public expects teachers to use technology in meaningful ways and the pressure to use

Table 4.1. Attributes of Instruction and Construction Learning Environments

Change	Knowledge Instruction	Knowledge Construction
Classroom activity	Teacher centered (didactic)	Learner centered (interactive)
Teacher role	Fact teller (always expert)	Collaborator (sometimes learner)
Student role	Listener (always listener)	Collaborator (sometimes expert)
Instructional emphasis	Facts (memorization)	Relationships (inquiry and intervention)
Concept of knowledge	Accumulation of facts	Transformation of facts
Demonstration of success	Quantity	Quality of understanding
Assessment	Norm-referenced (multiple-choice items)	Criterion-referenced (portfolios and performances)
Technology use	Drill-and-practice	Communication (collaboration, information access, and expression)

technology for students of all abilities has reached an all-time high, evidenced in part by the National Education Summit of the Nation's Governors and Corporate Leaders (National Education Summit, 1996). Summit participants placed the hope for educational reform squarely on the shoulders of technology when the chairperson of the National Governors Association stated that *information technology is critical to improving the quality and diversity of education*. Thus, higher educational standards and technology are once again inextricably linked into one educational reform package.

This time around educators must be smarter in how technology is used, especially in inclusive classrooms, by carefully considering the constellation of school and community issues that are certain to influence technology use. Central among them is teacher professional development and support. Historically, expectations for teachers have been misaligned with line-item budget expenditures. In a recent report to Congress, the typical school district technology budget allocated 55% for hardware, 30% for software, and only 15% for training (U.S. Congressional OTA, 1995). Even this percentage for training is high compared with that found in many districts. For example, Utah allocated only 6% of its budget for training in the third year of their technology implementation plan (Mergendoller, Johnston,

Rockman, & Willis, 1994). It is doubtful that teachers would learn much about the utility of computers in classrooms with such small investments in professional development. Therefore, an important component of any technology plan must address the individual differences in *teachers'* ability to effectively manage and use computer technology in the classroom.

Besides support and professional considerations, a technology plan must also take into account differences in the technological capabilities of individual schools and districts. In 1994, again using Utah as an example, it ranked 25th out of 50 states in computer–student ratio. Statistics like these are often misleading because less than half (47%) of the computers in the high schools were considered capable of running sophisticated software (Mergendoller, 1996). Thus, plans should relate to the intended application of technology within the school's or district's capability to provide it.

In constructing a technology plan, the developers must make strong connections between purpose and use. For example, earlier we explained that drill-and-practice software did not significantly raise student achievement in the 1980s. This was not exactly true. Close inspection of these findings suggests that students who learned via drill-and-practice software fared no better than students who learned from teacher-directed lessons, but they did *no worse* either. The disappointment originated from the somewhat unrealistic expectation of drill-and-practice software to produce more significant fact-based learning than conventional teacher-directed methods. If the objective is to increase student fluency on basic skills, then drill-and-practice software may be a good option. If the goal is to teach students how to solve open-ended problems, a different application is needed.

This latter point is an important one. That is, learning goals must be clearly defined before deciding on the most appropriate technology application (also see Chapters 7 and 8). On the surface, this probably seems obvious. However, the nature of technology applications, such as the Internet, can lead educators to make instructional decisions that appear quite different from the ones originally intended. For example, if the goal of an assignment is for students to write a research report about a country of their choice, students should know that their report will be judged on clarity of expression, attention to detail, and proper language mechanics. Students who hand in a colorful, brochure-like report and pay attention to these criteria will probably earn a high grade. Students who hand in a colorful report that lacks organization or substance can expect to receive a low grade. Thus, teachers who use technology in their teaching must be more careful than ever to convey to their students the specific criteria for judging quality work. Without these specifications, students may assume that appearance without substance can substitute for quality.

Understanding the Array of Technology Uses

In our view many educators apply technology in ways that are too often focused on rudimentary and discrete skills, which sometimes leads to inappropriate uses with students who have special needs. This can be attributed, in part, to technology plans that fail to address classroom issues related to inclusion practices. Thus, as we

Individuals can use computers to enhance the acquisition and fluency of basic skills. (Photograph by Carolyn F. Woods)

begin our discussion of the development of technology plans for the inclusive classroom, we think that it is important to provide an overview about what is known about the uses of technology with special needs populations.

Basic Skill Acquisition and Fluency

Most special educators believe that it is important to develop basic skills and that this development occurs in two stages: *acquisition* and *fluency* (also see Chapters 1 and 6). Acquisition refers to the initial learning of a skill, whereas fluency refers to the ability to access this skill (such as math facts) in a quick and effortless manner. It is important for students to learn basic skills at a fluent level or the learning process is incomplete. Students who do not reach fluency are anticipated to experience difficulty in adult roles.

The development of basic skills has been an integral part of technology use in special education over the decade. When used appropriately, technology offers educators the opportunity to help students with special needs develop acquisition and fluency skills. Unfortunately, for a large number of these students, the promise for more efficient learning has not yet been realized. Although some research studies have demonstrated learning advantages resulting from using technology for instruction, others have not (see Bottge, in press; Bottge & Hasselbring, 1993; Carnine, 1989; Hasselbring, Goin, Taylor, Bottge, & Dailey, 1997). In cases where technology-based instruction has been successful, the research suggests that it is most often the result of using the computer to deliver well-designed and well-managed instruction. When results were not as positive, they had very little to do with the technology, per se, and were more directly associated with the inappropriate use of technology.

Thus, the uncertainty of these findings has left many teachers, parents, and administrators confused and uncertain about how technology can help enhance the development of basic skills. However, despite the apparently disparate findings, research has uncovered important ways that technology can help students learn basic skills.

Acquisition

Direct instruction is a teaching method used by many special education teachers when initial learning, or acquisition, of a skill or knowledge is taught. Direct instruction provides the student with clear models of the desired skill or behavior, along with frequent corrective feedback and reinforcement. When a teacher enlists technology to assist in teaching a new skill, the same teaching strategies should be incorporated.

Traditionally, teachers have selected two types of applications, drill-and-practice and tutorial, to assist in the acquisition of a skill or knowledge. Although there is no question that the nature of a drill-and-practice application makes it ideal for providing endless practice in almost any curricular area, the use of drill-and-practice is inappropriate when a student is in an acquisition phase of learning. As the name implies, computer-based drill and practice is designed to reinforce *previously learned information* rather than provide direct instruction on new skills. Perhaps Alan Hofmeister (1983) said it best when he wrote, "Drill-and-practice activities that are used as a substitute for the necessary teaching of the under-

lying concepts, and drill that is not followed by meaningful applications of the skills are inappropriate uses of drill-and-practice, regardless of whether a computer is used or not" (p. 4-2).

If technology is to be used during the acquisition phase of a new skill or concept, the tutorial is the most appropriate type of program. A technology-based tutorial differs from a drill-and-practice application by assuming the surrogate role of a teacher and providing direct instruction on a new skill or concept. The tutorial presents the student with new or previously unlearned material in an individualized manner, providing frequent corrective feedback and reinforcement.

Much more is known about how to develop good tutorial programs than is evidenced in many of the commercial packages on the market today. For example, an effective tutorial program should do the following:

1. Require a response that resembles the terminal skill being taught

2. Limit the amount of new information presented at one time

3. Provide review of recently learned information

4. Provide corrective feedback

5. Provide management component that monitors student progress through the learning stages

Increasingly, much of the appeal of technology has come from the variety of graphics and game formats that have been available. One reason for this emphasis on graphics and gaming is that it keeps the student's attention. However, simply keeping the child's attention on the computer screen does not guarantee learning. When selecting a tutorial program, it is important to analyze the nature of the response that the tutorial requires of the student. Do not be influenced by flashy graphics or games that do not add to the instructional value of the program.

Well-designed tutorial programs should present the skill in such a way that the student response approximates the terminal skill the educator wants to teach. For example, in a spelling tutorial, the student should be required to type the correct sequence of letters from memory as opposed to simply selecting the correct spelling from a list of choices, copying, or rearranging letters to spell a word.

Interference in learning new skills can be avoided by carefully limiting the size of the "information set" to be learned and gradually increasing it as material is acquired. A good math tutorial might present a few facts at a time (e.g., all the number pairs that sum to 10) rather than in large groups. The student should receive instruction that is spaced over a number of days rather than massed instruction in 1 or 2 days. As new material is acquired, a well-designed tutorial should provide for appropriately spaced review. Further, the program should provide the student with specific corrective feedback when incorrect responses are given. Corrective feedback prevents the student from learning an incorrect strategy or information set that must be unlearned at a later time, a common problem with many paper-and-pencil materials.

Finally, a common error in teaching new skills involves the continued use of acquisition-type techniques after the student is ready to progress to the fluency stage. A good tutorial should include a management component that tracks student performance and at the very least signals when the student is ready for fluency training on the skill. In selecting tutorial software, the educator must make sure that the principles of effective instruction are incorporated into the program.

Fluency

A significant amount of research suggests that fluency in basic skills is a necessary condition for proficient performance on higher order learning tasks (LaBerge & Samuels, 1974; Torgesen, 1984). Fluency in basic skills reduces the amount of attention required to carry out these skills. Because all people have a limited capacity for information processing, attaining a level of fluency reduces the cognitive demand and increases the capacity for understanding higher level concepts. Thus, it appears that the ability to succeed in higher level skills is directly related to the efficiency by which lower level processes are exe-

cuted. This is not a new revelation. For example, LaBerge and Samuels (1974), Lesgold (1983), and Torgesen (1984) have all suggested that fluency in decoding is a necessary prerequisite to higher level functioning in reading. If excessive attention is required on the part of the student for decoding words, there is a reduction in the amount of attention that the student can devote to higher order skills such as the comprehension and synthesis of the material. This point becomes obvious when one works with a child who cannot recognize words by sight. As the child reads along, he or she must devote excessive attentional resources to the decoding task by sounding out each word that is encountered. This tedious process leaves few mental resources available for thinking about the meaning of the passage. Thus, by the time the child reaches the end of the passage, he or she has virtually no understanding of what has just been read. Attentional resource problems are not limited to reading; similar problems are encountered in other academic areas, such as math and language arts.

Once a student can demonstrate a skill at the acquisition level, it is essential that the student develop fluency in that skill if it is to become functional. The goal of fluency training is to increase the rate and accuracy with which the student performs the skill, and the activities should emphasize the speed of performance. Thus, technology-based programs used for developing fluency should appear different from tutorial programs used for acquiring skills. Well-designed programs for developing fluency should accomplish the following:

1. Provide practice on acquired skills or knowledge only

2. Provide practice on the desired terminal skill

3. Provide ample opportunities for practice

4. Emphasize speed of responding

5. Provide a management component that monitors student progress

Generally, drill-and-practice type programs lend themselves nicely to developing fluency on a skill. The research findings of Hasselbring, Goin, and Bransford (1988) suggested that when a student is in the fluency stage of learning, the use of drill-and-practice software will result in positive student gains. However, educators must be cautious and examine each program for the features listed above before assuming the program will be effective.

Perhaps the importance of these features can be shown most clearly by an example in mathematics. Many teachers who have tried to increase students' fluency in the basic math facts using drill-and-practice software have been unsuccessful. There are several reasons for this failure. First, a student is usually given drill-and-practice routines before the terminal skill is acquired that leads to practice on the nonterminal skill. For example, math facts such as $7 + 5$ and $12 - 7$ can be solved in two ways: the student can (1) retrieve the answer from memory or (2) reconstruct the answer using a counting method. Although the preferred terminal skill is to retrieve the fact from memory, most people place students on drill-and-practice programs before the student has this skill. This results in students employing laborious counting strategies for arriving at correct answers. Research shows that when this occurs, the only behavior that becomes more fluent is counting. There is no indication that students using counting strategies to solve basic math facts will begin recalling the answers from memory as a result of using drill-and-practice software (Hasselbring et al., 1988).

A second problem is that many drill-and-practice programs in math, as well as in other academic areas, do not emphasize rapid responding. Too often, the students are given an unlimited amount of time in which to respond. For example, giving students an unlimited amount of time to respond encourages the student to use counting strategies to solve problems rather than retrieving the answers from memory. For fluency to be developed, the student must be encouraged to respond as quickly as possible. Any fluency program should be designed to encourage high rates of responding.

Finally, much of the existing drill-and-practice software does not have a management system that monitors student progress. When software has no management system, the computer does not know which problems students should practice. This leads to providing the student with inappropriate practice sets, again encouraging nonterminal skills to be practiced. Chapter 8 presents strategies for managing and monitoring students' technology activities.

In summary, technology-based drill-and-practice programs have an important place in building fluency. However, as with any teaching method or material, drill-and-practice programs must be used appropriately. Drill-and-practice software should help build fluency but never be used to teach a skill.

Exploratory Technologies

The use of exploratory technology differs from that used to develop basic skills because the student is primarily responsible for directing his or her own learning. In an exploratory application, the student is presented with tasks that are often complex and engage the student's inactive problem solving or knowledge synthesis across a variety of domains. There are three broad types of technology used for exploratory learning with students who have special needs: (1) simulations or microworlds, (2) multimedia or electronic databases, and (3) the World Wide Web. Although these uses of technology differ in several ways, each provides students with the opportunity to discover and construct knowledge through a self-directed learning process (also see Chapters 3 and 7).

Simulations

A number of reasons have been suggested as to why simulations are useful for developing thinking and problem-solving abilities. For example, a technology-based simulation can model or recreate a real-life event that cannot be carried out easily in a traditional teaching environment. Simulations allow the student to vicariously experience such real-life events as traveling in space, homesteading in the 1800s, conducting a science experiment, or living as prey or predator in a food chain. Simulations can be used to introduce a sense of realism into what are often frustrating and abstract subjects for the learner with special needs. Further, simulations provide the opportunity for learners to participate in the activity rather than to assume the customary passive role.

Certain guidelines have been established for the appropriate use of technology-based simulations. Simulations are most appropriate as substitutes for real-life experiences when

1. The learning objectives are complex and students are unlikely to be able to develop the needed skills in a real-life environment (e.g., work skills).

2. The time scale of the real-life event is too long or too short to allow efficient learning (e.g., money management).

3. The real-life experience involves danger and/or high cost (e.g., driver training).

4. The real-life event cannot be carried out in a normal teaching environment (e.g., voting).

Many simulations are described as programs for developing decision making, which is unquestionably an important aspect of thinking and problem solving. However, several noted authorities on thinking and problem solving believe that students can solve and master a simulation without developing effective problem-solving skills (Bransford, Stein, Delclos, & Littlefield, 1986). Bransford and his colleagues argued that decisions made in many simulations can be based mainly on trial-and-error guessing rather than on systematic analysis of the available information. The risk of using simulations is that they encourage guessing and trial-and-error responding because, initially, students have very little information about the simulations. Bransford et al. also argued that a more effective procedure would be to teach information-gathering skills by first helping students to consult external sources of information that could assist them in making more rational decisions during the simulations.

Thus, it appears that technology-based simulations can be used to extend the boundaries of the traditional teaching environment in a safe and cost-effective manner. Although simulations provide students who have special needs with the kinds of learning opportunities not found in traditional learning environments, caution in their use must be observed. As Bransford et al. (1986) pointed out, people often fail to use appropriate concepts and strategies because they do not realize that this information is relevant. Teaching methods that bridge relevant pieces of information must be used to increase the probability that appropriate information will be used to improve decision making and problem solving through computer simulations. Although it appears that simulations may produce improved problem solving, this is likely to occur only when prior information is provided and can be used as part of the simulation.

Multimedia Databases

Simulations are not the only exploratory technology used in special education today. The use of exploratory technologies in special education has evolved more recently with the development of hypermedia or multimedia platforms and software. As reported in Chapter 2, the recent advances in computing and communication technology have opened flexible connections between formerly distinct media such as text, photographs, television, video, sound, graphics, and computing. The means to interweave written language, static and dynamic images, and sound under computer control has been called *hypermedia*. Although the ability to create hypermedia environments is relatively new, the concept of hypermedia is not. As early as 1945, Dr. Vannevar Bush, then the science adviser to President Franklin Roosevelt, published "As We May Think," a speculative article about a device that would leap through vast amounts of textual information with the speed and freedom of human thought (Bush, 1945). Bush realized that the world was on the verge of an information explosion and devices had to be developed to allow for the rapid access of this information.

In the 1960s Ted Nelson and others realized that Bush's vision of accessing information in much the same way the human mind thinks was theoretically possible because of advancements in computer technology. In discussing the concept of hypertext, Nelson (1967) described it as "nonsequential forms of writing that branch on request." Nelson argued that although text is printed linearly, it is a web conceptually, with complex interdependencies among its nodes. This fact is perhaps most evident in definitional documents, such as dictionaries, encyclopedias, and training manuals. Nelson suggested that computers could be used to establish electronic links between documents (or document parts) and to define associative paths through such linked materials. This linking process affords students more effective learning experiences than traditional linear texts, which literally send readers off to bookshelves or library stacks.

For an idea of how hypertext works, consider the following example. Suppose you are reading this book but, instead of being printed on paper, it is stored electronically and is printed on a computer screen. As you read along, you encounter a reference to another work that you are interested in reading. Normally, you would turn to the bibliography to get the complete reference and then head to the library to locate it. However, in a hypertext document things are different. Using a mouse or other pointing device, you would simply move the cursor to the reference, select it, and instantaneously be placed in that referenced article. Your journey, however, would not have to end there. As you read along in this new document, you may encounter another reference that you wish to explore. You simply select that reference and the computer moves you immediately to that document.

In a hypertext world, jumping from document to document is not the only choice you have. Suppose that you encounter a word that you do not understand. After clicking on the word, you are presented with an electronic dictionary that provides a basic definition and offers several sentences in which the contextual features of the word are revealed. You also can jump to a thesaurus in which you can browse definitions of related words. This concept of "jumping to" related documents from within a central document—as if they exist in hyperspace in which all documents are equally accessible from any point

in any other document—begins to convey the full notion and power of hypertext.

Hypermedia is a natural extension of the hypertext concept. Hypermedia allows video, graphics, and sound to be linked with text in new and important ways. From a psychological perspective, a key aspect of such uses of media is that they greatly facilitate certain fundamental activities required for learning and thinking. In particular, hypermedia encourages knowledge elaboration and the provision of multiple paths into knowledge use. Thus, hypermedia provides an opportunity for offering students entirely new approaches to learning.

Perhaps the best current examples of exploratory technologies are the multimedia encyclopedias marketed by major encyclopedia publishers. These products are ideal for exploratory use by students with special needs. As they explore one topic, they can jump to related topics quickly and easily. Further, many of the electronic encyclopedias currently on the market can actually create a physical link between topics so when students return to the topics the links will be noted. Many researchers and educators believe that it is the creation of this type of linkage that will help students develop deeper understandings of topics and ideas.

For all students, but especially for students with special needs, the use of hypermedia has some potential disadvantages. It is easy for students to get distracted or lost in the hypermedia environment that is filled with interesting information. Although it is wonderful to have access to vast amounts of information by clicking and browsing, the usefulness of this information comes from developing a conceptual framework from which to make sense of that information. Students must develop meaningful linkages between discrete bits of information and larger information domains. Teachers must take an active role in helping students to construct a conceptual understanding of how this information is related.

World Wide Web

Perhaps the most extensive and pervasive hypermedia resource to date is the World Wide Web.

The Web, most simply, is a hypertext-based multimedia structure on the Internet. What this means is that the Web is a way of exploring the Internet by pointing and clicking to jump from place to place. But more important, each stop is filled with a variety of multimedia resources including text, pictures, sounds, and even movies. The fact that the Web is a visual environment makes it not only easy to use but also a valuable resource for students with disabilities.

To understand the usefulness of the Web, it is important first to understand the power of the Internet. The Internet began as a military project to allow Department of Defense research computers to talk to each other. Since its early days, the Internet has transformed the communications world, much as television did for the previous generation. However, there is a huge difference between television and the Internet. On the Internet there are as many "channels" as there are computers attached to the Internet, and, unlike TV, the user can talk back. The Internet, then, is basically a huge interactive network connecting millions of computers all over the world. Being able to talk to or "link" to so many computers puts an unprecedented amount of information at the user's fingertips.

The World Wide Web takes advantage of the huge network of computers on the Internet and consists of thousands upon thousands of *sites*, also sometimes called *home pages* or *Web pages*. Think of Web sites as tourist attractions on the information superhighway. Web sites can belong to individual users, schools, businesses, or public institutions (e.g., the Smithsonian Institute). Many Web sites provide links to other Web sites. Thus, traveling the Internet and Web is as easy as pointing and clicking to a link that allows the user to jump to a new location on the Web.

For students with disabilities, the Web offers unprecedented access to a wealth of information and services. Through sites on the Web, students can access resources as diverse as the Library of Congress, encyclopedias, and art museums, as well as information on virtually every topic imaginable. The concept of the Web is so expansive that entire books have been written on the subject, so there is no way that we can do justice to

the topic here. However, there are some guidelines that should be considered when using the Internet and Web with students.

1. Travel on the Web should be purposeful and goal directed. Although some random exploration might be useful, more often than not it leads to wasted learning time with few positive outcomes.

2. Student work on the Web should result in some product that demonstrates what he or she has learned, such as a multimedia presentation on a specific topic.

3. Students should be carefully instructed in *acceptable use*. This means that if the student encounters information on the Web that is inappropriate, then he or she should leave that site immediately and report it to the teacher.

4. School should have a written *acceptable use policy* that is signed by every student using the Web as well as their parents.

Like all technology, the Internet and Web offer great opportunities for learning. However, these opportunities can be realized only if they are approached with purpose and care. Meaningful use of the Internet and Web requires planning and skill on the part of the teacher (see Appendixes G and H).

Application Technologies

The ultimate goal of all teachers is to develop skills and knowledge in their students that can be used in real-world settings. Unfortunately, the application of skills and knowledge may be the most significant problem that children with learning difficulties face. Although educators can often teach academic skills to a high level of fluency, the knowledge remains *inert* and useless unless the students are able to use this knowledge to solve everyday problems. To overcome this problem, many educators have suggested that technology be used to develop the thinking and problem-solving skills of students with special needs.

Exceptional individuals can use computers in inclusive settings to access the latest in technology and manage needed information. (Photograph by Carolyn F. Woods)

A number of applications programs can be used to promote students' understanding of how the skills and knowledge that they learn in school can be used to address problems they face on a daily basis. Technology applications, such as the familiar word processor, spreadsheet, database, and multimedia presentation tools, provide students the opportunity to use reading, writing, spelling, and mathematical skills to create products and to address real-world problems (also see Chapters 3 and 7). With applications software the technology becomes a tool that students can use to incorporate the skills and knowledge that they learn in school to facilitate thinking and problem solving. These tools also allow the student to be a producer of information as opposed to simply a consumer of information. Perhaps the most obvious way for a student to produce information is through the writing process.

Word Processing

Over the past 20 years, much has been written about the use of the word processor for improving the writing skills of children with learning difficulties. Frequently authors have lauded the characteristics of word processors with respect to the positive effects they have on the writing process for learners with special needs. For example, the ease of text revision, production of a clean readable text, and a sense of "authorship" are mentioned most often as attributes of word processors that lead to improved writing. However, until recently, little was known about the effectiveness of using word processors with children with special needs (Graham & MacArthur, 1988; MacArthur & Graham, 1987).

The work of MacArthur and Graham (1987; Graham & MacArthur, 1988) has provided some insight into this area of technology-based instruction. As we stated previously, good instruction, regardless of the medium of delivery, will have a positive effect on student achievement. This applies to the principles of writing instruction as well. When teaching with a word processor, students should be taught effective strategies for writing. However, the characteristics of the word processor alter the writing process because the students' work is more visible and more easily revised or erased. This has an impact not only on student writing behavior but also on teaching behavior. Although there is much more to learn about how children with learning and behavioral problems can use a word processor for writing, we suggest the following:

1. Teach keyboarding skills prior to using a word processor.

2. Teach the mechanics of the word processor prior to writing.

3. Select teaching strategies that reflect the student's current stage of writing.

4. Teach strategies for generating ideas in conjunction with using a word processor.

5. Have students compose directly on the word processor.

6. Save editing until the text is fully composed.

7. Allow students to have control over their writing.

Again, for additional information on the use of application software such as word processors, spreadsheets, and databases, see Chapters 3 and 7.

Students as Multimedia Developers

Recently, special educators have begun to recognize the value of having students create authentic products that are viewed by other students, parents, and community members (see Chapter 6). The products are multimedia presentations about important and timely issues, such as drugs and alcohol, AIDS, driving safety, and environmental concerns. Student production teams do the research necessary to create products that can teach and inform others. In creating the products, the students learn about the topics in a meaningful way.

The multimedia products produced by students incorporate text, sound, pictures, graphics, and video. Visual images may be collected from the Internet or Web or a public domain source. Students combine these with text and narration that they supply, as well as with music that they select or create. Because the development of the student products involves a wide range of talents (e.g., music, drawing, writing), the process allows students to use talents that often are not emphasized in school. The fact that students are creating products that will be shown to others appears to be highly motivating. Researchers who have conducted similar types of authentic products report that the motivation of at-risk students improves markedly in these learning situations (Collins, Hawkins, & Carver, 1991).

Other noteworthy benefits of producing multimedia have been discovered. First, classmates are extremely interested in each others' presentations. Second, teachers often report surprise at the level of attention and detail exhibited by children with learning and behavioral problems. Third, the quality of student work often belies the fact that they are receiving special education services.

When completed, students' products can be displayed in their school. In addition, the products can be transferred to videotape so that the students can take them home for their parents to see. Also, once on videotape, students at different schools have opportunities to share their products with one another.

When working with students who are producing multimedia products, educators must monitor several things for the development process to be beneficial to the student:

1. The student should select the topic so that he or she is motivated to complete the project.

2. All of the research should be completed and the presentation planned before the student begins creating the product on the computer.

3. The multimedia presentation tool should be simple for students to learn and provide only a limited number of options. Otherwise students get consumed with the technology and forget the content of their presentation.

4. Teachers must take advantage of opportunities for teaching (e.g., grammar, writing, spelling) within a context that is meaningful and motivating for the student.

Students will not produce masterpieces the first time. Their texts will need to be rewritten and their supporting media (e.g., pictures, graphics, video) will need to be edited and polished. These types of improvements require effective teaching and practice followed by feedback. Nevertheless, over time the students will produce some interesting and professional products and learn while they are doing it.

Communication Technologies

Communication technologies are becoming more prevalent in special education settings and allow students to access and send information, in a variety of forms, literally around the world. Newer forms of communication technology include interactive distance learning and, more recently, electronic field trips.

Communication technologies represent a relatively inexpensive yet powerful form of technology for instruction. Through the use of computer networks, many schools are connecting their computers to other computers, often thousands of miles away (also see Chapters 2 and 5). By networking computers within a room, building, or larger geographic area, students can send and receive information from other teachers or students not in their physical location. By networking computers, teachers and students are freed from the constraints of location and time. For example, students can log on to a network at any time that is convenient to send or receive information from any location attached to their network. Also, given the heavy dependence on text in most networked systems, students have a reason to use text to read, write, and construct thoughts and ideas for others to read and respond to.

The nature of networked systems also makes collaborative learning easier. Through networks, students from many different sites can share ideas and activities and learn from one another. For example, *learning circles* have been used to create electronic communities of about eight classrooms where teachers and students collaborate over a network on a common project (Riel, 1990). These projects are based on common curricular objectives for the learning circle classrooms. Typically, a problem is posed and the students in the learning circle research the issues collaboratively by searching for relevant information, sharing ideas, and offering solutions.

The success of collaborative endeavors such as learning circles depends on a number of different factors. The successful use of networks was examined by Levin, Kim, and Riel (1990), who found that successful collaborative projects had at least four of the following five characteristics:

1. Students and teachers, even though not in the same location, shared an interest in the educational projects.

2. The projects were well defined and structured.

3. Sites had access to a reliable computer network.

4. Students and teachers had a sense of responsibility to the project as well as the electronic community at large.

5. Strong leadership and a final evaluation of the project were provided.

Providing students with special needs access to a larger world opens many opportunities previously unavailable to them. Further, not all communication using networks has to be collabora-tive. In many cases communications can be private between two individuals. Because communicating using electronic mail can be a private experience, many individuals with disabilities find this to be very rewarding. When communicating in this way, the person on the other end of the communication cannot see the sender and has no idea what he or she looks like unless the sender wishes this to be known. If the sender is blind, deaf, physically challenged, or learning disabled, this is really unimportant in the communication process. Often, the fact that a sender has a disability is never known. In one case a student who was deaf and blind used adaptive computer equipment to communicate with people all over the world and no one ever knew the student had a disability. Clearly, communicating in this way can be a great equalizer.

A vast array of communications services are rapidly becoming available to students with special needs. For example, desktop videoconferencing systems are now being used to allow students and teachers at remote inclusive and segregated sites to see and hear each other. In this way face-to-face interactions can take place over great distances in real time.

One-way video and two-way audio are also being used for providing instruction to remote sites, as well as for such special events as *electronic field trips*. Students can visit places around the world that, in most cases, they would not have had the opportunity to visit without communication technology. For example, programs have been set up where students can visit interesting, scientific sites with a scientist as a guide. Diving underwater off a coral reef and visiting an archeological dig are the types of experiences that students can have on electronic field trips. The advantage of this type of experience over watching a video is that it occurs in real time and through two-way audio connections; students can actually ask the scientist questions about what they are seeing and get an immediate response. Although these types of programs have been largely experimental, advances in communication technology are making these types of experiences more affordable and accessible to larger numbers of schools.

The use of communication technology in inclusive and special needs classes is growing. As technology becomes cheaper and more available, many more students will be able to take advantage of the learning resources that are available throughout the world.

Keep Them Flying!

From reading the previous sections, it should be apparent that there are many questions to consider when developing a schoolwide or district-wide technology plan: Who should be on the planning committee? What are the advantages and disadvantages of each technology application for inclusive classrooms? In what ways does the plan ensure that the learning activities afforded by the application will result in better learning opportunities? and Is the application one that teachers will use? The last question is especially important because, unless the computer is turned on, none of the technology applications that we described in preceding sections can be pursued. We point this out because we often visit classrooms where three or four computers either are turned off or are turned on but no students are using them. An important part of the technology plan involves time management and making sure that the technology is being used to the maximum extent possible (also see Chapter 8).

An analogy that might be useful for planning committees and teachers to consider when they are thinking about how to use technology is the airline industry. Airline executives know all too well that the only time they make money is when their airplanes are flying and there are people in the seats. If the airplane is not flying, or if it is flying but has empty seats, the airline is losing money. The same could be said for schools and computers. Computers are costly items, and the only time there is a return on this investment is when they are being used. Ideally, from the time students enter school until they leave at the end of the day, computers should have a student in front of them and some meaningful activity should be taking place. If this is not the case, schools are not getting a return on their dollar.

Developing a Technology Plan

In the remainder of this chapter, we describe the steps that we feel are necessary for developing and implementing a quality technology plan in an inclusive setting. The four general steps are (1) forming the planning committee, (2) reviewing the school district's mission and goals, (3) assessing current status and anticipated needs, and (4) analyzing results.

Forming the Planning Committee

The first step in the planning process should be to form a planning committee to develop and successfully implement the technology plan. Committee makeup is a critical consideration and tricky at best. For example, it is best to have a heterogeneous group that represents every constituency from the early adopter of technology to the technophobe, from early childhood to high school, from math and science to art and music. It is important that all voices are heard and that professionals feel that their ideas and opinions are being heard. However, the committee should not be so big as to make it impossible to function. Much thought should go into forming a committee that will be able to develop a reasonable and workable technology plan.

Reviewing School District Mission and Goals

Especially pertinent to our previous discussion, special attention should focus on issues related to curriculum, professional development, and inclusion. In the curriculum area, members of the committee should have ample opportunity to discuss what they want students to learn and be able to do, ways in which instruction can be delivered to accomplish this, and possible ways in which progress toward these goals can be assessed. These three topics of discussion can be labeled curriculum, instruction, and assessment (CIA).

Strands of technology goals should be woven into the fabric of these plans. Whenever possible, technology should be combined with CIA goals, not separate from them. A common error in technology planning is the practice that labels technology as a distinct and separate entity from CIA. In these cases, the school district ends up with a CIA goal document and a separate technology document, each with its own set of goals. This is a risky practice for several reasons. First, any program separate from the main function of schools (i.e., CIA) is liable to be cut or severely reduced during financially troubled times. Second, if technology is to support the goals of CIA, implementation of technology should be a prime consideration. Sometimes, however, technology is not embraced wholeheartedly by faculty or administrators.

For these reasons goals and applications must be one package. In other words the learning goals should be written in such a way that they cannot be attained without the application that goes along with it, such as the following:

- Students will solve a multistep mathematics problem using search capabilities of at least two technology applications.

- Students will use the worldwide network as a resource to develop an argument for or against a problem of national concern.

Technology tools facilitate the planning, implementation, and assessment of curriculum and teaching–learning outcomes. (Photograph by Caroline F. Woods)

- Students will demonstrate their understanding of a topic of national concern by creating a multimedia production and presenting it to the class.

This is not to suggest that a separate technology committee should not be formed. However, if at all possible, this committee should be a subcommittee of the larger CIA planning group.

Assessing Current Status and Anticipated Needs

Once there is agreement on what students should learn, how they should learn it, and how to measure how much they have learned, attention should shift to the current status of these goals. Most often, this involves a survey or status report that assesses progress toward each goal. The planning model provides a handy reference tool from which to develop the survey questions. For example, a survey based on our model would ask professionals to respond to questions in three major areas:

1. What is your degree of technology literacy in each function?

2. How accessible is technology to you?

3. How do you use technology in your teaching?

We suggest that the survey ask professionals, in addition to assessing their current situation, for their opinion about the status of technology deployment in their school, the amount and type of staff development they have received, and their anticipated teaching and technology needs over the next 3 years. To assess current status and future wants, each item on the survey would ask for two responses: *what is now* and *what should be in 3 years*. A prototype of this kind of survey is provided in Figure 4.1. It is important that each committee constructs a survey based on the unique characteristics in its school or school district.

Analyzing Results

Although our sample technology questionnaire (Figure 4.1) is only a model for ones that

Technology Questionnaire

Directions: Please help us plan for the appropriate use of technology over the next 3 years by completing this questionnaire. For each item, please indicate what you think the current status of technology is in your classroom (what is now). Then indicate what you think it should be in 5 years (what should be).

Technology includes such things as a TV, videodisc players, and computers.

1 = never   2 = rarely   3 = sometimes   4 = usually   5 = always

My students use technology to:	**What is now**	**What should be**
1. develop basic skills such as reading, math, and spelling.	1 2 3 4 5	1 2 3 4 5
2. as tools to help them conduct research.	1 2 3 4 5	1 2 3 4 5
3. receive information from and send information to persons in other communities.	1 2 3 4 5	1 2 3 4 5
4. create multimedia presentations.	1 2 3 4 5	1 2 3 4 5

I am confident in my abilities to:

	What is now	**What should be**
5. select software that matches my instructional objectives.	1 2 3 4 5	1 2 3 4 5
6. access and navigate computer search tools (e.g., Internet).	1 2 3 4 5	1 2 3 4 5
7. find technology applications to help my students develop problem-solving skills.	1 2 3 4 5	1 2 3 4 5
8. help my students produce multimedia presentations.	1 2 3 4 5	1 2 3 4 5

To the following questions, select the most appropriate response:

9. About how many times a week do your students use a computer?
   a. Once a week
   b. Twice a week
   c. Three or more times a week
   d. Never

10. How many total minutes *a week* do your students use a computer?
    a. Less than 15 minutes
    b. 15–29 minutes
    c. 30–60 minutes
    d. More than 60 minutes

11. How many computers do you have in your classroom?
    a. None
    b. One
    c. Two
    d. Three or more

12. If you have computers in your classroom, what kind are they?

_____

_____

(continues)

Figure 4.1. Sample technology questionnaire.

13. I teach in a(n):
    a. Elementary school
    b. Middle school
    c. High school
    d. Alternative school
14. **(For middle school and high school teachers only)** I teach the following subjects:

_____
15. I would like to learn more about _____
_____

Figure 4.1. (*continued*)

committees will develop, it can help us demonstrate how the model and questionnaire responses provide clear direction for planning. Each *what is now* and *what should be* question provides three pieces of information: current status, future wants, and the size of the discrepancy between the two. For example, Question 2 asks to what extent students use technology applications when conducting research. If the teacher marks the 1 under *what is now*, the committee knows that, for some reason, students in that class do not use technology to help them conduct research. Further, if that teacher circles 5 under *what should be*, he or she thinks that students should use technology in their research. Suppose that the teacher chose 2 under *what is now*. That combination of responses would indicate that the teacher is not providing technology opportunities to his or her students and, perhaps more important, does not wish to.

If a computer is used to score and tabulate the responses, the discrepancies between *what is now* and *what should be* on each item can be plotted on a grid like the one in Figure 4.2. The vertical axis displays a continuum of response values for current status (*what is now*) from 1 at the bottom of the grid to 5 at the top. The horizontal axis displays the same values for future status (*what should be*). If some paired scores fall into Quadrant I, the activity described by the survey item is happening much of the time, but the respondent does not want it to happen in the future. Items that are in Quadrant II suggest that the activity is not happening now and the respondent does not

want it to occur in the future. In Quadrant III, the activity occurs frequently and the respondent wants it to continue. Quadrant IV is perhaps the most important of the four. If scores fall in this quadrant, the activity is not occurring but the respondent wants it to happen in the future.

For example, again using Question 2, suppose that teachers thought that the current status of that activity in their building averaged 2.1 and the average score for their future expectations was 4.5. That item would fall into Quadrant IV, which clearly indicates that the activity is not commonly occurring but that teachers want it to occur more often. By plotting each paired value on the grid, decision makers can get a visual representation of the results.

Most often, CIA goals and objectives are grouped according to grade levels (e.g., K–2, 3–5, 6–8, 9–12). To reduce the masking effects that may occur by totaling all responses across grade levels, we suggest that the results be disaggregated according to whatever grade-level groupings seem appropriate. This will enable planners to tailor general statements about the use of technology to more age-appropriate learning activities.

After the district has established a current level of technology use, it must decide how technology applications can contribute to the CIA goals. A time frame for implementing these applications should extend no longer than 5 years into the future. With the rapid expansion and sophistication of technology, plans that extend beyond 5 years may quickly become out of date. Again,

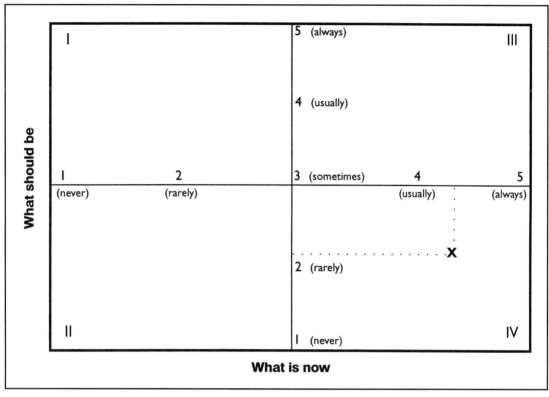

Figure 4.2. An agreement-discrepancy grid to help analyze questionnaire responses.

using the framework as a format for planning, decide on a reasonable 5-year goal. Close inspection of each cell combined with an estimate of the district's resources should help in formulating this goal.

For example, suppose that a district's curriculum and instruction goals emphasize all of the row functions indicated in the framework: computer-based instruction, exploration, communication, and production. The planning committee must then consider how much capital outlay monies can be directed toward the purchase of computers and installation of networks to accommodate those functions. If the goal is to install one computer per classroom in the next 5 years, committee members can identify specific learner goals, instructional applications, and assessment activities for that condition.

As we mentioned earlier, plans often fail because they do not take into account professional development issues. In our example, the goal is to incorporate curriculum-based instruction, explo-

ration, communication, and production functions into every classroom. Thus, teachers must learn the potential benefits of all three functions, ways to integrate them into lessons, classroom management strategies for the use of a single computer, and ways to match each student's individual needs with the benefits of each function. To address each of these topics adequately will require large amounts of time. Because the success of the plan depends on these implementation issues, investment in teacher training is critical.

Summary

The purpose of this chapter has been to provide a framework for successfully developing and implementing a technology program for inclusive settings. We began by reviewing what is meant by the inclusive classroom and by discussing the current expectation in education that all students need to perform better, whether or not they have a disability. Clearly, these changes in expectations have caused educators to rethink how instruction should be delivered. To many, technology offers students with disabilities an opportunity to level the playing field. However, before this becomes a reality, it is important that technology be used to support learning in a meaningful way. Simply making technology available is not enough. Thus, the development of any technology plan must make strong connections between purpose and use. A major part of the chapter reviewed what we have learned about making technology a useful and meaningful tool for learning. These lessons must be taken to heart if the technology plan is going to make a difference. Finally, we discussed the development of the plan itself. The successful technology plan must be thought of as a *work in progress*. The effective technology plan is never really completed, but rather is constantly being evaluated, updated, and reevaluated. The successful technology plan cannot be viewed as a static document, but rather as a dynamic and constantly changing plan that must adapt to the inevitable changes that technology presents.

Resources

Organizations

The Council for Exceptional Children (CEC) is the largest international professional organization dedicated to improving educational outcomes for individuals with exceptionalities. The CEC advocates for appropriate governmental policies, sets professional standards, provides continual professional development, advocates for newly and historically underserved individuals with exceptionalities, and helps professionals obtain conditions and resources necessary for effective professional practice. *Contact:* CEC, 1920 Association Drive, Reston, VA 20191-1589; Voice: 703/620-3660; TTY: 703/264-9446; Fax: 703/264-9494; E-mail: service@cec.sped.org; Web: http://www.cec.sped.org/

The Technology and Media Division of the Council for Exceptional Children (TAM) promotes the availability and effective use of technology and media for exceptional individuals. *Contact:* See previous CEC information. Web: http://www.ucc.ucon.edu/~tam/

The Trace Center is an interdisciplinary research, development, and resource center on technology and disabil-

ity. It is part of the Waisman Center and the Department of Industrial Engineering at the University of Wisconsin–Madison. The mission of the center is "to advance the ability of people with disabilities to achieve their life objectives through the use of communication, computer and information technologies." *Contact:* Trace Research and Development Center, University of Wisconsin–Madison, S-151 Waisman Center, 1500 Highland Avenue, Madison, WI 53705-2280; Voice: 608/262-6966; TTY: 608/263-5408; Fax: 608/262-8848; E-mail: web@trace.wisc.edu; Web: http://www.trace.wisc.edu/

The Center for Applied Special Technology (CAST) was founded in 1984. CAST is a not-for-profit organization whose mission is to expand opportunities for individuals with disabilities through innovative computer technology. This mission is achieved through research and product development that further universal design for learning. *Contact:* CAST, 39 Cross Street, Peabody, MA 01960; Voice: 978/531-8555; TTY: 978/538-3110; Fax: 978/531-0192; E-mail: cast@cast.org; Web: http://www.cast.org/index.html

International Society for Technology in Education (ISTE) promotes appropriate uses of technology to support and improve teaching and learning. Representing more than 40,000 educators, ISTE provides (a) curriculum for learning about technology and integrating it into the classroom, (b) research results and project reports, and (c) leadership for policy affecting educational technology. *Contact:* ISTE, 1787 Agate Street, Eugene, OR 97403-1923; Voice: 541/346-4414; Fax: 541/346-5890; E-mail: cust_svc@ccmail.uoregon.edu; Web: http://www.iste.org/index.html

The National Center to Improve Practice in Special Education Through Technology, Media, and Materials (NCIP) seeks to improve educational outcomes for students with disabilities by promoting the effective use of assistive and instructional technologies among educators and related personnel serving these students. *Contact:* NCIP, Education Development Center, Inc., 55 Chapel Street, Newton, MA 02158-1060; Voice: 617/969-7100 (2387); TTY: 617/969-4529; Fax: 617/969-3440; Web: http://www.edc.org/FSC/NCIP/

Journals

Educational Technology. This international journal addresses a variety of technology issues, including telecommunications in education and training; new forms and techniques of instructional design and development; multimedia software and interface design; and internet electronic performance and learning support technologies.

Contact: Educational Technology Publications, Inc., 700 Palisade Avenue, Englewood Cliffs, NJ 07632-0564; Voice: 201/871-4007; Fax: 201/871-4009; E-mail: edtec pubs@aol.com

Educational Technology Review. This periodical is devoted to the issues and applications of educational technology to enhance learning and teaching. This publication is designed to provide a multidisciplinary forum to present and discuss all aspects of educational technology at the school and college levels. *Contact: Educational Technology Review,* Association for the Advancement of Computing in Education (AACE), P.O. Box 2966, Charlottesville, VA 22902; Voice: 980/973-3987; Fax: 804/978-7449; E-mail: aace@virginia.edu

Electronic School. This journal chronicles technological change in the classroom, interprets education issues in a digital world, and offers readers practical advice on a broad range of topics pertinent to the implementation of technology in elementary and secondary schools. *Contact: Electronic School,* 1680 Duke Street, Alexandria, VA 22314; Voice: 703/838-6722; Fax: 703/549-6719; E-mail: electronic-school@nsba.org

Journal of Special Education Technology. This journal is devoted to the proliferation of information, research, and reports of innovative practices regarding the application of educational technology for the development and education of exceptional children. *Contact: Journal of Special Education Technology,* 306SZB, The University of Texas at Austin, Austin, TX 78712; Voice: 512/471-4161; Fax: 512/471-4061; E-mail: reith.Herb@mail.utexas.edu

Learning and Leading with Technology. This journal provides practical ideas for using technology where it can make a difference—making the teacher's job easier; saving time; motivating students; helping students with varying learning styles, abilities, and backgrounds; and creating educational environments that are unique. *Contact: Learning and Leading with Technology,* International Society for Technology in Education, 1787 Agate Street, Eugene, OR 97403-1923; Voice: 541/346-2400; E-mail: anita_best@ccmail.uoregon.edu

T.H.E. Journal: Technological Horizons in Education. This journal reports on the world of computers and related technologies, with a focus on their applications to improve teaching and learning for all ages. Published since 1973, the magazine consists of news, product info, case history stories, plus academic features written by educators, for educators. Features in the 11 annual issues provide professional educators with a forum to describe what they are doing to achieve educational success. *Contact: T.H.E. Journal,* 150 El Camino Real, Suite 112, Tustin, CA 92780-3670; Voice: 714/730-4011; Fax: 407/730-3739.

Laboratory–Practicum Activities

▶ 1. List three goals you will achieve in the next 3 months to enhance your inclusive-education knowledge base. Use technology to develop your goals, to describe how you will achieve these goals, and to manage the achievement of the goals.

▶ 2. List three goals you will achieve in the next 3 months to enhance your understanding of planning and implementing technology programs in inclusive settings. Use technology to develop your goals, to describe how you will achieve these goals, and to manage the achievement of the goals.

▶ 3. Search the Internet and World Wide Web for technology plans posted by different school districts. Compare and contrast these plans, evaluating them based on the principles outlined in this chapter, and share this information with your course instructor and peers.

▶ 4. Collaborate with your peers to compile a list of technology-related resources (organizations, printed materials, Web sites and pages, etc.) that can be used by professionals in an inclusive setting for meeting the needs of individuals with disabilities. Use the information listed above and in other chapters as a starting point but identify additional sources. Create a database to store this information and share it with your course instructor.

▶ 5. Collaborate with your peers to interview elementary-level general educators, special educators, and other professionals working in two different inclusive settings. Have these professionals describe (a) how they are planning and implementing technology programs and the programs' strengths and weaknesses and (b) what resources they use to achieve collaborative teaching–learning outcomes. Compare and contrast the descriptions. Share your findings with your course instructor.

▶ 6. Collaborate with your peers to interview secondary-level general educators, special educators, and other professionals working in two different inclusive settings. Have these professionals describe (a) how they are planning and implementing technology programs and the programs' strengths and weaknesses and (b) the resources they use to achieve collaborative teaching–learning outcomes. Compare and contrast the descriptions. Share your findings with your course instructor.

References

Baker, J., & Zigmond, N. (1990). Are regular education classes equipped to accommodate students with learning disabilities? *Exceptional Children, 56,* 515–526.

Bottge, B. A. (in press). Effects of contextualized math instruction on problem solving of average- and under-achieving students. *The Journal of Special Education.*

Bottge, B. A., & Hasselbring, T. S. (1993). A comparison of two approaches for teaching complex, authentic mathematics problems to adolescents with learning difficulties. *Exceptional Children, 59,* 556–566.

Bransford, J. D., Stein, B. S., Delclos, V. R., & Littlefield, J. (1986). Computers and problem solving. In C. K. Kinzer, R. Sherwood, & J. D. Bransford (Eds.), *Computer strategies for education* (pp. 147–180). Columbus, OH: Merrill.

Bruner, J. S. (1960). *The process of education.* New York: Vintage Books.

Bush, V. (1945). As we may think. *Atlantic Monthly, 176*(1), 101–108.

Carnine, D. (1989). Teaching complex content to learning disabled students: The role of technology. *Exceptional Children, 55,* 524–533.

Clark, R. E., & Salomon, G. (1986). Media in teaching. In M. C. Wittrock (Ed.), *Handbook of research on teaching* (pp. 464–478). New York: Macmillan.

Collins, A., Hawkins, J., & Carver, S. M. (1991). A cognitive apprenticeship for disadvantaged students. In B. Means, C. Chelemer, & M. S. Knapp (Eds.), *Teaching advanced skills to at-risk students* (pp. 216–243). San Francisco: Jossey-Bass.

Dwyer, D. C. (1996). The imperative to change our schools. In C. Fisher, D. C. Dwyer, & K. Yocam (Eds.), *Education and technology: Reflections on computing in classrooms* (pp. 15–33). San Francisco: Jossey-Bass.

Education for All Handicapped Children Act of 1975, 20 U.S.C. § 1400 *et seq.*

Graham, S., & MacArthur, C. (1988). Improving learning disabled students' skills at revising essays produced on a word processor: Self-instructional strategy training. *Journal of Special Education, 22,* 133–152.

Hasselbring, T. S., Goin, L., & Bransford, J. D. (1988). Developing math automaticity in learning handicapped children: The role of computerized drill and practice. *Focus on Exceptional Children, 20*(6), 1–7.

Hasselbring, T. S., Goin, L. I., Taylor, R., Bottge, B., & Dailey, P. (1997). The computer doesn't embarrass me. *Educational Leadership, 55*(3), 30–33.

Hofmeister, A. M. (1983). *Microcomputer applications in the classroom.* New York: Holt, Rinehart and Winston.

Individuals with Disabilities Education Act of 1990, 20 U.S.C. § 1400 *et seq.*

Kavanaugh-Brown, J. (1999). It's how you use it. *Government Technology, 12*(2), 28.

LaBerge, D., & Samuels, S. J. (1974). Toward a theory of automatic information processing in reading. *Cognitive Psychology, 6,* 293–323.

Lesgold, A. (1983). A rationale for computer based reading instruction. In A. C. Wilkinson (Ed.), *Classroom computers and cognitive science* (pp. 167–181). New York: Academic Press.

Levin, J. A., Kim, H., & Riel, M. M. (1990). Analyzing instructional interactions on electronic message networks. In L. M. Harasim (Ed.), *Online education: Perspectives on a new environment* (pp. 185–213). New York: Prager.

Lieberman, L. M. (1992). Preserving special education . . . For those who need it. In W. Stainback & S. Stainback (Eds.), *Controversial issues confronting special education: Divergent perspectives* (pp. 13–25). Needham Heights, MA: Allyn & Bacon.

Lipsky, D., & Gartner, A. (1992). Achieving full inclusion: Placing the students at the center of educational reform. In W. Stainback & S. Stainback (Eds.), *Controversial issues confronting special education: Divergent perspectives* (pp. 2–12). Needham Heights, MA: Allyn & Bacon.

MacArthur, C., & Graham, S. (1987). Learning disabled students' composing with three methods: Handwriting, dictation, and word processing. *Journal of Special Education, 21,* 22–41.

Mergendoller, J. R. (1996). Moving from technological possibility to richer student learning: Revitalized infrastructure and reconstructed pedagogy. *Educational Researcher, 25,* 43–46.

Mergendoller, J. R., Johnston, J., Rockman, S., & Willis, J. (1994). *Exemplary approaches to training teachers to use technology* (Report prepared for the U.S. Office of Technology Assessment). Novato, CA: Buck Institute for Education.

National Commission on Excellence in Education. (1983). *A nation at risk*. Washington, DC: U.S. Government Printing Office.

National Council of Teachers of Mathematics. (1989). *Evaluation standards: Curriculum and evaluation for school mathematics*. Reston, VA: Author.

National Education Summit. (1996). *Final policy statement: Technology is the equalizer in educational advancement* [On-line]. Available: www.summit96.ibm.com/brief/finaltech.html

Nelson, T. (1967). Getting it out of our system. In G. Schecter (Ed.), *Information retrieval: A critical view*. Washington, DC: Thompson Books.

Riel, M. (1990). Cooperative learning across classrooms in electronic learning circles. *Instructional Science, 9*, 445–466.

Stainback, S., Stainback, W., East, K., & Sapon-Shevin, M. (1994). A commentary on inclusion and the development of a positive self-identity by people with disabilities. *Exceptional Children, 60*, 486–490.

Stainback, S., Stainback, W., & Jackson, H. J. (1992). Toward inclusive classrooms. In S. Stainback & W. Stainback (Eds.), *Curriculum considerations in inclusive classrooms: Facilitating learning for all students* (pp. 3–17). Baltimore: Brookes.

Torgesen, J. K. (1984). Instructional uses of microcomputers with elementary aged mildly handicapped children. *Special Services in the Schools, 1*(1), 37–48.

U.S. Congressional Office of Technology Assessment. (1988). *Power on! New tools for teaching and learning* (Rep. No. OTA-SET-379). Washington, DC: U.S. Government Printing Office.

U.S. Congressional Office of Technology Assessment. (1995). *Teachers and technology: Making the connection* (Rep. No. OTA-EHR-616). Washington, DC: U.S. Government Printing Office.

U.S. Department of Education. (1996). *Getting America's students ready for the 21st century: Meeting the technology literacy challenge*. Washington, DC: U.S. Department of Education.

Walczak, F. R. (1999). Technology integration redux. *Converge, 2*(1), 52–53.

Ysseldyke, J. E., Thurlow, M. L., Wotruba, J. W., & Nanaia, P. A. (1990). Instructional arrangements: Perceptions from general education. *Teaching Exceptional Children, 22*, 4–8.

Chapter 5

ᔥ   ᔥ   ᔥ

Access to Technology: Removing Hardware and Other Barriers

Susan E. Garber
Technology Consultant, Baltimore

Judy J. Rein
Johns Hopkins University, Baltimore

Providing exceptional individuals with access to technology by identifying and removing barriers has been (see Lindsey, 1989, 1993) and continues to be (see King, 1999; Lewis, 1998) a primary objective. In this chapter we address access to computers and other assistive and instructional technologies from perspectives correlating with the multiple meanings of the concept of access. By first exploring *adapted access,* we examine overcoming the input and output barriers, the more technical aspects of how students with physical, sensory, or cognitive challenges can access or interface with a computer or other specialized technology. In our subsequent exploration of *gaining access,* as in acquiring or getting to use what exists, we examine overcoming environmental, financial, political, and attitudinal barriers.

In the late 1970s and early 1980s, when microcomputers were first bursting onto the scene, the early adapters (i.e., those special education and rehabilitation professionals first to view the potential of technology for students with special needs) were concerning themselves primarily with applications for one of two population groups (Behrmann, 1988). One recognized potential subset of users was the population of individuals with learning disabilities for whom computers were regarded as in infinitely patient and motivating instructor. The second subset of the population to receive attention was individuals with physical or speech disabilities, for whom computers were regarded as a compensatory or prosthetic device. For both groups, microcomputer technology and other forms of assistive technologies were viewed as tools to equalize the playing field with nondisabled peers.

Early research into the state of the art and the state of the practice emphasized finding a means to interface the student with a disability to a microcomputer. Practitioners were enamored with technology's potential, with the belief that no matter how severe a student's disability, a means could be developed for him or her to access a computer. Even if only an eye blink or a puff of breath were reliably available, an interface method and software to economize on activations could be developed.

The question being asked was, "*What* adapted input or output devices will enable this student to

Individuals can use technology tools to remove barriers. (Photograph by Carolyn F. Woods)

use a computer?" It took several years before the questions had more proper emphasis: "*To what* will this computer interface provide access? *For what* purpose will it be used?" It seemed to take even longer before even better questions were asked: "*How* best will I train the student (and staff) to use it? *How* will I integrate this technology into the student's curriculum and Individualized Education Program?"

Gaining Access: Barriers Limiting Access to Technology

The barriers limiting access to technology for individuals with special needs are many, although not all of those barriers may be readily apparent. The more obvious barriers, which we address first, are those related to hardware access. How do individuals with disabilities—whether physical, sensory, or cognitive—overcome the barrier of the keyboard and screen? How do they navigate the Internet, function on networked computers, or access augmentative communication devices?

Other significant barriers could be categorized as "people barriers," those in which finances, politics, and attitudes impede the availability of or access to technology. Environmental or "barrier-free" access in the home, school, and community constitutes another observable consideration. These people and environmental barriers, as well as general principles for an evaluation process to eliminate barriers, will be addressed following discussion of the hardware issues.

Adapted Access: Removing Hardware Barriers

The design of early microcomputer systems had tremendous potential for adaptation. This allowed computer hackers and software developers a golden opportunity to customize the microcomputer system to meet individual needs. Its open architecture allowed even non–computer "geeks" to pop the lid and insert necessary peripherals,

such as the Adapted Firmware Card or Echo speech synthesizer, allowing a student to use a switch as a means of access or to get auditory feedback to his or her responses.

By using an open architecture approach, Apple and IBM encouraged the development of third-party technology that supported options to add memory, enhance speed, use different types of disk drives for storage of data, control games by input devices other than the standard keyboard, and send information output to a variety of devices, such as dot matrix printers, daisy wheel printers, speech synthesizers for software that "talked," and eventually braille printers. These modifications were accomplished by the addition of circuit boards plugged into slots on the motherboard (main circuit board) of the computer. Professionals who designed and engineered assistive devices began to document their strategies for adaptation by the early 1980s, describing how to modify computer technology to help persons with sensory or physical disabilities (Vanderheiden, 1981).

During the 1980s the use of computer technology to enable persons with disabilities expanded dramatically. When the Macintosh platform emerged, it had several modifications for individuals with disabilities already built in, including screen magnification and the ability to adjust the repeat keys and speed of the mouse. However, the release in 1984 of the Macintosh, with its closed architecture, represented a new direction in computer design that had the potential to limit options for adaptation. The first Macintosh computers did not provide open slots to support the addition of circuit boards. Advocates for universal design began to seek opportunities to meet with representatives from the computer industry to develop guidelines for the design of future computer technology (Vanderheiden, 1991). Although there have been no legal mandates about computer design for manufacturers in general, Section 504 of the Rehabilitation Act of 1973 mandates that computers purchased by companies that receive government funds must be made accessible. Because major computer manufacturers sought large government contracts, the 504 mandates served as a strong catalyst for adaptation of the concept of universal design.

Universal design means that products and environments are designed for use by all people to the greatest extent possible (Connell et al., 1995). A classic example of universal design is a sidewalk curb cut with texture strips across it that signal a change in elevation to persons who are visually impaired or blind. In addition, the curb cuts allows persons in wheelchairs to safely navigate the transition from sidewalk to street, but it also assists those who use strollers, bicycles, wagons, skateboards, shopping carts, and delivery carts. In 1984 universal design advocates submitted to representatives of the federal government and major computer corporations a set of guidelines for "electronic curb cuts" that increased the accessibility of computer technology for persons with disabilities (Vanderheiden, 1991). As a result of this effort, there were some small but significant changes to the design of microcomputers currently in use. The power switches were moved from the back or side to the front of the computer console. Most important, hardware developers began to incorporate simple accessibility features into operating system software. This allowed users to adjust specific keyboard operations to meet individual needs.

Current Apple and Windows operating systems include features that allow adjustment of keyboard features (see Table 5.1). There are similar features for adjustments of the rate of mouse movements and mouse button clicks. Ironically,

these features can create some barriers of their own. One potential barrier is that these keyboard features are intended to work with specific versions of operating system software. This means moving from one operating system to another may result in the loss of an adaptation on which the person with a disability relies (Anson, 1996). Another potential barrier can be a lack of knowledge. Although these keyboard adjustments are designed to be simple and easy to use, it is not necessarily common knowledge that they are available or where they are found. Limited knowledge or lack of training to provide adequate knowledge can pose significant obstacles.

Although such principles for removal of hardware barriers have become integrated into the design of computer technology, many individuals with disabilities are unable to use standard computers as they are set up "out of the box." The barriers that these persons encounter may be attributed to factors outside the realm of hardware. There are human factors involved in the successful use of technology for persons with disabilities that warrant further discussion before returning to the discussion of hardware barriers.

Human Factor Barriers to Access

The human factor is one of several essential elements to consider in addition to technology, as cited in various models for assistive technology

Table 5.1. Adjustable Keyboard Features on Current Operating Systems

Feature	Function
Key Repeat Rate	Frequency at which key repeats when pressed down continuously
Delay Until Repeat	Duration between initial key press and start of automatic repeat feature
Sticky Keys	Electronic key latching for users who type with a single finger or pointer to press more than one key at a time
Slow Keys	Adds time delay between key press and transmission of signal to the computer to reduce the likelihood of accidental key presses by users with tremulous movements
Mouse Keys	Converts the numeric keypad to a keypad for controlling mouse movements by keystrokes

evaluation (Cook & Hussey, 1995; Scherer, 1996). Each person with a disability brings a set of "intrinsic" capabilities to using technology (Cook & Hussey, 1995). Although these capabilities are usually measured in terms of human performance on functional skills for self-care, school and work, and play and leisure, Scherer (1996) discussed additional personality characteristics in her Matching the Person to Technology model. These personality characteristics include degree of comfort with using technological devices; level of cognitive skills for understanding how to use complex technology; personality traits for adapting to new information and situations; judgments and preferences related to the motivation for using technology; and response to or ability to cope with disability. Persons are also significantly influenced by their environments or the milieu in which technology is used (Scherer, 1996). Different environmental settings can support or discourage exposure and opportunities for using technology, especially when funding is difficult to obtain. Similarly the degree to which social expectations are realistic or unrealistic can encourage or interfere with technology use. As a result, it is possible to find computer technology in schools that is accessible but not used. This reinforces the notion that removal of hardware barriers is only one of the many requirements for making computer technology accessible for children with disabilities in schools.

To summarize, the removal of barriers for persons with disabilities who want access to computer technology goes beyond the consideration of hardware design alone. Development of potential "bridges" or solutions must incorporate examination of the human factors involved in using technology (also see King, 1999). For this reason, the organizational structure for analyzing hardware issues suggested here follows the human performance perspective, giving consideration to physical, sensory, and cognitive needs. This approach is consistent with that of other experts who have been involved in the development of decision support systems for determining computer access strategies (Anson, 1996; Deterding, 1996).

Environmental Barriers to Access

The Americans with Disabilities Act of 1990 (ADA) demands barrier-free schools just as it does other barrier-free public facilities. However, schools, particularly in financially strapped urban areas, often lag behind what is legislated. Removing environmental barriers entails getting either the student physically to the technology or the technology physically to the student.

There are usually multiple solutions available to problems presented by the environment. The goal should be to find a reasonable accommodation that best meets the overall needs of the student. The following scenario illustrates multiple solutions or approaches to an environmental access barrier: A student who uses a wheelchair requires access to a computer, but all of the school's computer resources are centralized in a lab on the second floor of his neighborhood school building with no elevator access. Alternatives include the following:

- transporting the student to a building where he can get to the computer lab in his wheelchair

- installing an elevator in his neighborhood school

- moving the computer lab downstairs

- moving one or more computers downstairs as a distributed network

Computerized portable braillers can be used in the home, school, and community. (Photograph by Jimmy D. Lindsey)

- putting the computer, wherever it is located, on a height-adjustable table

- providing the student with a laptop computer

Although each alternative provides a potential solution, there are obvious pros and cons to each. We do not discuss them; we leave it for consideration in Laboratory–Practicum Activity 5 at the end of the chapter.

As schools develop plans for computer technology (see Dockstader, 1999), they need to plan for and implement accessibility measures. Because approximately 10% of students present with some type of disability, a suggested rule of thumb might be to earmark 10% of computer equipment and resources for accessibility (Berliss, 1991). Computing structure and disability demographics may dictate whether equipment is permanently housed in a particular location, shared among labs or classrooms as necessary, or checked out to individual students. The environment should include height-adjustable tables to accommodate both wheelchair users and persons of differing statures. Similarly adjustable chairs that provide support and stability should be included. The physical arrangement of the lab or classroom should include sufficiently wide aisles to accommodate wheelchair or mobility aid users. Consideration should also be given to lighting. Monitors should be positioned in such a way that glare on the screen is minimized. If natural light is a factor, positioning monitors at a 90-degree angle to windows will help (Berliss, 1991). The provision of noise-blocking earphones will assist individuals who require a quiet atmosphere in which to work.

Financial Barriers to Access

A very real barrier to technology access for individuals with disabilities, especially for students, is funding. If an Individualized Education Program (IEP) team determines that a particular assistive technology device or service is required for a free appropriate public education, then the assistive technology must be provided at no cost to the parents [34 C.F.R. § 300.1 and § 300.17 (a) (1) & (2)]. While districts may use alternative funding sources for the provision of assistive technology devices or services, such funds cannot be used if purchasing technology would result in a reduction of medical or other types of assistance available to students with disabilities. Furthermore, the use of private insurance proceeds must not pose a realistic threat of financial loss to parents of children with disabilities (see http://www.ucpa.org/html/innovative/atfsc/insur.html).

Although Medicaid is a frequently discussed funding alternative for assistive technology for students with disabilities, there are specific criteria to qualify for eligibility, including a need based on medical necessity, family income level restrictions, and considerable paperwork. In addition, there is frequently a considerable delay between application and acquisition. Such a delay in implementing an IEP is not permissible (Carl, Mataya, & Zabala, 1994). The growing trend of moving Medicaid recipients into managed care organizations may create further complications for this potential funding stream.

Although the Individuals with Disabilities Education Act of 1990 (IDEA) clearly defines a school system's obligation to provide access to assistive technology as special education, related services, or supplementary aids and services, in reality many systems successfully delay or avoid this obligation through a variety of tactics. Historically, special educators and related service providers have been "cautioned" by concerned administrators not to put technology in an IEP because the school will subsequently be obligated to provide it (B. Romich, personal communication, 1993). This is increasingly a problem as school-based management becomes more prevalent. Individual schools are hesitant to provide technology for a student with disabilities because they must shoulder the financial burden from their own rather than the school district's budget. One resulting question might be, "Should we buy new uniforms for the football team or get that costly augmentative communication device for Fred?" While the law is clear that meeting Fred's needs is mandated and football is not, it does nothing to cushion the resentment of allocating scarce resources to an individual or small group (see later section on attitudinal barriers).

It is significant to note that, although it is assumed that all adapted technology must be highly expensive, the Job Accommodation Network World Wide Web site in 1996 (http://jan web.icdi.wvu.edu) stated that 80% of job accommodations suggested by them cost under $500. There is no reason to believe that accommodations for education would be significantly different. Ironically, it is not the highly specialized devices for low-incidence populations that administrators fear the most (Golinker, 1995). Rather, it is the threat of numerous requests for laptop computers or portable word processors for students with learning disabilities that is causing the greatest financial concern among many administrators.

An additional and significant financial consideration facing administrators is that access to technological devices also means access to technological *services* (Goodman, 1995). There is nothing more wasteful of scarce dollars than to provide for the purchase of a device but not provide for appropriate training of the student, his or her parents, and service providers in the operation and integration of that device into the home, school, and community environments. However, this not uncommon occurrence frequently contributes to device abandonment (Phillips & Zhao, 1993).

Although schools shy from the perceived potential high cost of devices, the more significant expense may be incurred in providing the services to support and integrate that technology. Ultimately, however, the greatest expense to society may lie in *not* providing access to the devices and services needed. There is a popular bumper sticker that reads, "If you think education is expensive, try ignorance." A variation might be, "If you think technology for students with disabilities is expensive, try permanent dependence."

School systems could protect themselves from making costly purchase mistakes by employing trained personnel who can both assist in the appropriate recommendation of devices and support the student's and staff's needs for fully maximizing the benefit of that technology (see the technology evaluation section at the end of this chapter). Rather than regarding a technology resource person or, more appropriately, a technology team as an additional expense, school districts should consider them a strategy for saving money. By having the team select the best (not necessarily the most expensive) solution, they protect the interest of the student *and* the district.

By having a trained team or central resource person knowledgeable about the continuum of low-tech to high-tech devices and strategies, a special education department assures itself of appropriate choices (see Chapter 1). By building relationships with instructional computing personnel, they assure a more equitable distribution of financial obligations.

Political Barriers to Access

Much of the financial conundrum involved in making technology available to students with disabilities is the result of the separation, real and perceived, between special education and general education. Politically, the "special education" student is often not perceived as one of "ours" by building and system administrators. There is frequently a mindset that all needs of special education students will be funded and provided through the district's special education budget rather than from the general instructional budget. A mindset must be built that technology is for *all* students and, therefore, that *all* students should have access to *all* available instructional technology. While highly specialized peripherals may rightly be the responsibility of special education departments, the base computer might be viewed as deserving funding through the general instructional budget. Conversely, there is a need to identify software and peripherals that will be useful to many "mainstream" students, not only those identified as having special needs. These programs and peripherals should be part of a school's basic collection. For example, putting talking word processors, spell checkers, or screen enlargement programs on computer networks, whether in a lab or distributed throughout the building, could benefit numerous students, not only those with IEPs. Similarly, the use of touch screens or alternative keyboards, such as those discussed in Chapter 2, would make computers more accessible to all early childhood students.

As states and school districts develop their comprehensive multiyear plans for technology, they would be wise to follow Maryland's example. Rather than two separate plans for providing technology in the schools (one for general and one for special education), Maryland developed a single plan for all students. When schools apply for state grant funds, their technology plans must address how *all* students will be assured access to the requested technology (Maryland Blue Ribbon Committee on Technology in Education, 1994).

Attitudinal Barriers to Access

As noted in Chapter 1 and described in this chapter, negative attitudes toward the provision of adapted technologies have been sustained by unwise or inappropriate purchases. However, additional factors contribute to prevalent attitudes about the provision of technology to students with special needs.

Historically, special education classrooms have frequently been housed in or equipped with the "castoffs" of general education. Many special educators maintain that there are significant equity issues regarding computer technology for students with disabilities. Special education classrooms frequently receive the castoff computers as new labs are installed for general education students. This places those students with special needs several "generations down" from what is in current use by their peers and the business world. It is sometimes assumed that students with special needs only need slower computers (i.e., that fast processors, good sound and graphics, and modem access are not necessary). This situation constitutes a double irony. For example, the need for multimodality input by students with learning difficulties may actually warrant the most current in equipment. Similarly, the student who cannot physically turn the pages of a book independently may have access to resource materials necessary to complete assignments only through on-line access to library collections or to the Internet.

An ambitious statewide inventory of public schools by the Maryland State Department of Education in 1996 confirmed an overabundance of older computers within special education class-rooms throughout the state: 69.2% of the computers in special education programs in elementary schools and 71.7% of the computers in special education classrooms in secondary schools were older models (defined as pre-80286 PCs or pre-Mac LCII). The survey also indicated that less than 5% of the total inventory of computers in Maryland's schools reside in special education classrooms, and a disproportionately high number of those computers were donated (new or used) or obtained from fund-raising or supermarket promotions.

Special education professionals and advocates must change their pitch from "This poor disabled student deserves a computer" to "This student with disabilities requires a computer to maximize his more limited employment options" or "to participate fully in the educational process." Whereas able peers have myriad employment opportunities open to them, students with disabilities are more limited in their choices. While their nondisabled peers have the option of selecting either a technology-based career or one that requires physical labor, such as construction, students with physical and other challenges have a reduced range of choices.

Access to Desktop Technology

Physical access to any hardware requires adequate posture for controlling physical movements with precision, accuracy, and endurance (Deterding, 1996; Fraser, McGregor, Arango, & Kangas, 1994). Positioning a person so that all the components that must be manipulated to operate the computer are placed within reach is the first step in this process. This includes not only careful positioning of the keyboard or mouse, but also any power switches, disk drives, and output devices, including paper from printers that the user needs to control. Fundamental to this process is determining the body part that the person will use to control the technology (Cook & Hussey, 1995). Supported by research, there are guidelines for following a naturally preferred order for control sites, starting with the hands, then the head, and finally the feet (Cook &

Hussey, 1995; Glickman, Deitz, Anson, & Stewart, 1996). Once the body part or control site is decided, a series of questions is needed to investigate how the person interacts with the input devices for the computer system (Anson, 1996; Deterding, 1996). Table 5.2 presents a list of questions that could be asked.

A few of these questions can apply to any input device that a person with a disability may be interested in exploring. For example, the first and last questions about reaching the area of the input device and performing the control movements consistently, reliably, and with adequate endurance can apply to the use of voice recognition systems or activating switches. The other remaining questions are specific to using a keyboard, mouse, or graphics tablet (see Gowan, 1999).

A complete investigation of computer access usually begins by reviewing these questions with reference to using the standard keyboard and mouse, the input control devices common to the majority of computer users. If a person is obviously not a good candidate for a standard key-

Table 5.2. Questions To Guide Decision Making About Physical Access to Computers

Is the person able to:

1. Reach the entire area (all four corners) represented by the keyboard or input device?

2. Accurately press with smooth, refined control the size of keys contained on the keyboard or input device?

3. Press more than one key at a time for shifted characters and commands?

4. Avoid producing frequent unintended keystrokes by accidentally pressing nearby keys, by bouncing on keys, or by slow or delayed release of key presses?

5. Control the movement of the mouse to point to or move objects on the screen?

6. Control the click buttons on the mouse in coordination with mouse movements?

7. Repeat movements required for control consistently, reliably, and with sufficient endurance to complete the desired task?

board, the investigation proceeds to alternative keyboards and alternatives to a mouse. Because many keyboard and mouse alternatives are available, this phase of the investigation takes time and requires consideration of commercially available "off-the-shelf" input devices for the general population, alternate input devices designed for individuals with disabilities, and composite forms of control. The following examples illustrate the range of options available in this phase of the investigation: ergonomically designed keyboards and mice that minimize the risk for developing cumulative trauma disorders; special-purpose input devices for giving presentations or for precision in computer-assisted design applications; alternative input devices for individuals with disabilities; a mouse or mouse emulator to control an on-screen keyboard; or a voice recognition system that supports direct selection of commands for word processing but requires use of the military alphabet code to make corrections letter by letter.

Only when all other alternatives are exhausted is consideration given to switch-operated methods for keyboard and mouse control (Anson, 1996; Cook & Hussey, 1995; Deterding, 1996). Switch-operated methods include use of (a) one, two, or three switches for Morse code (an encoding system in which switches send a series of "dots" and "dashes" that are translated to characters) or (b) a scanning system (the computer presents a series of choices that the user selects by timing switch presses to type desired characters).

Sensory access to computer technology requires consideration of the type and quality of feedback generated by the computer (see Chapter 12). This feedback is essential for the user to monitor performance and produce the desired outcome with the computer. Because a wide variety of computer output adaptations are available, it is essential to ask discriminating questions that determine appropriate access methods for persons with sensory disabilities (see Table 5.3). Although the investigation begins with asking whether the person has normal vision and normal hearing, with or without correction, there are additional questions to explore (Anson, 1996; Deterding, 1996).

Examination of these questions needs to occur in the context of adaptations that are available

Table 5.3. Questions To Guide Decision Making About Sensory Access to Computers

Is the person able to:

1. Use partial vision or partial hearing?

2. Use an alternative sensory mode to compensate for total loss of vision or hearing?

3. Discriminate significant foreground from the rival background by use of screen contrast and brightness controls, strong color contrasts available, reorganization of information into more predictable visual format, or visual cues given simultaneously with auditory cues?

4. Read enlarged or magnified text instead of standard size?

5. Read closed captioning on videos?

6. Understand machine-generated speech?

7. Demonstrate good tactile discrimination or read braille?

for persons with sensory impairments. Persons who experience a partial hearing loss can take advantage of options for changing the system beep (used to give auditory feedback when the user attempts illegal actions) to a sound that is more audible. For those with total hearing loss, an option called See Beep (available in MS-DOS and Windows) pairs visual cues simultaneously with auditory cues.

Persons with partial vision can use a screen enlarger provided through hardware or software modifications. Another visual enhancement for these users is cursor enlargement modifications. Those who are blind can use a screen reader for speech output alone or in conjunction with refreshable braille displays. The screen reader is a combination of software and hardware called a speech synthesizer. While the software translates the text on the screen to spoken words, the speech synthesizer performs the "talking." The refreshable braille display converts the text on the screen one line at a time to braille on a separate display. Some persons with visual disabilities may use hybrid combinations of screen enlargers with screen readers, depending on the nature of the task to be performed. One advantage to using

a screen reader is that people can usually listen to text at a rate faster than they can read magnified text or braille. The benefit gained by combining a screen reader with a screen enlarger or braille display is the ability to review text with greater accuracy than possible with speech alone.

Cognitive access refers to performance of those functional tasks associated with perceptual and cognitive skills required for using computers. At a minimum, the user needs to understand that a switch or key press triggers a response from the computer that is displayed on the screen, spoken aloud, or both. Children as young as 6 to 7 months demonstrate an understanding of the relationship between a switch press and its associated computer response (Swinth, Anson, & Deitz, 1993). Once the user gets the computer response, he or she must understand what it means and what to do next. This implies that the user must be able to perceive, discriminate, and analyze information generated by the computer whether it is displayed in graphics, pictures or symbols, or text. In addition, the user may need to recall the sequence of actions required to get the desired results, initiate a response, and problem solve what to do if the desired outcome is not obtained. In other words, the level of perceptual and cognitive processes required for using computers ranges from simple to complex.

Another aspect of perceptual cognitive functioning is involved when a user incorporates or adds software programs that are designed to work in conjunction with standard application

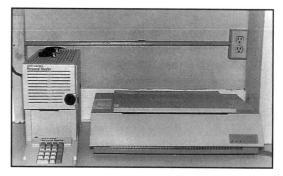

Kurzweil Reading Machine uses synthesized speech to orally read almost any book. (Photograph by Jimmy D. Lindsey)

programs. Some persons with severe disabilities must rely on input devices that are inherently slow, as evidenced by a scanning system in which the user must wait while the computer "highlights" or blinks through an array of choices. There are three major types of "add-on" or utility programs that are designed to enhance performance rate and accuracy or simplify task requirements (Anson, 1996). These utility programs work in the background simultaneously with major application programs, such as word processors, databases, and spreadsheets.

The first type, macro programs, allows the user to record and replay a series of frequently repeated keystrokes or mouse actions, including commands (Anson, 1996). The use of macros requires the ability to remember the keystroke and mouse actions that have been recorded or to refer to a cheat sheet to assist with recall. A second class of performance enhancement programs includes those that provide abbreviation expansion. Similar to macros in operation and memory requirements, an abbreviation expansion program lets the user assign a letter pattern (abbreviation) to a longer series of letters, words, or phrases (expansion) (Anson, 1996). When the person types an abbreviation, the computer automatically replaces it with an expansion. This type of performance enhancement is most effective when programmed to assist with typing high-frequency words or phrases.

Programs in the third group provide word prediction capability. When a user starts to type, a word prediction program provides a list of guesses about the word being typed. If the word prediction program generates a correct choice, the user selects the desired word and the computer automatically finishes typing the word. However, if the word prediction program does not display the desired word, the user continues to type letter by letter. Word prediction programs offer advantages for those who use switches for computer control or have difficulty recalling how to spell words or remembering abbreviations (Anson, 1996). The challenge for those who use word prediction is to split attention between what is being typed in the word processor and the list of predicted words.

Table 5.4 presents some key questions to explore when considering perceptual and cognitive capabilities for successful computer use (Anson, 1996; Deterding, 1996). Through careful selection of software and hardware, users who are cognitively young can effectively interact with computers and benefit from their use. However, when a person with a disability needs to be a completely independent user, then a high level of problem-solving skills is required. One investigation of the relationship between cognitive measures and computer input control skills found that a combination of measures was the most effective method of evaluating the appropriateness of computer-based assistive technology (Cress & French, 1994). Moreover, measures of device control potential were more informative when taken during training than when collected as static skill measurements prior to training.

The consideration of hardware access should extend beyond the stand-alone desktop computer. One must also consider whether any of the smaller, lighter, portable devices provide additional solutions or barriers. Similarly, the rapid increase in the use of networked computers and the Internet warrants further exploration.

Table 5.4. Questions To Guide Decision Making About Cognitive Access to Computers

Is the person able to:

1. Understand the concept of cause and effect?

2. Apply literacy skills for understanding information presented on the screen in a variety of formats: graphics, symbols, text, or numbers?

3. Demonstrate ability to split attention between the keyboard and screen or between two different activities occurring on the screen (e.g., when writing with a word processor in one window and using a word prediction program in another window)?

4. Remember sequences of keystrokes or codes (as required in abbreviation expansion)?

5. Demonstrate ability to solve problems that occur routinely with computer use?

Access to Laptop, Notebook, and Personal Digital Assistants

The advent of portable computer technology in the mid-1980s offered new freedoms for persons with disabilities. Portable technology meant that a user with a disability had access to the functions and capabilities inherent in a computer wherever he or she traveled. Students with limited vision were able to take their portable computers adapted with speech output systems or software-based screen enlargers to all their classes. Similarly, students who faced challenges to the physical aspects of writing were able to write via portable computers with adapted input controls.

Engineers designed the first portable computers to be more rugged and reliable because they were intended to withstand frequent movement from place to place. The major drawback to using portable computer technology is the need to recharge batteries periodically. For students with disabilities who attend older schools where one or two electrical outlets per classroom is the norm, this is indeed an annoying burden. Although one alternative is to carry extra batteries, this means additional weight and merely extends the time before batteries need to be recharged. Other disadvantages associated with portable computers are discussed in the following paragraphs.

Laptops, the first truly portable computers to appear on the market, were designed to be easy to carry for short periods of time. They were preceded by machines that were not always affectionately referred to as "luggables." Although they combined all the components of a desktop computer into a single "unit," they often weighed over 25 pounds, an uncomfortable weight to have in one's lap for any amount of time. Although laptops performed most of the functions possible on desktop computers, the only monitors available in these early models were monochrome liquid crystal displays (LCDs). The lack of a color display did not impose a barrier to most persons with disabil-

ities; however, some persons with visual impairments were unable to clearly discriminate foreground text from the background on the LCD displays. Recent improvements in portable monitors have enhanced the visibility and contrast. Similarly, as the size of computer components has shrunk, laptop computers have given way to notebook-size computers (e.g., Macintosh iBook).

Notebooks were designed to be smaller and lighter than laptops. Advancements in notebook technology have resulted in significant improvements in the quality of displays (from LCD to gas plasma displays); inclusion of modems, fax modems, and CD-ROM and DVD drives; and enhanced connectivity with other external peripheral devices (e.g., high-resolution monitors, LCD projection panels, and additional external hard drives or laser disk drives). Improvements in notebook computers have resulted in more persons with disabilities taking advantage of the portability offered by this technology. Unlike laptops, notebook computers are sufficiently small and lightweight for mounting on wheelchairs. Although some wheelchair users choose to place laptops on their wheelchair trays, a more secure alternative in terms of wheelchair safety and balance is to use specially designed mounting systems that can swivel the notebook from a tabletop position to alongside the wheelchair.

Personal Digital Assistants (PDAs) or palmtop computers are electronic devices designed to support common personal organization needs, such as a calendar, alarm, address book, and memo pad (Cohen, 1996). Initially, PDAs were intended to supplement, not duplicate, standard computer functions. Now some PDAs accommodate word processing, game playing, scheduling, managing finances, and other advanced capabilities. Generally, the input methods are limited to tiny chiclet-style keyboards or primitive handwriting recognition systems that require use of a special stylus. Most PDAs also rely on monochrome LCD technology to keep the display size small. Only the more expensive models offer connectivity to computers and communication technologies. The application of PDAs for persons with disabilities has been limited by major constraints in the visibility of the small LCD displays and the few options for input. Indeed many persons who are "temporarily able bodied"—people who do not have disabilities—find barriers to using PDAs and reject their usage.

Access to Networked Computers

Accommodations for persons with disabilities must play a catch-up role as technology rapidly advances. This is particularly true when making computers on local area networks (LANs) accessible (Center for Information Technology Accommodations [CITA], 1995). Although there are successful network users among individuals with disabilities, network access with adapted hardware and software usually requires careful planning and is more likely to be successful when more than one device is available that meets a user's needs. The most common barriers encountered are related to memory conflicts between the LAN software and the software that provides access for the person with a disability (CITA, 1995). Some LANs include memory management programs that provide options for different memory configurations in order to resolve memory conflicts. Other LANs automatically terminate any programs that conflict with LAN memory usage. The problem is most difficult to address when it takes a combination of software products to provide access because there are simply more software programs competing to use available memory.

There are also hardware-based barriers encountered with using networks. These occur when the LAN circuit board and the circuit board for the accommodation product are designed to plug into the same slot on the motherboard (CITA, 1995). Although some boards have configuration options that can solve these hardware conflicts, such solutions are not always available. One resource that can be particularly helpful when confronting the challenge of network accessibility is the inclusion of a network technician on the evaluation team. Similarly, school districts' instructional computing coordinators need to

carefully question retailers of large network software packages to assure that they are designed to operate in a manner that is compatible with the use of the more common alternative input and output devices.

Access to the Internet and World Wide Web

The Internet, or "information superhighway," is an expansive network that connects computers across the world to exchange information in a gigantic communications system (Ryder & Hughes, 1997). Those who use the Internet can browse for information, post or publish information on a World Wide Web page, and send and receive messages in seconds via e-mail. The Internet has been likened to the "mother of all libraries" in the vastness of its resource capabilities. On the other hand, no standards are required for putting information on the Internet. The only components required for accessing the Internet are the hardware (a computer with a modem or network connection), browsing software (such as Netscape Communicator, or Microsoft Internet Explorer), and an account with an Internet provider. The rapidly increasing popularity of the Internet, in combination with intense competition among major telephone, cable, and electronic corporations, led to the release in 1996 of Internet terminals designed to work with televisions (Langberg, 1996). Given the lack of standards, educators and parents have prepared for passage to the information superhighway by developing acceptable use policies or guidelines to protect young students from the ethically challenging information found on some pages of the Internet. In addition, many districts are interested in getting schools wired for Internet access as a resource to support learning.

For persons with disabilities, the Internet has offered new possibilities as well as new frustrations. When the Internet operated in primarily a text-based mode, it was relatively easy for users to translate text to speech or braille. With the recent shift to a graphical user interface (the Windows approach to software navigation), the Internet has become known as the World Wide Web. The use of graphical software for browsing also provides multimedia capabilities for displaying text with pictures, text in table format, audio clips, video clips or movies, and image maps. Current adapted access technologies have difficulty with the translation of multimedia information. Therefore, the Trace Research and Development Center has launched the development of guidelines to make Web pages accessible to persons with disabilities (Vanderheiden, Chisholm, & Ewers, 1996). These guidelines focus on making source material written in HyperText Markup Language (HTML) accessible. HyperText is the underlined text found on Web pages that a user clicks on with a mouse to link to a new Web page or topic. In general, the Trace guidelines present a variety of strategies for Web page design, supplementing graphics and sound with text descriptions or providing alternate text-only pages.

Access to the Internet for persons with disabilities has been a tremendous equalizer because it is not possible to discern that users or publishers have disabilities unless they report this personal information. In addition, the Internet has provided a means for improved dissemination of information relevant to disabilities, augmented research and learning, increased job opportunities, and enhanced social opportunities without the burden of making transportation arrangements. Every day there are growing numbers of success stories about persons with disabilities who

Computer hardware such as braille printers can be used in collection and database management. (Photograph by Jimmy D. Lindsey)

benefit from access to using a computer and the Internet.

Evaluation of Technology Needs

It goes without saying that the evaluation of technology is a key concept in this book. As stated in Chapter 1 and in this chapter, IDEA mandates that assistive technology be considered in the IEP process. Regrettably, the legislation does little to define what "considered" means, much less what constitutes a technology evaluation or who is a qualified examiner.

After years of preparation, the Rehabilitation Engineering and Assistive Technology Society of North America (RESNA) began administering a credentialing examination in the fall of 1996. The credentialing procedures were developed for assistive technology (AT) practitioners and suppliers as a means of providing quality assurance to consumers of AT devices and services (RESNA, 1996). Central to the RESNA effort is acceptance of a code of practice which includes practicing only in one's area of competence, engaging in no conduct that constitutes a conflict of interest, and holding paramount the welfare of persons served professionally. The credential is a voluntary, entry-level certification necessary to pursue more specialized credentialing in different aspects of AT, such as augmentative communication and rehabilitation engineering.

Guiding Principles for Technology Evaluations

Although previous sections of this chapter included specific suggestions for items to consider when prescribing computer-based technologies, there are certain principles to technology evaluations that guide the selection of other assistive and instructional technologies as well. Technology evaluation should be considered a process, not an event (Garber, Cassett-James, & Derrickson, 1989; Reed, 1995; Zabala, 1994). It is an ongoing endeavor best accomplished in an individual's natural environment by a team of professionals collaboratively combining their skills and knowledge.

Similar yet distinct models for technology evaluations have developed across the country (*Assistive Technology in the Classroom*, 1992; Clark, 1992; Cook & Hussey, 1995; Parette, Hourcade, & Van Biervliet, 1993; Reed, 1995; Scherer, 1996; Zabala, 1994). Whereas school system–based evaluations were initially conducted in centralized facilities by a core team of professionals, the trend has been to move evaluations closer and closer to the environment in which the student is most familiar (i.e., their own school or home) (see Reed, 1995).

The Center for Technology in Education has been utilizing a model for evaluations that began its evolution in 1988 (Garber et al., 1989). Collaborative problem solving, focused on the needs of an individual student, is used to train personnel as well as to select devices and strategies for the individual. Unlike a medical or "expert" model, the center's Statewide Technology Assistance and Training model is based on the belief that it is the child's parents and school team who are "experts" on the individual child. It is the role of the AT team to add members' expertise about technology and human dynamics to assist the child's team to develop a technology action plan. In this collaborative process, the child's team assumes responsibility for the actions recommended because they have helped develop the plan of action, rather than having it dictated to them by outside consultants.

The parents, the school team, and the student (where able) should actively contribute to the process. The school team should include, as appropriate, special and general educators; related services personnel, such as occupational therapists, physical therapists, speech–language pathologists, and vision or hearing consultants; as well as administrators and annual review and dismissal chairpersons (Carl et al., 1994; Garber et al., 1989). By including parents throughout every step of the process, realistic expectations as well as an understanding of the parents' role in the use of the technology can be established. Many potential conflicts can be avoided as strong rapport is built between the parents and school personnel. Similarly, involvement of administrators throughout the process helps them see the value of the technology for the student and keeps them informed of potential financial obligations.

Ideally, the school system will have a team of professionals with a broad knowledge of both the technologies available and the proven instructional strategies to implement their use in the needed environments. If a school system does not have such personnel available internally, it may have to rely on outside sources, such as medical or rehabilitation facilities, for evaluations. In this case, it is absolutely critical that members of the local school team, including the parents, have an opportunity to provide input and feedback to the professionals at the external evaluation facility (Shuster, 1996). This can greatly improve the likelihood of appropriate technology selections for the school environment.

Medically based clinics and rehabilitation facilities may be staffed by personnel highly trained in their particular disciplines. However, these persons may lack a working knowledge of the school environment, academic expectations, and "school society," all of which have an influence on successful use of technology (Shuster, 1996). Without input from school-based personnel and parents, well-meaning experts may recommend a technology that is simply not workable in the school environment.

Student, Environment, Tasks, and Technology (SETT) Framework

Joy Zabala, educational specialist for Region IV Educational Service Center in Houston, Texas, has a succinct way of defining the evaluation process. She utilizes the SETT Framework as a means of clarifying the process (Zabala, 1994). Professionals are advised to examine questions in this order:

- Student: What does the student need to do? What are his special needs and current abilities?

- Environment: What equipment and materials are currently available in the environment? What is the physical arrangement? Are there likely to be changes? What supports are available to the student? What resources are available to the people supporting the student?

- Tasks: What activities take place in the environment? What activities support the student's curriculum? What are the critical elements of the activities? How might the activities be modified to accommodate the student's special needs? How might technology support the student's active participation in those activities?

- Technology: What no tech, low tech, and high tech options should be considered when developing a system for a student with needs and these abilities doing these tasks in these environments? What strategies might be used to invite increased student performance? How might these tools be tried out with the student in the customary environments in which they will be used?

This framework properly places the technology last in the process. Once the other elements have been clearly defined, it is appropriate to look for the best match of available technologies to the criteria defined. The evaluation process should seek to define the characteristics of the device needed, rather than name a specific device. In selecting the device, one must also consider the social and cultural acceptability to the user and his or her family. By locating the most "transparent" means of interfacing the individual and his or her technology, further separation or isolation can be avoided.

As stated previously, IDEA mandates that technology be considered in the IEP development process. Until knowledge of the potential of assistive and instructional technologies is widespread, there will be no way to assure that appropriate referrals for technology evaluations will occur. An understanding of the changes that can result for a student through the use of technologies should not reside only in the hands of a few trained "specialists." Annual review and dismissal chairpersons, administrators, parents, and classroom-based personnel must all have a basic familiarity with technology's ability to assist students with special needs in order to assure that devices and services are considered, and provided where appropriate.

Summary

While seeking to remove the many barriers to technology access for individuals with special needs, we as educators must remember the reasons for advocating on their behalf. We constantly expand our thoughts on *who* can benefit, but in our zeal we must not lose sight of for *what* purpose, *where* and *when* it is appropriate to use the technologies, and *how much* technology should be used.

Since the early days of technology integration into school environments, the objective of educators has been to "even the playing field," to integrate students with special needs into a least restrictive or inclusive environment, to make them fit in, and to have them perceived as more like the next kid. Unfortunately, students are sometimes mainstreamed into classrooms that are not yet using computers, where technology is not yet integrated into the curriculum. Unless educators exercise good judgment, the adapted computer or other technology can become yet another "difference," yet another barrier that reduces acceptance by teachers untrained in even basic computer operation, much less trained to deal with adapted peripherals. Overzealous but well-meaning parents and advocates must avoid outfitting a student with too much technology. The technology should not create barriers it was intended to eliminate.

Resources

Books

Alliance for Technology Access. (1994). *Computer resources for people with disabilities: A guide to exploring today's assistive technology*. Alameda, CA: Hunter House.

Beukelman, D., & Mirenda, P. (1992). *Augmentative and alternative communication: Management of severe communication disorders in children and adults.* Baltimore: Brookes.

Church, G., & Glennen, S. (1992). *The handbook of assistive technology.* San Diego: Singular.

Enders, A., & Hall, M. (Eds.). (1990). *Assistive technology sourcebook.* Washington, DC: RESNA Press.

Glennen, S. L., & DeCoste, D. C. (1997). *The handbook of augmentative and alternative communication.* San Diego: Singular.

Lazzaro, J. J. (1996). *Adapting PCs for disabilities.* Reading, MA: Addison-Wesley.

Lewis, R. B. (1993). *Special education technology: Classroom applications.* Pacific Grove, CA: Brooks/Cole.

Male, M. (1994). *Technology for inclusion: Meeting the special needs of all students.* Needham Heights, MA: Allyn & Bacon.

Reichele, J., York, J., & Sigafoos, J. (1991). *Implementing augmentative and alternative communication: Strategies for learners with severe disabilities.* Baltimore: Brookes.

Smith, R. (1994). *Course guide: Introduction to assistive technology and rehabilitation technologies.* Madison, WI: Trace Research and Development Center.

Trefler, E., Hobson, D. A., & Shaw, C. G. (1993). *Seating and mobility: For persons with physical disabilities.* Tucson, AZ: Therapy Skill Builders.

Wright, C., & Nomura, M. (1988). *From toys to computers: Access for the physically disabled child.* Wauconda, IL: Don Johnston, Inc.

Periodicals

Assistive Technology
RESNA Press
1700 North Moore Street, Suite 1540
Arlington, VA 22209-1903
Voice: 703/524-6686

Augmentative and Alternative Communication
Closing the Gap
P.O. Box 68
Henderson, MN 56044
Voice: 507/248-3294
Fax: 507/248-3810

TAM Connector and *Journal of Special Education Technology*
Technology and Media Division
The Council for Exceptional Children
1920 Association Drive
Reston, VA 20191-1589

Laboratory–Practicum Activities

▶ 1. List three goals you will achieve in the next 3 months to enhance your understanding of environmental barriers that negatively impact individuals with disabilities as they "move about" the home, school, and community functions. Use technology to develop your goals, to describe how you will achieve these goals, and to manage the achievement of the goals.

▶ 2. List three goals you will achieve in the next 3 months to enhance your understanding of environmental barriers that negatively impact access to technology by individuals with disabilities. Use technology to develop your goals, to describe how you will achieve these goals, and to manage the achievement of the goals.

▶ 3. Search the Internet and World Wide Web for plans to promote technology access for individuals with disabilities posted by different school districts. Compare and contrast these plans, evaluating them based on the principles outlined in this chapter, and share this information with your course instructor and peers.

▶ 4. Collaborate with your peers to conduct an environmental access survey of your site. Develop an action plan for overcoming any physical barriers. Share this plan with your course instructor and those persons responsible for environmental access at your site.

▶ 5. Identify the pros and cons of the possible solutions identified for accommodating a student in a wheelchair presented in the section on environmental barriers to access. Share your comparison findings with your course instructor and peers.

▶ 6. Collaborate with your peers to create a database of keyboard adjustment features available for home, school, and community systems. Use technology to provide your course instructor and future students with a copy of this database.

▶ 7. Identify the political and attitudinal barriers to technology access for students with special needs that you encounter in your setting. Use technology to develop a database of action steps for overcoming these barriers. Share this database with your course instructor and peers.

References

Americans with Disabilities Act of 1990, 42 U.S.C. § 12101 et seq.

Anson, D. K. (1996). *Alternative computer access: A guide to selection*. Philadelphia: F. A. Davis.

Assistive Technology in the Classroom. (1992). Lincoln, NE: Meyer Rehabilitation Institute.

Behrmann, M. (Ed.). (1988). *Integrating computers into the curriculum: A handbook for special educators*. Boston: Little, Brown.

Berliss, J. (1991). *Checklists for implementing accessibility in computer laboratories at colleges and universities*. Madison, WI: Trace Developmental Center

Carl, D., Mataya, C., & Zabala, J. (1994). *What's the big IDEA? Assistive technology issues for teams in school settings*. Paper presented at Closing the Gap, Minneapolis, MN.

Center for Information Technology Accommodations. (1995). *Managing information resources for accessibility* [On-line]. Available: http://www.gsa.gov/coca/front.htm

Clark, M. C. (1992). Augmentative alternative communication assessment team guidelines and procedures for system selection for the motor disabled child. *Seminars in Speech and Language, 13*(1), 70–82.

Cohen, M. L. (1996). How to buy personal digital assistants. *Computer Life, 3*(10), 93–94.

Connell, B. R., Jones, M., Mace, R., Mueller, J., Mullick, A., Ostroff, E., Sanford, J., Steinfeld, E., Story, M., & Vanderheiden, G. (1995). *The principles of Universal Design* [On-line]. Available: http://trace.wisc.edu/te...n/ud_princ/u_princ.html

Cook, A. M., & Hussey, S. M. (1995). *Assistive technologies: Principles and practices*. St. Louis: Mosby.

Cress, C. J., & French, G. J. (1994). The relationship between cognitive load measurements and estimates of computer input controls. *Assistive Technology, 6*(1), 54–66.

Deterding, C. M. (1996). Computer access option. In J. Hammel (Ed.), *Technology and occupational therapy: A link to function* (pp. 1–35). Bethesda, MD: The American Occupational Therapy Association.

Dockstader, J. (1999). Teachers of the 21st century know the what, why, and how of technology integration. *T.H.E. Journal, 26*(6), 73–74.

Fraser, B. A., McGregor, G., Arango, G. A., & Kangas, K. (1994). *Physical characteristics assessment: Computer access for individuals with cerebral palsy*. Wauconda, IL: Don Johnston, Inc.

Garber, S., Cassett-James, E. L., & Derrickson, J. (1989). *Evaluating for technology: A team approach*. Baltimore: Center for Technology and Human Disabilities.

Glickman, L., Deitz, J., Anson, D., & Stewart, K. (1996). The effect of switch control site on computer skills of infants and toddlers. *The American Journal of Occupational Therapy, 50*(7), 545–553.

Golinker, L. (1995). *Myth #1: Assistive technology is a new benefit under the IDEA*. Washington, DC: Consortium for Assistive Technology Leadership and System Change.

Goodman, S. (1995). *Policy development in assistive technology and IDEA*. Washington, DC: Consortium for Assistive Technology Leadership and System Change.

Gowan, M. (1999, March). USB graphics tablets debut. *Macworld*, p. 30.

Individuals with Disabilities Education Act of 1990, 20 U.S.C. § 1400 et seq.

King, T. W. (1999). *Assistive technology: Essential human factors*. Needham Heights, MA: Allyn & Bacon.

Langberg, M. (1996). Web TV flattens a tollgate on the information superhighway. *Mercury News* [On-line]. Available: file://Al/WebLangberg.htm

Lewis, R. B. (1998). Assistive technology and learning disabilities: Today's realities and tomorrow's promises. *Journal of Learning Disabilities, 31*, 16–26, 54.

Lindsey, J. D. (Ed.). (1989). *Computers and exceptional individuals*. Columbus, OH: Merrill.

Lindsey, J. D. (Ed.). (1993). *Computers and exceptional individuals* (2nd ed.). Austin, TX: PRO-ED.

Maryland Blue Ribbon Committee on Technology in Education. (1994). *The Maryland Plan for Technology in Education*. Baltimore: Maryland State Board of Education.

Maryland State Department of Education. (1996). *1995–96 technology inventory of Maryland public school systems*. Baltimore: Author.

Parette, H. P., Hourcade, J. J., & Van Biervliet, A. (1993, Spring). Selection of appropriate technology for children with disabilities. *Teaching Exceptional Children*, pp. 18–22.

Phillips, B., & Zhao, H. (1993). Predictors of assistive technology abandonment. *Assistive Technology, 5*, 36–45.

Reed, P. (1995). *Assessing students' needs for assistive technology*. Madison, WI: Department of Public Instruction.

Rehabilitation Act of 1973, 29 U.S.C. § 701 et seq.

Rehabilitation Engineering and Assistive Technology Society of North America. (1996). *Reference on credentialing.* Arlington, VA: Author.

Ryder, R. J., & Hughes, T. (1997). *Internet for educators.* Upper Saddle River, NJ: Merrill.

Scherer, M. J. (1996). *Living in the state of stuck.* Cambridge, MA: Brookline Books.

Shuster, N. E. (1996). Addressing assistive technology needs in special education. *The American Journal of Occupational Therapy, 50,* 993–997.

Swinth, Y., Anson, D., & Deitz, J. (1993). Single-switch computer access for infants and toddlers. *The American Journal of Occupational Therapy, 47*(11), 1031–1038.

Vanderheiden, G. C. (1981). *Practical application of microcomputers to aid the handicapped.* Madison, WI: Trace Research and Development Center.

Vanderheiden, G. C. (1991). Guidelines for the design of consumer products to increase their accessibility to persons with disabilities. *Proceedings of the 14th Annual RESNA Conference.* Washington, DC: RESNA Press.

Vanderheiden, G. C., Chisholm, W. A., & Ewers, N. (1996). Design of HTML pages to increase their accessibility to users with disabilities. *Strategies for Today and Tomorrow* [On-line]. Available: http://www.trace.wisc.edu/text/guidelines/htmlgide/toc.html#TABLE

Zabala, J. (1994). *The SETT Framework: Critical questions to ask when making informed assistive technology decisions.* Paper presented at Closing the Gap, Minneapolis, MN.

Chapter 6

✌   ✌   ✌

Software Evaluation and Development

Florence M. Taber-Brown

Florida Diagnostic and Learning Resources System/South
Dade County Public Schools, Miami, Florida

General and special education professionals and clinicians often delude themselves into thinking that they write curricula. In reality, educational material producers in general, working with or without professionals, establish the scope and sequence of instruction in their development of products. This statement is as true today as it was for the first and second editions of this book (Lindsey, 1989, 1993). However, with the advent of technology there is the possibility, if educators and clinicians take the opportunity, for professionals to take the leadership in developing appropriate curricula to meet the changing needs of children, youths, and adults (i.e., software program *users*) and of society. With storage units for electronic media gaining more and more memory and programs becoming considerably more interactive and allowing for more creativity on the part of both the professional and the user, control of education now has the opportunity to be in the hands of the educator where it belongs (Szul & Woodland, 1998). Evaluation to select appropriate software for interactive education, including software that stimulates the teacher, clinician, and user to create their own programs, is now taking on an even more important role than it has in the past (see also Appendix D). Although professionals continue to purchase software primarily through catalog advertising (Gardner, Taber-Brown, & Wissick, 1992), more and more educators are taking an interest in selecting software that meets their needs (Palin, 1992). Professionals are increasingly selecting software based on published reviews of software, presentations at conventions, and review of software by centers within school districts.

There has also been a move for software producers to develop software that is based on consumer input, research, and results of collaborative-type grants supported by the federal government and private agencies and organizations. For example, Intellitools, makers of the Intellikeys alternative keyboard, has been working under an extensive grant with the National Science Foundation to determine appropriate keyboard overlays to meet the specific needs of users. The company has evaluated the effectiveness of various features available on overlays, including color, size of cells, texture, placement of cells, types of cells, shapes of cells, and the icons or pictures

Professionals should personally evaluate software if possible. (Photograph by Carolyn F. Woods)

placed on the cells. This project was done in collaboration with a number of software companies and the Alliance for Special Education Technology. The overlays were extensively evaluated by using them and the software for which they were developed with many users, including those involved with the Alliance for Technology Access. The data collected were then subjected to analysis by various statistical instruments to determine the most effective overlays used with each program and the type of users with which the various types of overlays were most beneficial.

Other companies, such as Skills Bank, have been industry leaders in conducting research on their products. The Little Planet Literacy Series (Little Planet Publishing) was created based on over 3 years of development and research headed by Ted S. Hasselbring from Peabody College at Vanderbilt University. This program is highly interactive and is a complete literacy series relating all areas of language arts for early grades. Laureate Learning Company has developed its language development software based on extensive research with two highly respected speech–language pathologists as president and vice president of the company. Their software can be used not only for instruction but also for assessment of user abilities necessary for augmentative communication.

Although many programs are based on research, there is still a need for evaluating software prior to purchase. Some companies continue to base their program development more on financial gain than on research or sound educational principles. Some of these companies are aware of what features should be in programs but choose not to incorporate features based on cost instead of educational effectiveness. Even if all producers develop proven educationally sound software and include the expense of comprehensive validation studies, professionals must evaluate possible software purchases to determine if the software (a) is appropriate to specific users' needs as stated in the Individualized Education Program (IEP), Individualized Transition Plan (ITP), or Individualized Family Service Plan (IFSP); (b) fits into the core curriculum strands; (c) complements the approaches and teaching styles of the educator;

and (d) meets the learning styles and addresses the learning intelligence(s) of the user (also see Chapters 3 and 9 and Appendix D).

Although software is becoming more responsive to good pedagogical theories and practice (see Chapters 1, 7, 8, 9, and 13), professionals still need to know how to evaluate software for their exceptional users. Some of the considerations for evaluation have changed over the past few years, based on changes in software that allow for considerably more interaction on the part of the user. When appropriate software is not available or if the educator desires, programs can be used that permit professionals not only to add content and make other instructional changes but also to create extensive interactions. These programs, categorized as authoring systems, can be especially important for special educators and clinicians who work with low-incident populations because software is often unavailable due to economic reasons. Some companies, however, such as R. J. Cooper and Associates, do design programs targeted for these populations.

This chapter is designed to provide professionals responsible for exceptional individuals with information that will aid in evaluating instructional software, to determine if it meets the needs of the educator and the individual instructional needs of the user; knowledge to assist in evaluating for assistive devices; a system for designing appropriate software when none is available; and a philosophy that encourages the use of this evaluative information in the selection of emerging technologies (Holden, Holcomb, & Wedman, 1992).

Software Evaluation

Evaluation and validation should be of primary concern to the educator of exceptional persons, if selection and use of software and any assistive or adaptive device are to be effective. Too often software (e.g., games or drill-and-practice programs) has been used only as a reinforcer for completing assignments. Higher level programs causing users to analyze, synthesize, or evaluate have been used less often, although with the advent of multimedia programs, more and more teachers are using software for these higher level thinking skills. Software is often used without an evaluation as to the appropriateness of the information and concepts it presents or whether it addresses thinking skills or the learning modality of the specific user. Special care must be taken to assure not only that the reading and interest levels are matched to those of the user, especially for those with disabilities and those who are gifted or talented, but also that the type of learner (McCarthy, 1991) or the type of intelligence through which the user learns most effectively (Gardner, 1982, 1993) is considered. In addition to considering the needs of users, the educator should select software that matches his or her teaching style, especially when teaching individuals with lower cognitive functioning. For individuals who are gifted and talented, as with all users, care must be taken to stimulate the learner and to employ methods that cause the individual to employ higher cognitive–thinking processes (see Chapter 13).

External Evaluation

General and special educators and clinicians cannot evaluate all software personally. Their school systems need to undertake some type of external means of evaluation. Evaluation centers are available in some school centers, although many of these centers house software for teachers to view and evaluate on their own. A number of these centers, however, have staff to evaluate a particular program and write a description of the program plus opinions about the use of the software with particular populations. This is the case in many of the specialized exceptional user education centers across the state of Florida. Florida is divided into 19 centers, called Florida Diagnostic and Learning Resources Systems (FDLRS), of which many house software, provide training on that software, and distribute newsletters that include information regarding software. In addition, Florida has an approved software list, which is developed through nomination by users, including special educators.

Many of the software evaluation centers across the United States that were available at the pub-

lication of earlier editions of this book are no longer available. Letters were sent to all addresses listed in the prior edition to verify their existence. A number of letters were returned indicating that the addressees either no longer exist or left no forwarding address. Two of the letters were answered, indicating that the centers either no longer publish software reports or have little information relating to special education. The sources listed in Table 6.1 provide information on special education technology, including software. A number of Web sites on the Internet also provide information on software and uses of that software not only in special education but in an inclusive environment in which special education users are included in general education (also see Chapters 3, 4, and 9). Often the software that is evaluated has been provided to a preview center by the publisher or the center has heard about the program through word of mouth or seen it at a convention. Therefore, for a number of reasons, special educators should investigate software from many sources and determine if that software will meet their particular needs. In other words, special educators who receive information from various sources should conduct a meta-evaluation to determine the validity of those evaluations as the software relates to their own use.

To conduct an effective meta-evaluation, the professional working with the special education user should consider a number of questions addressing various aspects of the evaluation:

1. Did the evaluation follow a precise process, and what was that process?

2. Was the evaluation carried out by a team or by one individual?

3. What is the educational background of the evaluator(s)?

4. What type of users were considered during the evaluation (e.g., disability area, level of disability, age)?

The evaluators should have had experience teaching users for whom the program was developed or for whom the program is being considered. For example, if an evaluator is an educator

Table 6.1. Evaluation and Information for Special Education Software Sources

Alliance for Technology Access
2175 East Francisco Boulevard, Suite L
San Rafael, CA 94901
Voice: 415/455-4575
Fax: 415/455-0654

Apple Computer, Inc.
Apple Education Division MS 198-K12
2420 Ridgepoint Drive
Austin, TX 78754
Voice: 800/800-2775

ConnSENSE Newsletter
Special Education Center Technology Lab
U-64, 249 Glenbrook Road
University of Connecticut
Storrs, CT 06269-2064
Voice: 203/486-0172

High/Scope Educational Research Foundation
600 North River Street
Ypsilanti, MI 48198-2898
Voice: 313/485-2000
Fax: 313/485-0704
E-mail: XWKJ18A@prodigy.com

IBM Corporation
IBM Special Needs System
11400 Burnet Road
Austin, TX 78758
Voice: 800/426-4832

Resource Directory
Closing the Gap
Box 68, 526 Main Street
Henderson, MN 56044
Voice: 507/248-3294
Fax: 507/248-3810

Trace Research and Development Center
Room S-151 Waisman Center
1500 Highland Avenue
University of Wisconsin
Madison, WI 53705-2280
TDD: 608/263-5408
Fax: 608/262-8848

and has extensive experience teaching high school algebra, this person may not necessarily be qualified to evaluate the effectiveness of a social studies program written for elementary users with gifts or talents, or to evaluate mathematical programs written for secondary users with learning disabilities. On the other hand, this person may be well qualified to evaluate other mathematics programs written for general education secondary-level users.

Individuals who have had teaching experiences with the subject matter and the audience for whom the software is intended must evaluate the software. Judgments on software designed for users with mild disabilities should not be made from the point of view of secondary regular education. Such a situation might occur if a secondary-level mathematics teacher evaluated a program designed to teach mathematical concepts to secondary users in a special education program, and the teacher's evaluation report indicated that the concepts were too basic or simple. Comments such as this may be predicated upon the evaluator's teaching experiences and not on the intended audience for the program. An evaluator not only has to be qualified as a classroom or therapy room professional, but also must have had experiences in understanding the dynamics of computing technologies. Further, a team evaluation eliminates the bias that occurs when judgment is made by only one person (also see Chapters 5 and 14).

If possible, an audience similar to the one for which the program was designed should be asked to evaluate the program. Programs considered to be exceptionally stimulating and informative by adults, regardless of their characteristics, may receive the opposite reaction from the intended group of users. Field studies conducted by a software developer who writes software primarily for secondary users with learning problems found that some programs considered to be highly educationally effective by an adult can be boring to a user. On the other hand, software designed for one population may also be appropriate for other populations, as demonstrated by the program Mind Castles, developed by Lawrence Productions. Although this program had been designed to develop logic and reasoning in users with mild cognitive disabilities at the secondary level, it was found during field testing to be equally effective with upper elementary nonexceptional users.

The key to the appropriateness of a specific program for a particular audience should be based on the specific objectives of the program plus the interest, reading, and presentation levels as validated by each possible audience. The fact that programs developed for specific audiences may be equally appropriate for other audiences supports the idea that there really is no such thing as "special education software." Again, the determination of possible effectiveness for a certain individual or group of users should depend on matching the software to the needs of the individual or group. The section later in this chapter on internal software evaluation discusses possible individual or group needs in much greater detail.

The extensiveness of the external evaluation is an extremely important factor in the educator's meta-evaluation. The evaluative process should permit a sufficient amount of time to follow the steps necessary to make valid and reliable judgments (see Figure 6.1). Initially in the process, software should go through screening. If the software is considered likely to be an effective instructional program, qualified educators should then thoroughly evaluate the software based on accepted educational principles and the dynamics of the computer. This is a time-consuming process, because every segment of the program must be evaluated based on all possible responses on input frames. In some programs, users type in "yes" or "no," select from multiple choices, or type in variable free short inputs. In others, especially those involving multimedia, the user defines his or her own program path or creates

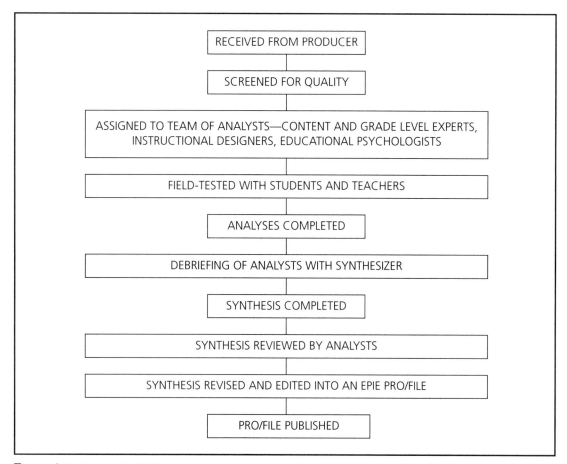

Figure 6.1. Steps in the EPIE courseware evaluation procedure. From Educational Products Information Exchange (EPIE), 103-3 W. Montauk Highway, Hampton Bay, NY 11946. Used with permission.

programs as he or she goes. These latter programs are more complex to evaluate but can be very educational for the user either working individually or in small groups. As indicated previously, once the program has been evaluated on specified criteria by qualified evaluators, the program should be used with members of the intended audience to determine if the specified goals and objectives can be reached by their interacting with the program.

Often the professional cannot locate evaluation information for a particular piece of software. This is especially true because no one source could possibly evaluate the multitude of software programs available. When no evaluation information is available, the professional may wish to read about the software in vendor catalogs, call the vendor to discuss the needs of users to determine if the software is appropriate, or ask others in the school system if they know anything about the program. Incidentally, calling vendors is an excellent idea. Many of them have special educators on staff and will provide valuable information to help with decision making.

Another excellent source for securing software evaluations is accessing Web sites such as Global Education Partners (http://www.global-ed.com). In addition to providing general information about software, the Global Education site has a myriad of links to sites with software previews (e.g., Educational Software Preview Guide— http://www2.sanjuan.edu/preview.guide/index. html) and software evaluations (e.g., Children's Software Review—http://www2.childrenssoftwa re.com/childrenssoftware/). Software reviews in national Macintosh magazines (e.g., McClelland, 1999), PC or Windows-based publications (e.g., McDonald, 1999), and local computer club newsletters (e.g., Smith, 1999) can also assist professionals in the software evaluation process.

Because searching for information from which the professional can make decisions about software can be tedious and time-consuming, it is a good idea for local education agencies (LEAs) and clinical centers to develop criteria to evaluate software and then keep information on file when professionals have evaluated a particular software program. For example, general and special educators should work with central office

personnel to decide their own specific criteria for evaluating software and then use these criteria to develop an evaluation form. Although there is some disagreement in special education circles concerning the development of LEA software evaluation forms, there are a number of reasons for school systems to take the time to develop such forms. If local professionals are involved in implementing the software evaluation procedures, they will be more likely to use those procedures. They will also be more knowledgeable about software evaluation principles and the form itself. Software evaluation generated by both general and special educators can be stored in a database program or on hard copy. The method selected for storing evaluation results should be based on "ready access" so professionals can easily retrieve needed information. It is also important that regular and special educators share information on software programs, especially with the inclusion movement, which includes special education users in general education. Educators are now collaborating, sharing the same classroom and user responsibilities, as in the inclusive approach to instruction where general and special education teachers and other professionals are working as a team.

The evaluation form should include the evaluator's name, position or role, and contact information, since colleagues may need further information on the program to determine if it will meet their needs. A number of models of evalua-

Software as well as related printed materials should be evaluated and findings catalogued. (Photograph by Carolyn F. Woods)

tion forms have been developed in the past (see http://www.seamonkey.ed.asu.edu/emc300/software/evalform.html; http://www.ht.gc.cc.fl.us/socsci/ireview/; http://www.sunbelt-software.com/convofrm.htm). However, most of these forms were developed prior to programs that involve multimedia and extensive decision making on the part of the user. On the other hand, the educational principles presented by the evaluation forms found in Appendix G at the back of this book continue to be appropriate in forms used by LEAs.

Internal Evaluation

Internal evaluation of software is completed by the professional for use in his or her own classroom. An appropriate internal evaluation model should be comprehensive and cover instructional information, educational adequacy, technical adequacy, and related technical information (see also Appendix D). Each of these areas should be based on the intended audience and the intended use of the program.

Instructional Information

Instructional information should include all factors external to the program that deal with implementing the program. The professional evaluating a program should determine if the software fits into the curriculum and if it introduces material, provides direct instruction, reinforces the instruction, or enhances the concepts learned. Many older programs introduced material, provided instruction, or reinforced what had been taught in the classroom, but few enhanced concepts providing stimulation to higher level thinking skills—analysis, synthesis, and evaluation—using skills and concepts learned for analysis, decision making, and creativity. Many of the programs on the market today are motivating higher level thinking skills, including programs for users who may have cognitive deficiencies and who were previously considered unable to succeed at this level. Although recent software may stimulate innovative thinking, the professional still

should consider if the software is appropriate for teaching using the computer, if it matches the teacher's style of instruction, and if it meets the user's individual needs. Matching the teaching style of the professional is especially important for users with lower functioning levels in initial instruction and for a controlled instructional style during the maintenance stage of instruction, when teaching transference of learning.

In addition, the software selected must consider the users' learning styles. Many models of instruction should be considered. For example, McCarthy's (1987) 4MAT System considers learning styles, including how educators perceive and process information in setting up instruction. It "is an open-ended teaching method . . . [that] is adaptable to the developmental level of the users, the content being taught, and the artistry of the moment" (McCarthy, 1992, p. 3). In essence all instruction should approach users based on their individual learning styles (Pracek, 1994b). This can be accomplished by dividing the instruction into four hemispheric modes or major identifiable learning styles with "combinations formed by [each user's] own perceiving and processing techniques which form [his or her] unique learning style" (p. 4). Each of the four major learning styles is divided into right and left brain approaches. Instructional plans are then created using the four major learning styles divided into right and left brain approaches so that the instruction reaches all users, thus directing that instruction to individual learning style.

Gardner's (1985, 1993) seven intelligences must also be considered when selecting software and organizing instruction. These seven intelligences—linguistic, logical–mathematical, spatial, musical, bodily–kinesthetic, interpersonal, and intrapersonal—can determine not only instructional approaches but also software selected, as well as any other instructional material (see Table 6.2). Technology specialist Eileen Pracek (1994a) took Gardner's intelligences and analyzed numerous software programs for the intelligence to which it directs instruction. Her descriptions of these learners and the types of software are as follows:

- *Linguistic learners* think in words; learn by listening, reading, and verbalizing; benefit from discussion; enjoy writing; like word games. These users enjoy word processing programs; programs that require them to read and answer questions; and those that encourage them to create poetry, essays, and other literary forms of expression.

- *Logical–mathematical learners* think conceptually; reach conclusions by reasoning logically; look for abstract patterns and relationships; like brain teasers, logical puzzles, and strategy games; enjoy using computers; enjoy experimenting; like to classify and categorize. These users enjoy database and spreadsheet programs, problem-solving software, programs that teach in a logical way, simulations that allow them to experiment, computer programming, and strategy programs.

- *Spatial learners* think in images and pictures, like mazes and jigsaw puzzles, like to draw and design things, like to build models, like diagrams and charts. These users enjoy draw and paint programs; graphic production software; reading programs that use visual clues; programs that require them to solve mazes or puzzles; programs that require them to create a picture and then write about it; programs that allow them to visualize information such as maps, charts, or diagrams; and hypermedia programs.

- *Bodily–kinesthetic learners* process knowledge through bodily sensation; communicate through gestures; learn by touching, manipulating, and moving; like role playing, creative movement, and any physical activity; enjoy fixing machines, building models, and hands-on art activities. These users enjoy software requiring alternative input such as joystick, mouse, Touchwindow or graphics tablet; keyboarding and word processing programs; instructional games, especially arcade format with fire buttons; graphics programs that produce blueprints for making three-dimensional models; science and math programs with accompanying manipulatives and probes; software that includes animated graphics; and programs that allow them to move objects around on the screen.

- *Musical learners* think in tones; learn through rhythm and melody; play musical instruments; remember melodies; notice nonverbal sounds in the environment; and learn by singing, tapping out a cadence, or whistling. These users enjoy programs that combine stories with songs, reading programs that associate letters and sounds with music, programs that use music as a reward or let them create their own music, programs designed to teach music concepts and skills, hypermedia, and programs that add music to their computer presentations.

- *Interpersonal learners* understand and care about people; like to socialize; learn more easily by relating and cooperating; enjoy playing group games; are good at teaching other children; like being involved with groups. These users enjoy telecommunication programs, programs that address social issues, programs that include group participation or decision making, games requiring two or more players, programs that allow them to interact with characters in a simulation or adventure format, and programs that turn learning into a social activity.

- *Intrapersonal learners* display a sense of independence; like to be alone; seem to be self-motivating; learn more easily with independent study, self-paced instruction, and individualized projects and games; need their own quiet space; and tend to "march to the beat of a different drummer." These users enjoy programs that are tutorial and self-paced, instructional games in which the opponent is the computer, programs that encourage self-awareness or build self-improvement skills, and programs that allow them to work independently.

Cynthia Magnus (1998) reported that an eighth intelligence—Naturalist Intelligence—has been discovered by Gardner. Magnus stated that persons with this intelligence notice relationships in nature and are ultrasensitive to the natural world. They see connections and patterns within the plant and animal kingdom.

An additional factor to be considered in internal software evaluation, which was mentioned

Table 6.2. Gardner's Multiple Intelligences in the Classroom

Linguistic Intelligence

The capacity to use written or oral words effectively. These students have the ability to manipulate the structure, sounds, and meaning of language. They use language in practical ways to remember information, convince others to take a specific course of action, inform, and talk about themselves. Students who are strong linguistic learners may become storytellers, orators, politicians, poets, playwrights, editors, and journalists.

Logical–Mathematical Intelligence

The capacity to use numbers effectively and reason well. These students are sensitive to logical patterns and relationships, cause–effect, if–then, functions (how things work), and related abstractions. These students relate effectively to the processes of categorization, classification, inference, generalization, calculation, and hypothesis testing. Students who are strong logical–mathematical learners may become scientists, computer programmers, logicians, mathematicians, tax accountants, and statisticians.

Spatial Intelligence

The capacity to perceive ones visual–spatial world accurately and perform changes and adjustments based on those perceptions. These students have a sensitivity to color, line, shape, form, space and any relationships that exist between these elements. They have the ability to visualize, to graphically represent visual or spatial ideas, and to orient appropriately in a spatial matrix. Students who are strong learners may become artists, map makers, interior decorators, guides, explorers, architects, and inventors.

Bodily–Kinesthetic Intelligence

The expertise of using one's whole body to express ideas and feelings, and using one's hands to produce or transform things. These students use the skills of coordination, balance, dexterity, strength, flexibility, and speed. They need to move and touch. Students who are bodily–kinesthetic learners may become actors, athletes, craftsmen, sculptors, mimes, mechanics, surgeons, and dancers.

Musical Intelligence

The capacity to perceive, discriminate, transform, and express musical forms. These students have a sensitivity to rhythm, pitch or melody, and interpretation of a musical piece. This may include figural, global, and intuitive understanding of music and/or a formal, analytical, and technical understanding of music. Students who are musical learners may become music critics, composers, performers, piano tuners, conductors, and music therapists.

Interpersonal Intelligence

The ability to perceive and make distinctions in the moods, motivations, and feelings of other people. These students are sensitive to facial expressions, voice, gestures, and other interpersonal clues. Based on the discrimination of these clues, they can respond effectively to influence a group of people to follow a certain line of action. Students who are interpersonal learners may become politicians, administrators, counselors, nurses, salespersons, public relations personnel, and arbitrators.

Intrapersonal Intelligence

Endowed with great self-knowledge and the ability to adapt based on that knowledge. These students have great understanding of their strengths, limitations, inner feelings, and desires. They have a great capacity for self-discipline, self-understanding, and self-esteem. Students who are intrapersonal learners may become psychologists, clergymen, philosophers, and entrepreneurs.

earlier in this chapter but needs to be emphasized again, is the effectiveness of the program with the intended audience. Field-test information should either accompany the program or be available upon request. If this information is not available, the educator can attempt to find out from the manufacturer the names and contact information of other educational professionals who are using the program with similar users. Contacting other professionals who have used the program can provide valuable information for decision making.

Information on other factors to be evaluated under the area of instructional information should be found in the documentation. At a minimum, documentation should present the information necessary to operate the program effectively in a form that is easy to understand. The instructional overview must provide general information about the program, as well as information about the goals and behavioral objectives of the program, which can be matched with those in the exceptional user's IEP. If the software does not provide a management program that includes information about the user's progress in the program, with both on-screen results and hard copy available, the documentation should provide an evaluation plan for assessing the user's progress toward meeting the objectives. Other vital information included in the documentation should be the prerequisite skills, concepts, and vocabulary necessary for the user to be successful with the program, including reading and interest levels. This information is necessary for the professional to determine not only whether the program will be used but, if selected, what modifications may be necessary in how the program is presented and in the teacher's instruction. For example, the professional may wish to preteach the prerequisite concepts and skills prior to program use or may wish to use a program for enhancement that was originally designed for direct instruction (see also Chapters 1 and 3). Also, if the program was designed to operate independently, the professional may wish to have users interact with the program in pairs or small groups.

Another instructional information consideration involves possible operation of the software using adaptive devices. A number of programs on the market, such as those from Laureate Learning, allow the professional to make a number of changes in adapting how the user inputs information. Laureate programs can be changed for scanning or mouse input, the size of the cursor, speed of scanning, and more. Programs that cannot be modified for different methods of input can also be modified but require an adaptive interface, such as Ke:nx from Don Johnston, which provides input by scanning, on-screen keyboard, alternative keyboard, assistive keyboard, Morse Code, or touch screen. In these programs the adaptations run in the background and are available while other software programs are operating at the same time.

Educational Adequacy

Another important evaluation area is educational adequacy, or issues involved with the instruction or program presentation. With the advent of multimedia programs that involve primarily the enhancement of skills, a different way of evaluating programs must emerge because these programs are holistic rather than sequential, providing multiple pathways that often require expansive higher level thinking skills.

Programs that are based on awareness and knowledge levels, should follow basic educational principles, some of which involve proceeding from simple to complex, progressing from concrete to abstract, and chaining to develop skills and concepts. When skills and concepts are being introduced, the task analysis must be appropriate for the intended audience and examples should be provided. Transference of learning should be programmed into the presentation, as should evaluation of comprehension. This appropriateness should include a sufficient number of questions or exercises to determine if the concept has been learned, questions of appropriate content to determine competency, and question types from the appropriate level of cognitive functioning based on Bloom's (1956) taxonomy (see Chapter 13).

With computer tutorial programs, the method in which the program responds to user input should be carefully considered based on reinforcement principles and branching capabilities. These programs should reinforce both correct responses and concepts. Reinforcing the correctness of the response and the concept is important because on many input frames users can obtain the correct answer by chance alone.

With tutorial or instructional programs and when user responses are incorrect, the program should either branch for reteaching or allow the user another opportunity to self-correct the response. If the program branches, the task analysis should be broken down into smaller steps and the conceptual or reading level may be lower. Users should not merely repeat the program sequence. If the concept or skill was not learned the first time, it will not be learned with subsequent identical presentations. Further, wrong responses should not be punished or, as is sometimes the case, reinforced. Obviously, in programs where responses that are incorrect are reinforced, users will respond incorrectly to obtain the exciting replies, thus reinforcing the incorrect responses. In other programs users are punished for incorrect responses ("Wrong answer, you dummy!"), and this type of negative reinforcement may even be accentuated with a loud noise that can be heard by all users in the classroom.

Software must consider responses that indicate whether users do or do not comprehend what is expected of them. These frames or error messages are necessary because they instruct the user about input expectations. "Type Yes or No" is one example of an error message. Another might be the appearance of a help screen with additional instructions. Although these error messages are necessary, their use can be minimized if the user can access directions or help screens whenever desired. Not only should help be available when needed or because the user inputs information indicating lack of comprehension, but the directions and help screens should be evaluated by the professional for clarity.

For software to be motivating, it should provide variable types of input, allow for user–computer program interaction, and branch within the program based on user choice or input. Software must be motivating and based on learning principles, rather than force feeding with regurgitation of information. In fact the more control users have over what they learn, and when, the more likely they are to retain that with which they have been involved.

With users who have emotional disabilities, typing in free inputs can be a double-edged sword. Software should allow users to interact with the program by allowing them the freedom to type in words and phrases, but the teacher should be aware of reaction by the class or users should profanity be entered, especially if that program provides speech synthesis (i.e., "talks").

Besides the variable input capabilities of the computer, programs must be personal, interacting with the user by using his or her name. The psychological value of the user's name entered into the program is obvious.

Too many professionals believe that the more graphics, animation, and QuickTime movies in a program, the better the program. This is not always true. These additions must enhance the skill or concept being taught, not detract from it. For users who function at low cognitive levels, the material must be concrete and, therefore, more realism should be employed. The needs of the audience must be considered to determine the necessity for any of these possible enhancements. These features should always be of high quality with high resolution and represent what is to be taught in a way that is most educationally effective for the user.

Other factors include the use of capabilities inherent in the computer, such as blinks, flashes, scrolling, and stimulating backgrounds. Consider the individual who will be using the program. For instance, flashing and other stimulating additions on the screen can stimulate seizures. For that matter, the constant changes that occur on the screen can also affect some users.

The advent of multimedia requires some additional features to evaluate. Although multimedia educational adequacy evaluation also should consider educational principles, it is not as straightforward. Many of these programs use voice, music, movie clips, graphics, art, moving text, and so on, to provide the user with a "virtual reality" environment for learning. Simulations, interactive games, problem-solving activities, and creative hypermedia are all used to make the program more "real" and provide the user with the stimulus necessary to use higher level thinking skills to develop creative solutions (Bloom's, 1956, taxonomy; see Chapter 13). For many users with disabilities, however, the methods and amounts of stimulation must be considered when evaluating programs. On the other hand, some users whom the professional would believe could not benefit from such a program, will do so. An unknown variable in the type and amount of stimulation has an unexpected effect and the user reacts.

Technical Adequacy and Related Technical Information

Technical adequacy and related technical information is another major issue to consider in software evaluation. The format of the frame, or what is seen on the screen at one time, is extremely important, especially for individuals who are cognitively challenged. For these individuals, the frame should be uncluttered and involve little if any text but have graphics, pictures, or video. The more realistic the frames, the more effective they will be with this population. For users with reading difficulties, phrases should be broken appropriately, and sentences should be of appropriate length for the audience. Single spacing of lines should be avoided because of the difficulty in reading lines placed too closely together. The presentation or format should be variable for this latter group to increase the program's ability to get and hold their attention. For lower functioning users, however, the format should be constant so they know what to expect. For users with cognitive challenges and reading difficulties, sound is very important. In addition, for those who have difficulty reading the screen but who cognitively can comprehend contents, screen reading of the text is vital. Many programs have this feature, but for those that do not, a screen reading program can be installed in the background to read the text. Pictures, video, and other realistic representations are important to supplement any text for comprehension purposes. When user inputs are recorded, the assess-

ment of these should be based on the concept and not on typing (or keyboarding) or spelling ability. Furthermore, the software program must take into consideration any probable input (e.g., all synonyms for the correct response must be accepted as correct).

The professional must be assured that the program will run to completion, regardless of user inputs. This may sound like an obvious factor to consider, but too often it is overlooked. In one instance, a number of software products found in a media center would not run to completion, and because they had been purchased earlier and never used, the condition was not noticed. Because they were no longer under warranty, the companies were not obligated to replace them, although in this case most of the companies were understanding and sent new programs.

One factor to consider in the purchase of software, then, is the warranty and replacement policy. Another is the update policy. Some companies automatically send update disks while others do so at a minimal charge. Therefore, it is very important that the information cards be completed and returned as soon as software arrives. It is also important to make sure the software is compatible to run on the available computer. For example, even if the catalog says the program "Runs on Macintosh," it does not mean it will run on every Macintosh. The professional should check the memory and RAM requirements. The professional will also want to check on peripherals that are required or optional for use of this program (e.g., a printer or CD-ROM or DVD-ROM) and functioning requirements for these devices.

Recent and emerging technologies add another dimension to evaluating for technical adequacy (see Jerome, 1999). Knowing the features that can be available will help the professional evaluate these technologies, as they are available on the market, of which many already are. For example, many classrooms not only have a computer and printer, but also CD-ROM (DVD-ROM), interactive video, special disk drives for extensive memory storage, computer cameras, and attachments for VCRs, all attached to the computer for use with multimedia instructional and multimedia presentation software. These additions not only make programs realistic but also, through a type of virtual reality, bring environments into the classroom, within which users can interact and learn. Features to evaluate include use of graphics or still pictures when video clips would be more effective; use and quality of pictures, art, and photographs; use and quality of sound; effective use of music; and type of instruction—simulations, interactive games, puzzle-solving exercises, creative product development, and ways to save and present the product. When selecting any program that is driven using computer technologies, the following should be considered:

1. Can this technology enhance the learning of the user?

2. Can this technology expand the ease with which the professional teaches the skill or concept?

3. Does this medium enhance the reality of the skill or concept?

4. Does this medium increase the involvement of the user?

5. Does this medium permit instruction to allow and encourage the user to employ higher level thinking skills (according to Bloom's, 1956, taxonomy)?

6. Is the use of this medium cost and time effective, based on the first five considerations?

There is also a whole other set of considerations when using utility programs (e.g., word processing, database, spreadsheet, multimedia presentation) (also see Chapters 3 and 5). The ease with which these programs are used is very important. Help sequences and tutorial programs should be readily available for most of these types of programs. The use of utility programs is usually to reinforce and enhance instruction and should be considered as such in teaching as well as the evaluation process. The professional should consider (a) the format, color, and size of cells or text; (b) the availability of speech synthesis to produce "orally" what is on the screen; and (c) the addition of "prediction" capabilities.

In word processing programs for individuals with physical disabilities, word prediction lets the user type long words and phrases with a minimum of keystrokes (e.g., one or two). Many programs not only predict the word the user is typing based on one or two letters but also predict the next word based on context. In addition, some programs have abbreviation expansion, where the user types a few letters, resulting in an entire phrase, sentence, or block of information appearing on the screen. The main question, as in Question 1 listed previously, should be asked: Can this program enhance the learning of the user? For example, quite often spreadsheet and database programs help keep the user organized and, with spreadsheet programs, permit data input without having to do calculations. Word processing programs are helpful for all users but especially for those with fine motor problems. These users can now be creative and write without having to think about how to form letters, thus increasing both speed and quality of work. The correct word processing program is very important, however, and must be evaluated to meet the user's needs. Does the user need reading back of text to help find errors (speech output)? Is the text the right size? Are the text and background colors helpful for the user's functioning? Is the program easy for the user to use? Some programs, such as Write:OutLoud (Don Johnston), include icons for commands for those who, because of reading or other cognitive disabilities, cannot use the text-based status bar across the top of the screen. Multimedia presentation software is discussed in the next section of this chapter. It is mentioned here because users use this type of software to enhance their learning and to expand considerably the function of word processing software by allowing users to add video clips, photos of themselves and others, art, pictures, sound, music, and speech. One user with a physical challenge, who could only use slight movement of her thumb to move a switch and operate a computer, used a multimedia presentation program to write a report for her class that included numerous pictures, sound, and speech. Without selection of the most effective program for her based on ease of operation and size of all text on the screen, along with the appropriate adaptive equipment, this user could not have been successful.

Teacher-Developed Software

The more the professional is involved with evaluation of software, the more he or she learns about the capabilities of the computer and learns that software for some populations, especially low-incidence populations, is extremely limited. This appears to be more of the situation today because the Apple IIe computer has become a "dying breed" and most of the low-level software available is designed for this platform. Limited software for the low-incidence populations has been programmed for MS-DOS, Windows, or Macintosh platforms, although three companies primarily address these populations: R. J. Cooper & Associates (24843 Del Prado, Suite 283, Dana Point, CA 90629, 800/RJCOOPER), UCLA Intervention (1000 Veteran Avenue, Room 23-10, Los Angeles, CA 90095, 310/825-4821), and Poor Richard's Publishing (P.O. Box 1075, Litchfield, CT 06759, 860/567-4307). Some companies, such as Laureate Learning Systems and Little Planet Publishing, that specialize in language development and emerging literacy software have programs that could be appropriate for these populations. For many of these exceptional individuals, however, software that could meet their functioning needs may not have been developed at the appropriate interest level, may involve extensive reading, and may not have the task broken down into the appropriate number of steps.

For many low-incidence exceptionalities, the software may not (a) address the appropriate level of functioning based on Bloom's (1956) taxonomy, (b) have appropriate control of stimuli, (c) have sufficient interactive qualities, or (d) have other necessary factors required to meet the needs of individuals within specific areas of exceptionality. Considering the level of functioning according to Bloom's taxonomy is a function not only of ability level but of where individuals are in the learning sequence: acquisition, fluency,

or maintenance (also see Chapters 1 and 8). At the acquisition stage, tutorial or direct instructional software may be appropriate; at the fluency stage, drill-and-practice would be appropriate; and at the maintenance stage, problem-solving software or software that uses and expands the skills and concepts learned would be required (see Chapters 1 and 4 for additional information concerning stages and types of software). Stages of learning and levels of functioning are important features to consider not only when selecting software but also when designing and developing software for use with users. Professionals need to be able to design software that meets the needs of individuals within identified audiences, especially in exceptional user education and especially for populations that do not encompass a large part of the general public.

When the use of computers for instructional purposes was in its infancy, special educators of low-incidence populations needed to be able to do some actual software programming using computer languages such as BASIC (Beginners All-purpose Symbolic Instruction Code). Today, however, with the advent of multimedia authoring systems, these professionals need to know more about designing programs that meet specific needs and how to use authoring systems to create programs. In addition to creating programs for users, general and special education professionals and clinicians need to be able to teach students and clients how to use these programs so that they can design and develop their own multimedia programs.

Software Development Considerations

To design educationally effective software, the professional needs a background in pedagogy, computer capabilities, use of multimedia peripherals, and content. Besides the learning theory discussed under program evaluation and the specific functioning levels of the user (Bloom's taxonomy) and the stage of learning (acquisition, fluency, or maintenance), a number of specific learner characteristics should be considered:

1. What is the learner's major learning modality: auditory, visual, or kinesthetic?

2. Is there a need to block a specific modality for input or output?

3. What adaptive device, if any, is necessary to meet the individual's specific needs?

4. If the user needs an adaptive device, how does that affect how the program is structured and the required inputs and control features of the program?

5. What are the individual's cognitive functioning levels (reading, writing, mathematics, reasoning, etc.)?

6. What is the individual's interest level (considering chronological age)?

7. What is the individual's optimal discrepancy for learning? Consider instruction between the user's frustration level (too difficult for success) and his or her boredom level (too easy).

8. What prerequisite skills will be necessary for the user to successfully use the program, or

how can the software be developed for the user who does not have these prerequisite skills?

Other considerations include considering right and left brain approaches to learning when developing software or having users develop their own software that fits into the various learning styles, as in McCarthy's (1991) 4Mat System. The 4Mat System involves dividing the lesson into four sections, which are then divided into right and left brain learning. The type of software developed should depend on which of the eight cells is most comfortable for the user. In the case of developing software for an entire class, all eight cells would be considered or the software would be designed to address one or more of the cells. A brief description of the eight cells is presented in Figure 6.2.

In addition to considering right and left modes of learning, Gardner's (1982, 1993) seven intelligences (Table 6.2) should play a major part in how software is developed (see Pracek's, 1994a, intelligence definitions and types of software programs presented earlier; also see Sarouphim,

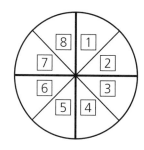

Section 1
  Cell 1 Creating an experience (Right Mode)
  Cell 2 Reflecting, analyzing, experiencing (Left Mode)

Section 2
  Cell 3 Integrating reflective analysis into concepts (Right Mode)
  Cell 4 Developing concepts, skills (Left Mode)

Section 3
  Cell 5 Practicing defined "givens" (Left Mode)
  Cell 6 Practicing and adding something of oneself (Right Mode)

Section 4
  Cell 7 Analyzing application for relevance, usefulness (Left Mode)
  Cell 8 Doing it and applying to new, more complex experience (Right Mode)

Figure 6.2. McCarthy's 4MAT Model. Adapted from *The 4MAT System: Awareness Workshop Materials, Part B: Introduction to Right/Left Processing and the 4MAT Model*, by B. McCarthy, 1991, Barrington, IL: Excel, Inc.

1999). Also, Gillentine (1996) has analyzed the multimedia program Little Planet Literacy Series for how it addresses each of the seven intelligences (see Table 6.3).

Other questions involving learning theory that should be considered include the following:

1. How can I use assessment before instructional or interactive segments both within the program and external to the program to determine the instructional path taken in the program?

2. How can I best evaluate progress periodically while the user interacts with the program as well as at the conclusion of the program?

3. How can I make this program motivating while considering learner needs?

4. How can I apply appropriate reinforcement principles that meet the needs of the specific user(s)?

5. How can I make this program both personal and interactive?

Table 6.3. Multiple Intelligences Learning Styles and Little Planet Literacy Series

Intelligences	Learning Style	Learning Activities	Little Planet
Linguistic	in word	telling stories, reading, writing, listening to stories	Feature Stories, Starting From Scratch, ReadAlong, Story Starters, Book Buddies
Logical–mathematical	by reasoning	questioning, sequencing, logical problem solving, experimental	Feature Stories—story mapping, sequencing ReadAlong—word families StoryStarters—story conclusion Starting From Scratch
Spatial	in images and pictures	video, drawing, designing, story boarding	Feature Stories—multimedia StoryStarters—illustrating conclusion Starting From Scratch— illustrating, story mapping Art Only
Bodily–kinesthetic	through somatic sensations	hands on, role playing, computer activities	All experiences—CD-ROM and multimedia, Acting out Little Planet characters, Feature Stories—StoryBoard cards
Musical	via rhythms and tones	singing, music listening, music playing	All experiences involve music for interpretation of print
Interpersonal	by bouncing ideas off other people	friends, relating, working in groups, E-mail	All experiences can be done cooperatively; stories can be created collaboratively; Little Planet Web site
Intrapersonal	deeply inside of themselves	choices, planning, self-paced, literature with deep meanings, journals, diaries	All experiences can be done individually, and self-paced Feature Stories—content StoryStarters and Starting From Scratch—creating stories and conclusions

Besides learning theory, the professional will need to have sufficient background in the use of computers for instruction to determine the purpose of the program, including drill-and-practice, tutorial or concept instruction, simulation, and problem solving, as these purposes relate to learning the stages of acquisition, fluency, and maintenance. In other words, the professional will want to be able to determine if the program is to provide original instruction, reinforce what has been learned, or enhance skills or concepts already learned. In addition, for low-incidence populations, program design should be determined by the professional's individual instructional approaches because these approaches will be the ones employed when using other materials and approaches for teaching. Using different approaches to learning can be confusing, especially for initial instruction for some low-incidence groups.

Additional experiences necessary for the development of effective educational software can be obtained through evaluation of already developed software, either commercial or public domain. The more professionals use and evaluate software, even informally, the more proficient they become in the skills necessary to design software that meets the needs of specific exceptional users. Elements to consider in evaluation and designing of software include but are not limited to the following:

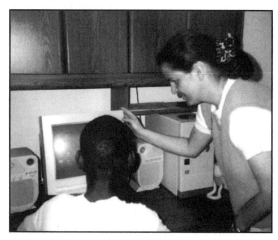

Professionals and students can work together to evaluate and develop software. (Photograph by Carolyn F. Woods)

1. Subject matter must be appropriate and appropriately programmed for the computer. If actual situations are available, they are the most effective teaching situations. Second best is virtual reality, which is rapidly becoming very popular. For example, the MindDrive program (Other 90% Technologies), entertainment software, enables people to command machines by thinking. Other programs use paraphernalia such as goggles, gloves, and special suits to provide the illusion of reality.

2. Software must be interesting, motivating, and appropriate for the interest level of the individual. This is especially true for individuals with severe disabilities, who need age-appropriate software not only to maintain interest but also to provide appropriate behavior models.

3. Software should be nonthreatening. It is important to challenge the individual without the program becoming frustrating and leading to failure.

4. Software must actively involve the individual using the program and provide interactive situations. Much of the newer software involves the individual significantly more than in the past; for example, in the Imagination Express Series from Edmark, users explore various geographic areas and use their creativity to create their own electronic books, including animation, scenery, narration, sound, and music. For younger users software such as Little Planet's emergent literacy programs provide software, video, CD-ROM (DVD-ROM titles may be available), and print materials to involve users in learning and then creating their own books.

5. Feedback and reinforcement should be appropriate and not punishing. For some users the reinforcement should be immediate, external locus of control. For other users the reinforcement comes from completing a routine or developing a product or program that provides reinforcement through an internal locus of control.

6. Software should be personal and involve interaction with the individual using the program.

This feature is especially important with younger users and those who have low functioning levels.

7. The lower the functioning level of the individual, the greater the importance for control of all stimuli—auditory, visual, and tactile. Text should be limited, read to the user, or in some cases nonexistent. For individuals with mild disabilities, the use of extensive auditory or too much visual stimuli can be distracting. In some situations, however, individuals with physical challenges have "true" potential functioning levels that have been depressed. These individuals may become bored with the lower level programs and lose interest, causing caregivers to believe they cannot function at the level of these programs, when in fact they could be successful if they wanted or were motivated to do so. These individuals often become motivated by programs thought to be too difficult for them.

8. The higher the functioning level of the individual, the more choices of direction and control of the program should be in the hands of the user. Care should be taken that higher functioning individuals with reading problems should be provided with considerable choices in direction. Also, as individuals with severe disabilities understand the control they have over what is on the screen, they should be provided with more choices or options.

9. The format of the screen should reflect the functioning and needs of the individual. Placement of text, QuickTime movies, graphics, and animation should be carefully considered because the individual's eyes should go from top left to bottom right.

10. Correct, wrong, and inappropriate responses of users should be appropriately handled. In other words, the frame sequences should be checked to be sure they follow as designed.

11. Error catching must be available. Regardless of the user's input, the program should not easily bomb or quit.

12. Management systems may also be important for some types of programs where the results can be used for evaluation of Individualized Education Plan (IEP) educational objectives.

13. The functioning level and instructional needs of the individual within Bloom's (1956) taxonomy should determine the level of the presentation. Instruction at all levels, including the individual's thought processing, involves task analysis and use of other educational principles.

One program frequently used by teachers to create instructional programs for users and by users to enhance what they have learned (maintenance stage) is HyperStudio (Roger Wagner Publishing). This program is excellent for addressing different learning styles and intelligences while using the 4MAT teaching approach. It permits teachers and users alike to create presentations, games, reports, and books. This program has been used with persons who function at all levels because of the ease of its use and capabilities. Users can also be encouraged to collaborate in the creation of a program and to explore the various effects based on what they do while programming. HyperStudio is easy to use with limited training because it does not involve scripting or using any programming language. Lynn (1994) from Poor Richard's Publishing, in his workshops involving this program, also instructs teachers on how to create programs for switch use, thus opening this program for easy use by individuals with physical or cognitive disabilities. Besides switch use, this program can easily be used with alternative keyboards and the Touch Window. A StudioWare Catalog described HyperStudio as having the following multimedia elements:

- Integrated Color
- QuickTime Movies
- Frame and Path-Based Animation
- Laserdisc and CD-ROM Support
- Easy-to-Create Buttons
- Live "Real-Time" Video Digitizing
- Lots of Clip Art and Sounds
- "Ready-Made" Templates

- Complete Paint Tools
- "StoryBoard" Stack Editor
- And Much, Much More!

Initial Design Stage

The following stages should be completed when developing effective software: initial design, specific design, programming, and formative evaluation. The two design phases are especially important because they provide the plan for success. All of the elements of appropriate software discussed in this chapter should be considered when designing software and, depending on the needs of the intended audience for the software, should be incorporated into the program under development. The designing phases, therefore, are vital to the goal(s) of the software being developed and often take more time than the actual programming. This phase is the professional's plan, a type of road map, without which the software developed will be like the trip taken with no planning: the travelers will not know where they are or where they are going, or even when they get there. Therefore, the first determination in the design or plan is to determine the goal(s) of the program based on the intended audience.

Besides all of the pedagogical considerations, the professional designing and developing software should obtain accurate and in-depth information on the content. Assistance may be obtained from content specialists within the community; from colleges and universities; and from databases, libraries, and on-line searches of the Internet and World Wide Web (see Appendixes D, F, and H).

After the professional has acquired the background necessary to develop effective software, the professional either needs to draw or outline what the software program will look like, which should be completed prior to any programming. At this point the shell package's features should be used to help decide how these features can best be used to meet the needs of the learner(s), needs that have been previously determined. The shell package used could be as comprehensive as HyperStudio or as simple as the MACs Software package developed for individuals with severe disabilities at Johns Hopkins University. In other instances, the professional who has done the designing can contact a person who programs software or a user who can program software as part of a classroom assignment to do the actual programming. If a programmer has been considered, he or she should be brought in at this point to help create the final design and the script because he or she has extensive knowledge on the capabilities of the computer.

The programmer's input, from the inception of the project, just after the goals and objectives are established, is essential because the programmer can give advice relating to the capabilities of the computer and the professional's plan for the program design. After discussing implementation ideas with the programmer, the professional can develop a general design for the program, similar to that shown in Figure 6.3.

Along with the general or initial design, the professional may wish to develop a standard outline for the program in which the professional uses roman numerals to develop the major objectives of the program and capital letters to designate specific frames. Arabic numerals are then used to describe what is to happen to each frame and any other necessary information, such as which frame or frames follow based on the input from the user or what animation is to occur. If a standard outline is not used, another type can be used as long as it organizes the frame sequence. If the program is providing instructional content, as in the initial stage of learning, one major caution to the professional at this point is to limit the content covered in one program. Programs of this type tend to grow after the initial design stage if the developer or professional is not careful. Prior to leaving this early developmental stage of the program, the programmer, if used, is again consulted to ensure that the content can be programmed and to obtain further ideas based on computer capabilities.

Specific Design Stage

Following the initial design stage, the educator develops the specific design of the program. As

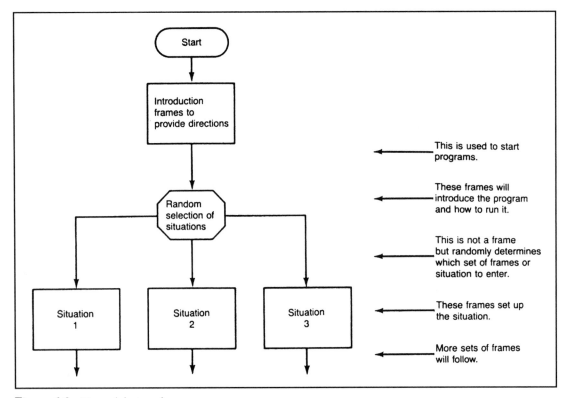

Figure 6.3. General design of program.

frames (what is seen on the screen at one time) are created, an educational flowchart may be developed on unlined paper or on other plain paper that can be obtained in rolls, and frames are placed on the flowchart in the appropriate order. The frames could also be developed on 4 × 6 inch cards or graph paper. For programs that have multiple options or pathways for the user to follow, using cards usually works best because they can be moved around more easily when designing the flow of the program. Each frame or card needs to indicate where media (e.g., text, graphics, animation, video input) will appear. Besides what will be seen on each frame, directions for programming need to be included. These directions should be placed on the reverse side of the card. For example, included on the back could be the frame sequence for a video, from what direction animation should occur, how the graphic will build, how the text will enter the screen, when and what the audio will be, and what the transition should be from this frame to the next. Figure 6.4 is an example of a simplified frame that also provides instructions to the programmer. Note that the cards or frames are numbered indicating the preceding and following frames, as well as any specific information for programming. The type and complexity of the flowchart that is developed will depend on the type and complexity of program developed. Figure 6.5 represents an example of parts of a relatively simple flowchart. With programs in which many choices are developed, it likely is easier to have each frame where multiple decisions are made be a circle instead of a diamond. Figure 6.6 represents an example of a more complex flowchart for a multimedia program with many choices of pathways through the program.

Programming Stage

With the plan completed, the person doing the programming is ready to proceed with the actual programming of the software. Prior to starting,

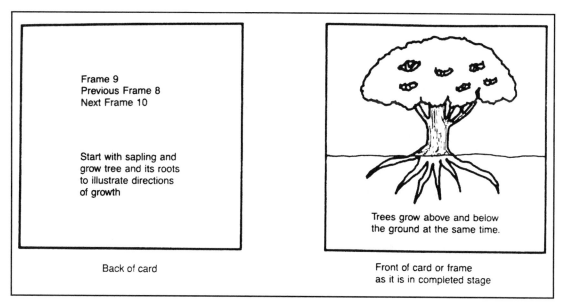

Figure 6.4. Example of a frame.

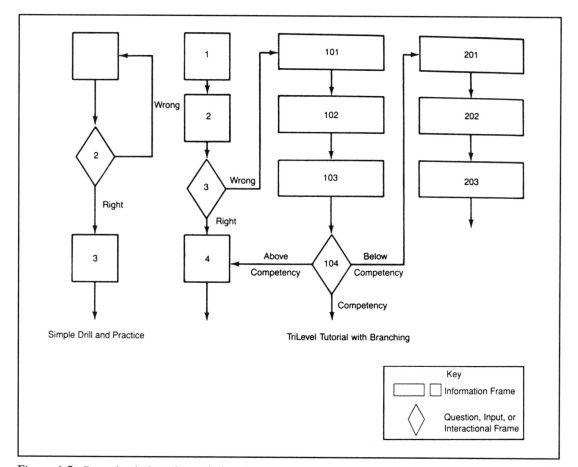

Figure 6.5. Example of relatively simple flowchart.

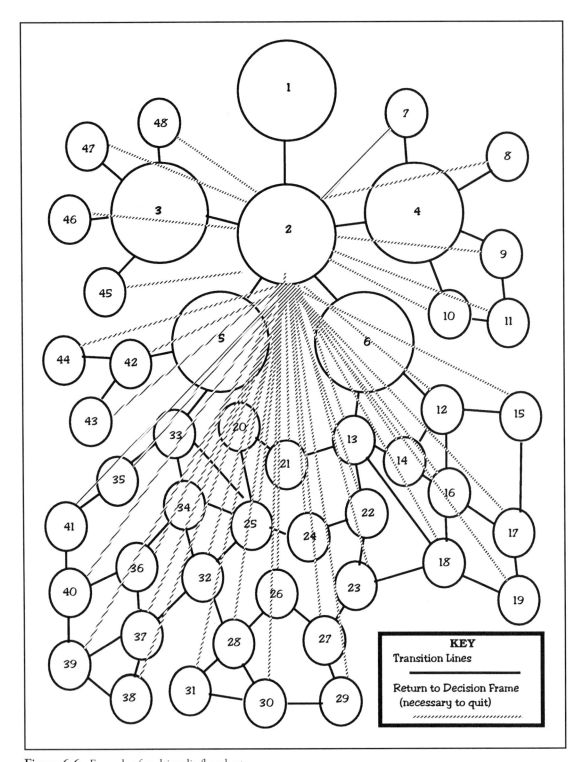

Figure 6.6. Example of multimedia flowchart.

however, if the professional is doing the programming, he or she may wish to share the plan with other professionals, the users for whom the program is being developed, or someone experienced with programming, for any suggestions that would add to the educational effectiveness and interest value of the program.

The actual programming is either written in a programming language by a programmer who is skilled in using that language or by the special education professional using a shell-type program. If using a shell-type program, the professional should become familiar with that program before starting to program software for specific purposes. Becoming familiar with the programming software can include reading the manual, running through a tutorial program, "playing" with the program, or taking a class in how to use the program. Many school systems have classes in using shell programs, such as HyperStudio, which teach using the program to develop software. Few, however, have the time or expertise to provide total program development instruction that includes software design. If courses are not available with the school system, the professional should find another avenue (e.g., a session at a local, state, or national conference) to receive instruction and hands-on guided tutorials on the use of the shell program.

Formative Evaluation Stage

When the programming is complete, the newly developed software should be formatively evaluated to determine minor changes that would enhance the program. In addition, it is wise to validate the program with the proposed audience and to allow other educators to interact with the program. Companies that develop software refer to this as the beta testing stage. This is also the stage when unforeseen errors are detected, those that cause the program to crash or to go to unintended places within the program. Therefore, the importance of this formative evaluation or testing stage cannot be stressed too greatly, because making minimal programming changes can make the difference in a software program's being successful with the intended audience.

Documentation Development

After the program is virtually completed, the educator should develop documentation incorporating the areas covered previously in the documentation discussion (see Internal Evaluation—Instructional Information). The documentation will be of assistance not only to the professional who developed the program but also to other professionals with whom the program can be shared. Sharing is highly suggested because of the time involved in developing programs and because the public domain (free programs) increases the availability of software programs to low-incidence populations as well as to other populations, both general and special education, thus expanding the software libraries within many schools and clinics.

Other Types of Programs

Developing programs that are designed for management requires all of the same stages of development, but instead of delineating instructional objectives, the professional should list all the outcomes expected from the program and the form in which those outcomes should be accessible. In general, it is important in designing management software to consider such factors as (a) the number and types of inputs; (b) the amount of space for each input; (c) the amount of space or memory for the total number of inputs, using the rule of thumb to triple that number; (d) the type of sorts or how inputs should be assessed in order to obtain the desired combination of outputs for reporting (e.g., sorting by disability categories based on chronological age); (e) user friendliness, including easy-to-operate menus, error catching, easily understood status lines, and help balloons and screens where possible; (f) a method for automatically saving data inputs; and (g) the form of the outputs, both hardcopy (report generation) and screen formats.

In general when developing software programs to operate assistive devices, the same stages and principles apply. For example, when developing an overlay for an alternative keyboard, it is important to determine the goals of the overlay (e.g., to run a specific program, to communicate, to generally access or run all software programs). Then, the professional must determine the layout of the overlay (what the user sees) based on the user's or users' specific physical and cognitive functioning needs. If the overlay is being designed to run a particular software program, the professional must run that program ahead of time and record every keystroke the user will need to operate the program using the alternative keyboard. In planning what the overlay will look like, every keystroke to run the program must be made available, except in cases where the professional only wants the user to have access to particular keystrokes. For example, if teaching users to share is an instructional goal and two alternative keyboards are available, one user could have a set of possible keystrokes as indicated by the cells on one overlay and the other keyboard could have the remainder of necessary keystrokes to run the program. Therefore, the layout will be determined by such factors as the ability level and physical needs of the user(s); cell size; color scheme; texture cell; placement of cells; print/text size, font, and style; objects, pictures, or icons needed; and so on.

After determining what the overlay will look like, the availability of sound or speech (i.e., what the computer "says" when a cell is pressed) should be determined. In addition, what function the computer will perform must be determined (e.g., typing a key, moving the mouse, changing to a different overlay). In the development of a communication overlay, when most cells are pressed, they provide the user an auditory stimulus. With this type of overlay, the computer performs no other function than to speak. After designing the overlay and determining what pressing or accessing each cell will do based on the specific needs of the user(s), this software should be tested (formative evaluation) to make sure it does what is expected. In other words, the overlay and the software that works in conjunction with that overlay should be used to run the program for which it was designed.

The same procedure must be used when programming other types of setups for other assistive devices. For example, when developing a scan-ning array, the professional would have to determine what size to make the cell, where to place the cell on the screen, what icons to use to represent concepts, what will be "said" when the cell is selected by pressing a switch, and what the computer will do.

When programming communication devices, the professional must carefully design each cell to say or use speech expressively at the appropriate receptive language and functioning levels of the user. The cognitive needs of the user determine whether an object is attached (usually by Velcro) or a picture, line drawing, or abstract icon is used to identify the cells on the communication device. The size of the cells and ways to access the cells must be determined by both the physical needs and the cognitive level of the user. As indicated earlier, only what the user "sees and hears" is what is primarily programmed. However, when the professional is programming levels on a communication device, the computer must be "told" to change the overlay program, which is done by programming what the computer will do when a key is pressed. It should be noted that the actual overlay or what the "user says" must be changed either electronically (by programming) or by changing a paper overlay. To change levels electronically, a standard place or set of cells on the face of the device or on the overlay (e.g., the top row of cells) should be used for this purpose.

Related Issues

Most of the issues surrounding software involve the purchase of educationally effective software and packages. All too often professionals make purchases without appropriate evaluation. They either do not know how to evaluate software or lack interest in doing so. In addition, many teacher-education training and other professional programs do not train their students in the area of special education technology—that is, how to integrate this technology into the teaching–clinical process and to use this technology to meet the educational needs of individuals with disabilities and challenges. Even recent graduates who have taken a technology course may not

Evaluation of adaptive devices is important to ensure proper fit. (Photograph courtesy of Prentke Romich Co. of Wooster, OH)

know how to operate a computer. In addition to this course, technology should be integrated into all of the core courses demonstrating the integration of technology into the education process.

Besides not knowing how to evaluate or use software effectively, professionals do not always have access to software prior to purchase. Some school districts have preview centers that are not used extensively because teachers do not have the time or the interest to avail themselves of this opportunity. Professionals could preview software at educational conferences, although relatively few attend these functions. Periodicals publish software reviews, but if professionals have a subscription to these periodicals, it is usually something they do on their own and is not supported by the school. There is a trend, however, for more and more professionals to join computer committees and be active in group selection of software, especially in the schools that have retrofit grants.

Another related issue involves illegal copying of software. In the early 1980s the software industry estimated that up to 80% of software used in and out of the classroom had been illegally copied. This led to mistrust on the part of the producer regarding preview of programs, a mistrust that is still a concern in the software industry today. When schools first used computers in the classroom, software companies spent thousands of dollars putting a protection system miniprogram on software so that it could not be copied.

However, this concern is somewhat different today because software can be copied onto hard drives and easily shared. However, more educators are realizing that making more than a backup copy of software is illegal and many school systems have issued statements regarding this issue. In addition, companies are cooperating with software preview labs by placing copies of software in these labs for teachers to review prior to purchase. This illegal copying issue has been instrumental in driving up the cost of software.

Another issue surrounds the field or beta testing of software. Often producers do not extensively field-test their software because the marketing window, or the amount of time the software will be profitable on the market, is extremely short. This is especially true for software that does not involve multimedia and because of the rapid changes occurring in what is considered to be state-of-the-art software. Developments in the software industry are occurring so rapidly that if producers do not release products in a timely manner, the software will be outdated before it reaches the market. On the other hand, producers have collaborated with professionals during the developmental and evaluation stages of software development. This collaboration seems to be more prevalent than previously, although some companies do not consider educational relevance high enough and are fixated on the profit margin. For example, professionals advised one company that develops software for the special education market to add sound, speech, and video to their skill development software. Because this company was anxious to get the product on the market, however, these suggestions were totally ignored.

Other issues involve the need to adapt technology to the learner and not the learner to technology. All too often software is purchased and cannot be used effectively with a user without modifications. In many instances modifications can be made in the way the software is presented or implemented into the instructional process (i.e., using the software in small groups, preteaching the goals of the software, adding a utility program that reads the text on the screen). Actual changes in the software usually are not possible because of its complexity. Because software should be designed to meet the needs of individual users, professionals and producers need to expand their avenues of communication to learn more about the modifications necessary to meet the specific needs of individuals (e.g., changes that can be easily accomplished within the program so that many users can use the same program). This communication is especially important in the area of exceptional education, where the students are not learning at the same rate or using the approaches successful with many of their nonexceptional peers in general education settings.

The final issue to be presented is compatibility, both with peripherals and assistive devices and between the various platforms. Peripherals, such as printers, touch windows, mice, graphics tablets, duo dock computers, and other devices, should all be standardized within the hardware industry. This would necessitate that the hardware be standardized as to ports, cables, and software compatibility. A few companies are working toward this end, but progress has been slow because of political and economic reasons. Assistive devices should also be compatible with multiple platforms as well as with each other. Too often when using one assistive device, another assistive device ceases to operate because both devices are trying to access the same memory area, both devices use the same input port, or some other reason for incompatibility. Because many individuals with disabilities require the use of more than one assistive device to empower them to communicate, control their environments, and learn, this issue is one that should be addressed immediately. The IBM Corporation's Special Needs System has been investigating the assistive device compatibility issue when using their computers.

Summary

This chapter has discussed the major reasons for software evaluation and has provided the professional with a plan for evaluative purposes. Two types of evaluation were discussed, external and internal. External evaluation requires the professional to gain evaluative information from sources such as periodicals, centers, and other people. Internal evaluation refers to the process professionals follow to determine if the software they are previewing is appropriate to meet their needs and the needs of their users. The three areas covered that are necessary for effective evaluation are instructional information, educational adequacy, and technical adequacy. With the emergence of multimedia, evaluation requires some changes in the areas to be evaluated because of the advanced multiple features for providing stimulation to the learner.

Often, even with specific evaluation techniques, the software necessary to meet the particular needs of users, especially those from low-incidence exceptionalities, is limited, and the professional needs to find ways to get that software created. In addition, a number of multimedia programs are on the market that permit users to create their own programs. Therefore, classroom and other professionals are creating software for their users and allowing their users to create software by "programming" their own using authoring systems or shell programs. Some educational professionals continue to design programs, but have someone proficient in more complex programming languages program for them. Regardless of whether professionals program the software or have the software completed by a programmer, they must be able to design effective software and communicate that information, when necessary, to the person who will do the programming. For effective designing of software, the professional must have a background in pedagogy, experiences involving the capabilities of the computer, and information on the content to be covered. Whether educational professionals or users are developing software, they should go through the same stages of software development to create an effective program: initial design, specific design, programming, and formative evaluation.

A number of issues related to evaluation of software and assistive devices and to program development were discussed, as were issues related to compatibility. Collaboration between business–industry and education appears to address all of these issues.

Resources

Organization

Florida Diagnostic and Learning Resources System–TECH
2700 St. Johns Street
Melbourne, FL 32940
Voice: 407/631-1911
Fax: 407/633-3520

Journal

ConnSENSE Newsletter
Special Education Center Technology Lab
U-64, 249 Glenbrook Road
University of Connecticut
Storrs, CT 06269-2064
Voice: 203/486-0172

Laboratory–Practicum Activities

▶ 1. List three goals you will achieve in the next 3 months to enhance your software evaluation knowledge. Use technology to develop your goals, to describe how you will achieve these goals, and to manage the achievement of the goals.

▶ 2. List three goals you will achieve in the next 3 months to enhance your software development knowledge. Use technology to develop your goals, to describe how you will achieve these goals, and to manage the achievement of the goals.

▶ 3. In Chapter 3 you found a recent journal article reviewing a tutorial, simulation, or drill-and-practice software package in your interest area (e.g., math, science, social studies). Using the 13 evaluation criteria listed in this chapter, evaluate this review and share your evaluation with your course instructor and peers.

▶ 4. Access a World Wide Web site where software evaluation information is presented (e.g., http://www.edsoft.com). Make a list of the software evaluation criteria described in this chapter that are used and not used at this site. If you were asked to coordinate the software evaluations presented at this site, delineate the changes you would make, provide a rationale for each change, and share your changes and rationales with your course instructor and peers.

▶ 5. Use a search engine (e.g., Lycos) and the search words "software (development)" to conduct a search of software development information on the World Wide Web. Describe the quantitative and qualitative findings of this search.

▶ 6. Interview the coordinator of the technology center for the local education agency. Ask this individual to describe the software evaluation system used for general education, special education, and other professions (speech pathology, physical therapy, etc.); the advances and disadvantages of this system; and changes he or she would make to improve this system.

▶ 7. Interview two professionals who use an external evaluation system to secure software evaluations. Ask these professionals to describe their systems and the strengths and weaknesses of these systems.

▶ 8. Use both the *Sector Courseware Evaluation Form* and the *UConn Educational Software Evaluation Form* in Appendix G to evaluate two software programs, one literary related and one mathematical. How were your two literary program evaluations similar and different? How were your literary and mathematical program evaluations similar and different?

▶ 9. Collaborate with peers to develop a list of software evaluation and development guidelines based on the concepts presented in Appendix D. Share this list with your course instructor.

▶ 10. Collaborate with your peers to describe a very specific exceptional individual from a low-incidence population and create a software program for this individual using a shell program such as HyperStudio. Use the four software development stages and provide evidence for each stage. Share this program with your course instructor.

References

Bloom, B. (1956). *Taxonomy of educational objectives.* New York: Longmans, Green.

Gardner, H. (1982). *Frames of mind: The theory of multiple intelligences.* New York: Basic Books.

Gardner, H. (1993). *Multiple intelligences: The theory in practice.* New York: Basic Books.

Gardner, J. E., Taber-Brown, F., & Wissick, C. A. (1992). Selecting age-appropriate software for adolescents and adults with developmental disabilities. *Teaching Exceptional Children, 24*(3), 60–63.

Gillentine, L. (1996). *Multiple intelligences learning styles and little planet literacy series.* Unpublished document, Little Planet Publishing, Nashville, TN.

Holden, M. C., Holcomb, C. M., & Wedman, J. F. (1992). Designing Hypercard stacks for cooperative learning. *Computing Teacher, 19*(5), 20–22.

Jerome, M. (1999). The perfect PC for me. *PC Computing, 12*(3), 134–148.

Lindsey, J. D. (Ed.). (1989). *Computers and exceptional individuals.* Columbus, OH: Merrill.

Lindsey, J. D. (Ed.). (1993). *Computer and exceptional individuals* (2nd ed.). Austin, TX: PRO-ED.

Lynn, B. (1994). *Switched-on HyperStudio: Creating switch accessible software for the Macintosh: A workshop.* Northfield, CT: Simtech.

Magnus, C. (1998). *Introduction to 4MAT for Teachers.* Presentation at Florida Diagnostic and Learning Resources System–South, Miami.

McCarthy, B. (1987). *The 4MAT system.* Barrington, IL: Excel.

McCarthy, B. (1991). *The 4MAT system: Awareness workshop materials, Part B: Introduction to right/left processing and the 4MAT model.* Barrington, IL: Excel.

McCarthy, B. (1992). *The 4MAT system: Awareness workshop materials, Part A: Introduction to learning styles.* Barrington, IL: Excel.

McClelland, D. (1999, March). Paint with vectors in Illustrator 8. *Macworld,* p. 97.

McDonald, G. (1999, March). Do Web accelerators work? *PC World,* pp. 145–154.

Palin, L. (1992). Examining the emperor's new clothes: The use of existing video in multimedia packages. *Computing Teacher, 19*(6), 5–7.

Pracek, E. (1994a). *Gardner's multiple intelligences and types of software.* Unpublished document, Florida Diagnostic and Learning Resources System–South, Miami.

Pracek, E. (1994b). *Introduction to 4MAT.* Presentation at Florida Diagnostic and Learning Resources System–South. FDLRS–Tech, Melbourne, FL.

Sarouphim, K. M. (1999). Discovering multiple intelligences through a performance-based assessment: Consistency with independent ratings. *Exceptional Children, 65,* 151–161.

Smith, S. (1999). Atomic clock. *Cajun Clickers Computer News, 11*(1), 13.

Szul, L. F., & Woodland, D. E. (1998, February). Does the right software a great designer make? *T.H.E. Journal,* pp. 48–49.

Chapter 7

☙   ☙   ☙

The Use of Technology To Enhance Personal Productivity

Dave L. Edyburn
University of Wisconsin–Milwaukee

J. Emmett Gardner
The University of Oklahoma, Norman

I n this chapter we examine the use of technology to enhance the professional productivity of special educators. We suggest that a variety of technologies, media, and materials can be used to enhance the professional productivity of these professionals. To initiate the journey involved in capturing the potential of technology, we explore the productivity demands special educators face. Using the productivity demands as a framework, we describe the creation of a technology toolkit and illustrate the connections between the technology tools with common tasks. Finally, we examine the professional development challenges that must be addressed to ensure the continuous improvement of the special educator's technology skills and productivity strategies.

Schiffman, 1986). As educators gained a glimpse of the possibilities that computers and productivity software held, the middle to late 1980s were characterized by widespread interest in inservice workshops, university courses, and conference presentations on the use of technology to enhance both personal productivity (e.g., creating a database for storing addresses of friends and relatives and then using this information to print mailing labels for holiday cards) and professional productivity (e.g., creating letters for parents, field trip permission slips).

The cornerstone of efforts to enhance educators' productivity has been to introduce teachers and administrators to "integrated software packages" or "software suites," products containing a

Technology and Productivity

The widespread availability of computers and productivity software, and access to the Internet and World Wide Web afford new opportunities for preparing special educators to work more effectively and efficiently than in the past (Carp, 1999; Willis, 1998). Since the early 1980s, numerous authors have described the potential of technology to free teachers from many of the clerical and repetitive record-keeping tasks associated with teaching (Bitter, Camuse, & Durbin, 1984; Office of Technology Assessment, 1995;

Professionals using computers must consider curricular goals, teaching–learning principles, user characteristics, and hardware and software attributes. (Photograph by Ed Washington)

word processor, database, spreadsheet, painting and drawing tools, and telecommunications (see also Chapter 3). Specific attributes of these tools captured the attention of many educators, who immediately recognized the practical applications in their workday:

- By learning to use a word processor, an individual could type anything, fix errors by simply pressing the delete key, check the spelling of a document, save files so they can be reused or modified, and print multiple copies.

- By learning to use a database, an individual could keep, organize, and store information in a manner that made it easy to locate information, as well as alphabetize it, sort it, and selectively print it.

- By learning to use a spreadsheet, an individual could store and sort grades in an electronic gradebook. Most important, however, grade averages could be calculated in seconds.

This last example, the electronic gradebook, has served as an icon of how technology enhances the productivity of educators: A teacher can enter vast numbers of student grades and, at the touch of a key, obtain an up-to-date average for every student. This single example captured the imagination of educational professionals, the public, and policymakers. As a result, calls for placing a computer on every teacher's desk have been increasingly common (Dockterman, 1989; Jacobson, 1993; McCarthy, 1993; National Foundation for Improvement of Education, 1989; Office of Technology Assessment, 1995). These initiatives were based on the assumption that preparing teachers to use new, powerful tools would alleviate clerical and managerial responsibilities that prevented teachers from spending more time engaged in instruction with students.

A logical target to impact the educator's use of technology for enhancing personal and professional productivity is the university-based teacher education program. Nationally, this has been accomplished by influencing the accreditation process. The National Council for Accreditation of Teacher Education (NCATE) redesigned its standards and processes in 1987 so that standards were approved by each field's professional association. The standards that guide the use of computers and technology in education were developed and validated by the International Society for Technology in Education (ISTE). Subsequently, these standards were used in the development of the Council for Exceptional Children's (CEC) Common Core of Knowledge and Skills Necessary for all Beginning Special Educators (Swan & Sirvis, 1992). Table 7.1 outlines the most recent Technology Foundation Standards guiding the preparation of special education teachers to use instructional technology. In this chapter we address the competencies outlined in Section B of the ISTE standards. In Chapter 8 we address the competencies outlined in Section C of the ISTE standards.

The power and influence of the accreditation process has resulted in the ISTE standards' becoming the current benchmark of what teachers need to know and do relative to instructional technology. Nevertheless, schools of education have been criticized for their failure to graduate beginning teachers with the knowledge and skills that K–12 schools need to utilize the technology they *already* own (Barksdale, 1996). As a result, school districts have been developing their own lists of what teachers need to know and be able to do. An example of one district's effort to create a self-assessment is illustrated in Figure 7.1. Initiatives like this are important, as they serve to make expectations explicit. In addition, competency checklists enable teachers to evaluate their current skills, contemplate their professional goals, and select appropriate staff development opportunities to meet their needs.

While the potential of technology to reduce the time spent in clerical tasks associated with teaching is clear, in retrospect, this potential has proven elusive to capture. Many educators, through university courses or district inservice workshops, have been introduced to the mechanical operation of programs, with minimal attention to developing specific productivity strategies. As a result, general and special educators are often left on their own to determine how multipurpose tools such as a word processor, database, and spreadsheet can provide practical gains in

Table 7.1. Technology Foundation Standards for All Students

The technology foundation standards for students are divided into six broad categories. Standards within each category are to be introduced, reinforced, and mastered by students. These categories provide a framework for linking performance indicators found within the Profiles for Technology Literate Students to the standards. Teachers can use these standards and profiles as guidelines for planning technology-based activities in which students achieve success in learning, communication, and life skills.

1. **Basic operations and concepts**

   • Students demonstrate a sound understanding of the nature and operation of technology systems.
   • Students are proficient in the use of technology.

2. **Social, ethical, and human issues**

   • Students understand the ethical, cultural, and societal issues related to technology.
   • Students practice responsible use of technology systems, information, and software.
   • Students develop positive attitudes toward technology uses that support lifelong learning, collaboration, personal pursuits, and productivity.

3. **Technology productivity tools**

   • Students use technology tools to enhance learning, increase productivity, and promote creativity.
   • Students use productivity tools to collaborate in constructing technology-enhanced models, preparing publications, and producing other creative works.

4. **Technology communications tools**

   • Students use telecommunications to collaborate, publish, and interact with peers, experts, and other audiences.
   • Students use a variety of media and formats to communicate information and ideas effectively to multiple audiences.

5. **Technology research tools**

   • Students use technology to locate, evaluate, and collect information from a variety of sources.
   • Students use technology tools to process data and report results.
   • Students evaluate and select new information resources and technological innovations based on the appropriateness to specific tasks.

6. **Technology problem-solving and decision-making tools**

   • Students use technology resources for solving problems and making informed decisions.
   • Students employ technology in the development of strategies for solving problems in the real world.

Note. From National Educational Technology Standards, World Wide Web: http://www.cnets.iste.org/ (January 29, 1999).

professional productivity. It is becoming increasingly clear that isolated technological skills do not easily transfer to educators' daily routine of teaching, learning, curriculum development, and professional growth (Office of Technology Assessment, 1995; Willis, 1993).

Despite the continuing interest in technology-enhanced productivity and its perceived benefits, the impact of information technology on the professional productivity of special educators has been limited. In our view, three factors operate individually and collectively as obstacles:

Whitnall School District
Technology Competencies for Certified Staff

Beginning Level—Tools for the Teacher

Computer Aided Learning

Competency 2: The certified staff member will use an integrated software package that will include word processing and graphics.

Check level of knowledge for each item below, indicating your assessment of your technology level.

		Knowledge Level			
		Awareness	Knowledge	Functional Knowledge	Advanced Knowledge
1	I can use the keyboard as a simple input device.				
2	I can demonstrate proper keyboarding skills.				
	Correct posture				
	Technique				
3	I can access a file using an integrated software program.				
4	I can create a document using the word processing program.				
5	I can save a document to my disk.				
6	I can print a hard copy of a document.				
7	I can access/open a saved file.				
8	I can create a word processing document which includes:				
	Boldface print				
	Underlined print				
	Centered print				
	Two or more type styles/fonts				
	Single and double spacing				
	Use of a spell checker				
	Use of a thesaurus				
	Use of tabs				
9	I can create and use computer graphics.				

You are encouraged to work with a peer to reach competency on items you have not yet achieved or seek the assistance of the Technology Coordinator.

SELF-EVALUATION
Name _____
Date _____

PEER EVALUATION
Name _____
Date _____

TECHNOLOGY COORDINATOR
Name _____
Date _____

PRINCIPAL
Name _____
Date _____

Figure 7.1. Example of a self-assessment from Whitnall School District. *Note.* "Technology Competencies for Certified Staff," by A. M. Goode, 1997, Hales Corner, WI: Whitnall School District. Reprinted with permission.

1. Commitment to supporting core productivity tools is weak.

2. Access to technology and appropriate tools is limited.

3. Teacher training is insufficient or inadequate.

Therefore, to fully realize the potential of technology, in our opinion, special education professionals need to reconsider the options. We contrast two perspectives on how technology enhances professional productivity in Table 7.2.

Technology-Enhanced Professional Productivity

Although the importance of using technology to support the productivity of special educators has been recognized, the applications tend to be described in technological terms rather than in terms of tasks to be accomplished. A significant transformation occurs, however, when the primary focus is on tasks associated with teaching and learning, which are then linked with tools. Consider the difference between these two perspectives:

1. Demonstrate mastery of selected features of a word processor (i.e., cut and paste) that will make writing exams easier.

2. To assess student understanding more efficiently, create worksheets, exams, and quizzes using a word processor.

a. When it comes time to make an exam, open the word processing file with your study guide or quiz and copy selected items. Navigate to the file with your exam template and paste the items so that you don't have to retype the selected items that you announced to your students would be on the exam.

b. Edit activity sheets to reflect alternative formats. Using a two-column list of states and their capitals, edit every other state and capital to become a fill-in-the-blank question (_____ = Lansing; Ohio = _____). Depending on the level of individual students, create a different level of prompting by editing both the states and capitals using the cloze procedure (e.g., M_c_i_a_ = _a_s_n_)."

In both cases, teachers learn about the mechanics of operating their word processor. In the first case, teachers are left to their own devices to discover the many applications of specific techniques while going about their work. In the second case, teachers gain clear insight into how to utilize tools in ways that have immediate practical value and contribute to enhanced productivity as a result of using technology.

In order to advance a new perspective on technology-enhanced professional productivity, special educators must refocus their efforts to reflect a sound understanding of what they do and the array of information technologies that might be applied to such activities. We favor the strategic perspective (see Table 7.2) because of three factors: It advances a vision of how information

Table 7.2. Contrasting Perspectives on How Technology Enhances Professional Productivity

Traditional View of Enhancing Productivity	Strategic Perspective of Enhancing Productivity
Learning to use a single integrated program	Assembling a small number of products that work together as an integrated desktop
Shopping for the "best" tool	Learning how to exploit the power of a small number of tools
Learning the mechanical operation of a program	Developing insight into the effective use of a collection of tools

technology is used as an essential tool for special educators in their work, it improves understanding of the productivity demands made on educators, and it causes educators to rethink how they work in light of available information technologies. In the sections that follow, we describe the strategic perspective in greater detail.

Vision and Commitment to Essential Professional Productivity Tools

Is technology essential to the work of special educators? Advocates argue that new times require new tools and, as a result, technology and media are essential teaching tools. Others argue that teaching is essentially a social activity and that a "good" teacher does not need to use technology to be effective. Leadership is sorely needed within the profession to build consensus on this fundamental issue. We argue that technology *is* an essential tool in the toolkit of special educators, given our work with students who have special learning and behavioral needs.

After resolving the philosophical question of whether technology is essential for educators, the focus shifts to understanding the types of electronic tools that should be used. Carnine (1992) observed that the hallmarks of a profession are the professionals' knowledge base and effective tools. To date, the benefits of technology-enhanced productivity have been limited largely to individuals. Individual teachers with a vision of the possibilities that technology affords their professional life have worked tirelessly to explore how technology makes them more effective and efficient. Yet, these benefits tend to be isolated. Seldom is technology-enhanced productivity implemented in a programmatic or systematic manner. In practical terms, educators have yet to move beyond individual visions to shared visions. While individuals advocate and groups (e.g., professional organizations) endorse specific tools as useful and valuable for educators, the essential tools of the trade have yet to be identified or validated by the profession.

Indeed, a primary obstacle that has limited the use of technology for enhancing professional productivity stems from the fact that the educational community has yet to systematically examine the available range of information technology tools and articulate a commitment regarding the fundamental and essential nature of these tools for enhancing the work of special educators. As a result, little effort has been devoted to identifying and validating core electronic tools. Without such a review, it is unlikely that special educators will be able to develop consensus concerning the essential electronic tools of their trade and subsequently make the necessary commitments to their implementation.

Finally, advances in technology-enhanced professional productivity will not occur without resolving the problem of access to technology. If a tool is essential, it must be readily available to support one's work, which is a reasonable assumption and modest goal, but limited access has been a difficult barrier to overcome. Recent state and national initiatives that seek to provide a computer in every classroom with Internet access appear promising.

Productivity Demands: Understanding What Special Educators Do

To fully consider the possibilities that technology affords for enhancing the productivity of educators, it is necessary to understand the productivity demands made on educators: How do teachers spend their time? What tasks are teachers commonly expected to complete?

Most people think teaching is an easy job: a 6-hour workday, frequent holidays, and vacations in the winter, spring, and summer. Most of what prospective educators know about teaching is the result of their years of experience as students, estimated at over 13,000 hours during their K–12 careers (Cuban, 1993, p. 258). However, as many first-year teachers will attest, being on the other side of the desk is considerably different. Arends (1991) observed that teachers do many things that are not readily apparent beyond the obvious classroom interactions with students: "They meet with students about nonacademic tasks; they meet with fellow teachers and specialists within the school; they go to meetings; they work with parents; and they attend to their own learning" (p. 388).

Cuban (1993) described the differences in the workday between elementary and secondary classrooms:

> The self-contained [elementary] classroom remains the dominant form of delivering instruction. Generally, teachers spend 5 or more hours with the same 30 or more students. They see far more of a child's strengths, limitations, capacities, and achievements than a high school teacher who sees five groups of 30 or more students for less than an hour a day. Over a year, the elementary school teacher sees a class of 30 children for nearly 1,000 hours; a high school teacher sees any one class for no more than 200 hours during the year, or about one fifth of the time that elementary school colleagues spend with pupils. (p. 258)

Experienced teachers know the intense time demands that occur as a result of the daily schedule coupled with the vast numbers of students they see each day. In one research study on this topic, Cypher and Willower (1984) reported that "a foremost mark of the work of teachers is its intensity of action and interaction. Activities are brief and fragmented. The world of teachers is a verbal one that is full of students" (p. 23). The researchers found that teachers spent their time as follows:

- 34.4% of their time in school was devoted to instructional activities. This included direct instruction (lecture, question–answer, and demonstration activities), reviewing homework assignments, giving tests, and various interactions concerning schoolwork that took place with students outside of regular classes.
- 27.8% of their time in school was devoted to classroom support, including organizing (dis-

tributing or collecting materials), desk work (school-related activities like correcting tests and recording grades, writing lesson plans, taking notes from readings, composing quizzes, or simply studying a lesson), routine tasks carried out to further teaching (taking attendance, reading notes and mail, getting out or putting away materials, and running off tests), and interactions with others regarding instruction.

- 19.3% of their time was devoted to pupil control activities. These included activities such as study hall supervision, control and supervision activities, monitoring student in-class work, and monitoring assemblies and student club meetings. The majority of the pupil control activities took the form of exchanges with students and involved giving the students permission or directions.
- 11.6% of their time in school was devoted to private–personal activities. These were times when the teacher was alone or isolated, interacting with other teachers about nonschool matters, or not engaged in school-related tasks. Most interactions during teachers' lunch periods were classified as personal.
- 5.3% of their time in school was consumed by travel, time spent going from place to place during the school day.
- 1.8% of their time in school was devoted to extracurricular activities. Although the actual time spent in extracurricular activities was recorded in their diaries, this category represents the activities that spilled over into the workday.

The teachers' days were dominated by students and the schedule and were typically composed of many brief verbal contacts. Over 96% of the teachers' contacts were verbal; less than 4% were written. Of the verbal contacts, more than 90% were with students, indicating a very small amount of time spent in adult-to-adult interactions. Sustained uninterrupted time was rare as interruptions were frequent. Secondary teachers interact with over 100 students a day and were involved in a new activity every 3.6 minutes.

Additional insight into the productivity demands made on teachers can be gained from a study of teachers' use of time. Wang (1985) studied 28 classrooms using the Academic Learning Environment Model as it was implemented in general education classrooms as part of a mainstreaming program for students classified as mildly handicapped and academically gifted. Teacher behaviors over an entire day were recorded and yielded a mean of 199.3 minutes of observation time for the 28 teachers in the study. Wang's research indicated that teachers spent 81.1% of their time on instruction-related activities and the remaining 18.8% of their time on noninstructional activities. The following is Wang's breakdown of the overall patterns of the distribution of teacher time:

Instruction-Related Activities

Instructing   93.4%
(providing instruction to individual students in small-group or whole-class settings and giving task-specific, procedural directions)

Planning   3.8%
(e.g., prescribing learning tasks, keeping records)

Evaluating Student Work   2.8%

Noninstruction-Related Activities

Behavior Management   44.1%

Other Activities   39.1%
(not defined)

Conversations   16.8%
(personal conversations with students)

In addition, Wang's research revealed a profile of the amount of time spent in different instructional groupings: whole class (18.3%), small group (5.2%), and working with individual students (76.5%).

Creating a Toolbox

Understanding the productivity demands made of teachers and how they spend their time sug-gests a framework for understanding how technology can be used to enhance professional productivity. As a result, we used the two studies presented in this chapter (Cypher & Willower, 1984; Wang, 1985) and our own observations of teachers to create a list of tasks commonly completed by special educators (see Table 7.3). Although experienced teachers will recognize many of the activities, the list is hardly the definitive framework on how special educators spend their time. Nonetheless, a list of this nature allows educators to systematically identify an integrated collection of tools that will support the entire range of productivity demands.

The framework outlined in Table 7.3 provides an organizer for assembling the tools that will facilitate such work. We use the term *technology toolbox* as a means of thinking about a set of technology tools that will facilitate educators work while completing routine tasks and special projects. The concept of a toolbox is borrowed from the trades that identify a core set of tools as fundamental to their work.

The toolbox is a valuable strategy for enhancing professional productivity. First, the tool gathering process is initiated and guided by a clear understanding of the nature of educators' daily activities. Educators should choose electronic tools to support their work, rather than succumbing to the pressure of the marketplace to acquire "cool new stuff." Second, tools should be selected with an explicit focus on identifying those that will enable specific tasks to be completed with increased efficiency, effectiveness, speed, and accuracy. Third, once a given set of tools has been identified, a significant time savings is realized from the opportunity to forego the lengthy search process to find "good" products. Fourth, professional training should be provided not only in the mechanical operation of the tools but in the conceptual and practical applications. Fifth, once the tools have been mastered, the skills are portable (i.e., the user will know how to operate similar products while at other schools or home). Finally, this approach deemphasizes single tools in favor of focusing on assembling a set of tools and the synergy that results from having an integrated desktop.

Table 7.3. Tasks Commonly Completed by Special Educators

Scheduling
  Daily classroom schedule
  Special schoolwide events
  Bus schedules
  Special schedules (i.e., student special services)
 	
Instruction
  Preparing
    Deciding what to teach
    Deciding how to teach
    The classroom environment
    For instruction (lesson plans)
  Delivering instruction (presenting)
  Instructional materials
    Text
    Text/images
    Authentic source materials (i.e., electronic
      newspaper)
  Monitoring student understanding
  Recording student progress
 	
Grading papers
 	
Record keeping
  Attendance
  Achievement
  Grades
  Book orders
  Field trip permission slips
  Fund-raising events
	Absences/makeup work
	
	Correspondence
	  Memos (internal)
	  Communication with parents
	    Letter of introduction (background, philosophy)
	    Letter at beginning of school year (expectations,
	      supplies needed, etc.)
	    Letter announcing a new unit and seeking
	      parent participation
	    Letter regarding mid-term progress
	    Letter regarding discipline procedure
	    Personal letter regarding significant student
	      achievement
	    Invitation to attend parent–teacher conference
	    Reminders
	  Other correspondence (requests, writing for more
	    information, etc.)
	
	Extracurricular responsibilities
	  Coaching
	  Special interest groups
	  Theater
	
	Professional responsibilities
	  Site-based management
	  Curriculum committees
	  Membership in professional association
	  Ongoing professional development

In conceptualizing the components of the special educator's electronic professional productivity toolbox, three primary information functions seem to capture the tasks commonly performed by special educators: creating, communicating, and managing. Special educators create information in a variety of formats: activity sheets, lesson plans, instructional materials, and visual designs. Although communicating information in the classroom frequently occurs orally, technology has particular value when communication is in print or electronic formats. The importance of storing and manipulating information for future reference and decision making comprises the managing information aspect. A template of the Special Educator's Professional Productivity Toolbox is illustrated in Figure 7.2. An additional category, Miscellaneous and Specialized Tools, is also included as a means of representing tools and

utilities not covered by the other three categories.

Given the template in Figure 7.2 as a framework for selecting an integrated set of tools, special educators next turn their attention to identifying specific professional productivity tools. Their goal is to enhance their understanding of the productivity demands and the possible tools that might be used while engaging in the common tasks of the profession. The section that follows provides an overview of the possibilities associated with designing a professional productivity toolbox.

Professional Productivity Tools

As noted earlier, the marketplace presents the consumer with many choices. Until the special

Special Educator's Professional Productivity Toolbox

CREATING INFORMATION	Possible Programs	Publisher
Text Word Processors Electronic Writing Aids		
Graphics Graphing and Charting Programs Paint Programs Desktop Video		
Instructional Materials Print Computer-based		

COMMUNICATING INFORMATION	Possible Programs	Publisher
In Print Desktop Publishing		
Orally/Visually Presentation Software		
Electronically Work Group Programs Telecommunications Information Services		

MANAGING INFORMATION	Possible Programs	Publisher
In Print Label Programs Form Generators		
Electronically Databases Financial Management Gradebooks Spreadsheets Statistical Analysis		

Figure 7.2. Special Educator's Professional Productivity Toolbox.

MISC. AND SPECIALIZED TOOLS	Possible Programs	Publisher
Desktop Productivity Calendars/Planners Screen Savers		
Miscellaneous Utilities File Exchange General Purpose Utilities Virus Protection		

Figure 7.2. *(continued)*

education community validates specific tools as essential, the task of creating a technology toolbox remains largely a "do-it-yourself project." In this section we provide an overview of the types of professional productivity tools that may be included in the special education technology toolbox. Although each special educator may not need each tool we discuss, we present information to help educators identify a core set of tools and learn to use them effectively. The discussion is based loosely on the list presented in Figure 7.2.

Creating Information

Education professionals spend a considerable amount of time creating information. In many respects, this is the most basic but essential unit of professional productivity. Technology tools for creating information have widespread application and are important building blocks for learning to use the tools for communicating and managing information. Common tasks that illustrate the creation of information include writing letters, creating flyers, developing instructional handouts and exams, and designing computer-based activities. Tools for creating information include word processors, electronic writing aids, graphics tools, and programs for creating instructional materials. This cluster provides the educator with a set of tools that will enable him or her to create information in multiple formats: text, graphics, or instructional materials (see Table 7.4).

Word Processors

A word processor is the first and perhaps most important program in a productivity toolbox. Productivity studies (e.g., Beaver, 1989) have found that students spend the bulk of their time in front of personal computers engaged in word processing. Whereas many users are introduced to the word processor as a means of typing papers, it is important to understand how the computer is much more than a typewriter (Williams, 1990, 1992).

As described in Chapter 3, a word processor allows the user to create electronic text. Once information is in the computer, it can be edited, saved, printed, or copied and pasted into a variety of other programs: e-mail, desktop publishing, or

Table 7.4. Creating Information: Linking Tasks and Tools

Types of Tasks	Types of Tools
Create a letter for parents	Word processor
Design a flyer	Word processor
Design a logo	Paint program
Create a multipage instructional handout	Word processor and clip art
Create an exam	Word processor
Create a computer-based activity	HyperStudio, KidPix

World Wide Web publishing. The word processor is the gateway to electronic information and is the fundamental tool supporting the work of educators because of the ease of correcting errors and the fluidness of editing and formatting text. The ability to delete and correct errors (by backspacing, using the cursor keys, or using the mouse to click–drag and highlight a block of text) provides an error correction environment not possible with a typewriter. The option of saving work to either a floppy or a hard disk, to be recalled in seconds, printed, or modified, makes electronic text extremely valuable. In addition, because the task of word processing is essentially the same regardless of the type of document being created (e.g., letters, instructional materials, notes), the word processor is a very flexible tool. Finally, features that allow the user to change the font, style, and size of type provide the user with significant power in the visual design of his or her message.

Despite all the positive features of word processors, other alternatives have been developed because sometimes people need to write when they do not have access to an electrical outlet as is needed for a desktop computer. *Smart keyboard* is the generic term for a battery-operated portable keyboard with memory (see Figure 7.3). Smart keyboards are designed to allow the user to enter and save text and feature a small screen (usually four lines of 40 characters). These keyboards weigh under 3 pounds and are extremely portable. By unplugging the computer's keyboard cable and connecting it to the smart keyboard, the user can transfer a text file to the computer by simply pressing an upload key. Then the text appears in the word processor as if the user has stayed home all day. Well under $300, smart keyboards have become a low-cost alternative to laptop computers for some writers.

Another option, particularly useful for writers who demand an extremely light and portable system (e.g., 1 pound) and prefer to enter text using handwriting rather than a keyboard, are Personal Digital Assistants (PDAs) such as the Apple Newton (Apple), the Psion Palmtop (Psion, Inc.), and the Sharp Wizard (Sharp Electronics) (also see Chapters 2 and 5). These products allow the user to enter text using a stylus. Handwriting recognition software translates the information into text, and infrared signals or cables are used to transfer the information between the PDA and the computer. Although PDAs may be a bit cumbersome for completing a large writing project, their portability makes them ideal for library research and for capturing writing ideas throughout the day. In the $300 to $1,200 range, these tools may be a bit too luxurious for most writers' budgets.

Another tool that extends the value of the word processor is a scanner. Frequently, writers will discover information that is available only in a paper format. Retyping this information into one's manuscript requires considerable time. Instead, the paper can be fed into a desktop scanner and the text captured by the computer software as if the user had typed the information at the keyboard. Once the information is in the computer, it is a simple matter to cut and paste it into a word processor, import it into a desktop publishing program, or e-mail it to a colleague. Desktop scanners can be found in the $99 to $300 range (also see Chapter 2).

Many factors contribute to selection and use considerations of a word processor. Some teachers prefer simple word processors with minimal functions, whereas others may prefer powerful full-featured products or an integrated suite of products. One important consideration in selecting a word processor focuses on compatibility with operating systems used by other teachers at the school. Although it is increasingly easy to

Figure 7.3. AlphaSmart. *Source:* AlphaSmart by Intelligent Peripheral Devices, Inc., Cupertino, CA.

transfer text from one program to another, having a word processing program that is supported by the school and colleagues means that a teacher will have a ready network for support and training as his or her technical prowess develops. Otherwise, given that most word processors work in a similar manner, it makes little difference about which word processor a teacher selects.

Electronic Writing Aids

Examples of electronic writing aids include programs classified as bibliographic tools; spelling, grammar, and style checkers; outliners; and reference works. Initially, the word processor was a stand-alone program that required the user to quit the program to use various writing aids such as spelling or grammar checkers. Now, various writing aids are built into the word processor, most notably spelling, grammar, and style checkers and a thesaurus.

Outliners also have moved from being stand-alone progams to being integrated into most word processors. However, to create and use an outline, the writer must fully understand the relationship among all the ideas. As a result, outlining tends to be underutilized as a writing strategy by many beginning writers. One alternative that has particular promise in special education is Inspiration (Inspiration Software), a product designed to support brainstorming. Ideas are randomly placed on the screen and, as order appears, can be moved and connected with various symbols. After the concept map is complete, the user simply toggles the view to see an outline of the ideas. Inspiration outlines and maps can be moved into the word processor for further development.

Another class of writing aids—reference tools and dictionaries—still tend to be separate products. Although it is more convenient to have these look-up functions available while writing, with operating systems that enable more than one program to be open at a time, looking up information may be only a few clicks away. After evaluating the writing aid features within the word processor, the user can consider what types of stand-alone programs to add to the hard drive.

Graphics Tools

Graphic images may be created and manipulated in a variety of products. Freehand illustrations can be designed with paint programs ranging in ease of use from Kid Pix (Brøderbund) to Adobe Illustrator (Adobe Systems). For users with less developed graphic skills, clip art is the solution. To make meaning from a variety of numerical data, spreadsheets can be used to create charts and graphs.

As desktop computers become increasingly powerful, tools such as QuickTime (Apple Computer) and PhotoShop (Adobe Systems) enable users to manipulate graphic images and movies with sophistication previously reserved for industry. As digital cameras continue to decrease in price, it is easy to capture photographic images and bring them into the computer to be manipulated. Indeed, most virtual reality images often begin with real-life images that are manipulated to create new images.

Graphic tools are powerful additions to desktop computers because they help users visually design information. Graphic images can be placed in a word processor to improve the quality of a message: a photo of the school can be used as part of a letterhead; achievement scores can be placed in a spreadsheet and plotted, and the graph inserted in a letter to parents explaining the groups scores; and so on. Graphics of all sorts

Electronic writing and graphics tools enhance professionals' personal productivity. (Photograph by Carolyn F. Woods)

improve the visual quality of desktop publishing regardless of whether a word processor or a powerful desktop publishing program is used.

When considering the purchase of graphic tools, the educator should consider the skill level of the user(s) and the amount of training required to master the product. Ideally, a range of options should be provided for teachers and students: clip art, paint programs, graphing and charting, and desktop video.

Programs for Creating Instructional Materials

Teachers frequently need a variety of programs to assist in creating instructional materials. A variety of tools offer assistance to teachers as they create practice activities, puzzles, fact sheets, cloze exercises, quizzes, and tests that students will complete on paper. Test generators allow teachers to create a test bank and create tests with a selected number of items randomly or purposefully selected. In addition, it is possible to print multiple versions of an exam to minimize the inappropriate exchange of answers between classes.

A second type of tool is available for the teacher interested in creating computer-based activities. Programs such as Digital Chisel (Pierian Spring Software) and HyperStudio (Roger Wagner) provide the user with a powerful development environment to create materials that students will use while at the computer (also see Chapters 6 and 9). Although some concerns have been raised about these types of tools as "programmer tools," in reality, when sufficient student access is available, they provide a practical means for interactively engaging students. The chief advantage of tools for creating computer-based materials is the power and flexibility they offer the teacher.

An important consideration in the selection and use of tools for creating instructional materials involves the preferred format. Predominantly, teachers have been interested in creating paper-and-pencil activities for their students. Computer-based development tools provide a powerful environment for creating interactive learning experiences. When forced-choice formats are used

for computer-based testing, the computer does the scoring. As a practical reality, however, most teachers find that the word processor is more than adequate in meeting their need to create classroom materials.

Communicating Information

Three types of technological communication tools extend the impact of the information educators create: presentation software and hardware, desktop publishing, and telecommunications. Because the distinctions between tools for creating and tools for communicating are beginning to blur, especially because some tools can be used for both, it may be useful to consider that communication tools focus on the way information looks or is presented after it has been created. It is also important to note that technology facilitates collaborative efforts, commonly referred to as workgroups. Table 7.5 illustrates the linkages between tasks and tools involved with communicating information.

Historically, communication has been accomplished orally. Indeed, much of teaching is based on an oral model of transmitting information. However, as communication options have expanded from oral, to print, to electronic, educators have become increasingly concerned with the persuasiveness of the message (style) in addition to concerns about content (substance). Pres-

Table 7.5. Communicating Information: Linking Tasks and Tools

Types of Tasks	Types of Tools
Publish a classroom newsletter	Desktop publishing
Publish a resource directory	Desktop publishing
Make a PTO presentation	Presentation software
Collaboratively develop a proposal	Workgroup software
Communicate with others	E-mail
Search for information	Web browser

ently, the technology tools are such that it matters little whether the content is text, graphics, or a combination.

Desktop Publishing

Although word processors are increasingly capable of producing materials with text and graphics, desktop publishing programs (e.g., Microsoft Publisher [Microsoft], PageMaker [Aldus], and Quark [Quark, Inc.]) are often used to produce newsletters and other documents that require a great deal of flexibility for style and placement of information. After the message is developed, the user is concerned about its looking good in print. With the power of the desktop printing process, the right of all voices and perspectives to have their views presented is increasingly exercised.

Many features of sophisticated desktop publishing programs are now available in word processors. As a result, the power and the challenge of looking good in print is now available to teachers simply wanting to create a weekly two-page newsletter to keep families informed about classroom events. Many factors contribute to considerations in selecting a desktop publishing program: ease of use, ease of learning, power, flexibility, and price. Mastering a desktop publishing program is a significant undertaking but a logical step after mastering tools for creating text and graphics.

Presentation Software

Presentation software products enable a teacher to create a visual presentation (e.g., a slide show on the computer) or print materials that can be made into overhead transparencies. This technology has been widely adopted in education as it cements the position of teacher-centered instruction and supports the oral tradition in education. However, it is increasingly possible not only to create presentations that provide text information but also to dynamically illustrate data or access current events information that is not available in any other form of printed instructional materials. To use presentation software effectively in the classroom, a projection system is required so that the group can view the information.

Slide show features are the primary purpose of dedicated programs such as PowerPoint (Microsoft), but can also be found within other programs such as ClarisWorks (Claris) and Kid Pix (Brøderbund). As a result, it is now possible for children of all ages to have the opportunity to gather information, organize it, and share it with an audience. Considerable anecdotal data suggest that these skills are and will be valued in a variety of educational and business contexts.

When considering which presentation program to use with students, most decisions focus on developmental factors (i.e., computer power required) and ease of learning issues. As with word processing products, the mechanics of presentation products are fairly similar across products.

Collaborative Work

With the development of local area and wide area networks, software has been designed to support the collaborative efforts of groups. Known as groupware, Lotus Notes (Lotus Development) is one example of a product that allows a group of users to share calendars, messages, and documents with each other. As schools have sought to foster cooperative learning environments, tools that support collaborative work are an important and necessary tool.

One example of a collaborative tool designed specifically for special educators is CoPlanner (Slipstream Software Systems), a product designed to support resource teachers as they work collaboratively in inclusionary settings through shared decision making (Robertson, Haines, Sanche, & Biffart, 1997). As a team explores key questions regarding a child's instructional program, decisions are documented in worksheets, goals are defined as timelines, and team responsibilities are determined. The system serves as a collaborative repository for the Individualized Education Program (IEP) team and provides e-mail capabilities so that team members may advise each other about developments. This tool embodies a process that enables a team to form a consensual vision which emerges from an initial concern about a student, through a recursive process of information gathering, reflection, teaching, monitoring, and reporting on the activities associated with implementing the child's IEP.

Workgroup software has yet to make a significant impact in education. However, as educational decision-making processes become increasingly collaborative, tools like these will be essential.

Telecommunications

Telecommunications is a broad term to cover most uses of technology that involve the computer and a phone line to enable a user to interact with another computer in a remote location (see also Chapters 2 and 3). At a practical level this means things like electronic mail (e-mail), searching electronic databases, and interacting on the World Wide Web. The essence of these applications is connectivity; users have discovered that single stand-alone computers are not as interesting as being connected with others.

E-mail is rapidly becoming one of the core applications of technology. The opportunity to send and receive messages when it is convenient is a powerful time-shifting strategy that allows users to be more productive. In addition, as more information is available in electronic format, access to information on any imaginable topic means that the ready-reference power of the desktop computer is mind boggling.

A variety of considerations are necessary to select the "best" or most economical telecommunications package. Colleagues may have advice on available packages in the community.

Managing Information

Educators may be concerned with two aspects of managing information: storing it and using it to make decisions. Locating information when it is needed is critical to effective decision making. Tools used for creating and managing information come in two formats: print and electronic. Table 7.6 outlines some sample tasks and tools for managing information.

Table 7.6. Managing Information: Linking Tasks and Tools

Types of Tasks	Types of Tools
Create forms	Word processor, Form generator
Create labels	Label printer
Keep track of grades	Electronic gradebook
Keep track of finances	Quicken (Intuit)
Basic statistical analysis	Statistics program
General record keeping	Database
Repetitive calculations	Spreadsheet

Increasingly, technology is being looked upon as a means of collecting, gathering, and reporting information. Some of these developments are driven by a concept referred to as a "paperless office" (Landcaster, 1978), in which paper is not needed because all records are created, stored, and accessed electronically. Some schools have made important strides toward implementing this concept in the area of purchasing. By creating an electronic purchase order form, staff use a computer to enter the information on a form, which is forwarded to the business manager for approval and then to the vendor for fulfillment. Other schools are exploring similar systems for tracking student attendance. Professionals, however, must remember that electronic storage is not always permanent or fail-safe and that some storage media have a relatively short "shelf life." For example, as noted in Chapter 3, some CD-ROM disks become unreliable after 5 years (Tangley, 1998).

Managing Information in Print Formats

A wide variety of form generator programs are available that allow users to create forms for their paper-based information system. In practice, many teachers use word processors to generate forms used in their classroom. Indeed, many school districts have adopted this approach to standardizing the forms used for collecting and managing information. Another common example of the use of technology to manage information in schools is to use labels or bar codes.

Databases

A database program is useful for storing and retrieving specific factual information, such as student information records and inventory lists. Databases are one of the modules in an integrated productivity package or may be purchased as a stand-alone product (e.g., Access by Microsoft or FileMaker Pro by FileMaker Claris). In addition, databases are being merged with the Web to provide sophisticated searching capabilities in an on-line environment.

Database creation involves thoughtful planning. While the development is not difficult, the commitment to maintaining the data is often a hidden cost to most novices. However, when properly designed, a database provides invaluable information for decision making. In addition, databases are increasingly flexible, are able to store both text and graphics, and have connections to the Web to monitor specific data. Databases can be simple or complex. The critical factors in the success of database development involve a response to a clear need, a commitment to maintenance, and ease of use.

Programs for Managing Numeric Data

Developed initially for business, a wide range of tools are available for managing numeric data. Administrators and faculty with duties involving the management of funds find financial management programs such as Quicken (Intuit) or QuickBooks (Intuit) invaluable for tracking income and expenses. Dedicated gradebook programs are available, as well as spreadsheet templates, for tracking student grades. When detailed analysis of numeric data is needed, statistical analysis programs are useful (e.g., SPSS/PC+).

Many of the considerations about the use of databases—accuracy, commitment to update, and

ease of use—also apply to programs that monitor numeric data. Decision makers who rely on these types of tools for managing their data seldom return to the primitive tools they once used.

Specialized Tools

Three types of specialized tools also may be needed in the productivity toolbox: IEP development tools, desktop productivity tools, and miscellaneous tools. Table 7.7 illustrates the link between common tasks and tools in this category.

IEP Development Tools

The paperwork associated with the development of IEPs is a significant demand on the productivity of special educators. Some districts have attempted to capture their IEP forms in a series of word processing files so that the special educator and IEP team can simply type the information, save it, and print it out. Other districts have used commercial IEP programs that have been evaluated for compliance in their state (see Chapter 3). In both cases, the strategy is to reduce the amount of handwriting required and take advantage of technology to store documents for easy updating. The 1997 reauthorization of the Individuals with Disabilities Education Act (IDEA) will result in a significant number of changes in computer-based IEP programs. Nonetheless, teacher satisfaction with these tools is generally favorable given the assistance these tools offer.

Table 7.7. Specialized Tools

Types of Tasks	Types of Tools
Create Individualized Education Programs (IEPs)	IEP development tools
Desktop productivity	Calendars/planners, screen savers
Miscellaneous tools	General purpose utilities, virus protection

Desktop Productivity

Examples of desktop productivity programs include calendars–planners and screen savers. Calendars and planners allow users to track time commitments. Although it is difficult to argue about the productivity value of screen savers, as a source of distraction and amusement they are hard to beat!

Miscellaneous Tools

Examples of miscellaneous tools for professional productivity include file exchange utilities, general purpose utilities, and virus protection programs. File exchange utilities (e.g., Can Opener [Abbott Systems] and Adobe Acrobat [Adobe Systems]) enable users to view or print disk files that originated in programs that the user does not own. Acrobat is a significant development because it allows a developer of information to save it in a universal file format (.pdf) that can then be viewed by anyone with Acrobat Reader (a free utility). As a result, educators can create information and other users can view it regardless of the computer system they are using.

One common utility that many computer owners have is Norton Utilities (Symantec). This series of modules provides a variety of diagnostic, troubleshooting, and repair functions. Although the feedback may be a bit technical, these utilities are lifesavers when a disk is unreadable or has been accidentally erased.

Computers can be used by professionals to write Individualized Education Plans. (Photograph by Carolyn F. Woods)

Another type of program that is common to include in the toolkit is a virus protection program. Viruses are programs designed to damage or annoy other users. Viruses can be transmitted on disks or via the Web and work by attaching themselves to programs on the hard drive. Virus protection software works by scanning any disk placed in the drive and monitoring the activity on the hard drive to alert the user to any suspicious activity. There are many myths surrounding viruses so it is a good idea to consult a local resource regarding questions and concerns.

Creating an Electronic Toolbox

A technology toolbox is a personal collection of electronic tools that support the productivity of its owner. As previously discussed, a number of tools can be used individually and collectively to contribute to the productivity of educators. In this section, we offer some thoughts on how you can begin assembling and using a technology toolbox to support your professional productivity.

▶ **Step 1. Consider access and availability.** Perhaps the first issue to address in creating an electronic toolbox involves identifying the type of computer system to be used. It is common to find DOS-, Windows-, and Macintosh-based computers, and even still some Apple II computers, in schools. Although there is considerable debate as to which system is the "best," such discussions overlook an essential point. Technical merit aside, the best computer is actually the one that the user has regular and convenient access to. Unfortunately, computer envy often infects a school, dividing the faculty into first- or second-class citizens based on CPU processing speed or hard drive size.

As an analogy, consider that each year the automobile manufacturers announce new models. Although, these marketplace developments affect the value of the car you are currently driving, they hardly require everyone to purchase a new car. Typically, you continue to drive your current car because of reasons related to not needing or wanting a new car, not being able to afford a new car, or the old car in fact works quite nicely. If the old car consistently gets you to where you want to be without problem (i.e., it accomplishes all the fundamental transportation needs you have), it matters little whether you have a 2000 model or a 1990 model. If, on the other hand, you cannot use your car to accomplish the tasks you desire or you rarely have convenient access to it and have to rely on other means to get where you want to be, then maybe it is time for a new model. The same can be said for computers. The best computer for you is the one that is accessible and meets your productivity needs. Having a computer that is not your first platform choice is still better than not having one or having limited access to your preferred platform.

▶ **Step 2: Identify and prioritize your productivity tasks.** Establish and rank-order what you do and how you spend your time. Given the many things you do, which activities require the greatest proportion of your time?

▶ **Step 3: Inventory your existing collection of tools.** Review the specific tools that are already available to you and decide whether additional tools need to be purchased. For example, you may already own a productivity suite that came preloaded or bundled with your system when it was purchased. Evaluate how each program meets your productivity needs. If you have little or no productivity tools available, or the current tools are not sufficient to meet your standards, you will need to prepare a shopping list for new tools to fill the gap in your toolbox.

▶ **Step 4: Conduct a search for productivity tools.** Armed with a list of your productivity needs, seek out reliable sources of information regarding specific tools in each category. Sources for this type of information include product descriptions in software catalogs, reviews in periodicals, colleagues using similar tools, and the Web (see also Chapter 3). It is important to make an informed decision

about which tool to select, ideally based on how well it will increase your productivity. Try to avoid selecting tools based primarily on initial cost. Rather, make decisions that represent investments in efficiency.

Figure 7.4 illustrates the choices one user made in identifying a set of tools that will support her productivity. Although the process of creating an electronic toolbox can be time-consuming, the result is that the user has the knowledge and skills to use each tool in the toolbox. Enhanced productivity can be demonstrated with individual tools, but the real power is displayed when information is manipulated using multiple tools. Only when the user begins to focus on the integrated desktop does the synergy become apparent.

Successful completion of the selection and acquisition process will mean your computer is now a powerful workshop. However, simple ownership of high-quality power tools does not transform a do-it-yourselfer into the master craftsperson. Indeed, there is a significant need for user training. If pride of ownership is going to be transferred into accomplishments, a commitment to acquire basic, intermediate, and advanced training in how to use and exploit the power of these tools is needed.

Professional Development

In this section, we address the professional development issues involved in utilizing technology in ways that enhance professional productivity.

Basic Training

Knowing the components of a toolbox and knowing how to use each tool effectively are two different matters. Indeed, having a keen understanding of the tasks involved in a project and being trained and skilled in using the tools are two factors that distinguish the do-it-yourselfer from a skilled craftsperson. By acquiring basic training on each of the tools in a toolbox, the user

Creating Information	Possible Programs	Publisher
Text Word Processors	Microsoft Word	Microsoft
Electronic Writing Aids	Microsoft Word	Microsoft
Graphics Graphing and Charting Programs	Quattro Pro	Borland
Paint Programs	Paint Shop Pro	JASC
Desktop Video	Quick Cam	Connetix
Instructional Materials Print	Microsoft Word	Microsoft
Computer-based	Print Shop Deluxe	Broderbund

Communicating Information	Possible Programs	Publisher
In Print Word Processors	Microsoft Word	Microsoft
Desktop Publishing	Microsoft Publisher	Microsoft
Orally/Visually Presentation Software	Power Point	Microsoft
Electronically Work Group Programs		
Telecommunications	Netscape Navigator	Netscape Corporation
Information Services	Mailserver	Microsoft

Figure 7.4. An example of a productivity toolbox. The programs above are not endorsed by MINDPLAY, a company promoting literacy. They are provided only as examples of the types of tools educators can use. This template was adapted from "Integrating Technology Into the Curriculum: How To Avoid Making It a Do-It-Yourself Project," by Dave Edyburn and Jim Gardner, April 12, 1997, presented at the 1997 Council for Exceptional Children Conference, Salt Lake City, UT. Source: http://www.mindplay.com/template2.html

ensures that he or she will be able to adequately use the tools when the need arises. Typically, the model has been to teach oneself. Although this may not be the preferred learning style of many individuals, the tutorial programs that come with many programs are extremely helpful in getting new users started. However, there are other ways to learn about the mechanics of operating a productivity program (e.g., classes, personal tutors, how-to books, and on-line study groups).

In our work, we have found it useful to create and use self-assessments (see examples in Tables 7.8, 7.9, and 7.10). Checklists are useful to teachers as a means of assessing their current skill develop-

Managing Information	Possible Programs	Publisher
In Print Label Programs	My Mail List	MySoftware
Form Generators		
Electronically Databases	Microsoft Office	Microsoft
Financial Management	Microsoft Office	Microsoft
Gradebooks	Grade Quick!	Jackson Software
IEP Management	IEP Works Pro	K-12 Micromedia
Spreadsheets	Quattro Pro	Borland
Statistical Analysis	Quattro Pro	Borland

Misc. and Specialized Tools	Possible Programs	Publisher
Desktop Productivity Calendars/Planners	Print Shop Deluxe	Broderbund
Screen Savers	Disney Collection	Berkeley
Misc. Utilities File Exchange		
General Purpose Utilities	Norton Utility Doctor	Symantec
Virus Protection	Norton AntiVirus	Symantec

Figure 7.4. *(continued)*

ment and mapping a series of statements about their technical competency. As we noted earlier, the process of making our expectations explicit is helpful for new users to understand what it is they need to learn and for experienced users to validate how much they already know while pointing out gaps in their knowledge and skills. Although we would like all training experiences to ensure that participants leave with more skills than they began with, additional research is needed to determine reasonable timelines for the process of expertise building required with various tools. In our experience, this is not necessarily a short-term learning experience.

Implementing Skills

After acquiring basic and intermediate skills with each tool, the user should try putting those skills into practice. The personal challenge involved in a skill test is important because it allows the user to determine if there are any gaps in his or her skills while providing clear reinforcement about the value and utility of what has already been learned.

Table 7.8. Example of Self-Assessment Checklist for Word Processing Skills

Name _____

Name of the Word Processing Program _____

Type of Computer:　☐ IBM compatible　　☐ Macintosh

Check the Pre column if you have the skill prior to this course. At the conclusion of the course, check the Post column if you have learned the skill.

Pre	Post	**BASIC SKILLS**
_____	_____	Prepare a blank disk for storing word processing files.
_____	_____	Demonstrate how to start your word processor and begin to enter text into a new file.
_____	_____	Demonstrate the ability to change fonts, text size, line spacing, and justification.
_____	_____	Demonstrate the ability to delete a character, word, and paragraph.
_____	_____	Demonstrate the ability to insert a character, word, and paragraph.
_____	_____	Demonstrate the ability to move quickly and easily through a document (up/down, by line, by screen, by page, by file).
_____	_____	Demonstrate how to access HELP within the word processor.
_____	_____	Demonstrate the ability to load a file from disk.
_____	_____	Demonstrate the ability to save a file from disk.
_____	_____	Demonstrate the use of the spelling checker.
_____	_____	Demonstrate the ability to print a document.

Pre	Post	**INTERMEDIATE SKILLS**
_____	_____	Demonstrate the ability to use block functions (move, copy, delete).
_____	_____	Demonstrate the ability to change margin and tab settings.
_____	_____	Demonstrate the ability to insert page numbers.

Pre	Post	**ADVANCED SKILLS**
_____	_____	Demonstrate the use of search and the search and replace functions.
_____	_____	Demonstrate the ability to add lines, boxes, or graphics.
_____	_____	Demonstrate the ability to use the mail merge features.
_____	_____	Demonstrate the ability to import text from other programs.
_____	_____	Demonstrate the ability to format text in columns.
_____	_____	Demonstrate the ability to use foreign language characters.

Table 7.9. Example of Self-Assessment Checklist for E-mail Skills

Name _____

Name of the E-mail Program _____

Type of Computer: ☐ IBM/compatible   ☐ Macintosh

Check the Pre column if you have the skill prior to this course. At the conclusion of the course, check the Post column if you have learned the skill.

Pre	Post	**AWARENESS**
_____	_____	I qualify for a free e-mail account through school or work.
_____	_____	I know how to obtain a subscription for an e-mail account.
_____	_____	I know where/how I could access e-mail at home or work.

Pre	Post	**BASIC SKILLS**
_____	_____	Demonstrate the ability to point and click.
_____	_____	I can locate the e-mail icon on the computer hard drive and initiate the program.
_____	_____	Demonstrate the ability to enter your user name and password.
_____	_____	Demonstrate the ability to check for new mail.
_____	_____	Demonstrate the ability to respond to a message.
_____	_____	Demonstrate the ability to compose and send a new message.
_____	_____	Demonstrate the ability to delete a message.
_____	_____	Demonstrate the ability to print a message.

Pre	Post	**INTERMEDIATE SKILLS**
_____	_____	Demonstrate the ability to send one message to multiple people.
_____	_____	Demonstrate the ability to create an entry in the address book.
_____	_____	Demonstrate the ability to save a message in a directory.
_____	_____	Demonstrate the ability to send an attachment.
_____	_____	Demonstrate the ability to open and view an attachment.

Pre	Post	**ADVANCED SKILLS**
_____	_____	Demonstrate the ability to customize your mail program.
_____	_____	I feel comfortable in teaching others how to use e-mail.

Table 7.10. Example of Self-Assessment for World Wide Web Skills

Name _____

Type of Computer: ☐ IBM/compatible   ☐ Macintosh

Type of Browser: ☐ America Online   ☐ Microsoft Internet Explorer   ☐ Netscape Navigator

Check the Pre column if you have the skill prior to this course. At the conclusion of the course, check the Post column if you have learned the skill.

Pre	Post	**AWARENESS**
____	____	I have heard of the World Wide Web.
____	____	I know someone who has "surfed the Web."
____	____	I have used a Web browser to "surf the Web."
____	____	I know where/how I could access the Web at home or work.

Pre	Post	**BASIC SKILLS**
____	____	Demonstrate the ability to point and click.
____	____	I can locate Netscape on the computer hard drive and initiate the program.
____	____	I know how to recognize a home page.
____	____	I know how to enter a www address into Netscape.
____	____	Demonstrate the ability to use scroll bars.
____	____	I can recognize the visual cues indicating a "link."
____	____	Demonstrate the ability to select and access a link.
____	____	Demonstrate the ability to use the "Back" button.

Pre	Post	**INTERMEDIATE SKILLS**
____	____	Demonstrate the ability to conduct a search on the Web.
____	____	I know how to obtain "copies" of selected information using the options for (a) Save As, (b) Mail Document, and (c) Print.
____	____	I have started collecting addresses of useful Web sites.

Pre	Post	**ADVANCED SKILLS**
____	____	I feel comfortable teaching others how to navigate the Web.
____	____	Demonstrate the ability to create a home page.
____	____	Demonstrate the ability to create working links.
____	____	Demonstrate the ability to copy selected portions of Hypertext Markup Language (html) code from a page and insert this code into a personal home page (e.g., graphic, animation, format).

In addition, skill tests are useful for creating that "teachable" moment for acquiring intermediate and advanced skills and productivity strategies.

In this section we outline a few ideas about how you might demonstrate your use of the tools you have selected for your productivity toolbox. We offer three skill levels: novice, intermediate, and advanced. In each case, ask yourself, "Can I do this?"

Word Processing

- *Novice:* Create a letter for parents introducing yourself as their child's new teacher.

- *Intermediate:* Create a letter for parents introducing yourself as their child's new teacher. Include appropriate clip art as part of the school's letterhead at the top of the page.

- *Advanced:* Use the mail merge feature of your word processor to create letters to parents that are customized with their name and address and that refer to the child by name.

Classroom Sign

- *Novice:* Use the program Print Shop Deluxe (Brøderbund) to create a sign for the door of your classroom.

- *Intermediate:* Create an original design that will be used as a logo for an upcoming instructional unit.

- *Advanced:* Integrate text and graphics from multiple sources into a single-page sign.

Classroom Newsletter

- *Novice:* Use a program such as Microsoft Publisher (Microsoft) to create a two-page newsletter for parents about events in your classroom.

- *Intermediate:* Use photos of students and images from the Web in your newsletter.

- *Advanced:* Use a desktop publishing program such as PageMaker (Aldus) or Quark (Quark, Inc.) to design your newsletter. Use student-generated text and import from disk.

E-mail

- *Novice:* Use the e-mail program of your choice to demonstrate how to send one message to multiple people.

- *Intermediate:* Demonstrate how to copy and paste a message from your word processor to an e-mail message.

- *Advanced:* Work with a colleague to create word processing files and send them back and forth as attachments.

Web Browsing

- *Novice:* Demonstrate how to reach a specific site (e.g., www.ed.gov).

- *Intermediate:* Save a text document or graphic image to your hard drive and demonstrate how to open the file in your word processor.

- *Advanced:* Create a bookmark collection of 10 sites that you believe your colleagues ought to explore.

Professional Development Challenges

As we conclude this chapter, we offer a few observations concerning the professional development challenges awaiting special educators as they seek to use technology to enhance their professional productivity. Four ideas seem useful to discuss at this point: apprenticeships, general productivity strategies, specific productivity strategies, and commitment to ongoing professional development.

Apprenticeships

Whereas many beginning special educators participate in induction programs in their school districts, similar mentoring programs do not exist for supporting new technology users. Despite the considerable literature on technology and staff development (Harp, Satzinger, & Taylor, 1997; Sandholtz, Ringstaff, & Dwyer, 1997; Tally & Grimaldi, 1995), educators often fail to recognize that the integration of technology is not a simple matter that results from attending a few workshops or training sessions. As a result, it seems appropriate to suggest that apprenticeships be considered one form of mentoring strategy for offering assistance to teachers as they face the challenges of acquiring tools and training.

Consider the following observation about the power of the desktop toolbox: Text that is captured on paper may be reproduced by copying or distributed by faxing. In contrast, a user can create electronic text in a word processor, modify it in seconds, print it if necessary, copy and paste it into an e-mail message and send it to a colleague, import it into a desktop publishing program to be made into a class handout, copy and paste it into a presentation program to illustrate a lecture or workshop, and publish it on a home page on the Web. This user's working knowledge of a core set of desktop tools transforms how he or she creates, manipulates, and distributes information. Productivity is enhanced as a result of the ease and efficiency with which common productivity demands are met. The extended training that molds an apprentice into a journeyperson, and ultimately a master craftsperson, is a story about tools, skill, and knowledge. Apprenticeships or some similar form of induction program may be a strategic initiative to foster the high levels of productivity the special education profession needs.

General Productivity Strategies

After the basic mechanics of using each tool are mastered, attention should focus on general productivity strategies. We discuss three general productivity strategies: work habits, templates, and keyboard shortcuts.

A number of work habits are associated with using technology efficiently. Perhaps the most important involves saving work frequently. One never knows when a power fluctuation or an unfortunate incident may cause the computer to lock up and result in the loss of current work. It is commonly recommended that a user save work every 10 minutes to minimize the loss of information. In a similar vein, the user should back up files on a regular basis to guard against loss should the hard drive become damaged.

Another series of good work habits involves naming and storing files for rapid retrieval. Rather than naming letters in series, such as "letter1," "letter2," and so on, the user should use descriptive names (e.g., "Welcome Letter") that will facilitate locating specific files in the future.

As a related suggestion, it is important to learn how to create and use folders or subdirectories for storing files (e.g., a folder for each subject and additional folders for each unit). Storing files titled "letter1," "letter2," and so on, in a folder titled "correspondence" will probably not facilitate the user's work later.

Templates are an important strategy for enhancing productivity by simplifying repetitive tasks. Essentially, a template is a file containing basic information, layout, and style. The user simply changes the date or makes other minor modifications to customize the information before printing. Templates that come with word processors may be relevant to an educator's work, or templates can be created by typing and saving a file and giving it a distinct name. As the need arises, the user opens the template file, makes the necessary changes, saves the changes if desired, and prints. By reviewing the activities of the work week, an educator can determine if any tasks could be completed more efficiently with a template.

Perhaps one of the most powerful examples of the value of word processing is copy and paste. This function allows the user to drag the cursor over a block of text and make a copy of it. Then, by placing the cursor in a new location and using the paste command, the block is repeated without retyping. The ultimate value of copy and paste is that it can be used in any application on the desktop. After creating an elaborate drawing in a paint program, the user can copy and move the design to the word processor for use as a logo in a letterhead. Text from a word processor can be moved to an e-mail message, and information from a Web page can be inserted into a handout for students. The options are endless.

One final general productivity strategy involves the use of keyboard shortcuts. Beginners are often taught how to select items from the menu bar (print, quit, bold, etc.). However, experienced users often memorize keyboard shortcuts as a more efficient means of doing the same command without taking hands away from the keyboard to move the mouse. Keyboard shortcuts can be found on the right side of a menu. For example, try this: Highlight a block of text in your word processor, pull down the edit menu, and select

The use of technology enhances personal productivity. (Photograph by Jimmy D. Lindsey)

cut. Now pull down the menu and again see what the keyboard shortcut is for paste. Release the menu and try the keyboard shortcut (on IBM and compatibles, hold control and press V; on Macintosh, hold command and press V). Over time, users learn keyboard shortcuts that make work more efficient.

Specific Productivity Strategies

In addition to acquiring general productivity strategies, educators can benefit from learning specific tips and tricks to use tools more efficiently. Experienced users often find that reading the manual for a software program yields all sorts of insights about how things work that they never took the time to explore or fully understood how to use.

The computer section in a bookstore has a wealth of information concerning each product in the productivity toolkit. Two companies that create the vast majority of self-help books are Que and IDG Books. Most users use only a fraction of the power their tools provide.

Commitment to Ongoing Professional Development

Learning to use technology effectively must be recognized as an ongoing responsibility. As the tools change, new possibilities emerge. As a result, we encourage readers to use the Laboratory–

Practicum Activities section at the end of this chapter to assess current skills and plan reasonable goals for moving to the next level of skill development and application. We look forward to participating in the evolving discussion about how technology enhances the productivity of special educators.

Summary

In this chapter we have advanced the concept of technology-enhanced professional productivity. We considered the activities and tasks commonly completed by special educators and used this information as a framework for examining the development of a technology toolbox. The productivity toolbox described in this chapter contains components for creating, communicating, and managing information, as well as specialized tools. Finally, we sought to underscore the importance of a series of professional development challenges that must be addressed as part of educators' commitment to continuing education.

Resources

Organizations

Council for Exceptional Children
1920 Association Avenue
Reston, VA 20191-1589
Voice: 703/620-3660 or 800/845-6232
Web: http://www.CEC.SPED.Org

International Society for Technology in Education
408 Charnelton Street
Eugene, OR 97401
Voice: 800/336-5191
Web: http://www.ISTE.Org

National Council for Accreditation of Teacher Education
2010 Massachusetts Avenue, NW
Suite 500
Washington, DC 20036-1023
Voice: 202/466-7496
Fax: 202/296-6620
Web: http://www.NCATE.Org

Books

Closing the Gap. (1997). *The 1997 Closing the Gap resource guide.* Henderson, MN: Author.

Emerging Technology Consultants. (1997). *The 1997 multimedia and videodisc compendium for education and training.* St. Paul, MN: Author. Available: http://www.emergingtechnology.com

Neill, S. B., & Neill, G. W. (1997). *Only the best 1997. The annual guide to highest-rated educational software from preschool–grade 12.* Alexandria, VA: Association for Supervision and Curriculum Development.

Sandholtz, J. H., Ringstaff, C., & Dwyer, D. C. (1997). *Teaching with technology: Creating student-centered classrooms.* New York: Teachers College Press.

Compact Disk

Educational Products Information Exchange (EPIE) Institute. (1997). *The electronic school* [CD]. Hampton Bays, NY: Author. [Phone: 516/728-9100]

Laboratory–Practicum Activities

▶ 1. List three goals you will achieve in the next 3 months to enhance your understanding of using technology to enhance personal productivity. Use technology to develop your goals, to describe how you will achieve these goals, and to manage the achievement of the goals.

▶ 2. Interview a technology-using professional to determine the productivity tools he or she uses. Record your findings on a chart similar to Figure 7.2. Probe to identify specific productivity strategies and examples of how technology improves this professional's productivity.

▶ 3. Visit a computer store. Create a shopping list of products you would like to purchase to enhance your productivity.

▶ 4. Create a seating chart for your classroom. Compare your results with others in the class. What tools did people use? What was easy about completing this task?

What was hard? What might you do differently next time? How might the class create a series of templates for this project?

▶ 5. Complete the checklist in Table 7.8 to illustrate your competence in word processing. Attach three to six examples of your word processor work.

▶ 6. Demonstrate your ability to manipulate information between programs on your desktop. For example, copy and paste information from a Web page into your word processor, use a graphic program to create a logo, and integrate these elements into a one-page sign.

▶ 7. Explore the use of a commercial IEP program or examine the use of a word processor and database program for managing IEP information.

▶ 8. Complete the checklist in Table 7.9 to illustrate your competence in using electronic mail (e-mail).

▶ 9. Complete the checklist in Table 7.10 to illustrate your competence in using the Internet and World Wide Web.

▶ 10. Identify 10 sites on the World Wide Web you believe would be useful for future students in this course to explore. Print this information, create a bookmark collection, or author a Web page to provide a legacy for future students.

Where possible, share your Laboratory–Practicum products with your course instructor and peers. Also, produce an archival record of your work for students who will be taking this course in the future (e.g., hardcopies or electronic files).

References

Arends, R. I. (1991). *Learning to teach* (2nd ed.). New York: McGraw-Hill.

Barksdale, J. M. (1996, April). New teachers unplugged: Why schools of education are still sending you staff you'll have to train in technology. *Electronic Learning*, pp. 38–45.

Beaver, J. F. (1989). *How are successful elementary schools allocating their instructional computing time?* Paper presented at the Annual Meeting of the Eastern Educational Research Association, Savannah, GA.

Bitter, G. G., Camuse, R. A., & Durbin, V. L. (1984). *Using a microcomputer in the classroom.* Boston: Allyn & Bacon.

Carnine, D. (1992). Expanding the notion of teachers' rights: Access to tools that work. *Journal of Applied Behavior Analysis, 25,* 13–19.

Carp, S. (1999). Telecommunications—Its future in education. *T.H.E. Journal, 26*(7), 4.

Cuban, L. (1993). *How teachers taught: Constancy and change in American classrooms, 1890–1990* (2nd ed.). New York: Teachers College Press.

Cypher, T., & Willower, D. J. (1984). The work behavior of secondary school teachers. *Journal of Research and Development in Education, 18,* 17–24.

Dockterman, D. (1989). *Teaching in the one computer classroom.* New York: Harper and Row.

Harp, C., Satzinger, J., & Taylor, S. (1997, May). Many paths to learning software. *Training and Development,* pp. 81–84.

Individuals with Disabilities Education Act Reauthorization of 1997, 20 U.S.C. § 1400 *et seq.*

Jacobson, R. L. (1993, May 5). As instructional technology proliferates, skeptics seek hard evidence of its value. *The Chronicle for Higher Education,* pp. A27–A29.

Landcaster, F. W. (1978). *Toward paperless information systems.* New York: Academic Press.

McCarthy, R. (1993). A computer on every teacher's desk. *Electronic Learning, 12*(7), 10–13.

National Foundation for Improvement of Education. (1989). *Images of potential.* Washington, DC: National Education Association.

Office of Technology Assessment. (1995). *Power on! New tools for teaching and learning.* Washington, DC: U.S. Government Printing Office.

Robertson, G., Haines, L. P., Sanche, R., & Biffart, W. (1997). Positive change through computer networking. *Teaching Exceptional Children, 29*(6), 22–30.

Sandholtz, J. H., Ringstaff, C., & Dwyer, D. C. (1997). *Teaching with technology: Creating student-centered classrooms.* New York: Teachers College Press.

Schiffman, S. S. (1986). Productivity tools for the classroom. *The Computing Teacher, 13*(8), 27–31.

Swan, W. W., & Sirvis, B. (1992). The CEC common core of knowledge and skills essential for all beginning special education teachers. *Teaching Exceptional Children, 25*(1), 16–20.

Tally, B., & Grimaldi, C. (1995, May–June). Developmental training: Understanding the ways teachers learn. *Electronic Learning,* pp. 14–15.

Tangley, L. (1998, February 16). Whoops, there goes another CD-ROM. *U.S. News & World Report,* pp. 67–68.

Wang, M. (1985). An analysis of program design implications for teacher and student use of school time. In C. W. Fisher & D. C. Berliner (Eds.), *Perspectives on instructional time* (pp. 237–262). New York: Longman.

Williams, R. (1990). *The Mac is not a typewriter: A style manual for creating professional-level type on your Macintosh.* Eugene, OR: International Society of Technology in Education.

Williams, R. (1992). *The PC is not a typewriter: A style manual for creating professional-level type on your personal computer.* Eugene, OR: International Society of Technology in Education.

Willis, J. (1993). What conditions encourage technology use. *Computers in the Schools, 9*(4), 13–32.

Willis, W. (1998). Speech recognition: Instead of typing clicking, talk and command. *T.H.E. Journal, 25*(6), 18–22.

Chapter 8

ぷ ぷ ぷ

Integrating Technology
To Support Effective Instruction

J. Emmett Gardner
The University of Oklahoma, Norman

Dave L. Edyburn
University of Wisconsin–Milwaukee

Given the challenge of integrating technology into the curriculum in instructionally meaningful and effective ways, this chapter examines the issues involved in the use of technology to support effective instruction. The chapter is organized around answering four questions: How does technology enhance teaching and learning? What does technology integration look like? How do I integrate technology into the curriculum? Are there specific strategies that may make technology integration more effective?

In each section, we present descriptions, illustrations, models, principles, and strategies for implementing technology in ways that enable teachers to enhance learning opportunities for their students. It is important to note at the outset that, while service delivery models in special education have become more inclusive, effective instruction is impartial to disabilities and most settings. Good instructional strategies do not apply to students' labels; they function as options for solving the learning problems presented by *any* student in general and special education settings.

How Technology Enhances Teaching and Learning

Educators are often told that technology has considerable potential for enhancing teaching and learning. However, educators' individual and collective efforts to capture the potential of technology for students with disabilities are often mediated by varied educational philosophies and influenced by an emerging understanding of what it means to use technology effectively in education.

Two writers in the mid-1980s provided insight regarding the perceived value of using computers in education. In *The Second Self,* Turkle (1984) described her research using extensive interviews and observations of computer users across the United States. Turkle suggested that perceptions of computers function much like a Rorschach inkblot test; an individual's beliefs regarding the effectiveness of a computer represents *whatever the user chooses to project onto it.* In a historical review of technological innovations in education since 1920, Cuban (1986) concluded that promises associated with the introduction of

Computers enhance technological access for exceptional individuals. (Photograph by Carolyn F. Woods)

computers in classrooms would largely remain unfulfilled unless significant attention was placed on the *instructional interactions* within the classroom, and the role technology will assume in these interactions.

A significant challenge for educators interested in creating technology-enhanced learning environments is to articulate a personal response to the question, How does technology enhance teaching and learning? There is no simple answer to this question.

During the past two decades, various analogies have shaped the instructional use of computers in education. One often cited analogy is Taylor's (1980) description of the computer as a *tutor* (i.e., an object that teaches), *tool* (i.e., an object students use to learn with), and *tutee* (i.e., an object that students teach). It is interesting to note that this metaphor places primary importance on the computer with secondary distinctions on how it might be used by teachers and students.

Later, Bunderson and Inouye (1987) observed that the use of technology in the classroom may alter the roles of a classroom teacher. They described these roles as *information processor* (e.g., lecturer, media user), *coach* and *tutor* (e.g., deliverer of feedback, organizer and director of learning and practice), and *lab instructor* (e.g., operator and monitor of computer equipment). This type of metaphor was common during a period of intense interest in educational reform and illustrated the belief that technology would contribute to efforts to fundamentally restructure education.

Russell, Corwin, Mokros, and Kapisovsky (1989) described the teaching roles that special education teachers using computers should be prepared to occupy. These roles include the teacher as an *introducer* (e.g., getting students started on new software), *technical adviser* (e.g., getting students through the mechanics of particular programs), *arranger* (e.g., building collaboration and cooperation skills between students), *visitor* (e.g., visiting students at the computer to check their work), *silent partner* (e.g., fostering student independence at the computer by refraining from action), *booster* (e.g., helping students when they are frustrated at the computer), *mentor* (e.g., requiring students to reflect and evaluate their com-

puter performance), and *learner* (e.g., accepting of the fact that students may learn things about or at the computer that the teacher does not yet know, and thus the teacher–student roles become reversed). This model reflects the complexity involved in creating a technology-enhanced learning environment and the importance of focusing on the metacognitive development.

Our collective understanding of how technology enhances teaching and learning has been greatly influenced by the perspectives of Taylor (1980), Bunderson and Inouye (1987), and Russell et al. (1989). We have come to understand that technology enhancement in special education was not to be identified through software and hardware applications but in the ways technology tools were used by teachers to facilitate student learning. This perspective was further reinforced in Okolo, Bahr, and Rieth's (1993) review of the literature on applications of computer-based instruction (CBI) with students with mild disabilities published from 1982 to 1992. They concluded that CBI in special education was no longer focusing on drill and practice but rather on the use of technology to promote effective learning in ways that emphasized students' learning of higher order thinking skills. Among the recent recommendations made in the *Report to the President on the Use of Technology To Strengthen K–12 Education in the United States* (President's Committee of Advisors on Science and Technology, 1997) pertaining to the instructional use of technology in education, two recommendations have particular relevance to the themes of this chapter. First, schools must focus on teaching students to learn *with* technology and not *about* technology. Second, educators must deemphasize hardware and focus on content and pedagogy. Educators can no longer view technology as simply a novel delivery system for information, but must consider how to apply technology across the curriculum to encourage students to become problem solvers and use higher order thinking skills in meaningful ways.

Jonassen and Reeves (1996) proposed that the goal for using technology in classrooms should move away from activities that tend to merely reproduce knowledge (e.g., using programs, such as drill and practice, where students more or less respond to computer prompts) to more meaningful, creative tasks in which students use computers as "cognitive tools," and teachers use computers to create environments where students learn *with* technology rather than *from* technology. Indeed, teachers' construction of events that promote students' higher order thinking skills, authentic learning, and creative problem solving are all outcomes articulated by a number of scholars examining the effectiveness of technology and learning in special and general education (e.g., Cognition and Technology Group at Vanderbilt, 1990, 1993a, 1993b; Grambinger, 1996; Hannafin, Hannafin, Hooper, Rieber, & Kini, 1996; Male, 1997; Russell et al., 1989).

What constitutes a meaningful learning environment, one that stresses higher order thinking skills? How do teachers design meaningful technology-enhanced learning environments for learners with special needs? One answer can be found by examining Grambinger's (1996) elements of REALs (Rich Environments for Active Learning): constructivist ideas, authentic learning, student responsibility and initiative, cooperative learning, generative learning activities, and authentic assessment (see Table 8.1 for additional elaboration). According to Grambinger, the elements of REALs reflect a variety of characteristics that teachers should strive to include when designing technology-based learning environments.

Grambinger (1996) reported that it is important to understand what REALs are, and what they are not. REALs do not emphasize using technology to deliver information; rather they represent "methods and ideas that help *cause* [italics added] learning" (p. 668). REALs do not simply provide technology-based learning environments that tend to promote or simulate a small-scale learning environment; rather they represent learning environments that are

> much more comprehensive and holistic than individual computer applications . . . [and when creating REALs] teachers must involve their students, parents, administrators, and colleagues in planning and implementing strategies that encourage student responsibil-

ity, active knowledge construction, and generative learning activities on a large scale and in a variety of methods and forms. (p. 668)

In a REAL, the *process* by which a student arrives at an outcome is as or more important than the product.

According to the North Central Regional Education Lab (NCREL) (1996), technology enhancement in teaching and learning occurs when students and teachers use technology to demonstrate one or more indicators of engaged learning and high technology performance (see Tables 8.2 and 8.3). NCREL's position is that teachers should compare their current instructional practices with the indicators found in Tables 8.2 and 8.3. While going through the comparison process, the teacher self-assesses what activities he or she is currently performing (or assesses what colleagues are performing to examine technology's impact on an entire school environment) and reflects on methods and strategies that might lead to increased indicators of students' engaged learning or high performance when using technology. The NCREL Web site provides a variety of on-line and downloadable tools that help prompt educators when considering technology integration (http://www.ncrel.org/).

When microcomputers were first introduced into schools, considerable efforts were directed toward understanding how to program the computer and developing computer literacy skills. Over time, experience and research regarding effective use of microcomputers has shown that this initial emphasis was somewhat misfocused. Indeed, the following quote by Clark (1983) is still relevant for focusing attention on the influence that educational technology has brought about on teaching and learning: "The best current evidence is that media are mere vehicles that deliver instruction but do not influence student achievement any more than the truck that delivers our groceries causes changes in our nutrition" (p. 445). As we have discussed, the use of technology to enhance teaching and learning is more than a preoccupation with hardware and software. Rather, it is the focused use of technology to achieve important instructional goals in learning

Table 8.1. Characteristics of Grambinger's (1996) Rich Environments for Active Learning (REAL)

Characteristic	Description/Perspective
Constructivist Ideas	Learning and instructional environments should include activities that allow a learner to generate or construct knowledge in a context that is meaningful to him or her. Student goals should emphasize developing meaningful skills that include problem solving, conducting research, analysis and synthesis to arrive at conclusions, and the generalization of knowledge and skills to other contexts.
Authentic Learning	Learning activities use contexts and tasks that draw upon realistic, age-appropriate uses of a learner's cognitive, physical, and social knowledge and skills.
Student Responsibility and Initiative	Learning is student centered and emphasizes the development of learning strategies and skills that promote self-initiation and lifelong learning. Students are intentional learners who are responsible for deciding goals and consciously working to regulate their subsequent learning toward meeting those goals. Specific skills to be developed include (a) questioning skills (students learn to ask teachers and peers higher order questions to help guide their knowledge construction and interpretation), (b) self-reflection (students learn to observe and interpret their actions, thoughts, and intentions), and (c) metacognition (students develop conscious control of their learning and their ability to make changes in learning strategies, such as planning and selecting strategies to learn, self-monitoring, analyzing and correcting errors).
Cooperative Learning	Peer groups of students achieve individual and group goals in ways that separate individuals could likely not achieve. Learning is often problem based, where the process of group problem solving, learning to display multiple roles, debate, cooperation and collaboration, and coteaching helps students gain or refine their knowledge base and insight regarding each others' individuality. Students' achieving of behavioral and social goals is as consequential as meeting academic goals.
Generative Learning Activities	Students are investigators, information gatherers, and problem solvers who learn by applying the information they have collected to generate new knowledge or alternative perspectives. Once generated, the knowledge is used in meaningful and authentic applications. Teachers serve as mediators of students' learning, helping students generate "fluid, flexible, usable knowledge" (p. 675).
Authentic Assessment	Learning should be evaluated based on how students organize knowledge and relate it to meaningful contexts. Assessment includes evaluating the mental process behind production of the product. Things to be evaluated include the students' ability to analyze, compare, and manipulate information; to perform authentic community-based and life-skill tasks; and to work with others.

Note. Adapted from "Rich Environments for Active Learning," by R. S. Grambinger, 1996, in *Handbook of Research for Educational Communications and Technology* (pp. 665–692), by D. H. Jonassen (Ed.), New York: Macmillan.

Table 8.2. North Central Regional Education Lab's Indicators of Engaged Learning

Variable	Indicator of Engaged Learning	Indicator Definition
Vision of Learning	Responsible for learning	Learner involved in setting goals, choosing tasks, developing assessments and standards for the tasks; has big picture of learning and next steps in mind
	Strategic	Learner actively develops repertoire of thinking and learning strategies
	Energized by learning	Learner is not dependent on rewards from others; has a passion for learning
	Collaborative	Learner develops new ideas and understanding in conversations and work with others
Tasks	Authentic	Pertains to real world, may be addressed to personal interest
	Challenging	Difficult enough to be interesting but not totally frustrating, usually sustained
	Multidisciplinary	Involves integrating disciplines to solve problems and address issues
Assessment	Performance-based	Involving a performance or demonstration, usually for a real audience and useful purpose
	Generative	Assessments having meaning for learner; maybe produce information, product, service
	Seamless and ongoing	Assessment is part of instruction and vice versa; students learn during assessment
	Equitable	Assessment is culture fair
Instructional Model	Interactive	Teacher or technology program responsive to student needs, requests (e.g., menu driven)
	Generative	Instruction oriented to constructing meaning; providing meaningful activities and experiences
Learning Context	Collaborative	Instruction conceptualizes students as part of learning community; activities are collaborative
	Knowledge-building	Learning experiences set up to bring multiple perspectives to solve problems such that each perspective contributes to shared understanding for all; goes beyond brainstorming
	Empathetic	Learning environment and experiences set up for valuing diversity, multiple perspectives, strengths
Grouping	Heterogeneous	Small groups with persons from different ability levels and backgrounds
	Equitable	Small groups organized so that over time all students have challenging learning tasks and experiences
	Flexible	Different groups organized for different instructional purposes so each person is a member of different groups; works with different people

(continues)

Table 8.2. *(continued)*

Variable	Indicator of Engaged Learning	Indicator Definition
Teacher Roles	Facilitator	Engages in negotiation, stimulates and monitors discussion and project work but does not control
	Guide	Helps students to construct their own meaning by modeling, mediating, explaining when needed, redirecting focus, providing options
	Colearner/ coinvestigator	Teacher considers self as learner; willing to take risks to explore areas outside his or her expertise; collaborates with other teachers and practicing professionals
Student Roles	Explorer	Students have opportunities to explore new ideas and tools; push the envelope in ideas and research
	Cognitive Apprentice	Learning is situated in relationship with mentor who coaches students to develop ideas and skills that simulate the role of practicing professionals (i.e., engage in real research)
	Teacher	Students encouraged to teach others in formal and informal contexts
	Producer	Students develop products of real use to themselves and others

Note. From "Designing Learning and Technology for Educational Reform," by B. Jones, G. Valdez, J. Norakowski, and C. Rasmusson, 1994, North Central Regional Education Lab. Available: http://www.ncrel.org/ncrel/sdrs/engaged.htm

environments where technology is essential rather than supplemental. Given these philosophical frameworks, we turn attention to a more practical matter: What does technology integration look like?

What Technology Integration Looks Like

Many discussions regarding the effective use of technology to enhance teaching and learning focus on the concept of integration. We believe that the term *technology integration* is often carelessly used to describe any situation in which students use computers. We must recognize a more precise meaning of the term technology integration. First, technology is much more than computers. Second, integration involves the purposeful selection and implementation of technology tools for the single purpose of enhancing instruction (Edyburn, 1997b). Unfortunately, educators often confuse the goals and activities of teaching *about* technology with integration efforts that result in teaching *with* technology.

A considerable body of literature documents the importance of integrating technology into elementary and secondary curricula (Hanley, Appel, & Harris, 1988; Morocco & Zorfass, 1988; O'Connor & Brie, 1994; Panyan, Hummel, & Jackson, 1988; Sheingold & Hadley, 1990), as well as into postsecondary education (Bitter & Yohe, 1989; Denk, Martin, & Sarangarm, 1993–1994; Hazari, 1991; Laurillard, 1993; U.S. Congress, Office of Technology Assessment, 1995; M. A. White & Righi, 1991). Sheingold (1991) aptly summarized the recurrent theme in the literature: "Technology is not likely to have a qualitative impact on education unless it is deeply integrated into the purposes and activities of the classroom" (p. 20). Surprisingly, there appears to be considerable consensus in the educational community that the effective use of technology involves integrating it into the curriculum and that this is a worthwhile goal.

Many discussions involving technology use the term *technology* as a synonym for *microcomputers*. Unfortunately, this unexamined assumption fails to recognize the fact that educators have access to an array of instructional tools that are

Table 8.3. North Central Regional Education Lab's Indicators of High Technology Performance

Variable	Indicator of High Technology Performance	Indicator Definition
Access	Connective	Schools are connected to Internet and other resources
	Ubiquitous	Technology resources and equipment are pervasive and conveniently located for individual (as opposed to centralized) use
	Interconnective	Students and teachers interact by communicating and collaborating in diverse ways
	Designed for equitable use	All students have access to rich, challenging learning opportunities and interactive, generative instruction
Operability	Interoperable	Capable of exchanging data easily among diverse formats and technologies
	Open architecture	Allows users to access third-party hardware and software
	Transparent	Users are not—and do not need to be—aware of how the hardware and software operates
Organization	Distributed	Technology and system resources are not centralized, but exist across any number of people, environments, and situations
	Designed for user contributions	Users can provide input or resources to the technology and system on demand
	Designed for collaborative projects	Technology is designed to facilitate communication among users with diverse systems and equipment
Engagability	Access to challenging tasks	Technology offers or allows access to tasks, data, and learning opportunities that stimulate thought and inquiry
	Enables learning by doing	Technology offers access to simulations, goal-based learning, and real-world problems
	Provides guided participation	Technology responds intelligently to user and is able to diagnose and prescribe new learning
Ease of Use	Effective helps	Technology provides help indices that are more than glossaries; may provide procedures for tasks and routines
	User friendliness/ user control	Technology facilitates user and is free from overly complex procedures; user can easily access data and tools on demand
	Fast	Technology has a fast processing speed and is not "down" for long periods of time
	Available training and support	Training is readily and conveniently available, as is ongoing support
	Provides just enough information just in time	Technology allows for random access, multiple points of entry, and different levels and types of information

(continues)

Table 8.3. (*continued*)

Variable	Indicator of High Technology Performance	Indicator Definition
Functionality	Diverse tools	Technology enables access to full diversity of generic and context-specific tools basic to learning and working in the 21st century
	Media use	Technology provides opportunities to use media technologies
	Promotes programming and authoring	Technology provides tools (e.g., "wizards") that are used to make other tools
	Supports project design skills	Technology facilitates the development of skills related to project design and implementation

Note. From "Designing Learning and Technology for Educational Reform," by B. Jones, G. Valdez, J. Norakowski, and C. Rasmusson, 1994, North Central Regional Education Lab. Available: http://www.ncrel.org/ncrel/sdrs/engaged.htm

much larger than computers. As a result, it is important to consider the many forms of instructional technology commonly found in schools. A classification system to assist educators in selecting appropriate technology tools is presented in Table 8.4. Despite the difficult economic times in many communities in the recent past, the financial investment in technology by school districts has been substantial.

The expanded definition of the term technology and the increased availability of technology tools generate important practical implications for equipping special and general educators with instructional toolboxes. For example, students who experience considerable failure in developing their writing skills represent an instructional challenge that involves creating a new learning environment to enable the students to develop and refine their writing skills. The traditional toolbox teachers have used to deal with these instructional problems includes tools such as textbooks, reference books, paper, and pencil. In contrast, a technology toolbox offers such extended possibilities as hand-held spelling checkers, predictive word processors, talking word processors, electronic thesaurus, electronic prewriting software, concept mapping software, graphic writing environments, telecommunications, desktop publishing, and video production tools. New tools provide new opportunities. Indeed, the im-

portance of reconceptualizing the teacher's toolbox is highlighted in a comment by educational researcher Linda Darling-Hammond: "in many places we still are preparing teachers for schools of the past rather than for schools of the future" (cited in Nicklin, 1994, p. A42).

Despite the clearly stated commitment to technology integration and recognition of the common barriers, the literature generally overlooks an essential component of the integration process, namely, what technology integration looks like or how it is achieved. Without models, principles, and strategies, the challenge of integrating technology into the curriculum can be an over-

Technology tools can be used to create new learning environments for exceptional individuals. (Photograph by Carolyn F. Woods)

Table 8.4. A Classification System To Select Appropriate Technology Tools

Portable Electronic Tools
  calculators
  spelling checkers
  personal organizers (e.g., Digital Diary, Newton, Wizard)
  instructional learning devices (e.g., Speak-N-Spell)

Microcomputers
  stand-alone computers
  workstations connected to a local area network
  integrated learning systems

Presentation Systems
  overhead projectors
  LCD panels
  videocassette recorders
  videodisc players
  tape recorders
  televisions

Distance Learning Systems
  instructional programming delivered via cable
  instructional programming delivered via satellite
  two-way interactive video teleconferencing

Video Production Tools
  camcorders
  video editing facilities

Communication Systems
  telephones
  message systems (e.g., Homework Hotlines)
  modems
  facsimile machines

Information Retrieval Systems
  electronic card catalogs
  CD-ROM or DVD-ROM based reference products (e.g., electronic encyclopedias)

whelming task with unpredictable results. For example, special educators are confronted with no shortage of educational software to use with their microcomputers; however, simply using math software for students who are below grade level in math skills does not constitute technology integration. There has to be more forethought.

The goal of integrating technology into the curriculum is to link software, media, and technology tools with specific instructional objectives in ways that enhance teaching and learning. This focus is referred to as the principle of *curriculum correspondence* (Edyburn, 1989; Gardner & Edyburn, 1993) and represents the importance of aligning instructional software with instructional objectives. Curriculum correspondence stipulates that a direct connection must exist between what a student does at the computer and the work he or she does at his or her desk. In other words, software must be matched to curriculum rather than curriculum to software. Application of the principle of curriculum correspondence results in classroom applications of the computer that are essential, important, meaningful, and substantially linked to curriculum and each student's Individualized Education Plan (IEP). The content area(s) and ability level reflected in classroom and deskwork materials must correlate directly with the content and educational challenge attributed to the software being used. Thus, part of the teacher's planning tasks requires the identification of specific objectives that have the potential to be enhanced through the use of microcomputers. One obvious method is to review students' IEPs. Another is to identify instructional objectives that appear to be consistently problematic or troublesome for particular students. These objectives, referred to as *targets of difficulty* (Pogrow, 1988), come to mind quickly for experienced teachers because students seem to have difficulty with these objectives day in and day out. Because these objectives appear to be consistently hard for students to master and perhaps difficult to teach using traditional classroom procedures, they make suitable targets for teachers to consider when planning for the use of technology to enhance teaching and learning (Edyburn, 1989).

Recent work by Fogarty (1991) illustrated that the term *integration* suggests at least 10 meaningful approaches for organizing curricula. Thus, it seems unwise and unproductive to believe that the development of a single definition will significantly advance a common vision of technology integration (Edyburn, 1997a). As a result, we propose two tactics for building consensus around a common vision about what it means to integrate technology into the curriculum: establishing what technology integration is not and fostering a common vision.

Establishing What Technology Integration Is Not

First, we wonder if educators can agree on what technology integration is not. Consider the scenario of walking into a classroom where the teacher is working with a group of students while one child is working at the computer in the back of the classroom. After a period of time, another child goes to the computer in an orderly exchange of seats and a new software program is initiated. Is this integration? It is hard to tell from the doorway. However, upon closer inspection we find that the students are using public domain software or selecting the educational game of their choice from a classroom collection. The management system that the teacher has established ensures that every student is allotted 15 minutes at the computer. In conversation with the teacher, we find that he has had little training in using the computer instructionally, receives little support or assistance in his efforts to implement technology-based instruction, receives no additional planning time or inservice opportunities, and has little or no budget for software or CDs for his classroom. Because he did not ask for a computer in his classroom but was given one as a result of PTO fund-raising, he feels compelled to keep it on as much as possible since the students enjoy it so much. In this situation, has technology been integrated? Not in our view. In that there are no apparent instructional goals, we prefer to call this *technology accommodation* rather than technology integration. When educators accommodate the computer in the learning environment, their intentions are simply to make it available to students, and as long as it is on, they will accomplish their ill-defined goals. When the instructional goals are focused on the technology, educators have supplemented the curriculum with new objectives to enhance instruction.

Fostering a Common Vision

Our second tactic for fostering a common vision about what it means to integrate technology into the curriculum focuses on examples individuals have provided as evidence of their integration efforts. We seek to foster discussion about the elements of several cases in an attempt to refine our personal and collective thinking about technology integration and contribute to consensus building within a group.

To date, the benefits of technology in special education have been limited largely to individual classrooms. Individual teachers and therapists with a vision of the possibilities that technology affords students with special needs have worked tirelessly to explore how to make technology work effectively for their students. Yet, the benefits of technology tend to be isolated. Seldom is technology implemented in a programmatic or systematic manner across a school system or special education program. In practical terms, educators have yet to move beyond individual visions to shared visions.

The ability to foster a common vision about technology integration is limited by the fact that few forums exist for developing consensus. Without the opportunity to make visions explicit, parents, teachers, and administrators are carrying around their own notions of what integration might look like. Although many teachers and administrators claim to have integrated technology into the curriculum, many individuals wonder, "Just because I *say* I have integrated technology into the curriculum, have I?"

How does one know when technology is being used effectively to enhance instruction for students with special education needs? What criteria must be considered to substantiate a claim that technology has been integrated into the curriculum? Is it possible to achieve consensus about what technology integration is and is not? Read the claims of technology integration presented in Box 8.1. In your opinion, which examples illustrate the integration of technology into the curriculum?

In our work with teachers, administrators, and teacher educators, these cases have caused spirited

---

Box 8.1. Self-Assessment: Visions of Integration

Invite a group of technology leaders (i.e., teachers, parents, members of the technology planning committee, administrators) to a discussion group. Present each of the following claims one at a time. Each speaker claims that technology has been integrated into the curriculum. Ask the group to discuss the following questions: Has the technology been integrated into the curriculum? Why? Why not? What additional information would you like to have before you make a decision? What principles support your position and help us understand the continuum of efforts to integrate technology into the curriculum?

• Claim 1: The headline in the local paper says, "Rockville Schools to spend five million dollars to wire school buildings for Internet access."

• Claim 2: An announcement in the school newsletter reports, "The Williamson School Technology Committee has been working with the district technology coordinator to establish a comprehensive plan that defines the technology needs of Williamson's students and staff. We have completed our mission statement and are currently considering the many questions involved in such areas as grant writing, developing partnerships with the computer-literate community, outlining maintenance guidelines, working on building infrastructure, integrating technology into the curriculum, and providing computers and other types of technology to students and staff." The committee chair says, "These efforts prove we have a commitment to integrating technology into the curriculum and providing the best possible educational experience for our children."

• Claim 3: "Sure, I've integrated technology into my class. I won't accept any assignment that is not word processed."

• Claim 4: "All students in my class use Alpha-Smart to draft their papers before moving onto the word processor to revise and print their work. Sometimes, students will even check out AlphaSmart to finish a writing project at home."

• Claim 5: "I use technology in my class all the time. I've placed all my lecture notes in Power-Point. Since I teach the same class five times a day, I can be sure that the students in my last hour class are getting the same information that those in my first hour receive."

• Claim 6: "We adopted a new science textbook this year. Each chapter features a technology activity that I have students complete."

• Claim 7: "Because some students in my classes have difficulty reading the social studies textbook, I scanned the chapter summaries into the computer and placed the files into a talking word processor. During study periods, students go to the computer, open the appropriate file, put on the earphones, and listen as the computer reads the summary."

• Claim 8: "I have submitted a request to purchase the following geography programs: 3-D Atas, Street Atlas USA, and Where in the USA is Carmen San Diego? which I plan to use as part of two different units later this year."

• Claim 9: While reviewing the weekly lesson plans from teachers in her building, a principal sees that Ms. Anderson plans to introduce a unit next week in which students will use the Internet to participate in a virtual field trip, conduct research with several electronic reference products in the library, and prepare a report using a word processor or presentation software. The principal comments, "This is exactly how I wished all teachers would integrate technology into the curriculum."

---

debate about whether the example is indeed integration, and how to know if it is or is not. Just because one person claims to have integrated technology, has he or she? Given the current status of the field—that is, no agreed-upon definition of the term *integration*, few models of technology integration in special education teacher education, and the necessity of developing personal plans for technology integration—it seems prudent that educators begin to define some principles for evaluating the various efforts to integrate technology into the curriculum. Toward this end, we have found it useful to ask questions and probe for evidence in four areas:

- *Teacher Thinking and Planning*—Is the teacher able to articulate a meaningful purpose for using technology and describe why the technology tools are essential for achieving the intended learning outcomes?

- *Emphasis of Objectives and Learning Outcomes*— Is the emphasis of the instructional objectives on instruction and learning, or on the technology? In other words, are the objectives phrased in computer literacy terms (i.e., students will copy information from one document and paste it into a second document; students will learn how to use a database; students will learn to use HyperStudio), or are they phrased in instructional terms (i.e., students will brainstorm ideas for their papers using the software program Inspiration; students will locate information for their report using three primary and three secondary sources)? Is the use of technology transparent in the pursuit of curricular goals but at the same time an important catalyst?

- *Student Engagement*—Are students using technology in ways that are essential, important, meaningful, and substantially linked to curriculum (i.e., characteristics associated with Grambinger's [1996] Rich Environments for Active Learning or NCREL's [1996] indicators of engaged learning)?

- *Technology Definition and Indicators*—In designing the integration plan, is the definition of technology broad (i.e., hand-held devices, presentation systems, video production tools, information retrieval tools, communication systems, distance learning, etc.) or narrow (i.e., computers)? Is the definition of technology robust enough to include indicators of high-technology performance (e.g., NCREL, 1996)?

Readers are encouraged to present the claims found in Box 8.1 to a group of school-based technology leaders and advocates for debate and discussion. The challenge for each group is to see if they can reach some level of consensus about what technology integration is and is not and explicitly define some principles that support their decisions. As a common vision of technology integration begins to take form, attention can be turned to the task of identifying a process that will direct educators' efforts to capture the potential of technology while seeking to integrate it into the curriculum.

Integrating Technology into the Curriculum

Despite many efforts and the perceived importance of technology in teacher education, technology has not yet become a central component in the teacher preparation experience in many colleges of education (U.S. Congress, Office of Technology Assessment, 1995). In the field of special education, there has been little discussion among teacher educators to foster a vision of (a) why technology should be integrated into the teacher preparation program and (b) how it could be utilized to enhance teaching and learning.

Although technology can be a valuable resource for improving teaching education, the process of technology integration is not easily or quickly accomplished in either K–12 or postsecondary education. The difficulties that one will encounter are well documented: lack of teacher time, access or hardware, software, and support; limited leadership and lack of a common vision or rationale for technology use; limited training and support; impact of current assessment practices on defining what teachers must teach; and the fact that what students learn with technology may not be readily measured on standardized tests (U.S. Congress, Office of Technology Assessment, 1995). Willis (1993) added a number of other interesting dimensions of the problems teacher educators confront: curricular integration is a complex, difficult-to-learn process; many educators feel isolated and alone; time to experiment, explore, and study innovations is essential but rare in schools; top–down projects tend to fail over time; resentment and resistance destroy projects; ownership is critical to success; bottom–up projects tend to fail over time; administrative support is critical; nonexistent, inadequate, or inconsistent support is a major reason for failure; and theories of change are useful planning guides for change. Finally, experienced technology-using teachers conclude, at least initially, that most uses of computers make teaching more challenging (U.S. Congress, Office of Technology Assessment, 1988).

A Model of the Technology Integration Process

Most integration models found in the literature are based on system change and top–down involvement. As a result, little information and guidance are available for individuals willing and interested in initiating technology integration. The model of the integration process presented in Table 8.5 was developed by Edyburn (1989) to (a) describe the various tasks involved in integrating software into the curriculum, (b) provide a planning guide for individuals interested in technology integration, (c) serve as a tool for discussing the process among the major stakeholders, and (d) assist in the identification of methods and resources for facilitating the process.

The process outlined in Table 8.5 describes the major tasks involved in selecting, acquiring, implementing, and integrating instructional technologies into the curriculum. The process appears generic in the sense that the process is the same regardless of ability level, subject matter, or type of technology. The process is divided into four phases, each comprised of three to four tasks that must be completed in working through the activities of a given phase. The model is described briefly here.

Selection

Phase 1, Selection, focuses on planning for the use of technology, media, and materials to enhance teaching and learning. These tasks can be completed cooperatively with other colleagues in the context of program planning, or individually. Upon completion of Phase 1, educators will have a comprehensive, prioritized listing of products that support the teaching and learning of a specific instructional objective.

Planning involves identification of instructional objectives and goals for using technology. The concepts of "curriculum correspondence" and "targets of difficulty" provide a way to think about where to start: What goals and objectives are in the student's IEP, and what skills have been consistently difficult for the student to learn? There is no need to know whether software or hardware products are available to teach these topics, because the intent is simply to create a list of goals and objectives and prioritize them regarding students' instructional needs. What is important about this step is the recognition that the learning needs of individual students drive the selection process, rather than the availability of software or hardware. Figure 8.1 provides an example of two planning forms, one designed to address multiple curriculum areas and the other designed to focus on a single curriculum area with multiple goals and objectives in mind.

Locating involves the search for appropriate technologies, media, and materials to support the specified objective. An exhaustive multifaceted search is done to identify multiple products that purportedly could be used to enhance instruction for the objective. The educator constructs a comprehensive list to avoid having to repeat the

Table 8.5. Edyburn's (1989) Model of the Technology Integration Process

Phase 1: Selection	Phase 2: Acquisition	Phase 3: Implementation	Phase 4: Integration
Planning	Previewing	Organizing	Linking
Locating	Evaluating	Teacher Training	Managing
Reviewing	Purchasing	Student Training	Assessing
Deciding			Extending

Software Integration Planning Form

Teacher's Name _____   Date _____

Number	Curriculum Area	Major Objectives	Program Name (Publisher)
1			
2			
3			
4			
5			
6			
7			
8			
9			
10			

Student Planning Form

Curriculum Area	Goals	Hardware Requirements	Software in Existing Collection	Potential Software To Review
	1.			
	2.			
	3.			

Figure 8.1. Sample software integration planning forms.

Box 8.2. Seven Search Strategies for Locating Technology, Media, and Materials

The following are some common approaches for searching for instructional technology, media, and materials.

Strategy 1. Review an existing technology collection. Examine the technology resources of your local school. Often, school districts have media resource centers or computer labs in designated schools or locations. Examine resource collections in your local public library.

Strategy 2. Seek recommendations from technology coordinators or other knowledgeable "technology gurus." Recommendations from knowledgeable individuals will assist you tremendously in locating useful, interesting, new, and effective materials.

Strategy 3. Ask other teachers for their suggestions about "what works." Recommendations from others about what they have tried, what they have discarded, and what they have continued to use can provide invaluable information.

Strategy 4. Go browsing. Browse catalogs and other print resources (e.g., software guides, resource books). (See Resources section later in this chapter.)

Strategy 5. Review electronic resources. Many CDs and software databases are available to allow you to search for software for a specific objective. If you have access to a CD player, consider ordering the K–12 Preview CD-ROM from Educational Resources (800/624-2926; it works on both Windows and Macintosh platforms; preview over 100 top-selling educational titles). Also, consider using Netscape to conduct a search of the Internet for information on commercial software.

Strategy 6. Consult educational technology magazines. A number of educational technology journals and magazines review new products and provide comparisons of similar products. Some common periodicals are listed in the Resources section at the end of the chapter.

Strategy 7. Go shopping. This approach is sometimes problematic if you are perceived as just browsing and not a serious customer. However, several national chains provide extensive software collections: Best Buy, COMPUSA (800/COMP USA), Computer City, (800/THECITY), and Egg-Head Software (818/881-7870).

---

search after beginning to evaluate a few products. Strategies and resources often used for locating include those described in Box 8.2.

Reviewing involves assigning a ranking to the possible products listed in the locating task. This is accomplished by seeking out and examining various reviews and consulting other evaluative tools to determine what products most likely are useful. Strategies often used for reviewing include locating software or hardware reviews in educational computing magazines, searching the World Wide Web for on-line reviews, and seeking advice from colleagues or participants in an on-line discussion group.

The task of *deciding* involves determining what to do with the list of products that has been assembled. Given the limits of time and effort to

devote to the process, the educator must decide how many products to examine (e.g., all the products, the top five, only the top one).

Acquisition

The tasks involved in Phase 2, Acquisition, focus on acquiring and personally reviewing products for the purpose of assessing whether a program will meet the needs and expectations of the teacher and students (also see Chapters 2 and 6). Successful evaluation results in a decision to purchase a product. At the end of this phase, the educator will own a product that can be used to enhance teaching and learning.

Previewing involves the process of personally reviewing a specific product, prior to purchasing, to determine whether it meets the students' or the educator's needs. It makes no sense to order software or hardware sight unseen. Often this step requires contacting a vendor to arrange for a free preview copy to be used for 30 days, or downloading a demo copy from the Web. Previewing may also entail traveling to another school site, university computer lab, or large computer or software store that serves as a preview center.

The task of *evaluating* involves assessing whether a program will meet the needs and expectations of the teacher and students. A variety of perspectives and issues must be considered regarding the concepts of software evaluation (e.g., Gardner, Taber-Brown, & Wissick, 1992; Hoffman & Lyons, 1997; J. M. Johnson, 1996; McDougall & Squires, 1995; Reiser & Kegelmann, 1994). Traditionally, educators have been taught to use evaluation forms to determine whether a software program is worth buying and keeping. Although such forms may be useful for sensitizing teachers to perspectives and issues, in our opinion, forms have an overrated impact on the selection of effective media. We suggest that educators put aside forms, compare three products, use them with students, consider how they would be used instructionally, and then decide to either look at additional products or purchase the favored one. Evaluation is a subjective process and an evaluation form does not make it any less so.

The cycle of previewing and evaluating may continue down an extensive list generated in the locating task. Only after the evaluation results in a decision to purchase a product does the integration process move to the next task.

Purchasing involves the administrative details involved with acquiring sufficient copies of a given product. Educators may or may not be involved in the purchasing process.

Implementation

Phase 3, implementation, advances educators' attention from decisions regarding selecting and acquiring software and hardware to examining factors involved in making the technology work. At the end of this phase, a new product will have been assimilated into the system and teachers and students will have been trained to use it.

The acquisition of new technology, media, and materials often creates a challenge for teachers to organize and manage their educational materials effectively. The task of *organizing* recognizes that there are managerial components associated with maintaining one's software and hardware inventory. Decisions include whether to place software on individual machines or on a network, and what procedures should be followed when students need to access software or related items (e.g., the single copy of software documentation).

Another important factor to consider is the degree and manner in which a new software or hardware product will influence the circumstances surrounding students' need to access certain software programs or personal files located in shared computer files or directories. Whether they are considering the principle of confidentiality as characterized by the Individuals with Disabilities Education Act of 1990 or the commonsense strategy of keeping each student's work separate for the purposes of maintaining privacy and organization, teachers need to consider what organizational strategies will best coordinate this process (see Box 8.3).

The task of *teacher training* requires that teachers attain the training necessary to fully use the products they plan to integrate. Teachers and classroom aides need to acquire the skills and knowledge to operate a program or hardware product, conduct basic troubleshooting, and be aware of methods and ideas for using the product in the classroom. Because the integration model presented in this chapter focuses on the individual teacher's seeking to meet each student's specific instructional and learning needs, the means by which teacher training is typically realized is via a "teach yourself" process.

Software that is easy to use often means that reading the manual is not necessary to begin using a program. In fact, there seems to be an unwritten law: "The less I have to use the instructional manual, the more I like the program." Self-teaching works well some of the time, but can be frustrating with a complex software program. In such cases, teachers can seek workshops on how

---

Box 8.3. Confidentiality and Computer Records

The Individuals with Disabilities Education Act of 1990 requires that teachers must employ appropriate methods to ensure confidentiality of records. Therefore, it is important to treat any form of computerized information containing confidential student information as one would a written document. Disks should be stored in a locked desk drawer or file cabinet. Information stored on a hard disk may need either to be encrypted or to employ a password protection system or scheme to control access. Also, computerized records directly associated with individual students must be considered part of their formal education record, and are subject to parental inspection (Jacob & Brantley, 1987). Additional discussion regarding ethical and legal considerations for microcomputer use in special education can be found in Jacob and Brantley's (1987) chapter.

---

to use the program or consult colleagues and friends who recommended a program. Sometimes the experience shared in a simple demonstration will save hours of frustration. Generally, an educator should not begin to integrate a program until he or she can sufficiently answer the following questions:

1. What are the major objectives of the program?

2. Have I mastered the mechanics of using the program?

3. What prerequisite skills and knowledge are required for my students to use the program?

4. Will special instructional strategies be required for my students to successfully use the program?

5. What basic troubleshooting skills will I need?

Student training recognizes the need for students to be introduced and trained on how to use a program or hardware. The goal is for students to be able to find and operate the programs and hardware easily enough that their time spent using these product(s) is focused primarily on learning, producing, and being successful, rather than on troubleshooting or being frustrated by not knowing what to do next. Key factors include teaching students access skills, basic navigation and mechanical use, and the purpose behind why they are using a particular technological application (i.e., what learning outcomes they are being asked to demonstrate or produce).

Some effective strategies can optimize training for students. Creating quick start-up sheets or guides of strategies and summaries of key commands will aid the process of training and subsequent use (see Box 8.4). It is probably useful to place related reference materials (e.g., atlas, fact books, software documentation) within reach of the computer, and to consider what additional cognitive adaptations (e.g., note paper, progress sheets, procedures for printing) will enhance a student's ability to independently and successfully operate a program. Considering all of these factors ensures that students are prepared to interact with the product when it is subsequently introduced in the curriculum.

Integration

The tasks involved in Phase 4, Integration, focus directly on using products in the classroom to enhance teaching and learning. Considerable time and effort has been expended to reach this phase. However, this is the phase where educators see the fruits of their labor. The following paragraphs summarize the tasks involved in this phase. Given their importance, we devote considerable attention to these issues in the final section of this chapter.

The task of *linking* involves examining the curriculum and determining when a product should be used, how the program can best be used to facilitate learning, and what activities would be useful both prior and subsequent to a product's use by students. Curriculum frameworks and calendars are important tools for this task.

The task of *managing* involves a variety of issues related to managing students' access to

---

Box 8.4. Tips for Designing Computer Activity Support Sheets

Exceptional students may encounter myriad difficulties associated with using particular software programs. Some students have problems reading software documentation because it is too elaborate or at a reading level too difficult for them to understand. Other students may shun using documentation or processing teachers' oral directions because of attention difficulties. Some students get stuck because they cannot remember key commands or tasks, and others forget important information revealed to them during the process of using software or make critical decisions or select certain attributes within a program that must be recalled at a future point in the program. Although some programs provide teachers with supplemental materials and activity sheets, the majority do not.

Creating supplemental activity or tip or cue sheets that support, abridge, summarize, or supplement relevant information found in software documentation often provides exceptional students greater opportunity to work independently on challenging computer tasks. A computer activity support sheet is analogous to a script or diagram of basic features and procedures needed to operate a program, and can also include strategies and tips to assist the process of interaction. Computer support sheets should be written at the lowest reading level and can contain one or more of the following types of information:

1. A summary of a program's main points, concepts, and objectives. This information can be provided either in print or by pictures of screens that highlight key commands or points.

2. Critical information regarding the content and design of the program based on functional categories (e.g., Starting for the first time, Tips, Commands, Definitions, Things to remember that you have *no* control over, or Important things to remember that only *you* can control).

3. A chronological "map" of the program that provides a flowchart of how the program works from beginning to end. Pictures of applicable computer screens may be reproduced.

4. Critical or frequently used key combinations (e.g., to get to the summary status screen from within the simulation do the following: Press Escape, Select option A, and press the 'S' key for summary information).

5. Sections or separate sheets to record relevant information, decisions, or data. While this strategy is rather self-explanatory, it may be helpful to consider the format in which you want the data entry fields to appear to the student. If you feel it would be easier for students to record information in a format that closely approximates the way it appears in the program, you could use a utility program to take a snapshot of the screen. You would edit its appearance in a drawing utility program so the student could write in his or her selection or possibly record a checkmark next to an attribute selected. For other students, it may simply be words and spaces on a worksheet to record information or an attribute selected.

6. Problem-solving strategies (e.g., "What to try, if . . ." or "If you can't get beyond X, ask yourself these questions . . .").

7. A reference list of supplemental books, articles, media, and materials that serves to clarify or provide further information about central or related concepts or factors presented in the software.

As with any self-made instructional material, the form and format of a clue sheet is up to the teacher. Information presented should be concrete and uncluttered. Avoid mixing information categories within an individual sheet, and be attentive to the number of clues and tips per sheet.

---

computers, monitoring and mediating students' computer performance, and considering ways to evaluate students' computer performance. Resolving the challenges involved in this task are critically important to the success of the technology integration process.

Assessing refers to the tasks involved in both formative and summative evaluation of the learning activities. Did students accomplish the intended learning objectives? If so, is the educator satisfied with the outcome or performance? If not, what steps should be taken to enable students to successfully achieve the established goals? Again, this is a critical task. In the final section, we consider multiple strategies for collecting and evaluating student performance data.

The final task, *extending,* recognizes that unless the educator can create additional instructional applications for a new tool, it will simply be returned to the shelf for storage until a future year. If the educator is able to identify methods of extending the value of the product, he or she resumes the technology integration process at the linking task in Phase 4 rather than starting the entire process over again.

In Summary

The technology integration process is recursive. That is, whereas Phase 1 results in a comprehensive list of products that address a specific instructional objective, Phases 2, 3, and 4 must be repeated with each new product. Thus, this process involves a significant commitment of time and effort. As a reasonable goal, we suggest that special educators initially work through this process until they have found 3 to 10 products that will support the varied needs of their students.

Strategies To Make Technology Integration More Effective

Blueprints for technology integration are hard to obtain. We operate under the belief that when the first three questions posed in the chapter's opening paragraph have been answered sufficiently, they serve as a solid foundation to provide special educators with a valuable perspective and sense of direction for integrating technology. By this point, educators should have already (a) acquired a vision for how to implement technology integration (Grambinger, 1996), (b) considered engaged student learning and high-technology performance (NCREL, 1996), (c) come to understand the integration process (e.g., Edyburn, 1989), and (d) developed a good sense of the types of teaching roles that can be promoted

within a technology-enhanced learning environment (Russell et al., 1989). What remains is to articulate a variety of strategies that may make technology integration more effective.

In contrast to the term *personal productivity,* which reflects the use of technology to enhance special educators' productivity with noninstructional tasks (Gardner & Edyburn, 1993), we offer the term *instructional productivity,* which describes those tasks that a teacher conducts that directly affect instruction. The use of technology for enhancing instructional productivity has generally received less attention than the area of personal productivity. In this section we examine specific tools and techniques to enhance the work of the teacher in his or her day-to-day planning, managing, and extending instruction for students with special learning or behavioral needs. The effective utilization of specific technology-related strategies for instructional productivity has significant potential for enabling a teacher to improve his or her teaching and facilitate student learning.

Planning and Linking to Instruction

Instructional planning is a daily task in which special education teachers engage as they assess, prepare, conduct, and evaluate lessons for their students. Special educators are well aware of the significant increase of time spent on these tasks due to their efforts to individualize instruction. The use of technology to assist in planning and linking to instruction can be described in several ways. Initially, identifying software to enhance instructional objectives (i.e., curriculum correspondence) is a key component to the process. This has already been discussed in a previous section. Once objectives have been established, outlining instructional strategies and developing computer lesson plans often serve as an effective blueprint for conducting instruction.

Instruction represents the deliberate organization of external events to support learning processes (Gagné, 1985; Gagné, Briggs, & Wager, 1992). In the applied context of the classroom, teachers deliberately arrange external events of instruction to support the internal processes of learning in their students (Gagné, 1985). Considering that the arrangement of particular events, their direct relevance, and the amount of information per event will vary with the circumstances of a particular lesson or lesson objective, Gagné (1985) described the process of instruction to generally include the following:

1. Gaining the learners' attention
2. Informing the learner of the objective
3. Stimulating recall of prior knowledge
4. Presenting the stimulus material
5. Providing learning guidance to the student
6. Eliciting student performance
7. Providing feedback to the student
8. Assessing student performance
9. Enhancing retention and transfer

When a teacher considers each of Gagné's events and organizes information, materials, and activities to fulfill the instructional purposes attributed to each event (see Gagné et al., 1992, pp. 185–204 for further discussion), instructional planning takes place. Typically, the most common form of instructional planning used by teachers is the lesson plan. Although Gagné's process of instruction echoes a universal format for considering instructional delivery, Jones and Jones (1986) incorporated instructional elements into a practical lesson plan format usable by teachers. By adapting the lesson design of Jones and Jones (1986, p. 252) and tying principles of instructional events (e.g., Gagné, 1985; Gagné et al., 1992) to teaching functions (e.g., Rosenshine & Stevens, 1986), we constructed an elaborated model of a lesson plan applicable to situations involving computer-based or computer-related instruction (see Table 8.6).

In practice the format of the computer-based lesson plan is selected by the individual teacher. Alternative versions of lesson plans applied to computer-based learning with exceptional students have been described by Male (1988), Male, Johnson, Johnson, and Anderson (1986), Malouf, Jamison, Kercher, and Carlucci (1991a, 1991b, 1991c), and Wood (1995).

The actual format of a computer lesson plan is less critical than appreciating how the format will facilitate deliberate consideration and guidance of how computer instruction is going to take place. For example, recognizing that some classroom teachers may not have time to develop elaborate computer lesson plans, Fields (1996) proposed that special educators should plan "computer-assisted activities" tailored to specific programs. Computer-assisted activities lack the embellishment of lesson plans but strive to maintain the connection between goals, software content, and an instructional assignment in a format easy for teachers to implement. Figure 8.2 provides an example of a completed computer lesson plan using the elaborated model (following Table 8.6 format) designed for students at Grade 4 and up, that emphasizes development of information management skills. Figure 8.3 provides an example of a computer-assisted activity based on Fields's (1996) model. Both examples use the same software program.

It is important to observe that the steps used in planning computer instruction also represent a model for conducting instruction. When a teacher actually performs Gagné's (1985) process of instruction, or the instructional events described in Table 8.6, instruction is deliberately and purposefully taking place. This is in sharp contrast to models that simply justify that exceptional learners should access computers because computer-based instruction is inherently beneficial (by virtue that it is motivating, fun, individualized, or designed to teach something).

Managing Instruction

The instructional models described in the previous section on planning computer instruction also represent models for conducting instruction. The distinction between using the models for planning versus practice is quite simple. As stated earlier, when a teacher considers instructional events separately, and organizes information, materials, and activities to fulfill instructional purposes attributed to each event, instructional planning takes place. When a teacher actively performs these instructional events, deliberate

Table 8.6. A Lesson Plan Design for Technology Applications with Exceptional Learners

Instructional Event	Function and Possible Applications
Anticipatory set	*Function:* To focus the student's attention and foster anticipation of the computer activity; to tie in previously learned information which can be used to facilitate new learning; to develop the student's readiness for instruction.
	Possible applications: Verbally, through statements or questions, relate individual or group interests to foster anticipation of the computer activity. Briefly describe interesting and salient features of the computer program to be used. Ask the learner to review what has been learned during previous computer sessions. Call attention to already designed written information (e.g., tip sheets or cue cards) that can serve to aid or refresh the student's memory. Review strategies that assist the student in accomplishing the computer tasks independently. Call attention to a bulletin board depicting the software program's theme(s) and objectives.
Informing the learner of the objective and its purpose	*Function:* To ensure that the learner is aware of what kind of computer achievement or performance (e.g., the conditions and criteria) is expected, why they will be doing the technology lesson, and what information or behavior indicates to the teacher and student that learning has occurred.
	Possible applications: Verbally state the objective of the computer activity (e.g., a short-term objective for one session, a long-term objective for an overall activity). Write the objectives down onto a checksheet and have the student take it to the computer. Post computer objectives on a bulletin board. Show the student a photograph or screen dump of how the computer screen appears when a particular objective is met. If an objective's conditions or criteria include a produced product (e.g., a story produced using a word processor, a computer-drawn picture), show the student an example of the finished product. *Note:* According to Gagné, Briggs, and Wager (1988), communicating an objective "takes little time, and may at least serve the purpose of preventing the student from getting entirely off the track." It "also appears to be an act consistent with the frankness and honesty of a good teacher" (pp. 183–184).
Instructional input	*Function:* Active instruction (a) facilitates students' perception of distinctive features of the computer, software, and supplemental materials that directly apply to the learning task and objective; (b) represents a deliberately planned organization of the instructional information, teaching procedures, and materials necessary to complete the computer assignment; (c) presents instructional information and procedures about the computer activity broken into small concrete steps, concentrating on one factor at a time; and (d) provides or demonstrates specific examples of how computer-related information will be presented to the student and what student behaviors represent correct performance.
	Possible applications: Task-analyze the computer activity. At each step, have specific feedback, events, or supplemental information prepared to present to the student. Prepare all materials to be discussed ahead of time. Maintain a library of sample printouts or screen pictures that help convey information to students.

(continues)

Table 8.6. (*continued*)

Instructional Event	Function and Possible Applications
Modeling	*Function:* Modeling can be a subset of instructional input. Delivering instruction is a fluid and dynamic process. Modeling is based on Bandura's (1977) theory of observational learning. When modeling is used in an instructional context, such as using a particular software program or performing a computer-related activity, teachers should demonstrate the appropriate computer behavior, and verbalize aloud the strategies and steps that are to be performed (Bell-Gredler, 1997). *Possible applications:* Physically demonstrate to the student how the software is to be used. During the demonstration, "think out loud," describing the thoughts, strategies, and actions that you are performing, relative to using the computer, software, and support materials. Make sure the student observes an example that demonstrates the criteria for correct computer performance.
Monitoring to check for understanding	*Function:* Frequent assessment of a student's computer performance is conducted to make sure that the student understands the content, skills, and procedures required to successfully perform the computer activities. Checking for understanding is essentially a precondition of guided practice. *Possible applications:* During instructional input and modeling, pause to ask students whether they are following and understanding the information being presented regarding computer activity. Ask students to verbally restate or physically perform key factors related to using the software.
Guided practice	*Function:* To monitor students' computer performance, provide feedback and guidance to facilitate the encoding of the information being learned and to ensure the accuracy of learning, especially during initial stages of the computer learning. *Possible applications:* Generate a variety of questions, hints, and prompts for each factor outlined via task analysis under the Instructional Input section. In the presence of the student, model appropriate computer behavior and strategies, and remain with the student to prompt him or her through the same sequence. Emphasize what information needs to be remembered, and what strategies are useful to facilitate learning. After modeling appropriate computer behavior and strategies, remain with the student to provide feedback and then guide him or her through computer performance using a sequence that gradually fades teacher assistance until the student assumes most, if not all, of the responsibility directing his or her computer learning.
Summary	*Function:* To achieve closure, students state or summarize, write about, or demonstrate on the computer what they have learned from the lesson (key factors/skills/concepts covered under the instructional input section). Each student or the teacher records the progress made toward the computer learning objective(s). *Possible applications:* Review and discuss the key factors or concepts addressed under the Instructional Input section.

(*continues*)

Table 8.6. *(continued)*

Instructional Event	Function and Possible Applications
Independent practice	*Function:* When students can perform particular computer tasks with little error and confusion, and are provided time to work on the computer with a minimum amount of teacher supervision, they acquire increased independence and responsibility in their learning activities. *Possible applications:* Reserve a block of time at the end of the lesson to allow for independent computer practice. Assign two or three problems or tasks, consistent with the lesson's objectives, that the student must complete using the software independently. Depending on the setting (classroom or computer lab) adapt Philips's (1983) scheduling strategies to allow the student access to time for independent practice during unstructured school time.

instruction takes place. Whereas planning instruction focuses on a broader model of instruction in a computer-based environment, the concept of managing instruction tends to focus on factors related to the incident-by-incident managerial issues and social interactions that take place between teachers and exceptional students once computer instruction has begun. Managing involves providing time for students to use a product and ensuring that all students are successfully achieving the objectives. For example, whereas access to a lab is useful, creative strategies must be used for managing the one-computer classroom.

Managing the Presentation of Computer-Based Information

The use of projection systems in conjunction with a computer enables a teacher to effectively use a computer in the classroom as a tool for presenting information to students. The LCD (liquid crystal display) panel connects to the computer and lays on top of an overhead projector to project the entire computer screen on the wall. This technology is quite effective in assisting a teacher with whole class instruction to demonstrate how to operate a new software program, to show the results of an interactive simulation, and in the writing classroom to illustrate both composition and revision strategies (Barbata, 1988; Moyer, 1988).

Certain products have been intentionally designed for whole class instruction. Tom Snyder Productions designs software to be used in the one-computer classroom. With the aid of a projection system, the Tom Snyder software seeks to have the teacher manage the classroom discussion while the computer displays and records the decisions of the class and presents new challenges to engage students in thinking and problem solving. Other examples where projection systems facilitate computer activities exist in conjunction with classroom applications of videodisc instruction. Systems Impact has created a series of videodiscs in math and science that ingeniously incorporate effective instruction into whole group instruction by presenting instructional lessons and mastery checkpoints. Based on the performance of the class, the teacher is directed to branch to the appropriate next chapter on the videodisc. The Learning Technology Center at Vanderbilt University created a videodisc-based series titled The Adventures of Jasper Woodbury (Cognition and Technology Group at Vanderbilt University, 1992) that seeks to improve students' problem-formulation and problem-posing skills through realistic and interesting real-life problem-solving adventures. In both cases students' abilities to observe a much larger picture enhance and help focus their observational skills and attention toward using meaningful knowledge (Cognition and Technology Group at Vanderbilt University, 1990, 1993b).

Lesson Plan

Curriculum Area: Information Skills   **Program Name: Sammy's Science House**

Objectives:

1. Students will identify and locate a variety of information sources.
2. Students will sort and use information in various formats.
3. Students will record and organize information to meet a stated need.

Computer Lesson Plan

Anticipatory Set

1. Read a book to the class about animals in springtime. Suggested titles: *At the Frog Pond* by Tilde Micelles or *What Happens in the Spring* by Kathleen Beer.
2. Discuss the different types of animals in the books and how they might be affected by the different seasons.
3. Brainstorm sources students can use to learn more about various animals and list ideas and sources on a chart. Make sure computers end up on the list!

Informing Learner of Objective and Plan

1. Show students the research form (*Research Planner,* published by The Education Center).
2. Explain to the students that they will be using Sammy's Science House as a source for locating information about various animals, and that they will select three to five animals, shown at Acorn Pond (one of the Sammy's Science House activities), to research.
3. Advise students that they should make notes on the back of their forms about changes that the animals experience in the different seasons of the year. Tell them that this information will be used to write a report about their favorite animal from those available at Acorn Pond.

Instructional Input and Modeling

1. Demonstrate Sammy's Science House using an LCD projection panel and overhead display. Make sure all students observe and understand how to access Acorn Pond and how to move through the seasons.
2. Depending on the number of computers available and the student grouping arrangements you wish to use (i.e., individuals, pairs, small groups of three), allow students to explore Acorn Pond and discover the changing seasons. Inform the students they are to observe and take notes about what changes they observe in the animals as the result of seasonal changes.
3. Have the students select three to five animals on which to focus their research.
4. After all students have selected their animals, call for their attention. Using the projection system (or large-screen monitor), demonstrate how to access the notebook pages in Acorn Pond that provide information on the animals.
5. Model how to fill out the Research Planner form using overhead transparencies. Think "out loud" about the changes noted in each season and how those changes affect a selected animal. Demonstrate note taking about seasonal animal changes, using the overhead.
6. Explain to the students that Sammy's Science House provides *some* of the information, but that *additional* information on animals can be found in many of the other sources previously brainstormed and listed on the chart (make sure you take the chart when you move from the classroom to the lab).

Figure 8.2. Sample computer lesson plan using Acorn Pond to enhance researching information about animals by students with mild or moderate disabilities, written by V. Wood, 1995, University of Oklahoma, Norman.

Monitoring To Check for Understanding

1. The teacher and assistant should rotate among the students to check information being recorded, answer questions, and provide assistance as needed. Pay particular attention to the students' ability to access and organize available information, and provide feedback when needed.

Prepare Research Forms

1. Have the students identify one animal and begin filling out their research forms with information obtained on the notebook pages in Acorn Pond.
2. Have the students independently access the Acorn Pond in Sammy's Science House, with monitoring and feedback by the teacher and assistant.
3. Allow time for students to complete their research forms to the maximum extent possible, for one animal, using only the information from Acorn Pond.
4. Check the research forms for accuracy and provide feedback.

Review

1. Summarize the key steps in gathering information from Sammy's Science House. Review the function and process associated with completing the research planner, both front and back.
2. Inform the students that they can use the same strategies and tasks to obtain and record information from other sources (e.g., library books) in addition to Sammy's Science House.

Independent Practice

1. Instruct the students to continue collecting information on two to five other animals. Now, in addition to gathering information from Acorn Pond, *they are also to go to the school media center* where they are to locate one or two additional resources to complete their research.
2. The students will organize their information into a three- to five-paragraph paper.
3. The students will present their information to the class and use the LCD projection system to demonstrate the changes shown for their animal in Acorn Pond.
4. The students will answer a variety of teacher-made riddles, or math problems, or both, by locating information in Acorn Pond.

Additional Activities

1. Students will produce an art project depicting their selected animals during each of the four seasons.
2. After all students have explored Acorn Pond and experienced each others' research presentations, the students will have an "Animal Academics Bowl" with two teams competing to see which team can correctly answer the most "who" questions asked by the Acorn Pond Owl.

Figure 8.2. (*continued*)

Managing Students' Computer Access

According to Berliner (1988), "time must be controlled after it is allocated or it is lost" (p. 13). Given the diversity of computer access conditions that can exist in a given school (e.g., one classroom computer, two or three available computers, no classroom computer but access to a lab), a number of management strategies for accessing computers should be considered. For example, Geisert and Futrell (1995) identified four computer-use paradigms that are likely to result in teachers' needing to consider different scheduling accommodations (see Table 8.7). According to this model, the amount of access provided to students is based on time or the type of outcome sought.

COMPUTER-ASSISTED ACTIVITY PLAN

STUDENT: Jonathan

GOAL(S):   Investigate and identify animal habitats and characteristics. Explore varying conditions and seasonal changes as applied to animals. Communicate answers.

SOFTWARE: Sammy's Science House

ACTIVITY: The Acorn Pond

ACTIVITY LEVELS: Use the discovery level to introduce this activity. Then move to the Question and Answer level. (*Note:* Click on the magic mirror to change levels.)

DELIVERY OPTIONS: One-switch scanning. After you have entered the software, press [command-option-A] to open Adult Options. Choose "single switch input" and click on "options." Set progression to "automatic" and scanning rate to "3" (larger numbers indicate a slower scan rate). Note: When using a software-driven scanning option, as in this program's case, set KE:NX/Discover to "no setup."

BEHAVIORAL INFO: Talk to Jon about what is happening on screen. Help him follow directions. Prompt him to return to task when attention wanders. Give assistance when necessary to facilitate the task. Let him make autonomous choices and experience wrong answers as well as right answers.

ASSIGNMENT: Using the Question and Answer level, go through at least one set of pond animals. Work on this activity for ____ minutes, or set a more concrete goal, such as "look up information about rabbits and print it out."

                     Then "read the information from your notebook. Tell me where rabbits live."

DATE: PERFORMANCE NOTES:

———   ——————————————————————

———   ——————————————————————

———   ——————————————————————

———   ——————————————————————

———   ——————————————————————

———   ——————————————————————

———   ——————————————————————

———   ——————————————————————

———   ——————————————————————

———   ——————————————————————

Figure 8.3. Sample computer-assisted activity plan. From *Augmentative Communication: Using the Macintosh Computer To Facilitate Speech, Language, and Communication Goals*, by S. Fields, 1996, workshop presented at the annual conference of the Technology and Media Division of The Council for Exceptional Children, Austin, TX.

When only one computer is available, Philips (1983, p. 32) described the following management strategies:

1. *Total Class Instruction Using Simulation Programs.* Connect the computer to a larger second monitor (21 inches or greater) or a LCD projection system so all students can view the output. Responses to the program are made by the class as a group with the teacher or a selected student entering information into the computer for the group. All students experience and participate in the instruction. Assessment of student learning is obtained through the use of follow-up commercial or teacher-made question sheets at their desks.

2. *Timed-Use Relay Utilizing One Program.* When the teacher requires multiple students to access a single program, the teacher begins by loading a program into the computer. Each student's time at the computer is scheduled for a specific interval and kept by a timer set by the student. When the bell rings, a new student goes to the computer, resets the program and timer, and begins his or her session.

3. *Block-Time Format.* Each student in the class receives a weekly prescheduled allocation of computer time. The day and time of each student's access is posted next to the computer.

4. *Nonscheduled Format.* Computer time before, during, and after school is blocked out. Sign-up sheets and procedural rules are maintained by the teacher to manage and prevent scheduling problems that might arise.

5. *Judicious Use of Systematic Procedures.* If the number and availability of computers vary (as additional computers are shared or acquired), to maximize efficiency and enforcement of access rules, the teacher can employ varia-

Table 8.7. Some Paradigms of Computer Use

Name	Paradigm	Discussion
Milestone	Distinct events or endpoints within the program are used as markers to determine how long a program session should be. The student works until reaching the milestone. Then the next student repeats the process.	This pattern is an appropriate one for learning programs in which something new is being learned or something previously learned is being practiced. Best used with tutorials or drill and practice.
Timed	Each student (or team) is assigned a set amount of time to work on a specific task.	Use caution with this option. Although it appears to be the fairest method of dividing up the computer's time, it hides the fact that the quicker students will learn more than the slower.
Task-defined	The student (or team) is assigned a task to complete and given as much time as necessary to do the job. Generally applicable to projects, newsletters, and other "broad" tasks.	Differs from Milestone in that the criterion for how much time is spent on the computer is external to the computer program. What is learned is not the endpoint in this pattern; rather, what is accomplished is.
Open time	The students (or teams) are allowed to use the computer at their discretion (within some broad set of limits).	This pattern fits well for recreational or reward use of the classroom computer. It must be watched carefully, because the more aggressive and interested students will tend to monopolize the available time.

Note. From *Teachers, Computers, and Curriculum: Microcomputers in the Classroom* (p. 179), by P. G. Geisert and M. K. Futrell, 1995, Needham Heights, MA: Allyn & Bacon. Reprinted with permission.

tions in the format and procedures listed in Items 1 through 4 above.

Whereas Philips (1983) presented managing students' computer access from a pragmatic scheduling perspective, Dockterman (1990) conceived of management in the one-computer classroom from a perspective emphasizing teaching applications. According to Dockterman, managing microcomputer-based instruction should involve use of the computer as one or more of the following:

1. *Smart Chalkboard.* The use of the computer as a smart chalkboard seeks to capitalize on the ease with which computers can present information, draw and redraw illustrations, and animate movement. Through the use of an LCD panel or projection system connected to the computer, software activities that were originally available to only one user are now projected for the whole class to interact with. For example, students could edit word processing documents or participate in a problem-solving simulation such as Where in the World is Carmen Sandiego? (Brøderbund).

2. *Discussion Generator.* The use of the computer as a discussion generator involves using software that causes the students to engage in discussion and problem solving that is moderated by the teacher. The role of the computer is to simply raise questions and issues and present new challenges based on students' choices.

3. *Group Activator.* The use of the computer as a group activator is integrally tied to the use of cooperative learning in the classroom. As students work in groups, the computer is used as a tool to enable the group to carry out specific tasks that relate to their role in achieving a classroom project goal. For example, in order to publish a classroom newsletter, students work together at the computer in a variety of tasks and focus their work on a specific tool (e.g., word processing program for composing text, drawing program for illustrating, desktop publishing program for page layout).

4. *Discovery Tool.* The use of the computer as a discovery tool involves a number of programs that enable students to engage in self-directed learning. This may be computer-assisted instruction software that allows students to explore new topics or it may involve telecommunications to enable students to conduct their own on-line searches. The value of this type of application tends to be underutilized in many classrooms.

5. *Teacher Secretary.* One important use of the computer, especially in the one-computer classroom, is as a teacher's assistant or teacher secretary. The previous section of this chapter on personal productivity discussed the value of this application.

Hodges (1997) described yet another way to manage a single-computer classroom. Hodges suggested that an effective strategy is to implement the concept of "task computing," where each student, on a daily or weekly basis, is assigned one or more academic tasks that require a computer to complete the assignment. According to Hodges, students check an assignment board to ascertain their specific task(s) at the beginning of a school day or week. Some students may be asked to search and retrieve information from specific Web sites (such as CNN's top news story or the temperature in Athens, Georgia), research a topic using a CD- or DVD-ROM encyclopedia, send e-mail to a "TeleMentor," or create

Professionals must work together to facilitate the use of technology in the classroom. (Photograph by Carolyn F. Woods)

a flyer for an upcoming school or home event. Clearly, Hodges's methods have strong implications for the student with special needs, given that teachers can consider assigning specific, individualized tasks that elicit performance of remedial, compensatory, and curriculum or IEP aligned tasks. From another vantage task computing provides each individual access to the computer to perform a minor or major task over the course of an established period of time.

Managing students' access to computers can also be considered to involve multiple variables, such as the number of computers available and the number of students who have to be served. Geisert and Futrell (1995) described a variety of advantages and disadvantages to using computers in this context (see Table 8.8). In this model, considering efficient ways to provide single and multiple groups of students access to a limited number of computers is the predominant goal. It also helps characterize the perspective of the one-computer classroom as a misnomer—it represents a set of effective instructional practices that work efficiently when not enough computers are available to guarantee students one-to-one access whenever they desire. In other words the classroom need not be limited to having one computer to use these instructional strategies.

Many schools believe it is cost-effective to group a large number of computers and software in a central classroom that functions as a computer lab. Often enough computers are available so that each student from an entire classroom can have a computer, or smaller groups (e.g., half a class at a time) are scheduled to maintain a one student to one computer ratio. Typically, access to computer labs is shared between general and special education classes, where little or no distinction is made between special education and general education software (in most cases, teachers use the grade level identified with software to "match" the grade-level skills of the learners with special needs). Generally, lab software is shared by *all* students in a school so teachers have no guarantee that features of software adjusted for specific students (e.g., rate and amount of information presented, level of difficulty, response criteria, type and amount of feedback and reinforce-ment) have remained unchanged since last used. Imagine the routine involved in arriving at a lab and passing out programs to 15 students, but subsequently having to readjust features in 10 of those programs before students can begin working. Therefore, when exceptional learners' access to computers takes place in lab settings, the following strategies can be considered.

1. Teachers should try to schedule access to the lab to coincide with the end of their planning period or at a time when students are away at other activities. Students report directly to the computer lab, where the teacher has already begun setting up programs for the period.

2. Use a classroom aide or encourage a student, parent, or grandparent volunteer to arrive ahead of the class to assist with setup and remain as a computer counselor.

3. Get students started on their computer work as quickly as possible. Create computer assignment sheets for each student that provide clear instructions of what short-term computer objectives are to be accomplished during the lab session. Create specialized "cue" or "tip" sheets (see previous Box 8.4). Maintain a computer progress notebook with sections for each student that can easily be carried to and from the lab.

4. Entrust the students with the responsibility of adjusting and individualizing software features. Whenever a new program is started, instruct the students in how to set custom features. For subsequent lab sessions students' assignment sheets should also include what software features are to be set for that day's lab session. The teacher monitors each student to ensure that self-adjustments are accurate.

5. Use proximity control. Locate closest to you those students who may need assistance when setting up programs. Grouping students who need more frequent verbal prompting or physical assistance when getting started or during computer use will result in more efficient teacher movement and availability.

Table 8.8. Considerations Regarding the Number of Users per Station

Users per Computer	Advantages	Disadvantages
One	The computer has the undivided attention of the student and can tailor tutorial lessons and drill and practice to the needs of the individual.	This is a rather expensive use of computer time. If each of 30 students spends 10 minutes a day at the computer, 5 hours of constant use result.
Two or three	This option has been given good reviews by the educational research literature. With many programs, two or three individuals can actually learn more than one at a time, due to interaction during the learning processes.	Not suitable for programs that are designed to address the specific needs of an individual user (typing, tutorials, etc.). May lead to domination of the activity by one student.
Small groups	Four or five students can use the computer at one time. This is fine for simulation programs where a team can discuss and plot strategies and try out the results. Best used within some cooperative learning format with individuals being given specific responsibilities, and with a clear designation of one role as "computer operator."	Tasks and assignments must be very clear or valuable computer time will be spent in discussion and off-task behaviors. The decision to use small groups must be made on the basis of the type of program being used and not simply because computer power is scarce. Programs that enhance the concepts of small group learning are needed, along with adequate space near the computer to arrange for comfortable screen viewing by all participants.
Large groups, but less than the entire class	Project work can be employed nicely with groups of almost any size. Programs such as desktop publishers lend themselves to the delegation of a subgroup within the large group to do the computer portions of the broader task.	In large group work the computer is a tool to augment the group's task accomplishment, so teams or individuals need to be assigned the computer aspect(s). Plans must be laid so that various groups are appropriately sharing the computer.
Whole class	An entire class can be engaged with one computer if only one or two members of the class are handling the operation aspect at any one time. The operator(s) could make project presentations, facilitate data analyses for the class, or use the computer to conduct some other class-based event.	Difficulties arise in seeing the screen, so such use requires either multiple screens, a large and clear monitor, or a projection monitor (although it may be monochrome and not as interesting as a color monitor). Physical arrangement to permit keyboard operation and screen viewing by the operator and the simultaneous classwide viewing of the entries is necessary.

Note. From *Teachers, Computers, and Curriculum: Microcomputers in the Classroom* (p. 180), by P. G. Geisert and M. K. Futrell, 1995, Needham Heights, MA: Allyn & Bacon. Reprinted with permission.

Managing Through Cooperative Learning

The combination of cooperative learning and computer-based instruction represents an effective management strategy when computer resources are scarce or the quantity and quality of positive interactions between students represent as significant an educational goal as achieving instructional objectives at the computer. According to Male (1988), once the basic components of a cooperative computer learning environment have been established (see Table 8.9), teachers can use the following steps as a model for a cooperative learning lesson:

1. Assign students to heterogeneous teams and do team-building as necessary to establish trust and friendship.

2. Present the group goal (the "payoff" for working together).

3. Review the group skills to be emphasized (checking, praising, summarizing, etc.).

4. Make sure at least one student in each group can operate the software program.

5. Explain how each student's understanding or contribution to team effort will be evaluated.

6. Observe the group working both at the computer and at a table as they plan their strategies and complete their assignment at the computer. The teacher keeps track of who should receive special recognition points for social skills during the "processing" discussion.

7. Review the group product.

8. Check for individual participation, understanding, and contribution.

9. Recognize outstanding group performance.

10. Lead the processing discussion. (Male, 1988, pp. 128–129)

More extensive discussion and examples regarding the application of computer-based cooperative learning strategies with exceptional learners can be found in Male (1988, 1991, 1997) and Male et al. (1986). Figure 8.4 is an example of a lesson plan designed by Male et al. (1986) to promote cooperative learning.

Why promote cooperative learning and the use of technology? According to D. W. Johnson and Johnson (1996), given the growing technologically rich society and the workplace changes that promote teamwork and collaboration, it is both a challenge and an obligation of educators to address cooperation and the use of technology in school programs (see Box 8.5).

Monitoring and Mediating Students' Computer Performance

Instruction is an active process. A teacher's management responsibilities during computer instruction should be much like those of a "mentor," where the teacher acts as a guide, counselor, and leader of instruction (White & Hubbard, 1988) and a coach and tutor (Bunderson & Inouye, 1987). At the same time, a second management responsibility of the teacher is that of a "formative evaluator," where the teacher must be able to observe a student's performance during computer work and determine whether the student is making progress toward a given objective and is not in need of further assistance, or whether the student is having difficulty learning and needs teacher intervention and mediation.

One concern expressed by Reith, Bahr, Polsgrove, Okolo, and Eckert (1987) was that special education teachers were overly optimistic regarding computers' capabilities as independent tutors. Reith et al. (1987) discovered that many teachers used a model that placed exceptional learners at computers for the purpose of independent work only. Although the evidence was clear that students were highly engaged in computer activity, teachers remained at their desks and did not interact with their students and software. Little monitoring and teacher mediation were taking place. Similar deficits in teacher–student interaction during computer work were cited by Cosden, Gerber, Semmel, Goldman, and Semmel (1987).

As with any instructional activity, computer learning should be built around an active process that is outcome based and includes the student, the computer, and the teacher. It is essential not only that student performance be monitored to ensure academic learning time but also that the teacher be prepared to mediate computer learning when students encounter difficulty at the computer or when the software lacks sufficient content or design compatible with specific learner characteristics or stated learning objectives. A major objective related to monitoring students' computer activity is for the teacher to be able to acquire enough information in as short a period

Table 8.9. Essential Components of Cooperative Computer Learning

---

1. Assign students to heterogeneous teams.

Cooperative learning represents a conscious effort to create computer learning teams that represent a mix of students who vary with respect to such characteristics as achievement, language and communication skills, gender, cultural background, problematic behaviors, and computer literacy (e.g., keyboarding skills). Groups can be assigned randomly, or purposely structured to ensure heterogeneity.

2. Establish team identity.

Building team spirit, trust, friendship, and a group identity through preparation activities provides an incentive for future teamwork and collaboration. Students in each group work on a variety of getting-acquainted activities that may or may not be computer related. Examples of activities include naming the group, naming the computer, using a drawing program to design a team logo and banner, and values clarification tied to computer use and working relationships.

3. Establish positive interdependence between team members.

Members of the group must believe that group success is dependent on *all* members of the group being successful. Interdependence between team members can be facilitated by requiring one or more of the following:

a. **Goal interdependence.**

The criteria for successful completion of a group goal is when every member of the group can demonstrate mastery of the targeted computer task being learned. For example, every member of the group is able to cut and copy text in a word processor or copy a graphic from the World Wide Web.

b. **Task interdependence.**

Each member of the group is responsible for performing a specific subtask that no other individual performs. The overall computer task can be accomplished only when members combine or "chain" their subtasks. For example, the group task is to design and display a story. One student creates the setting, another the characters, and a third the plot. In another context, one student enters the text into a word processor, another creates illustrations using a painting program, and a third edits and merges the text and illustrations into a book format. Group members must be in agreement about the story's overall content and appearance.

c. **Resource interdependence.**

Group members share computer-related supplies and resources. The group turns in a single, shared product (e.g., one worksheet, or one progress report) to summarize and represent the group's thoughts and output.

d. **Role interdependence.**

Each member of the group has a specific role that he or she is asked to perform. The group receives credit for how well each member performs his or her role. For example, one student's job is to be the facilitator, to prompt and ensure opportunities for each member to express his or her thoughts and ideas.

e. **Reward interdependence.**

Certain rewards that individual members receive are linked only to the performance of the group as a whole. For example, when all members score 80% or above on the quiz, everyone gets 10 bonus points, or each individual's grade on the assignment is the average of the individual group members' grades.

(continues)

Table 8.9. (*continued*)

4. Provide direct instruction of social skills.

A principal rationale for using cooperative learning is to provide students a learning environment in which positive social skills are facilitated and reinforced. However, teachers should not assume that their students possess all of the prerequisite social skills needed for successful cooperation and collaboration. Thus, students will likely need direct instruction in a variety of the social skills necessary for cooperative learning (e.g., praising, encouraging, listening, waiting for one's turn, explaining, clarifying). Direct instruction of social skills can include defining the skills, modeling the skills, discussing with students why the target skills are important, having students practice the skills through role playing or brainstorming, and monitoring to make sure that students continue to use the skills during the cooperative computer activities.

5. Establish individual accountability for each team member.

Establishing individual accountability increases the likelihood that each individual will contribute to the group learning process. It provides the teacher with a way to evaluate an individual student's contributions to the group as his or her personal mastery of learning objectives. At the beginning of cooperative learning activities, it is important that all students are made aware that they individually must demonstrate mastery to the teacher.

6. Provide students opportunities to discuss and process the social elements of their collaboration.

Students will benefit from structured activities that provide them with the opportunity to discuss and process the social elements that took place within their group. Topics of discussion can include how the group helped each member learn, problems solved by the group, particular things the group or individuals did to facilitate the problem-solving process, and things the group members think they need further assistance with.

Note. Adapted from Male (1988, 1991, 1997).

of time to determine whether a student is academically on task (and in need of little teaching assistance) or whether a student may be encountering difficulty that requires additional teacher support and intervention. If intervention is needed, it should be direct and timely. Effective monitoring by the teacher during computer activities can include one or more of the following strategies:

1. Be physically available and prepared to interact with students during computer work. Teachers should be up and about, frequently observing and formatively evaluating students' computer performance. Providing assistance to students and eliciting information about their performance are as much a part of computer instruction as in other areas of instruction.

2. Observe students' performance frequently to check for understanding. Specifically, con-

centrate on observing a student's computer work for a minute or two. For example, with drill-and-practice programs, wait for a summary screen and note the number attempted and number correct. If an unacceptable error rate is occurring and the program has a pause feature, invoke this function and intervene.

3. Be familiar with and perceptive to particular programs' auditory or visual feedback features that indicate correct or incorrect performance. Teachers should listen for sounds or watch for familiar screen layouts that cue them from across the room that a particular student may deserve praise or need assistance.

4. Be perceptive to and ready to interpret particular statements that students make regarding their computer performance as cues to whether they need assistance. For example, if a student is overheard saying, "Why can't I get out of the store?" or "This wasn't happening to me the last time I used this program,"

Learning Together Lesson Plan
(Where in the World is Carmen Sandiego?)

Description: Students are detectives using clues to catch a thief who is hiding in one of 30 cities. The World Almanac helps in exploring cities and countries.

Subject Areas: Problem solving and logical thinking; geography

Grade Level: 5 and up

1. **Objectives:**

    A. Students will be able to use problem solving and logical thinking skills while working with clues to solve a mystery.

    B. Students will be able to use the dictionary and World Almanac as reference tools.

    C. Students will gain information to enlarge their understanding of geography.

    D. Students will be able to ask team members why they are advocating an action and will be able to listen for the response.

2. **Materials Needed.** Where in the World Is Carmen Sandiego? program manual, World Almanac, dictionary, police dossiers in software booklet, paper and pencil, marbles, jar, job cards, evaluation forms

3. **Time Required:** One class period per activity

4. **Procedures**

    A. Preparation

        1. Assemble needed materials.

        2. Practice program of Where in the World Is Carmen Sandiego?, solve several cases.

    B. Set

        1. Ask students what mystery programs they have seen on TV. Ask what the role of the detective is.

        2. James Bond always started with an assignment. Today you have an assignment to catch a thief. You will use clues about Carmen Sandiego's gang, and clues about cities and countries to solve the mystery. Your team will work together in the investigation.

    C. Input

        1. As a total class, use the program Where in the World Is Carmen Sandiego? to solve a case. Ask three random questions to decide on a menu option. Then use another three students for the next option.

        2. Ask three students what to do next; ask each for their reason for this decision, and listen to the response. Get agreement on their next action for the case. Repeat with additional decisions and additional ideas from three students.

        3. Assign students to heterogeneous teams.

Figure 8.4. Sample lesson plan to promote cooperative learning. From *Cooperative Learning and Computers: An Activity Guide for Teachers* by M. Male, D. Johnson, R. Johnson, and M. Anderson, 1986, Santa Cruz, CA: Educational Applecations. Reprinted by permission of Mary Male.

4. Set the group goal. "Your team will work together on a case assignment today to catch a thief. You may use the Almanac, the dictionary, the police dossiers in the manual, and the hints that you get as you run the program. As you decide what to do next, you are to ask each member for his or her idea and then listen carefully to the response. Then you are to agree on your course of action."

5. To help you accomplish your task there are job cards at each computer. Please distribute these among team members. You may make suggestions to the reference people and the recorder. All of you are to use the social skill of asking for a reason and listening to the response.

6. Every group that catches a thief will be permitted to put a marble in the jar. When the jar is filled we will have a class party. In the meantime, every group that puts a marble in will have a day when they are first in the lunch line.

D. Guided Practice

1. Students will work in their teams to catch a thief.

2. Teacher observes and records instances of team members' asking others for the reason behind their ideas. Teacher also records students' listening for the responses of others.

E. Closure

1. Each individual fills out an evaluation form.

2. With the total class together, the teacher calls on students to give comments on work in their group. Afterwards the teacher gives comments with examples of what asking for a reason sounded like and what the behavior of listening to a response sounded like.

F. Independent Practice

1. Teams work on additional cases in succeeding days, adding marbles to the class jar as they are solved.

2. Teams can get together their members and work on cases before or after school or during unscheduled times.

Note-Taking Guide for Where in the World Is Carmen Sandiego?

Country	Capital	Population	Geography	Flag	Money	Products

Figure 8.4. (*continued*)

closer monitoring and intervention may be needed. It all goes without saying that teachers need to know their software well to discriminate these sorts of statements.

5. Collect brief but descriptive anecdotal records or observational data about students' computer performance on a consistent basis. As this information is accumulated, particular

---

Box 8.5. A Rationale Supporting Cooperative Learning and Technology in Special Education

How would you respond to the following questions: Is there a place for technology and cooperative learning in the special education classroom? What is the rationale behind using technology and cooperative learning?

In their chapter titled "Cooperation and the Use of Technology," appearing in the *Handbook of Research for Educational Communications and Technology* (Jonassen, 1996), D. W. Johnson and R. T. Johnson (1996) provided a comprehensive discussion regarding technology and cooperative learning. The following excerpts serve to provide some insight, and certainly a strong rationale, behind why cooperative learning and technology can provide learners with special needs with a variety of opportunities that enhance or promote social and academic learning outcomes in functionally beneficial ways.

▶ **Is there a place for technology and cooperative learning in the classroom?**

According to Johnson and Johnson (1996),

> We live in an age that needs people who can work collaboratively designing, using, and maintaining the tools of technology. These tools pervade every aspect of our lives, from automatic teller machines, to bar codes on the things we buy, to copy machines, computers, and fax machines. Our society has moved from manufacturing-based work on which individuals generally competed or were independent from each other to information and technological-rich work on which individuals generally work in teams. Technology and teamwork will continuously play a larger role in our lives. [Special needs learners, including] children, adolescents, and young adults have no choice but to develop and increase their technological and teamwork literacy. There is no better place for them to start than in school. Learning in cooperative groups while utilizing the tools of technology should occur in all grade levels and subject areas.
>
> Because the nature of technology used by a society influences what the society is and becomes, individuals who do not become technologically literate will be left behind. Influences of a technology include the nature of the

medium, the way the medium extends human senses, and the type of cognitive processing required by the medium. (Johnson & Johnson, 1996, p. 1017)

▶ **What is the rationale behind using technology and cooperative learning?**

According to Johnson and Johnson (1996),

> In order to enhance learning, technology must promote cooperation among students and create a shared experience. *Technology assisted cooperative learning* exists when the instructional use of technology is combined with the use of cooperative learning groups. Students, for example, may be assigned to cooperative groups of two or three members and given a cooperative assignment to complete a task for which a technology is to be utilized. Positive interdependence is typically established at the terminal so that students are aware of their dependence on other group members in accomplishing their learning goals.
>
> Adding technology to a lesson inherently increases the lesson's complexity. When students participate in technology-assisted instruction, they have the dual tasks of (a) learning how to use the technology (i.e., the hardware and software required by the lesson) and (b) mastering the information, skills, procedures, and processes being presented within the technology. When cooperative learning groups are used, students have the additional task of learning teamwork procedures and skills. The complexity may be worth it. Technology-assisted cooperative learning tends to be a cost-effective way of teaching students how to use technology, increasing academic achievement, giving learners control over their learning, creating positive attitudes toward technology-based instruction and cooperative learning, promoting cognitive development, and increasing social skills. (Johnson & Johnson, 1996, p. 1031)

Note. Johnson and Johnson quotation from "Cooperation and the Use of Technology," by D. W. Johnson and R. T. Johnson, 1996, in *Handbook of Research for Educational Communications and Technology*, D. H. Jonassen (Ed.), p. 1017–1044. Copyright 1996 by Simon & Schuster, Inc. Reprinted with permission from Macmillan Library Reference USA.

performance trends not previously spotted may emerge that accentuate a student's need for supplemental instruction in computer-related skills.

Another of the more pervasive aspects of monitoring computer instruction also exists in dialogue that takes place between learner and teacher when a student is in need of assistance or information that software fails to provide. As in any instructional situation, factors associated with effective teacher-to-student communication during computer instruction represent important variables to consider. Effective feedback and effective praise are important to use.

The ability to deliver immediate feedback is one of the common features attributed to the efficacy of using computers with exceptional learners. In considering elements of feedback as they pertain to the display of computer-based information, Flemming (1987) and Mory (1996) observed that feedback generally serves to reward or inform, and that feedback principles assume that an agent mediating feedback (the computer or teacher) is responsive and available. Generally, much of the educational software that exists adequately functions in the category of immediate feedback and reward. However, the informative components of computer software leave something to be desired. Therefore, when software provides only minimal feedback in situations where students require feedback that is more informative, teachers must be prepared to supplement with specific academic praise and feedback that is descriptive and corrective in nature.

While monitoring computer instruction, teachers should ask students questions about their computer work and be prepared to respond to questions or statements students make about their computer performance. When presenting corrective feedback regarding students' computer performance, it is recommended that teachers (a) keep directions simple and concrete, using explicit step-by-step statements; (b) emphasize and repeat main points, sometimes to the degree of being redundant; and (c) intersperse questions as a means to monitor understanding (Rosenshine & Stevens, 1986).

Praise is one of the most obvious forms of feedback. Effective praise for computer work should not only reinforce the exceptional learner's behavior but also focus descriptively on what is task relevant about the computer performance. Praise should be given in moderation, and ideally should be specific rather than general (Rosenshine & Stevens, 1986). Certain aspects of Brophy's (1981) features of effective praise can be adapted and applied to the context of exceptional learners working on computers:

1. Give praise contingent upon computer performance versus performance in general.

2. Praise specific components or criteria of computer performance versus general aspects of computer performance. It is better to call attention to a student's speed and accuracy when using a drill-and-practice program than to praise only for making the hall of fame at the end.

3. Praise the student for effort and competence shown in performing computer-related tasks.

4. Praise students for endogenous attributions and focus attention on task-relevant behaviors. That is, attribute accomplishment of the computer task to intrinsic student factors of effort and ability rather than focusing recognition of accomplishment largely on less student-oriented external features attributable to the computer or software. For example, saying "Super, you are writing more organized paragraphs since you have been using word processing, and your spelling has improved since you've begun editing your work! You're really making good use of the computer," is better than the vague statement, "Wow, I can see how the word processor has helped your writing."

We conclude this section with a discussion that emphasizes the bigger picture as it pertains to feedback and technology-enhanced learning: Educators must not limit themselves to giving feedback that pertains to what is being learned but rather must provide feedback that contributes to the entire learning experience that takes place in the context of learning with technology.

According to Mory (1996) the role of feedback from teachers is to provide a means of scaffolding behaviors that represent higher order learning. Applying Mory's perspective to students' use of computers, it becomes apparent that teachers must strive to provide feedback that also serves to (a) modify the learner's perspectives through feedback (e.g., providing feedback to students during computer activities for the purposes of improving their self-efficacy and positive expectancies); (b) provide feedback as part of the constructivist perspective (e.g., providing elaborative feedback to students during computer activities that helps them see and use multiple perspectives to solve problems and generate new perspectives); and (c) facilitate students' self-regulated learning (e.g., providing feedback to students during computer activities that mediates or reinforces their conscious monitoring and control of their own knowledge generation, beliefs, motivations, and cognitive processing).

When using technology as part of instruction, teachers should provide instruction and feedback that recognizes the fact that there are multiple student learning goals. These goals include cognitive, social, and metacognitive outcomes, which, while not directly affiliated with the curricular theme of a given technology application, nevertheless may be equally important components of a student's developing repertoire of knowledge, attitudes, and skills.

A hardware system with a scanner facilitates technology integration, record keeping, and program evaluation. (Photograph by Carolyn F. Woods)

Evaluating Instruction

Managing instruction applications using computers also includes formative and summative evaluation. Frequently, formal assessment of student performance is a critical factor in successful student achievement. Unfortunately, many software programs have marginal record-keeping features. Because different software programs incorporate a range of record-keeping features, one or more of the following strategies may be appropriate as alternative ways to evaluate and maintain data regarding students' computer performance:

1. Create a classroom atmosphere that stresses the importance and routine of collecting specific information about students' computer performance. Make students aware that this information is used for the purpose of teacher review, feedback, and problem solving, but at the same time stress that this information will not be used against them. As Papert (1980) suggested, inferior learning models stress a "got it" or "got it wrong" approach rather than encouraging a "fix it" approach. According to Papert, computers are objects that students use to think with. Exceptional learners' computer performance should include evaluations for learning progress rather than mastery alone.

2. If a software program stores performance information that is useful, adopt a routine that provides sufficient time to access and interpret this information (Malouf et al., 1991c).

3. If a program displays performance data but does not have a permanent record-keeping function, design custom forms onto which a teacher, aide, or student can transcribe information from performance summary screens.

4. When programs provide no permanent record-keeping functions, establish consistent procedures for collecting and recording performance data. For example, when students arrive at summary screens, they must raise their hand and wait for the teacher to record their scores before being allowed to begin another trial.

5. Have students assume the responsibility for recording their own performance. For example, when students check out programs to use, they also take to the computer a personalized progress folder. Whenever they reach a particular stage in the program where performance information is displayed or accessible via a command, they access this information and record it onto customized forms that have been developed by the teacher. Periodically, the teacher reviews this information and transcribes it onto a spreadsheet for graphing or charting and then places this information into students' folders for visual analysis and student feedback.

6. Create and stick by a schedule to formally or informally collect progress data. For example, student performance data are always recorded after a set number of sessions or on the same day of the week. A schedule is set that requires each student to be observed at the computer for 5 minutes once a week, with an anecdotal record written immediately after the observation.

7. Design paper-and-pencil tests to measure students on skills and information learned at the computer. Design tests that can probe for process errors, and consider these tests as a way to obtain information regarding the generalization of learning from the computer medium to another (Malouf et al., 1991c).

8. Elicit students' self-reports. After observing a situation where a student seemed to have problems, ask the student to describe what he or she found hard or why he or she was having difficulty. Student self-reports can also be extremely important in clarifying whether a student has mastered a particular skill or concept, especially when computer solutions can be achieved through trial and error. Another self-report method that can be used is the "think-aloud" procedure, often used to assess students' application of cognitive strategies or thinking skills. An example of a think-aloud application would be to ask the student to work at the computer and talk out loud about how he or she is thinking and problem solving to complete the task.

9. Use portfolios. Collect materials, permanent products, and electronic products that can be assembled in a folder, notebook, storage box, or electronic format and that provide evidence of computer-based learning. Examples might include screen prints of summary screens or printouts of status reports identifying key computer-based accomplishments or milestones; checklists or certificates indicating mastery of technology-based knowledge or skills; samples of work produced on the computer (e.g., a drawing, records or a report generated by a database, copies of computer-generated slides or a multimedia presentation used in a class report). Both the teacher and student should be able to place things into the portfolio. In addition, when constructing portfolios, teachers should keep in mind Pike and Salend's (1995) reminder that their purpose is not to be used as a repository for daily work but rather a collection of work samples that assist the student, teacher, and parent in documenting and evaluating a student's progress, process, and development over time.

Extending Instruction

The task of extending recognizes that, unless teachers can create additional instructional applications for a new tool, it will simply be returned to the shelf for storage. By identifying methods of extending the value of the product, teachers continue the technology integration process at the linking task in Phase 4 rather than starting the entire process over again.

The process of integrating technology into the curriculum for students with special needs and enabling teachers to use technology in support of their professional and instructional productivity clearly involves a significant commitment of time, energy, and resources. It may be useful to reflect on the fact that most computers in U.S. classrooms have been in place less than 10 years. The efforts of the educational community during this time have been focused largely on selecting, acquiring, and implementing new applications of technology for the classroom. Although these activities are necessary prerequisites to integrating technology into the curriculum, considerably less attention has been focused on extending instruction—that is, maximizing and maintaining software's impact once it has been introduced into instruction and promoting continuing student interest in learning. We suggest that renewed efforts should be placed on instructional practices that creatively and effectively utilize existing technology for additional instructional impact. The remainder of this section addresses this concept with some additional thoughts.

One common concern about instructional software is that it is consumable. That is, after students have used a program and mastered its content, the program must be returned to the shelf. The concept of shelf life suggests that a program is more valuable in the classroom when it is *not* sitting on the shelf. For example, utility or tool programs such as word processors and graphic programs have a variety of flexibility and can be used on a daily basis, resulting in less shelf-time. Unfortunately, instructional software often tends to have a greater shelf life than utility or tool programs because of its correlation with the curriculum: Students either master the content or become bored with the presentation before the content is mastered.

The issue of shelf life suggests a number of strategies that should be considered in order to extend the effectiveness of instruction through technology. One strategy that teachers use to decrease the shelf life of a program is to schedule its reintroduction into the classroom for the purpose of reviewing the skills covered by a program and to check for the maintenance of skills. Reintroducing the software with new purposes and learning objectives that are qualitatively different from the software's original objective is another strategy. There are a variety of ways software can be creatively reused as a context under which alternative learning activities occur. Examples include cooperative learning (e.g., social skills), having students write journals or newsletter articles (e.g., written language skills) and give oral reports (e.g., communication skills) about their adventures in simulation programs, having students go through programs such as Where in the USA Is Carmen Sandiego? (Brøderbund) and then use Clarisworks (Claris) to create a database of cities and information found in the program (e.g., organizational skills), and having students select a program and draw a picture of their favorite computer screen (e.g., fine motor or perceptual–memory skills). Using a lesson plan format such the one described earlier in this chapter (Figure 8.2) will certainly facilitate the planning and implementation processes associated with using software for alternative purposes.

The effectiveness of extending instruction can also be increased when teachers remain current with the teaching and practice-oriented literature in technology. Presently, few forums are devoted specifically to the discussion of creative applications of software that encourage the exchange of teacher ideas and promising practices that serve to decrease the shelf life of software. Useful sources of this type of information are newsletters published by software publishers (e.g., Sunburst, Davidson, Mindscape, Tom Snyder), magazines that include creative technology and software applications (e.g., *Family Computing*), and publications that accentuate practice-oriented applications of technology in education (e.g., *Learning and Leading with Technology, Electronic Learning, Teaching and Computers, Technology & Learning,* and the *Newsletter of the Technology & Media Division of CEC*). Another information source is networking with one's peers. State and national conferences on technology and education often have a variety of sessions addressing instructional applications using specific software programs. Also, teachers can locate or establish a local computer user's group that focuses on educational applications or form an instructional computing teachers' user group in a local school district to share ideas and applications.

Finally, given the constant constraints caused by limited resources for purchasing new software, limited availability of staff development opportunities, and limited technical assistance for integrating technology into the curriculum, the instructional application of technology with exceptional learners can also be extended through teachers' recognition of the need to balance an instructional software collection with a variety of tool or utility programs. It seems increasingly essential that teachers recognize the value of tool programs as they build classroom software collections. After identifying a few basic tool programs, teachers can begin collecting and testing instructional strategies that effectively utilize these tools to enhance teaching and learning. Tool programs that equip and enable students to engage in learning to learn (e.g., word processors, databases, telecommunications, desktop publishing) can be used by students in pursuit of knowledge in *any* subject area. Once a teacher and student have the opportunity to obtain high degrees of proficiency with these tools, there is little they cannot study. The value, power, and flexibility of tool programs are further enhanced when considering that these programs have short shelf lives. While a software collection of productivity tools for learning clearly empowers creative teachers, the use of technology to provide instruction is still a critical need. Software that utilizes sound instructional principles will always be welcome in any classroom. More important, successful teaching applications of technology with learners with special needs will remain a function of teachers' personal and instructional productivity—that is, a function of *how* teachers use computers instructionally and not of how powerful the technology is or what the software presupposes to teach.

Russell et al. (1989) referred to this type of application as *learner-centered software*, which exemplifies the concept of placing students with special needs in control of computer learning activities that encourage them "to think and use information to solve problems—or to create new problems to solve" (p. 4). In essence, any program can become learner centered if the teacher uses the software to focus on active development and exercise of mental skills and to improve students' learning strategies.

Epilogue: Putting the Technology Integration Model into Practice

Brunner (1990) observed that, of the many ways to integrate technology into the classroom, each method requires major efforts. The report, *Technology and Teachers: Making the Connection*, noted that "integration is a difficult, time consuming and resource-intensive endeavor" (U.S. Congress, Office of Technology Assessment, 1995, p. 3). In our opinion, technology integration is a "do-it-yourself" project. Until professional consensus is reached about what it means to utilize technology well within the discipline of special education, each teacher must construct and rely on his or her own model and strategies. Technology integration is not simply buying an integrated learning system or following outlined steps over the course of a year. Each teacher must develop a personal vision of what technology integration looks like for his or her students and teach and use technology in the context that creates the meaningful, authentic, higher order skills proposed earlier in this chapter. Then, we encourage them to share their plans with colleagues (see example plan in Appendix 8.A). This benefits others in starting the integration process and contributes to thoughtful conversation about whether there is consensus concerning the designs made, the tools selected, and the types of outcomes desired.

We do not know if any given technology integration plan can generalize beyond the instructor or the institution where it was developed. Thus, it is important to consider a process for validating integration plans and developing strategies that will enable others to move into Phase 4 of the integration model (see Table 8.5) with greater ease and efficiency than if they had to engage in the entire process themselves.

The integration model described in this chapter offers an excellent map for do-it-yourself efforts to integrate technology into the curriculum. Readers are encouraged to explore ways in which the model may assist in evaluating their current technology integration practices by identifying tasks that receive too much attention or tasks that have been overlooked. In addition, faculty and technology support staff should consider how they might develop strategies to facilitate movement through Phases 1 through 3 and to celebrate the evolving local knowledge base concerning the tasks in Phase 4.

The conversation about the potential of technology for individuals with disabilities is evolving as professionals observe how technology is used, evaluate its effectiveness, and experiment with new products. Without models, principles, and strategies, the challenge of integrating technology into the curriculum can be an overwhelming task with unpredictable results. Ideally, the conceptual foundations, validation process, and specific strategies presented in this chapter will stimulate discussion within the field and serve to advance a collective perspective of what technology integration looks like and how it is achieved.

Resources

Periodicals

Electronic Learning
Web: http://scholastic.com/EL

Teaching and Technology
Web: http://www.techlearning.com

Learning and Leading with Technology
Web: http://isteonline.uoregon.edu

Family Computing
Web: http://www.zdnet.com/familypc/

Reference Guides to Instructional Media

Buckleitner, W. (1997). *1997 survey of early childhood software*. Ypsilanti, MI: High/Scope Press.

Closing the Gap. (1997). *The 1997 Closing the Gap resource guide*. Henderson, MN: Author.

Educational Products Information Exchange (EPIE) Institute. (1997). *The electronic school* [CD]. Hampton Bays, NY: Author.

Emerging Technology Consultants. (1997). *The 1997 multimedia and videodisc compendium for education and training*. St. Paul, MN: Author.

Neill, S. B., & Neill, G. W. (1997). *Only the best 1997: The annual guide to highest-rated educational software from preschool–grade 12*. Alexandria, VA: Association for Supervision and Curriculum Development.

Trace Research and Development Center on Control and Computer Access for Disabled Individuals. (1997). *Trace Resource Book: Assistive technologies for communication, control, and computer access*. Madison, WI: Author.

Laboratory–Practicum Activities

▶ 1. List three goals you will achieve in the next 3 months to enhance your ability to integrate technology to support effective instruction. Use technology to develop your goals, to describe how you will achieve these goals, and to manage the achievement of the goals.

▶ 2. Collaborate with your peers to search local libraries, material centers, the Internet, and the World Wide Web for general principles and lesson plans for integrating technology to support effective instruction. Use the information presented in this chapter and what you find to develop a resource book for integrating technology lessons across different levels (e.g., preschool, elementary, secondary) and subject areas (e.g., reading, mathematics, science). Use technology to provide the course instructor and future students taking the course with a copy of your resource book.

▶ 3. Collaborate with your peers to develop, implement, and evaluate an elementary-level (e.g., reading) and secondary-level (e.g., science) instructional lesson in which technology is integrated to achieve teaching–learning outcomes. Use technology to provide your course instructor and future students taking the course with lesson-related objectives, activities, timelines, materials, and evaluative findings.

Appendix 8.A
Sample Plan for Technology-Enhanced Instruction
A Technology-Enhanced Learning Environment for Supporting the Writing Process

by Jennifer Stiemsma and Gina Simos

1. Purpose

Our interest in putting together this unit stems from the continued resistance and struggles with writing that we see from students. The enthusiasm of Nancie Atwell in her book, *In the Middle*, as well as the monstrous choices of technology that can be integrated within the writing process inspired us. We believe teachers do have ways to increase the motivation of students and assist them to feel successful with their writing.

The objective in this unit is for students to successfully plan, draft, revise, edit, and publish clear and effective writing. This objective is a standard set by the state Department of Public Instruction. Writing occurs throughout all areas of school. This unit not only is meant to assist students within their English classes, but should be threaded throughout all content areas. This unit includes a few items that can be especially beneficial for students with disabilities. Gone are the days of using only paper and pencils. The technological resources available can prove to have successful outcomes for all students.

2. Teacher Resources

This section provides resources that teachers may find useful as they begin planning and preparing process writing activities.

Professional Books

In the Middle: New Understanding about Writing, Reading, and Learning
By Nancie Atwell

An excellent book for setting up a writing workshop. Provides information on getting started, teaching mini-lessons, conferencing with students, and evaluating work.

The Art of Teaching Writing
By Lucie McCormick Calkins

A valuable resource on how children learn to write and how to set up a writer's workshop. A few topics include assessment, thematic studies, writing throughout the day, and publishing.

The Blue Pages: Resources for Teachers from Invitations, Changing as Teachers and Learners K–12
By Regie Routman

Book includes professional resources for teachers, recommended literature by grade level, a multicultural book list, and appendixes filled with useful information.

Technology for Inclusion: Meeting the Special Needs of All Students
By Mary Male

The chapter most relevant to the writing process is Chapter 8: Reading, Language Development, and Written Expression with Word Processing and Desktop Publishing.

Classroom Ideas for Using Inspiration: For Teachers by Teachers

This guide will help integrate the software program Inspiration into all subject areas. This book includes lesson plans and step-by-step instructions for all grade levels.

Articles On-line

No Title
By Marjorie Simic

http://www.ed.gov/databases/ERIC_Digests/
ed363884.html

This article is on the importance of publishing
and suggestions for publishing children's writing.

Suggestions for Helping Learning Disabled
Students to Write
By Paul Kaiser
http://www.ldresources.com/suggestions.html

All Children Can Write
By Donald Graves
http://www.ldonline.org/ld_indepth/writing/
graves_process.html

Teacher Resources on the Web

Graphic Organizers
http://www.ncrel.org/sdrs/areas/issues/students/
learning/lr2grap.htm

This site contains nine different graphic forms,
descriptions, and examples of topics that could be
represented using each form.

Teacher Resource Page
http://grove.ufl.edu/~klesyk/

A site with links for writing as well as other subject areas.

Teachers and Writers Collaborative
http://www.twc.org

A site for teachers to collaborate with professional writers. It contains references, students'
writing, information on their magazine, and an
opportunity for membership.

Additional Web Site Resources

Storyspace
http://www.eastgate.com/Storyspace.html

Humanities Software
http://www.humanitiessoftware.com

LD Resources
http://www.ldresources.com

LD Online
http://www.ldonline.org

3. Educational Software

This section identifies products that are valuable
additions to a school's software collection to support the success of all student writers.

Software To Help Students with Disabilities

Co: Writer
(Don Johnston)

A writing tool used in combination with a word
processor to help students write sentences by
using word prediction. It reduces the number of
keystrokes and can be adapted to a student's individual needs.

Write: OutLoud
(Don Johnston)

A talking word processor that immediately lets
students hear if words are omitted or misplaced. It
includes a talking spell checker that reads misspelled words and reads a list of suggested words.

Inspiration
(Inspiration Software)

Helps students sort words, concepts, or facts by
using visual organization through webbing, concept maps, and other graphical organizers.

Motivational Software

Hollywood High
(Theatrix)

A writing tool that brings the real world of teens
to life by creating live shows with characters,
scenes, animations, and musical backgrounds.

Imagination Express: Rainforest
(Edmark)

A storytelling program from a series of six by
Edmark. Students can create simple picture books

or multimedia productions by using tools to create background, cast characters, record dialogue, and add text, narration, and sound effects.

Multimedia Software

HyperStudio
(Roger Wagner Publishing)

Software to create multimedia projects. Students can add graphics, movies and animations to any project. Projects can easily be linked to the Internet.

The Multimedia Workshop
(Davidson)

A tool to help students create printed documents and video presentations through the help of three workshops within one program. Students can create book reports, newsletters, or photo essays by using the writing, video, and paint workshops.

Publishing Software

Microsoft Publisher 98
(Microsoft)

Create publications in print or on-line with the use of step-by-step Page Wizards or templates, Create newsletters, brochures, Web sites, and more. Includes clip art, fonts, borders, and photos.

Student Writing Center
(The Learning Company)

A word processing and desktop publishing program that includes five different document types. A few features include easy page layout, letterheads, borders, clip art, process writing and grammar tips, bibliography maker, and more.

4. Internet Resources

This section outlines Web sites that offer valuable information for student writers.

Web Sites for Young Writers

Kidnews
http://www.kidnews.com

A site for students to submit their writing and express ideas and opinions for others to read. Students have the opportunity to connect with a KeyPal.

Inkspot
http://www.inkspot.com/young

This site is an excellent place for students to visit. They can receive writing tips from other kids, have discussions, participate in contests, submit writing, and explore lots of other links to writing sites.

Stonesoup
http://www.stonesoup.com

A magazine by young writers and artists ages 8 to 13. Provides the possibility to publish original work or enjoy the writing of others. Provides many resources and links.

KidPub
http://www.kidpub.org/kidpub

Stories submitted appear on-line within 3 to 4 days. Visitors will find more than 20,000 stories in the database. A counter lets you know how many times your story was read since posting. Classes can have a link created to show their work. Also features opportunities to connect with KeyPals.

Writes of Passage
http://www.writes.org/netscape/index.html

Described as the on-line source for teenagers, this site is for teens who have something to say. It publishes student work and focuses on topics important to teens.

Student Reference Online

Merriam-Webster Online
http://www.m-w.com/

An on-line resource that allows students to conduct a search using the dictionary or thesaurus. It includes many other features, such as word games, word of the day, and more.

Bartlett's Familiar Quotations
http://www.cc.columbia.edu/acis/bartleby/barlett/

Search for quotations by famous people or put key words into the search engine to find quotes.

Homework Hotwire
http://sioux-center.k12.ia.us/SixthGrade/HHelp/HHelp.htm

This site offers links to help students with homework. The links are rated as well as categorized into topics. A few topics include references, language arts, current events, and science.

Young Writer Critique Group
http://www.realkids.com/critique.Shtml

Enter this workroom and a student will have the opportunity to exchange work and get helpful suggestions for improving his or her writing.

5. Curriculum Links

This section briefly describes our thoughts about integrating the writing process into the curriculum.

The writing process will be implemented by a four-person special education team. The special education teacher will initially take the lead as she teaches the English class. Instruction will begin at the start of the year. We believe this process is critical for the success of students in all classes and will foster skills that will be used all year. The three other teachers will expect the students to use each step of the writing process when doing an assignment or project that involves writing in the content-area classes.

6. Managing the Technology-Enhanced Learning Environment

When planning this unit, considerable thought was given to the organizational and management factors that will foster student learning and success. This section describes some general ideas for structuring the learning environment.

This unit will be implemented in the fall as part of an assignment in which each student will develop an autobiography.

Lesson: *Planning*

Time Frame: 2 to 3 class periods of 50 minutes

Goal: Students will prepare and organize the topic they are writing on.

Activities: In the computer lab, teach the students to use the software program Inspiration. Practice using the program by brainstorming and organizing using the topic of music. Apply the skills by organizing thoughts concerning key life events that might be included in an autobiography. Prepare a printout of the Web organization and outline.

Lesson: *Drafting*

Time Frame: 1 to 2 class periods of 50 minutes

Goal: Students will use their Inspiration maps or outlines to create a rough draft of their autobiography.

Activities: Students are provided with time to create a rough draft of their autobiography using the technology of their choice. This may include paper and pencil, word processing software, other writing software, or AlphaSmart. Teacher emphasis is on content generation rather than mechanics.

Lesson: *Revising*

Time Frame: 1 to 2 class periods of 50 minutes

Goal: Students will engage in revision tasks and assess their value for improving clarity.

Activities: The teacher reads a sample autobiography and facilitates the group's discussion of ideas on how to revise the draft. Subsequently, students pair up and exchange rough drafts. Each student gives the other feedback on enhancements that could be made. Finally, students are provided with additional time to incorporate preparing a revised draft. Teacher emphasis during these sessions is on mechanics.

Lesson: *Editing*

Time Frame: 1 to 2 class periods of 50 minutes

Goal: Students will review their revised papers to identify and correct mechanical errors.

Activities: Provide students with dictionaries, thesauruses, and hand-held spell checkers as well as other reference materials to assist in editing. Students should be encouraged to self-edit and then pair up and exchange papers for peer editing. Finally, individual student–teacher conferences should be held to review the paper.

Lesson: *Publishing*

Time Frame: By the due date of the project

Goal: Students will publish their work so others may read what they have written.

Activities: Provide time for the student to prepare a final copy using a word processor or publishing program using the format and tool of their choice. Encourage students to examine many formats: read it to the class, post it in the classroom, publish in the school newspaper, or post at a Web site. Discuss the reactions of others who have heard or read the student's writing.

7. Assessing

Assessment is a critical part of the technology integration process. Assessment involves more than the teacher just giving out a grade. There is a need for a standard rubric for evaluation. We will develop rubrics to evaluate the students' use of the Inspiration program, development of ideas, use of mechanics, and the final product.

Students will evaluate themselves on each section of the project using the rubrics provided. This will be followed by a conference with the teacher. The conference will allow both the student and the teacher to talk about how the unit went as they compare and discuss their rubric ratings. They collaboratively decide on a final grade for the project.

8. Extending

Many possibilities exist to extend this unit through all content areas. Even though this unit is taught in an English class, it will be implemented by the four-person special education team who teach all subjects. Therefore, the skills the students learned in English can be extended in each of the other content-area classes. The core software tools (word processor, clip art, World Wide Web, publishing software) can be reused with each new project, thereby developing high-skill levels. We anticipate that over time students will find the steps of the writing process easier and that they will want to write more.

References

Bandura, A. (1977). *Social learning theory*. Englewood Cliffs, NJ: Prentice-Hall.

Barbata, D. (1988). Data projection panels: What are the choices? *The Computing Teacher, 16*(1), 19–20.

Bell-Gredler, M. E. (1997). *Learning and instruction: Theory into practice* (3rd ed.). New York: Macmillan.

Berliner, D. C. (1988). The half-full glass: A review of research on teaching. In E. L. Meyen, G. A. Vergason, & R. J. Whelan (Eds.), *Effective instructional strategies for exceptional children* (pp. 7–31). Denver: Love.

Bitter, G. G., & Yohe, R. L. (1989, March). Preparing teachers for the information age. *Educational Technology*, pp. 22–25.

Brophy, J. (1981). Teacher praise: A functional analysis. *Review of Educational Research, 51*, 5–32.

Brunner, C. (1990). What it really means to "integrate" technology. *Technology and Learning, 11*(3), 12–14.

Bunderson, C. V., & Inouye, D. K. (1987). The evolution of computer-aided educational delivery systems. In R. M. Gagné (Ed.), *Instructional technology: Foundations* (pp. 283–318). Hillsdale, NJ: Erlbaum.

Clark, R. E. (1983). Reconsidering research on learning from media. *Review of Educational Research, 53*(4), 445–459.

Cognition and Technology Group at Vanderbilt. (1990). Anchored instruction and its relationship to situated cognition. *Educational Researcher, 19*(6), 2–10.

Cognition and Technology Group at Vanderbilt. (1992). The Jasper series as an example of anchored instruction: Theory, program description, and assessment data. *Educational Psychologist, 27*, 291–315.

Cognition and Technology Group at Vanderbilt. (1993a). Anchored instruction and its relationship to situated cognition revisited. *Educational Technology, 13*(3), 52–70.

Cognition and Technology Group at Vanderbilt Learning Technology Center. (1993b). Integrated media: Toward a theoretical framework for utilizing their potential. *Journal of Special Education Technology, 12*(2), 76–89.

Cosden, M. A., Gerber, M. M., Semmel, D. S., Goldman, S. R., & Semmel, M. I. (1987). Microcomputer use within microcomputer–educational environments. *Exceptional Children, 53*, 399–409.

Cuban, L. (1986). *Teachers and machines: The classroom use of technology since 1920*. New York: Teachers College Press.

Denk, J., Martin, J., & Sarangarm, S. (1993–1994). Not yet comfortable in the classroom: A study of academic computing at three land-grant universities. *Journal of Educational Technology Systems, 22*(1), 39–55.

Dockterman, D. (1990). *Great teaching in the one computer classroom* (2nd ed.). Cambridge, MA: Tom Snyder Productions.

Edyburn, D. L. (1989). Using microcomputers in special education teacher training programs. *Capturing the Potential, 2*(2), 1–3.

Edyburn, D. L. (1997a). Ten models for integrating curriculum and technology. *Closing the Gap, 16*(5), 1, 9, 30.

Edyburn, D. L. (1997b). Visions of integration: Would you recognize it if you saw it? *Closing the Gap, 16*(4), 5, 38.

Fields, S. (1996). *Augmentative communication: Using the Macintosh computer to facilitate speech, language, and communication goals*. Workshop presented at the annual conference of the Technology and Media Division of The Council for Exceptional Children, Austin, TX.

Flemming, M. L. (1987). Displays and communication. In R. M. Gagné (Ed.), *Instruction technology: Foundations*. Hillsdale, NJ: Erlbaum.

Fogarty, R. (1991). Ten ways to integrate curriculum. *Educational Leadership, 49*(2), 61–65.

Gagné, R. M. (1985). *The conditions of learning*. New York: Holt, Rinehart, and Winston.

Gagné, R. M., Briggs, L., & Wager, W. (1988). *Principles of instructional design* (2nd ed.). New York: Holt, Rinehart, and Winston.

Gagné, R. M., Briggs, L., & Wager, W. (1992). *Principles of instructional design* (3rd ed.). New York: Holt, Rinehart, and Winston.

Gardner, J. E., & Edyburn, D. L. (1993). Teaching applications with exceptional individuals. In J. D. Lindsey (Ed.), *Computers and exceptional individuals* (2nd ed.) (pp. 273–310). Austin, TX: PRO-ED.

Gardner, J. E., Taber-Brown, F. M., & Wissick, C. A. (1992). Selecting age-appropriate software for adolescents and adults with developmental disabilities. *Teaching Exceptional Children, 24*(3), 60–63

Geisert, P. G., & Futrell, M. K. (1995). *Teachers, computers, and curriculum: Microcomputers in the classroom*. Needham Heights, MA: Allyn & Bacon.

Grambinger, R. S. (1996). Rich environments for active learning. In D. H. Jonassen (Ed.), *Handbook of research for educational communications and technology* (pp. 665–692). New York: Macmillan.

Hanley, T. V., Appel, L. S., & Harris, C. D. (1988). Technological innovation in the context of special education systems: A qualitative and structured research approach. *Journal of Special Education Technology, 9*(2), 98–108.

Hannafin, M. J., Hannafin, K. M., Hooper, S. R., Rieber, L. P., & Kini, A. S. (1996). Research on and research with emerging technologies. In D. H. Jonassen (Ed.), *Handbook of research for educational communications and technology* (pp. 398–402). New York: Macmillan.

Hazari, S. (1991, October). Microcomputer training for higher education faculty. *Educational Technology*, pp. 48–50.

Hodges, B. (1997). Task computing. *Learning and Leading with Technology*, 25(2), 6–9.

Hoffman, J. L., & Lyons, D. J. (1997, October). Evaluating instructional software. *Learning and Leading with Technology*, pp. 52–56.

Individuals with Disabilities Education Act of 1990, 20 U.S.C. § 1400 *et seq.*

Jacob, S., & Brantley, J. C. (1987). Ethical and legal considerations for microcomputer use in special education. *Computers in the Schools*, 3(3,4), 185–194.

Johnson, D. W., & Johnson, R. T. (1996). Cooperation and the use of technology. In D. H. Jonassen (Ed.), *Handbook of research for educational communications and technology* (pp. 1017–1044). New York: Macmillan.

Johnson, J. M. (1996, December/January). Software for an evaluation workshop. *Learning and Leading with Technology*, pp. 48–49.

Jonassen, D. H., & Reeves, T. C. (1996). Learning with technology: Computers as cognitive tools. In D. H. Jonassen (Ed.), *Handbook of research for educational communications and technology* (pp. 693–719). New York: Macmillan.

Jones, V. F., & Jones, L. S. (1986). *Comprehensive classroom management: Creating positive learning environments* (2nd ed.). Boston: Allyn & Bacon.

Laurillard, D. (1993). *Rethinking university teaching: A framework for the effective use of educational technology.* New York: Routledge.

Male, M. (1988). *Special magic: Computers, classroom strategies and exceptional students.* Mountain View, CA: Mayfield.

Male, M. (1991). Cooperative learning and computers: Maximizing instructional power with minimal equipment. *ConnSENSE Bulletin*, 8(1), 1, 10–11.

Male, M. (1997). *Technology for inclusion.* Needham Heights, MA: Allyn & Bacon.

Male, M., Johnson, D., Johnson, R., & Anderson, M. (1986). *Cooperative learning and computers: An activity guide for teachers.* Santa Cruz, CA: Educational Applecations.

Malouf, D. B., Jamison, P. J., Kercher, M. H., & Carlucci, C. M. (1991a). Computer software aids effective instruction. *Teaching Exceptional Children*, 23(2), 56–57.

Malouf, D. B., Jamison, P. J., Kercher, M. H., & Carlucci, C. M. (1991b). Integrating computer software into effective instruction. *Teaching Exceptional Children*, 23(3), 54–56.

Malouf, D. B., Jamison, P. J., Kercher, M. H., & Carlucci, C. M. (1991c). Integrating computer software into effective instruction. *Teaching Exceptional Children*, 23(4), 57–60.

McDougall, A., & Squires, D. (1995). A critical examination of the checklist approach in software selection. *Journal of Educational Computing Research*, 12(3), 263–274.

Morocco, C. C., & Zorfass, J. M. (1988). Technology and transformation: A naturalistic study of special students and computers in the middle school. *Journal of Special Education Technology*, 9(2), 88–97.

Mory, E. H. (1996). Feedback research. In D. H. Janassen (Ed.), *Handbook of research for educational communications and technology.* New York: Macmillan.

Moyer, J. (1988). Using a data projection panel for computer applications. *The Computing Teacher*, 16(1), 17–18.

Nicklin, J. L. (1994, January 5). A big boost for reform. *The Chronicle of Higher Education*, p. A42.

North Central Regional Education Lab. (1996). Welcome to Pathways to School Improvement. Available: http://www.ncrel.org/ncrel/sdrs/pathways.htm

O'Connor, J., & Brie, R. (1994). The effects of technology infusion on the mathematics and science classroom. *Journal of Computing in Teacher Education*, 10(4), 15–18.

Okolo, C. M., Bahr, C. M., & Rieth, H. J. (1993). A retrospective view of computer-based instruction. *Journal of Special Education Technology*, 12(1), 1–27.

Panyan, M. V., Hummel, J., & Jackson, L. B. (1988). The integration of technology in the curriculum. *Journal of Special Education Technology*, 9(2), 109–119.

Papert, S. (1980). *Mindstorms: Children, computers, and powerful ideas.* New York: Basic Books.

Philips, W. R. (1983). How to manage effectively with twenty-five students and one computer. *The Computing Teacher*, 10(7), 32.

Pike, K., & Salend, S. J. (1995). Authentic assessment strategies: Alternatives to norm-referenced testing. *Teaching Exceptional Children*, 28(1), 15–20.

Pogrow, S. (1988, May/June). How to use computers to truly enhance learning. *Electronic Learning*, pp. 6–7.

President's Committee of Advisors on Science and Technology, Panel on Educational Technology. (1997). *Report to the President on the use of technology to strengthen K–12 education in the United States.* Washington, DC: Author.

Reiser, R. A., & Kegelmann, H. W. (1994). Evaluating instructional software: A review and critique of current methods. *Educational Technology Research and Development*, 42(3), 63–69.

Rieth, H., Bahr, C., Polsgrove, L., Okolo, C., & Eckert, R. (1987). The effects of microcomputers on the secondary special education classroom ecology. *Journal of Special Education Technology*, 8(4), 36–45.

Rosenshine, B., & Stevens, R. (1986). Teaching functions. In M. C. Wittrock (Ed.), *Handbook of research on teaching* (pp. 376–391). New York: Macmillan.

Russell, S. J., Corwin, R., Mokros, J. R., & Kapisovsky, P. M. (1989). *Beyond drill and practice: Expanding the computer mainstream*. Reston, VA: Council for Exceptional Children.

Sheingold, K., & Hadley, M. (1990). *Accomplished teachers: Integrating computers into classroom practice*. New York: Bank Street College of Education, Center for Technology in Education. (ERIC Document Reproduction Service No. ED 322 900)

Taylor, R. (Ed.). (1980). *The computer in the school: Tutor, tool, tutee*. New York: Teachers College Press.

Turkle, S. (1984). *The second self: Computers and the human spirit*. New York: Simon and Schuster.

U.S. Congress, Office of Technology Assessment. (1988). *Power on! New tools for teaching and learning*. Washington, DC: U.S. Government Printing Office.

U.S. Congress, Office of Technology Assessment. (1995). *Teachers and technology: Making the connection*. Washington, DC: U.S. Government Printing Office.

White, C. S., & Hubbard, G. (1988). *Computers and education*. New York: Macmillan.

White, M. A., & Righi, C. (1991, October). Software tools for students in higher education: A national survey of use. *Educational Technology*, pp. 45–47.

Willis, J. (1993). What conditions encourage technology use? It depends on the context. *Computers in Schools*, 9(4), 13–32.

Wood, V. (1995). *A computer lesson plan teaching information skills using Sammy's Science House*. Unpublished lesson plan.

Section III

⅋ ⅋ ⅋

Specific Inclusive and Categorical Applications

This section builds on the concepts presented in Sections I and II and describes specific technological applications for use with and by individuals with disabilities, gifts, and talents in inclusive and other settings.

Technology can facilitate teaching–learning outcomes. (Photograph by Carolyn F. Woods)

Chapter 9

᙮   ᙮   ᙮

Technology for Individuals
with Mild Disabilities

Cynthia M. Okolo
University of Delaware, Newark

In recent years education has been an increasing focus of public speculation and scrutiny (Riley, 1999). In response, educators, politicians, and public interest groups have promulgated numerous proposals for reform (e.g., National Commission for Excellence in Education, 1983; National Council of Teachers of Mathematics, 1989; National Education Commission on Time and Learning, 1994; National Education Summit, 1996). Key features of these reforms are an emphasis on more rigorous academic standards, challenging curricula, equal opportunities for all children to learn, inquiry- or project-based learning, and the cultivation of problem-solving and thinking skills. Many advocates of reform have emphasized that these expectations and standards must apply to *all* students. Although special educators have challenged the feasibility of recent reform movements to the education of learners with severe disabilities, most agree that they are worthy and feasible goals for students with mild disabilities.

Characteristics of Students with Mild Disabilities

Students with mild disabilities are those students who are diagnosed as having learning disabilities, mild mental retardation, or emotional or behavioral disturbances. Approximately 72% of the students who receive special education services have a mild disability (U.S. Department of Edu-

cation, 1996). Regardless of how they are labeled, students with mild disabilities are usually performing below grade level in core academic subjects such as reading, written expression, and mathematics (Deshler, Schumaker, Alley, Warner, & Clark, 1982; Hallahan & Kauffman, 1986). Many students with mild disabilities must learn to compensate for cognitive deficits such as poor memory or short attention span (Hallahan, Kauffman, & Lloyd, 1996; Krupski, 1981). Often inefficient learners, these students seem unaware of strategies such as rehearsal or self-monitoring that can offset their cognitive deficits (Baumeister & Brooks, 1981; Wallace & Kauffman, 1986). Without explicit instruction, they may not use cognitive strategies and may be unable to generalize what they have learned to new situations

Collaborative technology activities can be both exciting and effective. (Photograph by Carolyn F. Woods)

243

(Belmont, Butterfield, & Ferretti, 1982; Ellis, Lenz, & Sabornie, 1987).

Students with mild disabilities often fail to develop automaticity in basic skill areas such as decoding and math facts, which may have a deleterious effect on their acquisition and use of higher order skills such as reading comprehension and math problem solving (Goldman & Pellegrino, 1987; Torgesen, 1984). Furthermore, these students may lack the vocabulary and background knowledge necessary for success in content-area subjects such as science and social studies (Cognition and Technology Group at Vanderbilt, 1990).

In addition to cognitive and academic deficits, students with mild disabilities also experience social and motivational difficulties that further interfere with their success at school. Research has indicated that students with mild disabilities often lack intrinsic motivation to pursue academic tasks, are easily frustrated, have low self-concept and self-efficacy, and do not believe they are responsible for their successes and failures (Chapman, 1988; Pearl, 1982; Schunk, 1989). Not surprisingly, these students often lack appropriate social skills and consequently have difficulty forming and maintaining interpersonal relationships (Vaughn, McIntosh, & Spencer-Rowe, 1991). Over their school careers, poor reading skills, inefficient learning strategies, and decreased motivation to pursue academic tasks help widen the achievement gap between students with disabilities and their nondisabled peers.

Inclusion and Students with Mild Disabilities

In the 1993–1994 school year, almost three quarters of students with disabilities received their education in a general classroom for 50% or more of the school day (U.S. Department of Education, 1996). All trends indicate that school districts will continue to replace pull-out special education programs with services that maintain students with disabilities in general classrooms. Thus, increasing numbers of students with mild disabilities will be educated in heterogeneous

classrooms with their nondisabled peers. The inclusion movement occurs at a time when societal trends have helped shape increasingly diverse classrooms in which teachers must meet a range of student characteristics and needs, and often with a decrease in resources.

Effective Instruction for Students with Mild Disabilities

As the previous discussion suggests, students with mild disabilities and their teachers face formidable challenges in meeting reform-oriented educational goals and standards, particularly in the diverse setting of general education classrooms. However, there is considerable reason for optimism. Researchers have developed effective techniques and materials for helping students master the basic skills that often limit their success in acquiring information and demonstrating competence (e.g., Ball & Blachman, 1991; Byrne & Fielding-Barnsley, 1993; Hasselbring, Goin, & Bransford, 1988; O'Connor, Notari-Syverson, & Vadasy, 1996). More than two decades of increasingly refined research about cognitive strategy instruction has stimulated the development of techniques and tools that can help students to succeed with complex tasks such as written expression (e.g., Englert, 1990; Graham, Harris, MacArthur, & Schwartz, 1991), reading comprehension (e.g., Palincsar & Brown, 1984), and learning how to learn (e.g., Deshler & Schumaker, 1986; Mastropieri & Scruggs, 1991). Also, ample research has shown that well-designed instruction can help students master complex content (e.g., Carnine & Kameenui, 1992) and reason effectively (e.g., Collins, Carnine, & Gersten, 1987). It is becoming increasingly apparent that the difficulties encountered by students with mild disabilities can be at least partially overcome through a combination of effective instructional methods and compensatory tools.

How Technology Can Help

Computers and other electronic technologies can be powerful tools for improving educational opportunities for all students, including those with mild disabilities. In this chapter I discuss two broad categories of technology applications that can promote more effective outcomes for students with mild disabilities. First, computers and other electronic technologies, such as interactive videodiscs, can be used to *support teaching*. Under this designation, I first consider ways in which technology applications such as computer software, CD-ROMs and DVD-ROMs, and video-discs, can be used to *deliver instruction and practice* in basic and higher order skills. Software programs developed for these purposes have been the mainstay of educational technology use in special education, in part because early computer systems were best suited to these types of applications and in part because students with disabilities often need extensive practice to attain skill mastery. Next, I discuss *electronic books*, a newer entry to the software market, which can deliver potentially rich reading experiences to students. Then I examine the concept of *anchored instruction*, in which technology applications such as videodiscs or simulation programs are used to provide a context or background for instruction. Finally, I consider *network-based learning*, in which students and teachers have access to a wealth of information and instructional opportunities on the Internet and other electronic networks.

A second broad set of technology applications is captured by the notion of *technology tools*, or applications that provide direct assistance to students in accomplishing important instructional tasks. Within this category I discuss five types of tools. I first consider *word processors* or programs that can help students compose text that is easier to revise and more legible, as well as other computer-based *writing tools* such as word prediction programs, prompting programs, and multimedia composing tools. These latter applications can help students overcome bottlenecks, such as poor motor skills or lack of mastery over conventions of writing, that can impede their text production and inhibit their expression.

Next, I discuss *tools for organizing content-area instruction*, such as concept mapping and outlining programs, which can help improve students' study skills and acquisition of content-area infor-

mation. In addition to helping students organize their ideas and investigate relationships among them during the writing process, these types of programs can help promote students' comprehension and mastery of content-area information. By enabling students to better discern relationships among ideas, these types of programs can discourage students' tendencies to view content-area information as a set of isolated facts.

Then I discuss *authoring tools and multimedia projects*. Project-based learning provides students with an opportunity to investigate topics in detail and to produce a product that represents their findings. Authoring software provides one tool to help students to represent and communicate what they have learned. Students can develop presentations and other products that can be shared with or used to teach others.

The next topic is that of *electronic reference materials*, including computer-based encyclopedias and dictionaries and hand-held technology devices such as electronic organizers, spelling checkers, and thesauruses. These tools can give students access to a wealth of information in potentially more accessible forms and can aid students with memory deficits, poor spelling skills, or weak vocabulary knowledge.

Finally, I consider *databases*, available through software and on-line sources, as tools that can help students organize, manipulate, and analyze information.

Absent from this chapter is a discussion of the many excellent technology applications that support teachers in their instructional and professional activities. Although these have an important impact on what and how well students with mild disabilities learn, they are addressed in Chapters 7 and 8 of this book. Table 9.1 reviews the technology applications discussed in this chapter and the ways that they can assist students with mild disabilities.

Review of the Literature

Over the past 20 years, hardware and software have evolved at a dizzying pace. Although educational

Table 9.1. Applications of Technology To Meet the Needs of Students with Mild Disabilities

Application	How Application Helps Students with Mild Disabilities
Technology To Support Teaching	
Delivery of instruction and practice	Students often need repeated and extended practice to master skills. Computer-based practice can be varied, provide immediate feedback, and help reduce students' response latency. Some students prefer the impersonal nature of computer-based practice, and gamelike formats may motivate some students.
Electronic books	Text can be read by the computer, providing access to information above a student's reading level. Access to information through oral and written modes may assist in learning and comprehension. Enhancements such as the ability to reread text or student prompting may encourage acquisition of new skills and more sophisticated strategies.
Anchored instruction	Provides an authentic context in which to learn and apply information. Gives students and teachers a shared background upon which to build instruction. Can help compensate for students' lack of background knowledge. Video-based anchors can be reviewed and revisited to gain information and fresh perspectives. Video stories are motivating.
Network-based learning	Provides access to a wealth of information about any conceivable topic. On the World Wide Web, availability of multimedia information can help circumvent text barriers for poor readers. Encourages students to write for authentic audiences and collaborate in the solution of authentic problems, which can be motivating and promote better learning.
Technology Tools	
Word processors	Relieve many logistical barriers to writing, revising, and editing that frustrate poor writers. Help produce a legible product in different formats for publication, which improves attitudes toward writing. Features such as spelling checkers, dictionaries, and thesauruses can provide assistance with spelling and vocabulary. Speech-to-text translation can help students "hear" what they write and draw attention to areas in need of improvement.
Other writing tools	Offer a range of features to support all stages of the writing process. Different tools have features that can help stimulate ideas prior to writing, help organize ideas, and provide on-line assistance with revision and editing. Word prediction software can help poor typists and spellers. Multimedia options can help students represent their ideas in multiple ways, thus stimulating thinking and providing a motivating context for writing.
Tools for organizing content-area information	Outlining and concept mapping programs can help students organize, synthesize, and comprehend content-area information. Can help students view relationships among ideas, rather than learning information as a set of separate, unrelated facts.

(continues)

Table 9.1. *(continued)*

Application	How Application Helps Students with Mild Disabilities
Authoring tools and multimedia projects	Projects permit students to collaborate in the solution of authentic and interesting problems. Encourage collaboration and sustained engagement. Authoring tools provide a way to represent information in a nonlinear manner, helping students to understand multiple perspectives. Opportunities to present project results encourage self-evaluation, revision, and self-esteem.
Electronic reference tools	Multimedia features help students gather information through avenues other than text. Multiple search options provide different ways to access information, enhancing the probability that students will locate desired content. Hand-held electronic tools are portable, inexpensive, and can provide assistance with spelling, vocabulary, and other tasks important for school success.
Databases	Provide an easy way to organize and obtain information. Database activities can help students understand the limitations of information and can encourage analytic thinking and problem solving.

settings are rarely the beneficiaries of state-of-the-art technology applications, the past decade has witnessed a modest revolution in the ways in which technology has been used for teaching and learning. Historically, special educators have used computers primarily to provide drill and practice in basic skills (Becker, 1991; Cosden, 1988; Cosden & Abernathy, 1990; Cosden, Gerber, Semmel, Goldman, & Semmel, 1987; Okolo, Bahr, & Rieth, 1993). The predominance of these activities is predictable, given that most of the software available to educators in the 1980s was designed for this type of instruction. Furthermore, this software met a legitimate need in that students with mild disabilities often require repeated practice to develop basic skill automaticity.

Recent surveys, however, have documented a shift away from technology as an instructional delivery vehicle. As noted by Becker (1991), the author of several national surveys of computer use, today's educators are more likely to view computers "as a tool of intellect-enhancement rather than as a machine for focusing student attention on routine fact and basic skill learning" (p. 406). For example, a survey of more than 600 computer-using teachers found that word processing is the most frequently used software in K–12 classrooms (Sheingold & Hadley, 1990). Fifteen percent of the respondents in this study reported that although they have tried drill-and-practice software in the past, they no longer use it. More recently, a survey of over 1,000 special educators showed that 60% of the respondents used word processing and writing tools such as spelling checkers; drill-and-practice software was reported in use by slightly fewer, or 56%, of the respondents (Robey, Burton-Radzely, & Kallas, 1997).

In this section, I review research about ways that technology can support teaching and ways to use technology as tools. Just as new applications of technology have burgeoned, so has the research. Thus, this review highlights representative studies in each area, with special attention to studies that have included students with mild disabilities and studies that are particularly relevant to the education of these students.

Although I have selectively chosen a sample of studies to discuss, this section of the chapter is lengthy. I hope readers are not deterred by this fact, or by the phrase "review of the research," which may conjure up visions of terse academic discourse with questionable relevance to practice. I believe that there is much to be learned from the rich array of research that has been conducted over the past 15 years, much of it classroom based. I outline studies and their findings below and then, in the next two sections of the chapter, attempt to expand on the implications of these studies for using technology effectively in classroom and clinical settings.

Technology To Support Teaching

Technology To Deliver Instruction and Practice

Basic Skills Instruction. Given the patterns of technology use described above, it is understandable that much of the existing research about the effectiveness of technology for students with mild disabilities has examined the impact of software designed to teach basic skills. In general, this body of research has shown that technology can deliver instruction that facilitates the mastery of basic skills, including math computation, spelling, decoding, word recognition, and vocabulary (e.g., Hasselbring et al., 1988; G. Johnson, Gersten, & Carnine, 1987; Jones, Torgesen, & Sexton, 1987; Lin, Podell, & Rein, 1991; Roth & Beck, 1987; Saracho, 1982; Stevens, Blackhurst, & Slator, 1991; Swan, Guerrero, Mitrani, & Schoener, 1990; Wise & Olson, 1994). The design of these programs is critical to their effectiveness, a topic that I take up in the next section of this chapter.

Several videodisc programs have also been developed and used effectively to teach basic skills in mathematics. For example, the Core Concepts Mathematics Series (Systems Impact) provides whole-class instruction in mathematical topics such as fractions, decimals, and percentages. A teacher operates the videodisc with a hand-held remote control device, through which he or she can access individual video segments and remedial loops and exercise control over the pace of the program. As the videodisc presents instruction, the teacher can circulate among students and assess their progress. When additional instruction is necessary, the teacher can easily access a video segment, freeze the frame, and annotate it with additional explanations or clarification. Research has shown that these programs are effective in helping students master difficult mathematical concepts (Grossen & Carnine, 1996). Their major limitation may be that instruction is so tightly controlled and sequenced that students have difficulty transferring what they know to novel problems and situations (Bottge & Hasselbring, 1993; J. Woodward & Baxter, 1997).

Higher Order Skills and Content-Area Instruction. Research also has demonstrated that technology-based instruction can help students acquire higher order skills. Computers, interactive videodiscs, and multimedia software have been used to deliver effective instruction in areas as diverse as reading comprehension; mathematics and health problem solving; reasoning and study skills; social studies; and community living (Babbit & Miller, 1996; Browning, White, Nave, & Barkin, 1986; Collins et al., 1987; Gleason, Carnine, & Boriero, 1990; Grossen & Carnine, 1990; Horton, Lovitt, Givens, & Nelson, 1989; J. Woodward et al., 1986).

In some school districts, videodisc-based curricula are acceptable alternatives to textbooks for content-area instruction. Some educators find that, in contrast to written text, the dynamic visual and auditory information available on videodiscs helps bring concepts and events to life. Video representations of events and problems enable students to form rich mental models of problem situations (Cognition and Technology Group at Vanderbilt, 1990). They can supply the background knowledge that students with disabilities often need to successfully construct meaning from text or to solve complex problems (Bransford et al., 1988; Van Hanegan et al., 1989). Furthermore, video enables students with reading difficulties to access rich and complex information (Hasselbring & Moore, 1996). Indeed, videodisc-supported instruction is purported to be more efficient than traditional teaching methods and to result in increased retention of information, increased motivation, and reduced behavioral problems (Bosco, 1986).

Computer-Managed Instruction and Integrated Learning Systems. Individualization of instruction to address a particular student's strengths and weaknesses is a hallmark of special education programs. Student achievement increases when teachers make data-based instructional decisions (Fuchs, Deno, & Mirkin, 1984). In addition, students' motivation and interest in their academic programs often improve when they have frequent and immediate access to information about their progress (Hunter & Dickey, 1990). However, the systematic collection and analysis of individualized information is time consuming, labor intensive, and hence infeasible for many teachers. Computers are excellent tools for collecting, recording, storing, and analyzing such data. Sophisticated computer-managed instruction programs increase the ease with which teachers can accomplish the above activities and can enhance the types of data-based instructional decisions they make.

Integrated learning systems (ILSs) are a variant of computer-managed instruction. These systems are often used in Chapter 1 and other instructional programs that target low achievers and at-risk students. The typical system contains both instructional and management components, and the instructional activities are drawn from a broad selection of reading, math, and language arts software that spans several grade levels. The management component collects information about student performance during instructional activities and assigns students to individual lessons based on these data. Integrated learning systems are designed to run on networked computers in a school lab.

Research about the impact of ILSs on student learning is equivocal. After reviewing 30 studies of ILS programs, Becker (1993) concluded that their impact on student achievement varies widely from study to study but is, overall, quite modest. He observed that most ILSs are based on outdated and questionable models of learning that assume all instruction can be broken down and delivered in a series of small, discrete steps. This approach may prohibit students from making connections among concepts and can become repetitive and boring.

Based on systematic observations of four ILSs, Hativa and Lesgold (1996) reported that higher achievers derived greater benefits from ILSs than the lower achievers for whom these systems were primarily designed. They found that high achievers were motivated to compete with each other and thus learned correct answer patterns quickly, albeit superficially. In contrast, low achievers' errors were often misdiagnosed by the system. Software interpreted keyboarding mistakes or misunderstood directions as substantive errors, therefore making incorrect assessments about students' knowledge and, consequently, keeping them mired at lower levels of the system. Furthermore, low achievers received frequent feedback from the computer system indicating failure, further dampening their motivation.

Becker (1993) concluded that ILSs can help low achievers if they are well designed and accompanied by related teacher instruction. Other researchers have suggested that ILSs have not lived up to their potential because they are often implemented incorrectly. Van Dusen and Worthen (1993) purported that, for ILSs to have a positive impact on achievement, educators must provide students adequate time on the system and there must be teacher involvement, curricular integration, and staff development. These criteria are rarely met. For example, in over 80% of the schools studied by Van Dusen and Worthen, students received less than 60 minutes per week on an ILS, with some of this time devoted not to practice but to logging on and waiting for help. Few teachers monitored students' progress or related their classroom instruction to the content of the ILS, making it doubtful that teacher involvement and curricular integration occurred. Teacher monitoring of student progress is especially important, given that Hativa's research found that ILSs may make inaccurate decisions about and prescriptions for students with disabilities (Hativa, 1988; Hativa & Lesgold, 1990).

Electronic Books

Electronic books, typically available in a CD-ROM format, represent a fast-growing segment of the instructional software market. Researchers have examined students' use of electronic storybooks, basal readers, and textbooks. Electronic reference materials, another form of electronic books, are discussed later as an example of a technology tool.

Electronic Storybooks. One popular category of electronic books consists of electronic versions of popular children's literature such as *Green Eggs and Ham* and *Sheila Rae the Brave*. The computer "reads" the text, often with a choice of more than one language. In addition, readers can click on different features of each page to cause specific actions. For example, in the Living Books series (Brøderbund), readers can click on any page or word to hear it reread, click on any item in a picture to view entertaining animation, and in many programs participate in games that reinforce elements of the story. As the computer reads text, words are highlighted, drawing the child's attention to the link between speech and text. Important literacy skills develop through repeated exposure to storybook reading, including an understanding of the purpose of reading; knowledge of print conventions, vocabulary, and story schemas; and interest in and motivation to learn to read. Furthermore, studies have shown that simultaneous visual and auditory presentation of text can improve poor readers' comprehension (Montali & Lewandowski, 1996) and word recognition (Wise & Olson, 1994).

Electronic books can make literature accessible to readers who struggle with print or for whom English is a second language. These children can now enjoy a wide variety of age-appropriate books that are above their reading level without having to depend on others to read for them. These independent reading experiences may enhance students' motivation to read and promote students' self-efficacy as readers.

Despite these potential advantages, there are some possible limitations of electronic storybooks. Students may fail to profit from them because they do not take advantage of the learning opportunities embedded in them. For example, students with mild disabilities may be unaware that they do not recognize a word or that they are failing to comprehend a passage. Thus, they may not request to hear a word or passage reread. Some researchers have found that poor readers and students with learning disabilities do not use electronic book features designed to promote comprehension as effectively or efficiently as their designers might have intended (Keene & Davey, 1987; Reinking & Schriener, 1985; Swanson & Trahan, 1992).

Okolo and her colleagues (Okolo, in preparation; Okolo & Hayes, 1996) have examined ways in which students with and without mild disabilities interact with and comprehend electronic storybooks. They compared students' interaction and comprehension under three conditions: while reading electronic books with extensive animation, while reading electronic books with minimal animation, and while listening to books read by an adult. The results they obtained were nearly identical for students with and without disabilities. Students spent significantly longer periods of time interacting and were more engaged with the electronic storybooks that contained extensive animation. However, comprehension was poorest for electronic books in which animation did not directly support the story. When electronic storybook animation was consistent with the text, students' comprehension was approximately equal across the three conditions. These findings supported previous research demonstrating that illustrations that do not support the text they accompany can be distracting and hinder comprehension (Rose, 1986). Furthermore, these studies showed that, despite prompting, students rarely use electronic features that enable them to reread words or sentences. Thus, they do not spontaneously take advantage of features that are hypothesized to support word recognition and facilitate reading comprehension.

Electronic Basal Readers. Researchers also have investigated the potential of electronic books that provide more extensive instructional support to students with mild disabilities. Higgins and Boone (1990; also see Boone & Higgins, 1993) developed an electronic version of a basal reading series in which students could view and listen to reading sections on the computer and receive a variety of different types of assistance. For example, they could select pictures and animated graphics sequences to illustrate and expand the written text; obtain definitions; learn strategies for decoding words, understanding vocabulary, and using context clues; and engage in activities to promote comprehension of material. The electronic version of the basal reading series was designed to supplement, not replace, traditional reading instruction. Research showed that it was effective in promoting the reading achievement of many of the low achievers who used it, and teachers reported that it enabled some students who are at risk to remain in the general classroom for reading instruction.

Electronic Textbooks. As students progress through the grades, they are expected to have developed sufficient literacy skills to learn from texts and other printed materials. To do so, students must read text that often contains many unfamiliar words and technical terms, uses complex sentence structures, addresses novel content, and assumes a high degree of prior knowledge (Anderson-Inman & Horney, 1998). Content-area textbooks, in particular, have been criticized for their "inconsiderateness," and thus can pose formidable difficulties for students with mild disabilities (e.g., Armbruster & Anderson, 1988; A. Woodward, 1987).

Several researchers have investigated ways in which text can be electronically enhanced to help students overcome the obstacles outlined above. MacArthur and Haynes (1995) developed *The Student Assistant for Learning from Text* (SALT), which permits teachers to develop hypermedia versions of textbooks. The system "reads" text to students and enables teachers to modify it with a variety of features that can enhance its comprehensibility. These include highlighting ideas, defining terms, providing explanations and summaries, adding supplementary text and graphics, and linking questions to their answers within the text itself. In addition, the program provides support for the use of strategies that have been demonstrated to improve comprehension, including previewing a chapter, outlining, and self-questioning. Initial studies of SALT demonstrated that it is easy for students to learn to use and can improve their understanding of content-area texts.

Higgins, Boone, and Lovitt (1996) developed hypermedia study guides based on two chapters from a Washington state history book. The study guides contained the original text linked to enhancements such as additional explanatory information, graphics, or clarification of a word or phrase. Students were required to answer a multiple-choice question on each screen of the text before they were permitted to access the next screen. An incorrect response rerouted the student to the original text. Results suggested that low achievers and students with disabilities learned more when they used the study guides, with and without an accompanying lecture, than they did when they listened to a lecture and took notes. The researchers also found that students were utilizing and reading a substantial number of the electronic enhancements.

Researchers at the Center for Electronic Studying at the University of Oregon (Anderson-Inman, Horney, Chen, & Lewin, 1994; Horney & Anderson-Inman, 1994) developed electronically enhanced versions of short stories taught in a middle school literature class. The at-risk readers who used these electronic books could access vocabulary support in the form of definitions, pictures, and digitized pronunciations of words. Timelines and graphic overviews were provided to help students summarize and synthesize information, and different types of comprehension questions were embedded in the text to encourage the use of more sophisticated reading strategies. Students' systematic and purposeful use of these electronic resources was correlated with their comprehension of the stories (Anderson-Inman & Horney, 1993). Students most often made effective use of the electronic stories, moving through the text systematically and using electronic enhancements in an integrated manner. However, some students were observed to make infrequent use of the electronic resources, accessing them on the first few pages and then abandoning them while moving more quickly through the text itself. Other students were classified as "resource junkies," spending most of their time accessing electronic supports that they enjoyed, such as digitized pictures or sounds, without apparent attention to the relationship

Individualized instruction can be accomplished with computers. (Photograph by Carolyn F. Woods)

between these supports and the text (Horney & Anderson-Inman, 1994). Not surprisingly, these students showed minimal comprehension of the text (Anderson-Inman & Horney, 1993).

Anchored Instruction

Instruction for students with disabilities has been criticized for its focus on teaching isolated skills apart from the contexts in which students will be expected to use them (Bransford, Sherwood, Hasselbring, Kinzer, & Williams, 1990). Decontextualized learning can seem meaningless and unmotivating to students. Students may fail to see the reason for the extensive time they spend in repeated practice of phonics principles, math facts, or grammar rules. Furthermore, decontextualized skill instruction does little to help students know when and how to apply what they have learned. To the frustration of teachers and students alike, knowledge remains inert (Cognition and Technology Group at Vanderbilt, 1990; Whitehead, 1929). Students do not use the knowledge they have practiced and memorized as a tool to help them solve problems in school or in their daily lives.

One way to address the inert knowledge problem is by teaching students skills and information in situations where they can put what they are learning to immediate use. When instruction is *anchored* in a meaningful problem-solving context that cuts across a variety of different curricu-

lar areas, students are more likely to transfer what they have learned (Bransford & Vye, 1989; Cognition and Technology Group at Vanderbilt, 1990).

Video-Based Anchors. Researchers at Vanderbilt University have discussed the benefits of using videodiscs and other video-based materials as anchors that provide broad and rich contexts to facilitate instruction in a variety of skills and content areas. For example, Bransford and his colleagues (Bransford et al., 1994) have articulated the limitations of traditional literacy instruction for students who are at risk or disabled. These include adherence to a purported hierarchy of instruction, decontextualized drills, activities that contribute to dependency and passivity among learners, and lack of attention to the development of comprehension. They contend that effective early literacy instruction must focus on authentic, meaningful problems; embed instruction in basic skills in the context of more global tasks; and make connections with students' out-of-school experiences and cultures. To support these goals, these researchers have developed Multimedia environments that Organize and Support Text (MOST). A major goal of MOST environments is to accelerate children's learning by organizing instruction around visually rich and meaningful video-based stories that students and teachers can explore and share. Supports are provided for listening comprehension, phonemic awareness, decoding, and other word recognition skills. These environments appear to have a positive impact on students' comprehension and on the development of mental models that can support literate behaviors (Bransford et al., 1994; Sharp et al., 1993).

In a series of studies, Hasselbring and colleagues (Bottge & Hasselbring, 1993; Hasselbring & Moore, 1996) have investigated how video-based stories can serve as anchors to promote mathematical problem solving. In one study (Bottge & Hasselbring, 1993), adolescents with learning difficulties in mathematics were taught to solve problems in the context of a video story of two boys who purchase and make a cage for a new pet. All data to solve the problems, such as the price of various pets and different plans for constructing cages, were presented in the video. In order to resolve the overall problem of which pet to purchase and how to house it, students were required to separate relevant from irrelevant information, define and solve subproblems, and apply their knowledge of money, measurement, whole numbers, and fractions. Students who solved the contextualized problems, in contrast to a group of similar students who solved textbook-based story problems, were better able to transfer what they had learned to traditional story problems and to novel video-based problems.

Kinzer, Gabella, and Rieth (1994) have investigated anchored instruction in the social studies. In a unit on justice, students began by viewing a videodisc of *To Kill a Mockingbird* and discussing the historical context of the film. They then studied how political, economic, social, and geographic changes of the past 60 years have shaped today's society. In addition to viewing and reviewing the videodisc, students used computers, technology tools such as databases and word processing, and telecommunications networks to engage in research and communication about the topic of justice. Data showed that students were highly motivated by these activities and engaged in significantly more sophisticated thinking than during more traditional social studies instruction.

Kinzer, Hasselbring, Schmidt, and Meltzer (1990) used segments of news reports as video-based anchors to teach students with mild disabilities reading comprehension and writing skills. In the context of viewing the video anchors, students first learned to identify parts of a news story, monitor story accuracy, and determine the story's point of view. Students then used the anchor to write news stories from different perspectives. Students' writing, in response to both video-based and more traditional writing prompts, showed improvement. Although students' comprehension of video-presented news stories did not change, students were better able to comprehend information in written and orally presented news stories. These results suggested that the skills students learned in the presence of video anchors transferred to more traditional text-based tasks.

Simulations as Anchors. Although the majority of research about anchored instruction has examined video-based anchors, simulation programs could also serve as potentially effective anchors for a unit of instruction. Simulation programs portray complex problems, such as an international crime, the ecology of a rain forest, or a pioneer's cross-country wagon train journey. Often students assume the role of a character, such as a detective, scientist, or pioneer, and work through a series of decisions and problems to reach a desired goal. Simulations can help arouse students' curiosity about a topic and provide a motivating introduction. Students can be active participants in a "slice of reality," which may help them to make connections between information and its application to authentic problems (Frye & Frager, 1996). Participation in and well-structured discussions about a simulation can provide a common background of knowledge to which teachers and students can refer, and return to reexamine, throughout a unit of study.

Leali (1995) investigated the impact of mathematics simulations with 75 high school students at risk for failing their mathematics courses. Students worked in cooperative learning groups with three simulations available from Sunburst: Hot Dog Stand, Budget for Success, and Comparison Shopping. Students alternated roles of team leader, observer, keyboarder, and accountant/recorder. They evaluated their team's work at the end of each session and set a goal for their next. Students' journals showed positive changes in attitudes toward simulations, mathematics, and cooperation. In contrast to a control group that engaged in traditional instruction, students who used the simulations showed greater improvement in mathematics performance.

Network-Based Learning

Over 27 million users in 165 countries have access to the Global Matrix, an international network of information networks, including the Internet (Quartermann & Carl-Mitchell, 1995a, 1995b). There have been extensive efforts to provide American teachers and students with the Global Matrix, via Internet connections, and with good reason. The Internet can support teaching through three types of activities described by Harris (1995a, 1995b, 1995c, 1995d, 1996): interpersonal exchanges, information exchanges, and problem-solving projects.

Interpersonal Exchanges. Through conversations and the exchange of personal information between students, electronic networks can facilitate social-interaction skills and the development of long-distance friendships. Ongoing correspondence with someone whom the student does not know can help him or her realize the importance of describing information and events in a clear and comprehensible manner. Students who are otherwise reluctant writers may be highly motivated by the collaborative and communicative activities that networks offer (M. Cohen & Riel, 1989; Newman, 1987). The opportunity to engage in on-line dialogues provides students with expanded time in which to think and construct responses, in contrast to the pressure of responding immediately in real-time discussions (Meskill, Swan, & Frazer, 1997). Furthermore, one's disability can remain invisible. Thus, interpersonal on-line exchanges may provide students with disabilities an appealing option for communicating with others and accomplishing important academic and social outcomes in the process.

Mueller (1992) described a project in which students who were hospitalized for psychiatric disorders corresponded via electronic mail (e-mail) with students in special education classrooms in four states and Canada. She noted that students' initial correspondences were characterized by superficial information, but their messages over time contained more personal and supportive themes. Furthermore, messages were longer and grammar improved.

Meskill et al. (1997), in a study of community college students, found that students who did not regularly participate in class discussions participated in on-line discussions about class topics. On-line dialogues promoted reflection and collaboration in a way that was impossible within the constraints of classroom discussion. Interestingly, students' on-line comments were longer when they were permitted to sign their contributions with pseudonyms, and they expressed appreciation for the opportunity to respond anonymously, stating that they felt they could be "more honest."

Information Collections. Information collections are telecomputing activities that help students collect, organize, and share information. Students and their teachers collect and share information with other teachers and students around the world on topics of mutual interest such as movie reviews or international eating habits. For example, Kimeldorf (1995) described an activity in which elementary school students compile recipes and put them in a text file. A high school marketing class then takes the text file and produces a desktop-published book, which they package, advertise, and distribute. Also, students can make a virtual visit to other locations via information posted on a network. Through MayaQuest (Scholastic), students and their teachers can participate in a tele-fieldtrip by following the Central American expedition of a team of bicyclists and archaeologists.

Information gathered and shared through an information collection may be organized into a database for further exploration and analysis. In some cases students may engage in pooled data analysis activities and collaborate to analyze patterns in the data and design appropriate solutions.

Problem-Solving Projects. Current views of education stress the social nature of learning. Technology offers unprecedented opportunities for developing communities of learners (Brown, 1994) who work together to complete collaborative activities, share expertise and resources, and learn from each other. Collaborative projects can be organized around authentic tasks, such as designing ways to recycle garbage from the school lunchroom or developing solutions to reduce industrial pollutants. As discussed above, meaningful problem-oriented tasks can enhance students' motivation and increase the likelihood that they will transfer what they learned to new situations (Bransford et al., 1990).

Technology Tools

Word Processing and Other Writing Tools

Word Processing. As described previously in this and other chapters, word processing has overtaken basic skill instruction as the predominant use of educational technology in today's schools. Word processing lends itself well to a process writing approach, which is characterized by the iterative stages of planning, writing, and revision. Because word processing functions such as delete, move, and copy relieve many of the logistical burdens of revising, word processing can make it easier for students to iteratively write and revise, as good writers are known to do.

Poor writers often view writing as a test-taking rather than communicative activity (Thomas, Englert, & Gregg, 1987). Word processing and desktop publishing programs can encourage students to write for a wider audience that includes peers, parents, and others in the community outside school. The computer itself may stimulate more social interaction during writing activities. Because text on the computer screen can be read by anyone passing by, students may be more likely to read and comment on each other's writing as they wait to use a computer or move about the classroom (Bruce, Michaels, & Watson-Gegeo, 1985). Computer-generated copies of compositions can be easily shared and discussed by groups of students. Peer editing activities can help focus students' attention on what is unclear or missing from their composition, thus helping them become more effective writers (MacArthur, 1994).

Although students may make more revisions when they have access to computers and word processing software, these tend to be surface-level changes in spelling, punctuation, and text length (Cochran-Smith, 1991; Daiute, 1986; MacArthur, 1988). However, students' written expression skills often improve when word processing is incorporated into a systematic program of written expression instruction (Morocco, Dalton, & Tivnan, 1990; Stoddard & MacArthur, 1993).

Numerous studies have found that students have positive attitudes toward writing with word processors, believe that their writing improves, are more relaxed about writing with word processors, and are proud of their finished compositions (Cochran-Smith, 1991). Word processing programs and other tools such as desktop publishing software make it possible for students to produce professional-looking documents, including books, newsletters, and posters. Consequently, students are more motivated to share their writing. These are important outcomes, for students who have more positive attitudes about writing will participate more willingly in writing activities and thus gain more practice and experience as writers.

Spelling Checkers. A wide variety of other technology-based tools exist to support students' writing. For example, almost all word processing programs contain a spelling checker to help writers locate and correct their spelling errors. MacArthur, Graham, Haynes, and De La Paz (1996) demonstrated that, in a sample of students with learning disabilities who were experienced computer users, students found only about 28% of their spelling errors and successfully corrected only about 9% of them without a word processor. However, when these students used a word processing program with a spelling checker, they found about 63% of their errors and corrected 37%. Although these data suggested that spelling checkers improved students' compositions, many errors remained, indicating that students may need to use error-correction strategies in addition to running compositions through a spelling checker.

Speech Synthesis and Word Prediction. Speech synthesis, which translates typed letters and words into speech, has been incorporated into many word processing packages. A few researchers have found that hearing their text read to them has positive effects on students' writing (Borgh & Dickson, 1992; Rosegrant, 1986).

Word prediction software, a tool developed to reduce keyboarding demands, typically incorporates speech synthesis (also see Chapters 5 and

11). As the user types a letter, the software predicts the intended word and presents a list of words from which the user can select. With each subsequent letter typed, the prediction is updated and the list is revised. These programs vary in the information they use to predict word choices, but most use some combination of spelling patterns, word frequency, syntax, and user preferences.

Although originally developed to facilitate text entry for individuals with physical disabilities, word prediction programs may assist students with mild disabilities who have not mastered keyboarding skills. Students with severe spelling difficulties who can type the first few letters of a word may then select their intended word, correctly spelled, from the prediction list, thus improving their written products. Speech synthesis features help support students who might have difficulty reading word choices (Heinisch & Hecht, 1993).

MacArthur (1997) investigated the impact of a word processing package that contained speech synthesis and word prediction. Five students with learning disabilities used this software package to participate in dialogue journals with their teachers. By responding to and expanding upon students' journal entries, initiating new topics, and asking for clarification, teachers used dialogue journals to model written language. In this study, students wrote about self-selected topics with the My Words (Hartley) software program. Teachers responded to their writing by typing entries into their My Words file. The speech synthesis feature of the program enabled students to "read" their teachers' comments and to benefit from language models that were above their reading levels. In addition, the intervention had a strong positive effect on the legibility and spelling of journal entries of four of the five students.

Writing Prompts. Some computer-based tools support writing by prompting students to engage in effective strategies. Prompts, in the form of questions or statements, may remind students to consider audience, purpose, and content; direct their attention to the elaboration, organization, and explicitness of their text; and assist them in addressing mechanical aspects of their writing. Several researchers have found that textual

prompts can improve the quality of students' writing (Daiute, 1986; Zellermayer, Salomon, Globerson, & Givon, 1991).

Other software programs offer students the opportunity to create pictorial writing prompts. Students can create pictures by selecting from existing backgrounds and objects available within a software program or they can use graphics tools to produce original illustrations. By creating pictures before or while they write, students may activate their prior knowledge about a topic and thus develop their ideas more fully (Golub & Frederick, 1970). Swan and Meskill (1997) observed that the illustrations available in some components of a software program they developed seemed to help students construct richer and more coherent stories and provided support for more extended writing.

In a sample of students with learning and language disabilities, Bahr, Nelson, and Van Meter (1996) found no differences between textual and pictorial prompts on the quality and length of students' written compositions. These researchers noted that pictorial prompts seemed to help students plan their compositions but also detracted from the time available to write. Some students spent so much time creating pictures that they had to rush to complete their compositions, resulting in more errors.

Multimedia Composing Tools. Daiute and Morse (1994) proposed that students with disabilities often make poor progress in writing because instruction is centered around their disabilities rather than strengths. They noted the potential mismatch between the ubiquitous text-based instruction of schools and the strengths that many students have in aural and visual media. These researchers helped eight poor writers, of whom five received special education services, create compositions with a multimedia writing program that integrated their pictures and sounds with text. Students were given cameras and tape recorders to capture pictures and sounds and had access to a scanner to digitize pictures of interest. Daiute and Morse provided in-depth case studies for three of the students in their sample, demonstrating that writing with pictures and sounds helped students produce longer and richer compositions, enhanced students' motivation to write, and improved students' beliefs about themselves as writers. The researchers also found that the opportunity to write about images and sounds of personal interest was a powerful strategy for individualizing instruction and building upon the children's cultures and interests.

Tools for Organizing Content-Area Information

Outlining and concept mapping programs are robust tools that can assist writers in organizing their thoughts prior to and during the writing process (MacArthur, 1996). These tools also can facilitate students' acquisition of content-area information. Anderson-Inman and her colleagues (Anderson-Inman, Horney, Knox-Quinn, Corrigan, & Ditson, 1997; Anderson-Inman, Knox-Quinn, & Horney, 1996) have developed a repertoire of electronic study strategies using electronic outlines and concept mapping software. In their studies students with mild disabilities have used these tools to plan assignments, brainstorm ideas, take notes on textbooks and lectures, and synthesize information and self-test their knowledge. The researchers found that these tools and strategies improved the text comprehension of average and below average students and boosted the test performance of students with learning disabilities (Anderson-Inman et al., 1996).

Authoring Tools and Multimedia Projects

Consistent with attempts to involve students in more meaningful, extended learning activities, project-based learning has enjoyed a resurgence of interest in educational settings. In project-based learning activities, students engage in an extended investigation of an authentic question or problem. They collaborate with peers and others in a community of learners (Brown, 1994) to share expertise and construct a socially mediated understanding of their topic. They develop artifacts that represent the results of their investigations and share these with peers and other audiences (Blumenfeld et al., 1991). Cognitive tools

such as multimedia technology and writing tools (Cognition and Technology Group at Vanderbilt, 1990; MacArthur, 1996) are used to support and extend students' activities. Multimedia authoring software permits students to develop nonlinear displays of integrated text, images, and sound and provides a tool for students to illustrate and present the results of their investigations. A growing literature has described the variety of topics that teachers and their students have explored, including autobiographies, studies of one's own culture or community, and investigations of history, social science, and science topics (e.g., Carver, 1995; Lehrer, Erickson, & Connell, 1993; Okolo & Ferretti, 1996, 1997; Prickett, 1992; Rembelinsky, 1997–1998; Smith, 1992; Turner & Dipinto, 1992).

In a 4-year investigation, Ferretti and Okolo (1996, 1997; Okolo & Ferretti, 1996, 1997) have found that students with mild disabilities, working together with their nondisabled peers in collaborative groups, can successfully design multimedia projects about topics in the social studies. Students' knowledge of social studies topics and their attitudes toward social studies learning and cooperation improve by virtue of participation in these projects. Furthermore, observational data suggested that students with disabilities participate in research and project design activities at the same level as their nondisabled peers.

Electronic Reference Materials

Previously I discussed electronic books and the ways in which students might use them to enhance reading and learning. Electronic reference books, typically available on CD-ROM (DVD-ROM titles are increasing), are another type of technology tool that helps students by offering expanded ways to access information. Several popular dictionaries and encyclopedias are available on CD-ROM, and electronic enhancements make them easier to use and understand than text-based versions. Electronic reference materials contain text, pictures, sounds, and selected movie clips. Although the text is often as sophisticated as and no easier to understand than print-based versions, access to pictures, movies, and sounds can enhance students' comprehension of information. Electronic references also offer multiple ways for a student to search for information because any entry can be linked to multiple entries in a hypertext format (e.g., students are no longer restricted to a table of contents). They can now search by multiple indices, keywords, media type (e.g., pictures, sounds), atlases, timelines, and topically arranged graphic metaphors.

Increased search options enhance the probability that students will locate the information they seek and form richer connections between concepts and ideas. Research has suggested that electronic versions of reference materials are more effective when users are searching for information not explicitly contained in a table of contents or chapter headings (Egan, Remadae, Landauer, Lochdaum, & Gomez, 1989; Lehto, Zhu, & Carpenter, 1995; Leventhal, Teasley, Instone, Rohlman, & Farhat, 1993). However, especially when tasks are simple or facts are easy to locate through a table of contents or other index, fact retrieval may be slower in electronic than paper versions of reference materials (Marchionni, 1989; Marchionni & Schneiderman, 1988). In addition, the text of electronic encyclopedias is often shown in a small text box, which increases the difficulty of reading it. Despite these limitations, several studies have shown that users prefer electronic reference materials to paper versions (Marchionni, 1989; Marchionni & Schneiderman, 1988).

Edyburn (1991) studied students with and without disabilities as they retrieved information from different types of electronic encyclopedias. He found that students were about equally successful in retrieving specific facts from print and electronic versions of encyclopedias. Students with disabilities were able to retrieve only 16% of the requested information, whereas students without disabilities retrieved 43%. Furthermore, students performed better when they were assigned specific tasks than when they were able to self-select a task. These data suggest that searching for information, regardless of the format in which it is stored, is a difficult task for many students, and teachers should allocate time for instruction in information retrieval skills.

Databases

Databases are flexible, open-ended tools that can be used to store information in many different forms, including print, sounds, and images. In a typical database, information is organized in records, in a manner similar to index cards in a Rolodex. Each record contains the same set of information, stored in fields. Users can search the database in various ways, looking for specific records or looking for fields that contain certain types of data. Fields can contain text-based and, in a growing number of instances, multimedia information, such as pictures, sounds, and movie clips.

Stearns (1992) described projects in which special education teachers used databases in social studies and science instruction for students with mild disabilities. In one classroom, students used a commercial database about world cultures to research a nation of their choice and write a report. According to their teacher, students' reports contained the best writing they had done all year. In a second classroom, students worked with a database of information about the 50 states, developed questions they wished to explore, and printed reports of their investigations. Students were eager to show these reports to their parents, and increased contact between the classroom and home was an unintended outcome of the project. In a third classroom, students investigated topics in a commercial database and then designed their own databases about topics of personal interest. Their teacher noted improved organizational skills, more coherent writing, and more productive classroom discussions as a result of the database activities. All three teachers reported that their students were enthusiastic about database activities and remained on task much longer during these than during traditional school activities.

Teachers should be aware that access to data, whether generated by students or prepackaged, does not guarantee that students will reason appropriately with those data. Hancock, Kaput, and Goldsmith (1992) found that students as young as 8 years of age could understand a database tool, Tabletop (Brøderbund), including the various data plots that it produced. However, students aged 8 to 15 years had problems using data plots to support conclusions about a question under investigation. They also engaged in faulty reasoning because they often focused on individual cases rather than examining the central tendencies computed and represented by the database's tools. Furthermore, students often held tenaciously to personal views about a question or issue, even in the face of data that proved another view was more plausible. For example, students developed graphs or diagrams to represent trends in the data, such as students' favorite cafeteria meals, and then ignored these completely while formulating a conclusion based on their own experiences, such as a personal fondness for pizza. Finally, students struggled with issues of objectifying and externalizing knowledge. They sometimes resisted putting specific fields, such as gender, in a database because they claimed they already knew this information and thus had no reason to explicitly record it. Without including information about gender, however, students were unable to use the database to see if gender-based trends existed. Students also experienced difficulties in developing objective and reliable ways to collect information to include in a database.

General Hardware and Software Considerations

As the research reviewed previously demonstrates, educators have examined a multitude of ways in which technology can be used to improve the educational experiences of all students, including those with mild disabilities. This research also has exposed many limitations of technology use and warns of factors that need to be built into technology-based activities to optimize their impact on learning and motivation. This section articulates seven general considerations about the use of technology, whether it serves as a support for teaching or as a tool. It goes without saying that the points presented below review or expand upon similar issues presented in other chapters because (a) chapter authors are trying to develop a shared vision with respect to technology and exceptional individuals and (b) the importance of these considerations dictates that they be kept in the forefront.

Technology Must Be Integrated with the Curriculum

In a perfect world educators would have classrooms equipped with as many computers and other technologies as needed. In the real world, however, students must share access to limited technological resources. Thus, educators must prioritize the goals and purposes for which they are used. It should be clear from the research discussed previously that there is no *one* best or most effective way to use computers and other technologies. However, research has shown that, if instructional technology is to have optimal impact, it must be used by teachers in a systematic manner as part of their ongoing instructional programs. In other words, instructional technology must be *integrated* with the curriculum (Macro Systems, 1989; Winkler, Shavelson, Stasz, Robyn, & Fiebel, 1985; see also Chapter 8). Educators should give first priority to technology activities that are consistent with their curricular goals and that can support students' attainment of those outcomes.

Technology will be more effective and easier to integrate with the curriculum when it helps educators meet multiple, simultaneous goals. Technology applications that cross curricular boundaries are a good example. Consider a network-based learning activity in which students are collaborating with other schools about the concentration of acid rain in local communities. Such a project entails writing skills (as students correspond with distant peers), reading skills (as students read about acid rain in textbooks and other sources), science (as students learn about ecosystems and factors, such as environmental pollutants, that impact them), and social science (as students discuss the social implications of, for example, reducing industrial pollutants by making changes in local industries). Rich activities, in the hands of skilled teachers, help students meet multiple goals, provide them with authentic experiences and skills, and help them to see the connections between knowledge and action.

Although there is no best way to use technology, there is a best way *not* to use it: *only* as a reward for students who complete their work or behave appropriately. Not only does this type of use represent a narrow view of technology's potential, but also it is the students with mild disabilities—those with academic and behavioral problems—who often do not "earn" their computer time. Yet, these are the very students who stand so much to gain from access to technology.

Instructional Software Must Embody Principles of Effective Instruction

Research about the use of technology to deliver instruction in both basic and higher order skills makes it clear that technology-based instruction is most effective when it incorporates principles of effective instruction (Okolo, Bahr, & Rieth, 1993). There is nothing magical about the technology itself that promotes student achievement; rather it is the design of the software and the way it is used that facilitate student learning (see Clark, 1983). Poorly designed systems of instruction, regardless of the media through which they are delivered, are unlikely to improve student achievement. Some criteria to consider when reviewing technology-based instruction are presented in Table 9.2.

In an attempt to capture students' interest, many software programs have incorporated video game features such as fantasy themes, fast-paced responding, auditory and visual embellishments, and variable levels of performance (e.g., Chaffin, Maxwell, & Thompson, 1982; Malone, 1981). Although the idea of embedding learning activities in video game formats has considerable intuitive appeal, research suggests that gamelike features be used judiciously. These may detract from the time available for practice and learning (Okolo, 1991) and distract students from the skill they are supposed to practice (Christensen &

Table 9.2. Features of Effective Instructional Software

What To Look For	What To Avoid	Rationale
Programs that provide high rates of responding relevant to the skill to be learned.	Programs that take too much time to load and run or that contain too many activities unrelated to the skill to be learned.	The more time students spend on task, the more they learn.
Programs in which graphics and animation support the skill or concept that is being practiced.	Programs with graphics or animation that are unrelated to the program's instructional objectives.	While graphics and animation may facilitate student interest in an activity, they may distract students, interfere with skill mastery, and reduce practice time.
Programs in which reinforcement is used sparingly and approximates the type of reinforcement schedule students encounter in the classroom.	Programs that provide a reinforcing graphic or activity after every correct response.	If students are reinforced too frequently for correct responses, they may no longer exhibit those responses when fewer or no reinforcers are offered. Furthermore, excessive time spent engaging in the reinforcing activities detracts from time to learn and interferes with the development of automaticity.

Table 9.2. (*continued*)

What To Look For	What To Avoid	Rationale
Programs in which reinforcement is clearly related to task completion or mastery.	Programs in which the events that occur when students are incorrect (e.g., an explosion) are more reinforcing than the events that occur when the student is correct (e.g., a smiling face).	Some programs may actually encourage students to practice the incorrect response in order to view the event that they find more reinforcing.
Programs in which feedback helps students locate and correct their mistakes.	Programs in which students are merely told if they are right or wrong or are told to "try again."	Without feedback that informs them of the correct answer after a reasonable number of attempts, students may become frustrated and/or make random guesses.
Programs that provide practice on a small set of carefully sequenced items.	Programs that provide practice on a wide range of diverse items or programs that draw items at random from a large set of potential items.	Students master information more readily when they are given a small set of items that are carefully sequenced according to difficulty and/or to reduce potential confusion among similar items.
Programs that provide practice in a variety of different ways.	Programs in which students always practice a skill in the same way or always practice the same set of items.	If practice is not varied, students are less likely to generalize what they learn to new settings and situations.
Programs that provide cumulative review.	Programs that drop items once students have mastered them.	Students need to review previously mastered skills on a regular basis if they are to retain what they have learned.
Programs that store information about student performance or progress that can be accessed by the teacher at a later time.	Programs without record-keeping features.	Students may encounter difficulties with the skills covered by a program that require teacher intervention. However, teachers often find it difficult to monitor students as they work at the computer. Access to records of student performance enables the teacher to determine if a program is benefiting a student and whether the student needs additional assistance.
Programs with options for controlling features such as speed of problem presentation, type of feedback, problem difficulty, and number of practice trials.	Programs that must be used in the same way with every student.	Options are cost-effective; they enable the same program to be used with a broad range of students. Furthermore, they allow a teacher to provide more appropriately individualized instruction.

Gerber, 1990). Gamelike features may be most appropriate for students who have low motivation for a particular activity (Malouf, 1987–1988; Okolo, 1992; Okolo, Hinsey, & Yousefian, 1990).

Regardless of the type of program a teacher selects, software designed to foster memorization of basic facts, as is often the case with drill-and-practice programs, should never be used with students who have not yet acquired a conceptual understanding of a skill (see also Chapter 6). Students should use timed drills to rehearse information they already know but retrieve slowly. Otherwise, computer-based practice will have minimal effects on students' automaticity, and in some cases only encourage the rapidity with which students use strategies that interfere with automaticity, such as finger counting (Hasselbring et al., 1988). Drill-and-practice activities are more likely to be effective if students engage in short, spaced practice periods that intersperse to-be-learned material with frequent review of mastered information (Salisbury, 1990). Finally, drill and practice in basic skills should not be utilized as a prerequisite for engagement in more complex and meaningful activities. Rather, drill-and-practice activities will be more effective and motivating when their practice is embedded in meaningful skill application (Pea, 1987).

Students Need To Be Taught How To Use Technology

Technology applications have the potential to help students learn more and perform better. First, however, students need to learn how to use these applications. Even simple applications, which may seem self-evident to a teacher or clinician, can be confusing to a novice user. Combine that confusion with the struggle to perform a difficult task, such as setting up a math problem or writing a composition, and technology becomes a liability rather than an asset to instruction. Thus, teachers must allocate sufficient time to teach students how to use any new application. This includes reviewing directions and instructional feedback in applications that provide basic skills instruction and demonstrating and providing

Technology tools should not be used in isolation to develop academic and other abilities. (Photograph by Carolyn F. Woods)

guided practice in the use of features of technology tools. Students with disabilities can learn to use these tools, but educators must allocate sufficient time for these skills to develop.

After instruction, easy-to-read instructions, posted by each computer, can help students recall specific procedures as they use technology applications. An initial investment in preparing a subset of the class to be the "computer experts" can provide a welcome payoff when students are clamoring for assistance. Teachers can rotate experts, depending on the particular technology applications in use in the classroom. Students with disabilities can fulfill the expert role quite capably, gaining an opportunity to appear competent to peers.

Collaboration Takes Teaching and Support

Many of the instructional applications I have reviewed, including anchored instruction, multimedia projects, and network-based learning, entail collaboration among students. Also, word processing activities, simulations, and many programs designed to provide practice in basic skills can be used profitably by small groups of students (e.g., Cox & Berger, 1985; Dalton, Hannafin, & Hooper, 1989). Decades of research about collaborative and cooperative learning have promoted several very important principles that warrant attention in designing group-based activities that employ technology.

First, groups should be selected with care. Although it may be tempting to let students select their own groupmates, this approach mitigates against some potential benefits of cooperative learning. For example, it is unlikely that students will choose to work with unfamiliar peers. Because self-selected groups tend to be homogeneous, some groups will always outperform others. Consequently, cooperative learning mutates into another form of classroom competition, in which students with disabilities and other low achievers are sure to lose. Rather, teachers should strive to maximize group heterogeneity. Each group should be composed of students whose performance levels range from high to low, so that the average performance level of all groups is about equal (Dockterman, 1994). We have used reading scores and pretest scores about a topic as a way to share expertise across groups (Ferretti & Okolo, 1996). Similarly, ethnicity, race, and gender should be distributed among groups.

Second, social skills are essential for effective group work. Research has shown that students with mild disabilities often have social skills difficulties (Hazel & Schumaker, 1988; Vaughn et al., 1991), and students without disabilities may be less than tolerant of their peers who experience difficulties with group activities such as reading, writing, and speaking. Thus, students need to be taught those skills that will help them collaborate, including the following (Dockterman, 1994):

- Do not speak when others are speaking.

- Listen to what everyone has to say.

- Give everyone a chance.

- Use voting when necessary. Let the majority rule when conflicts occur.

- Say something positive about others' contributions to the group before you offer constructive criticism.

We have found that it helps to build social skill guidelines around the existing classroom rules (Feretti & Okolo, 1996). We introduce one social skill at a time, model its application through examples and nonexamples, and then give students a brief group activity, during which we monitor their use of the target skill and after which we ask the group to evaluate its use of the skill. As skills are introduced, they are added to a checklist that the teacher and students themselves use to monitor group work throughout the year. Kagan's (1994) book contains many useful activities for developing social skills in cooperative groups.

Third, when students engage in ill-structured activities such as projects, researchers have found that the nature of group discussion is critical for achievement gains. E. G. Cohen (1994) characterized optimal group interaction as an interactive process in which students share ideas, hypotheses, and strategies. Webb and her colleagues (e.g., Webb, 1992) found that students learn more in cooperative groups when they provide explanations and justifications for their ideas. However, Cosden, Goldman, and Hine (1990) found that students with disabilities were more apt to acquiesce than defend their personal opinions when discussing controversial issues in a group. Also, we have found that the majority of group discussion during multimedia projects, for students both with and without disabilities, is of a relatively low cognitive level (Okolo & Ferretti, 1997). Students spend most of their time giving information, reading independently, or listening to another student. Without instruction in how to do so, students rarely offer explanations, ask for clarifications, or question each others' contributions—the types of behaviors that promote achievement.

To maximize learning during cooperative activities, it is important to teach skills that can promote higher levels of discourse. King's (1994) reciprocal questioning strategy can promote group discussion and achievement. Students are first taught to differentiate between "memory" questions, or those requiring them to remember and repeat information, and "thinking" questions, or those that require them to remember information *and* think about it in some new way. Thinking questions are further classified into "comprehension" questions, which check how well someone understands, and "connection" questions, which link together two or more ideas. Students also are taught the difference between providing descriptions ("telling the 'what' about it") and explanations ("telling the 'why and how' of it"). Students learn to give explanations and to ask thinking questions through extensive teacher modeling and discussion. They then practice these skills in group activities, with teacher scaffolding and additional instruction as needed. Prompt cards, with examples of thinking questions, are given to each group to remind them to use these techniques during group discussion. Other suggestions for promoting cognitive skills in collaborative groups are contained in Sharan and Sharan's (1992) book. As with social skills, teachers and students should continue to monitor the exercise of cognitive skills during all phases of group work.

Fourth, teachers need to build interdependence among group members (D. W. Johnson, Johnson, & Holubec, 1994; Nastasi & Clements, 1991; Slavin, 1984). Otherwise, there are few incentives for students to work together. This is especially important in heterogeneous groups, where high achievers may choose to do most of the work, slighting students who are less capable. Alternatively, some students may choose not to participate because of skills deficits, poor motivation, or anxiety about working with peers. Group activities can be structured so that students have to work together through:

- *Goal interdependence*—setting goals that everyone in the group must attain.

- *Reward interdependence*—rewarding the group on the basis of the group's overall achievement (e.g., percentage of improvement over the average initial score of the group).

- *Resource interdependence*—providing limited copies of materials, rather than one copy per student, so that students must share. Ironically, the fact that technology resources are scarce can help promote resource interdependence.

- *Role interdependence*—assigning specialized but complementary roles to each individual in

the group so that everyone has a job in completing a task.

In addition, to interdependence, individual students must be held accountable for learning or improving as a result of cooperative learning activities. Thus, teachers should devise some way to assess and evaluate individuals' contributions to the group and personal improvement.

Finally, group work requires considerable teacher support. As emphasized previously, teachers must choose groups carefully and invest a considerable amount of time in teaching the social and cognitive skills needed for effective collaboration. Although it then may be tempting to sit back and let the students proceed as they will, the teacher plays an essential role throughout group activities. He or she must continue to monitor behavior, provide assistance with substantive tasks, and provide support with students' use of technology. We have found that student groups do the best in classrooms where teachers are constantly circulating, asking provocative questions, giving feedback, and monitoring progress (Okolo & Ferretti, 1997).

Project-Based Learning Requires Time and Preparation

The astute reader will have noticed that anchored instruction, network-based learning, multimedia projects, and some of the database activities described previously can be variants of project-based learning. Although technology plays a slightly different role in each of these learning activities (i.e., providing a context, serving as a connection to people or information, offering a means for developing presentations, providing a data collection or analysis tool), all can involve students in extended investigation of problems or issues, with the end goal of producing a specific product. The fact that this chapter includes so many applications of project-based learning is not an accident—it is my contention that project-based learning activities offer the richest environments in which to use technology and the most effective ways of integrating technology into the curriculum.

Regardless of the type of technology used, projects have in common the fact that they all entailed extended student work over a period of weeks or months. One of the first things teachers should consider when contemplating project-based learning is that these types of activities require a larger time commitment than more traditional instructional activities. Sufficient time must be allocated to enable students to adequately investigate a topic and develop an artifact, whether it be a multimedia presentation, a database, or a report.

Teachers may be well advised to start with simple projects involving easy technology tools and then build up to more complex topics and technology. Keep in mind that project development entails a complex series of steps and the simultaneous consideration of multiple processes. Students must attend to the substance that they wish to convey in their project, the tools to present that substance, and the design of their artifact. Substance should have primary consideration in students' efforts, and educators must be sure that students are not skimping on time needed to research and understand their topic in deference to time spent on packaging their product (Madian, 1995). Furthermore, students need time and guidance to develop the research skills that drive project-based learning. These include the ability to locate information about a topic, gather sufficient data, analyze information from diverse sources, consider multiple perspectives, synthesize and organize information, decide how best to convey findings, and transform those findings into multiple representations. Lamb, Smith, and Johnson (1997) described an eight-phase learning model for teaching the process of completing a research project. This article may be helpful to teachers as they contemplate how to teach research skills.

We (Ferretti & Okolo, 1996) have found that, before students embark on projects, it is important to provide them with models of completed ones and with demonstrations of features of the software they will use. These activities can be accomplished through a whole-class demonstration with a computer and large-screen monitor or LCD (liquid crystal display) panel (see Chapter 8). We also have discovered that it is essential to provide students with a structure for their final product. We provide explicit guidance about the features that we wish students to include in their final project, including the substantive components and the media elements to support them. Paper-based planning forms and templates are extremely helpful as students plan and organize their presentations. These devices also help students make the most of their time at the computer, which often has to be limited because of less than optimal computer–student ratios. Several useful examples of templates are provided in the article by Monahan and Susong (1996).

Finally, opportunities to showcase students' work are important elements of project-based activities. Researchers have found that the receipt of feedback from other students or audiences outside the classroom helps students to gain a new perspective on their work and make improvements in their products (Carver, 1995). The opportunity to display projects to audiences such as parents or conference participants encourages students to be more accountable for their work and to take pride in their efforts.

Information Is Not Knowledge

Technology continues to become increasingly sophisticated and affordable, storage media advance in power and capacity, and algorithms for compressing and conveying information across distances continue to evolve. A combination of these factors helps contribute to the fact that information is readily available on just about any conceivable topic.

This widely touted advantage of technology is also a major liability of its use. Information is not knowledge. Consider the World Wide Web, a component of the Internet that is mushrooming daily. In an analysis of 1,140 randomly selected World Wide Web sites, Debashis (1995) found 22% of the material focused on public relations information and 21% was advertising. Or, consider the experience of Harris (1996), simulating the role of a student using the Internet to conduct research about whales. Her efforts yielded over

150 hits per search which, along with information of great use to a student researcher, included petitions, whale-watching tour schedules, a review of a graduate course, a description of the phrase "kicking dead whales down the beach," and e-mail that happened to include the word "whale" somewhere in a correspondent's remarks. Clearly, students must learn to sort through a morass of information available on the Internet and other networks, on databases, on CD-ROMs and DVD-ROMs, and in other formats. Much of this information is only tangentially related to a student's initial purpose for conducting a search, or is of dubious credibility. Thus, students and teachers must limit themselves to appropriate interpretations and applications.

To productively use networks and other technology-based applications as information resources, students will need to learn how to transform that information into knowledge (i.e., something that is meaningful and understandable to them and applicable to their purposes). To do this students first need to learn skills to gather available information. These include search strategies and use of specific search tools available on the Internet and World Wide Web and in local databases. No less important, students must learn to analyze and interpret the data they obtain from their information forays. Wilkinson, Bennett, and Oliver (1997) outlined categories of criteria they culled from a variety of Internet and library reference materials that could be used for judging the quality of Internet resources. These categories are presented in Table 9.3, along with sample questions one might ask about features of the information. If students can answer these questions about their own research, a teacher might have more confidence that they are engaged not only

Table 9.3. Criteria for Judging the Quality of Information Sources

Resource identification and documentation: What is the title of the document? For what audience was it designed? When was the document last revised?

Author identification: What is the author's name and professional affiliation? What is the author's training or experience with the topic? Was the development of the document funded or otherwise supported by an individual, group, or organization other than the author?

Authority of author: Is the author an authority on the topic of the document? Has the author published related materials dealing with the topic? Is the author's training and experience appropriate and related to the document?

Information structure and design: Is the scope of the document clearly stated? Are the limits of the document stated? Does the content fit the stated scope, purpose, and audience? Has an appropriate treatment been employed to meet the objectives? Can the treatment employed be generalized to a range of situations?

Relevance and scope of content: Is the information sufficiently current? Is the information sufficiently broad? Does the document provide any new information on the topic? Are there obvious gaps or omissions in the coverage of the topic?

Validity of content: Has the document been linked to or referenced by a recognized authority? Is the document peer reviewed? Is the document a primary or secondary source? Does the information contradict or confirm information from other sources? Does the author cite references or data to support information and conclusions?

Accuracy and balance of content: Are there any obvious errors or misleading omissions in the document? If the document deals with controversial issues, is the bias of the author clearly identified? Does the author or sponsor have a vested or commercial interest in the topic?

Note. Adapted from "Evaluation Criteria and Indicators of Quality for Internet Resources," by G. L. Wilkinson, L. T. Bennett, and K. M. Oliver, 1997, *Educational Technology, 37*(3), pp. 52–59.

in the process of collecting information but also in the transformation of that information into knowledge.

Teachers Must Find New Modes for Assessment and Evaluation

Assessment and evaluation of technology-based learning pose new challenges for educators. Criteria typically applied to traditional instruction may not capture the nature of "multimedia" learning that is no longer based only in text. Brunner (1996) provided a helpful list of criteria for evaluating students' multimedia projects that could be adapted for other types of student products in which information is not restricted to print. Examples of evaluation criteria are outlined in Table 9.4. These could form the basis for a checklist that teachers could use to evaluate student-produced multimedia compositions, projects, or other products.

Because many technology-based activities are spread across time, it is important *not* to wait until the end of an activity to evaluate students' work and provide feedback. Rather, formative assessment should be an ongoing part of technol-ogy-based learning and results used to help students improve their performance, process of research, and collaboration over the life of an activity. Teachers should consider evaluation strategies *before* undertaking technology-based activities and make evaluation criteria explicit and public. Then, teachers and students can monitor the inclusion of evaluation criteria over the course of project development. Group inter-action, planning, and decision making can be evaluated on an ongoing basis through logs of students' discussions, decisions, and progress; individual journals; daily debriefing sessions; and checklists.

Instructional Applications

Now that I have set the stage by reviewing research and discussing general considerations for technology use, it is time to get down to specifics and discuss examples of software, CD-ROMs (again DVD-ROM titles are increasing), laser-discs, and hand-held electronic devices that can be used to support teaching and that can be used as technology tools. I provide examples of titles

---

Table 9.4. Criteria for Judging Students' Multimedia Products

Preparation: Can students state the questions that motivated their research? Have the students defined the sections of their report and how they relate to each other? How clear and complete are the students' storyboards?

Sources: How varied are the sources on which the research is based? How appropriate are the sources? Are sources of text, images, sounds, animation, and so forth, properly referenced?

Organization: Is there an appropriate central metaphor, such as a book in which buttons are used to turn the pages, that ties together different parts of the report? How good is the screen design? How good is the design of the information? Can the audience find the information it needs? Is it clear what is central and what is tangential information?

Navigation: How clear are navigation signals? Are links conceptual as well as navigational?

Media integration: Do students understand that their choice of representations (e.g., quotations, sounds, videos) creates a point of view? Can they articulate assumptions behind the representations they chose? Can they explain why they selected some materials and not others? How appropriate is the choice of media? How does it relate to the content they wish to convey? Can students explain their editorial decisions?

Note. Adapted from "Judging Student Multimedia," by C. Brunner, 1996, *Electronic Learning, 15*(6), pp. 14–15.

that fit into each category of technology use outlined previously. The examples are not exhaustive but rather selective; they are some titles commonly used by special and general educators to accomplish specific instructional goals. Inclusion of a title does not imply that I am making a judgment about its quality. In the final analysis, what students derive from their experiences with any application will depend on how skillfully they are prepared to use it, how adequately it is integrated into the curriculum, and how well their teachers harness its potential to expand students' skills and understanding. Where appropriate, this section also highlights factors to consider when using specific applications and examples of activities in which they have been used.

Technology To Support Teaching

Technology To Deliver Instruction and Practice

A dizzying array of software has been developed to assist students in their mastery of basic academic skills. Some products focus on the early learning market by targeting preschoolers and readiness skills such as letter and number recognition. Others are designed to help students master basic skills in such areas as word identification, math facts, and spelling patterns. Because students with mild disabilities are often low achievers, the age range cited as appropriate for a particular program may be too restrictive (e.g., older students may be able to benefit from programs advertised for younger learners). However, teachers and clinicians should review programs to make sure that their themes, graphics, and other features are age appropriate.

Early Learning Software. With the growth in home computers, the number of software programs to support early learning goals has burgeoned. Most early childhood experts recommend that technology-based activities capitalize on young children's curiosity, emphasize interaction and discovery, and teach youngsters how to work independently and make choices (Haugland & Shade, 1988; Murphy & Thuente, 1995).

Special educators should be on the lookout for difficulties that young children will encounter, such as text-based directions, complex loading procedures, and slow response times that make it difficult to associate an action (e.g., a click of the mouse) with an effect (e.g., an animation sequence). Davidson (1989) offered many helpful suggestions for introducing computers to developmentally young learners. Most early learning programs work with little more than a click of the mouse, and one can purchase a mouse specially designed for little fingers. Then lack of keyboarding skills should not pose barriers (also see Chapters 5 and 11).

In The Playroom (Brøderbund), students can explore a playroom scene by clicking a mouse on different areas of a room. Features of the playroom change with the student's choice and the program presents activities related to early numeracy and literacy skills. Other programs in this series include The Backyard, which promotes outdoor science and social skills, and The Treehouse, with activities designed to encourage creativity and reasoning skills.

Edmark's Early Learning Series contains seven titles for children ages 2 to 7. In Millie's Math House, children explore numbers, shapes, sizes, patterns, addition, and subtraction. Bailey's Book House introduces sounds, letters, words, and sentences. Sammy's Science House provides practice in scientific skills such as sorting, predicting, and constructing. Trudy's Time and Place House contains activities in mapping, time telling, and direction skills. Two newer titles, Millie & Bailey Preschool and Millie & Bailey Kindergarten, support preschool learning goals and the kindergarten curriculum, respectively, by compiling activities from other Early Learning titles on a single disk. Stanley's Sticker Stories provides a supportive context for emergent writers with stickers of characters and objects, scenes, an easy-to-use word processor, and an on-line spelling book.

The JumpStart series (Knowledge Adventure) is designed to help young children learn the skills they need for preschool and the early grades. Each program, which can be purchased separately, is geared to a specific level from preschool to fourth grade and includes skills that students are expected to perform at that level. Optimum Resources publishes At Home with Stickybear and Stickybear's Early Learning Activities. Each disk helps preschoolers learn letters, numbers, and other preschool skills.

Basic Skills Instruction. Teachers and clinicians can choose from a wealth of programs designed to develop students' basic academic skills. Increasingly, these programs are available on CD-ROMs (or DVD-ROMs) and include animation, sounds, illustrations, and movie clips. Table 9.5 lists a sampling of programs that are designed to help students acquire and practice basic skills in mathematics, reading, spelling, and keyboarding. These range in scope from those providing practice on a specific skill (e.g., telling time) to those providing integrated systems of instruction in many different components of mathematics or language arts.

Table 9.5. Basic Skill Programs

Title	Company	Content	Recommended Ages or Grades
Mathematics			
Math Blaster Jr	Davidson	Counting, shapes, adding, subtracting	Grades PreK–1
James Discovers Math	Brøderbund	Concepts	Grades PreK–2
Math Rabbit	The Learning Company	Counting, numeral recognition, computation	Ages 4–7
Mighty Math Carnival Countdown	Edmark	Addition, subtraction, place value, early multiplication	Ages 5–8
Mighty Math Zoo Zillions	Edmark	Story problems, shapes, money, making change	Ages 5–8
Time Shop	Hartley	Calendars and clocks	Grades K–3
Numbers Undercover	Sunburst	Digital and analog time, measuring, counting, money	Grades K–3
Coin Critters	Nordic	Coins from penny to half dollar	Grades K–6
Clock Shop	Nordic	Digital and analog time	Grades K–6
Clock	Hartley	Analog and digital time	Grades 1–5
Turbo Math Facts	Nordic	Basic facts	Grades K–6
Math Workshop	Brøderbund	Computation, problem solving, pattern recognition, and spatial relations	Grades K–8
Math Shop Jr	Scholastic	Computation, estimating, money, time	Grades 1–4
Math Blaster: In Search of Spot	Davidson	Computation	Grades 1–6
Access to Math	Don Johnston	Computation (reads teacher-developed problems aloud)	Grades 1–8

(continues)

Table 9.5. (*continued*)

Title	Company	Content	Recommended Ages or Grades
Math Munchers Deluxe	MECC	Computation and geometry	Grades 2–6
Mighty Math Number Heroes	Edmark	Fractions, geometry, probability, graphs and charts	Ages 8–12
Mighty Math Calculating Crew	Edmark	Decimals, number line concepts, shapes, money transactions	Ages 8–12
Might Math Cosmic Geometry	Edmark	Geometry	Ages 12–14
Major League Math	Sanctuary Woods	Uses baseball facts and statistics to teach averages, decimals, fractions, percentages, and place value	Grades 4–6
Math Shop	Scholastic	Computation, ratios and proportions, percentages, fractions, decimals	Grades 4–8
Math Shop Spotlight: Weights and Measures	Scholastic	Calendar, money, measurement	Grades 4–8
Math Shop Spotlight: Fractions and Decimals 1	Scholastic	Computation with decimals and fractions	Grades 4–8
Algebra Shop	Scholastic	Algebra	Grades 7–10
Reading			
DaisyQuest	PRO-ED	Phonological awareness: rhyming; beginning, middle, and ending sounds	Preschool and up
Daisy's Castle	PRO-ED	Phonological awareness: two-part blending, whole-word blending, segmenting	Preschool and up
The Busy World of Richard Scarry: Best Reading Program Ever	Simon & Schuster Interactive	Early literacy, phonics	Ages 3–6
My First Amazing Words and Pictures	DK Multimedia	Word recognition and vocabulary	Ages 3–7
Simon Sounds It Out	Don Johnston	Letter recognition and phonics	Ages 3–10
A to Zap!	Sunburst	Letter recognition	Grades PreK–1
Reading Blaster Jr	Davidson	Phonics, matching pictures, forming sentences, reading and spelling vocabulary	Grades PreK–2
First 1000 Words	Scholastic	Word recognition, ESL (Spanish)	Grades PreK–3

(*continues*)

Table 9.5. (*continued*)

Title	Company	Content	Recommended Ages or Grades
Reader Rabbit's Interactive Reading Journey	The Learning Company	Word recognition, phonics, stories	Grades K–1
Reader Rabbit 1 Reader Rabbit 2 Reader Rabbit 3	The Learning Company	Phonics, spelling patterns, word recognition, vocabulary, grammar	Grades K–1 Grades 1–3 Grades 2–4
Reading Who? Reading You! Something Phonics, Something New!	Sunburst	Phonics games and puzzles	Grades K–2
First Phonics	Sunburst	Phonics, initial letters	Grades K–2
Reading Blaster 2000	Davidson	Phonics, vocabulary, spelling, reading comprehension	Grades 1–3
Kid Phonics	Davidson	Phonics games	Ages 6–9
Word Munchers Deluxe	MECC	Phonics, grammar, classification, vocabulary	Grades 1–5
Word Attack 3	Davidson	Vocabulary and spelling	Grades 4 and up
Sentence Master	Laureate Learning Systems	Word recognition, spelling, comprehension	All ages
Spelling			
Spell It Deluxe	Davidson	Spelling	Ages 6 and up
Simon Spells	Don Johnston	Spelling—Dolch vocabulary and frequently used words	Grades 1–3
Spellevator	MECC	Spelling	Grades 1–6
Super Solvers Spellbound!	The Learning Company	Spelling	Grades 2–6
Keyboarding			
Mavis Beacon Teaches Typing for Kids	Mindscape	Keyboarding	Grades PreK–3
Mario Teaches Typing	Brainstorm	Keyboarding	Ages 5 and up
Read, Write, and Type	The Learning Company	Phonics, writing, keyboarding	Grades 1–2
Type to Learn	Sunburst	Keyboarding	Ages 8 and up
Mavis Beacon Teaches Typing	Mindscape	Keyboarding	Grades 3 and up

Systems Impact has produced a series of interactive videodiscs for teaching basic skills often covered in the secondary mathematics curriculum. The Core Concepts in Mathematics series includes the following five titles: Mastering Fractions; Mastering Decimals and Percents; Mastering Ratios and Word Problem Strategies; Mastering Equations, Roots and Exponents: Signed Numbers to Operations; and Mastering Informal Geometry. As discussed above, the programs are designed for group instruction and require a consumer model videodisc player and a large-screen monitor. The videodiscs present concepts and exercises with graphics, motion sequences, and audio, and the teacher controls the videodisc presentation with a remote control device. Student workbooks accompany the videodisc series. The Core Concepts videodiscs are designed around principles of effective instruction and have been thoroughly field-tested (e.g., Kelly, Carnine, Gersten, & Grossen, 1986; Kelly, Gersten, & Carnine, 1990; Moore & Carnine, 1989).

Higher Order Skills and Content-Area Instruction.

A variety of software programs are designed to promote critical thinking and problem-solving skills. These programs present users with different types of activities, such as recognizing and completing patterns, or solving puzzles. Because they often teach general problem-solving skills in situations that have little relationship to real-life activities, it is not clear how well these programs help students to address typical situations encountered in daily life. Nevertheless, problem-solving programs are prominent titles in every software catalog. A few of the more popular titles are highlighted below.

Edmark's Thinking Things series offers three different software titles designed to help children ages 4 to 13 to develop problem-solving skills through active engagement in games and problem-solving activities. Focusing on the acquisition of problem-solving skills through game playing, the Strategy Series (Edmark) is designed to help students learn and apply strategies as they engage in games such as Mancala and Jungle Chess.

Sunburst produces a variety of software programs designed to promote mathematical problem solving, such as patterns and inference, number sense, and logic. These include Safari Search, The King's Rule, The Pond, Puzzle Tanks, Divide and Conquer, and Teasers by Tobbs. Other Sunburst programs designed to promote problem solving in math include What Do You Do with a Broken Calculator, in which students experiment with different ways to arrive at solutions to math problems because of a broken calculator key. In How the West Was One + Three × Four and How the West Was Negative One, students construct mathematical equations to win a race through the Old West.

The Core Concepts in Science Series (Systems Impact) contains two titles designed to address topics in the secondary science curriculum: (a) Understanding Chemistry and Energy and (b) Earth Science. These videodiscs are designed to be used in the same way as the Core Concepts in Mathematics series (discussed previously).

Optical Data's Windows on Science curriculum is available for primary or intermediate science teaching. The curriculum packages are designed for whole-class instruction (see Chapter 8) and include videodiscs, pictures, graphs, charts, and movie clips, such as that of a tornado, filmed by a Minneapolis helicopter news crew, as it snaps power lines and tosses trees into the air. This sequence more than justifies the adage that "a picture is worth a thousand words" in that it provides students with a vivid mental model of the ways in which tornadoes form and travel and the destruction they can wreak. The videodiscs are accompanied by bar-coded teacher's guides with scripts for lesson presentation, worksheets, and experiments.

Finally, a number of topical CD-ROMs and videodiscs are available that can support content-area instruction. For example, Scholastic's Magic Schoolbus CD-ROMs help students in Grades 2 through 6 explore science topics such as body systems and astronomy. Scholastic also publishes the Interactive NOVA series for students in Grades 5 to 12 that has a family of videodiscs about science topics such as an exploration of planet Earth, human reproduction, and environmental threats. A.D.A.M. software produces three CD-ROMs about the human body. Optical Data publishes a series of videodiscs composed of edited and narrated new footage about contemporary events (e.g., the presidential election of 1988). These publishers, and many others, provide numerous multimedia resources that can help teachers expand upon the textbook-based instruction that often frustrates students with disabilities.

Electronic Books

Electronic books hold considerable potential to help students with mild disabilities circumvent print barriers to gain access to a wide range of written materials. Furthermore, they often contain enhancements that promote reading skills and support comprehension. A burgeoning number of electronic storybooks are available, geared primarily to students in the elementary grades. A list of some popular titles and their characteristics is contained in Table 9.6.

As the findings of the research reviewed above suggested, there are no guarantees that students will make mindful use of electronic books in ways that will facilitate their access to information or

Table 9.6. Electronic Books

Series, Titles, and Publisher/Distributor	Characteristics of Books
Storybook Series: The Three Billy Goats Gruff, The Little Red Hen, There are Tyrannosaurs Trying on My Pants in My Bedroom, The Three Little Pigs, What Was That? (Hartley)	Students can read along with the narrator, record their own voices reading the book, and, in some titles, write their own story. Grades PreK–3.
The Wonders of Learning Series: A World of Animals, Our Earth, The Human Body, A World of Plants, Animals and How They Grow, People Behind the Holidays, Seasons, Exploring the Solar System and Beyond (National Geographic)	Each book includes stories and facts about social studies and science concepts. Grades PreK–3.
Living Book Series: Arthur's Birthday, Arthur's Teacher Trouble, Dr. Seuss's ABC, Harry and the Haunted House, Just Grandma and Me, Little Monster at School, The New Kid on the Block, Ruff's Bone, Sheila Rae the Brave, Tortoise and the Hare (Brøderbund)	These books are best known for the engaging and entertaining animation that occurs when the user clicks on items in the illustrations. Most books can be read in English or Spanish. Newer titles contain learning games to reinforce specific skills and story content. Grades PreK–4.
Disney Interactive: Winnie the Pooh and the Honey Tree, 101 Dalmatians, Toy Story, Hunchback of Notre Dame	Children can click on pictures to see animation. Most books include songs and games to develop beginning problem-solving skills. Some books contain Action Dictionaries that use animation to define key words. A parents' guide with related activities accompanies the disks. Ages 3–8.
Sitting on the Farm (Sanctuary Woods Multimedia Corporation)	Students can listen to the story in English, French, or Spanish. Includes four modes. In Listen-Along mode, students hear narrated story. In Read-Along mode, students can record themselves reading the story, explore pictures, and learn new words. In Sing-Along mode, children can hear songs, listen to different instrumental versions of the song, and record themselves singing. In Write-Along mode, students can fill in the blanks, write and illustrate, and print their stories. Ages 4–10.

(continues)

Table 9.6. (*continued*)

Series, Titles, and Publisher/Distributor	Characteristics of Books
WiggleWorks (Scholastic)	Interactive beginning literacy program that combines reading, writing, listening, and speaking activities. Incorporates children's literature such as *Wake Me in the Spring* and *Clifford the Big Red Dog*. Students can record themselves as they read and write or dictate their own books. Comprehensive lesson plans and teacher's guides. Grades K–2.
The Magic Tales Interactive Storybooks: Baba Yaga and the Magic Geese—A Russian Folk Tale, The Little Samurai—A Japanese Folk Tale, Imo and the King—An African Folk Tale, Sleeping Cub's Test of Courage—A Native American Folk Tale, Liam Finds a Story—An Irish Folk Tale, The Princess and the Crab—An Italian Folk Tale. (Davidson)	Stories include activities and animation. Grades K–4.
Aladdin and the Wonderful Lamp (Ultra Media, Inc., Distributed by Universal CD-ROM)	Students listen to the narration and are prompted to make choices that affect the outcome of the story. Students can click on pictures to obtain animation and sound effects. Ages 5–10.
Mixed-Up Mother Goose (Sierra On-Line)	Traditional Mother Goose rhymes have been scrambled, and the student must locate and return missing objects from each rhyme to hear the rhyme sung. Encourages reasoning and problem-solving skills. Ages 5–10.
What's My Story (Digital Pictures, distributed by Brøderbund)	Introduces students to eight stories representing cultures from around the world. Students can create their own stories by combining film clips from the stories they have heard with their own text. Grades 2–6.
P.J.'s Reading Adventures: How the Leopard Got His Spots, Koi and the Kola Nuts, Paul Bunyan (Microsoft)	Students can listen to the story and explore the author's life and culture. By clicking on words, students can hear pronunciation or learn definitions by sound, video, photos, and animation. Contains interactive activities that tie in with the stories. Grades 2–6.
Smart Books: Exploring the Titanic, Malcolm X—By Any Means Necessary, If Your Name Was Changed at Ellis Island, Favorite Greek Myths (Scholastic)	Integrates social studies themes with reading and language arts strategies. Students can access primary source materials, see videos of people and places, highlight text, and respond in writing to what they read. Grades 3–8.
Mieko: A Story of Japanese Culture (Digital Pictures, Distributed by Brøderbund)	Story of Mieko, a Japanese girl who lives in Los Angeles. Provides an introduction to Japanese culture and enables the student to hear text read and narrated in five different languages. Grades 4 and up.

(continues)

Table 9.6. *(continued)*

Series, Titles, and Publisher/Distributor	Characteristics of Books
Twain's World (Thynx, Inc).	Full-text versions of eight of Twain's works, including *Huckleberry Finn* and *Tom Sawyer*. Includes a comprehensive portrait of Twain's life and work presented through photos, narrations, animations, and video clips.
In My Own Voice (Sunburst)	Audio recordings of award-winning contemporary poems, read by the poets. Set in New York City's Greenwich Village, students can attend poetry readings, see pictures of the poets and read their biographies, hear poets discuss how and why a poem was written, see related artworks, edit poems or write their own, and record their thoughts about the poems they read. Junior/senior high school.
The Bookworm Collection: A Midsummer Night's Dream, The Adventures of Huckleberry Finn, The Adventures of Tom Sawyer, Frankenstein, Hamlet, Little Women, Macbeth, Romeo and Juliet, The Scarlet Letter, Selected Works of Edgar Allen Poe (CIT, Inc., Distributed by Educational Resources)	Original works of classic American and English literature are read and annotated with film, sounds, graphics, and relevant criticism. Students can customize each title, creating their own multimedia edition by linking sound, video, notes, and other text directly to the work or to other works. Tools are available for marking and highlighting text, adding notes, searching for specific information within the text, and accessing a dictionary. Grades 7–12.
Romeo and Juliet: Center Stage (Sunburst)	Set on a Verona street, students can meet Romeo and Juliet and visit sites: the Players' Guild, where they can ask questions of the actors; the Library, where they can read Shakespeare's text and watch the play as it is read; and the Writer's Guild, where they can compose original creations based on the play's theme. Grades 7–12.

promote their acquisition and retention of new skills. Educators and clinicians must resist the temptation to think of electronic books as activities that can teach or enrich learning independent of the curriculum. Rather, students will benefit the most when their experiences with electronic books are guided by their teachers and integrated with other curricular activities and themes. Just as teachers implement activities prior to, during, and after reading traditional texts in the classroom, similar sets of activities will help students get the most from electronic books. Matthew (1996) proposed that teachers must first introduce students to the topic or theme of an electronic book through structured activities or questions. For example, an educator might introduce the electronic version of The Tortoise and the Hare (Brøderbund) by discussing with students the characteristics of a fable. He or she might ask students to complete a K-W-L activity (Ogle, 1986): Students would first brainstorm what they Know about fables, filling in the first column of the K-W-L chart. They would then discuss what they Want to know and fill in the second column of the chart with these ideas. After reading The Tortoise and the Hare and other fables, they would complete the third, or what they have Learned, column. Students could work in groups to share fables and discuss what they have learned. The teacher would then lead a whole-class discussion about groups' conclusions about the characteristics of fables and their common features. Students would be encouraged to write their own fables, perhaps illustrating them with the use of some of the multimedia composing or authoring tools discussed later.

In addition to integrating electronic books with themes or topics being studied in the classroom, teachers and clinicians must show students how to make purposeful and systematic use of the enhancements they contain. Students should be shown how to hear a word or page reread, how to access a definition, how to move back and forth through the pages, and how to access other features of the program such as a notepad or a skill-building game. Teachers can demonstrate these features to the whole class with an LCD panel or large-screen monitor and discuss where and when it would be appropriate to make use of them. Teachers can preview specific vocabulary words and direct students to click on them when they occur in the story. Checklists or prompts, situated by the computer, can serve as reminders to access specific features of the book. Teachers should monitor students as they use electronic books to make sure students are using them in ways that support learning.

Brøderbund publishes the Living Books Frameworks, which contain integrated whole-language teacher support materials for its electronic storybooks. The Frameworks contain classroom activities that tie each book into the curricular areas of language arts, reading, math, science, music, social studies, and drama. Also included are outlines for thematic units, reproducible worksheets and illustrations, tips for teachers, and a list of books and cassettes on topics related to each book. Materials such as these can help educators make full use of electronic books.

Anchored Instruction

Video-Based Anchors. Researchers at Vanderbilt University's Cognition and Technology Group have developed a series of 12 videodiscs designed to promote problem-solving skills through anchored instruction. In The New Adventures of Jasper Woodbury (Erlbaum), students first view a video story of an adventure and challenge encountered by Jasper Woodbury and his friends (e.g., navigating a boat down the river before dark or flying an ultralight plane to rescue a wounded bird). Students then work in collaborative groups, revisiting the video, defining subproblems, and finding the information needed to solve them. Finally, students present their solutions to the class and discuss the effectiveness of different approaches. The series is oriented toward mathematical problem solving, but has links to science, social science, and history, thus facilitating generalization of problem-solving skills across the curriculum.

The Little Planet Literacy Series (Little Planet Publishing) is developed around the principles of MOST literacy environments, as discussed previously (Bransford et al., 1994). Students begin each set of learning activities by viewing an animated anchor story. Throughout a unit, they revisit the anchor's theme and plot through use of a storyboard. Students work in cooperative groups on curricular activities that promote comprehension, storytelling, reading, writing, and analogical thinking.

Simulations. Social studies and science classes can be enhanced by the use of computer-based simulations. Simulations can portray real-life situations, ranging from immigration to laboratory experiments to drug and alcohol use, in which students could not otherwise participate. Simulations help students to view all sides of a problem and experience the consequences of decisions or actions. Access to a projection panel or large-screen monitor enables simulations to become a central feature of whole-class instruction (see Chapter 8). Because simulations branch to different paths, depending on the prior sequence of events, the same simulation can yield many different outcomes.

Brøderbund publishes the Carmen Sandiego series, in which students act as detectives and collect clues to locate Carmen and her gang of thieves. Students must use reference skills, geographical and historical knowledge, and deductive reasoning to make sense of information offered by the program. Depending on the program purchased, Carmen may be tracked through the United States, Europe, the world, space, time, or America's past.

MECC produces a number of popular simulation programs available on CD-ROM. In the Oregon Trail editions students make decisions about traveling on an American westward journey in the 1800s; Yukon Trail is situated in the 1897 Klondike gold rush; Africa Trail simulates a bicycle trek of the African continent; and MayaQuest offers a bicycle expedition through Central America. These simulations are designed for students aged 10 through 16.

The Carmen Sandiego and MECC simulations provide opportunities for students to engage in meaningful and motivating learning experiences. These and other simulation programs are excellent formats for cooperative learning. Students can assume different roles during the simulation, including keyboarder, notetaker, map reader, and reference librarian. Keep in mind, though, that simulations require much more than a disc, reference materials, and student groups to be effective. They should be used within a meaningful context and related to students' prior and future knowledge. Students will need coaching in appropriate strategies for engaging in simulation activities. If left to their own devices, many students fail to discover the solution to a simulated problem, feel overwhelmed and frustrated, or find alternative ways to solve the problem that circumvent the learning opportunities embedded in the simulation (Duffield, 1990).

Tom Snyder Productions has developed simulations for the social studies classroom that attempt to address some of the drawbacks cited above by providing a combination of teacher-directed instruction, group discussion, role playing, classroom debates, print materials, and simulation activities. These simulations are called "groupware" because they are designed to be used with a whole class of students in Grades 4 through 12. In the Decisions, Decisions series, students role-play government leaders and make decisions in programs titled The Environment, Building a Nation, Ancient Empires, Feudalism, Colonization, Immigration, Revolutionary Wars, and Prejudice. In The National Inspirer and The International Inspirer, students engage in scavenger hunts for resources across the United States or the world. Three other titles, Rainforest Researchers, The Great Ocean Rescue, and The Great Solar System Rescue, challenge students to solve mysteries about rainforest plants or embark upon rescue missions.

Network-Based Learning

The Internet and other electronic networks can be rich sources of information. They also can provide a lively forum for student collaboration, the exchange of information, and authentic writing activities. Table 9.7 presents activities that illustrate the three types of network-based learning experiences described by Harris (1995a, 1995b, 1995c, 1995d): interpersonal exchanges, information collections, and problem-solving projects.

As educators gain more experience using electronic networks, they are finding some activities more effective than others. Collaborative projects that (a) require students to engage in a joint activity, (b) do not rely on the response of a particular person, (c) enable teachers and students to work off-line and then transmit files locally, and (d) are characterized by the interdependency found in cooperative learning groups seem to have the best chances for success and are the least costly (Laboratory of Comparative Human Culture, 1989; Newman, 1987).

It is advisable to start with small-scale projects. Although keypals permits individuals to correspond with individuals and seems like the simplest sort of project, it is often difficult to monitor and troubleshoot the individual correspondence of a classroom full of students. Thus, projects in which the class makes a group response are often easier to manage. To get an idea of how to begin, teachers can explore project examples by perusing on-line collections. According to Harris (1996), the following Gophers

Table 9.7. Network-Based Learning Experiences

Type of Activity	Purpose	Example
Keypals	Electronic correspondence takes place between individuals, individuals and groups, or groups and groups.	Students with serious emotional disturbance correspond on a regular basis with residents of a senior citizen center.
Global classrooms	Two or more classrooms study a common topic.	Eight-year-old students from New Zealand posted six questions to other classrooms, asking them to think about and define what it means to be a village.
Electronic appearances	A special guest is available for a limited amount of time with whom students can correspond.	Authors of children's books are available at scheduled intervals to answer students' questions about their books and their careers as writers.
Electronic mentoring	Specialists from universities, businesses, government, or other schools are available to assist students who are studying a specific topic.	The Electronic Emissary project at the University of Texas at Austin matches volunteer subject-matter specialists with interested classes to structure a mentoring project.
Question-and-answer services	Students can ask an expert questions about research topics or other issues of interest.	The U.S. Geological Survey offers Ask-a-Geologist services. Students can e-mail a general question about earth science to: ask-a-geologist@octopus.wr.usgs.gov. The geologist of the day will answer or provide information about a better source to contact for the requested information.
Impersonations	Any or all of the correspondents in a conversation communicate with each other "in character."	Mysterious Mel, an alien, appears on the network to correspond with students with disabilities who are attending a summer program. He asks students for more information about themselves, their lives, and notes they have written, claiming he cannot understand them because he is from another planet. Students are inspired to write clearer and more detailed responses.
Information searches	Students are provided with clues and must use reference sources (online, CD-ROM, paper, etc.) to solve problems.	High school students with learning disabilities posted a "Where Are We" challenge to others. The challenge included 10 clues about their geographic location. Respondents were asked to solve the mystery and send back 10 clues about their own location.

(continues)

Table 9.7. (*continued*)

Type of Activity	Purpose	Example
Electronic process writing	Students serve as peer editors and collaborate in writing.	In the "Writers in Electronic Residence" project at York University, students share their poems with other students and professional writers, who provide feedback and constructive criticism.
Sequential creations	Participants progressively contribute to a common written product, visual image, or computer program.	Students all over North America created a "Native American ChainStack" by developing HyperStudio stacks about Native American tribes in their region and organizing them into one common stack.
Parallel problem solving	A similar problem is presented to students at different sites, who share their problem-solving methods and solutions electronically.	In conjunction with Earth Day, students became "Eco-Entrepreneurs" and developed new products that could make a profit, would not have a negative impact on the environment, and used at least 50% recycled material. Students wrote and submitted sales pitches, which were compiled in an all-site catalog. Students used the catalog to "order" products, and sales statistics were reviewed and analyzed by participants.
Virtual gatherings	Students are brought together in real-time chats or "in the spirit" through common activities across different sites.	Over a 1-week period, students throughout the country designed a model of a virtual city in an event hosted by the San Francisco Exploratorium (http://www.exploratorium.edu).
Simulations	Students collaborate with others in simulated activities.	The National Educational Supercomputing Program lets students "explore" supercomputing activities at the Lawrence Livermore Laboratory via an on-line connection and engages them in solving problems in math and science.
Social action projects	Students work together in humanitarian, socially oriented action projects.	After reading Al Gore's *Earth in the Balance: Ecology and the Human Spirit*, students in three states and London cooperated to investigate problems caused by water runoff and designed a public awareness program that could be implemented in their own communities. Project results were televised nationally.

Note. Based on Harris (1995a, 1995b, 1995c).

contain a multitude of examples of previous or ongoing projects:

- Armadillo Gopher: chico.rice.edu 1170

- Boulder Valley School District educational resources, with ideas and links to science-related activites: bvsd.k12.co.us

- Consortium for School Networking Gopher: digital.cosn.org

- NYSERNet's Gopher: nysernet.org

- Technology infusion into the curriculum: sjuvm.stjohns.edu

- USCD Internet Lesson Plans: ec.sdcs.k12.ca.us

At the time this chapter was written, these gophers were in service, but some were migrating to Web sites, which are also sources of ideas for network-based learning. The following sites should provide a teacher with many ideas and opportunities to join ongoing projects. Teachers also can initiate a project by soliciting participants at many of these sites:

- Resource Village: A Place for Teachers (sponsored by Macmillan/McGraw-Hill School Division): http://www.mmhschool.com

- Education Place (sponsored by Houghton Mifflin): http://www.eduplace.com

- EdWeb (sponsored by the Corporation for Public Broadcasting): http://edweb.gsn.org

- Ralph Bunche School Web site (sponsored by Ralph Bunche School, Harlem): http://ralphbunche.rbs.edu

- Global Schoolhouse (sponsored by Global Schoolnet Foundation): http://www.gsn.org

- Intercultural E-Mail Classroom Connections: http://www.stolaf.edu/network/iecc

When designing an online activity, educators should first develop an explicit idea of what the project's outcome and goals will be, determine how much time will be necessary, decide how often participating classrooms will be in contact with one another, set target dates for project activities, and plan a common product or culminating activities. Riel (1992) recommended that teachers plan projects that involve more than one or two other classrooms. By involving 5 to 10 other classrooms on extended projects, teachers will maximize cultural and regional diversity and avoid having to shut down a project should networking or other logistical problems cause a few classrooms to terminate their participation.

Collaborating classes should begin by introducing themselves to one another through activities in which students share information about themselves, the community in which they live, and descriptions of their daily lives. Experts recommend that structured activities be planned to help participants maintain contact during any data-gathering phases of the projects. These may be e-mail notes between individuals, progress reports, exchanges of postcards or other information about one's home and culture, or miniprojects spun off the main project. Finally, the project should include a concluding event (e.g., a tangible product, that is shared with all participants and made available to a larger audience of interested people such as parents or school board members. If time allows, the opportunity to share thoughts about the process, evaluate each others' contributions, and reflect on strengths and limitations of the project can inform future network-based learning activities (Harris, 1996; Kimeldorf, 1995; McCullen, 1995).

Educators and clinicians should keep in mind the need to allocate time to teach students how to use network applications such as e-mail, Web browsers, and search engines. Research shows that students who are more comfortable with computer-mediated communication are more likely to use it, and students who are more anxious about written communication are less likely to participate in public and group-oriented discussions. Also, the teacher's own use of these tools provides an important role model for students, especially for novice learners (Fishman, 1997).

The gophers and Web sites listed above are available through the Internet. The National Geographic Kids Network is a specialized tele-

Computer concepts learned at school can be used at home. (Photograph by Robin D. Thibodeaux)

communications-based science network. Classrooms can participate in units of instruction that address natural science topics with important environmental and social implications. Students engage in authentic science activities, using methods and materials employed by professional scientists. They use the computer network to exchange ideas, questions, and results with other classrooms. The present series contains four different units:

- What is our soil good for?
- Are we getting enough oxygen?
- How loud is too loud?
- Is our water at risk?

Each unit proceeds in four parts. In Parts 1 and 2 students learn by observing and measuring. In Part 3 students exchange data over the network. Data are contributed to a larger database, and students analyze these data. In Part 4 students investigate a question that emerged during their local investigations (Vesel, 1996).

Technology Tools

Word Processing

Keyboarding Skills. It is important to keep in mind that writing is a complex task that requires the integration of many skills. The use of a computer and word processing software adds additional task demands. Without instruction and practice in keyboarding and word processing functions, students may focus on the mechanics of operating the word processor rather than on the content of their writing (Cochran-Smith, Kahn, & Paris, 1988; Daiute, 1986). Many educators have recommended that students learn to type at least well enough so that they do not have to hunt for each key on the keyboard (Morocco, 1987; Morocco et al., 1990), although available evidence suggests that students with disabilities may require a substantial amount of practice to develop keyboarding fluency (Okolo et al., 1990). Given that the average elementary school child receives little systematic keyboarding instruction (Sormunen, Adams, Berg, & Prigge, 1989), teachers may find it better to integrate keyboarding with a regularly scheduled subject such as language arts (Sormunen & Wickersham, 1991). In fact, keyboarding instruction may be more motivating and effective when taught as a skill that is useful for learning other subjects (Anderson-Inman, 1990).

Keyboarding fluency can be developed through short practice sessions that focus on the sequential introduction of and practice with key locations and sequences (Neuman & Morocco, 1987). Educators should avoid game software that encourages students to hit keys as rapidly as possible to fire missiles, shoot spaceships, and so on. These programs may encourage students to sacrifice technique for speed. In order to be effective, students' keyboarding practice should be closely monitored by the teacher, who can reinforce the use of proper technique (Neuman & Morocco, 1987).

Some software programs, such as Type to Learn (Sunburst) and Read, Write, and Type (The Learning Company), emphasize keyboarding across the curriculum. Other criteria that teachers may wish to consider when choosing keyboarding programs include (Knapp, 1984; McClean, 1987):

- Sequential introduction of keys in small sets

- Frequent feedback about typing accuracy and speed, referenced to previous performance

- Screen display of upper- and lowercase letters

- Options for students to correct their errors during practice activities

- Use of real rather than nonsense words in practice exercises

- Options for teacher-created lessons

Students' lack of keyboarding skills should not preclude their use of word processing or other technology-based programs. This caveat is especially true of young children and learners with disabilities, whose developmental maturity or lack of fine motor skills may limit keyboarding proficiency.

Word Processing. Many different word processing programs are in use in today's classrooms. A partial list of programs that function *primarily* as word processors is contained in Table 9.8. Most of these programs contain components such as speech synthesis, clip art, drawing and painting tools, and spelling checkers and thesauruses.

Table 9.8. Word Processing Programs

Name	Publisher	Features and Recommended Ages
Dr. Peet's Talk/Writer	Hartley	Easy-to-use talking word processor for young writers. Includes a spelling checker and letter recognition activities. Works with a Unicorn Board and Adaptive Firmware Card or Intellikeys. Grades PreK–12.
My Words	Hartley	Has word prediction functions: As words are typed, they are added to a word bank for future access. Reads text and contains small bank of sound effects, and recording tool for adding more. Grades K–4.
Write: Outloud	Don Johnston	Talking word processor with talking spelling checker. Grades 2 and up.
Write Away!	Sunburst	Word processor that allows teacher to configure options for four different writing levels by adding and removing tool bars and menu items and customizing word lists. Includes features for graphics and formatting, an idea notebook, and an outlining tool. Keeps data about student use of spelling checker and other features and prints spelling lists for misspelled words. Grades 2–8.
The Children's Writing and Publishing Center	The Learning Company	Word processors with over 150 pictures. Grades 2–9.
Bank Street Writer	Scholastic	Includes teaching guides, activity units, capability to add "frozen text" that students cannot modify, and student writing resources. Grades 3–12.
Student Writing Center	The Learning Company	Word processor and desktop publishing program with templates for different writing activities. Grades 4 and up.
Write This Way	Hartley	Designed for students with learning disabilities. Highlights and "speaks" spelling and grammar errors and suggests solutions. Dictionary based on 50,000 most widely used school spelling and word frequency lists, to which students can add new words. Grades 4 and up.

Keep in mind that students will require introduction to and practice with word processing functions (delete, move, etc.) and word processing components (spelling checkers, thesauruses, etc.). Although these features may seem self-evident to adults, students with disabilities may encounter considerable difficulties when using them. Spelling checkers are an illustrative example. Although research shows that students with mild disabilities locate and correct significantly more of their spelling errors when they have access to a spelling checker (MacArthur et al., 1996), up to one in three of the spelling errors made by these students may not be flagged. This is because students' misspellings are often substitutions of a correctly spelled word for the intended word (e.g., "rain" for "rein"). MacArthur et al. (1996) also found that students using a spelling checker do not locate errors unless they are flagged by the checker. Thus, without teacher instruction and support, many errors may go unnoticed and uncorrected by the student. Furthermore, spelling checkers vary widely in their ability to suggest the correct spellings of misspelled words, so students should be taught to learn to use backup strategies in conjunction with a spelling checker. The Center for Electronic Studying at the University of Oregon (Anderson-Inman & Knox-Quinn, 1996) recommended these stgrategies:

- *Guess and Check:* When the spelling checker identifies a word as misspelled but does not suggest an alternative, students can systematically alter letters in the word until possible alternatives are given, by making changes in vowels first and then looking for consonants that might have more than one sound.

- *Dictionary Definition Strategy:* This strategy helps students who have difficulty recognizing the correct choice from among presented alternatives. To use it, the student must have an electronic dictionary available on the computer's hard drive or on a CD-ROM (or DVD-ROM). The student selects a suggested alternative from the spelling checker, looks up its meaning in the dictionary, and compares that with the intended word. The process is repeated until the correct alternative is located.

- *Text-to-Speech Strategies:* With access to electronic synthetic speech (via the word processor, spelling checker, or computer's operating system), the student listens to the alternatives presented in the spell checker to locate the intended word. Students can also listen to their compositions, via speech synthesis options in the word processor, to help locate words that are pronounced differently than intended, and hence are misspelled.

- *Word-Pair List Strategy:* Using a list of commonly misspelled words, such as homonyms or commonly confused pairs (e.g., *affect–effect, conscience–conscious*), students use the search and replace function of the word processor to search for the words in each pair. When a word is located, students determine if they have used the correct word and make replacements as necessary.

Other Tools To Support Writing. A number of programs have been developed to enhance students' motivation to write and to augment their writing experiences. Some of these are described in Table 9.9.

As noted earlier, many of these programs have fully functional word processors and extensions such as clip art, backgrounds, and sound effects that enable students to create multimedia compositions. For example, book reports are a staple of the elementary school curriculum, and software programs that integrate text tools with multimedia features can offer motivating alternatives to traditional text-based reports. Two sets of authors have described projects in which students used Kid Pix 2 (Brøderbund) to create slide show book reports (Monahan & Susong, 1996; Taylor & Stuhlmann, 1995). The first step for elementary-school students with mild disabilities participating in Monahan and Susong's (1996) project was to read several books by an author of their choice and write a short review of one. They then collected biographical information by writing to the author and the author's publisher and then wrote a short author biography. In some cases, students were able to meet and interview an author at local

Table 9.9. Writing Tools

Title	Publisher	Features and Ages/Grade Levels
Stanley's Sticker Stories	Edmark	Children create animated storybooks with cartoon characters from Edmark programs. Includes stickers, objects, and backgrounds to illustrate stories. Students can record their own voices reading their stories. Ages 3–7.
Storybook Maker Deluxe	Hartley	Students can choose from a variety of backgrounds and hundreds of picture cards to illustrate their story and can record themselves reading the story. Grades PreK–3.
Kid Works 2 and Kid Works Deluxe	Sunburst	Provides vocabulary support for writers through "boxes" of words that can be placed into stories. Contains speech synthesis, so stories can be read and recorded, and drawing tools. A Player file permits stories to be viewed by those who do not own a copy of Kid Works. Bilingual editions are available for Spanish and English. Grades PreK–4.
Sunbuddy Writer	Sunburst	Picture and word processor for young children. Animated characters provide audio instructions and writing tips. Also includes a word finder tool to let children add to the story by selecting from a database of words and pictures. A recording feature lets students read aloud what they write. Grades K–2.
ClarisWorks for Kids	Claris Corp.	A children's productivity package that combines word processing, painting, graphing, and list tools. Comes with special penmanship fonts, clip art, movies, sounds, and more than 75 activities. Grades K–3.
Storybook Weaver Deluxe	MECC	A composing tool that allows children to create and publish illustrated stories. More than 650 images and 450 scenery combinations with sounds, songs, page borders, and various type styles. Students can write stories in English or Spanish. Ages 5–10.
Great Beginnings	Teacher Support Software	Helps stimulate ideas prior to writing by providing lists of topics, descriptive words, and over 250 graphics. Grades K–3.
Sentence Starters	Teacher Support Software	Sentence starters, sentence endings, and graphics to inspire writing. Grades K–3.
Make-A-Book	Teacher Support Software	Prints students' stories in book format. Grades K–4.
Kid Pix Studio	Brøderbund	Students can add text animation, video, sound effects, and music to any picture or slide show production. Paint tools, animation tools, and more than 800 animated stamps. Ages 5–12.
Dinosaur Days	Pelican, a division of Queue	Composing program that lets children create dinosaurs and write stories or create dialogue among them. Speech synthesis feature can speak and spell any typed text, and permit characters to talk. Ages 5–12.
The Amazing Writing Machine	Brøderbund	Writing, illustration, and idea generation program. Students can express thoughts in five forms: story, letter, journal, essay, and poem. It has predesigned page layouts, has areas for text and graphics, and permits illustrated stories with Kid Pix tools. Grades K–8.

(continues)

Table 9.9. (*continued*)

Title	Publisher	Features and Ages/Grade Levels
Easy Book	Sunburst	Helps students and teachers author and publish stories in book form. Includes stamps and a paint program for developing illustrations. Grades K–6.
Imagination Express	Edmark	Six programs organized by different destinations (e.g., castle, neighborhood, time trip, USA). Students begin by looking at a fact book about their destination, examining a sample story, and learning some story ideas. Students create fiction or nonfiction stories by choosing backgrounds and adding characters, text, and sound effects related to the destination. Students can animate characters and record themselves reading the story. Grades K–8.
Creative Writer 2.0	Microsoft	Desktop publishing program for children, with writing and drawing tools, clip art and musical themes, and templates. Includes a story starter section and mixed up sentences to help stimulate writing. A Web Publishing Wizard helps students create Web pages. Grades 2 and up.
The Ultimate Writing and Creativity Center	The Learning Company	Word processor with prompts related to each phase of the writing process. Contains projects and ideas to inspire writing, painting and drawing tools, clip art, sounds, animation, speech, an interactive spellchecker, and templates for newsletters, storybooks, and other writing projects. Grades 2–5.
Magic Media Slate	Sunburst	Full-featured word processor that enables students to incorporate clip art, sound, laser disc clips, drawings, animation, and QuickTime movies into their compositions. Includes a spelling checker and text-to-speech option. Grades 3–10.
Write, Camera, Action!	Davidson	Students edit a movie and write dialogue, promotional news stories, and other topics. Grades 4–8.
Diary Maker	Scholastic	CD-ROM combines writing tools with authentic diary entries from Anne Frank, Zlata Filipovic (Sarajevo), and Latoya Hunter (New York City). Students can create their own multimedia journals. Includes features for collaboration and assistance with "writer's block." Grades 5–9.
Writer's Solution	Prentice-Hall	Contains three major components. Language Lab component contains skill-building exercises that explain rules of grammar and various writing styles. Writing Lab component contains writing activities that allow students to carry out prewriting tasks, draft, revise, edit, and publish or present their work, with a feature for peer response. Writers at Work component contains videodisc or videotapes of accomplished writers talking about writing process and how it relates to their lives. Grades 6–12.
Language Experience Recorder	Teacher Support Software	Speech synthesis reads students' writing. Analyzes stories to provide readability level, individual and cumulative word lists, new vocabulary, and more. All grades.
Co:Writer	Don Johnston	Word prediction program with a wide variety of options, including scanning and speech. All ages.

bookstores. Students illustrated their work by creating drawings with the Kid Pix graphics tools and by importing scanned images and movie stills. They shared their book reports during a slide show at an after-school open house and during a state educational computing conference.

When considering programs such as Kid Pix 2, teachers should keep in mind that students will need time and instruction to master the many commands necessary for utilizing graphics and editing capabilities. Furthermore, grammar checkers and other features that provide error correction feedback may be of little use to students who do not know how to make revisions based on this feedback.

Tools for Organizing Content-Area Information

As discussed previously, outlining and concept mapping programs are valuable tools for helping students organize their ideas prior to and during the writing process. In addition, they are viable tools to help students organize, comprehend, and study content-area information. Inspiration Software publishes Inspiration, a concept mapping, webbing, and planning tool, and Sunburst produces Expression, a program with similar features. Both tools permit students to move back and forth between webs, outlines, and concept maps, providing different perspectives on a topic.

Electronic timelines such as Chronicle (Sunburst) and TimeLiner 4.0 (Tom Snyder) can help students visualize a sequence of events and relationships between them. These versatile tools can plot and easily revise a time scale and make it easy for students to annotate events with text, graphics, and even movie clips. Timelines can be expanded, contracted, and merged. All of these options would be difficult if not impossible to achieve with paper and pencil.

Multimedia Projects and Authoring Tools

With access to appropriate software and at least one computer in the classroom, multimedia design projects are limited only by one's imagination. The following examples illustrate a range of student projects and the authoring tools that can be used to create them:

- Sixth-grade inclusive classrooms, in which about one third of the students have learning disabilities, are organized into heterogeneous cooperative groups to investigate the topic of Spanish colonization of Latin America. Students are asked to examine colonization from the perspectives of the Spaniards and of the indigenous peoples. They are charged with developing a multimedia presentation that represents both sides and then comes to a conclusion about whether colonization was desirable. Students view videotapes, read and study books about the topic, and engage in extended discussions within their groups and as a whole class. They develop their presentations with Digital Chisel (Pierian Spring) and augment their text with scanned pictures, illustrations they have created, and sound clips. Presentations are shown to parents at an Open House (Ferretti & Okolo, 1997).

- A first-grade class develops a unit about animals. Students work in groups of three or four to research information about an animal, write several paragraphs based on their research, and draw pictures illustrating what they have learned. With help from their teacher and the media specialist, students enter their text into Linkway (IBM) and use its paint tools to draw an illustration of what they have learned. Students help their teacher select videoclips from a Windows on Science (Optical Data) videodisc, and the teacher assembles and links the pages to produce a Linkway presentation that is shown to parents and shared with other students (Roscigno & Shearin, 1995).

- Title I students in Grades 3 to 5 work in cooperative groups to develop multimedia projects about biomes. They formulate questions about a chosen biome and research information about its attributes, location, climate, and threats to its ecosystem. Students use HyperStudio (Roger Wagner) to create their stacks and supplement their text with photos from a Photo CD, illustrations created in Kid Pix (Brøderbund), student-created spreadsheets and graphs, and HyperStudio maps. Students present their work at a conference sponsored by their city's Office of Education, at two school assemblies, and at an evening meeting for parents (Bennett & Diener, 1997).

The authoring tools described in these examples—Digital Chisel, Linkway, HyperStudio, and Kid Pix—are some of the most commonly used tools for multimedia project creation. They contain powerful tools for creating text, illustrations, animation, sound effects, and links among pages, and are packaged with a wealth of features, such as clip art, sound and picture libraries, and templates. They are compatible with a variety of different multimedia technologies, including Photoshop CDs, Quicktime movies, and digital cameras. With the growth of the World Wide Web, recent versions help students create projects that can be published on the Internet. Another helpful feature is the inclusion of a player feature or routine which permits those who do not have access to a copy of the authoring program to view a student's project.

As discussed above, multimedia projects must be carefully planned and structured if students are to benefit fully from them. Students will need to learn to collaborate effectively, engage in high levels of cognitive discourse, employ an appropriate process of research, transform information into knowledge, and master an authoring tool. Fortunately, an investment in teaching these skills can yield big dividends for student learning and motivation, as well as provide a foundation for behaviors that students can use in many different situations.

Electronic Reference Materials

Computer-Based Tools. There seems to be no shortage of CD-ROM reference materials, and new titles are appearing daily on CD- and DVD-ROMs. A teacher can now choose from a number of high-quality electronic encyclopedias, some of which are reviewed in Table 9.10.

Electronic dictionaries are another useful reference tool for students with reading difficulties.

For example, the American Heritage Talking Dictionary (Softkey, The Learning Company) pronounces over 72,000 words and provides access to over a million synonyms. Users can view pictures and over 50 videos.

Electronic atlases represent tools that can assist students in locating and learning geographic information. The Map Room (Sunburst), World Atlas and Almanac (Mindscape), and Talking USA Map (Orange Cherry) contain searchable maps, facts and data related to those maps, and enhancements such as drawing tools, movie clips, and digitized speech.

As Edyburn's (1991) research suggested, students will benefit more fully from electronic reference materials if they learn appropriate and flexible search strategies. Teachers can introduce these strategies through structured questions and activities that students apply to the reference material, followed by discussion of the approaches used, how well they worked, and introductions to other search options.

Hand-Held Electronic Devices. Hand-held electronic devices are another class of electronic reference tools. Electronic organizers that can store calendars, schedules, addresses, and reminders in one device can be a boon for students with poor memory or organizational skills.

Franklin Learning Resources produces a number of hand-held devices that can provide students with ready access to information. The Bookman is a hand-held electronic book with a card slot. Users can snap in various cards to turn the device into a dictionary and thesaurus; encyclopedia; foreign language translator; health, food, or movie guide; or electronic text of *Bartlett's Familiar Quotations*. Several "speaking" devices are available and are especially appropriate for students with mild disabilities. These include the Speaking Language Master Special Edition, which speaks everything that appears on the screen and every letter typed. Its reference functions include a dictionary, thesaurus, spelling correction for over 100,000 words, and electronic grammar handbook. Although these devices are rather expensive, Franklin also makes a variety of useful devices for under $50. These include the

Table 9.10. Electronic Encyclopedias

For Ages 3–8

My First Encyclopedia (Knowledge Adventure): Contains 575 brief entries organized by a "Tree of Knowledge" metaphor with 10 subject areas. Clicking on one of these takes students to a Learning Room, where they can click on pictures of objects to learn more. A video-recorded preteen supplies on-screen help and descriptions. Each learning area has an educational game and question-and-answer section.

First Connections: The Golden Book Encyclopedia (Hartley): Contains about 1,500 articles organized into four information paths. "World of Words" contains articles in nine categories. "Sights and Sounds" provides access to multimedia elements. "Seek and Find" has articles in nine categories. "ABC" has an alphabetical categorization of articles and is most useful for intermediate students. Students can click on hot links to cross-reference articles. Directions are spoken and text can be read. A Tracker tool keeps a list of all articles visited in the current session, permitting easy return to an entry.

Microsoft Explorapedia–The World of Nature: Microsoft Explorapedia–The World of People (Microsoft): Designed to present reference material in a playful manner for younger students. Thaddeus (Tad) Pole serves as a guide, helping students "leap" from the program to other writing or painting programs (for recording information), which can be clipped to the desktop before "leaping." Information is organized by locations, such as the Health Center, the Classroom, and Factory in The World of People, and lakes, rivers, and evergreen forests in the World of Nature. Students can explore each location or Tad can supply a list of topics contained in each scene. Material is based on the Random House Children's Encyclopedia.

For Ages 9–14

Compton's Interactive Encyclopedia (The Learning Company): Contains 38,000 articles, more than 8,000 photographs, 100 video clips, and over 4,000 Internet links. Includes an interactive timeline, dictionary, and thesaurus. Permits students to search for information through InfoLinks, which display a list of related entries around the main entry. Has a ShowMaker feature which students can use to create multimedia products from the encyclopedia's contents.

Microsoft Encarta 98 Encyclopedia Deluxe Edition (Microsoft): Contains 32,000 articles, 14,000 video photographs and illustrations, 150 video clips, and 2,300 music or sound clips. A Research Organizer tool assists students in writing reports and developing study habits. Provides links to over 10,000 World Wide Web sites and monthly on-line updates. Students can experiment with concepts during "InterActivities" and take virtual tours of historic sites.

1998 Grolier Multimedia Encyclopedia (Grolier Interactive): Contains 35,000 articles and accompanying multimedia information about a variety of topics. Includes maps and full-text historical documents. Guided tours help students investigate specific topics in depth. Provides Internet links to the Grolier Internet Index, which is updated monthly.

1998 World Book Deluxe (World Book Multimedia): Includes a Homework Wizard, which helps students create charts, graphs, and timelines and guides them through the creation of a written report. Provides Internet connectivity for weekly updates and access to archives dating back to 1922. Study Aids accompany major articles with outlines, questions, bibliographies, and lists of cross-referenced articles.

Guiness Encyclopedia (Grolier): Organized thematically into 11 categories with three information avenues which contain photographs, illustrations, languages, movies, and animation.

Collier's Encyclopedia 98 (Sierra): Contains the complete text of the print version of Collier's with 21,000 articles, plus thousands of photos, sounds, videos, and animations. Images and maps have zoom capabilities for closer examination. Twenty-four simulations encourage learning by experimentation. Includes an on-line dictionary and Internet access.

Table 9.10. *(continued)*

For Ages 14 and Up

Britannica CD (Encyclopaedia Britannica): Contains a large database that is searched with a search engine much like those available on the World Wide Web. Also permits natural language questions. Contains full text of the print version and more than 2,000 additional articles.

Britannica Online (Encyclopaedia Brittanica): On-line version of the Encyclopaedia Britannica, with links to 1,000s of sites on the Internet which are screened for their quality. Updated regularly, available for yearly or monthly subscription fee.

Encyclopedia Americana (Grolier): Uses a bookshelf metaphor that permits a user to search all of the books or a specific title. Dictionaries and a Chronology of World History are available for searching. Articles contain extensive bibliographies. Hypertext links are provided to selected Web sites.

Spelling Ace, which can help students correct over 80,000 words, and the Franklin Thesaurus, which contains over half a million synonyms and antonyms and spelling correction functions. These latter tools can be very useful for poor writers and spellers, as they are inexpensive, easy to use, and portable.

Databases

Extant databases, available on computer disks, on CD-ROM or DVD-ROM, and through networks, can be searched and analyzed by students for a variety of purposes. Students can obtain specific information about a topic (e.g., What is the average annual rainfall in Seattle?), examine trends in a set of data (e.g., Has average annual temperature risen or fallen in the past decade?), compare and contrast data trends (e.g., Is unemployment higher in the Northeast than the Midwest?), and examine relationships among different components of a data set (e.g., Are teachers' salaries higher in states where pupil–teacher ratios are lower?). The graphing and plotting tools available in some databases permit students to create visual representations that can help them discern and illustrate trends and patterns in the data.

Students also can create their own databases. Database creation activities include deciding what data to collect, designing a structure for organizing the data, and establishing systematic ways of measuring and categorizing (Hancock et al., 1992). As Hancock and his colleagues pointed out, data creation informs the analysis process because it helps students to see that conclusions are constrained by the set of data. Thus, teachers should consider both data creation and data analysis activities as they implement database activities in the classroom.

Authors have suggested that students be introduced to the concept of a database as a collection of cards. Initial activities, such as having students fill in a few fields of personal information in a teacher-created database and then searching for personal information about classmates, can familiarize students with the organization and purposes of databases. As with any other technology tool, mastering program operation will require time and practice (Stearns, 1992).

Norton and Harvey (1995) recommended that teachers organize database activities into the activities of searching, sorting, creating, and reporting. *Searching* involves gathering information relevant to a specific question or task in the database and elsewhere. *Sorting* requires students to judge the validity of information and evaluate it for its credibility, reliability, and validity. Creating and reporting are transformative processes. *Creating* involves combining information to generate insight, formulate solutions, make decisions, and ask why, what if, what is similar, what is different, and what inferences can be drawn questions. Students should share the products of their creations through *reporting*, which requires them to decide which information to include and to share their product with others.

As Hancock et al.'s (1992) research found, students will need instruction and guidance to learn how to reason with data. Although developed a decade ago, Watson's (1989) guide to developing thinking skills with database activities remains a great source of ideas for engaging students in activities that can promote analytic thinking.

Finally, many teachers use commercial databases such as FileMaker Pro (FileMaker-Claris), ClarisWorks (Claris), and Microsoft Works (Microsoft) for database activities. Only a few databases are developed specifically for the school-age market. The Tabletop (Brøderbund) comes in junior (Grades PreK to 5) and senior (Grades 4 to 12) editions. Students work with existing databases or create their own and then analyze and represent the data through various plots, graphs, and diagrams. The accompanying teacher's guides contain a variety of lessons to inform the program's use and integration across the curriculum. First Workshop and Information Workshop (Sunburst) are databases designed for Grades 2 to 5 and 4 to 10, respectively. They contain Wizard files that guide students through database creation, precreated topics, and graphing tools.

Summary

The research reviewed in this chapter has demonstrated that computers and other technologies can improve the education of students with mild disabilities. As technology becomes more sophisticated, it spawns an increasing number of uses in the classroom. There is no recipe for how best to use technology. Rather, technology can be used in many different ways to provide, support, and supplement a diversity of educational activities. Two broad categories of technology-based activities were presented in this chapter: technology to support teaching and technology tools. General considerations in using technology were outlined and guidelines, recommended activities, and commercial products related to each category were presented and discussed.

The large number of different applications examined in this chapter testifies to the power and flexibility of electronic technology and its potential for improving educational experiences for students with mild disabilities. Technological devices continue to become smaller without sacrificing their power or sophistication. Technology-based systems are becoming more user friendly. With the decreasing cost of mass storage devices, more information can be stored less expensively. The potential to represent ideas simultaneously in multiple media is a key feature of almost all recent technology applications. These factors will help increase the future availability of technology in both home and school settings and guarantee its use for an even wider variety of instructional purposes and student needs.

Visions of technology's potential for improving education have evolved from the programmed learning of the 1960s and 1970s to the computer-managed systems and expert systems of the 1980s to contemporary views of technology as one component of a complex learning environment in which students are engaged in authentic tasks. As such, technology serves as a tool that can facilitate more effective teaching and more sophisticated cognitive processes. It may also serve as a catalyst that encourages educators to try new approaches and spurs students to participate more fully (Okolo & Ferretti, 1996). Clearly, this vision of technology requires much more work on the part of educators, who now have to manage new complexities, orchestrate multiple activities, and find alternative ways to assess performance; however, I believe that this vision has the most potential for improving the educational experiences of *all* learners.

Even as technology becomes more sophisticated and the numbers of different ways in which it is used increase, two themes reiterated throughout this chapter are unlikely to change. First, instructional technology, in and of itself, is not the key to improved educational outcomes for students with mild disabilities. Rather, it is the way in which teachers use technology that matters. Technology use should be consistent with curricular goals and compatible with students' instructional needs. Its use should be integrated into ongoing instructional programs and directed toward accomplishing goals that are of importance to teachers and students.

Second, technology use must be accompanied by teacher-directed instruction, guidance, and monitoring. Rather than replacing the teacher, technology has underscored the supremacy of the teacher's role in the instructional process. Very few technology-based activities can introduce students to new skills and concepts as effectively as a teacher can. Students must be taught the prerequisite skills and knowledge necessary to take advantage of the opportunities afforded by tools such as word processing, network-based learning, and multimedia projects. Moreover, students must be taught functions and features of various technology applications and strategies to use them optimally. Students' understanding of technology-based tasks, their progress toward the acquisition and mastery of skills, and the products they produce must be overseen by a knowledgeable teacher who can clarify misunderstandings, provide additional instruction as needed, and encourage students to use more sophisticated strategies. Finally, the teacher must play a key role in helping students generalize information and models learned through technology to the classroom and to the world outside the school walls.

Resources

Organizations

International Society for Technology in Education is a nonprofit professional organization dedicated to the improvement of education through computer-based technology. They publish *Learning and Leading with Technology*, a large list of books and courseware on educational technology, and a Gopher/Web server ISTE-GOPHER. UOREGON.EDU. They offer distance education courses for graduate credit, special interest groups, and conferences. *Contact:* International Society for Technology in Education, 1787 Agate Street, Eugene, OR 97403-1923; Voice: 503/346-4414; Web: http://www.iste.org

LD Resources publishes a variety of resources for individuals with learning disabilities and an e-mail newsletter. Their Web site contains extensive information about technology and learning disabilities, including descriptions of software, articles and essays, and links to other resources. *Contact:* LD Resources, 202 Lake Road, New Preston, CT 06777; Voice: 860/868-3214; Web: http://www.ldresources.com

National Center to Improve Practice in Special Education through Technology, Media, and Materials (NCIP) sponsors a Web site that contains a wealth of information to assist educators in using technology with students who are disabled. Resources include facilitated discussions about technology topics, video profiles of technology use for students with disabilities, on-line workshops, virtual tours of exemplary programs, a library collection of resources about special education and technology, and links to other useful Web sites, including information about funding sources. *Contact:* NCIP, Education Development Center, Inc., 55 Chapel Street, Newton, MA 02158-1060; Voice: 617/969-7100 ext. 2387; Web: http://www.edc.org/FSC/NCIP/

Special Education Resources on the Internet (SERI) is a collection of Internet-accessible information resources of interest to those involved in the fields related to special education. The collection is organized topically (e.g., learning disabilities, behavior disorders, special needs and technology), and provides a comprehensive set of links that are related to each topic. *Contact:* Web: http://www.hood.edu/seri/serihome.htm

Technology and Media Division, a division of the Council for Exceptional Children, is an organization of professionals interested in the effective use of technology for individuals with disabilities. They publish a quarterly journal, *Journal of Special Technology,* and the *TAM Newsletter.* They also sponsor an annual conference. *Contact:* TAM, c/o Council for Exceptional Children, 1920 Association Drive, Reston, VA 22091; Voice: 703/620-3660. TAM's Web site includes a helpful set of links to resources about special education and technology: http://tamcec.org

Journals and Printed Materials

ConnSENSE Bulletin. The A. J. Pappanikou Center Technology Lab at the University of Connecticut sponsors the ConnSENSE annual conference about technology and special education and publishes the *ConnSENSE Bulletin,* a resource for people using computer technology in special education. Their Web site contains "Way Cool Software Reviews" of a variety of products and links to other software review sites. *Contact:* Chauncy N. Rucker, Ph.D., Director, A. J. Pappanikou Center Technology Lab, 249 Glenbrook Road, U-64, Storrs, CT 06269-2064; Voice: 203/486-0165; Web: http://www.ucc.uconn.edu/~wwwpcse/techlab.html

TECH-NJ. A comprehensive newsletter that describes uses of technology for students with disabilities and reviews software. *Contact:* Trenton State College, Department of Special Education, Hillwood Lakes CN4700,

Trenton, NJ 08650-4700; Voice: 609/771-2308; Web: http://www.tcnj.edu/~technj

Laboratory–Practicum Activities

▶ 1. Choose a software program or CD-ROM that is designed to deliver instruction or practice to a student. (You might choose one from Table 9.5 of this chapter.) Use the program as a student would, making the types of errors a student would make as he or she uses the program. Evaluate the program according to the criteria listed in the "What To Look For" column of Table 9.2. Write a software critique that describes the following:

1. How well the program meets each of the criteria

2. What your students need to know *before* they use this program

3. At least one activity that you could implement to help integrate the program with your curriculum

4. How you would evaluate what students learn from using this program

▶ 2. Develop a lesson that uses anchored instruction to teach vocabulary. Rent or choose a videodisc that would be of interest to your students. Preview the videodisc and locate five to eight vocabulary words that are thematically related, that are illustrated by scenes in the movie, and that would help promote your students' vocabulary knowledge. For example, in a videodisc of the movie *101 Dalmations*, you might choose the following vocabulary words: *cruel, hysterical, despondent, fortunate,* and *elated* (all words that describe ways the characters act or feel in the movie). Develop a lesson plan that uses segments of the videodisc as anchors to teach these words, including the following:

1. A description of how you would introduce the words

2. A discussion of how you would use the video to illustrate the words (including frame numbers of the scenes you would play)

3. Activities that would help the students practice the words in a variety of contexts *after* they have seen the video anchors

Note: This activity is based on Xin, Glaser, and Rieth (1996).

▶ 3. Access at least two of the gophers or Web sites listed in this chapter. Read about network-based learning projects in which other classrooms and students have participated. Choose a project that might be appropriate for your students. Describe the following:

1. Educational goals that this project could help you meet

2. Prerequisite skills that your students need before they can participate successfully in this project (consider both technical and substantive skills)

3. An outline of all project activities, including:

    a. How you will introduce participants to one another

    b. A list of activities in which students will engage

    c. A description of a final product

    d. A culminating activity

4. Logistical problems that might arise (e.g., difficulty providing enough time on-line, monitoring students' on-line correspondence, lack of response from other participating classrooms). Explain how you will address them.

▶ 4. Consider one of your students who has a severe problem with written expression. Choose two word processing or writing tools that might help this student. (You might choose from among the programs listed in Tables 9.8 and 9.9.) Explore each program's features thoroughly, using them as a student might. Write a plan for this student that discusses the following:

1. The writing difficulties experienced by the student

2. Features or characteristics of each program that specifically address these difficulties

3. Prerequisite skills that the student would need to use each program and how you would teach them

4. At least two sample assignments or activities that you would ask the student to complete using these programs

5. How you would evaluate what the student has learned or produced during each activity

▶ 5. Choose a topic that students might study in science or social studies. Design a unit plan for a multimedia project-based learning activity that could help students learn about this topic. In your plan, explain the following:

1. The title of the topic and what you hope students will learn about it during this activity

2. The final product that you want students to create

3. An outline of both the content and media elements that you want students to include in their final products

4. How you will place students in groups

5. Specific social and cognitive discourse skills that you will teach to students

6. How you will teach and monitor these skills

7. The resources you will use to help students gather information about the topic (in addition to textbooks)

8. The authoring program that students will use to develop their projects

Then, design a sample project that you could show to students as a model of what you expect them to produce.

▶ 6. Consider the types of difficulties that your students have in accessing, using, and organizing information in your class or in other classes. Experiment with three technology-based tools that could help them. These might be outlining or concept mapping programs; CD-ROM or on-line dictionaries, encyclopedias, timeliners, or atlases; and hand-held electronic devices. Write a report that describes the following:

1. The difficulties your students have in accessing, using, and organizing information

2. Specific ways that each of these tools could help students compensate for these difficulties

3. An activity that will show students how to use each tool *and* provide them with an appropriate model of situations in which the tool will be of most use to them

4. Limitations of each tool and how you will help students to overcome these limitations (e.g., by teaching alternative strategies)

▶ 7. Design a beginning of the year activity to help your students learn about databases. In this lesson, students will design, create, and use a database that will help them get to know their fellow classmates. In your lesson plan, describe the following:

1. The specific database software you will use in your classroom and why you have chosen this title

2. An introductory activity to acquaint your students with the concept of a database and its components

3. How the class will determine the content of the database—that is, how students will determine which fields should be included in the database

4. How the class will collect information for each record and enter information into each record

5. An outline of activities that you could use to teach students to
   a. Search the database they have created
   b. Sort the database they have created

References

Anderson-Inman, L. (1990). Keyboarding across the curriculum. *The Computing Teacher, 17*(8), 36.

Anderson-Inman, L., & Horney, M. A. (1993, April). *Profiles of hypertext readers: Case studies from the ElectroText project.* Paper presented at the annual meeting of the American Educational Research Association, Atlanta, GA.

Anderson-Inman, L., & Horney, M. A. (1998). Transforming text for at-risk readers. In D. Reinking, L. Labbo, M. McKenna, & R. Kieffler (Eds.), *Handbook of literacy and technology: Transformations in a post-typographic world* (pp. 15–43). Hillsdale, NJ: Erlbaum.

Anderson-Inman, L., Horney, M. A., Chen, D., & Lewin, L. (1994). Hypertext literacy: Observations from the ElectroText project. *Language Arts, 71*(4), 279–287.

Anderson-Inman, L., Horney, M. A., Knox-Quinn, C., Corrigan, B., & Ditson, M. (1997). *Computer-based study strategies.* Eugene, OR: Center for Electronic Studying.

Anderson-Inman, L., & Knox-Quinn, C. (1996). Spell checking strategies for successful students. *Journal of Adolescence and Adult Literacy, 39*(6), 500–503.

Anderson-Inman, L., Knox-Quinn, C., & Horney, M. A. (1996). Computer-based study strategies for students with learning disabilities: Individual differences associated with adoption level. *Journal of Learning Disabilities, 29,* 461–484.

Armbruster, B. B., & Anderson, T. H. (1988). On selecting "considerate" content area textbooks. *Remedial and Special Education, 9*(1), 47–52.

Babbit, B. C., & Miller, S. P. (1996). Using hypermedia to improve the mathematics problem-solving skills of students with learning disabilities. *Journal of Learning Disabilities, 29,* 391–401.

Bahr, C. M., Nelson, N. W., & Van Meter, A. M. (1996). The effects of text-based and graphics based software tools on planning and organizing of stories. *Journal of Learning Disabilities, 29,* 355–370.

Ball, E., & Blachman, B. (1991). Does phoneme awareness training in kindergarten make a difference in early word recognition and developmental spelling? *Reading Research Quarterly, 26,* 49–66.

Baumeister, A. A., & Brooks, P. H. (1981). Cognitive deficits in mental retardation. In J. M. Kauffman & D. P. Hallahan (Eds.), *Handbook of special education* (pp. 87–107). Englewood Cliffs, NJ: Prentice-Hall.

Becker, H. J. (1991). How computers are used in the United States schools: Basic data from the 1989 I.E.A. Computers in Education Survey. *Journal of Educational Computing Research, 7,* 385–406.

Belmont, J. M., Butterfield, E. C., & Ferretti, R. P. (1982). To secure transfer of training, instruct self-management skills. In D. K. Detterman & R. J. Sternberg (Eds.), *How much can intelligence be increased?* (pp. 147–154). Norwood, NJ: Ablex.

Bennett, N., & Diener, K. (1997). Habits of mind. *Learning and Leading with Technology, 24*(6), 18–21.

Blumenfeld, P. C., Soloway, E., Marx, R. W., Krajcik, J. S., Guzdial, M., & Palincsar, A. (1991). Motivating project-based learning: Sustaining the doing, supporting the learning. *Educational Psychologist, 26,* 369–398.

Boone, R., & Higgins, K. (1993). Hypermedia basal readers: Three years of school-based research. *Journal of Special Education Technology, 12,* 86–106.

Borgh, K., & Dickson, W. P. (1992). The effects on children's writing of adding speech synthesis to a word processor. *Journal of Research on Computing in Education, 24,* 533–544.

Borgh, K., & Dickson, W. P. (1992). The effects on children's writings of adding speech synthesis to a word processor. *Journal of Research on Computing in Education, 24*(4), 533–544.

Bosco, J. (1986). An analysis of evaluations of interactive video. *Educational Technology, 26*(5), 7–17.

Bottge, B. A., & Hasselbring, T. S. (1993). A comparison of two approaches for teaching complex, authentic mathematics problems to adolescents in remedial math classes. *Exceptional Children, 59,* 556–566.

Bransford, J. D., Hasselbring, T., Barron, B., Kulewicz, S., Littlefield, J., & Goin, L. (1988). Uses of macro-contexts to facilitate mathematical thinking. In R. Charles & E. A. Silver (Eds.), *The teaching and assessing of mathematical problem solving* (pp. 125–147). Hillsdale, NJ: Erlbaum.

Bransford, J. D., Sharp, D. M., Vye, N. J., Goldman, S. R., Hasselbring, T. S., Goin, L., O'Banion, K., Livernois, J., Saul, E., & the Cognition and Technology Group at Vanderbilt University. (1994, July–August). MOST environments for accelerating literacy development. Paper prepared for NATO Advanced Study Institute on the Psychological and Educational Foundations of Technology-Based Learning Environments, Kolymbari, Crete.

Bransford, J. D., Sherwood, R. D., Hasselbring, T. S., Kinzer, C. K., & Williams, S. M. (1990). Anchored instruction: Why we need it and how technology can help. In D. Nix & R. Spiro (Eds.), *Cognition, education, and multimedia* (pp. 115–141). Hillsdale, NJ: Erlbaum.

Bransford, J. D., & Vye, N. J. (1989). A perspective on cognitive research and its implications for instruction. In L. Resnick & L. Klopfer (Eds.), *Toward the thinking curriculum: Current cognitive research* (pp. 173–205). Alexandria, VA: Association for Supervision and Curriculum Development.

Brown, A. S. (1994). The advancement of learning. *Educational Researcher, 23,* 4–12.

Browning, P., White, W. A. T., Nave, G., & Barkin, P. Z. (1986). Interactive video in the classroom: A field study. *Education and Training in Mental Retardation, 21,* 85–92.

Bruce, B., Michaels, S., & Watson-Gegeo, K. (1985). How computers can change the writing process. *Language Arts, 62,* 143–149.

Brunner, C. (1996). Judging student multimedia. *Electronic Learning, 15*(6), 14–15.

Byrne, B., & Fielding-Barnsley, R. (1993). Evaluation of a program to teach phonemic awareness to young children: A 1-year follow-up. *Journal of Educational Psychology, 85,* 104–111.

Carnine, D., & Kameenui, E. (1992). *Higher order thinking: Designing curriculum for mainstreamed students.* Austin, TX: PRO-ED.

Carver, S. M. (1995). Cognitive apprenticeships: Putting theory into practice on a large scale. In C. N. Hedley, P. Antonacci, & M. Rabinowitz (Eds.), *Thinking and literacy: The mind at work* (pp. 203–228). Hillsdale, NJ: Erlbaum.

Chaffin, J. D., Maxwell, B., & Thompson, B. (1982). The ARC-ED Curriculum: The application of video game formats to educational software. *Exceptional Children, 49,* 173–178.

Chapman, J. W. (1988). Cognitive–motivational characteristics and academic achievement of learning disabled children: A longitudinal study. *Journal of Educational Psychology, 80,* 357–365.

Christensen, C. A., & Gerber, M. M. (1990). Effectiveness of computerized drill and practice games in teaching basic math facts. *Exceptionality, 1,* 149–165.

Clark, R. E. (1983). Reconsidering research on learning from media. *Review of Educational Research, 53,* 445–459.

Cochran-Smith, M. (1991). Word processing and writing in elementary classrooms: A critical review of related literature. *Review of Educational Research, 61,* 107–155.

Cochran-Smith, M., Kahn, J., & Paris, C. L. (1988). When word processors come into the classroom. In J. Hoot & S. Silvern (Eds.), *Writing with computers in the early grades* (pp. 43–74). New York: Teachers College Press.

Cognition and Technology Group at Vanderbilt. (1990). Anchored instruction and its relationship to situated cognition. *Educational Researcher, 19,* 2–10.

Cohen, E. G. (1994). Restructuring the classroom: Conditions for productive small groups. *Review of Educational Research, 64,* 1–35.

Cohen, M., & Riel, M. (1989). The effect of distant audiences on students' writing. *American Educational Research Journal, 26,* 143–159.

Collins, M., Carnine, D., & Gersten, R. (1987). Elaborated corrective feedback and the acquisition of reasoning skills: A study of computer-assisted instruction. *Exceptional Children, 54*(3), 254–262.

Cosden, M. A. (1988). Microcomputer instruction and perceptions of effectiveness of special and regular education elementary school teachers. *Journal of Special Education, 22,* 242–252.

Cosden, M. A., & Abernathy, T. V. (1990). Microcomputer use in schools: Teacher roles and instructional options. *Remedial and Special Education, 11,* 31–38.

Cosden, M. A., Gerber, M. M., Semmel, D. S., Goldman, S. R., & Semmel, M. I. (1987). Microcomputer use within microcomputer-educational environments. *Exceptional Children, 53,* 399–409.

Cosden, M. A., Goldman, S. R., & Hine, M. S. (1990). Learning handicapped students' interactions during a microcomputer-based group writing activity. *Journal of Special Education Technology, 10,* 220–232.

Cox, D. A., & Berger, C. F. (1985). The importance of group size in the use of problem-solving skills on a microcomputer. *Journal of Educational Computing Research, 1,* 459–468.

Daiute, C. (1986). Physical and cognitive factors in revising: Insights from studies with computers. *Research in the Teaching of English, 20,* 141–159.

Daiute, C., & Morse, F. (1994). Access to knowledge and expression: Multimedia writing tools for students with diverse needs and strengths. *Journal of Special Education Technology, 12,* 221–256.

Dalton, D. W., Hannafin, M. J., & Hooper, S. (1989). Effects of individual and cooperative computer-assisted instruction on student performance and attitudes. *Educational Technology Research and Development, 37*(2), 15–24.

Davidson, J. I. (1989). *Children and computers together in the early childhood classroom.* Albany, NY: Delmar.

Debashis, A. (1995). Adventure in cyberspace: Exploring the information content of World Wide Web pages on the Internet. *Dissertation Abstracts International, 56-09A,* 3358 (Dissertation Abstracts Online).

Deshler, D. D., & Schumaker, J. B. (1986). Learning strategies: An instructional alternative for low-achieving adolescents. *Exceptional Children, 52,* 583–590.

Deshler, D. D., Schumaker, J. B., Alley, G. R., Warner, M. M., & Clark, F. L. (1982). Learning disabilities in adolescent and adult populations. *Focus on Exceptional Children, 15*(1), 1–12.

Dockterman, D. A. (1994). Cooperative learning and technology. Watertown, MA: Tom Snyder Productions.

Duffield, J. A. (1990, April). *Problem solving software: What does it teach?* Paper presented at the annual meeting of the American Educational Research Association, Boston.

Edyburn, D. L. (1991). Fact retrieval by students with and without learning handicaps using print and electronic encyclopedias. *Journal of Special Education Technology, 11,* 75–90.

Egan, D. E., Remadae, J. R., Landauer, T. K., Lochdaum, C. C., & Gomez, L. M. (1989). Acquiring information in books and superbooks. *Machine Mediated Learning, 3,* 259–277.

Ellis, E. S., Lenz, K. B., & Sabornie, E. J. (1987). Generalization and acquisition of learning strategies to natural environments: Part II. Research into practice. *Remedial and Special Education, 8*(2), 6–23.

Englert, C. S. (1990). Unraveling the mysteries of writing through strategy instruction. In T. E. Scruggs & B. Y. L. Wong (Eds.), *Intervention research in learning disabilities* (pp. 105–151). Greenwich, CT: JAI Press.

Ferretti, R. P., & Okolo, C. M. (1996). Authenticity in learning: Multimedia design projects in social studies for students with disabilities. *Journal of Learning Disabilities, 29,* 450–460.

Ferretti, R. P., & Okolo, C. M. (1997, March). *Designing multimedia projects in the social studies: Effects on students' content knowledge and attitudes.* Paper presented at the annual meeting of the American Educational Research Association, Chicago.

Fishman, B. (1997, March). *Student traits and the use of computer-mediated communication tools: What matters most and why?* Paper presented at the annual meeting of the American Educational Research Association, Chicago.

Frye, B., & Frager, A. (1996). Civilization, colonization, SimCity: Simulations for the social studies classroom. *Learning and Leading with Technology, 24*(2), 21–23, 32.

Fuchs, L. S., Deno, S. L., & Mirkin, P. K. (1984). Effects of frequent curriculum-based measurement and evaluation on pedagogy, student achievement, and student awareness of learning. *American Educational Research Journal, 21,* 449–460.

Gleason, M., Carnine, D., & Boriero, D. (1990). Improving CAI effectiveness with attention to instructional design in teaching story problems to mildly handicapped students. *Journal of Special Education Technology, 10*(3), 129–136.

Goldman, S. R., & Pellegrino, J. (1987). Information processing and educational microcomputer technology: Where do we go from here? *Journal of Learning Disabilities, 20,* 144–154.

Golub, L. S., & Frederick, W. C. (1970). An analysis of children's writing under different stimulus conditions. *Research in the Teaching of English, 4*(2), 168–180.

Graham, S., Harris, K. R., MacArthur, C. A., & Schwartz, S. (1991). Writing and writing programs for students with learning disabilities: Review of a research program. *Learning Disability Quarterly, 14,* 89–114.

Grossen, B., & Carnine, D. (1990). Diagramming a logic strategy: Effects on more difficult problem types and transfer. *Learning Disability Quarterly, 13,* 168–182.

Grossen, B., & Carnine, D. (1996). Considerate instruction helps students with disabilities achieve world class standards. *Teaching Exceptional Children, 8*(4), 77–81.

Hallahan, D. P., & Kauffman, J. M. (1986). *Exceptional children* (3rd ed.). Englewood Cliffs, NJ: Prentice-Hall.

Hallahan, D. P., Kauffman, J. M., & Lloyd, J. W. (1996). *Introduction to learning disabilities* (3rd ed.). Needham Heights, MA: Allyn & Bacon.

Hancock, C., Kaput, J. J., & Goldsmith, L. T. (1992). Authentic inquiry with data: Critical barriers to classroom implementation. *Educational Psychologist, 27,* 337–364.

Harris, J. (1995a). Educational telecomputing projects: Information collections. *The Computing Teacher, 22*(7), 44–48.

Harris, J. (1995b). Educational telecomputing projects: Interpersonal exchanges. *The Computing Teacher, 22*(6), 60–64.

Harris, J. (1995c). Educational telecomputing projects: Problem-solving projects. *Learning and Leading with Technology, 22*(8), 59–63.

Harris, J. (1995d). Knowledge making in the information age: Beyond information access. *The Computing Teacher, 23*(2), 57–60.

Harris, J. B. (1996). Information is forever in formation; knowledge is forever in the knower: Global connectivity in K–12 classrooms. *Computers in the Schools, 12*(1–2), 11–22.

Hasselbring, T. S., Goin, L. I., & Bransford, J. D. (1988). Developing math automaticity in learning handicapped children: The role of computerized drill and practice. *Focus on Exceptional Children, 20*(6), 1–7.

Hasselbring, T. S., & Moore, P. R. (1996). Developing mathematical literacy through the use of contextualized learning environments. *Journal of Computing in Childhood Education, 7*(3–4), 199–222.

Hativa, N. (1988). Computer-based drill and practice in arithmetic: Widening the gap between high- and low-achieving students. *American Educational Research Journal, 25,* 366–397.

Hativa, N., & Lesgold, A. (1990, April). *Computerized management of practice—Can it adapt to the individual learner?* Paper presented at the annual meeting of the American Educational Research Association, Boston.

Hativa, N., & Lesgold, A. (1996). Situational effects in classroom technology implementation: Unfulfilled expectations and unexpected outcomes. In S. T. Kerr (Ed.), *Technology and the future of schooling: Ninety-fifth yearbook for the National Society for Education* (pp. 131–171). Chicago: University of Chicago Press.

Haugland, S. W., & Shade, D. D. (1988). Developmentally appropriate software for young children. *Young Children, 43*(4), 37–43.

Hazel, J. S., & Schumaker, J. B. (1988). Social skills and learning disabilities: Current issues and recommendations for future research. In J. F. Kavanagh & T. J. Kruss, Jr. (Eds.), *Learning disabilities: Proceedings of the national conference* (pp. 293–344). Parkton, MD: York Press.

Heinisch, B., & Hecht, J. (1993). A comparison of six programs: Word prediction software. *TAM Newsletter, 8*(3), 4–9.

Higgins, K., & Boone, R. (1990). Hypertext: A new vehicle for computer use in reading instruction. *Intervention in School and Clinic, 26*(1), 26–31.

Higgins, K., Boone, R., & Lovitt, T. (1996). Hypertext supports for remedial students and students with learning disabilities. *Journal of Learning Disabilities, 29*, 402–412.

Horney, M. A., & Anderson-Inman, L. (1994). The Electro-Text Project: Hypertext reading patterns of middle school students. *Journal of Educational Multimedia and Hypermedia, 3*(1), 71–91.

Horton, S. V., Lovitt, T. C., Givens, A., & Nelson, R. (1989). Teaching social studies to high school students with academic handicaps in a mainstream setting: Effects of a computerized study guide. *Journal of Learning Disabilities, 22*, 102–107.

Hunter, M. W., & Dickey, J. (1990, January). *A computer-based information system to support ongoing academic adjustment by at-risk secondary students: Initial design and field test.* Paper presented at the Technology and Media Division Conference on Special Education Technology, Lexington, KY.

Johnson, D. W., Johnson, R. T., & Holubec, E. (1994). *The new circles of learning: Cooperation in the classroom and school.* Alexandria, VA: Association for Supervision of Curriculum and Development.

Johnson, G., Gersten, R., & Carnine, D. (1987). Effects of instructional design variables on vocabulary acquisition of LD students: A study of computer-assisted instruction. *Journal of Learning Disabilities, 20*(4), 206–213.

Jones, K. M., Torgesen, J. K., & Sexton, M. A. (1987). Using computer guided practice to increase decoding fluency in learning disabled children: A study using the Hint and Hunt I program. *Journal of Learning Disabilities, 20,* 122–128.

Kagan, S. (1994). *Cooperative learning.* San Juan Capistrano, CA: Kagan Cooperative Learning.

Keene, S., & Davey, B. (1987). Effects of computer-presented text on LD adolescents' reading behavior. *Learning Disability Quarterly, 10*, 283–290.

Kelly, B., Carnine, D. W., Gersten, R., & Grossen, B. (1986). The effectiveness of videodisc instruction in teaching fractions to learning handicapped and remedial high school students. *Journal of Special Education Technology, 8*(2), 5–17.

Kelly, B., Gersten, R., & Carnine, D. (1990). Student error patterns as a function of curriculum design: Teaching fractions to remedial high school students with learning disabilities. *Journal of Learning Disabilities, 23*, 23–29.

Kimeldorf, M. (1995). Teaching online—Methods and techniques. *The Computing Teacher, 23*(1), 26–31.

King, A. (1994). Guiding knowledge construction in the classroom: Effects of teaching children how to question and how to explain. *American Educational Research Journal, 31*, 338–368.

Kinzer, C. K., Gabella, M. S., & Rieth, H. J. (1994). An argument for using multimedia and anchored instruction to facilitate mildly-disabled students' learning of literacy and social studies. *Technology and Disability, 3*(2), 128–139.

Kinzer, C. K., Hasselbring, T. S., Schmidt, C. A., & Meltzer, L. (1990, April). *Effects of multimedia to enhance writing ability.* Paper presented at the annual meeting of the American Educational Research Association, Boston.

Knapp, L. R. (1984). Finding the best typing tutorials. *Classroom Computer Learning, 5*(4), 70–71.

Krupski, A. (1981). An interactional approach to the study of attention problems in children with learning handicaps. *Exceptional Education Quarterly, 2*, 1–11.

Laboratory of Comparative Human Culture. (1989). Kids and computers: A positive vision of the future. *Harvard Educational Review, 59*, 73–86.

Lamb, A., Smith, N., & Johnson, L. (1997). Wondering, wiggling, and weaving. *Learning and Leading with Technology, 24*(7), 6–13.

Leali, S. (1995). Using computer simulations with at-risk students. *Learning and Leading with Technology, 23*(2), 8–9.

Lehrer, R., Erickson, J., & Connell, T. (1993, April). *The restless text: Student authoring with hypermedia tools.* Paper presented at the annual meeting of the American Educational Research Association, Atlanta, GA.

Lehto, M. R., Zhu, W., & Carpenter, B. (1995). The relative effectiveness of hypertext and text. *International Journal of Human–Computer Interaction, 7*(4), 293–313.

Leventhal, L., Teasley, B., Instone, K., Rohlman, D., & Farhat, J. (1993). Sleuthing in HyperHolmes? An evolution of using hypertext vs. a book to answer questions. *Behaviour and Information Technology, 12*, 149–164.

Lin, A., Podell, D. M., & Rein, N. (1991). The effects of CAI on word recognition in mildly mentally handicapped and nonhandicapped learners. *Journal of Special Education Technology, 11*, 16–25.

MacArthur, C. (1988). The impact of computers on the writing process. *Exceptional Children, 54*, 536–542.

MacArthur, C. A. (1994). Peers + word processing + strategies = a powerful combination for revising student writing. *Teaching Exceptional Children, 27*(1), 24–29.

MacArthur, C. A. (1996). Using technology to enhance the writing processes of students with learning disabilities. *Journal of Learning Disabilities, 29,* 344–354.

MacArthur, C. A. (1997, March). *Speech synthesis and word prediction for students with learning disabilities.* Paper presented at the annual meeting of the American Educational Research Association, Chicago.

MacArthur, C. A., Graham, S., Haynes, J. B., & De La Paz, S. (1996). Spelling checkers and students with learning disabilities: Performance comparisons and impact on spelling. *Journal of Special Education, 30,* 35–57.

MacArthur, C. A., & Haynes, J. (1995). The Student Assistant for Learning from Text (SALT): A hypermedia reading aide. *Journal of Learning Disabilities, 28*(3), 150–159.

Macro Systems, Inc. (1989, November). *Evaluation of the integration of technology for instructing handicapped students (high school level)* (Final Report, Executive Summary). Silver Springs, MD: Author.

Madian, J. (1995). Multimedia—Why and why not? *The Computing Teacher, 22*(7), 16–18.

Malone, T. W. (1981). Toward a theory of intrinsically motivating instruction. *Cognitive Science, 4,* 333–369.

Malouf, D. B. (1987–1988). The effect of instructional computer games on continuing student motivation. *Journal of Special Education,* pp. 27–38.

Marchionni, G. (1989). Making the transition from print to electronic encyclopedia: Adaptation of mental models. *International Journal of Man-Machine Studies, 30,* 591–618.

Marchionni, G., & Schneiderman, B. (1988). Finding facts vs. browsing knowledge in hypertext systems. *IEEE Computer, 21,* 70–80.

Mastropieri, M. A., & Scruggs, T. E. (1991). *Teaching students ways to remember: Strategies for learning mnemonically.* Cambridge, MA: Brookline Books.

Matthew, K. I. (1996). Using CD-ROMs in the language arts classroom. *Computers in the Schools, 12*(4), 73–81.

McClean, G. (1987). Criteria for selecting computer software for keyboarding instruction. *Business Education Forum, 41*(5), 10–11.

McCullen, C. (1995). World Wide Web in the classroom: The quintessential collaboration. *Learning and Teaching with Technology, 23*(3), 7–10.

Meskill, C., Swan, K., & Frazer, M. (1997). *Tools for supporting response-based literature teaching and learning: A multimedia exploration of the Beat Generation* (Report Series 2.29). Albany: National Research Center on English Learning and Achievement, State University of New York.

Monahan, S., & Susong, D. (1996). Author slide shows and Texas wildlife. *Learning and Leading with Technology, 24*(2), 6–11.

Montali, J., & Lewandowski, L. (1996). Bimodal reading: Benefits of a talking computer for average and less skilled readers. *Journal of Learning Disabilities, 29,* 271–279.

Moore, L., & Carnine, D. (1989). A comparison of two approaches to teaching ratios and proportions to remedial and learning disabled students: Active teaching with either basal or empirically validated curriculum design material. *Remedial and Special Education, 10,* 28–37.

Morocco, C. C. (1987). *Teachers, children, and the magical writing machine: Instructional contexts for word processing with learning disabled children* (Final Report, The EDC Writing Project). Newton, MA: Education Development Center.

Morocco, C., Dalton, B., & Tivnan, T. (1990, April). *The impact of computer-supported writing instruction on the writing quality of 4th grade students with learning disabilities.* Paper presented at the annual meeting of the American Educational Research Association, Boston.

Mueller, F. (1992). Telecommunications: A tool for developing writing and communication skills. *Teaching Exceptional Children, 25*(1), 8–11.

Murphy, V., & Thuente, K. (1995). Using technology in early learning classrooms. *Learning and Leading with Technology, 22*(8), 8–10.

Nastasi, B. K., & Clements, D. H. (1991). Research on cooperative learning: Implications for practice. *School Psychology Review, 20,* 110–131.

National Commission for Excellence in Education. (1983, April). *A nation at risk: The imperatives for educational reform.* Washington, DC: U.S. Department of Education.

National Council of Teachers of Mathematics. (1989). *Curriculum and evaluation standards for school mathematics.* Reston, VA: Author.

National Education Commission on Time and Learning. (1994, April). *Prisoners of time.* Washington, DC: U.S. Government Printing Office.

National Education Summit. (1996, March). (Available from http://www.summit96.ibm.com).

Neuman, S. B., & Morocco, C. (1987). Two hands is hard for me: Keyboarding and learning disabled children. *Educational Technology, 27*(12), 36–38.

Newman, D. (1987). Local and long distance computer networking for science classrooms. *Educational Technology, 27*(7), 20–23.

Norton, P., & Harvey, D. (1995). Information–Knowledge: Using databases to explore the tragedy at Donner Pass. *Learning and Leading with Technology, 23*(1), 23–25.

O'Connor, R. E., Notari-Syverson, A., & Vadasy, P. F. (1996). Ladders to literacy: The effects of teacher-led phonological activities for kindergarten children with and without disabilities. *Exceptional Children, 63,* 117–130.

Ogle, D. M. (1986). A teaching model that develops active reading of expository text. *The Reading Teacher, 39,* 564–570.

Okolo, C. (1991). Learning and behaviorally handicapped students' perceptions of instructional and motivational features of computer-assisted instruction. *Journal of Research on Computing in Education, 24,* 171–188.

Okolo, C. (1992). The effect of CAI format and initial attitude on the arithmetic facts proficiency and continuing motivation of students with learning disabilities. *Exceptionality, 3,* 195–211.

Okolo, C. (in preparation). *"You click on it and things happen": Students' interactions with and comprehension of electronic storybooks.*

Okolo, C. M., Bahr, C., & Rieth, H. (1993). A retrospective view of computer-based instruction. *Journal of Special Education Technology, 12,* 1–27.

Okolo, C. M., & Ferretti, R. P. (1996). The impact of multimedia design projects on the knowledge, attitudes, and collaboration of students in inclusive classrooms. *Journal of Computing in Childhood Education, 7,* 223–252.

Okolo, C. M., & Ferretti, R. P. (1997). Knowledge acquisition and multimedia design projects in the social studies for children with learning disabilities. *Journal of Special Education Technology, 13*(2), 91–103.

Okolo, C. M., & Hayes, R. (1996, April). *The impact of animation in CD-ROM books on students' reading behaviors and comprehension.* Paper presented at the annual meeting of the American Educational Research Association, New York.

Okolo, C. M., Hinsey, M., & Yousefian, B. (1990). Learning disabled students' acquisition of keyboarding skills and continuing motivation under drill-and-practice and game conditions. *Learning Disabilities Research, 5,* 100–109.

Palincsar, A. S., & Brown, A. L. (1984). Reciprocal teaching of comprehension-fostering and comprehension monitoring activities. *Cognition and Instruction, 1,* 117–175.

Pea, R. D. (1987). Cognitive technologies for mathematics education. In A. H. Schoenfeld (Ed.), *Cognitive science and mathematics education* (pp. 89–122). Hillsdale, NJ: Erlbaum.

Pearl, R. (1982). LD children's attributions for success and failure: A replication with a labeled LD sample. *Learning Disability Quarterly, 5,* 173–176.

Prickett, E. M. (1992). The multimedia classroom. In R. Boone & K. Higgins (Eds.), *Multimedia: TAM Topical Guide #1* (pp. 56–65). Reston, VA: Council for Exceptional Children.

Quartermann, J. S., & Carl-Mitchell, S. (1995a). Matrix size update. *Matrix News, 5*(1), 6.

Quartermann, J. S., & Carl-Mitchell, S. (1995b). MIDS press release: New data on the size of the Internet and the matrix. *Matrix News, 5*(1), 1, 5.

Reinking, D., & Schriener, R. (1985). The effects of computer-mediated text on measures of reading comprehension and reading behavior. *Reading Research Quarterly, 20,* 536–552.

Riel, M. (1992). Telecommunications: Avoiding the black hole. *The Computing Teacher, 17*(8), 16–17.

Rembelinsky, I. (1997–1998). "Us" and "them": Multimedia explorations of prejudice and intolerance in American history. *Learning and Leading with Technology, 25*(4), 42–47.

Riley, R. W. (1999). High quality teachers for every classroom. *Teaching PreK–8, 29*(4), 6.

Robey, E. P., Burton-Radzely, L., & Kallas, A. (1997, April). *Examining special educators' current use of technology in instruction.* Paper presented at the Annual Convention of the Council for Exceptional Children, Salt Lake City.

Roscigno, S., & Shearin, L. (1995). Animals! Animals! Animals! *The Computing Teacher, 22*(7), 27–29.

Rose, T. L. (1986). The effects of illustrations on reading comprehension of learning disabled students. *Journal of Learning Disabilities, 19,* 542–544.

Rosegrant, T. J. (1986, April). *It doesn't sound right: The role of speech output as a primary form of feedback for beginning text revision.* Paper presented at the annual meeting of the American Educational Research Association, San Francisco.

Roth, S. G., & Beck, I. L. (1987). Theoretical and instructional implications of the assessment of two microcomputer word recognition programs. *Reading Research Quarterly, 22,* 197–218.

Salisbury, D. F. (1990). Cognitive psychology and its implications for designing drill and practice programs for computers. *Journal of Computer-Based Education, 17,* 22–30.

Saracho, O. N. (1982). The effects of a computer-assisted instruction program on basic skills achievement and attitudes toward instruction of Spanish-speaking migrant children. *American Educational Research Journal, 19,* 201–219.

Schunk, D. H. (1989). Self-efficacy and classroom learning. *Psychology in the Schools, 22,* 208–223.

Sharan, Y., & Sharan, S. (1992). *Expanding cooperative learning through group investigation.* New York: Teachers College Press.

Sharp, D. L. M, Goldman, S. R., Bransford, J. D., Moore, P., Brophy, S., Vey, N. J., & Cognition and Technology Group at Vanderbilt. (1993, April). *Developing strategic approaches to narrative structures with integrated-media environments for young, at-risk children.* Paper presented at the annual meeting of the American Educational Research Association, Atlanta, GA.

Sheingold, K., & Hadley, M. (1990). *Accomplished teachers: Integrating computers into classroom practice.* New York: Bank Street College of Education, Center for Technology in Education.

Slavin, R. E. (1984). Students motivating students to excel: Cooperative incentives, cooperative tasks, and student achievement. *Elementary School Journal, 85,* 53–62.

Smith, K. J. (1992). Using multimedia with Navajo children: An effort to alleviate problems of cultural learning style, background of experience, and motivation. *Reading and Writing: Overcoming Learning Difficulties*, 8, 287–294.

Sormunen, C., Adams, M., Berg, D., & Prigge, L. (1989). *A national study of instructional practices and perceptions of elementary teachers about typewriting/keyboarding.* Little Rock, AR: Delta Pi Epsilon.

Sormunen, C., & Wickersham, G. (1991). Language arts and keyboarding skills development: A viable approach for teaching elementary school students. *Journal of Research on Computing in Education*, 23, 463–469.

Stearns, P. H. (1992). Preparing students with learning disabilities for information age success. *The Computing Teacher*, 19(7), 28–30.

Stevens, K., Blackhurst, A., & Slator, D. (1991). Teaching memorized spelling with a microcomputer: Time delay and computer-assisted instruction. *Journal of Applied Behavior Analysis*, 24, 153–160.

Stoddard, B., & MacArthur, C. A. (1993). A peer editor strategy: Guiding learning disabled students in response and revision. *Research in the Teaching of English*, 27, 76–103.

Swan, K., Guerrero, F., Mitrani, M., & Schoener, J. (1990). Honing in on the target: Who among the educationally disadvantaged benefits most from CBI? *Journal of Research on Computing in Education*, 22, 381–403.

Swan, K., & Meskill, C. (1997). *Multimedia and response-based literature teaching and learning* (Report Series 2.32). Albany: National Research Center on English Learning and Achievement, State University of New York.

Swanson, H. L., & Trahan, M. F. (1992). Learning disabled readers' comprehension of computer mediated text: The influence of working memory, metacognition, and attribution. *Learning Disabilities Research and Practice*, 7, 74–86.

Taylor, H. G., & Stuhlmann, J. M. (1995). Creating slide show book reports. *Learning and Leading with Technology*, 23(1), 8–10.

Thomas, C. C., Englert, C. S., & Gregg, S. (1987). An analysis of errors and strategies in the expository writing of learning disabled students. *Remedial and Special Education*, 8, 21–30.

Torgesen, J. K. (1984). Instructional use of computers with elementary aged mildly handicapped children. *Special Services in the Schools*, 1(1), 37–48.

Turner, S. V., & Dipinto, V. M. (1992). Students as hypermedia authors: Themes emerging from a qualitative study. *Journal of Research on Computing in Education*, 25, 187–199.

U.S. Department of Education. (1996). *To assure the free appropriate education of all children with disabilities: Eighteenth annual report to Congress on the implementation of the*

Individuals with Disabilities Education Act. Washington, DC: Author.

Van Dusen, L., & Worthen, B. (1993). Factors that facilitate or impede implementation of integrated learning systems. In G. Bailey (Ed.), *Computer-based integrated learning systems*. Englewood Cliffs, NJ: Educational Technology Publications.

Van Hanegan, J., Barron, L., Young, M., Williams, S., Vye, N., & Bransford, J. D. (1989). *The Jasper series: An experiment with new ways to enhance mathematical thinking* (Tech. Rep.). Nashville, TN: Vanderbilt University, Learning and Technology Center.

Vaughn, S., McIntosh, R. M., & Spencer-Rowe, J. (1991). Peer rejection is a stubborn thing: Increasing peer acceptance of rejected students with learning disabilities. *Learning Disabilities Research and Practice*, 6, 83–88.

Vesel, J. H. (1996). Using teleconversations to explore social issues. *Learning and Leading with Technology*, 23(5), 27–30.

Wallace, G., & Kauffman, J. M. (1986). *Teaching children with learning problems*. Columbus, OH: Merrill.

Watson, J. (1989). *Teaching thinking skills with databases*. Eugene, OR: International Council for Computers in Education.

Webb, N. (1992). Testing a theoretical model of student interaction and learning in small groups. In R. Hertz-Lazarowitz & N. Miller (Eds.), *Interaction in cooperative groups: The theoretical anatomy of group learning* (pp. 102–119). New York: Cambridge University Press.

Whitehead, A. N. (1929). *The aims of education*. New York: Macmillan.

Wiburg, K. (1995). Integrated learning systems: What does the research say? *The Computing Teacher*, 22(5), 7–10.

Wilkinson, G. L., Bennett, L. T., & Oliver, K. M. (1997). Evaluation criteria and indicators of quality for Internet resources. *Educational Technology*, 37(3), 52–59.

Winkler, J. D., Shavelson, R. J., Stasz, C., Robyn, A. E., & Fiebel, W. (1985). Pedagogically sound use of microcomputers in classroom instruction. *Journal of Educational Computing Research*, 18, 285–293.

Wise, B. W., & Olson, R. K. (1994). Computer speech and the remediation of reading and spelling problems. *Journal of Special Education Technology*, 12, 207–220.

Woodward, A. (1987). Textbooks: Less than meets the eye. *Journal of Curriculum Studies*, 19, 511–526.

Woodward, J., & Baxter, J. (1997, April). *Enhancing student understanding of decimals through multiple representations*. Paper presented at the annual meeting of the American Educational Research Association, Chicago.

Woodward, J., Carnine, D., Gersten, R., Gleason, M., Johnson, G., & Collins, M. (1986). Applying instructional design principles to CAI for mildly handicapped students: Four recently conducted studies. *Journal of Special Education Technology,* 8(1), 13–26.

Xin, F., Glaser, C., & Rieth, H. (1996). Multimedia reading: Using anchored instruction and video technology in vocabulary lessons. *Teaching Exceptional Children, 29*(2), 45–49.

Zellermayer, M., Salomon, G., Globerson, T., & Givon, H. (1991). Enhancing writing-related metacognitions through a computerized writing peer. *American Educational Research Journal, 28,* 373–391.

Chapter 10

Technology for Individuals with Speech and Language Disorders

Paula S. Cochran
Truman State University, Kirksville, Missouri

As computers became more common in business and education, the availability of powerful, creative, effective applications of technology for assisting persons with communication disorders was anxiously anticipated. Even though the advent of personal computers was exciting to some professionals from the start, it was acknowledged that early applications were often too primitive and too inflexible to be clinically useful. The lack of appropriate software in the early 1980s caused some experts to suggest that speech–language pathologists should learn computer programming for the purpose of writing their own software to meet the needs of individual clients (see, e.g., Ventkatagiri, 1987). Developers promised that more powerful, more affordable, more portable technology was coming soon.

The developers were right. Now the availability of powerful, creative, effective applications of technology for persons with communication disorders is a reality. Where once proponents of clinical applications of computers were armed with only anecdotal evidence and enthusiasm, now the results of controlled efficacy studies are available. Where once most clinical applications of computers appeared to be merely electronic workbook versions of traditional therapy activities, now computer applications serve a variety of useful roles in therapy. Where once the appearance of a computer was remarkable, computers are now a routine part of the landscape in homes, schools, hospitals, and clinics. For several years now the majority of the members of the American Speech-Language-Hearing Association (ASHA) have been using computers at work (Hyman, 1985). Where once few individuals with communication disorders had the opportunity to benefit from new clinical applications of computers, now many do so every day.

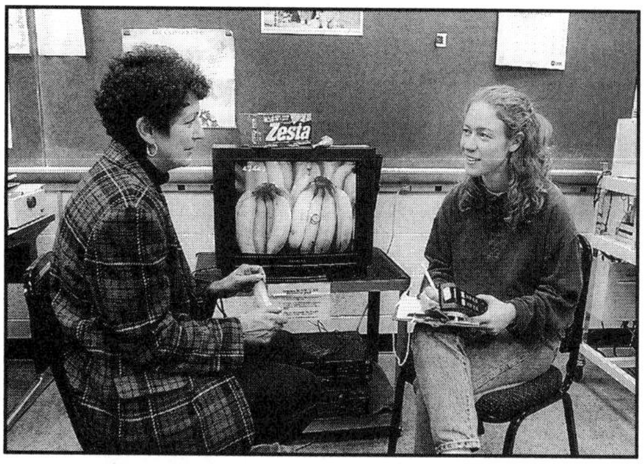

High-quality digitized images help language learners make the connection between real objects and pictures. (Photograph by Tim Barcus)

I would like to acknowledge the contributions and inspirations of Glen L. Bull and Gary E. Rushakoff, who together coauthored this chapter in the first edition. This chapter is dedicated to the memory of Gary E. Rushakoff, whose pioneering contributions to computer applications in communication disorders and patience with clinicians just starting to use them should not be forgotten.

Individuals with Communication Disorders

A communication disorder generally refers to any impairment of an individual's ability to use oral language to communicate with other people (Owens, 1999). Thus, communication disorders include problems with hearing, articulation (producing speech sounds), voice, fluency, or language. Speech disorders involve difficulty producing the actual sounds of a language intelligibly and fluently. In contrast, language disorders may include difficulty comprehending, planning, or producing communication appropriately. It is important to note that language disorders may go beyond difficulty with the form of language (sounds, grammar, vocabulary) to include difficulties with the use of language in various situations (body language, politeness, conversational conventions). Delays and disorders in speech and language often impact academic success. An important distinction exists between differences in communication style and disorders that impair communication development. Speakers of nonstandard dialects are not considered to have speech or language disorders unless their communication with other members of their own dialect group is impaired.

According to reports from the National Institute of Health, approximately 42 million people in the United States were affected by hearing loss or other communication disorders in 1991. During the 1992–1993 school year, 4,633,674 children with disabilities ages 6 to 21 received services under the Individuals with Disabilities Education Act of 1990 (IDEA) Part B and Chapter 1 of the Elementary and Secondary Education Act, State Operated Programs (U.S. Department of Education, 1995). Of these 4.6 million children, 21% received services for speech or language disorders and 1.3% received services for hearing disorders. In the 1991–1992 school year, 85.5% of students with speech or language disorders and 27% of students with hearing disorders were mainstreamed into general education classrooms (U.S. Department of Education, 1995).

Some communication disorders result from known organic causes. For example, a cleft palate or cerebral palsy may cause an individual to have difficulty producing intelligible speech. Often, however, no organic cause is apparent in the presence of a speech or language disorder. Mental retardation is one of the most common reasons that children fail to acquire language according to developmental expectations, but a variety of other reasons ranging from hearing loss to emotional disturbance may also be responsible. Thus, a communication disorder could involve delayed, arrested, or disordered acquisition of skills. Other communication disorders, such as adult aphasia resulting from stroke, involve the impairment or loss of previously acquired communication ability. Such a condition may be temporary (as in the case of a vocal pathology that can be surgically treated) or permanent (as in the case of a progressive neurological disease). In summary, persons with communication disorders may be any age and may be experiencing a temporary or permanent, sudden or gradual change in their ability to exchange information with other people through normal means. Intervention designed to assist persons with communication disorders, therefore, may have a very wide range of goals, including remediation, compensation, or rehabilitation.

Professionals who provide direct evaluation and intervention services for persons with speech and language disorders are called *speech–language pathologists*. Professionals who evaluate hearing and provide aural rehabilitation services are called *audiologists*. In nearly every state in the United States, a master's degree or equivalent is required to meet state licensure and teaching certification requirements in the area of speech–language pathology or audiology. Additional requirements, including 350 clock hours of supervised clinical practice, a national exam, and a clinical fellowship year in an employment setting, are necessary for obtaining national certification. This credential is called the Certificate of Clinical Competence and is granted by ASHA. Speech–language pathologists and audiologists provide services in a wide variety of work settings, including schools, hospitals, private and public clinics, rehabilitation centers, state residential institutions, nursing homes, and private offices.

This chapter focuses on the use of computers to aid in the evaluation and treatment of persons who have speech or language disorders, following a brief discussion of relevant administrative applications. Technology uses that are specific to managing individuals who are deaf or hard of hearing are emphasized in Chapter 12.

General Hardware Considerations

This section presents an overview of the ways in which professionals in communication disorders make use of new technologies. Opportunities for learning about new technologies and the competencies that speech–language pathologists and audiologists should try to attain are outlined.

Student Clinician Access to Technology Opportunities and Training

A recent national survey of public school speech–language pathologists found that 31% made use of computers at least weekly, especially for administrative purposes such as word processing reports (McRay & Fitch, 1996). Many respondents, however, noted that they felt ill prepared to make effective use of computers and other new technologies for evaluation and treatment of their students and clients. More than 95% of the 452 respondents indicated that they needed more technology training, with 71% considering their training needs to be moderate or extensive (McRay & Fitch, 1996). A 1996 national survey of directors of ASHA-accredited university programs in communication disorders presented a profile of the academic and clinical preparation that student clinicians typically receive regarding new technologies (Walz & Cochran, 1996). Use of computers for administrative tasks such as clinical report writing was common and had reached a level considered ideal only a

decade earlier (Lorendo, 1988). However, nearly 50% of program directors responding indicated that their students never or only occasionally made use of computers in clinical service delivery (Walz & Cochran, 1996). Clearly there is an ongoing need for more opportunities for working clinicians and clinicians-in-training to develop clinical computing competencies.

Technology-Related Competencies for Professionals

What clinical computing competencies do speech–language pathologists need? This question challenges the profession in part because technologies change so rapidly; skills that are narrow in focus may quickly become obsolete when technologies evolve. Therefore, competency with new technologies should be defined in a way that goes beyond what key to press. Clinical computing competency requires knowing why to use a certain technology, not simply *how*. In 1993 a group of technology leaders took on the task of describing a set of desirable computing competencies for clinicians (Cochran et al., 1993). The areas addressed by these competencies included using computers as productivity tools; awareness of technology-related ethical issues; awareness and use of technology-related resources; using computers as diagnostic tools; using computer-based materials as a context for conversation; using computers as instructors; using computers to record and analyze clinical data; using computers as biofeedback devices; and using computers to generate clinical materials. The authors stressed that education about new technologies must include hands-on opportunities and should reinforce good clinical practice.

A Model of Clinical Computing

The clinical computing competencies alluded to above suggest the wide variety of ways in which computers can assist the speech–language pathologist. Public school clinicians recently reported that 50% of their use of computers at work

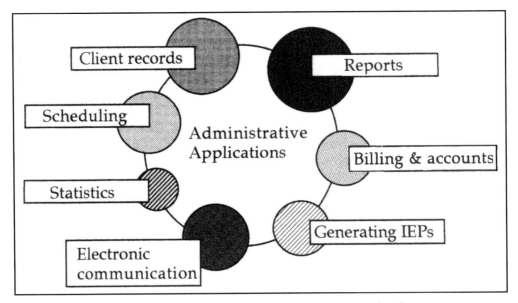

Figure 10.1. Administrative applications of computers in communication disorders.

consisted of word processing and report writing, with diagnostics (13%) and treatment (37%) making up the remainder (McRay & Fitch, 1996). Therefore, administrative applications will be considered separately from the clinical applications that directly impact evaluation and treatment of speech and language disorders.

Figure 10.1 shows that current administrative applications go well beyond word processing and report writing alone. Many other technology applications are valuable in the management of speech and language services, including Individualized Education Plan (IEP) generators, spreadsheets and billing software, client databases, statistical analysis, and electronic communication (Silverman, 1997). Figure 10.2 presents technologies that are used directly with persons who have communication disorders or disabilities. Note that although one traditional educational software category appears, using the computer as an instructor (computer-assisted instruction, or CAI), most of the uses of technology presented in Figure 10.2 do not match software categories that are traditional in education or business. Clinicians who are not yet using computers for evaluation and treatment of communication disor-

ders may not be aware of the range of possibilities, the ease with which new applications can be learned, or the research that suggests the efficacy of clinical applications (Cochran & Masterson, 1995). These specialized roles for technology in the field of communication disorders are described after a brief discussion of generic administrative applications.

Specific Technology Applications

Technology and Administrative Activities

Electronic Communication with Other Professionals

Many speech–language pathologists work in settings where they experience some degree of professional isolation, or at least limited access to consultation with colleagues who have similar expertise. Electronic communication in the form of electronic mail (e-mail), on-line discussion groups, and even videoconferencing can be used

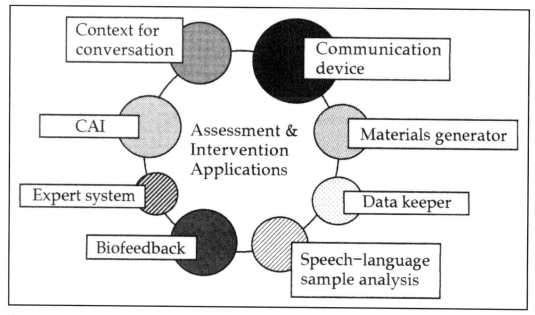

Figure 10.2. Computer applications for assessment and intervention in communication disorders. CAI = computer-assisted instruction.

to supplement face-to-face interactions (Bull, Bull, Garafola, & Sigmon, 1998). Clinicians who have access to the Internet can gain valuable insights into the feelings, attitudes, and experiences of persons with disabilities by reading or participating in electronic conversations with them (Stiegler & Currie, 1997). Dozens of on-line news groups and listservers that focus on topics related to communication disorders provide important professional support, information for the general public, parents, and persons with communication disorders themselves. More go on-line every day (see Resources at the end of this chapter).

Internet Resources for Communication Disorders

In addition to individual communications and interactions, speech–language pathologists use computers to access on-line resources pertaining to all aspects of communication disorders. The Internet, including the World Wide Web, is the international computer network through which most of this information is available (see Resources section for specific addresses). ASHA

maintains a Web site through which users can obtain information about professional issues, relevant legislation, grant opportunities, and research results. Internet users can readily access descriptive information about genetic disorders, diseases, and rare conditions. Most major publishers of tests, instructional materials, and clinical software maintain Web sites through which clinicians can quickly obtain ordering information and technical information. Some Web sites even provide materials that might be used directly in therapy, such as shareware games, activities, photos, movies, and sounds.

Report Writing, IEPs, and Client Record Keeping

The paperwork associated with providing services to persons with communication disorders sometimes seems overwhelming. Regardless of their work setting, clinicians must write evaluation reports, progress notes, and professional correspondence. Word processing facilitates the production of efficient, professional-looking documentation even when secretarial assistance is limited or absent. Clinicians often develop template files to speed report and letter writing, and may use personally developed databases of sample goals and objectives to facilitate IEP design. Special software for IEP generation in communication disorders has appeared on the market intermittently, but most school systems require that IEPs follow a certain, system-specific format that such products usually cannot replicate. Clinicians in some work settings, including private practice, use spreadsheet software to track billable hours, client billing records, and business expenses for tax purposes. Application software such as word processing, databases, and spreadsheets, can also have uses in direct clinical situations (also see Chapters 3 and 7). For example, a clinician might use a spreadsheet to track and graph client progress after each therapy session and to display progress to the client.

Glancing Ahead: Future On-line Activities

On-line resources are developing that will change the routine personal and professional interactions between speech–language pathologists. Electronic communication via e-mail and discussion groups will grow; as access becomes cheaper and easier, communication will become more frequent and more specialized. For example, continuing education opportunities such as college courses and professional workshops will become increasingly available over the Internet. Electronic journals will supplement more traditional print publications, and will likely include features such as author chat sessions, on-line search capabilities, and shorter submission-to-publication lag times. Clinicians for whom family responsibilities, finances, or transportation difficulties prevent regular participation in face-to-face conventions or conferences will have greatly expanded opportunities for continuing education.

Similar barriers prevent some clinical populations from obtaining adequate services. In the future, on-line opportunities may enhance face-to-face services for clients. Support groups may help persons with communication disabilities and their families establish long-term relationships with peers who face similar challenges.

Already, for instance, the parents of children with autism and other interested parties have been communicating with each other via a listserver, which resends all questions and comments to the e-mail address of each person on the subscription list. Subscribers use this mechanism to exchange information and anecdotes about behavior management, new interventions, nutrition, research findings, educational software recommendations, and any other news about autism. Although the information gleaned from such public listservers has not necessarily been reviewed for accuracy, parents and professionals clearly find the information exchange helpful. Increasingly, discussion forums on Web sites are replacing listservers as the medium of choice for such personal and group interactions. Examples of remote monitoring of medical status and patient recovery at home are already appearing (Swan, 1996). In the future, clinicians may use on-line communication in one form or another to monitor client "homework" activities and progress between sessions. According to a recent survey, clinicians in the United Kingdom and Ireland report that they would value the increased practice and morale boost that computer applications used by clients in home-based therapy programs could potentially provide (Petheram, 1992).

Technology in Remediation and Rehabilitation

The Computer as Instructor in Speech–Language Therapy

Most beginning clinicians and laypeople can readily envision a computer acting as an instructor during speech–language therapy. In this role the computer is assumed to be deliberately "teaching" the user something, or at the very least providing a structured opportunity for the user to practice a predetermined skill. Such applications are categorized as computer-assisted instruction (CAI) in traditional educational computing taxonomies. Generally, the pattern of interaction between the computer and the user during CAI goes something like this:

Computer presents information or stimulus question and waits for a response from the user. Example: Words on screen and synthesized speech says, "Which one is a vehicle?"

Person with speech or language disorder responds by pressing a key or using a keyboard alternative such as a touchscreen. Example: Presses number 2 to match the picture of a car on the screen.

Computer provides feedback about the correctness of the response. Example: Words on screen and synthesized speech says, "Yes, a car is a vehicle."

Thus a familiar stimulus–response–reinforcement pattern is used as the structure for two-way interaction between the computer and the user. Usually software designed to "teach" language in this manner also tracks correct and incorrect responses and provides individual performance records upon request.

Software designed to address language deficits in this way has been widely available as long as personal computers have been widely available. Unfortunately, there has been minimal research investigating the efficacy of CAI for improving communication skills, especially in children. Several studies have explored the use of language tutorials and drill-and-practice software by persons who have mental retardation. Researchers have used computers (vs. human teachers) to teach such skills as sight word recognition (Conners, Caruso, & Detterman, 1986; Wright &

The SpeechViewer provides immediate visual feedback about the speaker's voice. (Photograph by Tim Barcus)

Anderson, 1987) and picture recognition and categorization (Wilson & Fox, 1983). Usually, successful performance by subjects in such studies has been measured by their ability to respond correctly to very specific items during the computer trials. Generalization of new skills to real communication situations may be the criterion for success in the minds of teachers, clinicians, and parents. It has not, unfortunately, been a criterion for success in most experimental studies of CAI.

Recently, one team of researchers has been using computers in their investigation of the way children with language impairments hear and process spoken language (Merzenich, Jenkins, Miller, Schreiner, & Tallal, 1996; Tallal et al., 1996). Their work has resulted in a commercially available software product called Fast ForWord (Scientific Learning), which is accompanied by an extensive assessment and treatment protocol. The research and intervention program has received much media attention and sparked professional debate across several areas of expertise, including communication disorders, reading, and cognitive neuroscience (Brady, Scarborough, & Shankweiler, 1996; Rice, 1997). The researchers theorize that language impairment in children results from an inability to process the rapidly changing auditory signals in speech. Using technology to manipulate the speech in their software, the researchers claim that they can make the speech signal easier to discriminate. Intensive exposure to this acoustically modified speech occurs through participation in computer-delivered drill-and-practice games (3 hours per day, 5 days per week for 4 weeks in the first studies). This intervention resulted in significant improvements on several measures of language comprehension according to the researchers (Merzenich et al., 1996; Tallal et al., 1996). Other experts have criticized this research, including the basic theory of auditory processing it espouses. Additional points of concern have included the small number of children (18) treated in the studies reported thus far and the measures used to assess change.

Several experimental studies have considered the independent use of computers by adults who have acquired speech–language impairments resulting from stroke or traumatic brain injury (Katz, 1986; Katz & Wertz, 1997; Lynch, 1993; Mills, 1986). The computer has functioned successfully as an instructor when target behaviors involve improving written language skills (e.g., reading comprehension, spelling, sight-word recognition). The intervention plans for some adolescents and adults are designed to help them gain an increased sense of control and responsibility for their own rehabilitation. In such cases, independent use of computer applications capable of serving in the role of instructor may be particularly effective.

In summary, computer applications claiming to "teach" language concepts in the absence of a communicative context or a conversational partner are widely available and are commonly known as CAI. Software of this type assumes the role of the instructor and is designed to be used by an individual working alone. Generally, the software takes the user through a series of preprogrammed steps or practice items with a narrowly defined goal until a predetermined performance criterion is reached. Positive and negative feedback about responses is provided to the user and performance records are maintained. It is important to note the overall lack of empirical evidence to support the independent use of CAI by persons with speech or language disorders, if and when such use is intended to improve their comprehension or production of conversational language. Some evidence supports the independent use of a computer when such use is intended to improve literacy skills or overall independent learning habits.

The Computer as a Context for Speech or Language Therapy

Lee is a 5-year-old with delayed language who is working on the correct use of present and past tense action verbs in therapy (e.g., "The boy was walking. He walked"). Lee is pressing on the 'w' key and watching the face on the computer wink at her. Lee and the clinician have just finished creating the funny face by choosing the eyes, ears, nose, mouth, and hair from a collection of features that come as part of the computer program. Now they are causing parts of the face to move by pressing certain keys.

CLINICIAN: (pressing 'S' key) "Look! I'm making her smile. She's smiling. She's smiling at you."

LEE: "No, she's smiling at *you*. Let me do it." (Presses 'S' key)

CLINICIAN: (hiding her eyes) "What's happening?"

LEE: "She's smiling!" (presses 'W') "She's winking, too."

CLINICIAN: (peeking) "I saw her. She winked. She winked at me!"

Computer programs such as the classic Face-maker (Spinnaker) described in this example can function as context for a speech or language therapy session. In this role, the computer provides an ongoing focus for communication between the clinician and the person with a speech or language disorder. Open-ended, flexible software, which is guided by the input of the users, lends itself to this use of a computer in therapy. Such software has been labeled "learner-centered software" (Mokros & Russell, 1986). Learner-centered software is characterized by multiple, flexible outcomes, in contrast to the predetermined sequence of events typical of CAI. Users have control over goals and outcomes, such as whether to draw a picture, write a story, play a game, or rearrange items on the screen. A wide variety of specific speech or language goals can be addressed. Examples of specific learner-centered software programs used in speech and language therapy have been described elsewhere (Bozic, 1995; Bull, Cochran, & Snell, 1988; Cochran & Bull, 1991; King & Hux, 1995; McLeod & McLeod, 1994; Steiner & Larson, 1991).

As Lee's example illustrates, the value of learner-based software in therapy depends upon the occurrence of a three-way interaction between the student, the computer, and a clinician or teacher. In this case, the clinician provides the appropriate emphasis on action verbs to meet Lee's individual needs. Lee has the opportunity to hear and use the target language in the context of real communication with another person. Because the clinician's input during the use of the computer provides practice with specific language targets, many educational software programs *not* especially designed for this purpose can be successfully adapted.

Experimental studies have demonstrated the efficacy of the use of computer-based activities as a context for speech or language therapy with children (Bozic, Cooper, Etheridge, & Selby, 1995; Harn, 1986; O'Connor & Schery, 1986; Ott-Rose & Cochran, 1992; Prinz, 1991; Schery & O'Connor, 1992; Schetz, 1989; Shriberg, Kwiatkowski, & Snyder, 1989, 1990). Such studies have not attempted to replace the clinician with the computer; rather, the computer serves in the place of alternative materials or activities. Taken together, the results of these studies suggest that when a clinician and child use a computer together, a context for therapy exists that is at least as effective as that provided by more traditional materials.

In addition to concern about efficacy in achieving clinical goals, researchers share an interest in children's motivation and preferences regarding computer-based activities. Fazio and Rieth (1986) studied the free-play choices of preschoolers attending a nursery school program. They found that normally achieving preschoolers chose a computer activity 84% of the time, and their peers with mental retardation chose to use a computer 70% of the time, despite the presence of a wide variety of alternative activities. Both groups of children showed a marked preference for software categorized as user-controlled rather than drill-and-practice in format (Fazio & Rieth, 1986). In addition, two studies have tallied the preferences of preschool children using closely matched computer-based and traditional tabletop speech and language therapy activities (Ott-Rose & Cochran, 1992; Shriberg et al., 1989). In both cases, most children (15 out of 18, Shriberg et al., 1989; and 4 out of 5, Ott-Rose & Cochran, 1992) expressed a preference for the computer-based activities.

Using a Computer To Generate Materials for Speech–Language Therapy

Speech–language pathologists typically use a number of visual materials to help convey the meaning of words and to serve as stimulus items for a person working on improving speech or language skills. Stickers are taken home, worksheets are completed, and pictures are colored as reinforcement for good work. Computer programs that facilitate the development and individualization of consumable as well as reusable therapy materials have proliferated, although many clinicians remain unaware of the possibilities (see Chapter 7).

User-friendly, flexible software for quickly producing text and graphics (e.g., signs, greeting cards, calendars, banners, certificates) is available for all computers. Such software can also be used to create a context for therapy when the clinician and client use it together to accomplish a shared goal (Cochran & Bull, 1991). Schrader (1990) described hundreds of ideas for speech and language therapy activities that make use of graphics software, as well as other utilities such as word processing, spreadsheets, and database software.

Clip-art libraries, affordable scanners, and digitizing cameras have made it possible for clinicians to develop professional-looking therapy materials that are customized to match the needs of individual clients. For example, items from clip-art collections can be used to develop games or worksheets that include pictures of exactly the vocabulary targets chosen for a particular client. If a scanning device is available (see Chapter 2), images from printed pictures or photos can be transferred to the computer. The Internet is another source of high-quality images and sounds. The images captured or downloaded can be shrunk, expanded, rotated, or incorporated into other pictures. In this way, a clinician could build a library of images pertinent to particular clients and frequently addressed language objectives. These images could be printed to produce consumable materials or integrated into clinician-made computer activities.

Developing multimedia materials—documents or programs that include a combination of text, graphics, animation, music, speech, and video—is becoming easier and easier to do (see Chapter 6). Many school classrooms and labs have software such as Roger Wagner's HyperStudio that students or teachers can use as if it were multimedia "glue." That is, software like HyperStudio makes it especially convenient to incorporate graphics, sound, video, and "hot spots" for users to select in clinician-designed computer activities. Not quite so open ended are the multimedia tool kits produced by Edmark in their Imagination Express series. Each CD-ROM (DVD-ROM titles are increasing) in this series includes resource information, writing ideas, background scenes, characters, items, sounds, music, and animation related to a theme (i.e., neighborhood, castle, ocean, rainforest). Users may look up information in the resource section and then use the other components to develop an interactive page or book of their own design. Children can work individually or in teams on such projects, practicing all aspects of language: listening, talking, reading, and writing. Such software exemplifies how similar materials and activities can be used in speech–language therapy and classrooms to accomplish and reinforce complementary objectives.

It is important for clinicians to abide by all relevant copyright laws as they develop self-made therapy materials (Wynne & Hurst, 1995). The large quantity of high-quality downloadable graphics, photos, and text made possible by the Internet has resulted in new copyright law challenges. Authors and publishers relish the widespread, low-cost dissemination of their products, but also need to protect their ownership rights. Clinicians using materials obtained via an electronic source should be careful to cite the source in documents they later print, even for personal use and local dissemination. Besides being good practice, this provides an appropriate model for students and clients who may be obtaining similar materials.

The Computer as a Biofeedback Device in Speech–Language Therapy

A person who stutters may have trouble timing the movement of the vocal folds with initiation of airflow from the lungs when voice is produced. A businessperson making important presentations may bring the vocal folds together too abruptly and eventually develop a vocal pathology such as contact ulcers. A person with a hearing impairment may use inappropriate pitch or excessive nasality while talking. Often individuals with speech or language disorders are not aware of all the characteristics of their own speech. This is much the same difficulty as that encountered by students trying to master the production of a foreign language. It would be much easier for speakers to change undesirable habits and behaviors if they were able to identify them.

Sometimes auditory feedback—the *sound* of speech—is not enough to help the person make changes. Other forms of feedback include visual and tactile (touch). Attempts to develop instruments to analyze speech and provide improved feedback during the treatment of speech and hearing disorders span a century or more. Alexander Graham Bell attempted to create a device to make speech "visible" for persons with impaired hearing, but it was not until a half-century later that workers at Bell Laboratories devised a machine to translate speech into visible patterns (Potter, Kopp, & Green, 1947). Although only a few individuals were able to learn to read those visible speech patterns, such efforts have been followed by more than 50 years of ever-improving speech science instrumentation. As a result, instruments have been developed that can analyze certain aspects of a person's speech or voice and display those features visually. Such a visual display provides immediate information about a person's physical behavior, and is therefore labeled *biofeedback*. For example, it is possible for a speaker to watch a tracing of the pitch or loudness of his or her voice while saying a word or a phrase such as "Every good boy does fine." The addition of computers to speech science instruments has increased their power and flexibility and made them cost-effective for widespread clinical use.

There is a rich literature documenting the efficacy of computer-based speech and voice analysis in the evaluation and treatment of persons with speech and voice disorders (Blood, 1995; Bouglé, Ryalls, & Le Dorze, 1995; Dagenais, 1995; McGuire, 1995; Ruscello, 1995; Thomas-

Stonell, McLean, Dolman, & Oddson, 1992; Volin, 1991; Watson & Kewley-Port, 1989). In one of the earliest known examples, Rushakoff and Edwards (1982) described how a computer was used to significantly improve the attitude and speech performance of a 20-year-old college student receiving therapy for distorted sibilant (*s*-like) sounds. As therapy progressed for this client, she was shown how to use the computer for practice and feedback. She then scheduled herself to use the computer independently several times a week. Her reluctant attitude in therapy improved appreciably, and she was soon dismissed from the clinic.

According to Rushakoff and Edwards (1982), the computer's ability to provide appropriate biofeedback and self-paced practice was the primary reason for the successful outcome for this client. Computer-based methods of foreign accent reduction have been also been explored (Schwartz, Brogan, Emond, & Oleksiak, 1993). This is not to say, however, that such tools challenge the need for skilled clinicians. As Volin (1991) cautioned, "None of these machines knows how to choose a target; not one of them knows how to select an appropriate task" (p. 77). It should also be noted that the fine discriminations the human ear uses to recognize correctly produced speech sounds are extremely difficult to accomplish via computer. To date, computers cannot provide sufficiently reliable feedback about the articulation of most speech sounds to justify recommending them for independent use by persons with speech problems (Fitch, 1989; Thomas-Stonell et al., 1992). Nevertheless, the biofeedback and speech analysis capabilities of computers have simplified some previously complex clinical tasks (e.g., estimating a person's habitual pitch) and added to the number of potentially effective strategies for helping people improve their communication ability.

Although quite different in purpose, voice recognition technology is linked to speech biofeedback applications in the minds of many people. Everyone who has seen "Star Trek" has seen an enactment of the ultimate in voice recognition systems. The Captain says "Computer" to start the system, the computer says "Computer Ready," and the Captain dictates his requests as

he walks around the command deck. In this fantasy system, there is no keyboard, no mouse, no typing at a rate that is a fraction of the number of words per minute that most people speak. The impetus to perfect voice recognition has been development of an effective "hands-free" alternative input for computer control. Nothing available at present would make Captain Kirk jealous, but dramatically improved voice recognition capability is now within the financial reach of users who desire it.

Products such as Naturally Speaking (Dragon Systems, Inc.) and Via Voice (IBM) allow users to speak with a natural rhythm (continuous speech) into a microphone and have their words appear in a word processing program on the computer. Previously available voice recognition systems were significantly more costly and required speakers to pause after each word spoken (discrete speech), resulting in a slower rate of message transmission. For these reasons, and others, voice recognition products are finding a new level of acceptance by average computer users who may not have physical impairments but who need or desire some relief from keyboarding. Experts caution, however, that all such systems have important pros and cons when being considered for use by a person for whom regular keyboard and mouse control is limited. Many factors will influence whether a particular voice recognition system can be effectively employed as a sole, primary input method. Such factors include the user's cognitive abilities, literacy skills, vocal stamina, and patience, as well as the system's sensitivity, complexity, and flexibility. At the present time, voice recognition products vary a great deal in features such as degree of hands-free control, software applications compatibility, initial training, and visual display features (Tam & Stoddart, 1997).

The Computer as a Data Keeper in Speech–Language Therapy

Although using computers to record, summarize, and present clinical data seems like an obvious application, there is a lack of commercially available software designed primarily for this purpose. Most clinicians would agree that manual tracking of correct and incorrect responses is sometimes tedious or is difficult to accomplish without slowing down or interrupting ongoing communication with clients. Although computer-based data collection does not entirely eliminate the difficulties, it may have advantages in some situations.

The Pacer/Tally software developed by Beukelman, Yorkston, and Tice (1988) for use on Apple II computers was an early exemplar of this kind of application. It was designed to assist clinicians with two tasks in particular: the timing of the presentation of stimulus items and the tallying of client responses. Clinicians could develop lists of written stimulus items that were presented one at a time by the "pacer" component of the software, in accordance to the timing parameters chosen by the clinician. This feature was useful for speakers who normally used an inappropriately fast rate or who might skip or gloss over words. The clinician could pace the rate of stimulus presentation, and thereby cause the client to practice appropriate pausing, breath control, or whatever skills were of interest. The "tally" component of the software facilitated the accurate recording of correct and incorrect responses as judged by the clinician. This kind of application will likely be redesigned for a new generation of computers.

The Computer as an Expert System

Another clinical application of computers that may see greater development and use in the future is the *expert system*. Expert systems are usually discussed in the context of making very complex tasks (e.g., medical diagnosis, seismograph interpretation) more explicit to someone learning the task. The notion is that, by identifying the procedures and deductions of an acknowledged human expert, computer programmers can develop computer-based expert systems for use by persons who have less expertise. The computer would guide the learner through a series of questions or reminders, making sure that any important factors are taken into consideration.

Less elaborate but equally effective expert systems could be developed to assist persons with communication disorders (Bull et al., 1988). The computer could serve as an information retriever or reminder for persons whose ability to plan and carry out communication tasks is limited. Kirsh and Levine (1984) described an early example of such a computer-based reminder system used with a patient with a head injury. In many teaching contexts, text or picture-based cue cards have been used to help learners understand or recall the steps in a task (e.g., some cookbooks illustrate each step of a complex recipe). With increasingly portable computer technology becoming available, one can envision a computerized "coach" that would prompt a person with a language impairment to help the individual complete everyday interactions such as ordering lunch or making a phone call.

Technology and Assessment in Communication Disorders

New technologies have resulted in new methods of testing hearing, fitting hearing aids, and evaluating speech-reading abilities, among other advances (Hazan et al., 1995; Mendel, Wynne, English, & Schmidt-Troike, 1995). More information about technology and services for persons who are deaf or hard of hearing can be found in Chapter 12. Technology has several roles that aid in the assessment of persons who have speech or language disorders. Some applications are used during the assessment, as in the real-time

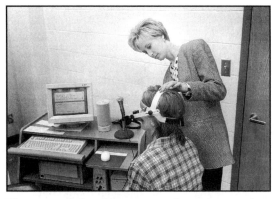

This computer-based instrument, the Nasometer from Kay Elemetrics, helps clinicians evaluate and treat speakers who have a cleft palate or other speech problems involving nasality. (Photograph by Tim Barcus)

analysis of a person's voice or test taking via computer. Others are indirect applications used by the speech–language pathologist for subsequent analysis of assessment data.

Computer-Assisted Voice Sample Analysis

The therapeutic role of biofeedback and the acoustic analysis of speech have been described briefly above. Such applications can also be invaluable in the evaluation or diagnosis of a communication disorder. For example, Kay Elemetric's Nasometer is a computer-based tool that has helped to quantify an otherwise subjectively judged aspect of speech called *nasality*. Nasality is a quality of speech perceived by a listener. In English, nasality is desirable when producing sounds like /m/ and /n/. When air escapes through the nose at inappropriate moments, however, too much nasality is perceived and the speech is judged to be hypernasal. Judging hypernasality reliably from moment to moment requires extensive experience and practice, not to mention endurance. The Nasometer assists the clinician by measuring physical attributes of speech production that are generally associated with nasality. The speaker wears a headpiece similar to a bicycle helmet, which is equipped with microphones situated on either side of a sound separator that rests on the speaker's upper lip. As the speaker talks, the computer calculates the relative proportion of nasal to nasal-plus-oral acoustic energy and displays the results on the monitor. This tool has been especially valuable in helping to quantify the impact of orofacial anomalies (e.g., cleft palate) and neurological impairments that affect speech. Other computer-based tools are available for estimating pitch range, habitual pitch during speech, vocal loudness, and other attributes of speech and voice production.

Computer-Assisted Phonetic Analysis of Speech Samples

Evaluation of a communication disorder frequently requires a clinician to phonetically analyze a speech or language sample recorded during communication between the clinician (or other communication partner) and the person with a possible communication disorder. Such analysis is often immensely time-consuming. Fortunately, new computer-based tools are streamlining such analysis and increasing clinician efficiency. Several "generations" of speech sample analysis software have been developed as computer capabilities have expanded (Masterson & Pagan, 1989; Palin & Mordecai, 1982). Not to be confused with programs that analyze the acoustic characteristics of speech directly, speech sample analysis software uses information about speech as it was transcribed by a clinician using special encoding rules. Thus, a mispronunciation of the word *got* by a child, who says "dot" instead, might be transcribed in phonetics as [dat]. Using the phonetic transcription of this word and many other examples, the computer can tabulate errors and help identify error patterns that have implications for remediation (Long & Masterson, 1993).

Computer-Assisted Language Sample Analysis

Language sample analysis software is available for assisting with the systematic examination of language produced during conversations, storytelling, and pretend play, among other oral events (Baker-Van Den Goorbergh, 1994; Long & Fey, 1992; Miller & Chapman, 1990). Language samples are used to supplement standardized test scores because they are presumed to represent a person's efforts during real communication, in contrast to the artificial and decontextualized tasks often used in tests. When a clinician analyzes a language sample "by hand," several hours may be required to transcribe the conversation from tapes and then analyze it in terms of grammatical structures, vocabulary, and conversation (discourse) rules. Long (1991) described the computer assisting the clinician in this evaluation as follows:

> Microcomputers can simplify clinical transcription by providing efficient methods for recording and editing responses. They can

process large quantities of client data, thereby relieving the clinician from many tasks that are both time-consuming and, because of their repetitiveness, mentally exhausting. Current software can also scan for subtle patterns within the data. Nevertheless, it is the clinician, not the microcomputer, who remains in charge of the assessment process; although technology can get the data to the clinician, only a clinician can derive information from that data. (p. 2)

Many clinicians dream of a day when technology will permit them to transfer samples directly from a tape into a computer for grammatical analysis, thus bypassing the tedious "transcription" phase. Voice recognition technology is not nearly this sophisticated yet. Even so, researchers remind us that a clinician's judgments about a speaker's intended message and appropriateness depend on the context of the conversation (Baker-Van Den Goorbergh, 1994). Computers as we know them will never understand why the expected answer to "Do you have the time?" is rarely yes or no. Nevertheless, available computer applications can assist in making language sample analysis a more efficient and thorough process (Long & Masterson, 1993; Miller, Freiberg, Rolland, & Reeves, 1992). Such support allows the clinician to focus less energy on mechanics and more energy on interpretations of assessment data.

Computer-Based Testing

Although not yet widely used, a few examples of software for computer-based test taking and computer-assisted test scoring in communication disorders have been available for several years. Preliminary research with children has attempted to compare the results of traditional administration to a closely matched computer version of evaluation instruments. Results have suggested that subtle differences between on- and off-computer tasks may be present and that careful evaluation is necessary (Shriberg, Kwiatkowski, & Snyder, 1986; Wiig, Jones, & Wiig, 1996). Wiig et al. (1996) administered the traditional and experimental computer versions of the *Test of*

Word Knowledge–Level 2 (TOWK–2) to 30 children with language-learning disabilities (LD), some of whom also had attention deficit disorders with or without hyperactivity (ADD/ADHD). When asked about their preferences, the majority expressed a preference for the computer version. Children with LD +ADD/ADHD were especially likely to prefer the computer version, and their teachers observed longer than usual attention to task. Children who self-reported reading slowly, problems with writing and spelling, or difficulties sounding out words, generally preferred standard administration. Interestingly, expressed test mode preferences were not necessarily matched by performance advantages. The authors reported an impressive time saving with the computer-based version, providing that available computer facilities permit multiple simultaneous administrations.

Technology and Augmentative and Alternative Communication (AAC)

What AAC Is and Who AAC Users Are

Countless individuals, for many different reasons, are not able to talk. For some people handwriting provides an alternative to talking, but writing a conversation is usually excruciatingly slow. For others with severe physical disabilities, even handwriting or sign language is not an option. Augmentative or alternative means of communication are sought when usual methods of producing speech or language are not possible. Individuals with severe communication disorders are those for whom gestural, speech, or written communication is temporarily or permanently inadequate to meet all of their communication needs. For these individuals, a hearing loss is not the primary cause for the communication impairment. Some of these individuals may be able to produce a limited amount of speech but require additional alternatives for meeting some communication needs (ASHA, 1991). Terms for persons with severe communication disorders that were initially used in the field but are now rarely mentioned include speechless, nonoral, nonvocal, nonverbal, and aphonic (Beukelman & Mirenda, 1992).

AAC Systems

Specialists in the planning and design of AAC systems are careful about how they use this term. They like to think of a person's AAC *system* as a combination of strategies, techniques, and devices or aids that facilitate 24-hour-a-day communication (Blackstone, 1987). Any and all means of expression on the part of the person with the disability or challenge are valued and encouraged. These may include eye contact, gestures, and vocalizations, as well as messages encoded through a special device. Each component of a person's system is designed to complement the rest. For example, because eye contact with other people is often a major avenue of communication for persons who cannot speak, a device that uses signaling methods other than visual focus may be preferred. In this way, one means of communication is not sacrificed for another unless absolutely necessary.

Many factors must be taken into account in planning an AAC system. Such factors include the person's most frequent communication partners, communication needs and opportunities, motor control and range of motion, current and potential ability to comprehend graphic symbols or text, memory and planning ability, visual acuity, and mobility. Ideally, a recommended communication system should also be compatible with the person's academic or vocational plans and activities. AAC experts have noted that high-tech devices are not always more effective than more traditional, low-tech solutions, which should also be given due consideration (Beukelman & Mirenda, 1992). Because evaluations and recommendations for AAC systems can be so complex, it is highly recommended that an experienced professional team undertake such services.

Importance of Team Assessment and Intervention

The exact membership of an AAC team will depend on the age, physical condition, and communication needs of the individual being served. For example, a child with cerebral palsy might work with an AAC team that includes a speech–language pathologist (communication skills and needs), physical therapist (wheelchair positioning), occupational therapist (optimal switch selection), special educator (literacy and other academic needs), and parents (needs at home and personal preferences). Case studies of AAC users suggest that substantial follow-up to an evaluation or recommendation is crucial in order to ensure that investments in time, energy, and specialized equipment result in real communication benefits (Beukelman, Yorkston, & Dowden, 1985). That is, expert recommendations alone cannot resolve the communication problems of an AAC user. A public school assistive technology team, for example, may work with a child, other school personnel, and parents over an extended period of time in order to establish an optimal AAC system for that child in an educational environment (see Chapters 1 and 5). As communication skills and needs change, opportunities, strategies, and devices must be adjusted accordingly (Blackstone, 1995).

Computers and AAC Devices

For many years teachers and clinicians have been modifying and adapting toys and instructional materials for children with special needs. For example, battery-operated toys can be modified so that children who cannot physically manipulate such toys can nonetheless control them by activating a properly positioned switch device (see Chapter 11). Similarly, for more than a decade, popular microcomputers have routinely been modified for use as AAC devices through the addition of special software, special access devices, keyboard emulators, or speech synthesizers (Beukelman et al., 1985; Blackstone, 1994; Lynch, 1993; Snyder, Freeman-Lorentz, & McLaughlin, 1994; Ventkatagiri, 1996). Modifying an existing computer in this way may result in a less expensive and more flexible device than one that is custom-built from specialized components.

Some AAC devices are termed dedicated because they can function only for the purposes of communication. A system making use of a general-purpose computer, in contrast, may give the user access to many other functions, such as mathematical calculations, electronic mail, writing and storing large amounts of text, producing art work, or using the same software as other people in a classroom or office. Dedicated devices tend to be more portable than most computers and the most sophisticated can be even more expensive. Some devices (e.g., the TouchTalker by Prentke Romich) can serve either as a dedicated device or can be attached to a personal computer for work or school. The advent of smaller, more reliable, more powerful notebook computers has greatly increased the possibilities in AAC system design.

Whether or not a personal computer becomes a long-term component of a person's AAC system, often a computer can be useful in the process of determining the best option. First, a computer can help a clinician estimate a person's prognosis for effective communication using an electronic aid. Many schools and clinics do not have a comprehensive selection of dedicated electronic communication aids available for assessments. Using a computer, special access devices, and a variety of communication software, clinicians can simulate the characteristics of some electronic aids to see how a user initially responds. Second, a computer with specialized software might be used to teach some of the skills that the potential user will require to make use of a more complex AAC device. Such skills might include symbol recognition, use of scanning arrays and switches, or direct selection with an adaptive device such as a head pointer.

Yet another use of computers is to provide clinicians a faster, more efficient way to accomplish tasks such as generating groups of pictures or symbols for device overlays or traditional communication boards. Several software programs for assisting in the design of communication boards are available. Such utilities make it possible to plan and produce multiple alternatives (i.e., vocabulary, labels, symbols, colors, and layouts) in less time than it once took to create a single version by hand. The Boardmaker program (Mayer-Johnson) could be considered a deluxe example

Student clinicians learn to modify battery-operated toys for single-switch control. (Photograph by Tim Barcus)

of such software. Consisting of an extensive clipart library of symbols and overlay templates, Boardmaker is used by clinicians not only for generating communication board overlays, but also for generating therapy materials such as worksheets, picture cards, and gameboards for their non-AAC caseload.

New technologies have made adaptive access to computers and other devices feasible for persons with even very severe motor challenges. Even the best of currently available technologies, however, usually results in a rate of message transmission that is painfully slow compared to normal speech. Many AAC users continue to eagerly anticipate technological advances that will speed message production, improve the quality and personalization of low-cost speech output, improve voice recognition capability, decrease cost, and increase the portability of AAC devices.

Technology, Communication, and the Classroom

Several touch-pad devices are commercially available that can digitize brief spoken messages and that cost under $500. These devices vary according to the features they offer, such as switch adaptation, number of possible spaces and messages, visual and auditory scanning, power, and volume control. The basic idea of these devices is to combine ease of recording with instant access to the recorded message by the press of a button or click of a switch. These inexpensive, easy-to-use devices are becoming indispensable tools in classrooms for children with multiple disabilities. Such speech output devices have the characteristics that are desirable in a new technology: affordability, flexibility, and ease of use.

Teachers and speech–language pathologists use these small speech output devices to help children with severely limited speech express their needs, indicate preferences, or participate in group activities. In most cases, these devices are not expected to meet all of a student's communication needs over an extended period of time; on the contrary, they are especially effective at meeting short-term or quickly changing needs, or as a bridge to more effective oral communication. Research in emergent literacy provides a perfect example of a scenario in which small speech output devices can be used to "include" children who do not speak.

Experts in literacy development recommend that teachers and parents choose stories with repeating lines to read aloud to young children (Musselwhite & King-DeBaun, 1997). Gradually, as children become familiar with the words in the story and can predict the repeating lines, they are encouraged to "fill in" lines at the appropriate moments in the story (e.g., "I'll huff, and I'll puff, and I'll blow your house down!"). Children are thrilled to participate and they become increasingly aware of how language works and what to expect when reading a story. In the past children with little or no intelligible speech listened to such stories but were passive participants at best. With the advent of small speech output devices, however, children can press a button or a switch and "speak" the desired line in the story, either alone or as part of a group. Because the devices are portable and easy to record on, teachers, clinicians, parents, and aides can readily rerecord brief messages that change with each new story or activity. Such devices are used to encourage participation from children who have all types of communication delays or disorders. Besides use with children, small speech output devices are also frequently used as temporary or beginning communication aides for adults with acquired

communication impairments resulting from vocal pathology, traumatic brain injury, or stroke.

Small speech output devices sometimes serve as a preparation for participation in computer-based activities that promote communication or literacy development. According to the popular press as well as professional publications such as *Reading Today* (e.g., "Technology and Reading," 1998), teachers in general education classrooms are increasingly making use of new technologies in all aspects of language arts instruction. This should make it easier to include students who need special technologies in order for materials to be appropriately adapted for them.

Some computer activities intended for general use lend themselves admirably to adaptation for children who have limited communication skills. For example, developers have employed CD-ROM technology to create "electronic books" based on many children's literature classics. Some of these CDs, such as the Living Books series (Brøderbund), include multiple language versions (e.g., Spanish, English, Japanese) and multiple modes (e.g., Read/Play). In Play mode, users not only hear the story but also have the option of clicking on objects on the screen to see animation, sounds, and events associated with the object selected. This mode disturbs some teachers who believe that it distracts children from the story and the task (reading). This is easily avoided by using the Read mode when the instructional focus should be on the story or when reading is the core objective. However, clinicians working with children who have speech or language deficits may find the Play mode useful during oral language activities. Children can be introduced to vocabulary, characters, and key story events while working with the speech–language pathologist. The same vocabulary, characters, and story events may later be encountered again during language arts activities. Several studies have identified computer-based activities that were effective in facilitating literacy in children with severe communication deficits (Blischak, 1995; Prinz, 1991; Steelman, Pierce, & Koppenhaver, 1993). Technology can be used to make all aspects of a language arts program accessible so that children with speech or language deficits are not further penalized by lack of exposure to reading and writing instruction (Musselwhite & King-DeBaun, 1997).

Funding for Communication Technologies

Obtaining funding for computers, adapted access devices, and dedicated communication aids has always been a challenge. To be in compliance with the Individuals with Disabilities Education Act of 1990, public schools are required to make assistive technology devices and services available to any child who requires them to receive a free and appropriate education (Exline, 1996). Because lack of communication ability has obvious educational implications, schools attempt to fill the gap and provide appropriate technology at least during school hours. However, all too often children are sent home at night, on the weekends, and even for summer months without the communication devices they have come to rely on at school. School officials feel that they cannot risk the possibility of school-owned technology being damaged or stolen when it is away from school property. Creative solutions are called for when a child's primary means of communicating with the world is at stake.

Public schools are often the sole provider of communication technology for children with severe communication disorders, a responsibility that can have significant financial impact. In addition to the initial investment in the technology itself, long-term provision must be made for staff training, maintenance and repair, and upgrades or replacement. It is important for school administrators to explore a variety of alternatives and develop strategies that make the most of public and private resources. For example, when the technology is deemed medically necessary, Medicaid or private health insurance may cover part or all of the cost. This may provide a partial solution to the problem of technology for noneducational purposes, such as communication and recreation away from school. Persons over 18 with a physical or mental disability may be eli-

gible for state vocational rehabilitation funds if there is a reasonable chance that they may be helped to obtain employment after the appropriate technology is obtained (Exline, 1996). In most communities, civic organizations and service clubs can be counted on to provide assistance in a case of extreme need and when the necessary technology is clearly specified and reasonably priced.

Schools face the challenge of obtaining funds to support many kinds of assistive technology and services. Successful financing of a public school assistive technology program requires an organized plan for applying for funding and persistence in appealing negative funding decisions. However, even as the role of computers and communication devices expands and the number of persons of all ages who need assistive technology increases, reliable public funding continues to be elusive.

Summary

New advances in technology have changed the way speech–language pathologists and audiologists manage the record keeping and communication necessary for organizing and administering services for individuals who have communication disorders. Among the most revolutionary influences is the Internet, which is expected to have even greater impact as access to it becomes more common and less costly.

Computers serve a wide variety of needs for persons who have speech or language impairments. For persons who cannot talk, a computer may provide part of an augmentative or alternative communication system. Computer applications also have an important role in the evaluation and treatment of persons who have impaired speech or language abilities. Computers assist with the analysis of speech and language samples obtained during assessment. During speech–language therapy, a computer may function in the role of instructor, materials generator, data keeper, biofeedback device, expert system, or as a context (topic) for interaction between the clinician and client. Computers and related new technologies can be used to facilitate not only oral language development but also literacy skills.

Resources

Organizations

American Speech-Language-Hearing Association. This organization certifies speech–language pathologists and audiologists, provides information to the public, and publishes several scholarly journals. *Contact:* ASHA, 10801 Rockville Pike, Rockville, MD 20852; Voice: 301/897-5700 or 800/638-8355; Web: http://www.asha.org

Closing the Gap. This organization publishes a newspaper-format technology update several times a year, which includes new product announcements, software reviews, and public policy information regarding technology and persons of all ages who have special needs for home, school, or the workplace. A national conference each fall is a major meeting of professionals, consumers, and developers of new technologies. *Contact:* Closing the Gap, P.O. Box 68, Henderson, MN 56044; Voice: 612/248-3294; Web: http://www.closingthegap.com

International Society for Augmentative and Alternative Communication (ISAAC). This organization sponsors an annual conference and publishes *The ISAAC Bulletin*. *Contact:* ISAAC, P.O. Box 1762, Station R, Toronto, Ontario M4G 4AC, Canada.

Trace Research and Development Center. One of the first major research centers focusing on AAC technologies, the Trace Center remains an important source of technical information. One recent product is a CD-ROM index and library of disability-related resources called Co-Net. DOS/Windows and Macintosh compatible, this fully accessible CD includes the full ABLEDATA database of over 20,000 products for people with disabilities. Pictures of more than 3,200 products are included. Services, information resources, and full text documents are included (Americans with Disabilities Act, legal rights, etc.). The CD is revised annually for subscribers. *Contact:* Trace Research and Development Center, Waisman Center, University of Wisconsin–Madison, 1550 Highland Avenue, Madison, WI 53705; Voice: 608/262-6966; Web: http://www.trace.wisc.edu/

International Society for Technology in Education (ISTE). This nonprofit organization is for professionals interested in the use of technology in all aspects and levels of education. Several notable publications include the *Journal of Research on Computing in Education* and smaller volumes related to special interest groups within the organization. The ISTE sponsors the annual National Educational Computing Conference and the annual International Conference on Telecommunications and Multimedia in Education. *Contact:* ISTE, 1787 Agate Street, Eugene, OR 97403-1923; Voice: 541/346-4414; Web: http://isteonline.uoregon.edu

Journals

Asha
10801 Rockville Pike
Rockville, MD 20852

Augmentative Communication News
One Surf Way, Suite 215
Monterey, CA 93940
Voice: 408/649-3050

Alternatively Speaking
A quarterly independent, consumer-authored publication for AAC users.
One Surf Way, Suite 215
Monterey, CA 93940
Voice: 408/649-3050

Closing the Gap
P.O. Box 68
Henderson, MN 56044
Voice: 612/248-3294

Learning & Leading with Technology (formerly *The Computing Teacher*)
ISTE
1787 Agate Street
Eugene, OR 97403-1923

Books

Beukelman, D. R., & Mirenda, P. (1992). *Augmentative and alternative communication: Management of severe communication disorders in children and adults*. Baltimore: Brookes.

Musselwhite, C., & King-DeBaun, P. (1997). *Emergent literacy success: Merging technology with whole language for students with disabilities*. Park City, UT: Creative Communicating.

Silverman, F. H. (1996). *Computer applications for augmenting the management of speech–language, and hearing disorders*. Needham Heights, MA: Allyn & Bacon.

Instructional Modules

Technology 2000: Clinical Applications for Speech–Language Pathology. This 1997 technology tutorial developed by a team of experts and sponsored by ASHA is available on-line at www.asha.org, or can be ordered softbound from ASHA Publications at 10801 Rockville Pike, Rockville, MD 20852.

Technology in the Classroom Series. This 1992 series includes four resource manuals and a 16-minute video-tape published by ASHA that can be purchased together or separately. The modules include *Technology in the Class-room: Education* by E. Lucinda Cassatt-James; *Technology in the Classroom: Communication* by Sarah Blackstone; *Technology in the Classroom: Listening and Hearing* by Carol Flexer; and *Technology in the Classroom: Positioning, Access, and Mobility* by Elaine Trefler. The excellent VHS videotape, *Assistive Technology: We Can Do It!* includes a wide variety of examples of assistive technology in actual use in educational settings and is an especially good value. Available from ASHA Publications, 10801 Rockville Pike, Rockville, MD 20852.

On-line Resources

Because Web addresses change frequently, if you try an address that no longer works, try using a Web search engine (e.g., Hotbot) to identify similar, current sites.

American Speech-Language-Hearing Association
Web: http://www.asha.org

Center for Disease Control
Web: http://www.cdc.gov/

Council for Exceptional Children
Web: http://www.cec.sped.org/

International Society for Technology in Education
Web: http://isteonline.uoregon.edu

American Association on Mental Retardation
Web: http://www.aamr.org/

Association of Retarded Citizens
Web: http://the arc.org/

Laboratory–Practicum Activities

▶ 1. Generate materials that could be used during speech or language therapy. Take advantage of specialized software if it is available; if not, word processing, paint programs, or software such as the popular Print Shop (Brøderbund) could be used. For example, you could make a reward certificate, a worksheet with pictures of words emphasizing a target sound, or a calendar with home practice reminders and assignments.

▶ 2. Visit the Web site of the American Speech-Language-Hearing Association (www.asha.org) to review information on current hot topics and issues or to look up detailed information on a specific disorder, syndrome, or disease that impacts a person's communication. Make a print-out of information of special interest, noting the Web site address so that you can cite it appropriately.

▶ 3. Visit the Web site of the National Center To Improve Practice in Special Education Through Technology, Media, and Materials (www.edc.org/FSC/NCIP). This site includes discussions, technology updates, and on-line examples of exemplary classrooms serving children who have communication disorders and other disabilities.

▶ 4. Simulate a simple AAC device using any computer with word processing software. With the help of a friend, have a conversation in which one of you talks and one of you types (no cheating!). What is it like to be the one who "talks"? Notice how your communication behavior changes in order to accommodate your partner who is using AAC. For example, try guessing whenever you think you know what is being typed, to save time. Does this speed up communication? Now switch roles. What is it like to be the one who "types"? Even if you type slowly, there is still a good chance that you are communicating more quickly than the average AAC user (5 to 6 words per minute). How does this change your attitude toward conversation? Do you find yourself leaving out unnecessary words?

▶ 5. Experience some low-tech biofeedback with the use of a small hand-held mirror. With a partner, evaluate what happens when you place the mirror under your nose while speaking. Take turns comparing the following sentences:

Every day the girl plays house with her doll baby.

My mother wants me to make her a malted milkshake.

What happens to the mirror? Which sentence has more nasal sounds in it? Can you say the second sentence without fogging the mirror? A person with hypernasal speech would also have difficulty saying the first sentence without fogging the mirror.

References

American Speech-Language-Hearing Association. (1991). Report: Augmentative and alternative communication. *Asha, 33*(Suppl. 5), 9–12.

Baker-Van Den Goorbergh, L. (1994). Computers and language analysis: Theory and practice. *Child Language Teaching and Therapy, 10*(3), 329–348.

Beukelman, D. R., & Mirenda, P. (1992). *Augmentative and alternative communication: Management of severe communication disorders in children and adults.* Baltimore: Brookes.

Beukelman, D., Yorkston, K., & Dowden, P. (1985). *Communication augmentation: A casebook of clinical management.* San Diego: College-Hill.

Beukelman, D., Yorkston, K., & Tice, R. (1988). *Pacer/Tally* [Computer program]. Tucson, AZ: Communication Skill Builders.

Blackstone, S. (Ed.). (1987). *Augmentative communication: An introduction.* Rockville, MD: American Speech-Language-Hearing Association.

Blackstone, S. (1994). Dynamic displays: An option for accessing language. *Augmentative Communication News, 7*(2), 1–3.

Blackstone, S. (1995). AAC Teams: How do we collaborate? *Augmentative Communication News, 8*(4), 1–3.

Blischak, D. M. (1995). Thomas the writer: Case study of a child with severe physical, speech, and visual impairments. *Language, Speech, and Hearing Services in Schools, 26*, 11–20.

Blood, G. (1995). A behavioral–cognitive therapy program for adults who stutter: Computers and counseling. *Journal of Communication Disorders, 28*, 165–180.

Bouglé, F., Ryalls, J., & Le Dorze, G. (1995). Improving fundamental frequency modulation in head trauma patients: A preliminary comparison of speech–language therapy conducted with and without IBM's Speechviewer. *Folia Phoniatrica et Logopaedica, 47*, 24–32.

Bozic, N. (1995). Using microcomputers in naturalistic language intervention: The trialling of a new approach. *British Journal of Learning Disabilities, 23*, 59–62.

Bozic, N., Cooper, L., Etheridge, A., & Selby, A. (1995). Microcomputer-based joint activities in communication intervention with visually impaired children: A case study. *Child Language Teaching and Therapy, 11*(1), 91–105.

Brady, S., Scarborough, H., & Shankweiler, D. (1996). A perspective on two recent research reports. *Perspectives, 22*(3), 5–9.

Bull, G., Bull, G., Garafola, J., & Sigmon, T. (1998). Mining the Internet: Virtual conferences. *Learning & Leading With Technology, 25*(5), 36–39.

Bull, G. L., Cochran, P. S., & Snell, M. E. (1988). Beyond CAI: Computers, language, and persons with mental retardation. *Topics in Language Disorders, 8*(4), 55–76.

Cochran, P. S., & Bull, G. L. (1991). Integrating word processing into language intervention. *Topics in Language Disorders, 11*(2), 31–48.

Cochran, P. S., & Masterson, J. J. (1995). NOT using a computer in language assessment/intervention: In defense of the reluctant clinician. *Language, Speech, and Hearing Services in Schools, 26*(3), 213–222.

Cochran, P. S., Masterson, J. J., Long, S. H., Katz, R., Seaton, W., Wynne, M., Lieberth, A., & Martin, D. (1993). Computing competencies for clinicians. *Asha, 35*(8), 48–49.

Conners, F. A., Caruso, D. R., & Detterman, D. K. (1986). Computer-assisted instruction for the mentally retarded. *International Review of Research in Mental Retardation, 14*, 105–134.

Dagenais, P. (1995). Electropalatography in the treatment of articulation/phonological disorders. *Journal of Communication Disorders, 28*, 303–329.

Exline, M. (1996). *Module two: Funding overview of augmentative communication.* Kansas City: Missouri Technology Center for Special Education.

Fazio, B. B., & Rieth, H. J. (1986). Characteristics of preschool handicapped children's microcomputer use during free-choice periods. *Journal of the Division for Early Childhood, 10*(3), 247–254.

Fitch, J. L. (1989). Computer recognition of correct sound productions in articulation treatment. *Journal for Computer Users in Speech and Hearing, 5*(1), 8–18.

Harn, W. E. (1986). Facilitating acquisition of subject–verb utterances in children: Actions, animation, and pictures. *Journal for Computer Users in Speech and Hearing, 2*(2), 95–101.

Hazan, V., Wilson, G., Howells, D., Miller, D., Abberton, E., & Fourcin, A. (1995). Speech pattern audiometry for clinical use. *European Journal of Disorders of Communication*, 30(2), 116–123.

Hyman, C. (1985). Computer usage in the speech–language–hearing profession. *Asha*, 27(10), 25.

Individuals with Disabilities Education Act of 1990, 20 U.S.C. § 1400 *et seq.*

Katz, R. C. (1986). *Aphasia treatment and microcomputers*. San Diego: College-Hill.

Katz, R. C., & Wertz, R. T. (1997). The efficacy of computer-provided reading treatment for chronic adult aphasics. *Journal of Speech and Hearing Research*, 40, 493–507.

King, J. M., & Hux, K. (1995). Intervention using talking word processing software: An aphasia case study. *Augmentative and Alternative Communication*, 11, 187–192.

Kirsh, N. L., & Levine, S. P. (1984, April). *A compensatory microcomputer intervention for patients with cognitive limitations*. Paper presented at the Conference on Models and Techniques in Cognitive Rehabilitation, Indianapolis, IN.

Long, S. H. (1991). Integrating microcomputer applications into speech and language assessment. *Topics in Language Disorders*, 11(2), 1–17.

Long, S., & Fey, M. (1992). *Computerized language profiling* [Computer program]. San Antonio: Psychological Corp.

Long, S., & Masterson, J. J. (1993). Computer technology: Use in language analysis. *Asha*, 35, 40–47.

Lorendo, L. C. (1988, May). *Educational technology: Computer implementation in communication sciences and disorders*. Unpublished doctoral dissertation, University of Mississippi, University.

Lynch, W. (1993). Update on a computer-based language prosthesis for aphasia therapy. *Journal of Head Trauma Rehabilitation*, 8, 107–109.

Masterson, J., & Pagan, F. (1989). *Interactive system for phonological analysis (ISPA) (Macintosh)* [Computer program]. San Antonio: Psychological Corp.

McGuire, R. A. (1995). Computer-based instrumentation: Issues in clinical applications. *Language, Speech, and Hearing Services in Schools*, 26(3), 223–231.

McLeod, D., & McLeod, S. (1994). Empowering language-impaired children through Logo. *Child Language Teaching and Therapy*, 10(1), 107–114.

McRay, L. B., & Fitch, J. L. (1996). A survey of computer use by public school speech–language pathologists. *Language, Speech, and Hearing Services in Schools*, 27(1), 40–47.

Mendel, L. L., Wynne, M. K., English, K., & Schmidt-Troike, A. (1995). Computer applications in educational audiology. *Language, Speech, and Hearing Services in Schools*, 26(3), 232–240.

Merzenich, M. M., Jenkins, W. M., Miller, S. L., Schreiner, C., & Tallal, P. (1996). Temporal processing deficits of language-learning impaired children ameliorated by training. *Science*, 271, 77–81.

Miller, J. F., & Chapman, R. S. (1990). *Systematic analysis of language transcripts (SALT) (MS-DOS, Macintosh)* [Computer program]. Madison, WI: Language Analysis Laboratory, Waisman Center on Mental Retardation and Human Development.

Miller, J. F., Freiberg, C., Rolland, M. B., & Reeves, M. A. (1992). Implementing computerized language sample analysis in the public school. *Topics in Language Disorders*, 12(2), 69–82.

Mills, R. H. (1986). Computerized management of aphasia. In R. Chapey (Ed.), *Language intervention strategies in adult aphasia* (pp. 333–344). Baltimore: William & Wilkins.

Mokros, J. R., & Russell, S. J. (1986). Learner-centered software: A survey of microcomputer use with special needs students. *Journal of Learning Disabilities*, 19(3), 185–190.

Musselwhite, C., & King-DeBaun, P. (1997). *Emergent literacy success: Merging technology with whole language for students with disabilities*. Park City, UT: Creative Communicating.

O'Connor, L., & Schery, T. K. (1986). A comparison of microcomputer-assisted and traditional language therapy for developing communication skills in nonoral toddlers. *Journal of Speech and Hearing Disorders*, 51(4), 356–361.

Ott-Rose, M., & Cochran, P. S. (1992). Teaching action verbs with computer-controlled videodisc vs. traditional picture stimuli. *Journal for Computer Users in Speech and Hearing*, 8(1–2), 15–32.

Owens, R. E. (1999). *Language disorders: A functional approach to assessment and intervention* (3rd ed.). Needham Heights, MA: Allyn & Bacon.

Palin, M. W., & Mordecai, D. R. (1982). *Lingquest 2: Phonological analysis (MS-DOS)* [Computer program]. Columbus, OH: Merrill.

Petheram, B. (1992). A survey of therapists' attitudes to computers in the home-based treatment of adult aphasics. *Aphasiology*, 6(2), 207–212.

Potter, R., Kopp, G., & Green, H. (1947). *Visible speech*. New York: D. Van Nostrand.

Prinz, P. M. (1991). Literacy and language development within microcomputer-videodisc–assisted interactive contexts. *Journal of Childhood Communication Disorders*, 14(1), 67–80.

Rice, M. L. (1997). Speaking out: Evaluating new training programs for language impairment. *Asha*, 39(3), 13.

Ruscello, D. M. (1995). Visual feedback in treatment of residual phonological disorders. *Journal of Communication Disorders*, 28, 279–302.

Rushakoff, G. E., & Edwards, W. (1982, November). *The /s/ meter: A beginning for microcomputer assisted articulation therapy*. Paper presented at the annual convention of the American Speech-Language-Hearing Association, Toronto, Ontario, Canada.

Schrader, M. (1990). *Computer applications for language learning*. Tucson, AZ: Communication Skill Builders.

Schery, T. K., & O'Connor, L. C. (1992). The effectiveness of school-based computer language intervention with severely handicapped children. *Language, Speech, and Hearing Services in Schools, 23*, 43–47.

Schetz, K. F. (1989). Computer-aided language/concept enrichment in kindergarten. *Language, Speech, and Hearing Services in the Schools, 20*, 2–10.

Schwartz, A. H., Brogan, V. M., Emond, G. A., & Oleksiak, J. F. (1993). Technology-enhanced accent modification. *Asha, 35*(8), 44–45, 51.

Shriberg, L. D., Kwiatkowski, J., & Snyder, T. (1986). Articulation testing by microcomputer. *Journal of Speech and Hearing Disorders, 51*, 309–324.

Shriberg, L. D., Kwiatkowski, J., & Snyder, T. (1989). Tabletop versus microcomputer-assisted speech management: Stabilization phase. *Journal of Speech and Hearing Disorders, 54*(2), 233–248.

Shriberg, L. D., Kwiatkowski, J., & Snyder, T. (1990). Tabletop versus microcomputer-assisted speech management: Response evocation phase. *Journal of Speech and Hearing Disorders, 55*(4), 635–655.

Silverman, F. H. (1997). *Computer applications for augmenting the management of speech–language, and hearing disorders*. Needham Heights, MA: Allyn & Bacon.

Snyder, T. L., Freeman-Lorentz, K., & McLaughlin, T. F. (1994). The effects of augmentative communication on vocabulary acquisition with primary age students with disabilities. *B.C. Journal of Special Education, 18*(1), 14–23.

Steelman, J. D., Pierce, P. L., & Koppenhaver, D. A. (1993). The role of computers in promoting literacy in children with severe speech and physical impairments (SSPI). *Topics in Language Disorders, 13*(2), 76–88.

Steiner, S., & Larson, V. L. (1991). Integrating microcomputers into language intervention with children. *Topics in Language Disorders, 11*(2), 18–30.

Stiegler, L. N., & Currie, P. S. (1997, August). Lurking and posting to gain clinical insight. *American Journal of Speech-Language Pathology, 6*, 15–18.

Swan, R. (1996). "Port-O-Tech": Technology on the home-health front. *Phi Kappa Phi National Forum, 76*(3), 6–7.

Tallal, P., Miller, S. L., Bedi, G., Byma, G., Wang, X., Nagarajan, S., Schreiner, C., Jenkins, W. M., & Merzenich, M. M. (1996). Fast-element enhanced speech improves language comprehension in language-learning impaired children. *Science, 271*, 81–84.

Tam, C., & Stoddart, P. (1997, October). *Selecting voice recognition systems: Considerations in making an informed choice*. Paper presented at the Closing the Gap Technology Conference, Minneapolis.

Technology and reading: Emerging consensus. (1998, February/March). *Reading Today, 15*(4), 3–5.

Thomas-Stonell, N., McLean, M., Dolman, L., & Oddson, B. (1992). Development and preliminary testing of a computer-based program for training stop consonants. *Journal of Speech-Language Pathology and Audiology, 16*(1), 5-9.

U.S. Department of Education. (1995). *Seventeenth Annual Report to Congress on the Implementation of The Individuals with Disabilities Education Act* [On-line document: www.ed.gov/pubs/OSEP95AnlRpt].

Ventkatagiri, H. S. (1987). Writing your own software: What are the options? *Asha, 29*(6), 27–29.

Ventkatagiri, H. S. (1996, November). The quality of digitized and synthesized speech: What clinicians should know. *American Journal of Speech–Language Pathology, 5*, 31–42.

Volin, R. A. (1991). Microcomputer-based systems providing biofeedback of voice and speech production. *Topics in Language Disorders, 11*(2), 65–79.

Walz, J., & Cochran, P. S. (1996, November). *Curricular integration of computers in graduate communication disorders programs*. A paper presented at the annual convention of the American Speech-Language-Hearing Association, Seattle.

Watson, C. S., & Kewley-Port, D. (1989). Advances in computer-based speech training (CBST): Aids for the profoundly hearing impaired. *Volta Review, 91*(5), 29–45.

Wiig, E. H., Jones, S. S., & Wiig, E. D. (1996). Computer-based assessment of word knowledge in teens with learning disabilities. *Language, Speech, and Hearing Services in Schools, 27*(1), 21–28.

Wilson, M. S., & Fox, B. J. (1983). Microcomputers: A clinical aid. In H. Winitz (Ed.), *Treating language disorders: For clinicians by clinicians* (pp. 248–255). Austin, TX: PRO-ED.

Wright, A., & Anderson, M. (1987). Does a computer system help to teach a sight vocabulary to children with severe learning difficulties? *British Journal of Educational Technology, 1*, 52–60.

Wynne, M. K., & Hurst, D. S. (1995). Legal issues and computer use by school-based audiologists and speech–language pathologists. *Language, Hearing, Speech Services in Schools, 26*(3), 251–259.

Chapter 11

❧   ❧   ❧

Technology for Individuals with Severe and Physical Disabilities

John Langone
University of Georgia, Athens

Technology solutions to daily problems are generated at an astounding rate (Walczak, 1999). In recent years individuals' lives at work and at home have changed significantly because of technology. Technological advances such as the personal computer and the microwave oven, for example, have changed work productivity and meal habits.

For persons with disabilities, technology has provided a freedom never before imagined. Today's technological advances can help persons with disabilities become independent and participate in lifelong learning. Advances in technology allow many people with disabilities to take control of their lives for the first time. For example, individuals with significant physical challenges can accomplish complex tasks such as independently managing the environmental conditions in their home, as well as simple tasks such as turning on an appliance.

An often cited statement regarding the effects of technology solutions on the lives of persons with disabilities was published in 1988 in the *Apple Computer Resources in Special Education Rehabilitation:*

> It's clear that the personal computer represents something very special to the disabled individual. Not a cure, not something that makes the disability any less real. But an equalizer of sorts. An enabler. A partner like no partner the disabled person has ever had before. (p. ix)

Although this statement was made some years ago and primarily referred to microcomputers, the message it conveys is as powerful today as it was at the time of its publication.

There are many examples of how technology can benefit people with severe disabilities and physical challenges. Technology solutions can help individuals with disabilities engage more naturally in leisure and recreation activities and as successfully as their typical peers (Langone, 1990). Technology applications can supplement the interactions between people with and without disabilities. Individuals with sensory deficits, physical challenges, or more severe cognitive delays can have access to high-technology devices that will allow them to communicate with others.

Technology can also set the stage for meaningful interaction with other people by providing individuals with disabilities opportunities for learning, exploring, and interacting with their environment. For people with significant disabilities, single-switch technology makes it possible to control and use a variety of electronic devices. Technology also allows people with disabilities to keep in touch with other people and professionals more efficiently so that they can have access to support and encouragement. Finally, technology opens doors for individuals with disabilities to quickly access information that may be beneficial to helping them develop and lead a more natural life.

This chapter presents information about technology that can enrich the lives of people with severe and physical disabilities. The emphasis is on how personal computers may be used to help persons with disabilities learn, become productive, and engage in leisure activities. Many individuals with severe disabilities can access the power of computer-based instruction through keyboards and mouse interface. For individuals with physical or motor disabilities, computer access will require use of single-switch technology and more sophisticated adaptive or alternative equipment. Devices and technology solutions for independent daily living are discussed throughout this chapter. The information in this chapter provides a similar focus to the other chapters of this text by stressing the relationship between integrating technology into daily learning, life, and leisure and recreation activities.

Many exceptional individuals with severe disabilities or physical challenges can access technology through the keyboard and the mouse. (Photograph by Carolyn F. Woods)

Characteristics of Persons with Severe and Physical Disabilities

Persons with severe and physical disabilities constitute a heterogeneous group of individuals (Turnbull, Turnbull, Shank, & Leal, 1999). Some of these individuals might have severe intellectual disabilities, whereas others might have intellectual abilities above the norm. Some individuals might be ambulatory and have full use of the limbs, whereas others might have little motor control, with movement confined to using a wheelchair. Any grouping of these individuals is artificial and done for the purposes of discussion related to technological devices that can improve the quality of their lives.

Understanding how technology can interact with the physical and learning characteristics of persons with disabilities is an important first step to using technology effectively. For professionals who work with these individuals, a precursor to the effective use of technology is understanding the importance of integrating technology into an intervention program. Because the types of technologies discussed in this chapter have applica-

tions for all persons with severe physical disabilities, a brief discussion of this group of individuals is important. Following is a presentation of the more salient characteristics of persons with severe cognitive and physical disabilities. A separate section follows presenting some salient and general characteristics of those individuals who have physical disabilities. These characteristics are presented to provide readers with a basis for seeking technology that meets the needs of specific individuals.

Persons with Severe Cognitive Disabilities

The term *severe disabilities* has been defined in a variety of ways by different professionals (Westling & Fox, 1995). This term suggests that individuals with more severe disabilities have considerably more debilitating problems than individuals with mild disabilities. Generally, persons with severe disabilities have multiple problems that could be manifested in a decreased ability to learn, deficits in social skills, sensory deficits, and possibly physical disabilities (Westling & Fox, 1995). Persons with severe cognitive disabilities may be categorized under specific disability labels. For example, these individuals might be categorized separately as having moderate to profound mental retardation, autism, or multiple (dual) disabilities (e.g., visual loss) and associated mental retardation.

Persons with severe disabilities may exhibit excessive behavior such as self-stimulation or tantrums (Dever & Knapczyk, 1997). Such behaviors can affect their attention span, thus interfering with their learning. They may also be deficient in areas such as self-help and often have significant deficits in language and communication. Individuals with severe disabilities do not effectively model the behavior of others and have difficulty processing information presented to them by parents and teachers. They also have difficulty with memory, attention, and perception. Learning more about these characteristics can help educators to better understand how technology can help these individuals to become more independent.

When individuals analyze and use information they have perceived, they have processed that information. For persons with severe cognitive disabilities, their difficulties in attention and perception exacerbate their problems processing information. Overcoming attention and perception problems while providing learners with new information are major goals for professionals. Technology solutions can enhance their efforts by providing learners with a variety of educational software and assistive hardware devices that allow learners access to the software. Integrated media holds the greatest promise for helping learners assimilate and accommodate new information. For example, CD-ROM or DVD-ROM technology allows software the ability to present many visual images as photos, videos, and graphics to reinforce important academic and social concepts. Along with sound, learners can be exposed to instruction that allows them interactivity. These programs expose learners to the information and provide them the opportunity to respond. CD-ROM and DVD-ROM software programs also branch learners to parts of the program where they can receive help or additional information if necessary.

Memory as a cognitive function is complex, and is tied to attention, perception, and information processing. Memory is the process whereby individuals store information they gather in their central nervous system and retrieve it for later use (Polloway & Patton, 1997). A key component to the process of memory involves peoples' ability to rehearse the material they perceive. When people efficiently rehearse (i.e., repeat or practice) information in their short-term memory, they can improve long-term memory (Polloway & Patton, 1997). When people analyze information in a more detailed way or pair the information with other knowledge, the better the chances for retention.

Most people with severe cognitive disabilities are not efficient in rehearsing information and need a considerable amount of repetition in order for them to store information for later retrieval (G. E. Thomas, 1996). As typical learners progress through school, they begin to develop rehearsal strategies that serve them in improving their memories. Learners with cognitive disabilities have considerable problems learning to use rehearsal strategies compared with their typical peers and have greater problems developing independent rehearsal strategies (Langone, 1990; Olson & Platt, 1996; Polloway & Patton, 1997).

High-quality computer-based instruction can help educators improve their attempts to teach their students the prerequisite tasks to using rehearsal skills. Many characteristics of technology are effective for helping students with memory deficits. For example, the ability of computer-based instruction to present many repetitions of the important information and to do so in different forms can be an asset to learners with memory deficits. When this information is paired with associated concepts or items, the learners have a better chance of storing the information for later use. Technology solutions allow teachers to present a variety of stimuli repetitively, with many examples accompanied by color, sound, and video.

Difficulties in maintaining attention to relevant details of a task and problems discriminating between important stimuli are commonly faced by learners who have cognitive disabilities (Olson & Platt, 1996; Rivera & Smith, 1997). For those children who do not have cognitive differences but have motor problems, less than optimum interaction with their environment can essentially create similar problems in attention and discrimination skills (Langone, 1990).

Technology solutions can help all learners with disabilities improve their attention to relevant stimuli. Computers equipped with speech synthesizers and accompanying software can, for example, help students focus their attention on important sounds, words, or phrases. When the software also includes visual or graphic cues, the students stand a better chance at improving in any skill area.

When stimuli are presented to the brain by an individual's senses, the ability to interpret information can be called perception (Polloway & Patton, 1997). Research suggests that infants can perceive visual and auditory stimuli and their perceptions provide a foundation for later learning (Cook, Tessier, & Klein, 1996). As colors, sounds, and smells become meaningful for learners, they can use the information they obtain to help them continue learning. People with severe cognitive disabilities are limited in their ability to perceive events around them (Olson & Platt, 1996).

Technology solutions now provide professionals with effective strategies for helping to supplement the instruction of learners with disabilities. Computer-based instruction can provide both visual images and sounds that may help students pay attention to the instruction and improve their perception to surrounding events. Computers can provide a large variety of stimuli to accompany important skills targeted for acquisition by the learner. Multimedia or integrated media instruction can help learners with disabilities experience events that may have previously been out of their reach (e.g., a visit to an art gallery in another country).

Persons with Physical Disabilities

Individuals with physical disabilities or challenges are a considerably more diverse group than those with severe cognitive deficits. These individuals may be born with a physical disability or acquire one anytime during their life. They may have associated cognitive disabilities that impede their ability to learn or may have cognitive abilities above the norm. Additionally, individuals with physical disabilities may have problems in all areas of learning characteristics (i.e., attention, information processing) discussed in the previous section or may have little or no problems in these domains.

Persons with physical disabilities have conditions that affect their mobility, gross or fine motor skills, and coordination. Their impairments may be a result of congenital conditions that are present at birth or acquired conditions that are the result of an accident or illness (Bigge, 1991). Many congenital conditions result in physical impairments. For example, cerebral palsy and muscular dystrophy are two of the more common disabilities that result in a variety of significant physical problems. Spinal cord and traumatic head injuries that result from accidents are examples of acquired injuries (Bigge, 1991).

The Individuals with Disabilities Education Act of 1990 (IDEA) identifies services for school-aged individuals who have physical disabilities and health impairments (Vaughn, Bos, & Schumm, 1997). Under IDEA students who may receive services are separated into three categories: orthopedic impairment, other health impairment, and traumatic brain injury. These designations that are part of IDEA expand the scope of this chapter. They demonstrate how technological solutions can be potentially helpful for individuals other than those identified as having motor and coordination problems. For example, a student with severe asthma, who has no problems with physical movement and coordination, may miss school a great deal. Distance education using technology (e.g., two-way real-time links to the classroom, e-mail) may help that individual succeed academically and keep up with classmates.

The definitions within IDEA are thorough and allow for the provision of services to learners who suffer from a variety of problems that adversely affect their educational performance. For example, persons with orthopedic disabilities may have problems adjusting socially, communicating with others, and learning (Vaughn et al., 1997). Similarly, persons with other health impairments may miss a considerable amount of school because of their condition, resulting in wide gaps in their educational progress. Individuals with traumatic brain injury (i.e., open or closed head injuries) may have impairments, for example, in cognition and language that adversely affect their social adjustment and educational progress.

The difficulty of discussing characteristics of individuals with severe and physical disabilities can be attributed to the heterogeneity of this group of people. Because individuals within each of these groups can also have a variety of associated disabilities (e.g., vision, hearing, and emotional problems), the task of providing general characteristics becomes complicated. In addition, the complex interaction between people with disabilities and their environments creates a variety of situations where the impact of the disability can be either lessened or enhanced. Therefore, it is essential that professionals assess the needs of individuals with disabilities in a case-by-case fashion (see Chapter 5). This fact is true for all aspects of program development including the selection or development of technology solutions.

For individuals with physical disabilities who have related cognitive or sensory deficits, the technology solutions mentioned previously have equal benefit. Technology solutions can help persons who because of physical disabilities cannot actively engage in a variety of daily living tasks, such as using kitchen appliances or turning on the television. Single-switch technology and adaptive keyboards allow these individuals to access microcomputers. Microcomputers and portable technologies can assist them in controlling their environment, communicating with others, and engaging in lifelong learning and recreation (see Chapters 2 and 5).

At times people with physical disabilities may not have optimal social and learning experiences, and thereby are susceptible to developing an outer-directed outlook on life resulting in "unresolved feelings of dependency and discomfort in dealing with dependence" (Bigge, 1991, p. 105). These behaviors sometimes manifest themselves in an outlook that causes the individuals to believe that they have little or no control over their own lives. Subsequently, these feelings may result in a lack of willingness to try anything but the simplest tasks. Some theorists believe that this unwillingness to try is a result of both a history of failure and other people's reactions to their disabilities (C. H. Thomas & Patton, 1994).

Many technology solutions are available that can help individuals with physical disabilities overcome the less productive behaviors associated with an external locus of control. Devices exist that can improve mobility for those who have physical challenges that impede movement. High-technology solutions to computer access and environmental control allow those persons with disabilities that affect their limbs to take control of their lives and become less reliant on others. The remainder of this chapter focuses on the use of technology solutions as tools that assist individuals with severe and physical disabilities to become independent in the true sense of the word. The next section presents information about hardware and software solutions that help individuals with disabilities overcome barriers to accessing computers. Following is a section on computer-based instruction and its uses for assisting individuals in becoming lifelong learners. The next section includes information about technology solutions for helping persons with severe and physical disabilities take control of their daily living. The final section presents resources for professionals, parents, and persons with disabilities who wish to learn more about technology solutions and to seek assistance in obtaining technology.

General Hardware and Software Technology

Many hardware and software solutions are available that allow persons with severe disabilities to take advantage of the power of technology for learning, communication, and recreation, among other of life's functions. This section first reviews the types of platforms or computers used today and then discusses hardware and software technology that persons with disabilities can use to access personal computers.

Computer Platforms

Personal computers used today by individuals with and without disabilities are typically based on one of two platforms, IBM and compatibles or Macintosh, but older Apple II series hardware (e.g., the e, c, and GS machines) are still found in many general and special education classrooms. The operating systems and software used by these platforms are also different—Apple DOS and ProDOS, PC/MS-DOS, Windows, and MacOS— but recent hardware and software innovations are making the IBM or compatible and Macintosh platforms more compatible. The new platforms not only are more powerful but also are more user friendly and come equipped with many solutions that make access easier for individuals with severe and physical disabilities. As discussed in Chapter 5, today's platforms come with software solutions for programs that promote access by adapting input and output functions (e.g., key stroke needs, voice input, speech synthesis, enlarged images). Because the newer platforms also offer multimedia capabilities, these machines have significantly increased the qualitative aspects of using technology for business, leisure, and instructional purposes (e.g., personal or instructional productivity.)

People typically purchase a computer system based on personal preference. Generally, the newest machines from either platform are comparable in every way. Comparable adaptive devices, peripherals, and software can be found for both Macintosh and IBM or compatible computers. Most manufacturers and software developers design versions of their products for both platforms. Before a consumer invests in a computer system, it is wise to spend time working with both platforms before deciding which one best fits the user's working style.

Whichever platform consumers choose, they should make sure their system comes with some basic, yet vital equipment. Computer systems should include a CD-ROM player, a modem (at least 14K bps, 56K recommended), a color monitor, at least eight megabytes (16MB recommended) of random access memory (RAM), and the largest hard drive one can afford. These spec-ifications allow the user to take advantage of the new multimedia programs and to link to the Internet. Many computers available today come with these features in the basic package.

Consumers would be advised to contact both Apple and IBM for information about their disability and special needs services. For example, Apple provides a series of disability-related information resources, one of which is an information packet that includes a comprehensive database of computer access products. This packet is called the Mac Access Passport (MAP) and is available free of charge by calling 800/600-7808 (voice) or 800/755-0601 (TTY). IBM Special Needs Systems also provides a wealth of information about their services and products for individuals with severe and physical disabilities. Information can be obtained from 800/426-4832 (voice) or 800/ 426-4833 (TDD), or www.austin.ibm.com/sns/snsmail2.html.

Environmental Modifications

Most people use their computers at standard workstations that include a desk or table modified to accommodate the machine. Preferably, the computer monitor is at eye height or slightly lower, and the keyboard is placed so the person's forearms are in a comfortable position. The work space surrounding the computer must be large enough to accommodate any peripheral devices that accompany the machine and still have ample room for other materials that may be needed (e.g., books, papers).

For individuals with severe disabilities and no motor problems, a standard computer workstation usually suffices. For persons with physical disabilities, however, more extensive environmental modifications might be necessary for them to adequately use their computers. Physical and occupational therapists should be consulted from the outset to determine the best position for each individual depending on his or her disability and the physical movement used to actuate the particular electronic device. For example, a physical therapist may use adaptive equipment (e.g., wheelchair attachments, bolsters) to get a person into a proper midline position that will facilitate his or her use of an alternate keyboard. People with physical disabilities have very different needs and professionals can develop the appropriate interventions to meet each individual's need.

Keyboard Adaptations

Low-technology and software solutions are available for those individuals with physical disabilities who have use of their hands but less fine motor control than required to use standard keyboards. Two low-tech hardware solutions for improving keyboard control are keylocks and keyguards. Keylocks are devices that assist the user with less able motor control to lock a specific key such as the "Command" key on Macintosh computers. This technology solution works well for people with use of only one hand by allowing them to activate multikey functions (e.g., Command + 'u' to start the underline command on some word processors). Keyguards are placed on top of the standard keyboard with raised holes that allow users with motor difficulties to locate the desired keys without accidentally actuating others. Keyguards are also useful adaptations for persons who require the use of head-mounted wands or mouth sticks to make keystrokes.

Most Macintosh computers come with onboard software called Easy Access (Apple Corporation) that allows users to convert the numeric keypad on the keyboard into a mouse simulator. A person with a physical disability who does not have the motor movements to control the circular motion of a mouse will find this feature valuable. Easy Access software allows the user to modify the speed at which the keys "send the message" when depressed. This Slow Keys feature of the Easy Access software is valuable for persons with physical disabilities who, because of control problems, may initially press the wrong key. By slowing down the reaction time of the keystrokes, the user is allowed additional time to correct an error by locating and depressing the desired key. Finally, the Sticky Keys feature of the Easy Access software program allows the user to lock specific function keys without the need for a keylock

Individuals with severe disabilities can use computers to improve their quality of life. (Photograph by Carolyn F. Woods)

device. Users can set a modifier key (e.g., Command) and other keys that activate functions to act when typed in sequence instead of when pressed simultaneously. In the example presented above, individuals might use the Sticky Keys function to activate the Command + 'u' keys to underline a word. When they wish to underline a word or phrase, they would press Command first and then the 'u' key to activate this function. Sticky keys are a great advantage for one-handed typists or typists who require a head wand or mouth stick to complete their work. The Easy Access software comes with the System 7 or later operating software for Macintosh or Power PC machines.

Similar software is available for IBM and compatible machines. Access DOS is software developed by the Trace Research and Development Center (more detailed information about Trace is presented in the Resources section at the end of this chapter) and is available free to persons with disabilities from IBM. Access DOS can perform the same functions as the Easy Access software.

Adaptive Hardware

Individuals with severe and physical disabilities may require other methods of computer access than a keyboard and mouse. Once they have access to personal computers, these machines can help them communicate, improve their knowledge through computer-based instruction, and allow them more opportunities for leisure and recreation. Sophisticated alternative keyboards and low-tech devices include head pointers, styluses, mouth sticks, and chin or head wands.

Students with severe disabilities often need assistive tools that allow them to interact with computers and other electronic devices. These assistive tools range in sophistication from simple switches that turn devices on and off, to alternative keyboards that have special characteristics that can be matched to individual needs. For example, a youngster who has physical disabilities might need a single switch to use and play with a toy. Another example is a student with poor motor control who uses an alternative keyboard with large keys or pads, increasing the size of the target and allowing access to a computer. A variety of adaptive hardware is available to assist individuals with severe and physical disabilities in accessing personal computers as tools for communication, learning, and leisure. In the following sections these devices are presented in three broad categories that represent the current products available.

Alternative Keyboards

There are many hardware alternatives to the standard keyboard and mouse setup for inputting information and commands into the computer. These hardware solutions have a variety of functions and can be programmed based on the needs of the individual users. For example, special keyboards or touch pads operating by means of touch-sensitive membranes can provide the user with larger targets to actuate or with the option of scanning several choices and picking the desired choice with one keystroke. These devices generally require some adaptations to the target device, usually the computer.

Before individuals with severe and physical disabilities can use the variety of alternative keyboards, additional hardware and software solutions called keyboard interface systems must be added to their machines. Keyboard interface systems enable various alternative input devices to be plugged into the computers so that standard software can be used by people with various disabilities who cannot use standard keyboards. The Apple IIe and IIGS can be equipped with an insert called the Adaptive Firmware Card (Don Johnston Developmental Equipment). This device allows the computer to respond to specialty keyboards designed for people with physical disabilities. The Adaptive Firmware Card is a hardware card that fits inside the computer and is attached to a control box on its exterior. This hardware and software solution allows other devices to act as a substitute for the standard keyboard (in the IIe) and keyboard and mouse (in the IIGS).

A similar device called the Ke:nx (Don Johnston Developmental Equipment), available for Macintosh computers, plugs into the mouse port normally reserved for the standard keyboard. When plugged into the Ke:nx, third-party alternative keyboards will control virtually any software that will run on the Macintosh computer. One brand of keyboard interface card for MS-DOS compatible computers is the P.C. SerialAid.

Computers such as the Apple IIe and IIGS and some older Macintosh machines can be equipped with an Echo Speech Synthesizer (Echo Speech Corporation) to make use of computer-generated speech. The Echo Speech Synthesizer allows the user access to software that can produce speech for communicating with others. Speech synthesizers can be used by individuals with severe and physical disabilities to improve their speech and language skills by providing them computer-generated models for speech. Speech synthesizer and software solutions can provide learners with severe disabilities access to a variety of language development exercises in which the computer prompts for responses, provides auditory feedback, and presents verbal reinforcement. Most newer models of computers come with the onboard ability to produce speech.

Many alternative keyboards are on the market that will provide persons with severe and physical disabilities access to computers. Alternative keyboards are electronic devices that interface with the computer to control its function. For persons with severe and physical disabilities, alternative keyboards have several advantages over the standard keyboard and mouse. Most of these devices can be programmed individually and customized to meet the needs of each user.

For example, the Unicorn keyboard (Intelli-Tools) is a programmable input device that has 128 touch-sensitive areas similar to keys that are each almost 1-inch square. These areas can represent the traditional keys on a keyboard or, for an individual with severe disabilities, be programmed to decrease the number of choices and include only the most important functions. Any key or group of keys can be defined to represent any string of characters up to 30 characters long. Once the keys are defined, they can be grouped in many different ways according to the user's needs and overlays can be created for the different uses. The Unicorn Model 510 is a smaller version with similar capabilities.

IntelliKeys (IntelliTools) is an advanced alternative keyboard that does not require an interface device such as the Adaptive Firmware Card, but plugs directly into the computer. This keyboard can be used with Apple, Macintosh, and IBM computers, thus allowing for more flexibility within programs that have multiple machines. The IntelliKeys includes "smart" overlays, which include a bar code that the board reads, allowing the user to begin typing immediately based on the functions represented on the particular overlay. The IntelliKeys can be used with IntelliTalk software, which allows individuals to type out messages they wish the computer to speak for them.

The Power Pad (Dunamis, Inc.) is a 12 × 12 inch touch-sensitive board that, when used with Power Pad software, allows younger students or those with more severe cognitive disabilities access to Apple II computers. This alternative input device provides access to software that helps students draw, communicate, and practice a variety of educational skills.

Single-Switch Technology

Switches are devices that allow individuals with severe and physical disabilities to control many electronic or battery-operated devices. They can also be used to actuate functions on a computer using a computer interface device such as the Adaptive Firmware Card or the Ke:nx. Some switches require the user to tap the switch to acti-

vate the device and tap it again to turn it off. Other switches require that the switch be held down or that pressure be applied to the switch the entire time a device is running.

The type of switch appropriate for persons with disabilities is matched to their skills. For example, people with two-way gross motor movement might best use a button-type single-switch device. People with gross motor pointing capabilities may need a large target switch. A variety of switches are available to meet the needs of many individuals with disabilities. For example, a ribbon switch is an extremely sensitive single-switch device that is a flat flexible strip, operated by applying pressure along any point of the ribbon. A button or platform switch sits on a platform, and pressure on the button activates the switch. Switches are available that allow a user with no hand control to operate devices by blowing into a tube to start the switch. Glove switches and pull switches are also available for helping individuals activate electronic devices. Switches are available that can be controlled by a hand, arm, foot, head, eyebrow, tongue, or any other muscle over which an individual with physical disabilities has control. Examples of commonly used switches are the Big Red Switch and Jelly Bean and Specs Switches (by Ablenet and available through Innocomp).

Software Solutions and Other Input Devices for Computers

As discussed in Chapter 5, there are many software solutions and other input devices that allow users to control the functions of computers. A number of word prediction programs are available for Macintosh, Apple, MS-DOS, and Windows environments that permit users to reduce the keystrokes to type words or phrases. For example, when a user types the initial two letters of a word, such as 'd' and 'e', the software program suggests options (e.g., 1. depress; 2. delete; 3. defend; 4. degenerate, 5. determine). If the desired word was *defend*, the user would choose the number three and the program would complete the typing of the word. This saves the user four additional keystrokes. If the desired word was not included in the five choices offered, the user would type the third letter and additional choices would be offered. Most prediction programs also advance two spaces after a period and capitalize the next letter automatically, saving additional keystrokes. Word prediction programs do a wonderful job of decreasing the amount of work individuals with physical disabilities have to do to accomplish their word processing tasks.

Many word prediction programs are available for all of the computer platforms. Predict It (Don Johnston) is a program for Apple computers that is both a word processor and a word prediction program. Co:Writer (Don Johnston) is an example of an add-on program for the Macintosh computer that works with word processors. For IBM and compatible computers, programs such as EZ Keys and Key Wiz (Word+, Inc.) provide excellent word prediction capabilities.

Talking word processors (word processors that can say letters, words, sentences, etc.) can benefit a variety of users with disabilities beyond those with visual disabilities. For users with spelling problems in addition to other disabling conditions, word processors that can provide auditory feedback can be extremely helpful. When talking word processors are used with word prediction software, the results can be quite beneficial for individuals with severe and physical disabilities.

Other input devices allow the user to enter data and commands into the computer. For example, TouchWindow (Edmark Corporation) is a thin, touch-sensitive overlay that fits over the computer screen and allows input into the computer by touching areas on the screen. This device is available for all computer platforms and operates similarly to a computer mouse. A great deal of quality software is compatible with TouchWindow. In addition, TouchWindow will often control the mouse functions of most software. Another innovative device is the Tongue Touch Keypad (newAbilities Systems), which can be used with both major computer platforms and fits into the roof of a user's mouth. The keypad includes nine keys that can be activated by the individual's tongue. By learning to activate two key sequences, the user can type letters.

HeadMaster (Prentke Romich) is a pointing device that allows users direct selection of their choice of commands to control computer functions or letters that are to be typed. With Head-Master individuals wear a headset that receives signals from an ultrasonic transmitting unit that sits on a Macintosh or IBM and compatible computer. The unit translates changes in the users' head position into changes in the cursor's position on the screen. Once the unit establishes the cursor's location, the user puffs into a tube connected to the headset, which is the equivalent of pressing the mouse button. When HeadMaster is used with the software ScreenTyper, a full keyboard is shown at the bottom of the screen (see http://kamprath.net/claireware/speech_typer. html). This feature allows users to type in characters by pointing the cursor to the desired keyboard image and puffing into the tube.

One other major input mechanism that has great potential for persons with disabilities is voice or speech input (Lewis, 1993). Controlling computer functions and typing by merely speaking the commands or words is a tremendous asset for persons with severe physical disabilities. Speech recognition is a hardware and software solution that works together to allow users to control their computers with speech. IBM and compatible users may choose from Dragon Dictate and the IBM Voice Type (both by Dragon Systems). Dragon Dictate, the more expensive and powerful option, can recognize and type 25,000-plus active words (230,000 total) and allows users the ability to add an additional 5,000-plus words common to their use. IBM Voice Type is a less powerful and less costly alternative that can recognize and type approximately 10,000-plus words (80,000-plus dictionary). The Voice Navigator (Articulate Systems) works with Macintosh computers and provides similar features as the systems designed for IBM machines.

Technology-Based Instruction

Once people with disabilities have access to technology, the hardware and software can be a tremendous benefit to their lives. Computers offer these individuals the ability to supplement their knowledge in most areas and the opportunity to share their ideas with others through word processing, e-mail, and voice production. Personal computers can enhance virtually every aspect of a person's life, including work, daily management, and leisure. The software available to help individuals with disabilities accomplish these tasks must be of high quality and adjustable to meet their needs. The quality of software is critical for individuals with severe cognitive disabilities whose significant learning problems require a multimodal approach to information presentation (also see Chapters 5 and 10).

Software or computer-based instruction (CBI) is available to help professionals in presenting a variety of language and academic skills to students who have severe and physical disabilities. These computer-based instructional packages can be used by individuals or in cooperative learning groups. This section presents a discussion of how CBI can improve the lifelong learning of persons with disabilities. The following sections present information concerning the importance of integrating technology into any educational program and information about selected CBI packages that have potential for these learners. Personal and instructional productivity concepts presented in Chapters 7 and 8 should also be considered as you read the sections below.

Integrating Technology into Instructional Programs

Technology in the form of CBI provides teachers, parents, and learners with tools that can increase learning and improve the quality of lives for persons with severe and physical disabilities. Like other tools, CBI can be misused when this form of instruction is not linked to instructional objectives (Langone, 1990). For example, a goal for a high school student with physical disabilities and learning problems may be to learn the skills necessary for him or her to pass a general mathematics course. A misuse of the tool exists if the teacher allows the student to practice advanced algorithms related to decimals using a computer program before being adequately instructed in

these skills (see Chapters 1, 6, and 8). Another possible misuse of technology beyond CBI might be when teachers instruct students with severe cognitive disabilities to communicate with electronic devices in isolated one-on-one activities (e.g., "May I have something to eat?"), then do not let them use the boards during snack and lunch.

All educational programs are based on goals and objectives. For students with disabilities these goals and objectives are formalized in Individualized Education Plans (IEPs) and commonly linked to skills taught in the general education classroom. Learners with physical disabilities and no cognitive deficits will have all of their goals and objectives linked to the general curriculum (Bigge, 1991). Students with severe cognitive disabilities will have their goals and objectives linked to activities in inclusive classroom settings and community-based instruction (Langone, 1990).

Teachers should link technology and CBI to the goals and objectives delineated on the students' IEPs or to their personal goals for independence. Teachers, parents, and consumers should carefully review any software program based either on IEPs or on personal goals. Then a thoughtful decision can be made regarding what role the software would play in the general plan to teach these skills.

Standard Computer-Based Instruction

There are many software programs available for "students" of all ages and that number is continually growing. Most of these programs focus on instructing language and academic skills. Persons with severe disabilities may require assistance in learning basic skills such as cause and effect, simple communication, or problem solving. Individuals with physical disabilities may not be able to experience or observe the number or variety of events that those without these challenges experience. Computer simulations and CD-ROM or DVD-ROM exploration software (e.g., visit to the National Gallery of Art) are available to assist individuals with severe and physical disabilities to broaden their experiences and to learn to solve problems.

For those individuals with severe cognitive disabilities, CBI can be an effective tool in helping them develop and use speech and language skills. Computer-based software used with speech synthesizers provides students with quality models for language and the means to express themselves (also see Chapter 10). For example, CBI can expose learners with cognitive disabilities to many high-quality examples of cause and effect concepts. Understanding cause and effect is important for language development and software programs are available that allow students to explore these relationships in gamelike environments that provide colorful graphics and reinforcing sound (speech and music).

High-quality CBI for assisting individuals in improving their oral language should include graphics and speech produced by the computer. These features highlight and reinforce important concepts and provide a frame of reference for words introduced during the instruction. Software programs are also available to help learners improve receptive language by introducing new vocabulary and language concepts. For example, when introducing the word *dog,* a photo or animation of a dog will appear on the computer monitor while the program using the speech synthesizer says "dog." The programs that may be the most productive for helping students to improve their language and communication skills are those that provide a variety of verbal, graphic, and pictorial cues. High-quality instructional software also provides learners with frequent feedback and reinforcement about their progress.

Laureate Learning Systems has designed and markets a variety of software for teaching cause and effect and receptive language skills. This company produces software based on sequences of language development for individuals without developmental delays. For example, the series called The Creature Games is for learners who have a functioning level below the age of 9 months. Six individual programs (Creature: Antics, Capers, Features, Cartoons, Magic, and Chorus) in this series help students to master skills of cause and effect relationships, the use of

single switches for input and program control, and turn taking. Laureate also produces The Early Vocabulary Development Series, which includes three programs: First Words, First Words II, and First Verbs. Basic levels of these programs allow users to activate a switch signifying that they recognize the picture on the screen. Advanced levels provide tests to evaluate whether the students have mastered the initial levels. These programs also have come in bilingual versions for young children from Spanish-speaking households. Other language and communication programs available from Laureate are the Exploring Early Vocabulary Series and The Early Vocabulary Development Series.

Laureate extends its receptive language programs by allowing learners access to words for constructing phrases and sentences. For example, the Talking Nouns program helps students to use "I," "we," "show me," "like," and other words or phrases for constructing simple sentences. These programs use overlays placed on the input device (i.e., alternative keyboard) that include pictures and words in combination. These combinations help students to choose the words or phrases they wish to use in a sentence they wish to develop. Laureate software includes a feature that corrects the student's grammar and produces the correctly spoken model of the sentence the learner constructed.

Other commercial enterprises have marketed software programs for helping students improve their expressive language skills. Don Johnston Developmental Equipment markets a variety of programs such as Day at Play, Eency and Friends, and Forgetful and Friends for helping students with severe cognitive disabilities to gain language skills. IntelliTools markets sophisticated alternative keyboards, as discussed previously, and software that supports these input devices and allows the computer to become a powerful communication device for expressive language. Laureate Learning Systems, in addition to the programs described above, markets other language programs including Talking Nouns II and Talking Verbs. Laureate also markets software for teaching word combinations, early syntax, and syntax mastery (e.g., First Categories, The Emerging

Rules Series, My Paint and Talking Color Books, Micro-Lads, Let's Go to the Circus, and The Words and Concepts Series).

Younger learners with severe cognitive disabilities can benefit from software marketed by PEAL Software. This company markets expressive language programs such as Exploratory Play, Representational Play, and Action/Music Play. Sunburst markets the Muppet Learning Keys (input device) and associated software for use in teaching early expressive language skills.

A major goal of educational programs for students with severe and physical disabilities is to encourage them to develop their cognitive skills and literacy. Computer-based instruction can be effective in helping learners develop basic cognitive processes such as attention, perception, discrimination, and memory (Lewis, 1993). Literally hundreds of companies market software designed to help students improve their academic skills. The scope of this chapter does not allow a complete listing of all software companies; however, the following discussion presents a sampling of companies and products that represent the larger universe.

Individuals who are physically challenged can use computers to facilitate learning. (Photograph by Carolyn F. Woods)

Educational Resources distributes software from a variety of publishers. Such a company can be helpful to professionals because it provides a comparison of a variety of products. Optimum Resource's Stickybear's Early Learning Activities allows young users to discover or be guided through six activities designed to help them gain basic skills for later success in academics (program is also available in Spanish). Its First Steps Counting and Thinking Games helps learners to practice counting and beginning learning number sets. Scholastic's Math Shop Series helps learners in gaining real world math skills. This software package is available for bilingual students and includes levels for students from first grade through high school. Educational Resources also markets software programs for assisting learners in gaining reading and language arts skills, such as Orange Cherry's Talking Vocabulary Builders, which teaches history, science, and social studies concepts.

Multimedia Instruction

Multimedia instruction that resides on interactive videodisc, CD-ROM, or DVD-ROM provides students with disabilities significantly greater opportunities for learning important information because of this technology's capabilities to store large amounts of data. Before CD-ROM based instruction and the ability to provide multiple visual examples, teachers always had difficulty placing important concepts and information in the context of meaningful events and activities. Teachers faced with this problem tend to present information that results in students learning skills that they are expected to recall upon command but that they are unable to use in problem-solving situations (Hasselbring, Goin, & Bransford, 1991). This phenomenon was described by Whitehead (1929) as the learning of "inert" knowledge and has been a subject for considerable debate among cognitive theorists. These professionals believe that educators, for the most part, present information to learners that proliferates the spread of knowledge that has little or no link to practical application (Brown, Collins,

& Duguid, 1989; Tripp, 1993). For children with disabilities, teaching any skills in isolation, with no link to common events or concrete applications, may serve to impede their ability to learn the skills and solve problems (Langone, 1990).

In an attempt to overcome the problem of teaching inert knowledge, the Cognition and Technology Group at Vanderbilt (CTGV) has developed a system called *anchored instruction*. Anchored instruction attempts to situate learning in videodisc or CD-ROM based environments by providing learners with examples of how experts use knowledge as tools to solve problems. The JASPER series developed at Vanderbilt and marketed by Optical Data School Media allows students and their teachers, who act as partners in learning instead of transmitters of learning, to explore video environments rich in information. Students use video examples cooperatively to solve increasingly complex problems (CTGV, 1993; Young, 1993). The research supporting the effectiveness of situated learning in general (Griffin, 1995) and anchored instruction specifically (CTGV, 1993, 1994) is promising. This instruction provides the opportunity for applying technology-based situated learning to other areas (Hedberg & Alexander, 1994).

Computer-based multimedia CD-ROM, DVD-ROM, and videodisc software extends anchored instruction by allowing students with severe and physical disabilities the opportunity to experience a variety of stimuli (e.g., sound, video, animation). These stimuli reinforce important ideas or transmit information in a way that allows the learners to experience concrete examples. CD-ROM and DVD-ROM technology allows software developers considerable storage capacity (see Chapter 2), which allows them to create more powerful instructional programs. Software developers can include digitized video, animation, sophisticated graphics, and sounds designed to enhance the learning.

For example, Science Elements (Mentorom, available from Educational Resources) provides students with the ability to study complex science concepts with the help of video, graphics, animation, slides, audio, and text. Complex concepts such as the periodic table, atoms, and radioactivity are paired with several multimedia

forms that provide students the opportunity to better understand the concepts and view applications that increase the probability for using the information in problem-solving situations. CD-ROM based software is available for most areas of academic study. For example, Discover the World (Entrex, available from Educational Resources) provides students with a wealth of social studies related information while solving problems in a game-based environment.

Videodisc technology allows teachers to quickly retrieve short video clips they wish to use for reinforcing words or ideas being introduced in a lesson by using a remote control or bar code reader available with videodisc players. This feature also allows teachers more freedom to retrieve short video clips multiple times if their students need more exposure to concepts supported by video. Additional trials may help the students to form a mental picture that can be associated with the target word or phrase. A VHS tape and VCR player require considerably more time to manipulate, breaking the flow of the lesson and possibly losing the attention of the children. However, videodisc technology is considered an old technology because of the limited storage capacity. With the recent innovations in CD-ROM and DVD-ROM technology, videodisc instruction will continue to be phased out over the next 10 years. Currently, videodisc players are still available and underused in the public schools. Videodisc instructional programs are available and often affordable, so teachers should use this technology in their work if access to more sophisticated forms of CBI are not readily available.

Many quality CD-ROM and videodisc-based instructional programs are available (DVD-ROM titles are increasing) that can be beneficial for students who have severe and physical disabilities. These instructional packages will support learning in any of the academic areas, and programs are also available for helping students gain social and vocational skills.

CD-ROM Based Instruction

Hartley offers many CD-ROM based instructional packages that can help students with severe and physical disabilities learn a variety of skills. Tapestry Language Development includes five stories designed to stimulate oral language development, sensory awareness, and problem solving. Tapestry Early Math includes five stories designed to help in developing problem-solving, decision-making, and emerging math skills. The Hartley Drug Education Series provides students with a variety of information supported by graphics and includes examples for dealing with the pressures to use drugs.

For younger students beginning to develop literacy and math skills, a variety of CD-ROM software is available. Let's Start Learning (The Learning Company) gives students the opportunity to follow Reader Rabbit through many exploration activities designed to strengthen letter and number skills. The Living Books Series (Brøderbund Software) including ABC's by Dr. Seuss and The Tortoise and the Hare, helps learners explore interactive environments they may have experienced in the text versions. Mr. Potato Head Saves Veggie Valley (Playskool) helps students learn to solve problems and strengthen basic language and preacademic arithmetic skills. A to Zap! (Sunburst) provides students with a sophisticated interactive environment that helps them to gain letter, number, and word skills.

Educational Resources distributes an outstanding collection of CD-ROM based instructional packages that could benefit students with disabilities in all areas of the school curriculum. For example, for teachers presenting information about African American accomplishments, the African-American History: Heroism, Struggle, and Hope CD (Clearvue) can provide their students sound and animation to support information about the history of African Americans in the United States from the slave trade through the Civil Rights movement.

Pierian Spring Software has developed a variety of innovative software that supports instruction in math, science, language arts, and geography. Their innovative Pierian CampOS is a virtual environment that allows students to explore buildings where they are challenged by lessons and problem solving activities. For example, Pierian's Interactive Geography software challenges students to go beyond memorization and

use skills to solve problems integrating knowledge and skills from other academic subject areas. This company's use of 3-D graphics that engage learners while providing visual illustrations of important academic concepts is outstanding.

Videodisc Programs

Laser Learning Technologies has a large collection of videodisc instructional packages (as well as CD-ROM software). Some of their social studies titles include Images U.S.A.; Maps, Globes & Directions; Africa: the Serengeti; STV: North America/ American History; Videodisc Colonial America in 1760's; Birth of a Nation Series Inventors; and the American Industrial Revolution. Their science and math topics include Your Active Body Series: Bones & Movement; Minds on Science Set; High Tech Reports; STV: Restless Earth; Life Computation Skills Math for Beginners–Add/Sub; and Math for Beginners–Mult/Div. They have many more titles in literature and other academic areas. Emerging Technology Consultants also has a variety of videodisc titles. One product they sell is the Multimedia and Videodisc Compendium that lists over 2,800 products. This resource is a valuable tool for educators.

Technology for Daily Living

Most of us look forward to driving because it translates into freedom; when we lose our ability to drive, we lose that sense of freedom. This analogy translates to other areas of our lives when we look forward to the freedom to be master of our environment. If people with severe and physical disabilities lead sheltered lives because of barriers that restrict their ability to control their environment, be mobile, communicate with others, and access information, they run the risk of losing their sense of freedom. Technology solutions can help individuals with disabilities to overcome most barriers of environmental control, mobility, communication, and information access. Many products are available to help people with disabilities to be more independent. In the following sections, a few of these products are discussed to provide a sampling of all that are available. Access concepts presented in Chapter 5 should also be considered as you read this section.

Technology Solutions for Environmental Control

Environmental control units allow individuals with severe and physical disabilities the ability to manage or control various functions in their living or working environment. These devices are sophisticated remote control systems that, when effectively matched to a user's needs and abilities, provide increased independence and productivity (Adams, Pon, & Blois, 1993). Environmental control units increase personal safety and productivity, improving a person's general quality of life (Adam, 1994; Adams et al., 1993). These technology solutions range from simple push-button systems to microprocessors that provide computer options for automating homes and for telemaintenance and other activities that can be conducted simultaneously (Stefanelli, 1994; Volunteers for Medical Engineering, n.d.). A variety of options on the market provide consumers with a choice of devices for virtually any need (Adam, 1994; Eubank & Latchman, 1992).

Environmental control units help persons with disabilities independently complete a variety of daily living tasks that persons without disabilities take for granted. For example, these devices can help to change climate control settings, open doors and draw the drapes, and operate TVs and stereo systems (Scheiderman, 1994). Environmental control units also allow people with disabilities complete use of their phone and, when interfaced with a computer, provide them with on-line banking, shopping, and access to distance education programs. These technology solutions also provide persons with disabilities increased opportunities for employment (Marsden, McGillis, & Murray, 1992).

Single-switch technology is a low-technology solution for environmental control. For example, appliances may be adapted to operate with a single switch when plugged into an electrical control unit. AbleNet markets a variety of single switches designed for people with physical limitations and the PowerLink 2 control unit that can work with appliances, electrical games, lights, and so on.

More sophisticated systems allow persons with disabilities to manipulate more than one device or function at a time. For example, radio-activated control units broadcast a signal that allows the user to operate appliances. This technology solution consists of a transmitter and a receiver unit. The electrical device is plugged into the receiver and can be turned on and off when the transmitter is activated. Some radio-controlled units are designed to activate several appliances.

Voice-activated control units are available to control phones, electric beds, VCRs, and other accessories. Some of these products can be programmed to turn appliances on or off at preset times (Stefanelli, 1994). They can detect the presence of intruders and retrieve data from a computer. Voice-activated environmental control units are trained to recognize the user's voice and are activated by speaking commands in a specific sequence. One such unit, the Vocal Link Cellular Module is a voice recognition telephone device that connects to a standard cellular telephone. Users can vocally re-call prestored telephone numbers either by key words they have selected or by vocally entering numbers. Mastervoice (Automated Voice Systems) is a voice-controlled environmental control unit that can control up to 42 devices by voice and 16 by timers. The Mastervoice is a comprehensive system that has a built-in speaker phone that can be dialed by voice command.

The environmental control of a person's home is an important skill that is often overlooked because it is such a natural occurrence. When electricity is interrupted because of a storm, a person suddenly realizes how important being able to control the temperature is. For persons with physical disabilities, barriers to controlling their living environment can be quite frustrating. One technology solution is the personal computer. With some additional hardware and the appropriate software, personal computers can be the control units that allow users to monitor and control their home's heating and air conditioning, lighting, alarms, phones, VCRs, and some electrical appliances. The Mastervoice system described previously is a stand-alone unit that works independently of a personal computer but is a powerful environmental control unit.

There are many other products that can help individuals control virtually every aspect of their daily lives. For example, the Robotic Work Station Attendant is an environmental control unit that, with the use of a robotic arm, can turn pages, operate office equipment, and handle files, diskettes, and telephone handsets. This unit includes multiple-hand designs that can provide different accommodations for different user needs. The arm is controlled by a computer and can be operated with voice input, standard or alternative keyboard, Morse Code, or row scanning. Technical Aids and Systems for the Handicapped markets environmental control units, such as the Relax system and the X-10 Controller unit. American Phone Products and AT&T National Special Needs Center market adaptive telephones that allow users with disabilities to simplify communication by telephone.

Technology Solutions for Mobility

Assisting people with disabilities to be more independently mobile becomes a major goal for any program that provides services. Many technology solutions exist for adapting vehicles that allow access for persons with disabilities. Vans can be equipped to have removable seats, allowing individuals to use a wheelchair as the driving seat. Wheelchair hoist lifts assist in placing folded wheelchairs into or out of the car or van after the driver has entered the vehicle. Newer van lift units can be operated independently by the user and some use a hydraulic suspension system that lowers the entire vehicle to reduce the angle of the ramp for easier wheelchair access. Hand controls can be permanently attached to the steering column of any vehicle, allowing users to control braking and acceleration. Head-operated controls are also available and can be used to operate lights, turn signals, and radios.

Wheelchairs have become quite sophisticated and offer many technological innovations to improve mobility. Technology has allowed for the development of lightweight manual wheelchairs, generally weighing about 28 pounds, that require significantly less energy to propel. Powered wheelchairs are technology solutions that provide independence for individuals unable to use a manual wheelchair and may be built or adapted to the needs of the user. Scooters are three-wheeled power mobility alternatives for individuals with physical disabilities who can sit upright. More locations in the community such as grocery stores and shopping malls are now offering scooters for use by older adults and individuals with disabilities.

Technology Solutions for Communication and Information Access

The ability to communicate with others and remain current with the rapidly growing flow of information is a critical determinant of independence. The personal computer equipped with adaptive devices that meet the user's needs and a modem allows the individuals to reach out from their homes and communicate with others via e-mail, to seek information about services and programs, to access educational opportunities, and to engage in employment and leisure pursuits. Probably the most significant technological advancement to enhance telecommunication and information dissemination has been the Internet and the World Wide Web. As noted in earlier chapters, the Internet and Web are accessible sources of information on technology solutions for persons with disabilities. Commercial services provide households with computers and modems access to the Internet and Web for a monthly fee. For those individuals without access, many public libraries are offering their patrons access to the Web's resources.

Teachers of students with disabilities can often find on the Internet and Web examples of lesson plans and sources for materials that can improve the quality of their work. Individuals with disabilities, parents, and teachers can also join listservers (groups of individuals who have a common interest who can post electronic messages to other members of the group) where they can discuss problems or share information of common interest (e.g., www.ability.org/server.html). The Web also presents information such as resources for funding assistive technology, product descriptions, services of organizations, and guidelines for developing accessible Web sites (www.w3.org/TR/WAI-WEBCONTENT).

Literally thousands of Web sites provide information dealing with technology solutions for persons with disabilities. The Web has the advantage of allowing the user to move quickly from one site to the other by clicking on a name or graphic highlighted in color. This feature allows Web site managers to link their sites to others that deal with similar topics.

A short list of potential sites of interest to individuals with disabilities, professionals, and parents is presented in Resources at the end of this chapter. I recommend beginning by visiting The National Center to Improve Practice (NCIP). This center (http://www.edc.org/FSC/NCIP/) promotes the effective use of technology for helping individuals with sensory, cognitive, physical, and social–emotional disabilities. A goal of the NCIP is to link a national community of professionals who use or want to use technology with advocates and consumers. The NCIP also has available materials in print and video, and an extensive collection of resources that are available on their Web site. The center, located at Education Development Center, Inc. (EDC), in Newton, Massachusetts, is funded by the U.S. Department of Education's Office for Special Education Programs (OSEP).

Augmentative and Alternative Communication

For some individuals with disabilities, the ability to produce intelligible speech may not be possible. Technology now provides powerful tools that help individuals overcome the barriers to communication and language development. Some individuals with disabilities have the ability to produce speech yet can benefit from the use of augmentative communication devices that support their communication attempts. Alternative communication devices can replace speech for those persons who may not have the ability to speak. Communication devices range from low-tech solutions (e.g., picture communication boards, photos, printed symbol systems) to high-tech solutions (e.g., microcomputers and stand-alone electronic boards). High-tech solutions can be critical devices for those individuals who cannot produce speech. They also can help others with severe cognitive disabilities who have the ability to produce speech by providing models for (a) pronouncing words and (b) the cause and effect relationship between requests and the actions of others (Suddath & Susnik, 1991). This section presents a brief description of some high-tech solutions available for augmentative and alternative communication (AAC) (see also Chapters 5 and 10).

Stand-alone electronic communication boards and computers with speech production capabilities enable individuals to respond to many day-to-day opportunities to communicate (Angelo & Goldstein, 1990). Electronic stand-alone units generally use touch-sensitive membranes as the target surface for pointing. Communication boards use either synthesized speech (computer-produced speech sounds) or digitized speech (digitally recorded natural speech). Digitized speech is immediately more recognizable for the listener,

Children who are physically challenged can use computers to facilitate learning. (Photograph by Carolyn F. Woods)

although listeners can learn to understand the synthesized speech.

A variety of stand-alone electronic devices are available. The type of device bought usually depends on the amount of money one can spend, the ability to adapt the device to the person's needs, and the device's durability and ease of use. The following list represents a number of devices that are available. For funding sources please refer to Parette, Hofmann, and VanBiervliet's (1994) article and volumes 20 (1990) and 25 (1995) of *Exceptional Parent* and the Abledata Web site (http://abledata.com/funding.htm).

Wolf Board (ADAMLAB)

- Screen can be divided into as many as 36 squares or rectangles.
- Uses lower quality synthesized speech.
- Limited memory of approximately 800 words.
- Can be activated by touch or be connected to switches.
- More sophisticated than the Intro Talker.
- Less expensive alternative to high-end devices.

Intro Talker (Prentke Romich)

- Touch-sensitive board offering 8 to 32 fairly large squares.
- Programmable with digitized recordings of natural speech.
- Suitable for younger children or more severe disabilities.
- Squares can be labeled with pictures or words.
- Often used as a student's first electronic communication board.

Touch Talker (Prentke Romich)

- Synthesized speech device with 8 to 32 small keys.
- Generates highly sophisticated synthesized speech.
- User learns to create words by combining specific keys in sequence.
- Requires more refined motor skills to access keys than Intro Talker.

- Includes an LCD display.

Liberator (Prentke Romich)

- Similar to Touch Talker in size and function.
- Uses advanced speech synthesis.
- Can save phrases and longer messages in memory for use at a later time.
- Can be adapted for use of head pointers or other devices.
- In addition to an LCD display, can generate a small paper printout of messages.

Macaw II (ZYGO Industries)

- Two models available, one with direct selection only, one with direct selection and scanning.
- Lightweight and small for easy use.
- Records communication messages.
- Enlarged key patterns with sensitive keys.

Big Mack Voice Output Communication Aid (Ablenet, available through Innocomp)

- Allows for 20 seconds of recorded speech.
- One large button activates the message.
- Easy to use for teaching beginning communication as well as cause and effect.

Speakeasy Voice Output and Communication Aid (Ablenet, available through Innocomp)

- Allows for 120 seconds of recorded speech.
- Can adapt for up to 12 switches for group work.
- Allows for auditory scanning and has a keyguard available.

DigiVox and DynaVox (Sentient Systems Technology)

- High-end systems that allow for complex communication.
- Multiple message levels.
- Uses digital recordings of human voice messages.
- Allows for custom keyboard layout.

Summary

This chapter has provided an overview of technology for persons with severe and physical disabilities. Technology is not a panacea, but advances can improve independence, learning, and the general quality of lives for these individuals. Like all tools, technology can be used effectively or misused, and professionals should be diligent in their search for ways to make technology work. Technology solutions are most effective when they are integrated into all daily life activities and when they conform to the needs of individuals.

Resources

Organizations

Association for Persons with Severe Handicaps (TASH). TASH is an international advocacy organization of approximately 7,000 professionals, parents, and other members with 38 chapters and members from 34 different countries and territories. TASH's mission is to eliminate physical and social obstacles that prevent equity, diversity, and quality of life. TASH publishes a quarterly journal (see below) and holds a national conference. *Contact:* TASH, 29 West Susquehanna Avenue, Suite 210, Baltimore, MD 21204; Voice: 410/848-8274; Fax: 410/828-6700; Web: http://www.tash.org; e-mail: info@ash.org

National Easter Seal Society. This organization of parents, professionals, and concerned citizens engages in research, publishing, and educational activities to improve the education and life of exceptional persons. *Contact:* National Easter Seal Society, 230 West Monroe, Suite 1800, Chicago, IL 60606; Voice: 800/221-6827

Trace Research and Development Center. This interdisciplinary research, development, and resource center specializes in technology and disability. It is part of the Waisman Center and the Department of Industrial Engineering at the University of Wisconsin–Madison. The main goal of the Trace Center is to put extensive disability-related information in the hands of consumers, professionals, and others in an easy-to-use, accessible form. Trace also designs software for persons with disabilities and organizes the Cooperative Electronic Library on Disability, disseminated on CD-ROM as Co-Net. The Trace Center is involved directly with research and development, and also responds directly to the information needs of consumers and their families, professionals, industry, government, and other researchers. *Contact:* Trace Research and Development Center, Waisman Center, University of Wisconsin–Madison, 1500 Highland Avenue, Madison, WI 57505; Voice: 608/262-6966; Web: http://www.trace.wisc.edu/

United Cerebral Palsy Association. This organization of interested persons supports a number of activities to improve the lives of individuals with cerebral palsy. *Contact:* United Cerebral Palsy Association, 1600 L. Street NW, Washington, DC 20036; Voice: 800/USA-5-UCP; TTY: 202/973-7197; Fax: 202/776-0414; Web: http://www.ucpa.org (or 7 Penn Station #804, New York City, NY 10001; 212/268-6655)

Journal

Journal of the Association for Persons with Severe Handicaps is published quarterly. Contact: TASH, 29 West Susquehanna Avenue, Suite 210, Baltimore, MD 21204; Voice: 410/828-8274; Fax: 410/828-6700; Web: http://www.tash.org.

Books

Beukelman, D. R., & Mirenda, P. (1998). *Augmentative and alternative communication: Management of severe communication disorders in children and adults* (2nd ed.). Baltimore: Brookes.

Hallahan, D. P., & Kauffman, J.M. (1998). *Exceptional learners: Introduction to special education* (7th ed.). Englewood Cliffs, NJ: Prentice-Hall.

Westling, D. L., & Fox, L. (1995). *Teaching students with severe disabilities*. Englewood Cliffs, NJ: Prentice-Hall.

World Wide Web Sites or Pages

http://www.edc.org/FSC/NCIP/SETT_home.html The SETT page of the National Center to Improve Practice's site is a virtual team meeting. This 4-week workshop provides information for selecting assistive technology for students with disabilities. The workshop is organized around the SETT Framework (Student, Environments, Tasks, and Tools), a framework for selecting assistive technology for students with disabilities, developed by the workshop leader, Joy Zabala.

http://www.edc.org/FSC/NCIP/Library_top.html The National Center to Improve Practice (NCIP) Library is organized into an expanding number of topical collections. NCIP staff have gathered and synthesized a rich collection of print, video, and on-line resources. These resources include overviews of the topical area, including classroom vignettes, illustrating how technology solutions are integrated into instructional practices or the lives of individuals. These profiles are available in two different formats: (a) the HTML format that allows users to read the profile on the computer screen, view pictures, link to related information, and print out the profile and (b) the Adobe Acrobat format that enables users to download a fully formatted version of this profile (text pictures) using Adobe Acrobat Reader software (Adobe Systems).

http://www.edc.org/FSC/NCIP/Library_EC_insights. html This NCIP Web page is dedicated to technology in early childhood education. The format of this page is to present conversations taken from NCIPnet (an on-line community of users interested in special education technology) and compiled into threaded messages for easier reading and viewing. For example, recent postings involve discussions about Boardmaker, a software program for the Macintosh computer used to develop communication board overlays. This Web page also provides an extensive resource list, such as the NCIP Profile: Technology Supports Inclusion in Preschool and Resource Files: Technology in Early Childhood Education.

http://www.edc.org/FSC/NCIP/Library_Early_Child. html This Web page is from the NCIP Library: Technology in Early Childhood Education Collection. It presents a variety of low- and high-tech tools for enhancing the learning of young children with disabilities. Information is presented about the use of technology for promoting growth in communication, social interaction, and cognitive development among preschoolers with special needs.

http://www.edc.org/FSC/NCIP/EC_TOC.html This Web page provides a listing of the resources currently contained within NCIP's Early Childhood Resource File. Resources are grouped into these categories: General, Practice, Products, Research, Vignette, and Publications.

http://www.rehab.uiuc.edu/pursuit/dis-resources/dis-resources.html Disability Information Resources is maintained by Project Pursuit, University of Illinois, and provides a wealth of information about all aspects of assistive technology. For example, an extensive description of environmental control units has been written to assist potential consumers in learning about the availability of these devices and in choosing the right device for their needs.

http://disability.com/ Evan Kemp Associates, Inc., is a commercial enterprise that provides products and services that enhance the quality of life for consumers with disabilities and chronic health conditions. Their Web page presents a variety of information and services for consumers, including their One Step Ahead Newspaper.

This electronic newspaper presents a variety of information of interest to persons with disabilities and their families. For example, this Web page offers a Solution Center that attempts to answer questions submitted by interested parties. Postings on this Web page have included "Tips on Parenting from a Wheelchair" and "What's New On the Legal Front with the ADA, IDEA, Fair Housing and Other Laws." This site also offers a service called Disability Links that allows users to link to the other disability-related resources on the World Wide Web.

http://www.mindspring.com/~accesshm/index.htm Accessible Homes, Inc., specializes in barrier-free environments. This group offers a complete range of services to help persons with disabilities design attractive barrier-free homes. This group states that their designs incorporate features that enhance the convenience, safety, efficiency, and accessibility for all residents.

http://cosmos.ot.buffalo.edu/aztech.html AZtech, Inc., is a not-for-profit, community-based enterprise by and for persons with disabilities. The name AZtech stands for A to Z assistive TECHnology. AZtech is operated by the Rehabilitation Engineering Research Center on Technology Evaluation and Transfer, which is supported by a grant from the National Institute on Disability and Rehabilitation Research, U.S. Department of Education.

http://www.rt66.com/catn.org/ The Consumer Assistive Technology Transfer Network (CATN) is funded through a grant from the National Institute on Disability and Rehabilitation Research with the New Mexico Technology Assistance Program (NMTAP), Division of Vocational Rehabilitation/State Department of Education NMTAP is operating the CATN as a model through Career Services for Persons with Disabilities, a consumer driven organization in Albuquerque. The CATN involves consumers, family members, entrepreneurs, researchers, and service providers in assistive technology transfer solutions networking.

http://www.nmia.com/~riattdev/ The Assistive Technology Resource Alliance (ATRA) is a resource for participants in the market for assistive technology. ATRA was formed by the Research Institute for Assistive and Training Technologies at the University of New Mexico, Sandia National Laboratories, and Laguna Industries, Inc., in conjunction with the New Mexico Technology Deployment Pilot Project. ATRA links assistive technology product developers and entrepreneurs with technologists, investors, policy makers, and consumers, and assists users in deciding needs, as well as finding new product ideas, new technologies, funding sources, and key market information.

http://users.aol.com/dreamms/main.htm DREAMMS for Kids, Inc. (Developmental Research for the Effective

Advancement of Memory and Motor Skills), is a nonprofit parent and professional service agency specializing in assistive technology related research, development, and information dissemination. DREAMMS shares information for facilitating the use of computers, assistive technologies, and quality instructional technologies for students and youth with special needs in schools, homes, and the community. The services of this group include newsletters, individually prepared Tech Paks, and special programs titled Computers for Kids and Tools for Transition.

http://www2.apple.com/disability/welcome.html This Web site by Apple Computer, Inc., presents MAP, the Mac Access Passport, a tool that helps consumers and professionals discover assistive technology solutions for Macintosh computers. MAP is an on-line version of the Mac Access Passport that provides information about the kinds of products that make it possible for persons who have a disability to use a Macintosh computer. Users can download the latest version of Apple's product database, link directly with major organizations and manufacturers, and find a collection of access software programs from Apple.

http://www.austin.ibm.com/sns/index.html or http://www.austin.ibm.com/sns/snsvision.html IBM Special Needs Systems developed this Web page to enhance the employability, education, and quality of life of people who have disabilities. Under their Independence Series trademark, IBM has developed a number of assistive devices and software tools that make the computer more accessible for persons with disabilities. Visitors to this Web page have access to information about the variety of products IBM has to offer and information on where to receive assistance with IBM technology tools.

http://interwork.sdsu.edu/ablenet.html This Web site is managed by ABLE.NET, whose goal is to foster a dynamic exchange of ideas and lifelong learning opportunities. This site provides a great deal of information covering a wide range of ability and disability management system components. This site also allows ABLE.NET to support its goal of providing networking among interested students, people with disabilities, and professionals. Examples of some topics of interest available at this Web site are "Forces that Sabotage Return to Work," a chapter from the book *Return to Work by Design: Managing the Human and Financial Costs of Disability* by Gene Dent (1990); "Creating A World of Opportunities Through Telecommunication Teleconference Text;" Links to On-line Disability Information Resources; Legal Issues, Americans with Disabilities Act Legislation; and Rehabilitation Options, i.e., Re-employment, Job Retention and Medical Separation.

http://www.aten.ocps.k12.fl.us/ The Assistive Technology Educational Network (ATEN) provides a variety of services and information, such as the ATEN CHAT ROOM, which allows users to leave messages, add messages, chat live with someone concerning assistive technology, and join monthly conferences on-line. It also provides a catalog of switches that includes specs, ordering information, and color pictures of the devices. Each month ATEN describes a new device that may be useful for persons with disabilities, including statistics, pricing, and ordering information.

http://www.ari.net/resna/ The Rehabilitation Engineering and Assistive Technology Society of North America (RESNA) is an interdisciplinary association for the advancement of rehabilitation and assistive technologies. This Web page provides a number of services, including RESNA Government Relations, which allows visitors to track legislation and e-mail congressional representatives about important disability legislation; Career Opportunities in Assistive Technology, which helps visitors find an assisitive technology job with the RESNA Job Bank or post a listing to find candidates for a specific job; and a technical assistance grant home page.

http://gopher.usdoj.gov/crt/ada/ada-home.html This Web page is a compilation of Web resources relating to the Americans with Disabilities Act. The information is categorized under the following 10 subject areas that are then linked to many other Web pages: Americans with Disabilities Act Home Page; Americans with Disabilities Act; Americans with Disabilities Act: Q&A; ADA Title II Technical Assistance Manual; ADA Title II Technical Assistance Manual Supplement; ADA Title III Technical Assistance Manual; ADA Title III Technical Assistance Manual Supplement; Nondiscrimination on the Basis of Disability in State and Local Government Services; Part 36–Nondiscrimination Based on Disability by Public Accommodations and in Commercial Facilities; and ADA Information on the Gopher.

http://abe.www.ecn.purdue.edu/ABE/Extension/BNG/ The Breaking New Ground (BNG) Resource Center is located in Purdue University's Department of Agricultural and Biological Engineering. It is internationally recognized as the primary source for information and resources on rehabilitation technology for persons working in agriculture. This Web page provides visitors with the following information: publications and resources available; information on the National AgrAbility Project; National Conference on Rural Assistive Technology; BNG programs and activities (Summary); and links to disability resources.

http://www.gsa.gov/coca/law_pol.htm This Web page is maintained by the Clearinghouse on Computer Accommodation. It provides information on legislation and policies important to people with disabilities. The managers of this site plan to post the text of all disability-related laws and policies.

http://www.closingthegap.com/rd.html Closing the Gap is an organization that focuses on technology for persons with disabilities through its newsletter, annual conference, and Web site. One publication, *The Resource Directory*, is a guide to thousands of commercially available hardware and software products and organizations that serve people with special needs. This print guide provides complete information for the consumer, such as product listings that include descriptions, price information, and system requirements. Other features of this directory include a software and hardware matrix and a producer directory containing contact information of the producers.

http://www.cais.net/naric//index.html The National Rehabilitation Information Center (NARIC) is a library and information center on disability and rehabilitation. This center is funded by the National Institute on Disability and Rehabilitation Research. NARIC collects and disseminates the results of federally funded research projects. The document collection, which includes commercially published books, journal articles, and audiovisuals, grows at a rate of 250 new documents per month. NARIC allows visitors to contact information specialists who can help them answer questions or locate information.

http://www.goodnet.com/~onaroll/ On A Roll is a live, weekly syndicated radio talk show on disability lifestyle issues. This program airs Sunday evenings from 7 to 8 p.m. Eastern time, and the Web page provides information on how to locate the broadcast in different parts of the country.

http://www.yuri.org/webable/index.html WebABLE! is a directory for disability-related Internet resources. The WebABLE! Web site is part of the Yuri Rubinsky Insight Foundation Web site and has a search engine that allows visitors to locate information in its directory of Internet resources.

http://www.ahs.uwo.ca/TETRA/ Tetra is an organization that recruits skilled volunteer engineers and technicians to create assistive devices for people with disabilities. It assists in providing solutions to daily living problems of persons with disabilities. Tetra recruits volunteer engineers, design technicians, and health professionals to work one to one with their clients who have disabilities and to make assistive aids or modifications to their environment.

Laboratory–Practicum Activities

▶ 1. List three goals you will achieve in the next 2 months to enhance your understanding of technology for individuals with severe and physical disabilities. Use technology to develop your goals, to describe how you will achieve these goals, and to manage the achievement of the goals.

▶ 2. Search the Internet and World Wide Web for technology plans for individuals with severe and physical disabilities posted by different school districts. Compare and contrast these plans and share your findings with your peers and course instructor.

▶ 3. Collaborate with your peers to compile a list of technology-related resources (e.g., organizations, printed materials, Web sites and pages) that can be used by professionals in special education and inclusive settings for meeting the needs of individuals with severe and physical disabilities. Use the information listed in this and other chapters as a starting point, but identify additional resources. Create a database to store this information and share it with your peers and course instructor.

▶ 4. Collaborate with your peers to interview elementary-level general educators, special educators, and other professionals working with individuals with severe and physical disabilities in special education and inclusive settings. Have these professionals describe (a) how they are planning and implementing technology programs and the strengths and weaknesses and (b) the resources they use to achieve collaborative teaching–learning outcomes. Compare and contrast the descriptions and share your findings with your peers and course instructor.

▶ 5. Collaborate with your peers to interview secondary-level general educators, special educators, and other professionals working with individuals with severe and physical disabilities in special education and inclusive settings. Have these professionals describe (a) how they are planning and implementing technology programs and the strengths and weaknesses and (b) the resources they use to achieve collaborative teaching–learning outcomes. Compare and contrast the descriptions and share your findings with your peers and course instructor.

▶ 6. Collaborate with your peers to identify two fellow students who are physically challenged and use technology for home, school, and community purposes. Ask these individuals if they would speak during a class period about the duration and nature of their challenge(s); the impact of their challenge(s), particularly in school settings; and a historical overview of their use of technology. If these individuals do not want to speak to the class, seek their permission and conduct interviews to secure the above information. Compare and contrast the presentation or interview descriptions and share your findings with your peers and course instructor.

References

Adam, J. A. (1994). Technology combats disabilities. *IEEE Spectrum, 31*, 24–26.

Adams, K. D., Pon, C., & Blois, T. (1993). An environment for control assessment. *Proceedings of Resna Conference: Engineering the ADA: From Vision to Reality with Technology, USA, 93*, 68–70.

Angelo, D. H., & Goldstein, H. (1990). Effects of a pragmatic teaching strategy for requesting information by communication board users. *Journal of Speech and Hearing Disorders, 55*, 231–243.

Apple computer resources in special education rehabilitation. (1988). Park Allen, TX: DLM/Teaching Resources.

Bigge, J. L. (1991). *Teaching individuals with physical and multiple disabilities* (3rd ed.), New York: Macmillan.

Brown, J. S., Collins, A., & Duguid, P. (1989). Situated cognition and the culture of learning. *Educational Researcher, 18*, 32–41.

Cognition and Technology Group at Vanderbilt. (1993). Integrated media: Toward a theoretical framework for utilizing their potential. *Journal of Special Education Technology, 12*, 71–85.

Cognition and Technology Group at Vanderbilt. (1994). The relationship between situated cognition and anchored instruction: A response to Tripp. *Educational Technology, 34*(8), 28–32.

Cook, R. E., Tessier, A., & Klein, M. D. (1996). *Adapting early childhood curricula for children in inclusive settings* (4th ed.). Columbus, OH: Merrill.

Dever, R. B., & Knapczyk, D. R. (1997). *Teaching persons with mental retardation: A model for curriculum development and teaching.* Madison, WI: Brown & Benchmark.

Eubank, C. S., & Latchman, H. A. (1992). Communication and control electronics for the disabled. *Proceedings of Resna Conference: Towering Achievements, USA, 92*, 507–509.

Griffin, M. M. (1995). You can't get there from here: Situated learning, transfer, and map skills. *Contemporary Educational Psychology, 20*, 65–87.

Hasselbring, T. S., Goin, L. I., & Bransford, J. D. (1991, May). *Integrated media: Toward a theoretical framework for utilizing their potential.* Paper presented at The Multimedia Technology Seminar, Washington, DC.

Hedberg, J., & Alexander, S. (1994). Virtual reality in education: Defining researchable issues. *Educational Media International, 31*, 214–220.

Individuals with Disabilities Education Act of 1990, 20 U.S.C. § 1400 *et seq.*

Langone, J. (1990). *Teaching students with mild and moderate learning problems.* Needham Heights, MA: Allyn & Bacon.

Lewis, R. B. (1993). *Special education technology: Classroom applications.* Pacific Grove, CA: Brooks/Cole.

Marsden, R., McGillis, G., & Murray, H. (1992). Adapting the Macintosh to become a flexible living and work aid. *Proceedings of Resna Conference: Towering Achievements, USA, 92*, 561–563.

Olson, J. L., & Platt, J. M. (1996). *Teaching children and adolescents with special needs* (2nd ed). Columbus, OH: Merrill.

Parette, H. P., Hofmann, A., & VanBiervliet, A. (1994). The professional's role in obtaining funding for assistive technology for infants and toddlers with disabilities. *Teaching Exceptional Children, 26*, 22–28.

Polloway, E. A., & Patton, J. R. (1997). *Strategies for teaching learners with special needs* (6th ed.). Columbus, OH: Merrill.

Rivera, D. P., & Smith, D. D. (1997). *Teaching students with learning and behavior problems* (3rd ed.). Needham Heights, MA: Allyn & Bacon.

Scheiderman, H. (1994). *Environmental controls* (Report No. EC 303 271). Washington, DC: Department of Education. (ERIC Document Reproduction Service No. ED 373 502)

Stefanelli, L. (1994). Defie: An intelligent and flexible integrated environment for disabled and elderly people. *Proceedings of Resna Conference: Tuning in to the 21st Century Through Assistive Technology, USA, 94,* 420–422.

Suddath, C., & Susnik, J. (1991). *Augmentative communication devices.* Reston, VA: Council for Exceptional Children, Center for Special Education Technology.

Thomas, C. H., & Patton, J. R. (1994). Characteristics of individuals with milder forms of retardation. In M. Beirne-Smith, J. R. Patton, & R. Ittenbach (Eds.), *Mental retardation* (4th ed., pp. 203–240). New York: Macmillan.

Thomas, G. E. (1996). *Teaching students with mental retardation: A life goal curriculum planning approach.* Columbus, OH: Merrill.

Tripp, S. D. (1993). Theories, traditions, and situated learning. *Educational Technology, 33*(3), 71–77.

Turnbull, A., Turnbull, R., Shank, M., & Leal, D. (1999). *Exceptional lives: Education in today's school* (2nd ed.). Upper Saddle River, NJ: Prentice-Hall.

Vaughn, S., Bos, C. S., & Schumm, J. S. (1997). *Teaching mainstreamed, diverse, and at-risk students in the general education classroom.* Needham Heights, MA: Allyn & Bacon.

Volunteers for Medical Engineering. (n.d.) *Future home: Independent living through technology.* Baltimore: Montebello Hospital.

Westling, D. L., & Fox, L. (1995). *Teaching students with severe disabilities.* Englewood Cliffs, NJ: Prentice-Hall.

Walczak, F. R. (1999). Technology integration redux. *Converge, 2*(1), 52–53.

Whitehead, A. N. (1929). *The aims of education.* New York: Macmillan.

Young, M. F. (1993). Instructional design for situated learning. *Educational Technology Research and Development, 41,* 43–58.

Chapter 12

✢   ✢   ✢

Technology for Individuals Who Are Deaf, Hard of Hearing, Blind, and Partially Sighted

Ronald R. Kelly
National Technical Institute for the Deaf
Rochester Institute of Technology, Rochester, New York

A remarkable evolution in technology applicable to education has occurred over the past 30 years (see "Anytime, anywhere" 1998, and http://www.microsoft.com/education/k12/aal/), particularly for educational programs serving students with hearing or vision loss. In discussing the technological advances in education for students who are deaf since the 1960s, Stepp (1994) described four stages or phases as a framework for understanding these changes. He categorized the first stage as Educators' Technology, during which it was primarily the policy makers of the schools—the administrators and supervisors who were usually the ones involved in selecting instructional materials—along with senior officials of state and national educational agencies who initiated an interest and awareness of the technology potential for both the teachers and students in programs serving learners who are deaf, hard of hearing, blind, and partially sighted. The second stage focused more on a Teachers' Technology, in which teachers actively selected, adapted, designed, and produced media and materials tailored to the particular needs of their students and to their own teaching methods. This trend was advanced by the development of instructional media centers in the schools. During this period, educators grew increasingly convinced that if substantive, long-term learning was the goal, then students must also be actively involved and encouraged to take a greater responsibility for their own learning.

Such thinking logically gave rise to the third stage, which Stepp referred to as Learners' Technology, where the profession began to focus realistically on the benefits of making the students more active partners in the educational process by having them use the media and initiate some of the directions of their own learning. Finally, Stepp referred to the fourth and current stage of technological change that is occurring in education as Communicators' Technology. This stage focuses on using the available technology as a means of self-expression and reaching out to other people to interact with ideas, information, and different knowledge bases.

The concept of students with hearing or vision loss as interactive communicators also fits the

Technology permits individuals with a hearing loss to access language-related text and graphics. (Photograph by Carolyn F. Woods)

changing philosophical approach to educational environments. Over the past 15 to 20 years, education has rapidly moved from a self-contained classroom or residential program approach for learners with hearing or vision loss to a mainstreamed concept where these students are integrated in part or fully into general education programs. More recently, the concept of full inclusive education has emerged, which goes beyond the concept of mainstreaming as practiced in the schools. The philosophy of inclusion is analogous to teaching a foreign language by immersion (Karmen, 1996). Total immersion in a language is achieved by actually "living the language" in a natural learning environment. Similarly,

> inclusion is immersion—a way to "eat, sleep and think" the language of childhood and development. Inclusion allows children to learn and practice appropriate skills and socially acceptable behaviors among other children, who are themselves ongoing learners. By providing a natural setting for the "language" of childhood and developmental growth, we offer all children the chance to learn together, to develop their own "vocabulary and idioms," and to be accepted because they have been part of the learning community all along. To acquire fluency in life, one needs practice with the rhythms, rules and sounds of life's dialogues. Instead of being misunderstood foreigners in a strange land, all children are natives in the culture of inclusion. (Karmen, 1996)

Clearly, a communicators' technology approach through the use of computer networking, on-line access to information, and interactive electronic messaging is a potential "equalizer" for all participants in a learning (or working) environment and offers excellent technical support to the educational implementation of inclusion and mainstreaming. Subsequent examples of technology applications in this chapter illustrate the equal participatory effects of interactive computer technology.

The advances in personal computers and software since the early 1980s have made the implementation of a communicators' technology a real-

ity in school environments and in the daily social and work lives of individuals who are deaf, hard of hearing, blind, or partially sighted. The personal computer is clearly the current technological vehicle of choice to deliver instruction and provide many important learning activities for students who have a hearing or vision loss. However, the use of the computer, like all other instructional delivery media, is not a panacea that will automatically solve the learning problems of individuals who experience substantial educational and developmental challenges. For example, in spite of the concerted educational emphasis on developing language and communication skills for individuals who are deaf, those who graduate from high school continue to have, on average, reading skills below fifth-grade level (Allen, 1986). Furthermore, Lowenbraun and Thompson (1989) concluded that students who are deaf "on the average do not perform at an academic level near or equal to that of their normally-hearing peers in any setting, and that the absolute magnitude of difference increases with age" (p. 53). The challenge for teachers, service providers, and parents is how to best use technology to address the developmental, educational, and interactive needs of individual learners who are deaf, hard of hearing, blind, or partially sighted.

The logical perspective for computer applications within an educational context is that a computer, like all other instructional and learning technologies, is a tool to be used according to a purposeful design and outcome. Thus, the selection and application of goals, purposeful intent, structure, content, objectives, and evaluative criteria within the context of a curriculum and related learning theories, as well as drawing from appropriate research knowledge bases, are critical to the successful implementation of computers as a useful educational tool. As Clark (1983, 1985, 1994), Lumsdaine (1963), and Schramm (1977), eloquently argued, it is the methods (i.e., instructional strategies, goals, objectives, and content) that influence learning and enhance achievement, not the delivery vehicle or medium.

Unfortunately, how to apply computer technology to the developmental and educational processes of individuals who have a hearing or vision loss in order to maximize the benefits for instruction and learning is not readily transparent (Cronin, 1992). Furthermore, the educational potential of computer technology may not offer equal benefits to individuals who cannot functionally read or process information readily. A successful match of a learner with appropriate instructional strategies and methodologies requires an understanding of both the individual's needs and the capabilities of computers. Successful applications of computer technology to meet the specific needs of learners who have a hearing or vision loss require the integrated insight, knowledge, and creativity of parents, teachers, instructional designers, service providers, and the individual learners themselves.

Individuals with a Loss of Hearing or Vision

Students in the same age range who are deaf, hard of hearing, blind, or partially sighted often have a wide range of abilities, which complicates the educational strategies for teachers and other service providers. For example, a classroom serving either a group of students who are deaf and hard of hearing or a group of students who are blind with a relatively small pupil–teacher ratio in the range of five to eight students to one teacher generally provides far more instructional complexity for a teacher than does a general education classroom with a larger number of students who can be organized into more heterogeneous groupings for instruction. For all students who are deaf, hard of hearing, blind, or partially sighted, the complexity of variables that influence individual performances include: (a) age at onset, (b) severity or degree of hearing or vision loss, (c) causal factor of hearing or vision loss, (d) multiplicity of exceptional conditions, (e) timing of earliest developmental or educational interventions, (f) type of family support and home environment, (g) cognitive potential, and (h) chronological age (see Lowenfeld, 1981; Myklebust, 1964; Warren, 1977). When educators of these students discuss the need for individualized instruction, their perspective is based on practical necessity.

Persons Who Are Deaf or Hard of Hearing

Hearing loss introduces complexity to the educational and developmental processes of an individual. The implications of a hearing loss varies "from person to person and from one circumstance to another. This makes it difficult to define rigorously what is meant by terms such as hearing loss, deaf, and hard of hearing" (Myklebust, 1964, p. 3). Furthermore, the usefulness of the various terms and definitions "depends on our purposes, and the important purpose for which those terms are useful are social, educational, and medical" (Davis, 1970, p. 84). In terms of hearing levels,

> we find a zone of uncertainty from 70 to 90 dB (ISO). . . . Within this zone some individuals are socially deaf, but more of them are merely very hard of hearing. . . . We propose to confine the term deafness to hearing-threshold levels for speech greater than 92 dB (ISO). A good reason for selecting this particular boundary is that the most authoritative medical rule . . . reads "if the average hearing threshold level at 500, 1000, and 2000 Hz is over 92 dB (ISO), the handicap for hearing everyday speech should be considered total." Our criterion thus has a medical sanction in a social and economic context. (Davis, 1970, p. 84)

A long-standing definition of hearing loss was provided by the Committee on Nomenclature of the Conference of Executives of American Schools for the Deaf (1938). According to this definition, the deaf are "those in whom the sense of hearing is non-functional for the ordinary purpose of life." This committee classified the deaf into two groups: (a) congenitally deaf; or those who are born deaf, and (b) adventitiously deaf, or those who are born with normal hearing but in whom the sense of hearing becomes nonfunctional later through illness or accident. However, when planning educational interventions, Myklebust (1964) recommended that educators adopt a more useful definition of students with hearing loss. According to Myklebust, persons who are deaf are those whose hearing loss has precluded normal acquisition of language, whereas persons who are hard of hearing are those whose hearing loss is not great enough to prevent language acquisition. Silverman and Lane (1970, p. 386) included in their functional definition of children who are deaf those who have not developed the expressive and receptive skills of communication before the onset of deafness. This means they cannot talk or understand the speech of others as do children of the same age with normal hearing. Also included in this definition are those children who have acquired some of these skills of communication before the onset of deafness but whose incomplete language skills still necessitate additional educational interventions and techniques.

The most obvious effect of a hearing loss is the negative impact on the development of expressive and receptive communication skills and patterns of language. Both are critical components of human development and the educational processes. Clearly, a hearing loss has considerable implications for learning, personal development, and social interaction. "The loss of hearing sensitivity in young children alters the character of their linguistic intake, which in turn interacts with their development and maturation and affects the acquisition of language (and speech) to the degree that many deaf children enter adolescence and adulthood without the ability to communicate effectively in English" (Bochner, 1982, p. 107). This situation, in turn, influences the educational experiences of individuals with hearing loss:

> Since academic subjects have required English as a mode of instruction, the greater instructional emphasis has always been placed on teaching English. As a result, deaf children have had less exposure to the amount and quality of school subjects than have their English-speaking peers. . . . The fourth-grade achievement levels exhibited by the average deaf high school graduate could be considered a result of both English deficits and a lack of knowledge and information about the world. (Hofmeister & Drury, 1982, p. 359)

Language skills, conceptual development, communication, and academic content are critical areas to consider in planning appropriate experiences for learners who are deaf or hard of hearing. There are also important implications for individualized instruction and independent study.

Persons Who Are Blind or Have Low Vision

The only common feature of individuals who are blind or partially sighted is vision loss. Jan, Freeman, and Scott (1977) noted that there is no universally accepted definition of blindness—over 65 different definitions of visual loss exist throughout the word. From an ophthalmologic perspective,

> visual impairment or visual disability can be used to describe a visual limitation of 20/70 or worse. The "20/70" refers to the diagnosis made by using the Snellen chart; it means that the person could see no more at a distance of 20 feet than someone with adequate vision can see at a distance of 70 feet. Those persons whose visual acuity falls between 20/70 and 20/200 are considered *partially sighted* and therefore, deserving of rehabilitative services. . . . The clients in a rehabilitation setting whose visual acuity falls between 20/200 and 20/500 are described as having *partial vision, low vision,* or *useful vision.* Clients with 20/500 or worse . . . are termed *totally blind or having no useful vision.* (Vander Kolk, 1981, p. 2)

An ophthalmologic definition is not always adequate for educational or rehabilitative purposes. Individuals with visual loss may vary in their abilities to use the existing sight they have (Lowenfeld, 1981). Vander Kolk (1981) observed that two persons with diagnosed 20/200 vision may function in different ways. One individual may be able to move about independently, read regular printed materials, and function similarly to a normally sighted person. The other individual, however, may have trouble reading regular print, will not be able to see at night, and may function as if totally blind. Individuals such as these two may also vary considerably in their ability to use low-vision assistive aids. Certainly, there is a discrepancy between measured vision and how an individual translates it into functional vision. Functional use of impaired vision is in part due to the interaction of the personal variables that influence performance. As Lowenfeld (1981) noted, success for people with visual loss "is basically dependent upon the strengths of each individual" (p. 229).

Planning appropriate educational experiences for people with visual loss requires individualization and independent learning activities. Six major concerns that Chorniak (1977) suggested should be considered in planning learning experiences for students with visual loss are individual differences, physical encounter, stimulation, structure (wholeness and relationships), reinforcement, and independence. Lowenfeld (1981) cited similar educational principles: individualization, concreteness, unified instruction, additional stimulation, and self-activity. Although technological advances in media, aids, tools, and equipment have made learning more efficient for students who are totally blind and partially sighted (Chorniak, 1977), there is a continuing need to improve the instructional and learning efficiency of the educational environment. Persons with vision loss need an extraordinary learning environment.

Individuals Who Are Deaf–Blind

The combination of losses of both hearing and vision creates even greater instructional complexity for parents, educators, and other service providers. The dual situation of blindness and deafness is relatively rare; it is estimated that there are fewer than 14,000 children who are deaf–blind below the age of 21 in the United States (see Hardman, Drew, & Egan, 1999). Multiple sensory losses, particularly from birth or prior to near-complete language acquisition, necessitate comprehensive and systematic educational interventions if even the slightest gains are to be made related to educational, personal, and social development. Educational planning is

complicated by the fact that functionally defining deaf–blindness is influenced by a variety of factors. Dinsmore (cited in Warren, 1977) suggested five possible categories:

> 1) those children who have had vision and hearing for several years, so that verbal and visual memory are available, 2) those who have been deaf from early in life but have had vision for some years, 3) those who have been blind from very early in life, but have had auditory function for some years, 4) those who have been both visually and auditorily impaired from early in life, and 5) those who have variously combined partial losses. (p. 174)

To further complicate matters, professional perspective influences one's understanding of deaf–blindness, and thus has the potential for affecting the educational planning and subsequent implementation. Warren (1977) observed that, because

> those who are primarily interested in deafness tend to view such children as deaf with the additional handicap of visual loss, while those primarily interested in blindness tend to regard the hearing impairment as secondary . . . the child with the dual handicap may fail to receive a program that is geared optimally to his capabilities. (p. 174)

It continues to be difficult to say whether computer applications offer the same potential for individuals who are deaf–blind as they do for persons who have only a hearing or a vision loss. The continuing problem is that the primary way people interface with a computer currently requires a combination of sight, sound, and touch, and the degree of functionality of either vision or hearing of a person who is deaf–blind will determine the potential use of a computer. Thus, rather than generalized applicability, computer applications to meet the needs of people who are deaf–blind fall into the realm of individual case situations.

Computer applications are particularly beneficial to individualization, structure, unified instruction, and independent learning. Because of continuing technological advances, personal computer applications provide benefit to people with vision loss in the educational, home, and work environments. Table 12.1 lists general computer applications for people with low vision or blindness and for those who are deaf or hard of hearing. Detailed information regarding these applications and concepts are provided later in this chapter.

Some Technological Considerations

Current, state-of-the-art software requires higher performing computers (also see Chapter 2). Although the technical definition of computer performance remains a fuzzy and debatable area, for educational applications the following areas of consideration are generally sufficient: (a) clock speed of the processor—select a computer with a processing chip with a clock speed of 300 MHz or faster; (b) amount of random access memory (RAM)—while 32 MB of RAM is currently adequate to run most software programs, more optimum software performance occurs by increasing RAM to 48 to 64 MB or higher (one should always check the software manufacturer's requirements for RAM); (c) storage capacity of the hard drive—select at least 3 to 5 GB of storage memory; (d) CD-ROM or DVD-ROM—select a CD-ROM drive of at least 24× or higher speed; (e) modem/fax—select an internal or external modem that is at least 56 kbps capable (even though current regulations limit download speeds to 53 kbps) with x2 technology; and (f) size of the display monitor—whereas a 15-inch monitor may be adequate for most applications, one should consider selecting a larger 17- or 21-inch display, particularly if enlarged fonts are to be used for individuals with visual loss. One should also consider an ergonomic keyboard if the physical needs of a specific individual warrant it. These considerations apply whether one is looking at a Macintosh PowerPC environment or a Windows PC environment. Finally, the operating systems should be as up-to-date as possible (currently, at least OS 8.1 or higher for a Macintosh and Windows 95 or 98 for a PC).

More specifically, when selecting computer equipment for individuals with visual loss, the prime considerations are the interface capabilities with the assistive devices required for the individual (e.g., speech synthesizer, large-print displays for the video screen and printer, and letter recognition for converting text to speech). The availability of appropriate software for the computer equipment under consideration should also be a principal criterion in hardware selection.

Table 12.1. General Computer Applications for Individuals Who Are Blind, Low Vision, Deaf, and Hard of Hearing

Individuals	General Computer Applications
Low Vision	Computer-assisted instruction (CAI), information access via Internet and CD-ROM, electronic messaging, fax, large print for both video displays and printers, and speech synthesis
Blind	Speech synthesis, hard copy braille, refreshable (paperless) braille, text to braille, braille to text, text to tactile equivalent, CAI, information access via Internet and CD-ROM, electronic messaging, and fax
Deaf or Hard of Hearing	Language development, writing skills, telecommunications, interactive video, C-Print real-time graphics, CAI, information access via Internet and CD-ROM, electronic messaging, multiuser conferencing, and fax

For individuals with hearing loss, interface and compatibility considerations are not generally necessary for educational computer applications because assistive devices are not often involved. Thus, selecting computer equipment for students with hearing loss is similar to selecting equipment for any typical user. Special considerations for computer applications with students who have hearing loss may be necessary if the implementation requires a sophisticated and complex systems design such as interactive video or specific research and related training.

The evaluation criteria for selecting computer hardware and software depend on each individual learner's specific needs (also see Chapter 5). In educational settings, selection could begin with the needs generated by the integrative educational plan and proceed from there. The computer applications illustrated in this chapter should serve as a point of departure for planning computer applications. However, the nature of serving educational needs of students with hearing or vision loss often necessitates extensive individualization.

Specific Technology for Persons Who Are Deaf and Hard of Hearing

With regard to learners who are deaf and hard of hearing, it is not surprising that computer applications continue to focus on their unique educational needs related to language and communication. Such computer applications also address the needs for independent learning, individual initiative, responsibility, and self-reliance. Specifically, the unique educational needs of learners with hearing loss are reflected in computer applications in the areas of basic skills (e.g., reading comprehension, writing techniques, mathematics instruction), sign language instruction and practice, speech reading activities, auditory listening skills, assessment of skill levels in the above areas, electronic messaging, fax, and telephone communication. Examples of computer applications with learners who are deaf and hard of hearing are described below.

Student Captioning of Video Content Using Computers

A recent innovative application of computer technology involves students who are deaf and hard of hearing in writing captioned text for video materials, an activity that enables them to practice and develop their writing skills, language, and content organization. From 1991 to 1996, the Corporation for Public Broadcasting WGBH National Center for Accessible Media (WGBH-NCAM) in Boston and the National Technical Institute for the Deaf (NTID) at Rochester Institute of Technology in Rochester, New York, were involved in two federally funded projects to examine the implementation feasibility and educational benefits of student-based captioning technology in the classroom for students who are deaf and other students with language needs. The initial student captioning project funded by the U.S. Department of Education, Educational Media, Research, Production, Distribution and Training (No. H026R10009) was conducted from 1991 to 1993, with elementary-level students who are deaf at the TRIPOD program in Burbank, California (see Kelly et al., 1994). The purpose of this project was to have the students translate a series of 40 American Sign Language (ASL) short video stories into English captions.

The second student captioning project funded by the U.S. Department of Education, Office of Special Education Programs (No. H180E30021), was conducted between September 1993 and August 1996 with six schools in the Northeast with students at the elementary, middle school, and secondary levels (Loeterman & Kelly, 1997). The purpose of the second project was to develop instructional units centered around student-based captioning activities. The student-based "do-it-yourself" captioning was done with a captioning workstation that utilized a special collection of technology that included word processing,

Two eighth-grade deaf students working at a captioning workstation. (Photograph courtesy of National Technical Institute for the Deaf)

video, and a character generator for captioning. The students who participated in this project were either deaf and hard of hearing or learning disabled. WGBH-NCAM and NTID collaboratively provided technical support and conducted both qualitative and quantitative evaluative research on the outcomes of these student captioning projects in the classrooms at six school sites (three schools serving students who are deaf and three serving students with learning disabili-

ties, with four school sites in Massachusetts and one each in Connecticut and Western New York).

The student captioning workstation was conceived and developed by WGBH-NCAM. It consists of a personal computer, two VCRs (one for playback and one for recording the student-captioned videotape), a captioning device that allows text to be superimposed onto video, a printer, a video monitor, and an optional camcorder. Briefly, the procedure for using this "do-it-yourself" captioning system is as follows. The students watched videotape material, pausing and reviewing at their own pace. They then used a word processing program to compose their own caption text, either narrating the video, inventing a new script, summarizing the information presented, or transcribing the audio. When finished, they combined their composed text with the video and, using the second VCR, created a captioned videotape. They synchronized and made the captions appear on the video by hitting a designated key on the computer keyboard. Figure 12.1 provides a diagram of the technology used in the captioning workstation. The accompanying photograph shows two students at the

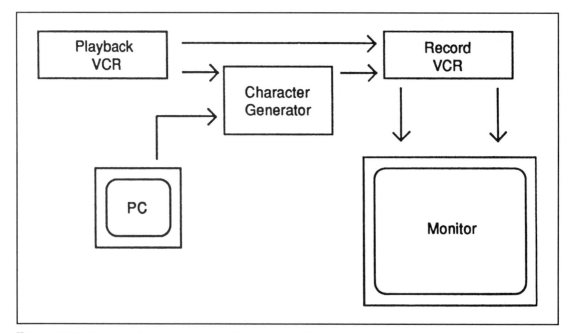

Figure 12.1. Diagram of the captioning workstation technology.

captioning workstation synchronizing and transferring their captioned text onto the video.

Loeterman and Morse (1996) discussed ways that the captioning workstation can be used with students at the upper elementary, middle school, or high school levels. Briefly, this included the following:

- Using precise, descriptive language to give directions

- Applying language learned in any content area to caption video materials in that area

- Translating and captioning a personal story

- Dramatizing and captioning math word problems

Teachers can use student captioning technology for numerous purposes that require writing and composition. The captioning suggestions listed above and the following examples can be modified for use with any students who can benefit from improving their written English skills. As you read about the various approaches to learning with captioning technology, consider the purpose of the activity, the actual tasks of the children, the teacher's role and the degree to which the activity promotes independence, and the active learning and interaction among peers or between students and their teacher.

For some of the student captioning activities, the production of a captioned videotape is critical to the approach and to the motivation of the students; for others, actually putting one's text over the video is secondary to the process of creating the text, and may even be unnecessary depending on a range of personal, instructional, and environmental factors in the classroom. The following examples of purposes for student captioning activities are also adapted from Loeterman and Morse (1996).

Use Text To Narrate

Captions can serve as a narration track in much the same way that audio is used to narrate a TV program. Students can also create their own video to narrate by working with the teacher to create a storyboard and plan the production. When the video provides a topic for writing and a loose organization of themes, students make their own decisions about what to say and what aspects of the video are pertinent and decide, for example, whether to describe the action as an outside observer or to provide editorial commentary. They also need to decide how much to focus on broad themes versus interesting details. At the beginning of the writing process, the students brainstorm with classmates or their teacher to help formulate and organize their ideas. They follow strategies typically used in process writing, including creating a draft, peer conference, and self-correction and revision, repeating the steps as necessary. Often students work collaboratively with a peer throughout the process, working on turn taking and cooperation. The teacher can use the captioning feedback session as an opportunity to focus on any aspects of language that individual students need to work on. When the videotape is to be shown to an audience (i.e., classmates, others in the school, or parents), the students are motivated to create the best possible product. The teacher can take advantage of this motivation to guide the students regarding the more mechanical aspects of their writing that need attention.

Invent a Script

Using silent video in which the dialogue among the characters is left to the imagination of the viewer, students are free to be quite creative with their captions. Their focus is twofold: to create a flow of written language that makes sense in the context of the video and to improve the mechanical aspects of writing including spelling, punctuation, and grammar. This approach works well when students are captioning for an eventual audience or working to produce a final product of which they can feel proud.

Summarize or Highlight

Unlike professionally produced captions for television, student-produced captions do not have to be complete sentences or concerned with a one-to-one correspondence between the video and text. Instead captions can be free-form, falling along a continuum. On one end is note taking, in which a student summarizes key information in a presentation (when the presentation is in sign or another oral language, they are instructed *not* to attempt to translate or write word for word but to summarize the meaning). At the other end on the continuum, a student creates captions as a reason to tune into key actions or events in the video (e.g., themes in a narrative from literature). The purpose for this approach is to help the student attend to critical information, retain the information presented, and make sense of it. After captioning, individual students can use their own tape for study purposes. An important role of the teacher is to model beforehand the type of information to be included in the captions. During the captioning process, the teacher is available to clarify information in the video on request. Finally, the teacher should assess whether the captions are on target and provide constructive feedback to the students.

Describe

Students watch the unfolding of an intricate process (e.g., a small structure made from children's colored building blocks). They must use unambiguous language to describe the process step by step so that someone who has not seen the video can understand the process and even re-create it. An important task for the students is to find the most accurate descriptive words that fit. When they work independently, they are forced to locate the appropriate language within their own knowledge bank. Targeted feedback from a teacher is critical to helping students attend to and understand inaccuracies, ambiguities, and inadequate detail in their writing.

Transcribe the Audio

Students with and without hearing impairments carry out audio transcription in different ways. When hearing students transcribe audio, they follow the same process that professional caption writers do when captioning programs for broad-

cast. The focus is on comprehension of the content of the video (e.g., a news program) and on the mechanics of writing. Students who are hard of hearing and oral deaf have also captioned the audio of video, as well as audio that they have written and spoken themselves. The focus of this approach to captioning is, more than other approaches outlined above, on the advance preparation of a script that the students follow as they produce their videotape. The same script is used for captioning, the main purpose of which is to provide access for viewers who may not understand the on-camera speech of the students who are deaf.

Translate from Sign or Other Native Spoken Language to English

Translation can follow one of two paths: students can create a narrative in their native language and caption into English, or students watch someone else's sign or native language presentation and translate this language into English. Either way, this approach to captioning creates opportunities for students who are deaf or who speak English as a second language to think about meaning, structure, and vocabulary in two languages of great importance to them. A primary purpose is to increase students' consciousness of their own language knowledge and enhance that knowledge. Because a student who is deaf can see his or her words superimposed over sign, captioning provides a rare opportunity to consider both languages in a deliberate way. When first introduced to this activity, some students question the purpose of captioning a sign language video when they already understand sign language. However, when given the opportunity to think about captioning the signs (i.e., captions can help others not fluent in understanding sign language) they are extremely proud to provide access to their own language for an English-only speaker. This can help to bridge the signing world at school and the English world at home. The teacher's role in the process is critical but varies in intensity, depending on the age and written English skills of the students. The teacher must be fluent in both languages or the classroom should include adults fluent in both languages. Some students have worked independently, receiving targeted feedback after the captioning session; students with very limited English knowledge have worked side by side with a teacher throughout the process. Either way, this approach to captioning provides fertile ground for dialogue about language.

Captioning technology is available for both the PC Windows and the Macintosh environments. WGBH-NCAM in Boston was collaboratively involved in the development of both captioning systems. For information on this do-it-yourself captioning technology for students and teachers, Universal Learning Technology in Peabody, Massachusetts, should be contacted with regard to software and hardware for both Macintosh and PC Windows. The address is provided at the end of this chapter in the Resources section on Hardware/Software.

Real-Time Graphic Display

Real-time graphic display of speech is another intriguing application of computers to the communication needs of the hearing impaired. Under the leadership of Ross Stuckless at the National Technical Institute for the Deaf (NTID), Rochester Institute of Technology in Rochester, New York, the real-time graphic display was initially developed in 1978 and has been in continuous implementation since 1982, particularly in convocation settings. The system uses a court

Captionist providing C-Print services to a deaf student in a mainstreamed class at Rochester Institute of Technology. (Photograph courtesy of WGBH)

stenographer who enters speech sounds in phonetic shorthand into a minicomputer that regenerates English. The spoken English is then displayed (almost instantaneously) on a television display. Hard-copy text of the spoken lecture or discussion can be printed out for student or participant use (Stuckless, 1983). The concept of real-time graphic display was the foundation for the C-Print technology, which provides computer text display and hard-copy notes for students who are deaf in the general education classroom and is discussed in the following section.

C-Print and Classroom Note Taking

Providing adequate communication for students who are deaf or hard of hearing in mainstreamed classrooms is a complex and challenging task. One recent innovative and practical form of support developed by researchers at NTID is a computer-aided system for transcribing speech to print, called the NTID Computer-Aided Transcription System or C-Print. As described by Stinson and Stuckless (1998), the C-Print system has a hearing operator who transcribes the spoken lecture on an IBM-compatible laptop computer using a commercially available word processing program, WordPerfect, and an abbreviation software program, Productivity Plus. As the lecturer talks, the operator types a combination of abbreviations and regular words. For the abbreviations, Productivity Plus searches the dictionary for the equivalent full word and displays it on the screen. The text is saved as a word processing file that can be corrected and printed later. As McKee, Stinson, and Giles (1996) reported, due to the speed of speech normally used by college instructors (approximately 150 words per minute), the C-Print system cannot provide word-for-word transcription. To use the C-Print system of word processing software and the abbreviation program, procedures for training classroom captionists have been developed. The evaluation procedures used for this practical classroom computer transcription system has been reported in detail elsewhere (see Everhart, Stinson, McKee, &

Giles, 1996). In addition to providing a hard-copy printout of the spoken text, the C-Print system also provides a real-time text display that a student who is deaf or hard of hearing can read on a second laptop computer or a TV monitor to understand what is happening in the classroom (McKee et al., 1996).

The C-Print system is a practical and affordable approach to providing information access for students who are deaf and hard of hearing in both inclusive and other classroom settings. It is more cost effective than a steno system for providing real-time text display in the classroom. With a steno-based approach, there are the limitations of having a small number of trained and qualified people in courtroom stenography and the high cost of paying for these individuals, especially when the service is being provided to a single student in a general education classroom (Stinson & Stuckless, 1998).

The initial development of the C-Print system with deaf and hard of hearing college students was supported by a 3-year grant for the period December 1993 to November 1996 (No. H180J 30011) from the U.S. Department of Education, Office of Special Education and Rehabilitative Services. A second grant for the period December 1996 to November 1999 from the U.S. Department of Education (No. H180U60004) is currently supporting the evaluation of the C-Print system with students in inclusive and mainstreamed high school settings.

For additional information on the C-Print system, contact the National Technical Institute for the Deaf at Rochester Institute of Technology in Rochester, New York. The address is provided in Appendix I.

Before leaving this topic, it should be noted that others have also used notebook computers for note-taking purposes in inclusive and mainstreamed educational environments. James and Hammersley (1993) reported the use of cable-linked computers in the classroom for both note-taking and interactive communication. Although the note-taking activities were initially implemented in 1991, they are based on the Phones for the Deaf Programme which has been successfully used in Australia since 1985. For the note-taking

process in the classroom, two computers were linked through a lap-link cable. The typist typed all that is said by the teacher or other students on one computer and the complete text is instantly transferred to the screen of the student's computer. If the student who is deaf or hard of hearing cannot understand a particular point, he or she can immediately seek clarification from the note taker via the link. If it is not a note-taking problem, it can be referred immediately to the teacher.

Computer Networks in the Teaching–Learning Environment

Computer networks for interactive communication and writing have been used in a number of educational environments to develop literacy skills. The Electronics Networks for Interaction (ENFI) Project began at Gallaudet University in 1985 under the leadership of Trent Batson and others in the English department (Peyton, 1991). This creative use of a computer network as the forum for interactive and collaborative writing by students who are deaf has been reported in a number of publications (Batson, 1988; Peyton, 1988, 1990, 1991). Briefly, ENFI involves the use of a local area computer network within a classroom for real-time written communication. Each student in the class, as well as the teacher, sits at a computer terminal and types what he or she wants to say into a private area at the bottom of the screen. When ready, students can transmit their message to the entire class with the press of a key, tagged with their name on it. Messages are passed back and forth emulating the dialogue and discussions that might occur in any typical classroom. The computer stores the entire interactive discussion of all participants in the class, and this discussion can be reviewed at any point during the class or printed out in its entirety at the end of class. Students who use ENFI enjoy the interaction and often feel motivated to work more than with other writing approaches (Batson, 1988). The ENFI system has been used with students who are deaf ranging from elementary level to college level. When discussing the elementary-level students, Peyton (1991) noted that writing development in students can be attributed to the conditions for communication that network writing creates. These conditions include the following:

- A nonthreatening social context for writing with other writers from whom students can draw ideas and language

- Both print and signed support for and extension of what students are attempting to write

- The use of print in this context is continuous (at least 40-minute time periods) and long term (for at least a year, and in many cases for several years)

Computer networking has also been used to immerse students at the Lexington School for the Deaf in a print environment devoted to the study of earth science (Reich, Matthews, Goldman, Brienne, & Matthews, 1991). The computer network was used both for instruction and for interaction among the students and with the teachers. E-mail was used to present and review information, as well as to communicate with the individual students. Students used a word processing system to write lab reports and other assignments. As a result of this interactive network approach, students improved their productivity in terms of completing the written assignments and improving the quality of their written work.

The process of writing and interacting via a computer network is clearly a practical and productive computer application, and has been successful with students who are deaf and hard of hearing from elementary through college levels. Furthermore, the utility of computer networks is not limited by topic or academic area. They can be used for interactive communication, exchange of information, and writing pertinent to any academic subject.

Telecommunications

Telecommunication capabilities of the computer and the Internet have provided valuable access and interactive communication benefits for individuals who are deaf and hard of hearing. Mackall (1996) described the uses of the Internet and World Wide Web, along with addresses of listservers relating to individuals who are deaf or hard of hearing. The on-line computer services, e-mail for messaging, and teleconferencing with multiusers have all provided considerable benefit to people with a hearing loss by increasing access to communication and information databases. If used to full advantage, the considerable array of telecommunications technology available to people who are deaf can have a profound effect on their lives (Jensema, 1994). The computer communication technologies not only have the potential to affect the work and social lives of people who are deaf but have language implications as well. Spillers, Heatherly, Kenyon, and Rittenhouse (1994) noted that with the computer environment students practice using written English in practical and highly motivating situations. Furthermore, they develop social skills by conversing with people beyond their own schools and communities and discover the fun of direct, written communication. Electronic forums and e-mail not only support access but also involve immersion into a writing environment.

Interactive Videodisc and CD-ROM (DVD-ROM) Discs

Computer technology has also been critical to advances in using video materials within the teaching and learning environments of learners who are deaf and hard of hearing. While interactive videodisc technology has been used with students with hearing loss for speech and language drill and for sign language instruction since 1978 (Sims & Clymer, 1986; Sims, Scott, & Myers, 1982; Newell, Sims, & Clymer, 1984), the advances in personal computer technology and software have improved educators' abilities to present instructional video materials in an interactive context for student-directed learning (Hanson & Padden, 1989). Videodiscs provide for high-density storage of visual and auditory information with rapid search and access capabilities.

Videodisc material can also be presented in slow motion or by single freeze frame at the direction of the computer software (also see Chapters 2 and 3).

Prinz (1991) used computer and videodisc interactive contexts to address the literacy and language development of young children who were deaf ages 3½ to 12 years of age. This approach involved an adult and child having interactive discourse about computer-presented video material. Through simple commands on an interface keyboard overlay, the corresponding words or phrases were printed and displayed on a large color monitor and appropriate graphics in pictures or signs also were displayed. As a result of this interactive discourse with an adult and videodisc materials, the children in the study demonstrated strong gains in reading and writing new words. They also learned to read and write new sentences and to relate these sentences both to pictorial animation and optionally to sign language.

In another interactive video approach, Hanson and Padden (1989) used a bilingual approach to teach written aspects of English to students whose first language was ASL. The students were all fluent in ASL and ranged from third- to sixth-grade levels. In this bilingual study, the computer software offered the students five activity options: watch a story, read a story, answer questions about a story, write a story, or stop the session. Later they added another option—to caption a story. The students in this study used the answer questions option most, presumably because of the high level of interactivity involved. Furthermore, this study demonstrated the feasibility of using interactive video as a viable format for bilingual language instruction.

Volterra, Pace, Pennacchi, and Corazza (1995) also used interactive videodisc technology for bilingual education of children who were deaf. This approach involved interactive video to access both Italian Sign Language (LIS) and standard written Italian. The Italian students ranged from 6.5 years to 16 years of age. They were initially allowed to freely explore the computer environment and then required to access information in two subsequent learning activi-

ties. The results showed that the ability to compare both LIS and written Italian on the screen simultaneously supported improved reading and writing skills, thus fostering learning processes that contribute to literacy development. Furthermore, the work done on this project enabled the authors to create a new version of this application on CD-ROM, which permitted the inclusion of activities that were initially done outside of the computer environment in the original effort.

Rittenhouse, Spillers, and Kenyon (1993) also discussed videodisc technology as a viable combination of video and computer-based instruction. With videodisc technology, students can readily access and interact with text, audio, and graphics. Furthermore, through software programming the system can talk to students, answer questions, and show video sequences for clarification.

However, the advent of CD-ROM technology and the growing DVD-ROM technology will undoubtedly replace the aging videodisc instructional systems. All the various educational applications of videodisc materials and computer technology that have been conducted to date can now be more easily accomplished with CD-ROM and DVD-ROM discs for use in a special drive installed in computers. The digitized information on these media presents images, sound, and text with the same ease of access as the videodisc technology, and CD-ROMs are increasingly available with a wide range of content material. Furthermore, CD-ROM burners are now available and economically within reach so that CD-ROMs can be produced locally for educational purposes.

An interesting use of CD-ROM technology to support language and communication of children who are deaf is described by Stewart, Heeter, and Dickson (1996). The Personal Communicator is a CD-ROM software program designed to enhance the interactions of children who are deaf and their hearing peers. The software includes a chat screen, dictionary, writer's notebook, conversation recorder, and sign language playroom. This CD-ROM software would seem particularly beneficial to an inclusive educational environment.

Specific Technology for Persons Who Are Blind or Have Low Vision

No easy technological solutions are available to meet the interactive and educational needs of individuals who are blind or have low vision. Although computers have been used to address a variety of unique communication and instructional needs created by a sensory loss, computer applications have not satisfactorily resolved all of the educational needs of learners with vision or hearing losses.

Individuals who are blind and have low vision use computers for the same purposes as sighted persons. Goodrich (1984) reminded readers that the primary application of computers is information processing. Access to and the management of information are the major advantages of computer applications for on-line services, electronic messaging, CD- and DVD-ROMs, word processing, databases, spreadsheets, and games. The key to successful computer use is the degree to which it enhances an individual's education, work, and leisure.

Kleiman (1984) described six computer capabilities that continue to meet some of the specific needs of individuals who are blind and have low vision:

1. *Computer speech synthesis*—The computer can state which line the cursor is on and speak the words on that line, which makes almost all of the computer's capabilities accessible to people who are blind.

2. *Large-print display*—The computer can display large, high-contrast print on the computer monitor or through the use of an appropriate printer.

3. *Tactile forms*—For people who cannot read any print regardless of size, various devices can convert printed letters to a tactile code of vibrating patterns or to braille.

4. *Braille word processing*—Special braille printers can interface with computers to take advantage of the word processing capabilities.

5. *Computerized letter recognition*—Speech synthesizers and text-to-speech programs can convert words stored in the computer to speech, large-letter displays, braille, or tactile signals.

6. *Conversion of print to speech*—Scanner and reader technology can convert print to speech by combining conversion capabilities.

As noted by Lazzaro (1994), many of the access and adaptive technologies are available with off-the-shelf software such as speech output systems that can verbalize keystrokes and read information displayed on the screen, all at the touch of a key. Voice recognition software is also available that permits users to access a computer via verbal commands, and braille printers that can easily interface to PCs allow many existing word processor software programs to print braille.

Because computers and access technology are critical to meeting the needs of individuals with vision loss, Mack, Koenig, and Ashcroft (1990) recommended that such knowledge and related skills should become part of the basic competencies required of educational programs for teachers. At the minimum, all entering teachers to the profession need to have an awareness and basic skills in access technology and computer applications. These include the following (Mack et al., 1990, p. 527):

- Awareness of accessible computer hardware and software

- Basic skills in determining whether a given student should use braille, print, large print, speech, or any combination of these to access computers

- Awareness of the range and variety of accessible word-processing programs

- Basic skills in the use of one or more accessible word-processing programs

- Awareness of the applications in telecommunications

Given the ever-changing applications of computers and access technologies, such objectives will need to be periodically reviewed and modified accordingly (Mack et al., 1990).

Some Computer Applications for Reading and Access

Access to reading material has been the primary focus of computer applications for individuals who are blind and have low vision. Dixon and Mandelbaum (1990) provided an overview of the ways the computer has been used for reading access. Their discussion covers computerized telephone reading services and using the computer as a reading machine. Also, the computer provides on-line access to a number of services and databases that include information searches; shopping services; banking; reading newspapers, magazines, wire services, and business or financial information; searching reference materials such as encyclopedias or on-line travel schedules; and sending e-mail (or having a hard copy printed for the recipient). Other capabilities of the computer include using the hard disk as a storage medium and accessing library information via varied media (e.g., CD-ROM). Such computer applications offer the potential for people with vision loss to be on an equal basis with their sighted peers for interaction and access to information. Jackson and Busset (1991) discussed the value of telecommunications and on-line services for students who are blind and partially sighted in general education classrooms. Not only do the students use computers and on-line access to information to prepare their school assignments and reports, but also they use e-mail for communication and social interaction. In addition to the utility of such access, these computer applications contribute to the students' development of independence and self-confidence. Another computer application for reading access is the use of telecommunications and speech synthesis to transmit a daily newspaper to peoples' homes (Hjelmquist, Jansson, & Torell, 1990). In this project, Hjelmquist et al. demonstrated the importance to people with vision loss of receiving a newspaper at the same time sighted people received theirs, as well as the chance to choose what to read easily.

Another interesting application of computer technology is to teach spatial locations to individuals who are blind using computer simulations. Zimmerman (1990) asked persons who were blind to learn a spatial location of a 5×5 block residential neighborhood through either a tactile graphic aid or a computer simulation. The results showed that the students' accuracy for spatial knowledge was equal for both conditions. This raises the possibility that persons who are blind could use computer-accessed information to become familiar with new spatial location knowledge, such as about a classroom building, college campus, or town before visiting or moving there.

With regard to telecommunications and distance learning, Coombs (1993) used the computer network to teach a college history course to students who were both deaf and hearing. Coombs, who was blind, used the electronic network to interact with students using a PC adapted for synthetic speech output. This distance learning project was unique in that the computer and electronic networking were used to provide equal access and interaction for a mix of participants who were blind, deaf, and hearing. Coombs's practical application of computer technology and telecommunications is an excellent demonstration of how to transcend both physical distance and interactive challenges that occur among people who are blind, deaf, and hearing.

In addition to access and interaction, the computer can also be used as an educational training aid. Cates and Sowell (1989, 1990) used computer-generated tachistoscope-like displays of electronic braille to explore the improvement of braille reading speeds by students who are blind. Such innovative applications can be used to address specific skill acquisition of any individual.

Speech Synthesis

From an educational perspective, synthesized speech offers excellent potential for computer applications (also see Chapters 2, 5, and 10). Its use means that individuals with vision loss will have access to a considerable portion of the commercially available software without extensive adaptation. However, speech synthesizers will not provide access to graphic information. Through speech synthesizers, learners with vision loss will be able to use the same software programs as sighted students (Hagen, 1984). Speech synthesizers allow a major improvement in resource use for general and special educators as well as individuals who are blind and partially sighted. Even more important, with these assistive computer aids, it is possible for individuals with vision loss to achieve almost complete independence in accessing the information electronically stored in the computer memory banks. Processing information independently and self-directed control in the learning process are critically important to the development and growth of all people.

Large Print

Large print can be generated either through software on a typical computer or by the use of specially designed equipment. A problem with large-print computers is that they reduce the amount of material displayed at one time and make review tedious and difficult (Goodrich, 1984). In spite of the limitations, such devices are workable alternatives for providing access to computers for persons who are blind and partially sighted who need this type of enhancement. When sufficient for the individual, low-vision aids such as magnifiers are less expensive and generally do not require

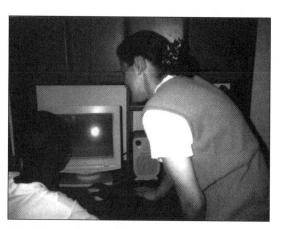

Individuals with vision loss can use computers to enlarge text or change text to braille. (Photograph by Carolyn F. Woods)

modification of the computer equipment, thus offering a wider range in the selection of computers and software. Low-vision aids for the computer are essentially the same as normally used magnification aids for reading print on paper or the computer monitor.

Braille Applications

Refreshable or paperless braille allows immediate feedback of information for editing purposes, whereas hard-copy braille provides a permanent record. Refreshable braille is a changeable tactile system that uses a series of pins that are raised or lowered to form braille characters. The refreshable braille systems are more expensive than voice synthesizers and have limitations such as the single-line display of the VersaBraille.

The OPTACON is one of the more widely used technologies for accessing print, including computer text (Ruconich, Ashcroft, & Young, 1986). The OPTACON system translates visual text into a raised, vibrating, tactile print that is not braille but a tactile counterpart of visible symbols. With appropriate camera lenses, the OPTACON can read either the paper printout or the electronic video display. The clear advantage of the OPTACON is its versatility for accessing print on either hard copy or video display, while one of its limitations is the slow speed of 20 to 60 words per minute.

VersaBraille

Another important educational application of computer technology for individuals with vision loss is the VersaBraille, a paperless braille machine. It is a portable stand-alone machine that functions like a word processor. Braille is displayed on a field of 20 cells containing six holes each through which rounded pins project to form the braille characters. The editing capability for braille, similar to word processing, is a key advantage. Information is stored on audiocassette tape for ease of retrieval. Furthermore, through the use of adapters, the VersaBraille can be interfaced with both computers or printers.

Tactile Graphics Display

The American Foundation for the Blind has developed and offers a Tactile Graphics Display under a grant from the National Science Foundation. As Maure (1984) reported, the Tactile Graphics Display:

> can be configured in single-line, multi-line, or full-page displays (Library of Congress standards). Because of its symmetrical dot configuration, multiple alphanumeric fonts, conventional six-dot braille, computer braille and graphics can be generated. Black pins on a white background provide a sharp contrast which enables the partially sighted to use the display, as well as the blind. (p. 139)

The design of this device using electronic control results in a low-cost assistive aid. The flexibility and relatively low cost offer considerable potential for educational applications.

Augmentative Writing Systems

In addition to the specific applications discussed previously for people with vision loss, there are more general and technical considerations pertinent to supporting their writing needs. Further considerations for implementing an augmentative writing system are keyboard support systems, switch systems, alternative interfaces, software, voice output, and enhanced print options. Shell (1989) provided an excellent overview of these areas, along with various implementation considerations (see Chapters 5 and 11).

Summary

This chapter has described some of the educational challenges faced by individuals who are deaf, hard of hearing, blind, and partially sighted. These challenges are the focus for most computer applications for learners with either a hearing or vision loss. For those with vision loss, computer applications primarily involve assistive aids to overcome the vision loss, including speech synthesizers, large-print computer displays and printers, text-to-speech conversion, tactile devices, and braille interfaces. For individuals who are deaf and hard of hearing, computer applications generally focus on language-related development, such as writing, reading, and literacy skills. Furthermore, the information access, electronic messaging, and interactive communication aspects of computer technology are important contributors to the implementation of inclusion in educational environments for learners who are deaf, hard of hearing, blind, or partially sighted.

Resources

Organizations

Alexander Graham Bell Association. This professional organization provides printed materials (e.g., *The Volta Review*) about hearing loss to special educators, parents, and persons who are deaf and hard of hearing. *Contact:* Alexander Graham Bell Association, 3417 Volta Place NW, Washington, DC 20007.

American Foundation for the Blind. This organization publishes numerous printed materials related to individuals who are blind and partially sighted, including the *Journal of Visual Impairment and Blindness. Contact:* American Foundation for the Blind, 15 West 16th Street, New York, NY 10011.

American Printing House for the Blind. This organization provides various materials (e.g., large-print books, braille) to individuals with vision loss as well as educators. *Contact:* American Printing House for the Blind, 1839 Franksort Avenue, Louisville, KY 40206.

National Association of the Deaf. This organization serves as a clearinghouse for information on education, communication, employment, and related topics for individuals who are deaf and hard of hearing. *Contact:* National Association of the Deaf, 814 Thayer Avenue, Silver Springs, MD 20910.

Journals

American Annals of the Deaf. This bimonthly journal publishes articles that focus on education and research with regard to people who are deaf and hard of hearing. *Contact:* Convention of American Instructors of the Deaf and the Conference of Executives of American Schools for the Deaf, 814 Thayer Avenue, Silver Springs, MD 20910.

Education of the Visually Handicapped. This quarterly journal publishes research and practical articles for teachers of students who are blind or partially sighted. *Contact:* Association for the Education of the Visually Handicapped, 206 N. Washington Street, Suite 320, Alexandria, VA 22314.

Journal of Visual Impairment and Blindness. This journal, published 10 times a year, focuses on topics related to the education and rehabilitation of individuals who are blind and partially sighted. *Contact:* American Foundation for the Blind, 15 West 16th Street, New York, NY 10011.

Volta Review. This journal, published nine times a year, focuses on topics related to educating individuals who are deaf and hard of hearing. *Contact:* Alexander Graham Bell Association, 3417 Volta Place, Washington, DC 20007.

Laboratory–Practicum Activities

► 1. List three goals you will achieve in the next 2 months to enhance your understanding of technology for individuals who are deaf, hard of hearing, blind, and partially sighted. Use technology to develop your goals, to describe how you will achieve these goals, and to manage the achievement of the goals.

► 2. Search the Internet and World Wide Web for technology plans for individuals who are deaf, hard of hearing, blind, and partially sighted posted by different school districts. Compare and contrast these plans and share your findings with your peers and course instructor.

► 3. Collaborate with your peers to compile a list of technology-related resources (e.g., organizations, printed materials, Web sites and pages) that can be used by professionals in special education and inclusive settings for meeting the needs of individuals who are deaf, hard of hearing, blind, and partially sighted. Use the information listed in this and other

chapters as a starting point but identify additional resources. Create a database to store this information and share it with your peers and course instructor.

► 4. Collaborate with your peers to interview elementary-level general educators, special educators, and other professionals working with individuals who are deaf, hard of hearing, blind, and partially sighted in special education and inclusive settings. Have these professionals describe (a) how they are planning and implementing technology programs and the strengths and weaknesses of these programs and (b) the resources they use to achieve collaborative teaching–learning outcomes. Compare and contrast the descriptions and share your findings with your peers and course instructor.

► 5. Collaborate with your peers to interview secondary-level general educators, special educators, and other professionals working with individuals who are deaf, hard of hearing, blind, and partially sighted in special education and inclusive settings. Have these professionals describe (a) how they are planning and implementing technology programs and the strengths and weaknesses of these programs and (b) the resources they use to achieve collaborative teaching–learning outcomes. Compare and contrast the descriptions and share your findings with your peers and course instructor.

► 6. Collaborate with your peers to identify a fellow student who is deaf or hard of hearing and uses technology for home, school, and community purposes. Ask this individual if he or she would serve as a resource person during a class period to describe the duration, nature, and impact of his or hearing loss (particularly in school settings) and to provide a historical overview of his or her use of technology. If the individual cannot serve as a resource person, seek his or her permission and interview him or her to find out the above information. Share your findings with your course instructor.

▶ 7. Collaborate with your peers to identify a fellow student who is blind or partially sighted and uses technology for home, school, and community purposes. Ask this individual if he or she would serve as a resource person during a class period to describe the duration, nature, and impact of his or her vision loss (particularly in school settings) and to provide a historical overview of his or her use of technology. If the individual cannot serve as resource person, seek his or her permission and interview him or her to find out the above information. Share your findings with your course instructor.

References

Allen, T. E. (1986). Patterns of academic achievement among hearing impaired students, 1974 and 1983. In A. N. Scheldroker & M. A. Karchmer (Eds.), *Deaf children in America* (pp. 106–206). San Diego, CA: College-Hill Press.

Anytime, anywhere learning with laptops: Results from a Microsoft/Toshiba Pilot Program. (1998). *T.H.E. Journal, 25*(8), 75.

Batson, T. (1988). The ENFI project: An update. *Teaching English to Deaf and Second Language Students, 6,* 5–8.

Bochner, J. H. (1982). English in the deaf population. In D. G. Sims, G. G. Walter, & R. L. Whitehead (Eds.), *Deafness and communication* (pp. 107–123). Baltimore: Williams & Wilkins.

Cates, D. L., & Sowell, V. M. (1989). Random access. *Journal of Visual Impairment and Blindness, 84,* 361–364.

Cates, D. L., & Sowell, V. M. (1990). Using a braille tachistoscope to improve braille reading speed. *Journal of Visual Impairment and Blindness, 84,* 556–559.

Chorniak, E. J. (1977). Education of visually impaired children. In J. E. Jan, R. D. Freeman, & E. P. Scott (Eds.), *Visual impairment in children and adolescents* (pp. 291–304). New York: Grune & Stratton.

Clark, R. E. (1983). Reconsidering research on learning from media. *Review of Educational Research, 53,* 445–459.

Clark, R. E. (1985). Confounding in educational computing research. *Journal of Educational Computing Research, 1,* 137–148.

Clark, R. E. (1994). Media will never influence learning. *Educational Technology Research and Development, 42,* 21–29.

Committee on Nomenclature of the Conference of Executives of American Schools for the Deaf. (1938). *American Annals of the Deaf, 83,* 1.

Coombs, N. (1993). Global empowerment of impaired learners: Data networks will transcend both physical distance and physical disabilities. *Educational Media International, 30,* 23–25.

Cronin, P. J. (1992). A direct service program for mainstreamed students by a residential school. *Journal of Visual Impairment and Blindness, 86,* 101–104.

Davis, H. (1970). Abnormal hearing and deafness. In H. Davis & S. R. Silverman (Eds.), *Hearing and deafness* (3rd ed., pp. 83–139). New York: Holt, Rinehart and Winston.

Dixon, J. M., & Mandelbaum, J. B. (1990). Reading through technology: Evolving methods and opportunities for print-handicapped individuals. *Journal of Visual Impairment and Blindness, 84,* 493–496.

Everhart, V., Stinson, M. S., McKee, B., & Giles, P. (1996, April). *Evaluation of a speech-to-print transcription system as a resource for mainstreamed deaf students.* Paper presented at the annual meeting of the American Educational Research Association, New York City.

Goodrich, G. L. (1984). Applications of microcomputers by visually impaired persons. *Journal of Visual Impairment and Blindness, 78,* 408–414.

Hagen, D. (1984). *Microcomputer resource book for special education.* Reston, VA: Reston Publishing.

Hanson, V. L., & Padden, C. A. (1989). Interactive video for bilingual ASL/English instruction of deaf children. *American Annals of the Deaf, 134,* 209–213.

Hardman, M. L., Drew, C. J., & Egan, M. W. (1999). *Human exceptionality: Society, school, and family* (6th ed.). Needham Heights, MA: Allyn & Bacon.

Hjelmquist, E., Jansson, B., & Torell, G. (1990). Computer-oriented technology for blind readers. *Journal of Visual Impairment and Blindness, 84,* 210–215.

Hofmeister, R., & Drury, A. M. (1982). English training for the primary and secondary level deaf student. In D. G. Sims, G. G. Walter, & R. L. Whitehead (Eds.), *Deafness and communication* (pp. 259–371). Baltimore: Williams & Wilkins.

Jackson, D. B., & Busset, P. (1991). Making information accessible to blind and visually impaired mainstreamed students. *Journal of Visual Impairment and Blindness, 85,* 228–229.

James, V., & Hammersley, M. (1993). Notebook computers as note-takers for handicapped students. *British Journal of Educational Technology, 24,* 63–66.

Jan, J. E., Freeman, R. D., & Scott, E. P. (1977). *Visual impairment in children and adolescents.* New York: Grune & Stratton.

Jensema, C. J. (1994). Telecommunications for the deaf. *American Annals for the Deaf, 139,* 22–27.

Karmen, L. (1996, October). *Jowonio philosophy on inclusion.* Homepage for Jowonio School in Syracuse, NY. Available: http://www.dreamscape.com/jowonio/jowoincl.html

Kelly, R. R., Samar, V. J., Loeterman, M., Berent, G. P., Parasnis, I., Kirchner, C. J., Fischer, S. D., Brown, P., & Murphy, C. (1994). CC school project: Personal captioning technology applied to the language learning environment of deaf children. *Technology and Disability, 3*, 26–38.

Kleiman, G. M. (1984, September). Aids for the blind. *Compute*, pp. 122–124.

Lazzaro, J. J. (1994). Adaptive computing and the Internet: One step forward, two steps back? *Internet Research, 4*, 2–8.

Loeterman, M., & Kelly, R. R. (1997). *Personal captioning for students with language-related learning needs*. Final Report of the Demonstration and Evaluation Project Funded by the Division of Innovation and Development Office of Special Education Programs, U.S. Department of Education (Grant No. H180E30021).

Loeterman, M., & Morse, A. B. (1996, April). *Captioning and the learning process*. Presentation at The WGBH Technology Fair, Boston.

Lowenbraun, S., & Thompson, M. (1989). Environments and strategies for learning and teaching. In M. Wang, M. Reynolds, & H. Walberg (Eds.), *Handbook of special education research and practice: Volume 3. Low incidence conditions* (pp. 47–69). Oxford: Pergamon Press.

Lowenfeld, B. (1981). *Berthold Lowenfeld on blindness and blind people: Selected papers*. New York: American Foundation for the Blind.

Lumsdaine, A. A. (1963). Instruments and media of instruction. In N. Gage (Ed.), *Handbook of research on teaching* (pp. 583–682). Chicago: Rand McNally.

Mack, C. G., Koenig, A. J., & Ashcroft, S. C. (1990). Microcomputers and access technology in programs for teachers of visually impaired students. *Journal of Visual Impairment and Blindness, 84*, 526–530.

Mackall, P. (1996). A wide world of Internet resources. *Perspectives in Education and Deafness, 15*, 22–23.

Maure, D. R. (1984). Tactile graphics display. In J. E. Roel (Ed.), *Computers for the disabled: Conference papers* (pp. 137–140). Menomonie: University of Wisconsin-Stout, Materials Development Center.

McKee, B., Stinson, M. S., & Giles, P. (1996). C-Print: Where have we been? What did we learn? Where are we going? *NTID Research Bulletin, 1*, 1–5.

Myklebust, H. R. (1964). *The psychology of deafness* (2nd ed.). New York: Grune & Stratton.

Newell, W., Sims, D. G., & Clymer, E. W. (1984). Meet DAVID, our teachers' helper. *Perspectives in Education and Deafness, 2*, 15–18.

Peyton, J. K. (1988). Computer networking: Providing a context for deaf students to write collaboratively. *Teaching English to Deaf and Second Language Students, 6*, 19–24.

Peyton, J. K. (1990). Technological innovation meets institution: Birth of creativity or murder of a great idea? *Technological Innovation Meets Institution, 7*, 15–32.

Peyton, J. K. (1991). Electronic communication for developing the literacy skills of elementary school students. *Teaching English to Deaf and Second Language Students, 9*, 4–9.

Prinz, P. M. (1991). Literacy and language development within microcomputer-videodisk–assisted interactive contexts. *Journal of Childhood Communication Disorders, 14*, 67–80.

Reich, C. F, Matthews, A., Goldman, S., Brienne, D., & Matthews, T. J. (1991). Teaching earth science through a computer network. *Perspectives in Education and Deafness, 9*, 4–7.

Rittenhouse, R. K., Spillers, D. S., & Kenyon, P. (1993). A technological teaching tool: Interactive videodisc systems. *Perspectives in Education and Deafness, 12*, 2–6.

Ruconich, S. K., Ashcroft, S. C., & Young, M. F. (1986). Making microcomputers accessible to blind persons. *Journal of Special Education Technology, 8*, 37–46.

Schramm, W. (1977). *Big media, little media*. Beverly Hills, CA: Sage.

Shell, D. F. (1989). Computer-based compensatory augmentative communication technology for physically disabled, visually impaired, and speech impaired students. *Journal of Special Education Technology, 10*, 29–43.

Silverman, S. R., & Lane, H. S. (1970). Deaf children. In H. Davis & S. R. Silverman (Eds.), *Hearing and deafness* (3rd ed., pp. 385–425). New York: Holt, Rinehart and Winston.

Sims, D. G., & Clymer, E. W. (1986). Computer assisted instruction for the hearing impaired. In J. L. Northern (Ed.), *The personal computer for speech, language, and hearing professionals* (pp. 157–175). Boston: Little, Brown.

Sims, D. G., Scott, L., & Myers, T. (1982). Past, present and future: Computer assisted communication training at NTID. *Journal of the Academy of Rehabilitative Audiology, 15*, 103–115.

Spillers, D., Heatherly, A., Kenyon, P., & Rittenhouse, R. K. (1994). Making connections: Students, technology, and language learning. *Perspectives in Education and Deafness, 12*, 6–9.

Stewart, D. A., Heeter, C., & Dickson, P. (1996). CD-ROM technology: Support for language and communication. *Perspectives in Education and Deafness, 14*, 16–17.

Stepp, R. E., Jr. (1994). A technological metamorphosis in the education of deaf students. *American Annals of the Deaf, 139*, 14–17.

Stinson, M. S., & Stuckless, R. (1998). Recent developments in speech-to-print transcription systems for deaf students. In A. Weisel (Ed.), *Deaf education in the 1990s: International perspectives*. Washington, DC: Gallaudet University Press.

Stuckless, E. R. (1983). Real-time transliteration for speech into print for hearing-impaired students in regular classes. *American Annals of the Deaf, 128,* 619–624.

Vander Kolk, C. J. (1981). *Assessment and planning with the visually impaired.* Austin, TX: PRO-ED.

Volterra, V., Pace, C., Pennacchi, B., & Corazza, S. (1995). Advanced learning technology for a bilingual education of deaf children. *American Annals of the Deaf, 140,* 402–409.

Warren, D. H. (1977). *Blindness and early childhood development.* New York: American Foundation for the Blind.

Zimmerman, G. J. (1990). Effects of microcomputer and tactile aid simulations on the spatial ability of blind individuals. *Journal of Visual Impairment and Blindness, 84,* 541–547.

Chapter 13

ᔓ   ᔓ   ᔓ

Technology for Individuals with Gifts and Talents

Evelyn J. Dale
California State University–Sacramento

In 1980 a pebble was dropped in the ocean of computer technology—Seymour Papert's book, *Mindstorms: Children, Computers, and Powerful Ideas*, was published. *Mindstorms'* ripples go beyond its specific focus on the computer language LOGO to address the broader aspects of computer education. The purpose of computer technology for students, Papert argued, is to empower them and, in so doing, to develop independence, critical thinking, and problem-solving skills. This is possible because computers put the tools of the professional into the hands of the young, enabling their intellectual explorations to become increasingly mature and profound. This chapter explores ways in which technology can open the doors of intellectual and creative discovery for individuals with gifts and talents. It is important that these exceptional individuals achieve their potential so that they can maximize their contributions to society (Shaklee, 1992).

Individuals with Gifts and Talents

Renzulli's (1978) three-ring concept of giftedness helps define individuals with gifts and talents (see Figure 13.1). This definition is based on past research that includes Terman's (1959) component of academic excellence, the United States Office of Education's component of multiple talent and criteria, and Witty's (1958) criterion of

remarkable performance. Renzulli's concept is based on two assumptions. First, giftedness is not something an individual either has or does not have but rather a mode of behavior. The idea that giftedness is a mode of behavior is significant because it questions the organizational structure of programs that identify and separate gifted students into special classes. Renzulli (1978) suggested exchanging this traditional configuration for his Revolving Door Identification Model (RDIM). With this plan students with gifted potential are identified but remain in a mixed-ability class working on an enriched and challenging curriculum. When students exhibit gifted behavior, they are "revolved" into a special program designed to meet their new needs and interests. Renzulli's RDIM model can be modified to

Young students who are gifted and talented can quickly master basic computer concepts. (Photograph by Jimmy D. Lindsey)

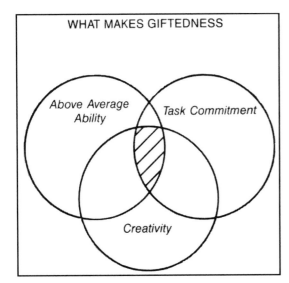

WHAT MAKES GIFTEDNESS

Above Average Ability

Task Commitment

Creativity

Figure 13.1. Renzulli's three-ring concept of giftedness. From *The Revolving Door Identification Model*, by J. S. Renzulli, S. M. Reis, and L. H. Smith, 1981, Hartford, CT: Creative Learning Press. Copyright 1981 by Creative Learning Press. Reprinted by permission.

accommodate different programs for gifted and talented students, but the main point is that the students move into and out of the program according to their needs (Renzulli, Reis, & Smith, 1981).

Renzulli's (1978) second assumption was that giftedness is composed of three equally important clusters of human traits—above average intelligence, creativity, and task commitment—and that gifted behavior is not present without all three. This is important because it is generally assumed that superior intelligence makes an individual gifted. The three-ring concept makes it clear that truly gifted behavior depends on all three traits.

Although above average intelligence is essential to giftedness, research has indicated that the connection between high intelligence quotients or aptitude test scores and some gifted and talented behavior (e.g., creativity) is only distantly related. As Wallach (1976) pointed out, academic skills assessments are not accurate in predicting future achievements. What they do predict is "the results a person will obtain on other

tests of the same kind" (p. 57). Whereas intelligence is not the only factor in determining giftedness, it is necessary. How high that ability needs to be depends on the performance area itself (MacKinnon, 1968b).

Terman (1959) noted that the gifted people in his study who were most successful were those who worked diligently to accomplish their goals. The work of Roe (1975) and MacKinnon (1968b) also underscored the importance of task commitment to gifted behavior. It is often easier to exercise the kind of task commitment required by special projects outside the traditional school environment. Unless programs for individuals with gifts and talents are changed to meet this need, the discrepancy that exists between in-school and out-of-school achievements for many gifted persons will continue (MacKinnon, 1968a).

Creativity, the third ingredient of giftedness, is difficult to discuss because a positive correlation between creativity tests and actual creative products has not been established (Crockenburg, 1972). Furthermore, the validity of creativity tests has been questioned (Getzel & Csikszentmihayli, 1975; Nicholls, 1972) because these tests do not probe the test taker's ability to identify and define the problem itself and may be measuring only one part of the total process. Wallach (1976) recommended other ways to assess creativity, such as judging samples of students' work and reading students' evaluations of their own creative accomplishments. Today, this kind of evaluation is known as portfolio assessment.

Renzulli's (1978) three-ring concept of giftedness works with many different types of gifted individuals; it helps to identify not only gifted artists, musicians, and scientists, but also individuals with special needs. For example, gifted students with learning disabilities (LD) are often overlooked (Senf, 1983). Baum (1984) provided an excellent discussion about how Renzulli's three-ring conception of giftedness and the RDIM model can be used to provide enrichment activities for gifted students with LD. More recently, Cohen (1996) addressed the need to broaden and diversify the criteria for giftedness and that gifted education needs to be part of mainstream education so it can be a positive influence for transforming the education of all students. Schack (1996) echoed Cohen's call for reform in gifted education, emphasizing the need to provide enriched and flexible curricula for all students so a broader range of talents, skills, and abilities is developed. Schack (1996) also suggested that technology should be used to reach resources and people outside of the classroom. Cohen's and Schack's position for inclusion, diversity, and mainstreaming is supported by an update of a 1991 needs assessment survey conducted by the National Research Center on the Gifted and Talented (Gubbins, 1996).

Possessing above average ability, task commitment, and creativity means nothing until these traits are applied to a specific performance area. The question, of course, is what specific performance areas are to be considered? Cartooning, poetry, ornithology, city planning, dancing, sculpting, or developing Web pages for the Internet are only a few of the vast array of possibilities. At first supporting so many interests seems impossible. Fortunately, computer technology helps meet the diverse needs and interests of persons with gifts and talents. Table 13.1 delineates the two types of exceptional individuals and general computer applications that enhance their development.

A Brief Review of the Literature

After more than a decade, research into the general impact of technology in education is still largely investigative. This is particularly true of the literature about gifted and talented education. In his article, "An Historical Content Analysis of Publications in Gifted Education Journals," Hays (1993) pointed out that technology represents less than 1% of all gifted education research. Discussions within this tiny 1% of the literature tend to focus on existing programs and their curricula, computer activities for learning, and a few reviews of software programs.

While traditional research into technology and individuals with gifts and talents seems to have been neglected, there has been tremendous growth in the resources available on the Internet. Web sites filled with resources for parents, teachers, and students abound. Some of the more established include the TAG (Talented And Gifted) Family Network, Armadillo, the Education Program for Gifted Youth, and the Johns Hopkins University's Institute for the Academic Advancement of Youth. The Educational Resources Information Center (ERIC) is also

Table 13.1. Individuals with Gifts and Talents and Computer Applications

Individual	Computer Applications
Academically gifted	Programming languages (e.g., HTML, Java, LOGO, Pascal)
	Computer-assisted instruction
	Computer tools (e.g., word processors, databases, spreadsheets, and charts)
	Telecommunications/Internet research
Creative and talented	Computer-assisted design (CAD), painting, drawing software to develop graphic images
	Music synthesis and Musical Instrument Digital Interface (MIDI)
	Multimedia Web pages and digital movies with animation, video, and sound
	Analysis and cataloging of athletics, dance, drama, and other kinesthetic activities

Note. Many individuals with gifts and talents are both academically and creatively strong and therefore use computer applications from both areas.

on-line and provides, among other things, 16 clearinghouses or ERIC databases including scholarly articles about gifted and talented education, although very few actually discuss technology's specific impact. Once at the ERIC site, searches can be conducted, abstracts read, and on-line articles or abstracts printed out. Other on-line resources include university and college libraries. Although these libraries provide access to their catalogs, access to an actual printed article or book is less often available. The Electric Library, however, permits subscribers to search, view, and print out articles. A subscriber simply conducts a search of the Electric Library's databases and then saves and prints out pertinent articles. Such easy access is especially useful when a topic is difficult to find or when publications may be located at several distant locations. See the Resources section at the end of this chapter for details about these and other on-line resources.

Programs for individuals with gifts and talents come in many configurations. For years schools have offered classes that enrich or accelerate the education of students who are gifted. With the Internet readily accessible, learning on-line becomes a genuine possibility. As a result, partial or total home schooling is now a viable option. Parents can use the Internet as a resource for developing a challenging curriculum that includes gathering sophisticated data, consulting with experts, and participating in on-line global projects. High schools offering a fast-paced college preparatory curriculum are establishing a presence on the Internet as well. Also, distance learning through universities provides opportunities for highly able students to take college-level courses regardless of where they live. Special academic programs outside of the usual school setting provide another avenue for young people with gifts and talents. Stanley (1991) described the development of such a program at Johns Hopkins University. It began in 1971 with the Study of Mathematically Precocious Youth (SMPY). Since then, this program has expanded to include a wide range of private and public universities, including Duke, Northwestern, and California State at Sacramento. Each institution retains its independent identity as the SMPY model is adapted to suit the needs of the population with gifts and talents in its surrounding community.

Kolstad and Lidtke (1983) compared two Illinois computer projects for students with gifts and talents. The purpose of both projects was to identify students' computer interests and use this knowledge to develop a computer curriculum. The first project began in 1972 in the elementary schools and was expanded in 1975 to include a more formal program for junior high school students. The second project started in the early 1980s and involved only junior high school students. Both programs used the University of Illinois's PLATO computer system to provide students with computer-assisted instruction (CAI) and programming experience. Both programs found that students were least interested in CAI and more interested in computer games. They also found that time and supervision were essential to student progress.

Rotenberg (1985) described two schools in Pennsylvania that used computers with students with gifts and talents. In these programs the emphasis was on integrating the computer into the total learning process by using it as a resource tool. Instead of concentrating on CAI and programming, students used computers for word processing, database management, communication, graphics, and speech development tools. The difference between the Illinois and Pennsylvania programs indicates a shift from the CAI and programming approach to one that recognizes technology's ability to act as a powerful learning resource (Hamlett, 1984). Additional research into the impact of computers on students with gifts and talents has been presented by Hersberger and Wheatley (1989), who investigated the impact of computers on the development of problem-solving skills among fifth- and sixth-grade students who were mathematically gifted and talented.

Over the years computer curricula have evolved from examining the computer as a machine to using the computer as a learning and research tool. For example, in 1988 Balajthy reported that the computer curriculum emphasized hardware and its operation rather than understanding how to use the technology effectively. Today the view is quite different. In "Confessions of an Internet Junkie," Lewis (1996) provided an excellent overview of the Internet and what it can do for learners with gifts and talents. Starting with how to get on the Internet, Lewis explained the Internet's basic communication and research tools and how individuals with gifts and talents can use them for a wide range of purposes. Troxclair, Stephens, Bennett, and Karnes (1996) described a multimedia course offered to students who were gifted in 7th to 12th grades through the University of Southern Mississippi's Saturday Gifted Studies program.

Ravaglia, Suppes, Stillinger, and Alper (1995) presented a carefully documented study of the success of students with gifts and talents with computer-based instruction. Beginning in the fall of 1990, three groups of middle and high school students participated in the Education Program for Gifted Youth (EPGY) at Stanford University. The first group (Calc91) studied Calculus AB. A year later a second group (Calc92) studied Calculus BC. In 1993 a third group, made up of students from Calc91 and Calc92, studied Physics C, Mechanics. Students worked at home with computer-based software that was designed to present multimedia lectures, on-line exercises, mastery quizzes, and problem sets. E-mail was used by the students to discuss ideas and to ask questions of their tutors. Off-line work included reading and exercises in traditional textbooks as well as examinations. Students learned at their own pace, with the software presenting concepts and immediately testing their understanding of the work. Additional computer instruction was then based on the students' diagnosed weaknesses. The results of these three groups were impressive. Most students scored 4 or 5 out of 5 on the Advanced Placement examinations for each course, and gender differences were nonexistent (i.e., boys and girls achieved equally high scores).

Stanford University's EPGY program continues to provide advantages for both students and schools. Gifted students work at home on their own, thus avoiding the awkwardness of attending college classes with older students. Furthermore, students are not restricted by time or place in that they can enroll in EPGY classes at any time of the year and can take them regardless of where they live. The advantages for schools are that the needs of their students who are gifted can be met while keeping them in the school setting and addressing their other social and educational needs. The courses discussed in the Ravaglia et al. (1995) article are designed for learners highly gifted in the areas of mathematics and science (the top 1% of the population). Current EPGY course offerings provide students with opportunities to acquire 29 quarter units of college credit, and plans are under way to add courses in multivariate calculus, linear algebra, differential equations, optics, thermodynamics, and modern physics.

In 1991 the National Science Foundation awarded a grant to the Technology, Science, Mathematics (TSM) Integration Project at Virginia Tech for the development of middle school instructional activities that incorporated science, math, and technology. Sanders (1994) discussed the purpose of these activities and provided a brief description of them and their content. These activities go beyond computers and calculators to include three basic categories of technology: communication, production, and power/energy/transportation. The 15 activities outlined in the article emphasize the technological problem-solving method, which involves students in building technological solutions to different problems with limited teacher guidance. These TSM integration activities provide an in-depth understanding of math, science, and technology through a cycle of development, assessment, and redevelopment. Students use this cycle to solve a specific problem by first designing a possible solution, then constructing it, and finally testing it. The product's operation is analyzed and ways to improve it are then developed. The redesigned product is then reassessed through observation and data collection. If there is time, students repeat this cycle of designing, producing, and testing for a third time. The repetition of this cycle is valuable to the development of students' knowledge and understanding of math, science, technology, and how they are interconnected.

Although technology is a tool for every learner, it is especially powerful in the hands of individuals with gifts and talents. Jones (1990) made this point quite effectively in describing the benefits of using technology to meet the special needs of students who are gifted. He pointed out that the computer has moved beyond the basic calculator to an "idea engine" or "tool for discovery, exploration and collaboration" (Jones, 1990, p. 2). Hicks (1993) made a compelling case for incorporating technology into the education of young people who are creative and talented as well. With an increasingly technological world, Hicks maintained that art has expanded to include the media arts; many artists use computer technology to generate images, animations, and video presentations. As an emerging area of aesthetic expression, the combination of art and technology offers increased opportunities to reach a wider range of creative young people. Hicks gave several reasons for incorporating technology and the media arts into the education of students who are creative and aesthetically gifted: (a) visual symbols are a part of the multidimensional world of communication; (b) the aesthetic design of technology itself is recognized as an important part of successful marketing; and (c) the creative and aesthetic synthesis of information and ideas is needed in today's age of global communication. Hicks concluded that there is a growing need for people with talents who can use technology to analyze and solve problems with creativity and aesthetic sensitivity.

Students who are academically gifted in computer science need to pursue their interests as well. Options for advanced programming and sophisticated applications of computer technology are available to many students with gifts and talents at secondary and postsecondary schools. Many high schools offer advanced placement computer science courses, and many colleges and universities give college credit to students who successfully complete these courses.

The Institute for the Academic Advancement of Youth (IAAY) at Johns Hopkins University has developed a range of programs for young people with gifts and talents. The Center for Talented Youth (CTY) is designed to identify and serve fifth, sixth, and seventh graders with exceptional mathematical or verbal reasoning abilities and provide academic programs and opportunities in the humanities, mathematics, and science for in-depth academic learning. The Center for Academic Advancement (CAA) serves students not eligible for CTY programs. CAA also offers workshops for parents, teachers, and administrators, and initiates and sustains programs and services for youth who are academically talented. IAAY also supports 12 sites at different university campuses across the United States where similar programs are offered, conducts research on K–12 gifted and talented education, and provides a variety of publications addressing gifted and talented issues.

California State University at Sacramento (CSUS) offers a program that is endorsed by Johns Hopkins's CTY but is based on a different approach. CSUS's Project Talent Search reflects the multiple needs and interests of the population with gifts and talents. For example, one course focuses on the use of word processing, spreadsheets, and database management for personal and academic enrichment. Another course uses the programming language LOGO to introduce students to computer science. A third course emphasizes using the tools of the information highway, such as e-mail, listservers, newsgroups, Telnet, File Transfer Protocol, and building home pages. Project Talent Search began investigating the effects of academic acceleration on students' social and academic achievement in 1985. Participating students were given a series of formal questionnaires over a 3-year period. The results of this study indicated that "bright, highly motivated early entrants to college can be quite successful in college and later in life" (Brody, Assouline, & Stanley, 1990, p. 138). The authors, however, pointed out that success is most likely when the verbal and mathematical SAT scores of the early entrants are the same or better than the means of the other entrants at the college that these young people are attending.

Books and articles about computers and people with gifts and talents have often focused on the how-to aspect. Terry's (1984) book focused on the practical aspects of developing and implementing an educational plan. Greenlaw and

MacIntosh (1988) presented a brief but excellent discussion of a K–12 computer curriculum for students with gifts and talents, and Sisk (1987) provided an analysis of technology's role in understanding intelligence. Swassing's (1984) book included a chapter by Trifiletti on using computers to teach the gifted. More recently, Niess (1990) discussed the need for professional educators to be computer competent and able to incorporate technology into their curriculum in meaningful ways.

The periodical *Gifted Child Today* (G/C/T) has published articles on computers for students with gifts and talents since at least the early 1980s. For example, the November/December 1983 issue includes articles on family computing, the application of computers to gifted education, and the development of a computer-based classroom. The January/February 1985 issue includes articles that discuss a curriculum guide for teaching computer literacy, using computers to solve math problems, and preschool computer games for learning. More recently the January/February 1996 issue included an excellent article by Lewis on the Internet. In the September/October 1996 issue, Troxclair et al. described the University of Southern Mississippi's 17th Saturday Gifted Program for kindergarten through 12th-grade students. This program included a multimedia course in which participants in 7th through 12th grades used technology to research, write, and present their ideas. Resources included access to the research databases ERIC (Educational Resources Information Clearinghouse) and OSCAR (Online System for Computer Assisted Retrieval). Reports were word processed with Microsoft Word and multimedia slide presentations were developed with Microsoft's PowerPoint. Using AVerMedia's Aver-Key, the students' computer presentations were then copied to videotape for home viewing. Technology was the means with which these young people enhanced their thinking and processing skills and developed multimedia products. Although participants in this course were identified as gifted, they came from different backgrounds and brought with them varying levels of technical knowledge. In spite of these differences, there was a high degree of support, cooperation, and sharing of ideas among this group of 7th to 12th graders.

With the new millennium fast approaching, it is wise to take stock of how gifted education fits into the technological future. Cohen (1996) presented a no-nonsense view of the strengths and weaknesses of gifted education today and provided a structure for thinking about future changes. Cohen maintained that gifted education is more vulnerable today than ever before. The desire for quick fixes and easy answers has produced research without direction and haphazard application of findings. Politics and competing paradigms have resulted in funding cuts and lack of support as well. The cumulative effect is that education of individuals with gifts and talents has been weakened in practice, research, and theory. To remedy this situation Cohen recommended (a) serious "stock-taking" of where the field is today; (b) thoughtful development of new theories and practices in gifted education; (c) research that considers the breadth, depth, and complexity of the field and the people it seeks to support; (d) inclusion of the political issues of equity as well as excellence; (e) changes in today's paradigm for gifted education; and (f) bringing gifted education into the mainstream arena where it will be able to transform it.

The role of technology in gifted and talented education is most closely related to Cohen's (1996) recommendation for paradigm changes. Cohen stated that in the information age, the world is so small and information is changing so quickly that a new, more dynamic, and complex world view is necessary. This new world view supports the notion that change is a given and that stability is an anomaly. A paradigm that reflects this new perspective began in the early 1990s and is reflected in the general educational policy as outlined in Goals 2000: Educate America Act of 1994, the development of new technologies, and changes in the workplace that require people to be able to quickly learn and apply information in new and creative ways. If gifted education is to remain viable, Cohen proposed that it needs to change its own paradigm to reflect this new world view and adjust today to the technological changes of tomorrow.

The winter 1996 issue of the semiannual newsletter for The National Research Center on the Gifted and Talented (NRC/GT) outlined the gifted education research agenda and specific proposals for 1995 through 2000. After a needs assessment survey, two basic areas emerged: (a) identifying individuals with gifts and talents within more economically and culturally diverse populations and (b) integrating gifted and talented programs and methods into mainstream education. What is surprising in the NRC/GT's outline for future research is the absence of any reference to technology and its connection to the education of individuals with gifts and talents. Only one research proposal, Robert Sternberg's "Giftedness and Expertise," even mentioned the word computer. From his abstract, he appears to suggest that computers will provide practice in complex reasoning tasks for both gifted and nongifted students. Nowhere in this newsletter are there proposals to investigate the use of technology as a tool for research, multimedia productions, or accelerated learning.

The question that must be asked is, "Where have these researchers been?" Cohen's (1996) new paradigm for gifted education emphasized the need to consider the fluid, fast-changing world. The fastest changing part of this very complex world is technology and most particularly the technology of multimedia telecommunications on the Internet. Why is it that this powerful force in an increasingly global society is addressed constantly by mainstream educational journals but much less so by publications dealing with gifted and talented issues? For example, Harp (1996) described how technology is changing the learning equation in ordinary classrooms by enabling students to reach beyond their bland textbooks to global resources on the Internet. Today's technology provides all students, gifted, talented, or otherwise, with opportunities to exercise higher, more complex levels of thinking as they evaluate resources and discuss ideas with experts on-line. Faced with students finding a wide variety of primary resources and discovering new perspectives on old topics, teachers are redesigning their curricula to help students sharpen their abilities to analyze, synthesize, and evaluate ideas. Surely technology is particularly well suited to serve the NCR/GT's research agenda described in the prior paragraph. The Internet is already the tool of many unidentified people with gifts and talents. They navigate the Net on school, library, or home computers and share information, discuss ideas, and learn from a global community. With access to technology and especially the Internet becoming increasingly available to people from all cultural and economic backgrounds, the pool of individuals with gifts and talents becomes significantly broader and more diverse. Furthermore, technology in general and the Internet in particular helps people from all cultural and economic backgrounds access a wide range of resources that can develop their own unique giftedness. Technology will also assist the NRC/GT in achieving its goal of supporting mainstream education because its multimedia, interactive nature appeals and motivates just about every student. It is equally obvious that all students need to learn how to apply higher levels of thinking to the information they find through technology. Gifted and talented programs have always emphasized the importance of such thinking and are, therefore, uniquely positioned to serve mainstream

Students can take their computers to and from class. (Photograph by Carolyn F. Woods)

education. Everyone needs to be prepared for the challenges that confront them in the increasingly complex world of global information. Gifted and talented research needs to address these issues and to help all individuals achieve their gifted and talented potential in the next millennium.

General Hardware and Software Considerations

Although many individuals with gifts and talents have computers at home, many others do not. To correct this imbalance schools need to provide these students with access to the technology. While computer labs continue to be a resource for whole-class computer activities, many classrooms have at least one workstation for small group or individual projects. An increasing number of classrooms, school libraries, and even entire schools provide access to the Internet as well. California's Net Day 1996, an effort to get a large number of schools connected to the Internet quickly and inexpensively, was so successful that many communities in other states have planned similar projects.

When computers are brought into the classroom, classroom management and student learning need to be considered. The overall purpose of computers in education should be to integrate subject areas, extend learning, and contribute to the total learning process. Teachers of students with gifts and talents need to keep in mind that technology is a powerful, multifaceted tool that can greatly benefit the powerful, multifaceted minds of their students. For example, a single computer can be used to word process new ideas, create visual images of extraordinary quality, record and produce original music, develop multimedia presentations on any number of topics, and, with access to the Internet, provide global exploration and communication. It is therefore essential that this versatile technology be available to all students with gifts and talents regardless of their gender, economic situation, or cultural heritage (Middleton, Littlefield, & Lehrer, 1992).

Educational Setting

Over the years there has been considerable debate about the best arrangement for computers in schools. Some educators believe the computer lab is best, whereas others feel computers belong in the classroom. Today, there is often a combination of both configurations. In general, the lab is best suited for whole-class computer activities and classroom computers for small group and individual activities (also see Chapter 8). For example, in a computer lab an entire class can be introduced to a software program and begin a new project. If the software used in the lab is also available on classroom computers, students can continue working on their projects when they return to their classroom. Networking can support these two configurations nicely when classroom computers are networked to the computer lab because student files can be transferred easily from one location to another. In fact, having computers in classrooms and labs networked not only provides the best of these two worlds but also adds greater flexibility than either configuration has alone.

Schools are linking computers in a variety of networked arrangements. A local area network (LAN) links computers within a lab, single building, or campus, whereas a wide area network (WAN) connects entire school districts. The mother-of-all-networks is the Internet to which independent computers or entire networks can be connected. Networks are powerful configurations for communication, and even limited intraschool networks, without access to the Internet, increase communication among students and teachers within a school or school district. Access to the Internet, however, means access to the world. The impact of this global connection is perhaps greatest in a classroom where students have little opportunity to share ideas with others. Once connected to the Internet, teachers and students communicate with others around the world, participate in projects involving different countries and cultures, and gather information from experts thousands of miles away. Today's global classroom is definitely not the classroom of the past.

Classroom Management and Teaching Resources

Off-line

The three most useful applications for classroom management are word processors, database managers, and spreadsheets. These programs can be used for writing and revising letters and reports, sorting and retrieving important data, and generating and monitoring budgets. Word processors help teachers with any task associated with written communication. Customizing layouts and adding graphics ensures a high degree of clarity, refinement, and interest. Database managers enable teachers to work efficiently with information related to class projects or learning resources. For example, a database of community mentors could be developed to store people's names, addresses, phone numbers, areas of expertise, and the time they can consult with students. Spreadsheets are wonderful resources for developing budgets and adjusting for fluctuations in funding. Charts from a spreadsheet can be used to present statistical data in an easy to understand format. For example, charts could be used to compare costs of different mentoring programs.

Software packages that include word processor, database, and spreadsheet applications (e.g., Microsoft Works or ClarisWorks) make writing and record keeping especially easy in that information can be easily transferred from one application to another. For instance, a mentor database could be used to identify experts in animal husbandry and the word processor to write personal letters requesting information and help from those who are selected. Integrated packages offer good value not only because it is easy to share data between different application files but, also because the applications can be used by students as well. (See later section on Computer Tools.)

On-line

Whether students with gifts and talents are in a special program or in a general education class-room, they are an intellectually challenging group of people who require support in many different areas. Providing meaningful and intellectually challenging activities for such rapid learners can be a difficult and arduous task. This is especially true for teachers who are responsible for the education of all students with gifts and talents in a school or an entire school district (Mills & Durden, 1992). Fortunately, telecommunications and the Internet and World Wide Web can help (Berman & Tinker, 1997). If a school is wired for direct access to the Internet, it is a simple matter of turning on the computer and opening the appropriate software. Schools that are unable to provide such ease of access can still have access to the outside world by purchasing a modem, the software to run it, a telephone line, and an Internet provider. An increasing number of school districts provide access to the Internet and World Wide Web by either becoming an Internet provider themselves or making arrangements with a commercial provider for such access.

The Internet and World Wide Web offer an amazing array of resources for teachers of young people with gifts and talents. Newsgroups provide opportunities to share ideas and concerns with groups of people who have similar interests, and electronic mail (e-mail) provides quick and efficient messaging between individuals. On-line newsletters and listservers help teachers stay current on gifted/talented issues as well. The TAG Family Network, for example, provides an electronic newsletter that can be read on-line or saved and printed out. This newsletter can also be delivered electronically to those who subscribe to TAG's listserver. Listservers are designed to automatically send files to those who request a subscription. Although they are meant only to send information to subscribers and not to receive it, the information sent from a listserver often includes ways to contact people or join special projects, so they do help teachers interact with colleagues and develop curriculum through special projects and resources. Requests to join a listserver are made via e-mail and require a specific message requesting the subscription. It is important to note that a listserver can quickly fill up a subscriber's electronic mailbox so it is important to remember how to unsubscribe as well. The Resources section at the end of this chapter lists a few listservers and newsgroups.

Curriculum ideas and actual lesson plans designed for gifted and talented education can be found at Web, gopher, and telnet sites on the Internet. The TAG Family Network and The National Research Center on the Gifted and Talented (NRC/GT) Web sites provide a range of resources. The parent-run TAG Family Network shares information, supports parents and educators, and monitors legal issues associated with youth who are gifted and talented. This site includes information about the organization and its goals, a TAG Hotline, articles, book reviews, extensive links to Web sites, reference tools for students and educators, and mailing lists. The University of Connecticut's NRC/GT offers newsletters, abstracts, and products for gifted and talented education. Rice University in Texas has a unique program: the Center for Research on Parallel Computation sponsored GirlTECH '96. Twenty teachers from the Houston area participated in this intensive technology training program where they explored innovative teaching strategies in an effort to develop ways to involve young women in the fields of computer technology, engineering, math, and science. The ERIC home page provides, among other things, access to ERIC, ERIC on the 'Net, AskEric, National Parent Information Network, Search the ERIC Database, and ERIC Systemwide Publications. From this site it is easy to find a wide range of information about gifted and talented topics.

Educational Web sites do not need to be labeled gifted and talented to contain valuable curriculum resources that are appropriate for young people who are bright and highly gifted. Two such sites are Classroom Connect and Web66. These on-line resources put teachers and their students in touch with others who have similar needs and interests by providing teaching ideas, lesson plans, and projects with which to build intellectually challenging curricula. It should be noted that there is also a *Classroom Connect* publication, which is one of the finest magazines for finding educational resources on the Internet. Begun in 1994, the publication provides teachers with up-to-date information on Internet resources, tips, projects, and lesson plans, as well as articles.

The Internet is an incredible tool for learning, but teachers need to manage student access to it as well. Decisions as to what is appropriate necessarily depend upon the maturity of the students, as well as school, community, and parent policies and attitudes. Unfiltered access to the Internet means students have unrestricted access to any topic. Although a great deal of information on the Internet is valuable, there are sites where the information is suspect, illegal, or profoundly disturbing (Quesada & Summers, 1998). There is also the potential for young people to be contacted by unsuitable or even dangerous individuals.

There are several ways to deal with this telecommunication problem. First and foremost, an acceptable use policy (AUP) needs to be written that clearly states the school's or district's Internet access rules. Many schools invite parents and others in the community to help design an AUP. When this is done, the AUP is more likely to have support because it reflects the values of the community. Essential to such a plan are clear student guidelines for what is and is not appropriate when on-line. Equally important is the clear articulation of the consequences for those who violate these rules. AUPs are also important because they help students to act responsibly and develop good judgment, and they help protect educational institutions and teachers from liability issues. It is therefore a good idea to have a written AUP that students and parents sign before students are provided access to the Internet.

Many schools also install filtering software on computers with Internet access. Such utilities maintain databases of specific inappropriate sites and lists of objectionable terms found in Internet addresses and site descriptions. These programs can also evaluate the context in which objectionable terms are found and, based on that evaluation, "decide" if the site can be accessed. Some filtering software permits sites to be rated by age appropriateness, whereas others allow system administrators to set graduated levels of access. The combining of Internet filtering with proxy server technology will offer a similar service for computers on networks (Mather, 1996; http:// n2h2.com/main_isps_bottom.html).

A simpler and less intrusive way to monitor student access is to use bookmarks to steer students to appropriate Web sites and model appropriate uses of the Internet. The Scholastic Network is a site that uses this technique. Hotlists of appropriate sites for educational activities, teachers, and students also provide efficient and safe paths for Internet users. Commercial on-line services such as America Online, CompuServ, and Prodigy provide more restricted and safe electronic environments. They have education areas of their own, include parental control options, and may include filtering software for restricting where young people can go (Mather, 1996).

Finally, Internet content providers have established a self-rating mechanism in response to the 1996 passage of the Communications Decency Act. The Recreational Software Advisory Council (RSACi) developed an Internet rating system based on ratings that webmasters assign to their own sites. By going to the RSACi site, teachers, parents, and students can make informed choices. Platform for Internet Content Selection (PICS) has developed technology that selects Web sites based on the rating codes that webmasters or third-party rating bureaus embed in the HTML code of web documents. PICS compatible software can then be used to block access to selected sites (Mather, 1996).

Student Learning: Classroom, Computer Lab, and Around the World

The purpose of computers in any educational program is to promote learning. With individuals with gifts and talents, it is especially important that hardware and software support independent learning in many different fields.

The first thing to consider is how technology can serve educational goals. Teachers should list their educational goals and then delineate the ways computers can be used in their gifted and talented programs. They should also include applications they know they need and those they

may need at some future date. Flexibility and expandability of hardware and software are important as well. Hardware should be flexible and expandable so it can be adapted to changes in technology and different projects. This is especially true in a multimedia environment. Purchasing less costly equipment that can be replaced or enhanced as needs arise helps to keep initial costs down (e.g., Sun's JAVA Internet Computer or Oracle's Network Computer). Later, when more funds are available or needs change, the new computers can be purchased or the old system upgraded (e.g., extra RAM, larger hard drives, audiovisual cards, digital cameras, scanners). Software that serves multiple purposes will also increase a computer's utility as well (e.g., integrated packages such as ClarisWorks, Microsoft Works and Office). Such software accommodates a wide range of abilities and interests and provides an excellent foundation for software resources for students with gifts and talents.

Access to computers is essential for students with gifts and talents. The question, however, is just how many computers are needed. As stated earlier, there are times when it is important for an entire class to work at one time on a project. When this is the case, computer labs are the most efficient configuration. At other times, a few computers in the classroom may be all that is needed. What is necessary, however, is for students with gifts and talents to have ready access to the technology when they need it so it becomes an integral part of the way they learn. It is worth noting that one multipurpose computer can serve students with diverse interests and talents. With the appropriate software and hardware, a single workstation can become a tool for composing and producing music, generating and printing architectural plans, creating and printing commercial or fine art, putting together video productions, or building and testing robots. Figure 13.2 illustrates some of the different ways students with gifts and talents might use a single classroom computer. Chapter 8 also addresses computer and student configurations.

Distance learning has long been a way to provide challenging curriculum to students with gifts and talents. Students and teachers involved in

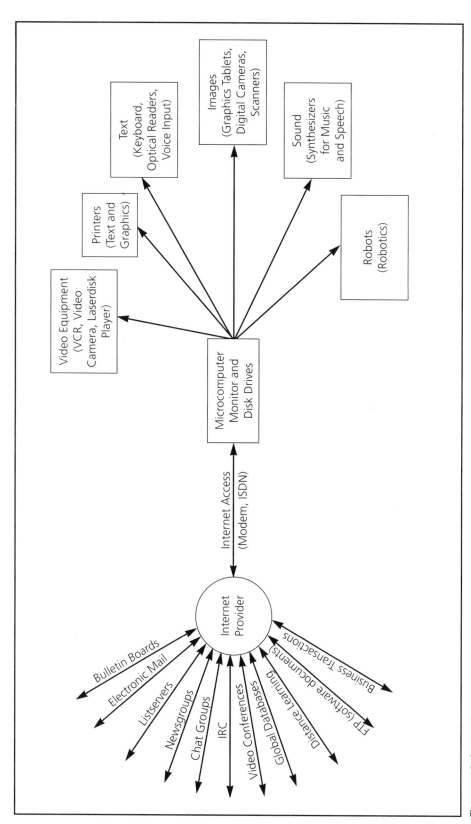

Figure 13.2. Single-computer concept.

AT&T's Long Distance Learning Network found the experience of working together across the miles intellectually invigorating and challenging. Information shared included knowledge about software and hardware, as well as ideas and curriculum (Lake, 1988–1989). National Geographic's Kids Network uses telecommunications to bring together students from all parts of the world to collaborate on scientific investigations that involve data collection and analysis. Distance learning includes college-level courses as well. Stanford University, for example, has the Education Program for Gifted Youth, which offers advanced mathematics, physics, and writing courses to highly capable middle and high school students. Using specially designed software and appropriate texts, these students learn complex material at their own pace on their own computers. Other universities and colleges across the country also offer courses via the Internet. For example, the School of Computer Science and Engineering at California State University in Sacramento (CSUS) offers an Internet course that is open to qualified high school students. Although access to the Internet is required, students without home access can use their school's access. This course is part of CSUS's program of study for high school students who wish to take college-level courses. The Accelerated College Entrance (ACE) Center at CSUS provides learning opportunities to highly able students who wish to further their academic growth during the school year. Qualified students may take courses at CSUS for a minimal fee. For those who cannot get to the campus regularly, general education courses are available through local cable companies. ACE students earn college credits that may be applied to degree programs at CSUS or transferred to other universities. Other distance learning opportunities can be found on the Internet at the Gifted and Talented (TAG) Resources Page. (See the Resources section at the end of this chapter for details about these and other Internet learning opportunities for individuals with gifts and talents.)

Computers are powerful tools for learning that can transport the education of individuals with gifts and talents to new heights (Hancock, 1997).

Today, computers are in more homes than ever before because many people recognize the significance of this versatile technology, and as prices fall, people can afford the technology. As a consequence, more and more students have computers at home and many are bringing portable devices (e.g., laptops) to school. Computers are especially useful for students with gifts and talents with special needs. Today, if a young person needs a computer to learn, he or she should have it. Technology that allows individuals to develop their gifts and talents fully is not an option, but a necessity.

Specific Technology Applications

Software provides the versatility that makes computer technology particularly appropriate for individuals with gifts and talents. To begin with, software can turn a computer into a tool for exploring a wide range of advanced subjects such as molecular biology, multivariate calculus, or thermodynamics and physics. Exemplary software also provides users with a motivating environment in which they can rapidly acquire knowledge and skills while developing their creativity and thinking skills.

In his Taxonomy of Educational Objectives, Bloom (1956) described six major categories of thinking: knowledge, comprehension, application, analysis, synthesis, and evaluation. Knowledge and comprehension, at the lower end of this scale, represent the most basic kinds of thinking, whereas synthesis and evaluation are the most advanced levels. According to Taylor (1983), learning for individuals with gifts and talents should begin at the application level. Unfortunately, 90% to 95% of all learning at the elementary school level and 95% to 100% of all learning at the secondary level emphasize only the two lowest levels, knowledge and comprehension. This is the case in many programs for students with gifts and talents as well. As noted at the beginning of this chapter, what makes individuals gifted and talented is their behavior—giftedness depends upon above average ability, task commitment, and creativity. Software that creates an environment in which all three of these behaviors come together is software for individuals who are gifted and talented.

Software Criteria

Although people with gifts and talents form a unique and intellectually demanding group with special needs and interests, little software is targeted for this population. As a result it is important to outline basic criteria for identifying software that is especially appropriate for these individuals. Finding common evaluative criteria to apply is especially difficult because of the diversity of abilities and interests of this group. For example, as part of a solar energy project for the California Science Fair in 1983, 6-year-old Jamie Lockwood built a computer to record each day's high and low temperatures and to calculate the day's average. This project required not only building a computer but reprogramming an electronically programmable read-only memory (EPROM) chip. Jamie was an exceptionally gifted child whose level of development can be measured by the remark he made to his mother after his first visit to the physics lab at the University of California, Davis, "I thought I'd have to wait years before I could talk to someone who'd understand me." Although the type of software Jamie needed for his scientific project was very different from the software needed for a gifted musician or artist, the basic criteria remain the same.

Because of the great diversity within the population with gifts and talents, it is important to remember that the first priority must be to consider who will be using the software and for what purpose. Some individuals with gifts and talents may need to build skills, whereas others may have special needs and disabilities. Finally, it is important to understand that ability and interest rather than age dictate when a specific package is appropriate. Bearing all this in mind, the following characteristics should be considered when selecting software for individuals with gifts and talents:

1. *Flexible*—Does it support different subject areas either in a specific field or in several fields?

2. *Modifiable*—Can the content, pace, or order of operation be changed? How much control does the user have?

3. *Expandable*—Can it be used to explore more than one subject?

4. *Responsive*—Does it offer different ways to alter the sequence of operation and speed?

5. *Imaginative*—Does it encourage and support diverse thinking and multiple solutions to intriguing problems?

Computer Applications

The following discussion of applications for individuals with gifts and talents is divided into three major categories: (1) computer-assisted instruction—how the computer can be used to teach specific skills and concepts; (2) computer tools—software packages developed to explore different fields (e.g., multipurpose tools for examining many subjects or single-purpose tools for a specific field); and (3) computer science—the practice and theory behind computer technology.

As stated in previous chapters, a software package is designed to run on a specific computer platform or operating system (Macintosh, DOS, or Windows). It is therefore important to know

A computer lab can be used to develop computer abilities of students who are gifted and talented. (Photograph by Carolyn F. Woods)

the system requirements of a particular software package. Today, most educational software can be purchased for either Macintosh, MS-DOS, or Windows environments. Software on CD-ROM or DVD-ROM often runs on multiple platforms because there is enough room on the disc to store several operating systems.

Computer-Assisted Instruction

Computer-assisted instruction (CAI) provides opportunities to acquire knowledge in a computer-controlled environment. Depending on needs, this type of software can be used to acquire new or to review old information in a self-paced environment. The basic CAI categories are drill-and-practice, tutorial, problem solving, simulation, and edutainment. Today's software often combines several of these categories. When evaluating specific software, it is important to consider, along with the five general criteria listed previously, whether it challenges the intellect, stimulates critical thinking, and develops problem-solving strategies.

Drill-and-Practice and Tutorial

Drill-and-practice and tutorial packages traditionally offer users little control but help introduce or review information and concepts. Whenever possible, these applications should be modifiable in both content and learning sequence (see Chapter 6). Such software packages offer opportunities for independent, self-paced learning or a chance to reinforce learning. For example, Number Munchers by MECC, which was originally written for the Apple II platform has withstood the test of time and is now available for both Macintosh and MS-DOS platforms. In this drill-and-practice game, students hone their skills with multiples, equivalent fractions, and prime numbers. Management options and the ability to vary the levels of difficulty are available. Sunburst Communication's How the West Was One + Three × Four for the Macintosh, MS-DOS, and Windows environments is another engaging and challenging drill-and-practice pack-

age. Following a gameboard format, students construct and then solve arithmetic expressions as they progress along a number line trail.

Problem Solving

Problem-solving software provides tools to solve and even create problems that focus attention on specific thinking skills. Sunburst Communication's The Factory and Puzzle Tanks supply intriguing challenges for young learners. The Factory builds spatial perception and flexible problem-solving skills associated with visual reasoning, pattern and sequence recognition, and prediction and analysis processes. Puzzle Tanks emphasizes number and logic puzzles with different levels of difficulty. Both of these products are available for Apple, Macintosh, MS-DOS, and Windows platforms. There are Spanish versions, La Fabrica and Tanto Tanque, for these programs as well.

Simulation

Simulation software usually includes a problem-solving component. However, this type of software creates an environment in which problems are solved by applying knowledge and testing hypotheses. Such environments are usually difficult or impossible to experience in today's world but are easy to experience with a computer. Flying an airplane, traveling west in the 19th century, or managing a nuclear reactor are all examples of such environments. Simulations are especially useful for students with gifts and talents because they provide a variety of opportunities for in-depth exploration. Tom Snyder Productions offers excellent problem-solving simulations for classrooms with only one computer. These simulations range from the S.M.A.R.T. Choices series, in which students discuss ways to deal with personal issues such as drugs, sex, and responsible behavior in and out of school, to Decisions, Decisions series, in which students participate in political or historical situations. These software packages not only develop problem-solving strategies and critical-thinking skills but also promote cooperative learning as students work in teams to make decisions.

Simulations can also enrich hands-on experience. For example, a science student can study human anatomy using A.D.A.M. Software's A.D.A.M. Essentials. This CD-ROM (DVD-ROM may be available) provides a comprehensive introduction to human anatomy and the body's 12 major systems, including more than 100 medically accurate layers of human anatomy with over 4,000 anatomical structures. Oregon Trail is among the best known and loved simulations. Over the years MECC has enhanced this software so that versions are available for all computer platforms and for stand-alone and networked computers. Oregon Trail is the classic version for single computers, whereas Oregon Trail II and later editions include three-dimensional graphics, video footage, and sound, as well as different trails to take. Wagon Train 1848 uses a network to link computers together to form wagon trains and enable students to confer and discuss matters as they travel the trail. Finally, MECC's Inter@ctive Explorer Series takes the simulation a step further by providing on-line adventures. Furthermore, Oregon Trail Online and MayaQuest both use the Internet to connect students and their teachers with experts around the world. A subscription kit needs to be purchased and time set aside in the curriculum to participate in such projects. The National Geographic's Kids Network series offers similar opportunities for global scientific investigations. It should be noted that similar activities organized by teachers are available on the Internet for free, and in many ways the Internet is the ultimate in electronic simulations.

Edutainment

Edutainment refers to computer games that have educational value. Quality edutainment combines intellectual challenge with the compelling format of a game to develop logical thinking, planning, and sequencing skills. These programs can also stimulate off-computer learning in that players may have to create maps or game plans, conduct research, and discuss strategies with others in an effort to win or achieve a higher level of success. In short, games have always been a source of intellectual challenge and pleasure for people with gifts and talents, and a computer simply provides a new game format (Hamlett, 1984).

Adventure games are a popular form of edutainment that brings together on- and off-computer learning. Perhaps the most famous of these games is Brøderbund's Carmen Sandiego series, including Where in the U.S.A. Is Carmen Sandiego? and Where in the World Is Carmen Sandiego? Playing these adventure games, students research, gather and analyze data, and then draw conclusions in an effort to track down Carmen and her notorious gang. The Learning Company's Super Solvers series and Logic Quest are captivating adventure games as well. For example, Super Solvers: Midnight Rescue! builds reading comprehension and deductive-thinking skills, and Logic Quest is a medieval adventure in which players are presented with challenging mazes, puzzle, and construction activities. Both Brøderbund and The Learning Company's game software are available for Macintosh, MS-DOS, and Windows environments in disk and CD-ROM formats (DVD-ROM titles are increasing).

Computer Tools

Software that turns the computer into a tool is powerful in the hands of individuals who are gifted and talented. While word processor, database, and spreadsheet applications are the three most commonly used tools, there are many other kinds of utility software such as programs to create works of art, design buildings, compose music, and produce full-motion video.

Word Processing

A word processor is an excellent tool for individuals with gifts and talents to develop writing skills because it frees the user from the mechanics of writing and rewriting drafts so they can concentrate on the content and organization of their prose. This is especially important for young people whose ideas often outstrip their ability to write on paper.

Even the most basic word processor is useful and some that are free have special features. For example, Simpletext comes with all Macintosh computers. Although this software does not have a spellchecker or thesaurus, it does have audio output so the computer can read text in a word processed file. Young writers delight in selecting a "voice" for the computer and then having it read their stories aloud. More complete word processors that include a spellchecker, thesaurus, and perhaps a grammar checker can be purchased. Among the many excellent packages available are Microsoft's Word, Corel's WordPerfect, and Softkey's Write Now. Some word processors can support non-English languages. For example, Apple Language Kits permit switching between the computer's main language and another language. Languages available with these kits include Japanese, Chinese, Hebrew, and Arabic. It is worth noting that these kits do occupy considerable hard drive space. In addition to the usual spelling and thesaurus options, word processors often include sophisticated features for page layout, graphics, outlines, tables, and even multimedia presentations. Many also provide easy ways to create Web pages. More advanced students with gifts and talents may wish to use desktop publishing tools such as Adobe's Page-Maker to put together elaborate publications for paper or cyberspace. In short, word processors have become powerful presentation and communication tools for publishing on- or off-line.

Although most word processors are more than adequate for basic writing tasks, there is also innovative software for young children including Write Away! and Magic Media Slate by Sunburst Communications, and Storybook Weaver by MECC. Write Away! includes special features such as four levels for individualized writing, teacher-defined wordlists, outline and notebook capability, and a standard spellchecker. Magic Media Slate and Storybook Weaver emphasize multimedia presentation features such as adding clip art and sound. Storybook Weaver Deluxe (MECC) and the Bilingual Writing Center (The Learning Company) are bilingual in English and Spanish. These multifaceted word processors help young learners create engaging stories with text, graphics, and sounds.

The major obstacle to successful word processing is keyboarding skills. There are, of course, software packages such as Mavis Beacon Teaches Typing or Mavis Beacon Teaches Typing for Kids by Mindscape, and UltraKey by Bytes of Learning. Keyboarding software should be used when the learner's hands are large enough to reach all keys comfortably and when the learner sees a real need to type quickly and efficiently. When these two factors coincide, this type of software becomes motivating and fun to use, and typing speed and accuracy develop quickly and naturally.

Electronic Spreadsheets

Like word processors and databases, electronic spreadsheets were developed for business purposes. While businesses use this software to keep track of financial matters that require recording and forecasting, researchers use it for mathematical analysis of numeric data. For instance, a social studies project comparing cities in the United States could use a spreadsheet to record and manipulate census data gathered from field research, government, or Internet sources about cities across the United States. The completed spreadsheet could then be used to produce a ranked listing of all the major U.S. cities according to their populations. Nonnumeric data could be evaluated as well by weighting it numerically. For example, categories for public transportation systems, levels of pollution, and numbers of parks and cultural centers could be ranked on a scale from 1 to 10. Cities could then be compared according to the value given each category. A final column totaling each city's points would provide a final quality-of-life score for each city. This grand total could be used to rank the cities according to their total scores. Analysis of such ranking is not only interesting in itself but could lead to a discussion of statistical ranking and a comparison of seemingly objective figures that may, in fact, produce biased results.

Electronic spreadsheets are easy to use. All that is needed is an understanding of basic arithmetic operations and grid layouts that use rows and columns. Dickinson and Hopping (1985) reported that average fourth graders enjoyed working with spreadsheets. Spreadsheets are also excellent for developing critical thinking skills because students can organize and analyze data and then hypothesize outcomes (Parker & Wider, 1989). Today, spreadsheets not only crunch numbers but generate charts and graphs to enhance statistical analyses. Microsoft's Excel and Lotus 1-2-3 are general-purpose spreadsheet applications that individuals with gifts and talents can use. Casady and Greene's Let's Keep It Simple Spreadsheet and Mathsoft's Mathcad PLUS 6 are two other packages that offer easy ways to create spreadsheets and produce graphs. Mathcad PLUS 6 integrates calculations, graphics, and text into one worksheet so it is easy to formulate ideas, set up problems, and develop solutions. Both the process and the solutions to such problems can then be shared through printed documents and e-mail. Whatever the package, spreadsheets are excellent tools for analyzing statistical data and answering "what if" questions based on numeric calculations.

Databases

Although databases were originally developed to help businesses keep track of a wide variety of information, they also are extremely useful for many advanced projects involving collection, analysis, interpretation, organization, and retrieval of information. Working with databases helps to develop the higher level thinking skills of analysis, synthesis, and evaluation. Such advanced thinking skills apply to all fields of learning and are useful in off-computer as well as on-computer projects (Watson & Strudler, 1989–1990).

Understanding how to search databases effectively is an increasingly important skill in today's age of information because so much of it is now stored electronically. The CD-ROM and CD-R (DVD-ROM and DVD-R) media can be used to store vast databases filled with text, images, and sounds covering many topics. Libraries, large or small, use CD-ROMs to provide access to databases filled with references and full-text resources (again, DVD-ROM titles are increasing). CD-ROMs for the classroom or home market offer entire encyclopedias or specialized databases filled with audio, visual, and textual information on specific topics such as rainforests. It should be noted that encyclopedias on a compact disc, especially low-cost home versions, are generally not as complete as the multiple-volume versions that libraries purchase. CD-ROMs for specific subject areas, on the other hand, can be excellent inexpensive or even free resources for in-depth research and explorations.

Although it is important for students with gifts and talents to be able to use databases, it is also important that they understand how to create their own. FileMaker Pro by FileMaker-Claris is an easy to use and sophisticated relational database that includes ScriptMaker for conditional branching and custom messages. Sharing File-Maker Pro databases between IBM or compatible and Macintosh computers is so easy that both platforms can work off the same network. Charts and graphs can be easily created as well. Once students know how to create databases, they can develop their own for a wide range of subjects. For example, students interested in astronomy can gather information about stars from a variety of resources including CD-ROMs and the Internet as well as the more traditional nonelectronic resources of printed periodicals and books. They could then create an astronomy database with the following categories: name, light-years from Earth, magnitude (brightness), color and type, constellation, and seasons. Once students finish this star database, they could use database search tools to find stars that are less than 10 light-years away, stars larger than the sun, the blue giants or red dwarfs, all stars in the Orion constellation, those stars visible only in spring, or the yellow main-sequence stars that are less than 50 light-years away (Bollinger & Hopping, 1985). For an excellent explanation of how to use databases with first through fifth graders who are gifted, see Brooks' (1990) article. Databases are powerful tools for research in all fields and can be used for school, job, or personal projects.

Integrated Packages

It is possible to purchase a single software package that integrates word processor, database, and spreadsheet applications into one software package (other applications could also be bundled). The advantages of such packages are that the commands are similar for all applications included in the package and the cost for the single package is considerably less than the total cost of purchasing each application separately. Claris-Works, Microsoft Works and Office, Corel Word-Perfect Suite, and Lotus SmartSuite are examples of such integrated packages. These packages may also include additional applications to create graphics and computer presentations, to engage in communications, to create multimedia presentations, and to send and read e-mail messages.

Reference Tools

In the Information Age knowing how to access vast quantities of information quickly and easily is essential. Computers are well suited to this task because they are multipurpose systems that can efficiently sort through information and then deliver it to the user quickly and easily. The most common media for providing large amounts of information are CD-ROM and DVD-ROM, videodiscs, and the Internet.

For individuals with gifts and talents, CD-ROMs, DVD-ROMs, and videodiscs are of greatest value when they provide vast databases of text, still images, and video clips for researching, learning, and developing projects. Today, most libraries, regardless of size, have databases of reference and full-text resources available on CD-ROMs. To keep such information current, libraries subscribe to different services. For example, InfoTrac provides periodical indexes as well as references and citations to microfiche and some full-text articles. NewsBank, on the other hand, provides full-text newspaper articles on a wide range of topics. Subscribers to InfoTrac or NewsBank receive CD-ROMs each month so information is kept current. Full-text articles on social issues, scientific developments, and global economic

and political events are all provided through a third service, SIRS Researcher CD-ROM.

Free CD-ROMs are often available through government or other special programs. For example, SIRCED02 (Shuttle Imaging Radar-C Educational CD-ROM 2) is a free compact disc developed for educators by NASA and the Jet Propulsion Lab. It is filled with lesson plans, science data collected from Earth Orbit on two Space Shuttle missions, radar images of the Earth from space, and movies about issues such as global warming. On a different topic, the California Indian Library put together two CD-ROMs, one each about the Pomo and the Miwok Indian tribes. Each CD-ROM is filled with archived materials about California's Native Americans, including photographs, sound recordings, and textual materials collected by University of California at Berkeley anthropologists in the early part of the 20th century. Each CD-ROM includes comprehensive bibliographies that can be searched by author, title, periodical, series, keywords, and holdings. This project was funded by the U.S. Department of Education with the understanding that the CD-ROMs would be free to libraries and educators.

Commercial CD-ROMs can be purchased as well. Since they easily support multimedia, they are especially good for fields of study that have visual and audio components, such as biology, genetics, music theory or composition, history, and geography. For young readers, wonderfully engaging interactive books are available on CD-ROM. For example, Brøderbund's Living Books series for Macintosh and Windows platforms includes *Just Grandma and Me*, *The New Kid on the Block*, and *Arthur's Teacher Troubles*.

As so many people have discovered, the Internet is a vast resource that can provide rich, up-to-date information about many topics. Once on the Internet, it is a simple matter of selecting a search engine such as InfoSeek, AltaVista, or Excite; entering key words; and clicking the "Search" button. Within seconds a scored list of on-line resources appears. The Electric Library is a special-purpose search engine that provides, among other things, an extensive, searchable database of on-line articles for those willing to pay for this service. The difference between Internet searches and CD-ROM searches is that of magnitude and immediacy. Databases on one or more CD-ROMs are necessarily more limited and less current than the combined global resources of the Internet that are regularly updated. Although electronic references provide quick and efficient access to vast amounts of information, there is still a need for traditional libraries that provide printed publications dating back many years. Such works are not likely to be available electronically for some time. There is also something to be said for bound books that can be carried about without the need for a computer to read them.

In addition to providing access to on-line research, statistical data, and scholarly articles, the Internet provides access to newsgroups for on-line discussions of specific topics, listservers for regular delivery of electronic information such as newsletters and publications, and e-mail for correspondence with scholars and other professionals and for participation in special projects. In the hands of individuals who are gifted and talented, the Internet can be a powerful and versatile research and communication tool. (See Resources at the end of this chapter for newsgroups and listservers that address gifted issues.)

Special-Purpose Media Tools

Word processors, databases, electronic spreadsheets, and research tools are general-purpose applications for exploring many different fields. Computer tools to investigate specific gifts and talents such as art and music are available as well. Many of these specialized applications require additional hardware.

Hardware is an important consideration for computer artists and musicians. For some applications a basic computer and its mouse is enough, whereas others require powerful multimedia computers capable of audio and video output as well as special peripherals. Having a computer workstation that is powerful enough to support the memory-hungry software needed for graphic and music manipulation and the hard disk space

Students who are gifted and talented can support as well as benefit from their schools' computer programs. (Photograph by Carolyn F. Woods)

to store these large files is important. In general, a computer should have a minimum of 32 megabytes (MB) of RAM and an operating speed of at least 300 Megahertz (MHz). Storage space of 6 gigabytes (GB) or more is important to have as well. Artists and musicians often find disk drives such as Iomega's Zip or Jaz drives to be useful for several reasons. First, these drives use removable cartridges so the capacity of the drive is limited only by the number of cartridges available. Second, these cartridges are more reliable and capable of storing many more data files than an ordinary floppy disk. Finally, transporting large art, music, or multimedia files is easy with these slim drives and their removable cartridges.

Special-purpose peripherals are important too. Many artists, for example, prefer a graphics tablet such as the Wacom Graphics Tablet to a mouse for creating their computer art. Scanners (e.g., Epson, Hewlett Packard) and digital cameras (e.g., Apple's QuickTake and Connectix's Quick-Cam color) convert two- and three-dimensional work into digital files. Finished artwork can be viewed from a computer's monitor or printed on paper or film. Computer artists can use affordable inkjet and color laser printers to print out their two-dimensional work. However, high-quality printing would be done by a professional on a powerful, expensive printer. Musicians need special peripherals as well. For example, a MIDI (musical instrument digital interface) translator and MIDI instruments are often required to run music programs. Add-on speakers can also be used to enhance the quality of sound produced by a computer and are generally easy to connect with cables. Again, high-quality recording would be done professionally. An increasing number of computer artists and musicians work in multimedia environments that incorporate animations, video clips, and sounds into their work. See later Multimedia Applications section for additional hardware considerations.

Graphic Art Tools

Computer art has become a distinct medium and a legitimate form of artistic expression. Graphic tools range from sophisticated software to special cards and computer peripherals.

A great deal of software is available for computer artists. Draw and paint programs such as Adobe's Illustrator and Fractal Design's Painter turn the computer into a canvas for artists to explore line, color, pattern, and texture on a two-dimensional surface of light. Creating three-dimensional art can be done with a variety of computer-aided design (CAD) applications. For example, MiniCad by Diehl Graphsoft is a drafting and modeling tool used by architects and mechanical designers. Adobe's PhotoShop is the software of choice for computer artists needing to retouch and add special filters to digital images. MetaCreations publishes several software packages for computer artists, including Kai's Power Tools and Bryce. Kai's Power Tools is a set of plug-in filters for software such as PhotoShop so artists can apply new special effects and filters to computer images. With Bryce three-dimensional landscapes and objects can be produced with ease (see Figure 13.3, Chris Grantham's "Pyramid of Dreams," for an example of what can be created with this software).

An increasing demand for computer artists is related to the rapid growth of technology and the changes that accompany it. The Internet, film, and television industries are all clamoring for people who have both artistic and computer talents. Businesses employ these individuals to create Web pages filled with dynamic digital art that can be viewed with graphical browsers such as Netscape's Netscape Navigator/Communicator and Microsoft's Internet Explorer. Visual images are increasingly important in the age of global communication where computer artists convey ideas in a nonverbal, visual format. The Internet and World Wide Web are exciting for computer artists because they make it easy to share ideas and to display and sell work.

Music Tools

Computer technology has opened up the world of music to both novice and accomplished musicians. Although multimedia computers with stereo speakers can play CDs or music composed by the user, quality sound requires special hardware and software.

Music software can accommodate a wide range of abilities. ARS Nova has developed two software packages for teaching music skills and concepts. A Little Kidmusic is for younger children who want to learn how to read standard music notation and write their own compositions. This package supports teacher-designed exercises and can be customized to meet individual needs. Practica Musica by ARS Nova is customizable software that offers music fundamentals at the college level and includes comprehen-

Figure 13.3. "Pyramid of Dreams" by Chris Grantham using MetaCreations Bryce 2. Reproduced with permission of Chris Grantham.

sive music theory and ear training. Macromedia's SoundEdit 16 and Deck II is among the more popular packages for editing sound. With this software, music for multimedia and Internet projects can be created and recorded. With a MIDI interface and MIDI instrument, musicians can use Musicshop by Opcode to record, play, and print their own music from a Macintosh computer. Multitrack recording is possible as well. DigiTrax by Opcode is recording software that supports up to six audio tracks for importing audio from CDs and QuickTime movies, tuning mixes, adding sound effects and voice-overs, and exporting soundtracks in either 8- or 16-bit format.

Musicians also use the Internet for a wide variety of purposes. Along with communicating with professionals through e-mail, newsgroups, and list-servers, there are Web sites where they can share compositions and even participate in on-line jam sessions by downloading music files, changing them, and then uploading them to share with others. This freewheeling exchange of ideas between diverse cultures with their own musical traditions is bound to have a profound impact on the future development of music.

Multimedia Applications

The computer is the controlling agent for multimedia explorations, enabling users to integrate music, voice, text, graphics, animation, and live-action video. Such productions can take many forms, such as a multimedia video or an informational telepresentation (D'Ignazio, 1990).

A computer-based inquiry center usually includes additional equipment such as a videodisc player for instant access to slides and films, a VCR player for recording and playing tapes, a camcorder for on-location live-action videos, and a cassette player for recording sounds and dialogue (D'Ignazio, 1990). Multimedia software on a computer controls these different pieces of equipment to create interactive multimedia productions. HyperStudio for Macintosh or Windows and HyperCard for Macintosh platforms are excellent software packages for developing multimedia productions. HyperStudio by Roger Wag-

ner Publishing is an easy-to-use yet powerful product for creating advanced and sophisticated presentations that include animations, Quick-Time movies, graphics, sound, and text, as well as access to compact discs, videodiscs, and even the Internet. HyperCard from FileMaker is another tool for creating multimedia presentations and customizing software. Like HyperStudio, it supports graphics, QuickTime movies, and sound. HyperCard can be used by novices to create a wide range of multimedia presentations or by professional developers to produce custom software. Both of these versatile packages include scripting languages for those with an interest in using programming skills to customize their productions. Microsoft's PowerPoint and Adobe's Premier are two other presentation software packages. Power-Point is part of Microsoft's Office package and is a basic tool for putting together attractive page-turner presentations. Premier, on the other hand, is a sophisticated presentation tool that uses files from other applications such as Adobe Illustrator and PhotoShop, QuickTime movies, and sound files.

Because multimedia uses both audio and visual file, it is important to have enough computer memory (RAM), storage space, and processing speed (megahertz) on the computer system. If sophisticated multimedia production is a goal, it is best to have a multimedia computer system that supports audio and video operations. Otherwise, special audio–video cards need to be purchased. In addition to the extra cost of these cards, they are often not as satisfactory as a system originally designed for multimedia production. Fortunately, computer manufacturers are responding to the increasing demand for multimedia machines at an affordable price.

In addition to a powerful computer with an internal CD-ROM or DVD-ROM drive, multimedia productions often involve a wide range of peripherals such as scanners, digital cameras, videodisc players, and camcorders. The Internet and World Wide Web contain a wealth of audio and visual files as well. Access to all this electronic material does not mean that it can be used. In fact, the issue of copyright is one that needs to be considered carefully. As a general rule, permission to use material from other sources should be given before using it unless it is clearly stated that the material is not copyrighted. This is particularly true when multimedia work is part of an Internet Web site where there is bound to be a wider audience than in the home or classroom. In short, when in doubt, get permission.

Internet Web pages are perhaps the ultimate multimedia production because they present text, image, and sound in a totally electronic environment. Using HyperText Markup Language (HTML) and Java coding, individuals with gifts and talents are already filling the Internet with their creative projects. There are many ways to create Web pages. Typing the HTML code into a word processor file and saving it as a basic text file requires no special software. This method also guarantees that the programmer will understand HTML. There is also software that helps in the construction of a Web page. With this software it is easy to learn how to construct Web pages and, in some instances, it is not even necessary to know how to use Web page code. Freeware, such as BBEdit Lite, is software that can be used without paying anything. Shareware, on the other hand, is not free. Users are expected to pay the programmer who developed it a nominal fee. Webweaver is a shareware application that can be downloaded from the Internet. BBEdit and Webweaver assume the user has a basic knowledge of HTML code and simply provide quick ways to do so. Finally, commercial packages such as Adobe's PageMill can be purchased. PageMill's advantage is that the user needs little or no knowledge of HTML code (see Computer Science section, which is next, for more about HTML programming).

Multimedia applications offer young people with gifts and talents opportunities to develop their multiple intelligences in new and stimulating ways. Opportunities are increasing for young people to develop their talents through special programs such as the Saturday Gifted Program at the University of Southern Mississippi (Troxclair et al., 1996); the Tower of Youth Project in Sacramento, California; MetaTools Teen Digital Movie Competition; and Internet competitions such as ThinkQuest and the Webstar Award Competition for Best Public Service Web Site from a K–12 Webmaster. With so many programs available, multimedia's future is bright with possibilities for individuals with gifts and talents.

Computer Science

Computer science involves the technical side of computing. Typically, it is divided into two basic levels: (1) controlling the computer through programming languages and understanding of the computer's internal architecture and (2) applying this knowledge to the field of artificial intelligence.

Programming

Because it is often assumed that individuals with gifts and talents ought to learn how to program, they are encouraged to learn how to do so on their computers at home, at school, or in special programs (e.g., Johns Hopkins's CTY). Whether the purpose of programming is to develop general problem-solving skills or technical knowledge for entering the field of computer science, it is important to consider which computer languages are most appropriate.

In the past BASIC was the most common programming language studied because most computers came with it so it was the primary programming language by default. Programming languages, however, should be selected on the basis of whether they support and develop students' interests, abilities, and needs. This is especially true for people with gifts and talents who have such diverse abilities and interests. The primary value of programming is to develop independence, self-esteem, critical-thinking, problem-solving, and communication skills. Programming to develop computer science knowledge is important as well for those who demonstrate an interest in the field itself.

LOGO first appeared on the educational market in the early 1980s. It continues to be used in classrooms today. LCSI and Harvard Associates are publishers of different versions of LOGO. LCSI's new version is Microworlds. Harvard Associates offers several LOGO packages for

Macintosh and PC computers. Originally developed for the concrete exploration of abstract mathematical concepts, LOGO promotes higher level thinking, problem-solving, and communication skills. It also supports individual learning styles and promotes problem-solving skills through its interactive and procedural structure. As an interactive language with clear error messages, LOGO helps programmers debug or locate problems. Its modular or procedural structure also helps pinpoint errors because a program can be run in its entirety, on a procedure-by-procedure basis, or even on a line-by-line basis. LOGO also supports both inductive and deductive reasoning. That is to say, a program can be developed either deductively from a general idea that is broken down into subgroups of code or it can be developed inductively from a basic idea that is teased into a full-blown and complex program (Dale, 1984). For these reasons LOGO continues to be an excellent programming language for individuals with gifts and talents to learn how to use.

It is also possible to develop programming skills with multimedia software. Both HyperCard and HyperStudio include scripting languages that can be used to produce sophisticated interactive programs. Along with the growth of the Internet and Web browser software, two multimedia programming languages have been developed: HTML and Java. HTML is the easiest to learn and many people with gifts and talents have used it successfully to create award-winning Web pages that include "hot" or linked text with color graphics and sounds. Although Java is a more complex language for the Internet, it is not beyond the grasp of individuals who are gifted and talented. In fact many Internet programmers have learned their craft on the Internet and World Wide Web by searching for HTML or Java sites, scrutinizing the source code of intriguing Web pages, downloading instructional guides and tips, and corresponding with experts.

Those who wish to study the field of computer science must also understand computer architecture and the theories and principles upon which computer technology is based. Learning assembly and machine language and knowing how to use compilers and interpreters help achieve this goal.

Appendix C presents additional information about computer languages.

Artificial Intelligence

The study of the field of artificial intelligence (AI) can develop quite naturally from programming and is particularly appropriate for many individuals with gifts and talents. The field of AI is the study of the nature of intelligence through the artificial or nonhuman means of a computer. Because the computer provides an environment in which all conditions can be controlled, a researcher can limit a machine to certain identifiable data and abilities. Specific problems or tasks are then presented to the computer and the results carefully observed. Free from social and psychological influences, a computer provides pure, limited intelligence with which AI researchers can test their scientific theories.

While a good number of programming languages are available, LOGO remains an excellent one with which to begin exploring the field of artificial intelligence because it is an intriguing and fairly easy language to learn and has a procedural and list-processing structure. Furthermore, it is the front end of LISP, a language used in artificial intelligence research. Thus, LOGO provides a natural beginning and a comfortable bridge to this complex field.

Additional Technology Issues

For two reasons, people with gifts and talents need to be aware of the impact of technology on the way people work, socialize, and govern. First, many are or will be decision makers. Although these positions may not involve direct use of technology, certain leadership positions may require an understanding of technology and how to use it. Second, technology represents intellectual challenges that, when overcome, give a sense of control and accomplishment. These challenges, in turn, may lead to inappropriate or even illegal uses of technology. It is therefore important for bright, inquisitive individuals to understand technology and what the consequences are, to themselves and society, when ethical and legal procedures are not followed.

Computer crime, the most prominent computer issue today, ranges from violation of copyright laws to espionage. Such criminal activity is especially tempting because it is often easy to do, difficult to detect, and, in the case of copying protected software, practiced by so many. To help prevent illegal uses of technology, it is important to discuss thoroughly the social and personal implications of such actions with young people with gifts and talents. Discussions should focus on real-life situations and help students arrive at thoughtful conclusions that support both the good of communities and the individuals who live in them. It is equally important for individuals with gifts and talents to understand how the law affects the computer world. Considering different options helps people make wise and informed decisions.

Opportunities for illegal or inappropriate behavior have grown along with the Internet and World Wide Web. Today there are several options for controlling student behavior on the Internet. Greatest control is achieved by keeping students off the Internet entirely and downloading appropriate sites for students to explore offline. A second option uses software designed to restrict access to certain Web sites. Least restrictive is full Internet and World Wide Web access for those who have signed an acceptable user policy (AUP). Usually, parents and students are required to sign such policies. Restricting access to information is controversial, and many see it as censorship. Do such restrictions represent inappropriate and intrusive control of intellectual freedom? Should schools or governments control what people can and cannot learn? On the other hand, what are the responsibilities and liabilities of institutions that permit full, unrestricted Internet access, when someone accesses information that is illegal? There is a delicate balance between intellectual restriction and freedom. Finally, does an institution bear responsibility for the behavior of all of its Internet and World Wide Web users? What happens when a user does something illegal or unethical while using an institution's Internet access? Schools and libraries are grappling with these very issues today. Why not include individuals with gifts and talents in this discussion as well?

Since everyone is affected by computer technology in one way or another, it is also important to consider technology's impact on the world itself. An awareness of how technology is used to accomplish ordinary tasks such as regulating the temperature of a microwave oven or extraordinary tasks such as navigating a satellite through outer space develops a sense of technology's current capabilities and future potentials. It is also important to understand the impact of technology on careers. How will jobs be changed? Which jobs are likely to be eliminated? How might careers change over the years? What skills are most important in a volatile job market?

Today our very lives depend on technology. It helps us drive cars, heat and cool homes, calculate variables in scientific experiments, construct safe buildings, administer medication to a patient, and communicate with others. It can also be used to observe people in the workplace, maintain blacklists of citizens, commit crimes, and invade people's privacy. What we know about technology and how we use it makes a difference to us and to the world we live in. For these reasons, it is especially important for the gifted and talented leaders of tomorrow to understand technology's multifaceted impact on our lives.

Summary

Computers present unique opportunities for expanding intellectual horizons in ways never before thought possible, and people with gifts and talents are among those who are most likely to benefit from the use of this technology. Identifying the best hardware and software for individuals with gifts and talents is difficult because of the varied abilities and interests of this group of people. Schools need to consider how best to distribute their often meager computer resources.

Learning by individuals with gifts and talents is greatly enhanced by all aspects of technology. Computer-assisted instruction enables them to complete missed work, develop weak skills, accelerate learning, and explore problem-solving strategies. They can also use computers as application tools for general purposes (e.g., word processing) or focus on specific tasks (e.g., art, music, multimedia). Persons with gifts and talents can also learn programming languages (e.g., LOGO or HTML) to develop creativity, critical-thinking skills, and problem-solving strategies and to investigate the field of computer science. Finally, people with gifts and talents need to be aware of the current and future legal, ethical, and social implications of the technology.

Resources

Organizations

Use a World Wide Web search engine (e.g., AltaVista or HotBot) to find the Web sites of the organizations below and explore these sites. Create a database with the snail and e-mail addresses, telephone and fax numbers, and other pertinent information about these organizations.

- Center for Academic Advancement (CAA) is part of the Institute for Academic Advancement of Youth at Johns Hopkins University, Baltimore

- Center for Academic Precocity (CAP) at Arizona State University, Tempe

- Center for Talent Development at Northwestern University, Evanston, IL

- Center for Talented Youth (CTY) is part of the Institute for Academic Advancement of Youth at Johns Hopkins University, Baltimore

- Council for Exceptional Children (CEC)

- Education Program for Gifted Youth (EPGY) at Stanford University, Stanford, CA

- Gifted Child Society, 190 Rock Road, Glen Rock, NJ 07452-1736; e-mail: admin@gifted.org

- Institute for Academic Advancement of Youth (IAAY) at Johns Hopkins University, Baltimore

- Jacob K. Javits Gifted and Talented Education Program

- National Research Center on the Gifted and Talented at University of Connecticut, Storrs

- TAG Family Network

- TIP Program at Duke University, Durham, NC

- UC Berkeley Academic Talent Development Program at University of California, Berkeley

- USA2100 CyberLearning Center

Periodicals and Publishers

Challenge. In five issues per year, this magazine provides reproducible information, articles from leaders in gifted education, schedules of upcoming conferences, and ideas to help parents of gifted children. Designed for preschool through Grade 8. *Contact:* Challenge, P.O. Box 55681, Boulder, CO 80322-5681; Voice: 800/264-9873.

Classroom Connect. A must for anyone interested in using the Internet for educational purposes. This publication for K–12 educators includes lesson plans, reviews of new educational sites, articles about new Internet developments, an Internet and e-mail project section, and valuable tips for using the Internet as an educational resource. You can also subscribe to the listserver or download files via FTP. *Contact* (for a free trial issue or more information): Classroom Connect, 1866 Colonial Village Lane, Lancaster, PA 17601-6704; Voice: 800/638-1639; Fax: 717/393-5752; E-mail: connect@classroom.net; Web: http://www.classroom.net

Communicator. Addresses pertinent and timely issues related to giftedness from a variety of viewpoints. *Contact:* E-mail: cbs2000@aol.com

Creative Kids Magazine. A 1996 Parent's Choice award winner, *Creative Kids Magazine,* includes games, art, stories, poetry, and opinion by and for kids ages 8 through 14. Get a free issue through Prufrock Press: http://www.prufrock.com

Gifted Child Quarterly. Published by the National Association for Gifted Children, the oldest professional journal in the field. Reports recent research and developments in gifted education. *Contact: Gifted Child Quarterly,* 1155 15th Street NW, Suite 1002, Washington, DC 20005.

Gifted Child Today. Practical and timely information for teachers and parents about children who are creative, talented, and gifted. Both Edpress and Parent's Choice awarded this publication for its editorial excellence. Get a free issue through Prufrock Press. *Contact:* Voice: 800/998-2208; Web: http://www.prufrock.com

Gifted Education Press. Publisher provides a strong advocacy forum for gifted education. Current materials emphasize humanities curriculum, but subject areas being developed include science. Publications include *Gifted Education Press Quarterly*, which publishes articles about advocacy for gifted programs and other topics related to educating children who are gifted in the humanities, literature, and science, and *Gifted Education News-Page*, a bimonthly periodical that reviews high-quality trade books and discusses other materials and topics related to educating the gifted. The News-Page will be sent free of charge. *Contact:* Gifted Education Press, 10201 Yuma Court, P.O. Box 1586, Manassas, VA 22110; E-mail: mdfish@pipeline.com

Gifted Education Review. Briefly summarizes the papers in journals that specialize in the field of gifted education. *Contact:* P.O Box 2278, Evergreen, CO 80437-2278; Voice: 800/643-2194; E-mail: pkeducre@aol.com

Imagine. Newsletter for students in Grades 7 through 12 interested in academic challenges and for those who work with them. Published five times a year, *Imagine* helps students identify options at home, in school, and in the larger community that will satisfy their intellectual curiosity and need for greater academic challenge. *Contact:* Johns Hopkins Press, P.O. Box 19966, Baltimore, MD 21211; Voice: 800/548-1784; E-mail: jlorder@jhunix.hcf.jhu.edu

Journal for the Education of the Gifted. The official publication of The Association for the Gifted (TAG), a division of the Council for Exceptional Children, and is published through a cooperative partnership with Prufrock Press. Articles include original research, theoretical position papers, descriptions of innovative programming and instructional practices, reviews of literature, and historical perspectives. *Contact:* Journals Department, University of North Carolina Press, P.O. Box 2288, Chapel Hill, NC 27515-2288. Get a free issue through Prufrock Press (http://www.prufrock.com).

Journal of Secondary Gifted Education. Publishes articles on the latest and most comprehensive research and critical theory concerning gifted adolescents. Get a free issue through Prufrock Press (http://www.prufrock.com).

MonTAGe E-Journal. Sponsored by the Families of the Gifted and Talented, this e-Journal has some great stuff! Visit their whole site: http://www.access.digex.net/%7Eking/tagfam.html

Prufrock Press. Largest publisher of materials in gifted education. Materials are designed to encourage diverse creative, leadership, and academic talents of children and adolescents. Publications include more than 100 book and software products as well as periodicals (*Gifted Child Today, Creative Kids Magazine, Journal for the Education of the Gifted,* and *Journal of Secondary Gifted Education*). Abstracts, magazine samples, and free catalog request at the Web site (http://www.prufrock.com).

Roeper Review. In-depth publication about gifted and talented education and research for scholars and educators. *Contact:* P.O. Box 329, Bloomfield Hills, MI 48305; Voice: 810/642-1500.

Understanding Our Gifted. An excellent bimonthly mini-journal for parents and professionals. *Contact:* Open Space Communications, Inc., P.O. Box 18268, Boulder, CO 80308-8268.

Listservers and Newsgroups

GIFTEDNET-L Primarily for educators of gifted students. To subscribe, send e-mail message to listserver@listserv.cc.wm.edu (leave the subject blank and write: subscribe GIFTEDNET-L "your first name" "your last name").

TAGFAM for parents (and teachers) of gifted students. To subscribe, send e-mail message to listserv@sjuvm.stjohns.edu (leave the subject blank and write: subscribe TAGFAM "your first name" "your last name").

TAG-L General discussion group for TAG parents, teachers, and others. To subscribe, send e-mail message to listserv@listserv.nodak.edu (leave the subject blank and write: subscribe TAG-L "your first name" "your last name").

World Wide Web Sites

Armadillo Gifted Education. Rice University's Web site offers mailing lists, discussion groups, and resource links to other Internet sites. Web: http://www.rice.edu/armadillo/Rice/Resources/gifted.html

Center for Academic Advancement (CAA). The newest of the two program centers at Johns Hopkins University's IAAY. CAA's mission is to offer students not eligible for CTY academic programs the opportunity to enroll in summer academic programs; to assist parents, teachers, and administrators through workshops and consultations in understanding and implementing the Optimal Match; and to initiate and sustain programs and services for youth who are academically talented. (See IAAY below.) Web: http://www.jhu.edu/~gifted/caa/caa.html

Center for Academic Precocity (CAP) at Arizona State University. Offers programs and courses for students who are gifted and talented in Grades PreK through 11, as well as services for parents, students, and schools; Web links; and CAP Kids Web pages. Web: http://www-cap.ed.asu.edu/index.html

Center for Research on Parallel Computation at Rice University. Provides education and outreach programs for K–12 educators and students, college students, women, and underrepresented minorities whose purpose is to help train scientists and engineers familiar with both scientific problem solving and parallel computation and to encourage students, particularly minorities and women, to enter programs of computational science and engineering. Web: http://www.crpc.rice.edu/CRPC/

Center for Talent Development at Northwestern University. Provides educational services to academically talented students. Web: http://ctdnet.acns.nwu/u.edu

Center for Talented Youth (CTY). Johns Hopkins University's program designed to identify and serve fifth, sixth, and seventh graders with exceptional mathematical or verbal reasoning abilities. Academic programs provide opportunities for accelerated yet in-depth learning. Qualified students choose from a wide range of courses in the humanities, mathematics, and science held at 12 sites in the United States.(See IAAY below) Web: http://www.jhu.edu/~gifted/cty.html

Classroom Connect. This excellent site makes keeping up with the ever-changing Internet easy. Lesson plans, Internet and e-mail projects, and reviews of educational sites and links to them are among the many resources available here. Useful files can be downloaded via ftp as well. Subscribe to the Classroom Connect listserver and receive information in your e-mail box on a regular basis. Web: http://classroom.net

Council for Exceptional Children (CEC). Largest international professional organization dedicated to improving educational outcomes for individuals with exceptionalities—students with disabilities or giftedness. CEC influences governmental policies, sets professional standards, provides continual professional development, advocates for newly and historically underserved individuals with exceptionalities, and helps professionals obtain conditions and resources necessary for effective professional practice. *Contact:* Council for Exceptional Children, 1920 Association Drive, Reston, VA 20191-1589; Voice: 703/620-3660; TTY: 703/264-9464; Fax: 703/264-9494. Web: http://www.cec.sped.org

Program Education for Gifted Youth. Continuing project at Stanford University offering computer-based courses in mathematics and the mathematical sciences for bright young students through the Stanford Continuing Studies Program. Web: http://kanpai.stanford.edu/epgy/pamph.html

ERIC (Educational Resources Information Center). ERIC is a national educational information system sponsored by the Office of Educational Research and Improvement of the U.S. Department of Education. This site provides links to all ERIC sites, which have educational materials including research and government reports, curriculum guides, conference papers, and projects or program reviews. ERIC databases can be searched via question–answer searching services. Use this site to link to all ERIC sites, as well as information about ERIC and Adjunct ERIC Clearinghouses, publishers of ERIC material and listservers, and names and addresses of ERIC components. Web: http://www.aspensys.com:80/eric/barak.html/

Electric Library. Excellent on-line resource for books, magazines, newspaper and newswire articles, TV and radio transcripts, maps, and images. Users pay a monthly fee to use this service. Web: http://www.elibrary.com/

Gifted and Talented (TAG) Resources Page. Comprehensive guide to on-line resources for gifted and talented education, including enrichment programs, talent searches, early entrance and scholarship programs, mailing lists, competitions, legal info, publications, catalogs, and vendors. http://edcen.ehhs.cmich.edu/~tvantlne/edgt.html

Gifted Child Society. Provides support for parents, teachers, and young people who are gifted. *Contact:* Gifted Child Society, 190 Rock Road, Glen Rock, NJ 07452-1736; E-mail: admin@gifted.org

Gifted Education Center. Resources for parents as well as teachers.

> Telnet to cap.gwu.edu
> Use login: guest
> password: visitor
> then, "go gifted"

IAAY. Established in 1979, the Institute for the Academic Advancement of Youth (IAAY) developed from a program for students with exceptional mathematical abilities to one committed to the pursuit of academic excellence and the worldwide reform and improvement of education. Today, this program offers young people opportunities to explore their individual academic talents as well as courses to accelerate their learning in specific subject areas. IAAY also provides publications and conducts research on K–12 gifted and talented youth. See also Center for Talented Youth and Center for Academic Advancement above. *Contact:* The Johns Hopkins

University, 3400 North Charles Street, Baltimore, MD 21218; Voice: 410/516-0337; Fax: 410/516-0804; Web: http://www.jhu.edu/~gifted/

Jacob K. Javits Gifted and Talented Education Program. Explains about this program for gifted and talented individuals from all cultural and economic groups. Find out about U.S. Department of Education grants ranging from $100,000 to $250,000 for states, local education agencies, institutions of high learning, and so on, that wish to develop programs for gifted students from diverse socio-economic backgrounds; leadership conferences, seminars and meetings, and curricula projects for high-ability students; and research through the National Research Center on the Gifted and Talented. Web site also includes access to related publications and resources and highlights from demonstration projects. Web: http://www.ed.gov/prog_info/Javits

National Research Center on the Gifted and Talented (NRC/GT). Located at the University of Connecticut, NRC/GT is a consortium including City University of New York/City College, Stanford University, University of Virginia, and Yale University. This Web site includes an overview of the NRC/GT program directed by Joseph Renzulli, newsletters, research abstracts, and product listings. *Contact:* University of Connecticut, 262 Fairfield Road, U-7, Storrs, CT 06269-2007; Voice: 860/486-4979; Fax: 860/486-2900. Web: http://www.ucc.uconn.edu/~wwwgt/nrcgt.html

Pitsco's Launch to Gifted and Talented Resources. Links to many sites focusing on gifted and talented individuals. Topics include counseling, distance learning, U.S. Department of Education, gifted education reform, lessons and curriculum alternatives, homeschooling resources, schools and special programs; and a link to CTD-Net Gallery where writing, art, music, and video files made by students who are gifted and talented in Grades K through 12 are available. Web: http://www.pitsco.com/p/gft.html

Platform for Internet Content Selection (PICS). Provides selected Web sites based on the rating codes that webmasters or third-party rating bureaus embed in the HTML code of Web documents. PICS-compatible software can then be used to block access to selected sites. Web: http://pics.microsys.com/

Prufrock Press. A major publisher for gifted education books, magazines, and research journals. Search through on-line catalog by title, author, or key word. Web: http://www.prufrock.com/index.html

The Recreational Software Advisory Council (RSACi). Provides Internet rating system based on ratings that webmasters assign to their own sites. Web: http://www.rsac.org

TAG Family Network. Parent-run Web site supports parents and monitors and influences legal issues for youth with gifts and talents. Provides links to Web sites of interest to parents, educators, and children, as well as articles of interest to parents and information on other resources. Disseminates quarterly packet of information to members and maintains a TAG Hotline. Web: http://www.teleport.com/~rkaltwas/tag/

TIP Program. Duke University's Talent Identification Program (TIP) Web site is designed especially for TIP participants. Site includes archived editions of the newsletter (Insights), information about Duke's PreCollege program, the latest scientific field studies, international study opportunities, TIP Scholar Weekends, the TIP Independent Learning Program, a College Guide Online for finding the right college, and FishNet, a place for students to share ideas, debate issues, gather information, and download shareware. Web: http://www.jayi.com/jayi/tip/

University of California, Berkeley, Academic Talent Development Program. Web site includes ATDPHome for information about summer program for academically talented youth, NewsBITS to keep students and families up to date about ATDP, WEBSites for Web pages created by ATDP students, and VirtualATDP for interacting with ATDP staff and mentors using digital media tools such as CU-SeeMe and CoolTalk. Web: http://www.atdp.berkeley.edu/

USA2100 CyberLearning Center. Core project of the nonprofit National Education Foundation whose mission is to help children and adults reach their lifelong learning potential by learning academic, computer, Internet, and language skills through hands-on exploration and interactive learning with the latest technologies and global communication, and support of professional mentors and teachers. Grades K through 12 math, science, reading, and writing courses and resources, as well as a free newsletter are offered. Web: http://www.usa2100.org/

Web66. Developed as a cooperative project by Hillside Elementary School and the University of Minnesota, this invaluable site is designed to help K–12 schools set up their own Internet servers; link K–12 Web servers and the educators and students who use them; and provide Internet K–12 educational resources through links and ideas. Join Web66's Mailing List for educators and share questions, problems, ideas, and successes. Web: http://Web66.umn.edu/

Yahoo Directory on Gifted Youth. Go to this Web page for links to new and interesting Internet sites or to search for even more gifted and talented topics. Web: http://www.yahoo.com/Education/k_12/Gifted_Youth/

Laboratory–Practicum Activities

▶ 1. Find and describe three Internet or World Wide Web resources that you can use to increase your understanding of using technology with individuals who are gifted or talented. Use technology to develop, revise, and share the descriptions with your course instructor and peers.

▶ 2. Find and describe three Internet or World Wide Web resources that can be used to enrich the learning experiences of students with gifts and talents. Use technology to develop, revise, and share the descriptions with your course instructor and peers.

▶ 3. Collaborate with your peers to create a Web page that reviews a favorite book and includes an illustration. Also, create an "Introductory" Web page and use it to link reviews together to form an electronic book. *Note:* Web pages can be viewed without being connected to the Internet. All that is needed is a computer with appropriate viewing software such as Netscape Navigator/Communicator or Microsoft Internet Explorer.

▶ 4. Visit a class for students with gifts and talents. Interview the students to determine (1) the hardware and software they use, (2) their favorite software and why, (3) their favorite Web sites and why, (4) their perceptions of their access to technology, and (5) their recommendations for improving their programs. Use technology to record their responses and provide an analysis, synthesis, and evaluation of your findings with your course instructor and peers.

▶ 5. Observe a group of students with gifts and talents as they create a multimedia production. Compare and contrast their developmental procedures with those you read in Chapter 6. Interview the students to learn what they would do to improve and expand the project.

▶ 6. Collaborate with your peers to use the Internet and World Wide Web to learn about a current topic of interest about which you have a limited knowledge base. Bookmark the most valuable sites and create a database that includes names, Web addresses, and brief description of these sites. Describe a Web site or page you *did not find* but wish existed (i.e., it would have assisted you in searching for or developing knowledge about the topic selected).

References

Balajthy, E. (1988). Results of the first National Assessment of Computer Competence. *Reading Teacher, 42,* 242–246.

Baum, S. (1984). Meeting the needs of learning disabled gifted students. *Roeper Review, 7*(1),16–19.

Berman, S., & Tinker, R. (1997). The world's limit in the virtual high school. *Educational Leadership, 55*(3), 52–54.

Bloom, B. (1956). *Taxonomy of educational objectives.* New York: Longmans, Green.

Bollinger, R., & Hopping, L. (1985). Research for the stars. *Teaching Computers, 2*(7), 12–19.

Brody, L. E., Assouline, S. G., & Stanley, J. C. (1990). Five years of early entrants: Predicting successful achievement in college. *Gifted Child Quarterly, 34*(4), 138–142.

Brooks, S. (1990). Using applications software with gifted students. *The Computing Teacher, 18*(3), 41–43.

Cohen, L. M. (1996, February 1). Mapping the domains of ignorance and knowledge in gifted education. *Roeper Review,* pp. 1–18.

Crockenburg, S. B. (1972). Creativity tests: A boon or boondoggle for education? *Review of Educational Research, 42,* 27–45.

Dale, E. J. (1984). LOGO builds thinking skills. In D. T. Bonnette (Ed.), *The Sixth Annual National Educational Computing Conference* (pp. 224–226). Dayton, OH: National Educating Computing.

Dickinson, C., & Hopping, L. (1985). Teach dollars and sense with spreadsheets. *Teaching and Computers, 2*(6), 12–17.

D'Ignazio, F. (1990). Multimedia sandbox. *Computing Teacher, 17*(6), 16–19.

Getzel, J. W., & Csikszentmihayli, M. (1975). From problem solving to problem finding. In I. A. Taylor & J. W. Getzel (Eds.), *Perspective in creativity* (pp. 741–775). Chicago: Aldine.

Greenlaw, M. J., & Macintosh, M. E. (1988). *Educating the gifted: A sourcebook*. Chicago: American Library Association.

Gubbins, E. J. (1996). NRC/GT through the year 2000. *NRC/GT Newsletter* (On-line). Available: http//www.ucc.uconn.edu/~wwwgt/wintr961.html

Hamlett, C. (1984). Microcomputer activities for gifted elementary children: Alternatives to programming. *Teaching Exceptional Children,16*, 153–157.

Hancock, V. (1997). Creating the information age school. *Educational Leadership, 55*(3), 60–63.

Harp, L. (1996). The history wars. *Electronic Learning, 16*(2), 32–39.

Hays, T. (1993, September 1). An historical content analysis of publications in gifted education journals. *Roeper Review*, pp. 1–8.

Hersberger, J., & Wheatley, G. (1989). Computers and gifted students: An effective mathematics program. *Gifted Child Quarterly, 33*(3), 106–109.

Hicks, H. (1993, November). Technology and aesthetic education: A crucial synthesis. *Art Education, 46*, 42 –47.

Jones, G. (1990). Personal computers help gifted students work smart. *ERIC Digest #E483*.

Kolstad, R., & Lidtke, D. (1983). Gifted and talented. In D. Harper & J. Stewart (Eds.), *RUN: Computer education* (pp. 222–226). Monterey, CA: Brooks/Cole.

Lake, D. (1988–1989). Telecommunications in the classroom. *The Computing Teacher,16*(4), 17–19.

Lewis, J. D. (1996). Confessions of an Internet junkie. *Gifted Child Today, 19*(1), 40–48.

MacKinnon, D. W. (1968a). Educating for creativity: A modern myth? In P. Heist (Ed.), *The creative college student: An unmet challenge* (pp. 147–160). San Francisco: Jossey-Bass.

MacKinnon, D. W. (1968b). Selecting students with creative potential. In P. Heist (Ed.), *The creative college student: An unmet challenge* (pp. 101–116). San Francisco: Jossey-Bass.

Mather, M. A. (1996). Exploring the Internet safely: What schools can do. *Technology and Learning, 17*(1), 38–46.

Middleton, J. A., Littlefield, J., & Lehrer, R. (1992). Gifted students' conceptions of academic fun: An examination of a critical construct for gifted students. *Gifted Child Quarterly, 36*(1), 38–44.

Mills, C. J., & Durden, W. G. (1992). Cooperative learning and ability grouping: An issue of choice. *Gifted Child Quarterly, 36*(1), 11–16.

Nicholls, J. C. (1972). Creativity in the person who will never produce anything original and useful: The concept of creativity as a normally distributed trait. *American Psychologist, 27*, 717–727.

Niess, M. (1990). Preparing computer using educators in a new decade. *The Computing Teacher, 18*(3), 10–15.

Papert, S. (1980). *Mindstorms: Children. computers, and powerful ideas*. New York: Basic Books.

Parker, J., & Wider, C. C. (1989). Using spreadsheets to encourage critical thinking. *The Computing Teacher, 16*(6), 27–55.

Quesada, A., & Summers, S. (1998). Literacy in the Cyber-Age: Teaching kids to be media savvy. *Technology and Learning, 18*(5), 30–36.

Ravaglia, R., Suppes, P., Stillinger, C., & Alper, T. M. (1995). Computer-based mathematics and physics for gifted students. *Gifted Child Quarterly, 39*(1), 7–13.

Renzulli, J. S. (1978). What makes giftedness? Reexamining a definition. *Phi Delta Kappan, 60*(3), 180–261.

Renzulli, J. S., Reis, S. M., & Smith, L. H. (1981). *The revolving door identification model*. Hartford, CT: Creative Learning Press.

Roe, A. (1975). Psychologist examines 64 eminent scientists. In W. B. Barbe & J. S. Renzulli (Eds.), *Psychology and education of the gifted* (pp. 119–126). New York: Irvington.

Rotenberg, L. (1985). Classroom happenings. *Teaching and Computers, 2*(6), 11.

Sanders, M. (1994, January 1). Technological problem-solving activities as a means of instruction; The TSM integration program. *School Science & Mathematics, 94*, 1–11.

Schack, G. (1996, February 1). All aboard or standing on the shore? Gifted educators and the educational reform movement, *Roeper Review*, pp. 1–19.

Senf, G. M. (1983). The nature and identification of learning disabilities and their relationship to the gifted child. In L. H. Fox, L. Brody, & D. Tobin (Eds.), *Learning-disabled/gifted children: Identification and programming* (pp. 37–49). Austin, TX: PRO-ED.

Shaklee, B. D. (1992). Identification of young gifted children. *Journal for the Education of the Gifted, 15*(2), 134–144.

Sisk, D. (1987). *Creative teaching of the gifted*. New York: McGraw-Hill.

Stanley, J. C. (1991). An academic model for educating the mathematically talented. *Gifted Child Quarterly, 35*(1), 36–42.

Swassing, R. H. (1984). *Teaching gifted children and adolescents*. Columbus, OH: Merrill.

Taylor, R. (1983). *Building a quality program for gifted students*. Paso Robles, CA: Bureau of Education and Research.

Terman, L. M. (1959). *Genetic studies of genius: The gifted group at mid-life*. Palo Alto, CA: Stanford University.

Terry, P. J. (1984). *How to use computers with gifted students: Creative microcomputing in a differentiated curriculum*. Manassas, VA: Reading Tutorium.

Troxclair, D., Stephens, K., Bennet, T., & Karnes, F. (1996). Teaching technology: Multimedia presentations in the classroom. *Gifted Child Today, 19*(5), 34–47.

Wallach, M. A. (1976). Tests tell us little about talent. *American Scientist, 64,* 57–63.

Watson, J., & Strudler, N. (1989–1990). Teaching higher-order thinking skills with databases. *Computing Teacher, 16*(4), 47–57.

Witty, P. (1958). Who are the gifted? In P. Witty (Ed.), *Education of the gifted. National Society for the Study of Education Series* (Vol. 57, Pt. 2). Chicago: University of Chicago Press.

Section IV

❧   ❧   ❧

Technology Evaluation and Research Concepts

This section presents principles and procedures for evaluating the technology program and conduct- ing research studies to add to the developing literature on technology and exceptional individuals.

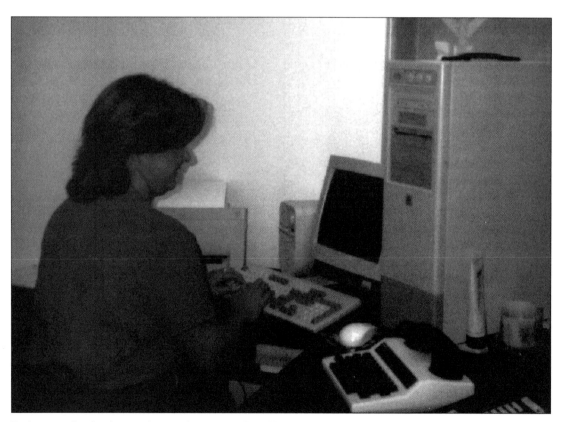

Evaluation of technology and research concepts should be conducted on a regular basis. (Photograph by Carolyn F. Woods)

Chapter 14

ᔓ   ᔓ   ᔓ

Evaluation Models for Technology Applications

Earl H. Cheek, Jr.
Louisiana State University,
Baton Rouge

R. Kenton Denny
Louisiana State University,
Baton Rouge

Gary E. Rice
University of Missouri–St. Louis

Perhaps the most applied research in education involves studies designed to address the impact of current practices and innovations (Kurtz, 1999). Evaluation has been defined as the systematic process of collecting data to facilitate decision making (Gay, 1996). Evaluation studies are those planned activities pursued to ensure that these data are not systematically biased and produce as unambiguous findings as possible. Technology applications reviewed in this book all require substantial commitments of human and fiscal resources and therefore warrant evaluation. As time and funds are invested into technology, the need for approaches to evaluate efforts gains new instructional and political significance (Bryant & Seay, 1998). We offer in this chapter an overview for evaluation of technology applications that includes evaluation as an integral part of a system of continual improvement.

Often, education has appeared to systematically avoid evaluation of its attempts to improve its product. Disagreement as to the nature of that product has existed for many years and continues to the current day. Education has often tended to move from innovation to innovation with little regard for the systematic collection of data to determine initial or relative effectiveness (Kavanaugh-Brown, 1999). This has culminated in a system that is largely divorced from its constituents, plagued with conflicting orientations within its system and often an extreme lack of consumer confidence. The current rush to provide technological capabilities and networking to schools in the absence of articulated outcomes faces danger of eroding the consumer's confidence in education's ability to change.

Purposes of Evaluation

Brinkerhoff (1979) proposed four main purposes of evaluation in educational settings: evaluation should (1) serve to clarify and communicate the expectations or standards for the program; (2) document the operation of the program; (3) assess the impact of the program on its intended recipients; and (4) provide information to revise and improve the program. Brinkerhoff described the evaluation process as consisting of three major phases. In the first phase, the expectations for the program are developed, specifying the intended outcomes and scope of operation for

The personal computer was a major factor in the technology revolution. (Photograph by Carolyn F. Woods)

411

the program. In the second phase, the evaluation questions are delineated for each component of the program operation. In the third phase, the data collection system for the evaluation is developed for addressing each of the evaluation questions from the preceding phases.

Cheek and Kelly (1993) identified the following purposes and scope of evaluation related to technology applications:

1. To supplement traditional instruction activities

2. To replace in whole or part the curriculum delivery system

3. To expand the involvement and quality of independent learning activities in specific skill or curriculum areas

4. To explore or develop innovative instructional strategies that are equal to or exceed the effects of traditional instructional methods in use

5. To influence the attitudes or motivation of students

6. To examine student performance and achievement using computer based delivery systems and traditional classroom activities

7. To compare the benefits and cost effectiveness of traditional classroom activities and computer based instruction (pp. 314–315)

As Cheek and Kelly indicated, the form of evaluation design is derived from the scope and purposes of the evaluation questions. In the following sections, we discuss the types and forms of evaluation procedures that are valid, are useful, and have the potential for being implemented by school districts.

Types of Evaluation

A great deal of discussion revolves around the most appropriate type of evaluation in applied settings. Two forms of evaluation most frequently addressed involve formative and summative evaluation. These two forms directly relate to the stated purposes of evaluation. Formative evaluation is used to determine if the program is operating as originally planned or if improvements are necessary before the program is implemented on a wide scale, whereas, the major concern of summative evaluation is the evaluation of the final product with the major emphasis being program appraisal.

When applied to technology applications, formative evaluation would stress the try-out and revision process, whereas summative evaluation uses specified outcome criteria, indicators, or benchmarks to appraise the impact of the technological innovation. Both forms of evaluation are required to meet the needs for instructional development and political support required for the widespread integration of technology applications.

Issues of Measurement

Perhaps the most difficult task in the development of a program of evaluation is the selection of the unit(s) of measurement. Identifying the outcomes desired from the integration of technology is a difficult process requiring consensus building by all potential consumers and participants. Individuals responsible for technology applications must delineate the proposed outcomes without unduly restricting the potential for innovation and serendipitous findings. In other words, individuals must attempt to identify their outcomes while measuring broadly enough to capture unanticipated impacts of their program interventions. To rely on serendipity is inefficient and foolhardy; the need to develop a measurement system that is broad enough to point to new and potentially productive evaluation areas is central to evaluation as a constructive process.

Typically, measurement ranges along a continuum of direct measures (e.g., behavior, problems solved, words read) to indirect measures (e.g., intelligence, self-concept), and the schedule by which the measurement is taken ranges from continuous (e.g., real-time collection by the software program) to discontinuous (e.g., an end of unit measurement; annual or semi-annual measures of achievement). The closer the measurement unit and schedule approximate the direct and continuous end of the continuum, the more likely the measures reflect the aspect being studied and the less chance of error due to problems of construct validity. A rule of thumb is to always select measures as close to direct and continuous as possible and move toward more indirect and discontinuous only when conditions (e.g., time, costs, personnel) make more accurate measures unfeasible (R. E. Shores, personal communication, August 19, 1997). A useful addition to this axiom is to move as quickly as possible toward the direct and continuous end of the continuum as technology, developing expertise, and resources allow. In this manner, as in the research process, evaluation becomes a self-improving system continually moving toward better and more accurate units of measurement.

Quantitative Designs for Evaluation

The conversion of information (data) into a numeric representation is the basis of positivistic approaches for understanding. This quantification has allowed the analysis of information in education using techniques commonly reserved for "harder" sciences. While the debates regarding the adequacy of the conversions for adequately representing the phenomena being studied will continue, it should be recognized that traditional quantitative analysis represents the predominant approach in education. In the following sections we provide an overview of the use of quantitative designs in education and the application of these designs to evaluation. The use of idiographic (single-case) designs and the quantitative case study as potential approaches to the evaluation of technological applications are also presented.

Group Designs

The tradition of educational research has been the nomothetic approach in which groups of students have been systematically exposed to or protected from the intervention of interest and mea-

surement of the impact of the intervention has been taken at various points in the process. The assumptions underlying the experimental approach reflect the notions of subject equivalence and the use of statistical tests to examine group differences for significant differences. The seminal work on group design is a short paper by Campbell and Stanley (1963) that described both experimental and quasi-experimental designs, as well as the potential threats to internal and external validity associated with each.

The impracticality of random assignment to interventions has limited much applied educational research to what Campbell and Stanley (1963) identified as quasi-experimental research. Educators are most familiar with the pre–post test designs identified by Campbell and Stanley. In this process, subjects are assessed on some dimension of performance or attribute prior to and following the introduction of the independent (treatment) variable. Statistical comparisons are then made between the first and second measurements to determine whether any difference exists, and, if so, whether the difference is statistically significant. Campbell and Stanley recognized the limitations of this approach in terms of controlling for extraneous variables and appropriately designated the simple pre–post design as a preexperimental design. To address threats to internal validity, a nontreatment control group must be included to demonstrate that performance changes occur only in the presence of the intervention or treatment variable.

Professionals must carefully evaluate computer systems for exceptional individuals. (Photograph by Jimmy D. Lindsey)

Single-Subject Design

Single-subject designs may trace their origins to the laboratory work of Skinner (1953) and Sidman (1960). This approach recognizes the utility of studying the individual (idiographic) under closely controlled conditions to establish statements of functional relationships between the individual's behavior and the environmental conditions (Johnson & Pennypacker, 1990). The goal of the single-subject research is to investigate the effect of an intervention (e.g., computer-assisted instruction; contingent access to computers) on the performance (behavior) of an individual. Single-subject research is characterized by frequent, often daily, repeated measurement of an individual's behavior under no-treatment and treatment conditions. If the individual's behavior changes systematically with the introduction or removal of the intervention, a functional relationship between the intervention and the behavior may be proposed. Designs, from this perspective, are derived from the experimental process of systematically controlling for threats to internal validity (e.g., maturation, multiple treatment effects) and external validity (i.e., generality of findings). Central to the understanding of single-subject approaches is the process of replication, where interventions are systematically withdrawn and reintroduced either by the same or different experimenters to demonstrate that the changes in performance are uniform.

The advantages of the single-subject approach lie in its congruence with the educational process (Alberto & Troutman, 1996) and the ability to offer a clear demonstration of the effect of an intervention. Disadvantages include the need to control for unplanned or unsystematic changes in the environment, the need for frequent measurement, and the problems of generalizing individual relationships to larger populations and differing environments. Several texts address the application of single-subject approaches in educational and clinical settings and are valuable resources for teachers and administrators (e.g., Alberto & Troutman, 1996; Kazdin, 1982; Sulzer-Azaroff & Reese, 1982; Tawney & Gast, 1984; Wolery, Bailey, & Sugai, 1987).

Case Study

The case study as a research or evaluation approach has often suffered from being misrepresented as inadequate quantitative design or strictly as qualitative approach. Yin (1984) provided a convincing argument for the case study as a distinctly unique approach to answering questions of interest when control of environmental events is not the aim of the research or when control is not possible. Although Yin indicated that case study methodology may employ either quantitative data or qualitative perspectives, it is uniquely suited for answering questions regarding the how or why. Yin defined the case study as "an empirical inquiry that investigates a contemporary phenomenon within its real life context, when the boundaries between the phenomenon and the context are not clearly evident; and in which multiple sources of evidence are used" (p. 23). Given that the application of technology will always constitute an emerging practice, the case study approach provides a viable supplement to standard model development and testing process.

The argument for studying emerging practices in existing sites as opposed to model development and evaluation rests on two major beliefs—(1) the belief that model program development may not be the most pressing need for contributing to the state of practice, our knowledge base, or ultimately the integration of technology to support individuals with disabilities in educational settings, and (2) the belief that a process that acknowledges the potential for "grounded theory" (Glaser & Strauss, 1967), which is the theory that emerges from examining many disparate pieces of evidence that are related to each other, has a great potential to impact the field and expand the current state of knowledge. Each teacher in a school site, each parent whose child with disabilities attends classes and interacts with classmates, the classmates, program developers, and others have a unique knowledge of experience. This experiential knowledge is too seldom seen in texts or journal articles and is not easily discoverable through quasi-experimental approaches. The discovery of the knowledge of the application of technology often requires a multidimensional approach. This approach should address technology application in a systematic and quantifiable process while recognizing that the Macro-Level variables proposed by the National Rehabilitation Research Center Panel on Indicators of Effectiveness in Special Education (1986) as important setting factors in which may lie the ultimate adoption and successful implementation of effective supports.

Educators should study existing exemplary or emerging practices to establish a benchmark for other programs. An excellent example of a benchmark was the development of an Individualized Education Plan (IEP) process called Choosing Outcomes and Accommodaations for Children, or COACH (Giangreco, Cloninger, & Iverson, 1993), which guides evaluation teams through the process of developing appropriate goals and objectives to meet the learning needs of students with exceptionalities. The development of appropriate benchmarks is seen as a critical step in school reform and school improvement (Carnine, 1996) that includes the integration of technology.

Qualitative Approaches for Evaluation

There is little question that the use of qualitative approaches for research has increased in popularity in education. The use of language (words) as the basic data for analysis and the related analyses of these data to produce or derive meaning have been proposed as both supplementary and replacement approaches for understanding or evaluating educational innovation. Although it is beyond the scope of this chapter to address the relative merit of qualitative approaches, we present them as a potentially viable approach for addressing technology applications.

The use of technology in analyzing qualitative research has become a topic of some discussion in recent years. As qualitative methods have become widely used in educational research, it is natural that researchers have looked for tools to assist in collecting and analyzing large and some-

what unwieldy amounts of data, especially massive amounts of field notes. This section provides an overview of qualitative methods in evaluative research, raises some concerns regarding the use of computers in analyzing qualitative data, and provides an overview of five types of software programs used for qualitative data analysis.

The notable differences between qualitative and quantitative methods may be understood by the simple question, "What is truth?" How one answers this question establishes a frame for "knowing" and then leads to question how one knows or what it means to know. This then establishes one's epistemology or theory of knowledge. There has been a great amount of debate regarding epistemologies and volumes have been written in this area. Educational research in the past two decades has begun to reexamine its most basic assumptions regarding learning and what it means to "know." Researchers have examined their methodologies for asking the most fundamental questions regarding education: "What is learning?" and "How do we know when it has occurred?" The debate regarding qualitative versus quantitative methodologies is concerned with these questions.

Quantitative methods define truth mechanistically. The main assumptions of the quantitative position are as follows:

1. There is one single reality that is composed of constituent parts that are both observable and measurable.

2. There is a separation between knower and known, observer and observed, researcher and subject.

3. All events that have an effect also have a cause, and all causes have an effect.

4. It is inherent within the methodology that all results are free from bias.

Quantitative methods are used to demonstrate causality, to predict, or to generalize findings to larger populations. This is accomplished by selecting identifiable variables and measuring relationships to reveal some amount of deterministic effect that one variable has upon another. The underlying principle of quantitative measures is that social phenomena have realities that are objective and, therefore, measurable. The role of the researcher is to objectify these social relationships as detached and neutral from the phenomena so as not to contaminate the data. The conditions are experimental (deductive) in nature and dispassionate of the results from the experiment.

Qualitative research methods are viewed as paradigmatically different from traditional quantitative methods. Whereas quantitative research situates itself within a positivistic paradigm, qualitative research is characterized by a naturalistic paradigm. It may be surprising for some readers to discover that the underlying assumptions of qualitative research are diametrically opposed to those underlying quantitative research, point by point and measure by measure.

Qualitative research is characterized as process oriented, building upon complex social interactions that occur in natural settings. The purpose of qualitative research is to examine these complex relations as they occur in an authentic context and to explore the various layers and dimensions of the processes of interaction rather than specifying outcomes or products. The researcher is an inexplicable part of the social milieu in which he or she is studying and is therefore able to inductively describe and explore the experiences of those being studied. It is only through these *emic* (inside perspective or subjective) experiences that truth and reality can be accurately observed, recorded, and interpreted as opposed to the *etic* (outside perspective or subjective) experiences of the quantitative method.

The following are the main assumptions of qualitative research:

1. Reality exists in combination with other realities (multiple realities) that are not subject to isolation or manipulation. To understand, to know, one has to examine phenomena in their natural state, without violating the circumstances under which they exist. Under these conditions it is not possible to control events or to predict a priori possible outcomes. Doing so would cause a change in the behavior of how these multiple realities are constructed.

2. Knower and known are inseparable from one another. The relationship that exists between the observer and the observed is the nature of qualitative research. It is not possible to separate the observer from the observed, and it is how the observer and the observed influence one another that is the focus of the inquiry.

3. The purpose of the research is to establish an understanding and describe a particular case, rather than to develop a set of truths that are context free. It is the appreciation of the complexity and richness of the context within which a phenomena occurs that is valued.

4. There is no causality, only an understanding that all events occur simultaneously with one another and therefore are impossible to explicate one from another.

In qualitative research, primary data collection techniques are observations, field notes, the use of key informants (those people providing critical insights about the participants and the research setting), student products, interviews, official documents such as cumulative records and report cards, and conversations with students, teachers, and parents. In gathering these data, the researcher is obligated to ensure individual rights to privacy, confidentiality, and avoidance of harm.

In qualitative research, data are analyzed inductively. The researcher begins with specific,

Notebook computers can be used to generate and manage quantitative and qualitative assessment data. (Photograph by Jimmy D. Lindsey)

raw units of information that are then classified or incorporated into a more comprehensive category or under a general principle (Lincoln & Guba, 1985). Analysis occurs both during and after data collection. A central feature of qualitative analysis is the constant comparative approach (Glaser & Strauss, 1967).

The steps in the constant comparative method enumerated by Glaser (as cited in Bogdan & Biklen, 1992) are as follows: (a) begin data collection; (b) search for important issues, recurring events, or activities in the data to develop categories of focus; (c) collect further data that provide examples of the categories of focus, looking to see the diversity of each category; (d) write about the categories by describing and accounting for all the incidents within the data while constantly searching for new incidents; (e) work with the data and emerging themes to discover basic processes and relationships; and (f) sample, code, and write as the analysis focuses on the core categories.

Although seemingly a step-by-step process, these procedures occur simultaneously, and the analysis continues in a complex recursive fashion where data are continually collected, coded, categorized, and analyzed until the completion of the research report.

Although qualitative researchers do not use the same methods for establishing validity and reliability of their data collection methods and conclusions as do quantitative researchers, these elements are no less important in qualitative research (Rowe, 1986). Qualitative researchers use the terms credibility, transferability, dependability, and confirmability to establish the trustworthiness of the findings (Lincoln & Guba, 1985). To persuade readers that the findings are legitimate and trustworthy, several procedures are followed. These include the techniques of prolonged engagement, persistent observation, triangulation, member checking, and peer debriefing (Lincoln & Guba, 1985). Through prolonged engagement and persistent observation, the researcher builds trust among the participants, establishes emerging themes, and determines irrelevancies and distortions.

As a second precaution to ensure credibility, triangulation is built into studies in two ways. By collecting data through a number of techniques (triangulation of methods), the limitations of one technique are compensated for, and the use of other methods strengthens the research. By collecting and confirming data through multiple sources (triangulation of sources), data are verified and emerging themes and patterns are better established. Through these two procedures, any proposition that was confirmed through the use of several methods or sources has its credibility greatly enhanced.

In educational research, the classroom teacher may serve as the member checker (Lincoln & Guba, 1985). He or she receives and reviews a copy of the field notes daily and discusses with the researcher any needed changes to accurately reflect the classroom situation and to eliminate any bias. As the final research report is completed, the teacher has a final opportunity to test the credibility of the research by completing a comprehensive member check.

The use of a peer debriefer (Lincoln & Guba, 1985) is another technique to establish credibility. Through the entire research process, the peer debriefer discusses and debates the working hypotheses, probes for biases, helps define coding categories, and assists the researcher with any questions and concerns.

The thick description present in a qualitative report enables someone interested in generalizing the information from the context of the study to reach a conclusion about whether transfer is possible to another context. Lincoln and Guba (1985) asserted that the degree of transferability depends upon the degree of similarity between the sending and receiving contexts. Because the original researcher cannot know the contexts to which transferability might be sought, it is the responsibility of the researcher only to provide sufficient descriptive data to make similarity judgments possible. Thus, determinations of the generalizability of research findings must be left to those researchers who wish to apply these findings to other settings.

Lincoln and Guba (1985) suggested the use of an external auditor to provide dependability and confirmability. Qualitative researchers use an auditor to examine the data after field notes are analyzed to carefully verify both the process and the product of the research. The researcher leaves an audit trail consisting of six types of documentation suggested by Halpern (as cited in Lincoln & Guba, 1985): raw data, data reduction and analysis products, data reconstruction and synthesis products, process notes, materials related to intentions and dispositions, and instrument development information. The auditor discerns whether the inferences are logical, and checks for bias. Schwandt and Halpern (1988) recommended six questions for the auditor to consider: Are findings grounded in the data? Are inferences logical? Is the category structure appropriate? Can methodological shifts and inquiry decisions be justified? What is the degree of researcher bias? What strategies were used for increasing credibility?

The increasing popularity of qualitative research in education has created something of a dilemma in terms of technological applications. Many qualitative researchers use computers for analysis of data, but have reservations about the ability of the various software programs to accomplish this task effectively. One reason for this apprehension relates directly to the nature of qualitative research, which does not lend itself easily to the well-ordered gathering and entering of data. For example, field notes, which are the heart and soul of qualitative research, are gathered through various means as previously discussed and may be very difficult to sort and load into a computer analysis program. Many of the researchers who avail themselves of these technological applications typically rely on code-and-retrieve software, rather than some of the more sophisticated programs.

Richards and Richards (1994) identified the following five types of specialist software for qualitative data analysis QDA:

1. *Code-and-retrieve software* was the first type of software developed for QDA. Its primary function is to allow the researcher to enter coding of specific text into a database, then collect and display all text segments marked by the same code. Examples of this software are QUAL-PRO (Impulse Development) and ETHNO-GRAPH (Scolari, Sage Publications).

2. *Rule-based theory-building systems* are fundamentally code-and-retrieve systems, but have the capacity to include pictures and audio- and videotapes among the documents it can index. One of its features is its ability to autocode text search finds. An example of this software is Hyper RESEARCH (Research-Ware).

3. *Logic-based systems* use if–then rules for their representation of hypotheses. These systems support code-and-retrieve but use clausal form logic and a sophisticated set of retrieval patterns called hypothesis structures to provide analyses of data. An example of this software is AQUAD (Ingeborg Huber Verlag).

4. An *index-based approach* features both a document system, which holds textual-level data about documents, and an index system, designed to allow the user to create and manipulate concepts and store and explore emerging ideas. An example of this software is NUD*IST (Scolari, Sage Publications).

5. *Conceptual network systems* represent conceptual information in a graphic manner, as opposed to production rules or the symbolic approach of formal logic. An example of this software is ATLAS (Scolari, Sage Publications).

Strategic Approach to Addressing Technology Applications

Schools are facing increasing pressure to integrate technology applications within their doors (Lewis, 1998). However, technology is a constantly changing and dynamic set of tools. Even the technology industry cannot predict what technology will "look like" in 3 to 5 years. Planning and evaluation in such uncertain circumstances require approaches and skills that are responsive to changing environments and still allow for determining fact from rhetoric (Cheek & Kelly, 1993). Strategic approaches have been popularized in the organizational changes while still pursuing a systematic and planned approach to business. The most notable work in education has been by William Glasser in his efforts to develop the "Quality School" (Glasser, 1992). Strategic approaches have been defined as the organization's (school's) activities and plans that are designed to (a) match the organization's objectives with its mission and (b) match the organization's mission with its environment in an effective and efficient manner. Byars (1984) suggested that the strategic process could be divided into strategic planning and strategic implementation. Planning includes developing a mission statement, developing policies to guide the organization to plan in a meaningful manner, establishing long- and short-term objectives, and determining which strategy to be used. Implementation includes the development of an organizational structure to achieve the strategy, monitoring the activities designed to implement the strategy, and monitoring the effectiveness of the strategy. Although our interests are in this chapter primarily in the evaluation activities associated with implementation, we recognize that effective program development and evaluation are interrelated processes. While several models for the creation of a strategic plan exist, they generally consist of (a) defining the organization's mission; (b) analyzing or scanning the external environment (e.g., market); (c) identifying strategic targets (long- and short-term objectives); (d) identifying and selecting strategic alternatives for reaching the targets; and (e) creating benchmarks or indicators for accomplishing the targets. Effective planning requires that evaluation needs and concerns be addressed early in the process and flow directly from the mission of the organization.

Developing a Mission Statement

The development of a mission statement is an integral part of clarifying the program's intent and proposed outcomes. A viable mission statement reflects the vision of teachers, administrators, parents, and students regarding the use of technology in their schools. Although mission statements are rather individualized at the

school, district, or state level, there are several examples of mission statements at the national level. The Office of Special Education Programs (OSEP) has engaged in a strategic planning process to guide program activities in technology, research, and programs for students with severe emotional disturbance. The process involved the identification of constituents, multiple focus groups representing various constituent groups, and the development and continual refinement of mission statements and strategic targets. To set forth an agenda for the Technology, Educational Media, and Materials Program, community members were asked to identify the advances needed for improving quality, use, and access of technology, educational media, and materials to achieve better results for children and youth with disabilities. To illustrate the outcomes of this process, we provide a copy of the Agenda for the Technology, Educational Media, and Materials Program in Table 14.1.

Conducting an Environmental Scan

As previously stated, the forecasting of technology applications is a rather uncertain enterprise. In conducting an environmental scan, planners and evaluators should work together to identify the contextual variables that will impact on technology adoption. They must address current and projected levels of trained personnel; fiscal resources for the purchase, maintenance, and replacement of hardware and software; attitudes toward technology; and other dimensions. The purpose of the environmental scan is to provide a baseline of current status and to identify trends (e.g., requests for computers, assistive technology required by students with disabilities). Two procedures for supplementing environmental scans are focus groups and delphi study procedures. In focus groups, consumers (defined broadly) are asked to respond as part of a group to broad guiding questions (e.g., How should technology be used in your school?). Standard practice is that focus group participants are relative strangers to each other and selected because they represent certain consumer groups (e.g., elementary school

Table 14.1. Office of Special Education's OSEP Agenda for the Technology, Educational Media, and Materials Program

---

Program Mission

To improve results for individuals with disabilities by advancing the creation, evaluation, and use of tools that enable students with disabilities for lifelong learning, inclusion, and productivity.

Strategic Targets for the Program

Enable the Learner.

The Program will foster the creation of state-of-the-art instructional environments, both in and out of school. Technology, educational media, and materials will be used to enable students with disabilities to access knowledge, to develop skills and problem-solving strategies, and to engage in educational experiences necessary for them to participate fully and successfully in our society.

Promote Effective Policy.

The Program will promote supportive policy making at all levels in government, schools, and business. Such policies should ensure accessibility, availability, effective application, and consistent use of appropriate technology, media, and materials. The policies will recognize that these tools are essential to achieving better lifelong results for individuals with disabilities.

Improve Use Through Professional Development.

The Program will encourage an investigation of approaches and strategies for training and supporting teachers, administrators, parents, and related service personnel on the uses of instructional and assistive technologies. This broad group of consumers needs to know what is available and how it can best be used for individuals with disabilities. Acting on such knowledge, they can increase productive use of instructional time; prepare students with disabilities for employment and citizenship; and promote their intellectual, ethical, cultural, and physical growth.

Create Innovative Tools.

The program will encourage and support development of varied and integrated technologies, media, and materials which open up and expand the lives of those with disabilities. This can be accomplished by individuals, corporations, or agencies dedicated to improving the educational, social, occupational, and cultural opportunities for all students. Their work should enable individuals with disabilities to achieve the results expected of all students—independence, self-determination, and a quality of life that is productive and personally satisfying.

Available: http://www.ed.gov/offices/OSERS/OSEP/OSEP97AnlRpt/pdf/appendc.pdf

parents, parents of students with disabilities). In a delphi technique, persons knowledgeable regarding a particular area (e.g., hardware, software, adaptation) are asked to forecast the trends in this area and project or predict the changes possible in a certain time period (e.g., 2 years, 5 years). Both techniques are supplements to an environmental scan process and should not replace quantifiable data when available.

Establishing Long- and Short-Term Objectives and Strategic Targets

Once the direction of the technology integration program has been established, the targets for the plan must be established. In general, long-term goals have a 5- to 10-year perspective, whereas short-term goals are usually for periods of an academic school year. These goals may vary greatly given the financial and personnel context of the school. For example, it may not be unreasonable for a school with high levels of community and industry support to have Internet access as a 5-year or even longer period target. The overall requirement is that the time period reflect the actual environment of the district in order for the objective to serve as a meaningful indicator for the district.

The purposes of the strategic targets are at least twofold. First, they provide a broad-based consensus for program development areas and evaluation activities. By sharing a vision of the direction for change, parents, policy makers, educators, and researchers can focus efforts toward innovation and development. The role of a strategic target should help to move everyone concerned from the question of "What to do?" to that of "How to do it?" Second, the purpose of the targets is to serve as a short-term "investment guide" for school personnel in terms of both fiscal and human resources. Each of the targets should represent substantial topical areas for research and development activities that can and should be pursued on local, state, and federal levels.

The development of indicators as a guide for program development is not without problems. There is danger in providing persons responsible for the design and implementation of programs for children with benchmarks that are too low, thereby stifling continued progress and innovation. In like manner to propose "exemplary practices" without understanding historical, cultural, and contextual factors related to their success can lead to frustration and disenchantment by individuals seeking replication (see also Chapters 1 and 5).

Reorganization To Achieve Strategic Targets

It is often necessary to rearrange existing organizational structures to support the implementation of technology programs. The use of technology cuts across disciplines and grades within schools. The ability to alter staffing patterns in a manner that supports the overall use of technology in a broad range of curriculum and instructional units is critical to maximizing the impact of technology. For example, a district or school may decide to develop an "expert" approach to technology adoption. A particular person or group of persons is given the primary responsibility and often the budget to identify and secure hardware, select software, provide training in its use, and evaluate its effectiveness. Another approach might be general training of all personnel in "generic" technology integration. That is, all of the instructional staff are provided training in the selection and integration of technology on a nonspecific subject basis and expected to generalize to their particular setting and needs. The successful integration of technology will require (a) instructional personnel to assume new roles and (b) an altering of staffing patterns to support achievement of long- and short-term objectives.

Monitoring the Strategic Plan (Formative Evaluation)

As we previously discussed, formative evaluation consists of procedures to assure that the project is on track in relation to effectiveness, timelines, and procedures. This evaluation is continuous.

Monitoring Effectiveness (Outcome Evaluation)

Indicators have been defined as a "statistic of direct normative interest which facilitates concise, comprehensive, and balanced judgments about the conditions of major aspects of society" (U.S. Department of Health, Education and Welfare, 1969). The purpose of an indicator is to provide information regarding the current functioning of a system for the purpose of predicting the future functioning of that system. Rockwell (1989) provided several characteristics or criteria for a measure to serve as an indicator, including

Technology makes learning fun for children, youth, and adults. (Photograph by Robin D. Thibodeaux)

timelines of reporting, the potential to facilitate decision making, a future orientation, collectability across time, validity, reliability, and accuracy. An indicator should have the potential to be reported within a time frame that makes the data current enough to be relevant. It should provide information that is useful not only to policy makers, but to others involved in the system such as administrators, parents, and teachers. It should be broad enough to anticipate and encompass changing situations so as not to become useless over time. It should be capable of being collected often so that a context is provided from one measurement to the next. Last, and certainly not least, it should possess adequate measurement properties of validity, reliability, and accuracy (Rockwell, 1989).

Criteria for the Adoption of Innovation

As we pointed out, technology applications represent a substantial investment of fiscal and human resources. As schools move toward the integration of technology, the need to identify approaches and options that will produce desired results becomes critical. Just as no one educational approach has been successful with all children in all settings, no one approach will work in every school system for every school. The "context" of the innovation (e.g., fiscal resources, level of commitment, available internal and external expertise) will certainly impact the effectiveness of proposed innovations.

Perkins (1993) suggested the following criteria for "going to scale" with an innovation:

1. A widescale innovation should not escalate a teacher's workload.

2. A widescale innovation should avoid extreme demands on a teacher's skills and talents.

3. A widescale innovation should include strong material supports.

4. A widescale innovation should not boost cost allotments.

5. A widescale innovation should fulfill many conventional educational goals and objectives at least as well as conventional objectives.

Perkins strongly suggested that any innovation that does not systematically address each of these criteria will ultimately fail to be adopted and maintained on a wide scale. While educators may look at each criterion in relation to the adoption of technology and forecast its ultimate failure, they may also look at each criterion as a roadmap for planning to assure the success of any technology efforts. Many of the implications of these criteria are evidenced in the Agenda for Technology, Educational Media, and Materials presented in Table 14.1, reflecting the need for advocacy for technology, as well as congruence of technology and innovation with the conventional goals of independence, access and equity, and the critical need for personnel preparation and support. If technological innovations applied to education are to take hold and flourish, educators must address each of these criteria in their planning and evaluation efforts.

Resources

Books

Alberto, P. A., & Troutman, A. C. (1996). *Applied behavior analysis for teachers* (4th ed.). Columbus, OH: Merrill.

Ary, D., Jacobs, L. C., & Razavieh, A. (1996). *Introduction to research in education* (5th ed.). Fort Worth, TX: Holt, Rinehart and Winston.

Bogdan, R. C., & Biklen, S. K. (1992). *Qualitative research for education: An introduction to theory and methods.* Needham Heights, MA: Allyn & Bacon.

Edyburn, D. L. (1999). *The electronic scholar: Enhancing research productivity with technology.* Upper Saddle River, NJ: Prentice-Hall.

Gall, M.D., Borg, W. R., & Gall, J. P. (1996). *Educational Research: An introduction* (6th ed.). White Plains, NY: Longman.

Harris, M. B. (1998). *Basic statistics for behavioral science research* (2nd ed.). Needham Heights, MA: Allyn & Bacon.

Heiman, G. W. (1996). *Basic statistics for the behavioral sciences* (2nd ed.). Boston: Houghton Mifflin.

Tawney, J. W., & Gast, D. L. (1984). *Single subject research in special education.* New York: Merrill/Macmillan.

Organizations

American Education Research Association (AERA) is an organization of 22,000 educators, administrators, and other professionals working or interested in education research. AERA is concerned with improving education through research and disseminating and applying these research results (e.g., holding conferences and publishing journals and newsletters, such as the *American Educational Research Journal*). *Contact:* AERA, 1230 Seventeenth Street NW, Washington, DC 20036-3878; Voice: 202/223-9485; Fax: 202/775-1824; Web: http://www.aera.net.

References

Alberto, P. A., & Troutman, A. C. (1996). *Applied behavior analysis for teachers* (4th ed.). Columbus, OH: Merrill.

Bogdan, R. C., & Biklen, S. K. (1992). *Qualitative research for education: An introduction to theory and methods.* Needham Heights, MA: Allyn & Bacon.

Brinkerhoff, R. O. (1979). Evaluating full service special education programs. In E. L. Meyen, G. A. Vergason, & R. J. Whelan (Eds.)., *Instructional planning for exceptional children: Essays from Focus on Exceptional Children* (pp. 351–373). Denver, CO: Love Publishing.

Bryant, B. R., & Seay, P. C. (1998). The Technology-Related Assistance to Individuals with Disabilities Act: Relevance to individuals with learning disabilities and their advocates. *Journal of Learning Disabilities, 31,* 4–15.

Byars, L. L. (1984). *Strategic management: Planning and implementation.* New York: Harper and Row.

Campbell, D. T., & Stanley, J. C. (1963). Experimental and quasi-experimental designs for research on teaching. In N. L. Gage (Ed.), *Handbook of research on teaching* (pp. 171–246). Chicago: Rand-McNally.

Carnine, D. (1996). *Creating smart schools.* Eugene, OR: National Center to Improve Tools for Educators (NCITE). Available: http://darkwing.uoregon.edu/~ncite/smart.html

Cheek, E. H., & Kelly, R. R. (1993). Evaluation models for technology applications. In J. Lindsey (Ed.), *Computers and exceptional individuals* (2nd ed.) (pp. 311–331). Austin, TX: PRO-ED.

Gay, L. R. (1996). *Educational research: Competencies for analysis and application* (5th ed.). Englewood Cliffs, NJ: Prentice-Hall.

Giangreco, M. F., Cloninger, C. J., & Iverson, V. S. (1993). *Choosing options and accommodations for children.* Baltimore: Brookes.

Glaser, B., & Strauss, A. L. (1967). *The discovery of grounded theory: Strategies for qualitative research.* Chicago: Aldine.

Glasser, W. (1992). *The quality school: Managing students without coercion* (2nd ed.). New York: Harper Perennial.

Johnson, J. M., & Pennypacker, H. S. (1990). *Strategies and tactics of human behavioral research* (2nd ed.). Hillsdale, NJ: Erlbaum.

Kavanaugh-Brown, J. (1999). It's how you use it. *Government Technology, 12*(2), 28.

Kazdin, A. E. (1982). *Single-case research designs: Methods for clinical and applied settings.* New York: Oxford University Press.

Kurtz, N. R. (1999). *Statistical analysis for the social sciences.* Needham Heights, MA: Allyn & Bacon.

Lewis, R. B. (1998). Assistive technology and learning disabilities: Today's realities and tomorrow's promises. *Journal of Learning Disabilities, 31,* 16–26, 54.

Lincoln, Y. S., & Guba, E. G. (1985). *Naturalistic inquiry.* Thousand Oaks, CA: Sage.

National RRC Panel on Indicators of Effectiveness in Special Education. (1986). *Effectiveness indicators for special education: A reference tool.* Lexington, KY: Mid-South Regional Resource Center.

Perkins, D. (1993). *Smart schools: Better thinking and learning for every child.* New York: Free Press.

Richards, T. J., & Richards, L. (1994). Using computers in qualitative research. In N. K. Denzin & Y. S. Lincoln (Eds.)., *Handbook of qualitative research* (pp. 445–462). Thousand Oaks, CA: Sage.

Rockwell, C. R. (1989). *Lessons from the history of the social indicators movement.* Washington, DC: Social Science Research Council, Washington Consulting Group.

Rowe, D. (1986). Literacy in the child's world: Young children's explorations of alternate communication systems. *University Microfilms International,* 870 7819.

Schwandt, T. A., & Halpern, E. S. (1988). *Linking auditing and metaevaluation: Enhancing quality in applied research.* Newbury Park, CA: Sage.

Sidman, M. (1960). *Tactics of scientific research*. New York: Basic Books.

Skinner, B. F. (1953). *Science and human behavior*. New York: Macmillan.

Sulzer-Azaroff, B., & Reese, M. P. (1982). *Applying behavior analysis: A program for developing professional competence*. New York: Holt, Rinehart, & Winston.

Tawney, J. W., & Gast, D. L. (1984). *Single subject research in special education*. Columbus, OH: Merrill.

U.S. Department of Health, Education and Welfare (USD-HEW). (1969). *Toward a social report*. Washington, DC: U.S. Government Printing Office.

Wolery, M., Bailey, D. B., & Sugai, G. M. (1987). *Effective teaching: Principles and procedures of applied behavior analysis with exceptional students*. Boston: Allyn & Bacon.

Yin, R. K. (1984). *Case study research: Design and methods* (2nd ed). Newbury Park, CA: Sage.

Epilogue

You have just read 14 dynamic chapters, and if you have not done so already, I hope you will take some time to read the appendixes that follow. Although there are a number of ways in which I could have provided a recapitulation or synopsis for the myriad of technological concepts presented, I found myself returning to one conclusion—the best way to end this edition was by listing some of the more poignant statements made by the chapter authors. I believe the following statements summarize important content from this latest edition of *Technology and Exceptional Individuals*:

The real . . . [technological] revolution is taking place in the area of software as people think up new tasks for computers to do and better ways to accomplish them.

General and special educators, other professionals, and exceptional individuals who are willing to master the general concepts of computer technology will be able to communicate their operational needs to hardware designers.

When considering applications for individuals with disabilities a useful perspective is to view various types of technology as tools . . . [and] to think about a continuum that ranges from "high tech" to "no tech" solutions to problems.

Technology solutions can help individuals with disabilities to overcome barriers of environmental control, mobility, communication, and information access.

Technology that allows individuals to develop their gifts and talents is not an option but a reality.

Until knowledge of the potential of assistive and instructional technologies is widespread,

there will be no way to assure that appropriate referrals for technology evaluations occur.

Evaluation and validation should be of primary concern to the educator of exceptional persons, if selection and use of software and any assistive device are to be effective.

. . . the use of . . . [technology], like all other instructional delivery media, is not a panacea that will automatically solve the learning problems of individuals who experience substantial educational and developmental challenges.

The process of integrating technology into the curriculum for students with special needs and enabling teachers to use technology in support of their professional and instructional productivity clearly involves a significant commitment of time, energy, and resources.

Although there is no best way to use technology, there is a best way *not* to use it: *only* as a reward for students who complete their work or behave appropriately. Also, technology use should be consistent with curricular goals and compatible with students' instructional needs.

"E-mail" . . . if the sender is blind, deaf, physically challenged, or learning disabled, this is really unimportant in the communication process . . . [and] is never known.

The current rush to provide technological capabilities and networking to schools in the absence of articulated outcomes faces danger of eroding the consumer's confidence in education's ability to change.

Successful financing of a public school assistive technology program requires an organized plan for applying for funding and persistence in appealing negative funding decisions.

Finally, the single most important technological development for individuals with disabilities, gifts, and talents that separates the 1993 and this edition of *Technology and Exceptional Individuals* was presented throughout this book using four words—Internet and World Wide Web (WWW). The International Internet has grown from just four computers connected in 1969 by the Advanced Research Projects Agency (ARPA) to more than 20 million computers linked throughout the world that offer users 250 million to 500 million Web sites (see The Internet: Weapon of the Cold War, 1999). This former weapon of the Cold War is now used for our most important peacetime activities including communication, entertainment, education, shopping, and business, and is significantly changing the lives of individuals with and without disabilities, gifts, and talents. Just think about your developing Internet experiences and the impact of this system on your life. What if the Internet did not exist? Yet, and paraphrasing the words of Carl Steinhof and associates you read in the Preface, what we have in the Internet today "is only a portent of what is to come."

Visit the portals developed by Netscape, Yahoo, Lycos, and others and think about the type of and format for information that these sites will have five years from now. Also, access the Internet, close your eyes or blindfold yourself, and use the search engine HotBot to find information about the American Foundation for the Blind. Then, visit IBM's Web site, download its Home Page Reader, and find the information you searched for with your eyes closed or blindfolded. How do you think these access, find, and output procedures will function 5 years from now? With total voice recognition and speech synthesis? In what ways do you believe developing technologies based on wireless communications, networked systems, and the integration of the computer, telephone, and television will change the Internet for individuals with disabilities, gifts, and talents? Will the fourth edition of this book introduce and describe how exceptional individuals are using the CompPhoneVision or NetPhone or smart chips woven into the fabric of their clothes for Internet and other technological purposes (Chmielewski, 1998; Krantz, 1999)? Will my epilogue for the next edition ask the starting date for the UniverseNet/UWW and whether or not exceptional individuals will access this planetary system through brain waves and will be able to use this network to generate holograms to benefit their lives? Remember, only 6 or so years ago very few of us knew about the Internet and World Wide Web, only a small percentage of that few accessed the system, and it looked and functioned quite differently.

References

Chmielewski, D. C. (1998, June 7). Wearable computers, phones foreseen. *Sunday Advocate*, pp. 2H–3H.

The Internet: Weapon of the Cold War. (1999, March 15). *The Advocate*, p. 7A.

Krantz, M. (1999, March 8). Tomorrow's gadgets. *Time Digital*, 4(1) 48–53.

Appendix A

⁊ ⁊ ⁊

Technology Glossary

Jimmy D. Lindsey
Southern University–Baton Rouge

Access time The time needed to get data from main memory or from a storage device (e.g., diskette, tape, Winchester disk).

Acoustic coupler A device used to transmit data over telephone lines by changing electrical signals into audio signals and vice versa.

Address The number used to identify a specific location in a computer's memory.

Advanced Research Project Administration Network (ARPANet) A wide-area network developed by the Department of Defense (circa 1960) to survive a nuclear war and was the forerunner of the Internet.

Algorithm A set of rules or procedures for solving a problem.

Alias A short and easy to remember name or term that is used for a longer and difficult to remember name or term.

Alphanumeric A term for alphabetic letters, numerical digits, and special characters (e.g., $, +, [ ]) that can be processed by computers.

American National Standards Institute (ANSI) The organization responsible for approving U.S. standards in computers and communications (i.e., ANSI standards).

Anonymous File Transfer Protocol (FTP) A protocol that permits users to secure publicly accessible files (e.g., programs and documents) on the Internet using "anonymous" instead of a user ID and password to bypass security checks.

APL A terminal-oriented and symbolic programming language that was specifically developed for interactive problem solving.

Applesoft A revised and extended version of the BASIC programming language developed for the Apple II family of computers.

Appletalk Apple's networking protocol for communication between Apple Computer products and other computers.

Application A particular task or program (e.g., manipulating student records) to which a computer solution can be applied.

Application program A computer program designed to address unique user needs (e.g., a program that monitors school or testing data).

Application software Computer programs developed to perform specific user applications.

Archie A software program used on the Internet with anonymous file transfer protocol to find archives or stored files (e.g., indexed directory by file name).

Architecture Often refers to the design or organization of the central processing unit (CPU).

Argument The value (number or variable) contained in parentheses following a function and on which a function operates.

Arithmetic expression A combination of arithmetic operators and numbers (e.g., $8 - 4 =$) that directs a specific operation to be conducted.

Arithmetic/logic unit (ALU) The area of the central processing unit where arithmetic and logical operations are performed.

Array A programming procedure in which a series of related items (e.g., vectors, determinants, matrices) are arranged to perform a specific task.

Artificial intelligence A branch in computer science that uses computers to solve problems that require knowledge, intuition, or imagination.

ASCII Acronym for American Standard Code for Information Interchange, which has assigned a binary number to each alpha and numeric character and several non-printing characters to control communication devices and printers. For example, the ASCII code for the letter 'a' is 01000001.

Assembler A program that takes a computer's nonmachine language and converts it into a form that the computer can use.

Assembly language A low-level symbolic language that permits a computer programmer or user to develop a program using mnemonics instead of numeric instructions.

Asynchronous A communication procedure whereby computer information and data are transmitted as soon as they are ready instead of at fixed intervals.

Backbone A series of connections or a high-speed line that provides the primary path for a network.

Background A programming procedure in which one or more noninteractive tasks are running on the computer while the user is using another interactive (foreground) task.

Background processing The automatic carrying out of a low-priority computer program when higher priority programs are not being executed by the computer.

Backup The copying of one or more disks, diskettes, tapes, or files on a storage medium to ensure safekeeping of the original.

Bandwidth A measure of the amount of information that can be transmitted through a network line or connection (e.g., bits per second or the difference in highest to lowest hertz).

BASIC Acronym for Beginners' All-purpose Symbolic Instruction Code, an interactive programming language developed at Dartmouth College.

Batch processing The automatic execution of a particular set of computer programs, usually without human direction or interaction during the execution.

Baud The modem unit of speed for data transmitting and receiving approximately equal to a single bit per second. Common baud rates are 300, 1,200, 2,400, etc.

Bidirectional The ability of a printer to print from right to left as well as from left to right or the ability to transfer data on a bus in either direction.

Binary The number system having two digits (e.g., 0 and 1) in which each symbol represents a decimal power of two. Also a system that has two functions or levels (e.g., off and on).

Bit The smallest unit of data (binary digit 0 and 1) recognized by a computer. For example, all letters, numerals, and symbols processed by a computer are digitized and expressed as a combination of bits or 0's and 1's.

Bit-map graphics Graphic technology that permits the control of individual pixels on a monitor to produce elements such as arcs, circles, sine waves, etc., of superior resolution that block-addressing technology cannot accurately display.

Bits per second (bps) A basic measure of speed for transferring information (e.g., 56 K is 56,000 bits per second).

Board A circuit or plastic resin board containing electronic components such as chips and the circuits needed to connect them.

Boot The act of starting a computer by loading a program into its memory from an external storage medium such as a disk, diskette, or tape.

Branch A programming procedure to send a program execution to a line or statement other than the next one in sequence.

Branch instruction The instruction used to transfer control from one sequence of a program to another.

Browser Software program (e.g., Netscape Communicator or Microsoft Internet Explorer) that can be used to access and inspect Internet properties (e.g., Web pages).

Buffer A temporary storage area used to hold data that is being passed between computers and other devices (e.g., printers) because the devices operate at different speeds or different times.

Bug A mistake in a computer program or a malfunction in a computer hardware component.

Bulletin Board System (BBS) A computerized system where individuals at different times logon to get BBS news, exchange communications, upload and download files, and play games, among other functions.

Bus A group of parallel electrical connections that carry signals or impulses between computer components or devices.

Byte The number of bits used to represent a character. For computers, a byte is usually 8 bits.

Campus Wide Information System (CWIS) A "system" that provides information and services on a campus via kiosks (e.g., directory information, calendars, bulletin boards, databases) and permits interactive computing and networking.

Capacity The number of items of data (e.g., words, bytes, characters) that a storage device is capable of containing.

Card A storage medium in which data are represented by means of holes punched in vertical columns in a paper card.

Card reader An input device that can transfer data punched into cards to a computer's memory.

Cathode ray tube (CRT) A vacuum tube that generates and guides electrons onto a fluorescent screen to produce such images as characters or graphic displays on video display screens.

Central processing unit (CPU) Electronic components in a computer that control the transfer of data and information. CPUs also perform arithmetic and logic calculations.

Character A single printable letter (A–Z), numeral (0–9), or symbol (e.g., $, &, %) used to represent data. Nonvisible elements such as spaces, tabs, or carriage returns are also characters.

Character code A code (e.g., ASCII) that assigns numerical values to characters.

Character printer A printer that prints one character at a time like a typewriter.

Chip The piece of semiconducting material (usually silicon) on which an integrated circuit is fabricated. The word *chip* correctly refers to the piece of silicon itself, but it is often used to mean an integrated circuit and its package.

Circuit The system of semiconductors and related electrical elements through which electrical currents are directed or flow.

Client A computer system (or process) that requests a service of another computer system (or process).

Client software A program that permits the user to access server software programs on another computer and obtains information from that computer.

COBOL Acronym for COmmon Business Oriented Language, a high-level programming language that is well suited to business applications involving complex data records (e.g., school records and accounts) and large amounts of printed output.

Code A computer program that translates a source program written in a high-level language into a series of machine language instructions.

Cold start The process of starting a computer when the power is already on (or as if the power had just been turned on) by loading the operating system into memory and then loading and running a program.

Column A vertical arrangement of graphics points or character spaces on the screen.

Command A user instruction to the computer (e.g., word, mnemonic, or character) that is generally given through a keyboard and that causes a computer to perform a predefined function.

Compact disc (CD) A disc-storage medium based on optical or laser technology and capable of storing millions of bytes of information (e.g., 550 MB or megabytes) in text, video, audio, and other media formats (e.g., graphics). CD-ROM offers read-only capabilities while CD-R permits both reading and writing (recording).

Compatibility The ability of computers to work with other computers that are not necessarily similar in design or capabilities. Also, compatibility can refer to the ability of an instruction, program, or component to be used on more than one computer.

Computer A programmable electronic machine that can store, retrieve, and process data for educational, scientific, business, and other purposes.

Computer language *See* Programming language.

Computer network An interconnection of computer systems, terminals, and communications facilities.

Computer program A series of commands and instructions that guide the activities of a computer.

Computer science The field of knowledge that includes all aspects of computer design and use.

Computer security The protection of computer hardware, software, and data from unauthorized access or use.

Computer system The combination of hardware and software used as a unit to receive, manipulate, store, retrieve, and transmit data.

Computing The act of using electronic equipment for processing data.

Configuration The assortment of equipment (e.g., disks, tapes, printers) in a particular system.

Control The sequence or order in which statements of a program are carried out.

Core The older type of nonvolatile computer memory, made of ferrite rings; that represents binary data by switching the direction of polarity of magnetic cores.

CP/M Abbreviation for Control Program for Microprocessors, an operating system used in the past by many computers.

Cursor A movable, blinking marker (usually a box or a line) on the terminal video screen that defines the next point of character entry or change.

Daisy wheel A print head shaped like a wheel with many spokes that forms full characters similar to those of a regular typewriter rather than characters formed of dots.

Data Facts, numbers, letters, and symbols used, created, processed, or stored in the computer.

Database A large collection of organized data (e.g., information on individuals, test scores) that is required to perform a task.

Database administrator (DBA) The individual responsible for the orderly development, operation, and security of a database.

Database management system (DBMS) A collection of related programs for loading, accessing, and controlling a database.

Data communication The movement of coded data (e.g., sending and receiving) by means of electrically transmitted signals.

Data diskette A diskette that is used entirely or primarily to contain data files.

Data processing The application in which a computer works primarily with numerical data, as opposed to text.

Debugging Detection and elimination of all mistakes in a computer program or in the computing system itself.

Deferred execution The saving of a program line for execution at a later time as part of a complete program.

Device A piece of computer hardware that performs some specific functions such as an input device (e.g., keyboard to get data into CPU), output device (e.g., printer or monitor to take data out of the computer), or input/output device (e.g., terminal or disk drive to perform both inputting and outputting of data).

Diagnostic A program that examines the operation of a device, board, or other component for malfunctions and reports its findings.

Dialup Temporary connections between computers over a regulation telephone line.

Digit One of the symbols of a number system (0–9) that is used to designate a quantity.

Digital computer A computer that manipulates digital data and performs arithmetic and logic operations with these data.

Digital printer An output device that uses an automatically controlled pen to graph data.

Digital video or versatile disc (DVD) A disc-storage medium based on compact-disc (CD) technology but capable of storing billions of bytes of information (e.g., 2.5 to 17 GB or gigabytes). DVD-ROM offers read-only capability while DVD-RAM or DVD+RW permits both reading and writing (recording).

Direct memory access (DMA) A method for transferring data to or from a computer's memory without CPU intervention.

Disk A rigid, flat circular plate of varying size and storage capacity with a magnetic coating for storing data.

Disk access time The time required to locate a specific track on a disk.

Disk/diskette drive A device (single or dual) used to read data from or write data onto one or more diskettes.

Diskette A flexible, flat, circular plate (usually 3½, 5¼, or 8 inches in diameter) permanently housed in a paper or plastic envelope with magnetic coating that stores data and software.

Disk operating systems (DOS) An optional software system that enables a computer to control and communicate with one or more disk drives.

Display A display device or monitor that exhibits information visually.

Display screen A device such as a cathode ray tube that provides a visual representation of data.

Distributed data processing A computing approach in which an organization uses computers in more than one location, rather than one large computer in a single location.

Distributed processing system A set of interacting computer systems or databases situated in different locations.

Domain name A name with two or more parts separated by dots that identifies a specific Internet site (e.g., proed inc.com). Some domains are commercial (.com), network (.net), organizational (.org), governmental (.gov), military (.mil), and educational (.edu).

DOS *See* Disk operating system.

DOS shell A user-friendly software program designed to make working with DOS easier.

Dot-matrix printer A printer that forms characters from a two-dimension array of dots.

Double density Recording procedure for diskettes that permits them to store twice as much data as in normal or single-density recordings.

Downtime The period of time when a computer is not working.

Draft-quality printer A printer that produces high-speed readable characters that are less than typewriter quality. This printer is typically used to generate internal office documents.

Drive A peripheral device that holds a disk or diskette so the computer can read data from and write data on it.

Edit To change or modify text by replacing, moving, or inserting data or information in a document.

EDP Abbreviation for Electronic Data Processing.

Electronic file cabinet A storage unit that stores data much like a regular file cabinet. However, the electronic filing cabinet can store a great deal of information in a small area, access and change this information quickly, organize information more efficiently, and store information more securely.

Electronic mail (e-mail) Messages typically in text format sent via a computer by an individual to one or more persons.

Electronic spreadsheet A type of software program that can perform in minutes complex financial tasks that would take hours to complete manually.

Emulator A program that allows a computer to imitate a different system, thus enabling different systems to use the same data and programs to achieve the same results but sometimes at different performance rates.

Encryption Network security used on the Internet and World Wide Web to "manipulate or code" electronic information or files to prevent unauthorized persons from reading the data.

E-rate The discount, ranging from 20% to 90%, that eligible libraries and schools receive for acquiring telecommunication services starting January 1, 1998 (Technology Act of 1996 and Universal Service Fund of approximately $2 billion per year). These services could include satellite delivery for distance learning, coaxial cable, telephone lines, and Internet access among other services. It does not include computers, facsimile machines, software, and staff or professional development.

Ergonomics The science of human engineering that combines the study of human-body mechanics and physical limitations with industrial psychology.

Error message The text displayed by the computer when an incorrect response is typed. The error message may also identify the problem and indicate what to do next.

Ethernet A popular way to connect similar or different computers in a local area network (LAN).

Execute To perform or carry out a specified action or sequence of actions such as those described by a program.

Expression One or more formulas in a program describing a calculation or calculations to be performed.

Extended Industry Standard Architecture (EISA) A computer bus system designed by several companies that extends the Industry Standard Architecture's (ISA) 8- and 16-bit bus to 32 bits.

Fanfold paper A continuous sheet of paper whose pages are folded accordion style and separated by perforations. This type of paper can be used to print lengthy documents without having to insert individual sheets of paper manually.

File A collection of logically related records or data treated as a single item. A file is also the means by which data and information are stored on a disk or diskette.

Filename The sequence of alphanumeric characters assigned by a user to identify or name a file that can be read by both the computer and the user.

File transfer The copying of a file from computer to computer over a system or network.

File Transfer Protocol (FTP) A network procedure to login from one host to another host or Internet site to retrieve or send files.

Firmware A program on a silicon chip that combines elements of both hardware and software.

Flexible disk *See* Diskette.

Floppy disk *See* Diskette.

Flowchart A form of algorithm that uses symbols and interconnecting lines to show the logic and sequence of specific program operations (program flowchart) or a system of processing to achieve objectives (system flowchart).

Font A complete set of letters, numerals, and symbols of the same type style of a given typeface (e.g., typefaces such as Baskerville, Century, and Helvetica; fonts such as Baskerville Italic, Baskerville Bold, and Baskerville Bold Italic).

Foreground processing Data or information processing that has top priority over background or lower priority processing.

Format (1) The form in which information is organized or presented. (2) To specify or control the format of information. (3) To prepare a blank disk to receive information by dividing its surface into tracks and sectors.

Form feed The capability of a printer to advance fanfold paper automatically to the top of the next page or form when the printer has finished printing the previous form.

FORTRAN Acronym for FORmula TRANslator. A widely used high-level programming language well suited to scientific problems and applications that can be expressed in terms of algebraic formulas.

Frequently Asked Questions (FAQ) Internet resources that provide a listing of and answers for the most frequently asked questions about specific topics (e.g., software).

Function A preprogrammed calculation that can be executed on request from any point in a program.

Function key A key that causes a computer to perform a function (e.g., clearing the screen) or carry out a program.

Gateway A term previously used for a software or hardware method to interface two different protocols. The term *router* is currently used.

General purpose computer system A computer system that has been designed to deal with or solve a variety of problems.

Gopher An early distribution information service or menu system for material on the Internet that is slowly being replaced by the World Wide Web.

Graphics The use of lines and figures, as opposed to the use of printed characters, to display data or information.

Graphics digitizer An input device that converts graphic and pictorial data into binary inputs for use in a computer.

Graphic user interface (GUI) "Gooey" is the communication link (e.g., pull-down menus, pictures/icons) between the user and the operating system.

Hand-held computer A portable computer that can be programmed to perform a wide variety of applications.

Hang For a program or system to malfunction and perform no useful work.

Hard copy Output in permanent form on paper or paper tape as opposed to input in temporary form as data on a visual display or CRT.

Hard disk A disk such as the Winchester disk that is not flexible. It is more expensive than a diskette, but it has the ability to store much more data.

Hardware The physical equipment that makes up a computer system.

Hardwired This refers to a permanent, as opposed to a switched, physical connection between two points in an electrical circuit or between two devices linked by a communication line. For example, local computer connections are typically hardwired, but all connections through a modem are switched because they use telephone lines.

Head A component that reads, writes, or erases data on a storage medium such as a disk or diskette.

Help service Messages displayed on the video screen that provide information on how to use applications and other system services.

High-level language A programming language, such as BASIC, Pascal, or FORTRAN, that is relatively easy for humans to understand. Typically, a single statement in a high-level language corresponds to several instructions in machine language.

Host A computer that allows users to communicate with other host computers on a network.

Hub A device used to connect several computers together. A "hub" also refers to the transfer messages across a system or network.

Hypercard An authoring software program that can be used to develop a multimedia program in a short time and permits the user to interactively look through the program (i.e., Hypercard stack or database) for specific purposes.

Hypercard Stack A computer program or database designed with Hypercard.

Hypertext Text that incorporates word or phrase "links," that permit accessing or displaying linked or connected text or resources.

Hypertext Markup Language (HTML) A coding language used by programmers and others to create hypertext resources for the World Wide Web.

Immediate execution The execution of a program line as soon as it is typed to try out a statement to see how it works.

Impact printer A printer that forms characters on paper by striking an inked ribbon with a character-forming element.

Indefinite loop A section of a program that will repeat the same sequence of actions indefinitely.

Information processing All the operations performed by a computer.

Information retrieval The procedures used to recover specific stored information and data.

Information services Publicly accessible computer repositories for specific or general information and data (e.g., literature bibliographies, stock exchange data).

Inkjet printer A printer that forms characters and images on paper by spraying ink from a printhead into the desired pattern.

Input The act of entering data, or data entered into the computer.

Input/output device A device that is used to get data from the user into the central processing unit and to transfer data from the compiler's main storage to an auxiliary storage medium or to an output device.

Instruction A command that tells the computer which operation to perform next.

Integrated circuit A computer electrical circuit on a silicon chip.

Integrated Services Digital Network (ISDN) A method of combining voice and digital service to increase the amount of information that can be moved over common telephone lines.

Interactive Capable of carrying on a dialogue through a keyboard with the user as opposed to simply responding to commands.

Interface An electronic assembly that connects an external device (e.g., a printer) to a computer.

Internet The present system of interconnected networks using Transmission Control Protocol/Internet Protocol (TCP/IP) protocols that started as the Department of Defense's ARPANet.

Interpreter A computer program that translates each source language statement into a sequence of machine instructions and then executes these machine instructions before translating the next source language statement.

Inverse video The display of text on the display screen in the form of dark dots on a light background instead of light dots on a dark background.

I/O Abbreviation for Input/Output. Pertaining to procedures for transferring information into and out of a computer.

IP number A number with four parts separated by dots that is used to identify a specific machine on the Internet (e.g., 291.721.371.345).

Job A program or task for a computer to execute (e.g., saving a file).

Joystick A device for entering X–Y coordinates by moving a lever to change the position of a cursor on a graphic display screen.

K The symbol for the quantity 2^{10}, or 1,024. K is always in uppercase to distinguish it from lowercase k used for "kilo," which is 10^3, or 1,000.

Kbyte (KB) 1,024 bytes.

Kermit A file transfer protocol that provides easy eclectic transfer in most operating systems (e.g., Bulletin Board System to home computer).

Keyboard The set of keys on a terminal that allows alphanumeric characters or symbols to be transmitted when keys are depressed. It inputs text and instructions to the computer.

Keystroke The act of pressing a single key or a combination of keys on the computer's keyboard.

Keyword A special word or sequence of characters that identifies a specific statement or command (e.g., SAVE, RUN).

Language A set of rules, representations, and conventions used to convey information.

Laptop computer A computer that runs on battery or alternating current and weighs 8 or more pounds.

Large-scale integration (LSI) The combining of about 1,000 to 10,000 circuits on a single chip. LSI circuits include memory chips, microprocessors, calculator chips, and watch chips.

Laser printer High-resolution printer that produces hard copy by using laser technology to fuse the ink to the paper.

Letter-quality printer The printer used to produce documents in print comparable to that of a typewriter.

Light pen An electrical device resembling a pen that can be used to write or sketch on the screen of a cathode ray tube to provide input.

Line number A number identifying a program line in a program (e.g., 10 PRINT "HELLO").

Line printer A high-speed printer that prints an entire line of characters at a time.

Liquid crystal display (LCD) A type of screen for notebook and laptop computers that reflects existing light (reflective LCD) or has its own light (backlit LCD).

List processing The word processing application that permits many copies of a form document to be produced, with certain information changing from one copy to the next (e.g., the production of personalized form letters).

Load To transfer information from a peripheral storage medium (e.g., a disk) into main memory for use or execution.

Local Hardwired connection of a computer to another computer, terminal, or peripheral device such as in a local area network.

Local area network (LAN) A system or network of computers and related devices (e.g., printers) to serve a small area or setting.

Loop A sequence of instructions in a program that can be executed repeatedly until certain specified conditions are satisfied.

Low-level language A programming language (e.g., assembly language) that is relatively close to the form that the computer's processor can execute directly.

Machine language The basic language of a computer.

Magnetic bubble storage A memory that uses locally magnetized areas that can move about in a magnetic material, such as a plate of orthoferrite. Because it is possible to control reading in and out of this magnetic material, a very high capacity memory can be built.

Magnetic disk A disk made of rigid material (hard disk) or heavy mylar (floppy disk) and used to hold magnetized material.

Magnetic tape or Magtape Magnetic tape used as mass storage media and packaged on reels. Since the data stored on magnetic tape can only be accessed serially, it is not practical for use with personal computers and is often used as a backup device on larger computer systems.

Mainframe A very expensive computer (e.g., IBM 4300) that is physically large and provides the capability to perform applications requiring large amounts of data.

Main memory The memory component of a computer system that can store information for later retrieval (e.g., random access memory and read-only memory).

Main storage The fastest general purpose memory of a computer.

Management information system An information system designed to supply organizational managers with the necessary information needed to plan, organize, staff, direct, and control the operations of the organization.

Mass storage A device like a disk or magtape that can store large amounts of data readily accessible to the central processing unit.

Medium The physical substance upon which data are recorded (e.g., magnetic disks, magnetic tape, punched cards).

Megabyte (MB) 1,048,576 bytes, or 1,000 Kbytes.

Memory The main high-speed storage area in a computer where instructions for a program being run are temporarily kept, or a device where information and data can be stored and from which they can be retrieved.

Memory location A unit of main memory that is identified by an address and can hold a single item of information of a fixed size.

Menu A displayed list of options a computer user can select from by typing a letter or by positioning the cursor.

Menu-driven A computer system that primarily uses menus for its user interface rather than a command language.

Micro channel architecture (MCA) IBM's 16- and 32-bit bus designed for the PS/2 personal computer that permits more than one CPU in a computer.

Microcomputer A computer based on large-scale integration that is physically very small and can fit on or under a desk.

Microcomputer system A system that includes a microcomputer, peripherals, operating system, and applications programs.

Microprocessor A single-chip central processing unit incorporating LSI technology.

Migration path A series of alternatives outlined by a computer manufacturer that enables new computer equipment to be introduced into the present system. This permits users to increase their system's computing power by adding or trading in components rather than giving up all their current hardware and software.

Minicomputer A once-popular type of computer (e.g., IBM System/36) whose physical size is usually smaller than a mainframe, but whose performance exceeds that of a microcomputer or workstation.

Mnemonic A short easy-to-remember name or abbreviation that can be used for many functions, including commands in programming languages.

Mode A state of a computer or system that determines its behavior (e.g., processing, waiting for command).

Modem Acronym for MOdulator/DEModulator. A device that converts computer signals into high-frequency communications signals, and vice versa, and sends and receives these signals over telephone lines.

Monitor A hardware television-like or CRT device that can be used as an output display screen. With respect to software, a monitor is a part of the operating system that allows the user to enter programs and data into memory and run programs.

MOS Abbreviation for Metal-Oxide Semiconductor, which is the most common form of large-scale integration (LSI) technology.

Mouse A device, attached to a computer by a cable, that can control the movement of a cursor by being rolled along a flat surface by hand.

Multikey sort Using more than one parameter to qualify a record for inclusion in a specified group or to order a set of records.

Multimedia Computer presentations incorporating two or more types of media, including text, audio, graphics, animation, still or motion video, and voice.

Multiplexer A device that permits more than one communication line to share one computer data channel.

Multiprocessing The execution of two or more programs by a computer that contains more than one central processor.

Multiprogramming A scheduling technique that permits two or more tasks to be in an executable state at any one time. When the computer has only one CPU, then more than one program can appear to be running at a time because the CPU is giving small slices of its time to each program.

Multitasking The execution of several tasks "at the same time" without having to complete one before starting another. Although computers can perform only one task at a time, the speed at which a computer operates is so fast that it appears as though several tasks are being performed simultaneously.

Musical instrument digital interface (MIDI) Standard for how musical instruments and computers communicate (e.g., keyboard synthesizers are input devices for MIDI-equipped computers).

Natural language A language (also called problem-oriented language) that permits computer users to prepare programs in English or other spoken languages.

Nested loop A loop contained within the body of another loop and executed repeatedly during each pass through the containing loop.

Network A group of computers connected to each other by communications lines to share information and resources.

Newsgroups The discussion groups that can be found on Usenet.

Node A single computer or addressable device connected to a network.

Nonimpact printer A printer that produces a printed image without striking the paper.

Nonvolatile memory Memory that does not lose its contents when a processor's power supply is shut off or disrupted.

Normal The video display format that is made up of light dots on a dark background.

Notebook computer A computer the size of a notebook that runs on battery or alternating current and weighs 1 to 8 pounds.

Numerical analysis The branch of mathematics concerned with the study and development of effective procedures for computing answers to problems.

OCR Abbreviation for Optical Character Registration. Characters printed in a special type style that can be read by both machines and people.

Off-line A term describing persons, devices, or equipment not in direct communication with a computer's central processing unit.

On-line Directly under the control or in communication with the computer. For example, data are introduced immediately into the central processing unit.

Operating system A collection of computer programs that controls the overall operation of a computer and performs such tasks as assigning places in memory to programs and data, processing interrupts, scheduling jobs, and controlling the overall input/output of the system.

Option module An add-on printed-circuit module that allows expansion of a system.

Output device A unit (e.g., monitor, printer) used for taking information from a computer and presenting it in the appropriate form to the user.

Packet A generic term for units of data sent across a network.

Paddle A hand-held device connected to the computer that can move the display cursor left/right or up/down.

Parallel transmission Sending more than one bit at a time.

Parity A one-extra-bit code used to detect recording or transmission errors by making the total number of 1 bits in a unit of data—including the parity bit itself—odd or even.

Pascal A high-level programming language that facilitates the use of good structured-programming techniques.

Password A code or access identification used to enter a secured or locked system (e.g., the alphanumeric GODAWGS).

Peripheral A device (e.g., printer, modem) that is external to the CPU and main memory but connected to them by appropriate electrical connections.

Personal computer A small and inexpensive microcomputer that can be used in the home for household tasks, business, education, and entertainment, among other activities.

Pixels Shortened form of "picture elements." Definable locations on a display screen that are used to form images on the screen. Higher resolution graphic displays can be produced by increasing the number of pixels.

Pocket computer A portable, battery-operated computer that can be programmed to perform a wide number of applications.

Point of Presence (POP) A site with pertinent hardware and software for telecommunication purposes.

Point-to-Point Protocol (PPP) A protocol that permits a computer user to use a modem and the public telephone line to connect to the Internet (i.e., make a TIP/IP connection).

Port A physical area for the connection of a communications line. This line can be between the CPU and anything external to it (e.g., a modem, a printer, a second computer, or another communications line).

Post Office Protocol (POP) A protocol that permits a single user (or host) to read "mail" from a server. POP3 is the most recent version of this standard protocol.

Power supply A transistor switch that converts AC power into DC power or steps down the power supplied to certain devices. A power supply also energizes components such as monitors, integrated circuits, and keyboards.

Print The act of transferring data from a computer's internal memory to a printing device.

Printer The printing device (e.g., dot matrix, inkjet, laser) that produces a paper copy or hard copy output of a document.

Print head The element in a printer that forms a printed character.

Printout A general term that is used to refer to almost anything printed by a computer peripheral device.

Processing Generally, the arithmetic and logic operations performed on data in the course of executing a computer program.

Processor The functional part of the computer system (the CPU or central processing unit) that reads, interprets, and executes instructions.

Program The complete sequence of instructions and routines needed to solve a problem or to execute directions in a computer.

Program disk A disk containing the instructions of a program.

Program execution The process of putting a program in the computer, along with any other information required, and instructing the machine to execute or run the program.

Program library A collection of available computer programs and routines.

Program line The basic unit of a written program that consists of one or more statements separated by colons.

Program maintenance The process of keeping a program operation at an acceptable level, including correcting undetected bugs and making appropriate revisions or changes to meet new requirements.

Programmer The human author or writer of a program.

Programming language The words, symbols, mnemonics, and specific rules that permit an individual to construct a computer program.

Program testing Executing a program with test information to determine whether or not the program can be executed.

PROM Acronym for Programmed Read-Only Memory. A memory that is programmed by the user, not the manufacturer.

Protocol The rules and formats for messages that computers must follow to exchange messages.

PS/2 Operating system developed by IBM and Microsoft to take full advantage of the capabilities of 80286 microprocessors and to do multitasking.

Punch card A cardboard card once used in data processing operations in which tiny rectangular holes punched at specific locations denote numerical values and alphanumeric codes.

Query language A set of commands used to extract from a database the data that meet specific criteria.

Radio-frequency modulator A device for converting video signals produced by computers to a form that can be used by a standard television set.

RAM Acronym for Random Access Memory. Memory that can both be read and written into (i.e., altered) during normal operation and is used in most computers to store the instructions for programs currently being run.

Read To get information from any input or file storage media.

Read–write memory Memory whose contents can be both read and written but that is erased and permanently lost unless saved when the computer's power is turned off.

Real time Refers to computer systems or programs that perform a computation during the actual time that a related physical process transpires so that the results of the computation can be recorded or used to guide the physical process.

Record A collection of related data items.

Remote Typically refers to peripheral devices (e.g., printers, video terminals) that are located at a site away from the CPU.

Reserved word A sequence of characters or a word reserved by a programming language for some special use. For example, the words CALL, END, GOTO, and SAVE, among other words, are reserved words in Applesoft BASIC and cannot be used as variable names in a program.

Response time The time it takes the computer system to react to a given input (e.g., the interval between the pressing of the letter 'a' and the visual displaying of an 'a').

Reverse video A feature on a display unit that produces the opposite combination of characters and background from that which is usually employed (e.g., black characters on a green screen if green characters on a black screen is normal).

ROM Acronym for Read-Only-Memory. Memory that is programmed on a solid-state storage chip at the time of a computer's manufacture and cannot be reprogrammed by the computer itself.

Rotational delay time The time required for the disk to attain the desired position at the read–write head.

Route The path or course that system or network "transmissions" take (e.g., host to host).

Router (formerly Gateway) A device that forwards "transmissions" between systems or networks.

Routine A part of a program that accomplishes some task subordinate to the overall task of the program.

Run The single and continuous execution of a program by a computer on a given set of data.

Screen The display surface of a video monitor or the pattern or information displayed on the screen.

Scrolling The changing of all or part of the content on a display screen by shifting information out one end (usually at the top) to provide room for new data appearing at the other end (usually at the bottom), which produces an effect similar to that of moving a scroll of paper past a fixed viewing window.

Self-test A procedure that permits a program or a peripheral device to check its own operation.

Semiconductor A material such as silicon with a conductivity between that of a metal and an insulator that can be used in the manufacture of solid-state devices (e.g., transistors, integrated circuits) that comprise computer logic hardware.

Semiconductor storage A memory device whose storage elements are formed as solid-state electronic components on an integrated circuit chip.

Serial access Refers to sequential devices (e.g., magnetic tape) that require data, information, or instruction retrieval only by passing through all locations between the ones that are currently being accessed and ones that are desired.

Serial transmission Sending one bit at a time. *See* Parallel transmission.

Server (computer or software) A machine, process, or program that can be accessed using client system, process, or software.

Signature The identification of a sender by lines at the bottom of e-mail or a Usenet article.

Simulation software A computer program (e.g., flight simulation) that has the instructions needed to represent the functioning of another system or event.

Single-density The normal or standard recording density for disks and diskettes. For example, 250,000 bytes can be stored on a single-density 8-inch disk.

Single thread A simple operating system (as opposed to a multitasking system) that carries out a specific task from beginning to end without interruption.

Snail mail Mail and other printed documents sent and received via standard postal service.

Soft copy Alphanumeric and/or graphical data presented in nonpermanent form (e.g., on a video screen).

Software The tasks (e.g., instructions in programs) that make computers perform particular functions.

Sort Rearranging the records in a file (e.g., alphabetically or numerically) so that the order is convenient to the user.

Special interest group (SIG) A group of individuals who interact to address a common interest or concern (e.g., Lotus Suite Users Group, Rain Forest).

Special purpose computer system A computer system capable of solving only a few selected types of numerical or logical problems.

Stand-alone graphics system A graphics system that includes a microcomputer storage, terminal, and other input/output devices.

Startup disk A disk containing software recorded in the proper form that is loaded into the computer's memory to set the system into operation.

Storage capacity The number of items of data that a memory device is capable of containing.

Storage unit A place (e.g., disk, diskette, tape) where files and documents can be saved for later use.

String A programming procedure whereby an item of information consisting of a sequence of data or instructions is put together (e.g., A/B*66 = 26).

Subroutine A programming procedure whereby a part of a program is carried out on request from any point in the program and control is returned to the point of the request on completion of the procedure.

Supercomputer A very large and expensive computer system, characterized by fast processing speeds, that is capable of executing many million instructions per second.

Symbol An element of a computer language's character set (e.g., mark, number, alphabet) that represents a numeral, operation, or relation.

System A combination of software and hardware that performs specific processing operations.

System board The main module (or motherboard) in a personal computer system box that contains the CPU, memory, and the interface circuitry for the keyboard, a printer port, and a communications port.

System unit The unit or structure that houses the system board, disk drives, power supply, and modules.

Tape A recording medium for data or computer programs. Tapes are available in permanent form (e.g., perforated paper tape) and are used as a mass storage medium because they store more data than disks. However, it takes much longer to write or recover data from tapes than from disks.

Task A program in execution.

Telnet A software program that permits a computer user remote communication connections (e.g., to be at one "Internet site" and login at another).

Terminal An input/output device used to enter data into a computer and record the output either as hard copy (e.g., printers) or as soft copy (e.g., video terminals).

Terminal emulation A communication whereby a terminal acts as a terminal of a different design so that it can be used on various systems.

Thumb wheels Dials that provide input into a computer system.

Time-sharing The providing of computer service to more than one user by working on each user's task part of the time.

Token ring A type of local area network (LAN) with nodes wired into a ring and constantly passing a control message (or token) one to the next.

Top–down program design The process of breaking a large and complicated problem into a series of smaller and easier to solve problems.

Touch-sensitive panel An input device that is made up of sets of horizontal and vertical wires mounted on a thin plastic sheet that is then combined into a grid separated by a third plastic sheet and mounted on a display screen.

Track The portion of a moving storage medium (e.g., a disk or a tape) that is accessible to a given read–write head position.

Track ball A device that can be used to move the cursor on a video display. It consists of a box-shaped mounting that holds a ball that moves at the speed and in the direction of the ball's motion.

Tractor feed An attachment used to move paper through a printer. The roller that moves the paper has sprockets on each end that fit into the fanfold paper's matching pattern of holes.

Transmission Control Protocol/Internet Protocol (TCP/IP) A software program or bundle of protocols for Internet functions.

Turnaround time The time between the initiation of a computer job and its completion.

Turnkey system A computer that is ready to be used without adding any hardware or software because it is complete as packaged for a particular application.

Uniform Resource Locator (URL) The specific address of a World Wide Web resource on the Internet (e.g., Council for Exceptional Children: http://www.cec.sped.org).

Universal Product Code A machine-readable code based on parallel bars used for labeling products in a point-of-scale automation system (e.g., grocery items).

Upgrade To reconfigure a personal computer as new features are developed or when existing features are enhanced.

Usenet A system of discussion or "newsgroups" around the world where hundreds of thousands of individuals read and/or send messages over hundreds of thousands of machines.

User-defined key A key that can remember and store a number of keystrokes needed to execute a particular operation. When the key is pressed, it carries out the keystrokes in the proper sequence, thus saving the user from having to press each key in the sequence.

User-friendly A term that implies the computer system or software is easy to use.

User group Individuals who use similar hardware and/or software and meet in person or via computers to share ideas.

Very large-scale integration The accumulation of hundreds of thousands of electronic circuit elements (VLSI) on a single semiconductor chip.

Video disk A disk (also called optical disk) that can store both text and pictures.

Video graphics array (VGA) The display standard for 640 × 480 resolution color displays with a refresh rate of 60 hertz (i.e., the time needed to redraw a display screen) and 16 colors or 256 colors capability. A super VGA display has an 800 × 600 resolution (14-inch monitor) to 1,600 × 1,200 resolution (20-inch or larger monitor) and supports millions of colors.

Video terminal A terminal that displays data on a CRT.

Virus A harmless or harmful program within software or on a disk that is hidden and executes unwanted commands (e.g., changes date and time) at specific signals.

Volatile memory Memory that loses its contents when power is removed unless battery backup is available.

Warm start The restarting of the computer after the power is already on without reloading the operating system into main memory and often without losing the program or data already in main memory.

What you see is what you get (WYSIWYG) The match between computer interface and printer that results in what is seen on the screen being produced in the hard copy.

Wide area network (WAN) A system or network that covers a large geographic area (e.g., more than one site, building, or setting).

White pages Databases on the Internet that can be accessed to secure user information (e.g., telephone numbers, e-mail addresses).

Winchester disk A hard disk capable of storing larger amounts of data than a diskette that is permanently sealed in a drive unit to prevent contaminants from affecting the read–write head.

Word processing system A system that processes text by performing such functions as inserting, deleting, moving, replacing, and printing text, among other activities.

Word wrapping The automatic shifting of words from a line that is too long to the next line.

Workstation A type of computer falling between a microcomputer and minicomputer that is used for engineering, desktop publishing, and software development because of its power, memory capabilities, and high-resolution graphics.

World Wide Web (Web, WWW, or W3) The hypertext or HTTP servers that permit creating, editing, and browsing hypertext documents and engaging in multimedia activities (e.g., text, graphics, sound).

Wraparound The automatic continuation of text on a display screen or printer from the end of one line to the beginning of the next.

Write The process of transferring data and information from the computer to an output medium.

Write-enable notch The square cutout in one edge of a disk's jacket that permits information to be written on the disk. If there is no write-enable notch, or if it is covered with a write-protect tab, information can be read from the disk but not written onto it.

Write-once-read-many (WORM) Optical drive that permits the user to write permanently to a disk until it is full and then read the disk as many times as necessary.

Write-protect To protect data and information on a disk by covering the write-enable notch with a write-protect tab. Write-protect procedures also prevent new information from being written onto the disk.

Write-protect tab A small adhesive sticker used to write-protect a disk by covering the write-enable notch.

Yellow Pages A database on the Internet that can be accessed to secure information about businesses (e.g., telephone numbers, addresses).

Appendix B

჻   ჻   ჻

A Brief History of Computer Technology

Chhanda Ghose and Barbara L. Guillory
Southern University–Baton Rouge, Louisiana

Anatomy of a Microcomputer

A computer is a machine that can be programmed to accept data (input) and process it into useful information (output). A computer system has four main areas: input, processing, output, and storage. Input devices accept data in a form that the computer can use and send to the central processing unit. Input may be achieved by typing on a keyboard, clicking a mouse, or scanning. The brain of the computer is its central processing unit (CPU), where most calculations take place. In terms of computing power, the CPU is the most important element of a computer system. On personal computers the CPU is a single chip called the microprocessor. Two typical components of a CPU are the Arithmetic Logic Unit (ALU) and the Control Unit. The latter extracts instructions from memory and decodes and executes them, calling on the ALU when necessary. Two characteristics differentiate microprocessors —bandwidth (number of bits processed in a single instruction) and clockspeed (given in MHz or the number of instructions per second that the processor can execute). The higher the value, the more powerful the CPU. For example, a 32-bit microprocessor that runs at 50 MHz is more powerful than a 16-bit microprocessor that runs at 25 MHz.

The ROM (read-only memory) chips have permanently etched instructions. In other words it is computer memory on which data have been prerecorded. Once data have been written on a ROM chip, it cannot be removed; it can only be read. ROM retains its contents even when the computer is turned off. Most personal computers contain a small amount of ROM that stores critical programs such as the program that boots the computer. The RAM (random access memory), on the other hand, is computer memory that can be accessed randomly and is the main memory. However, it is volatile, meaning the contents are lost when the computer is turned off.

Processed data become information or data that are organized and meaningful. Two common output devices are screens (monitors) and printers. A most common storage media is a magnetic disk. A magnetic disk is a flat, oxide-coated disk on which data are recorded as magnetic spots. A disk can be a diskette or hard disk. Diskettes look like small stereo records and come in two diameters: 5 1/4 inches (floppy) or 3 1/2 inches (firm). Hard disks hold more data and have faster access than diskettes. Disk data are read by disk drives, which may be housed within the computer or in a separate box that connects to the computer. Disk drives not only read data but write data onto a disk. The most recent storage technology is the optical disk, which uses a laser beam to store large volumes of data inexpensively.

The operating system is the most important program that runs on the computer. It runs other programs, performs basic tasks of housekeeping, and provides a software platform for running applications programs. For IBM and compatible personal computers, the most popular operating systems are DOS, OS/2, and Windows. Macintosh computers use MACOS. The choice of operating system determines the applications that can be run.

The History of Computers

The Computer Revolution, like the Industrial Revolution, has dramatically changed the ways people live and think. The computer is not merely a fad, but a major trend that is shaping society in fundamental ways. Despite what appears to be widespread use of the computer, some people continue to be uneasy about the mathematical sound of the word *computer*, which means "one who computes or calculates" (*The New Webster Dictionary*, 1993, p. 80). Initially, the word computer seemed to suggest that only those with strong analytical and quantitative skills could understand and use the machine. However, the number of persons suffering from computer anxiety has begun to decline due to the availability of cheaper, easier to use personal computers and the rise of a generation of children growing up in the information processing age who are very comfortable with the computer.

Historically, developments leading to the modern computer have been slow. However, during the last 50 years, there have been tremendous developments leaping through six generations of technology.

The Mechanical Age

Modern computer technology has its roots in the works of Charles Babbage (1791–1871), an Englishman who is widely regarded as the father of computing. When solving certain equations, he found that mathematical tables constructed manually were prone to error. In 1823 he developed what he called the "Difference Engine," a machine that would solve the equations better by calculating the differences between them. However, many imperfections in the machine made it unreliable and the British government withdrew its financial support. Despite this setback, Babbage conceived of another machine, the "Analytical Engine," which he believed would perform a wide range of calculating tasks. Although Babbage's Analytical Engine could not be built because parts could not be made for it, his concept was workable and embodied the five key features of modern computers: (1) an input device; (2) a storage place to hold the number waiting to be processed; (3) a processor, or number calculator; (4) a control unit to direct the tasks to be performed and their sequence; and (5) an output device.

If Babbage was the father of computing, then Ada Byron, the Countess of Lovelace, was the first computer programmer. The Countess collaborated with Babbage on instructions for doing computations on the Analytical Engine, and it was her published notes that eventually led others to accomplish what Babbage had envisioned.

The manual tabulation of the 1880 United States Census took 7 ½ years to complete. A contest was held to find a device to speed the counting process. Herman Hollerith's tabulating machine won the contest and was used in the counting process of the 1890 U.S. Census. As a result, an unofficial count was reported only 6 weeks after the Census was taken. Hollerith's machine used electric rather than mechanical power, and processed punched cards on which the location of each punched hole represented coded information (age, sex, race, etc.). In 1896 he founded the Tabulating Machine Company, which merged in 1924 with two other companies to form the International Business Machines Corporation (IBM).

The Electronic Age

In the 1930s many inventors contributed to the development of the modern desktop personal computer. Germany's Conrad Zuse designed an electric calculator that used a binary rather than a decimal system. Besides being simpler, the binary system permitted the incorporation of Boolean logic. This system of logic, worked out by George Boole, enabled one to code propositions as either true or false. In 1940 George Stibitz and Samuel Williams of Bell Labs together constructed a device that could add, subtract, multiply, and divide using electronic rays.

Although the calculating technologies available in the 1930s served business and scientific users, they fell short of the demands of the military during World War II. The military wanted to break codes, prepare firing tables for new guns, and design atomic weapons. The old technologies were too slow in calculating, and the military was willing to spend whatever it would take to develop the kinds of calculating machines it needed. In 1936 Howard Aiken, a Harvard mathematician, after reading Lady Lovelace's notes, began to think that a modern equivalent of Babbage's Analytical Engine could be constructed. As a result, the gigantic Mark I was developed. It stood 8 feet tall, was 51 feet wide, and contained 750,000 components. Unveiled in 1944, the Mark I used the decimal rather than a binary system and was not very efficient.

Also, during World War II, the British Intelligence's need for cracking German codes led to the development of a new type of computer called the Colossus. At the same time, the need for the U.S. military to rapidly calculate trajectories for artillery and missiles led to the development of the ENIAC (Electronic Numerical Integrator and Calculator) by John Mauchly and J. Presper Eckert of the University of Pennsylvania. They used the ABC (Atanasoff-Berry Computer) as the basis for the development of their electronic digital computer. The ENIAC was 18 feet tall and 80 feet wide, and computing was speeded up by the use of 17,000 vacuum tubes and 100,000 electronic components.

Reprogramming the ENIAC involved rerouting thousands of wires; to overcome this limitation, Mauchly and Eckert designed the EDVAC (Electronic Discrete Variable Computer). The EDVAC was a major improvement as it employed mathematics and programs stored electronically without rewiring. John Von Neumann, a Hungarian-born mathematician, joined the EDVAC team and is credited with publishing the first document on electronic digital computers. In 1951 Maurice Wilkes, a British scientist, developed the EDSAC (Electronic Delay Storage Automatic Calculator) based on the lectures of Mauchly and Eckert. The EDSAC could switch from one task to another by entering new instructions into the computer's memory. This stored-program concept is used in modern desktop computers to shift from one task to another.

The Computer Age

The first three generations of the computer age can be pinned to three technological developments—the vacuum tube, transistor, and the integrated circuit—each of which drastically changed the nature of computers. Timing of each generation is defined according to the beginning of commercial delivery of the hardware technology. Defining the later generations has become complicated because of the complications of the entire industry.

The first generation of computers (1951–1958) used vacuum tube technology. In 1951 the UNIVAC (Universal Automatic Computer) was delivered to the U.S. Census Bureau for tabulating the previous year's census. Thousands of electronic tubes about the size of lightbulbs were used as internal components, and this led to excessive heat, frequent burnouts, and problems in temperature regulation and climate control. Another drawback was that the language used in programming was machine language, which uses numbers rather than modern higher level languages, and this made programming more difficult and time consuming. The first-generation computers were enormous in size and expensive, required air conditioned environments, and were used primarily for scientific and engineering calculations, rather than for business data processing applications.

The development of the transistor revolutionized computer technology and led to the second generation (1959–1964). Transistors were smaller than vacuum tubes, needed no warm-up time; consumed less energy; and were faster and more reliable. Another important development during this time was the move from machine language to assembly or symbolic languages, which used abbreviations for instructions (e.g., L for Load). Development of symbolic languages led to the development of higher level languages, such as FORTRAN (1954) and COBOL (1959). In 1962 the first removable disk pack was marketed. Disk storage enabled users to have faster access to data. All of these developments made the second generation computers less costly to operate. During this time computers were used mainly by businesses, universities, and government organizations.

The introduction of integrated circuits characterized the third generation of computers (1965–1970). An integrated circuit is a complete electronic circuit on a small chip of silicon. The silicon chips, each with a complete circuit, were tiny (half the size of a fingernail), reliable, compact, and low cost, and used less power. In 1969 Intel Corporation, an integrated circuit manufacturer in Silicon Valley, California, was asked to build a set of chips for a calculator. The company designed a programmable chip for the calculator; it was actually a primitive microcomputer.

During the 1970s computers increased in speed, reliability, and storage capacity. Entry into the fourth generation was evolutionary rather than revolutionary as it was an extension of the technology used in the third generation. The microprocessor became commercially available in 1971. In 1974 the magazine *Radio Electronics* featured plans for a do-it-yourself computer for $250. Six months later *Popular Electronics* featured a kit for building Altair 8800 for $400. Many companies sprang up to cater to the needs of home computerists. Steve Wozniak and Steven Jobs created Apple Computer I in 1975 and Apple II in 1977. In 1981 IBM entered the market with its personal computer or PC.

In 1980 Japan announced that it would take the lead in computer technology and take it to the fifth generation. The key areas of research were to be artificial intelligence, expert systems, and natural language. Artificial intelligence involves determining how computers can be used for tasks requiring human characteristics, such as intelligence, imagination, and intuition. An expert system involves software that allows the computer to be an expert on a particular subject and be available for "consultation." Normal language refers to everyday language (e.g., English). Fifth generation technology involved research on robotics, vision systems (where the computer acts based on what it "sees"), and new types of hardware for greater computer speed and power. The fifth generation was viewed by some as a race for world computer supremacy between Japan and the United States.

During 1980 dozens of spreadsheet and word processing packages appeared on the market and the potential of the personal computer as an office machine was recognized. At this point traditional business machine manufacturers such as IBM began to take an interest. Because IBM lacked the interest in developing the software needed for personal computers, company executives approached Bill Gates and Paul Allen's Microsoft office in Seattle. The operating system PC- or MS-DOS was installed in every IBM personal computer and compatible machine, earning Microsoft a large royalty. Microsoft's Windows 1.0 was launched in 1984 and was based on the Macintosh interface. Version 2.0, released in 1987, was compatible with IBM as well as Macintosh. The rapid growth in the software industry was due to the increasing sophistication and updating of applications packages. In 1990 Windows 3.0 was launched around the world. The early 1990s were characterized as the period of great software wars between Microsoft, IBM, and Apple. In 1995, Microsoft launched Windows 95, and Windows 98 is now available.

The Internet and World Wide Web

The early 1990s saw the emergence of the Internet, which is a network linking millions of computers around the world. In the fall of 1990 there were 313,000 computers on the Internet; by 1996 there were close to 10 million. The networking idea was politicized by the 1992 Clinton–Gore campaign, and "information superhighway" became a household term. Although computer technology has made the Internet possible, its importance is economic and social as it gives computer users access to information sources and the ability to communicate. The Internet is most widely used for electronic mail (e-mail), which reaches its destination within a few minutes of sending it.

However, the use of the Internet has created the most excitement because it gives ordinary people access to the world's store of knowledge through the World Wide Web. The joys of "surfing the net" were at first limited to computer networks in government, higher education, and big business. Computer hobbyists or private firms that did not have access to a host computer could not access the network. To fill this void a number of firms, such as CompuServe, Prodigy, America Online, AT&T, Premier, and Eatel sprang up to provide low-cost network access. There are several applications to access the World Wide Web. Two of the most popular are produced by Netscape (Navigator and Communicator) and Microsoft (Internet Explorer).

Recent and Evolving Computer Developments

As you have read throughout this text, technology has revolutionized the workplace, education, and the home for individuals with disabilities, gifts, and talents. Computers are now smaller, faster, and more user-friendly, and children know more about the Internet than their parents as a result of personal and instructional experiences. Individuals with physical and other challenges can use technology and the touch of a button to turn off a light, turn on the television, play a videotape, and shop and bank without moving out of their chairs. Technological innovations have definitely changed the way in which everyday tasks are executed, and as we move into the next millennium, the changes will be more dramatic and encompassing. Consider the following current and evolving concerns about technology:

There are ongoing issues or controversies relative to the program that makes the computer a computer—its operating system (OS, see Chapter 3). Microsoft continues to dominate the personal computer OS market with Windows and NT, but other operating systems are available including the powerful Unix and the developing Unix-like Linux (a free program that requires an 80386 or higher microprocessor). Apple's Macintosh computers (e.g., desktops, notebooks, and iMacs) continue to use the accepted and reliable Macintosh OS, but Mac users could have a new and more powerful operating system in the future (e.g., Rhapsody, see http://www.apple.com/macros/rhapsody). Also, the growing popularity of the Internet and the movement to use it for all computing purposes (e.g., inexpensive computers downloading needed programs from the Internet as needed) has led to the discussion for one easy, fast, and efficient OS. The Java programming language developed by Sun Microsystems for consumer electronics (e.g., TVs, VCRs, toasters) may become this OS for inexpensive Internet computers and platforms based on Windows, NT, Unix, Linux, and other operating systems.

Other advances in computer hardware technology, particularly microprocessors, have evolved. Currently, the advent of Intel's Pentium III, AMD's K6-3 and K7, Cyrix's MII and MIII, and Apple's PowerPC G3 and G4 hold much promise for changing our lives (see Chapter 2). For example, in addition to significantly increasing computing speed, the Pentium III processor is configured to improve speech-recognition and Internet capabilities. Its new instruction set results in crisper images and 3-D graphics, and Intel plans to introduce Pentium IIIs that run at 600 MHz or higher in the coming months. Interestingly, desktops are becoming more powerful with random access memory (RAM) approaching one gigabyte (GB), hard drives are capable of storing over 25 GBs, DVD drives are replacing CD-ROM drives, multimedia peripherals and 56K modems are standard, and monitors are becoming larger and flatter. CD and DVD "format jukeboxes" are also available that integrate the latest storage technologies to hold 120, 240, or 480 discs and store 78 GB, 156 GB, and 312 GB respectively (see http://www.plasmon.co.ukproducts/dseries.htm). The latest entry in desktops, Apple's iMac, has also provided the consumer with an interesting perspective—choice of colors such as tangerine, lime, strawberry, grape, blueberry, and bondi blue. Also, laptop and notebook computers (e.g., the Macintosh iBook) are becoming lighter and more powerful with state-of-the-art microprocessors and enhanced memory, graphics, and sound peripherals, and handheld or palm-size computers are offering users major application programs, access to the Internet, and wireless capabilities.

Even more impressive than changes in processing, input, and output hardware, speed, and capacity is the latest breakthrough that delivers a fast, wireless Internet. As Levin (1999) reported:

> The infra-com Red Beamer establishes a wireless infrared connection from a phone outlet to a transceiver located atop an Internet TV, PC, or notebook computer. Unlike conventional infrared technology, which requires a direct line of sight, the Red Beamer uses a safer, omnidirectional infrared light that fills the room and bounces off of walls, ceilings, floors, and objects until it reaches its partner. The technology works within a radius of 8.5 yards. Future applications may include wireless keyboards and toys. (p. 36)

The evolving development of hand-held computers and satellite technologies will provide a totally mobile computing system comparable to telephone cellular uses.

As with all technology, the concept of the television has continuously evolved over the years. There is now a new way to broadcast programming. This new service, called digital television (DTV), is a new way of transmitting information over the airwaves. Similar to what is seen in a theater, the DTV picture will be widescreened with CD-sound quality. Not only has television broadcasting evolved, but so has the size of the television. The big bulky sets now have a skinny twin; the flat-panel TV is only about 4 inches deep. Amazingly, this television can hang on the wall just like the family portrait.

The integration of telecommunication systems that connect the telephone, computers and the Internet, and digital cameras and televisions will greatly expand the capabilities and services these devices provide. Eventually, we will have one system that is designed to keep everyone connected 24 hours a day for personal communication and access to information.

Multimedia systems that provide a wide array of services are also becoming available. These services include interactive entertainment, distribution of news and information, on-demand video services, home banking and shopping, interactive multiuser games, and digital multimedia libraries accessible from home. Also, cable and phone companies, as infrastructure providers and companies owning content to populate the infrastructure, have realized that a capable network coupled with improved computing and compression techniques can soon deliver interactive services in a profitable manner. For example, many universities offer courses via distance learning using the compressed video technology. This enables students who are able to meet at the same time but not at the same place to take a course via distance learning. Courses are taught using compressed video technology and two-way real-time video and audio; this is known as interactive television.

A number of entertainment, cable, phone, and computer companies recently have formed alliances to architect a wide-area information infrastructure. Universities and industrial laboratories have been intensively working to define this architecture. A number of standard groups have also emerged to bring some order to the undertaking. Out of all these activities, a picture of future information infrastructure is emerging. These standards are also being established for individuals with disabilities, gifts, and talents so that they will have the opportunity to access and use these evolving infrastructures and technologies (e.g., Microsoft's Active Accessibility technology and IBM's talking or home page Internet speech synthesis system). This technology, as noted by Steinhof and others (see Preface and Chapter 2), is just a portent of what is to come.

Finally, technology has changed and will continue to change the way people live, shop, conduct business, access data, and learn. Computer hardware size, speed, and capability and the innovations in integrated multimedia are developing so rapidly that current access is becoming obsolete as we speak. Currently, the Affective Computing Department at MIT Media Lab is researching how computers can be used to detect our emotions (see http://www.media.mit.edu/projects/affect/index.html). Furthermore, the applications and implications of these "multimedia smart tools or cards" are affecting people's homes, lifestyles, dress, transportation, access to and use of computers, banking and shopping, access to medical information, use of the telephone and the Internet (Krantz, 1999).

References

Krantz, M. (1999, March 8). Tomorrow's gadgets. *Time Digital, 4*(1), 48–53.

Levin, C. (1999). The Web, now in infrared. *PC Magazine, 18*(4), 36.

McCullagh, D. (1999, March 8). IRS vs. Y2K. *Time Digital, 4*(1), 46–47.

The New Webster Dictionary. (1993). Danbury, CT: Lexicon.

Resources

Books

Campbell-Kelly, M., & Aspray, W. (1997). *Computer: A history of the information machine.* New York: Basic Books.

Kalmback, J. R. (1996). *Computer and the page: The theory, history, and pedagogy of publishing as social process.* Norwood, NJ: Ablex.

Shurkin, J. (1996). *Engines of the mind: The evolution of the computer from the mainframes to microcomputers.* New York: Norton.

Williams, M. R. (1997). *A history of computing technology* (2nd ed.). Piscataway, NJ: IEEE Computer Society.

Web Sites

http://www.studyweb.com

http://www.cs.gmu.edu/~amarchan/history.html

Appendix C

ॐ   ॐ   ॐ

Computer Languages

Stephen J. Puster
Traffic Products, Inc., Atlanta, Georgia

It has been said that computers are the smartest machines that humans have ever invented. Computers are not really smart; in fact, they can perform only the functions that a computer operator instructs them to do. These instructions are transmitted to the "brain," or central processing unit (CPU), through software programs. These programs are written in a language that can be recognized by the computer. This language actually transmits instructions to the CPU that turn switches on and off inside the computer. Contrary to popular opinion, one does not need to be a skilled scientist or mathematician to develop a computer program. Even elementary school children are writing computer programs. For the most part, and as would be expected, all programming languages available today were developed for the convenience of the user and not the computer.

The two major types of programs that can be used with computers are based on low-level and high-level computer language, respectively. A low-level language can be used to write programs or instructions that are directly and easily understood by a computer's CPU. Machine language is an example of a low-level language. Low-level languages are more difficult than high-level languages for programmers to learn and use because commands and structures do not correspond to English vocabulary and structures. However, one advantage of a low-level program is that it is able to run faster in a computer than a program written in a high-level language; a high-level language program (e.g., RPG, or Report Program Generator) must be translated to a low-level language so that a CPU can understand it.

High-level languages are easier to learn and understand because they more closely resemble the English language. A high-level language makes communications between humans and computers easier because it permits programmers to identify information-handling routines in a language convenient for human use. However, as stated previously, a high-level language program must be translated into a low-level language before a computer's CPU can understand the instructions. This translation is done by an interpreter or a compiler. The distinction between the two translators is based on the time of the actual conversion to machine language. An interpreter translates a high-level language program into a low-level language when the program is actually running in the CPU. A compiler, on the other hand, translates the entire high-level language program into machine code before program execution begins. Compiled programs do not have to be interpreted during each execution, and therefore run very fast. The primary advantages of high-level language programs are ease of operation, reduced programming time, reduced documentation costs, program language commonality, elimination of specialists, real-time processing, and program consistency.

Machine Language

Machine language is a low-level language that is readily recognized by computers and is based on the raw sequence of 1's and 0's. In machine language each letter of the alphabet, every number, and various symbols are made up of a set of eight

1's and/or 0's in a preset sequence. For instance, "10000011" in machine language could represent the capital letter 'A,' and another sequence could represent the lowercase letter 'a.' Because machine language is rather cumbersome to use in writing lengthy programs, most programs are written in another language and either compiled or converted into machine language. The majority of programs still written in machine language are done so to take advantage of the processing speed afforded by bypassing the need for using a compiler or an interpreter, or to include a routine that is not readily available in another language.

Assembly Language

Assembly language, a low-level language that is one step away from machine language, is used where performance is important and there is no reason for modification by the user. Word processing is a good example because this application in a software program takes a lot of computer resources. Assembly language keeps the computer resource use of a word processing program to a minimum. Unlike business application programs that require the user to modify the program itself to address particular business changes, word processing programs are such that programmers or users do not need to make changes in the program structure.

Assembly language is sometimes inserted into high-level language programs to increase their performance. The following program, written in Assembly Language, prints a grid of 156 rows by 198 columns of dots on the Apple Computer's high-resolution screen. The dots are stepped by 3 both horizontally and vertically.

```
:DOTSCREEN listing
770A900      LDA00      load accumulator with zero
7728D0003    STA0300    put zero in row count
775A200      LDX00      starting column is zero
7778E0103    STX0301    save the starting column
780A000      LDY00      need a zero in the Y
  register
7822057F4    JSRF457    plot the point
785AE0103    LDX0301    get the column count
788E8        INX        increment column
789 E8       INX            count
790E8        INX                    by 3
```

```
7918E0103    STXX0301   save new column count
794AD0003    LDA0301    get row count
797EE0C6         CPXC6  is column count 198?
799D0EB          BNEEB   if not 198 then finish
row
801AD0003    LDA0300    get row count
80418        CLC        clear the carry flag
8056903          ADC03   increment row count by 3
8078D0003    STAA0300   save new row
810C99C          CMP9C   is row count 156
812D0D9          BNED9   if not 156 then start
another row
81460        RST        return to BASIC

45 BYTES TOTAL LENGTH
```

FORTRAN

FORTRAN (FORmula TRANslation) was developed by IBM in 1956 as a scientific programming language. It is used for a variety of mathematical applications, varying from simple addition to complex problems involving higher mathematics and complicated algorithms. FORTRAN was the first widely used high-level computer language and is the best defined and standardized high-level language available today. FORTRAN, the earliest of the non–machine-specific high-level languages to be used, is a procedure-oriented language and at one time was the most widely used language for scientific and engineering applications. In FORTRAN a complex computation such as "V is equal to the square root of P squared plus (R-1) squared" would be written in FORTRAN as V=SORT(P*2+(R-1)*2). What follows is a program in FORTRAN for finding the area of a circle with a diameter of 4 using the Monte Carlo technique:

```
$JOB  CUR PAGES=10
C$NOEXTEN
      APPROX=AREA(2.,1000,-2.,2.)
      WRITE(6,10)APPROX
      STOP
10 FORMAT (/////10X,'THE AREA OF THE CIRCLE SQR(4-
   X**2)IS ',F10.2)
      END

      FUNCTION AREA(HIGH ,N,A,B)
         INTEGER HITS
         REAL INTVAL
         F(X)=SQRT (4-X*X)
         INTVAL=B-A
         HITS=0
```

```
        I=1
    WHILE(I.LE.N) DO
        Y=RAND(HIGH)
    X=RAND(INTVAL)=a
        IF(F(X).GF.7)HITS=HITS+1
        I=I+1
    ENDWHILE
    AREA=2.*(HIGH*INTVAL*(FLOAT(HITS)/N))
    RETURN
    END

    FUNCTION RAND(RMAX)
    DATA IRAND/137462873/,MULT/65539/,LARGE/
2147483647/
    IRAND=IRAND*MULT
    IF(IRAND .T. 0)IRAND=(IRAND+LARGE)+1
    RAND=RMAX*(IRAND-1)/(LARGE-1)
    RETURN
    END
```

COBOL

COBOL stands for Common Business Oriented Language and was developed in 1959 by a committee formed by the Department of Defense. The primary purpose of this committee was to provide a programming language that was compatible between machines made by different manufacturers. Until 1968 when a new "standard COBOL" was introduced by the United States National Standards Institute, several versions of COBOL had been written. In 1969 this new standard COBOL underwent a name change to become the American National Standards Institute (ANSI) COBOL. Whereas FORTRAN was developed for use in the scientific community, COBOL was the counterpart for the business community. COBOL is not a particularly easy language to learn to use, although it uses commands such as "add pay-raise to old-salary giving new-pay."

There are four distinct divisions in a COBOL program. The Identification Division is a small set of statements serving to identify the program name, the author, the date written, and the company name. The Environment Division is two subsections, "configuration" and "input–output." The configuration program subsection describes the type of computer on which the program is designed to run, and the input–output defines which input and output devices are being addressed. The Data Division also has two sub-

sections: "file" and "working storage." The file subsection is concerned with each of the files and the data used in the program. The working storage subsection describes all pertinent information that is not contained in any of the input–output records. The heart of a COBOL program is contained in the Procedure Division, which defines the steps required to perform the functions of the program. These steps include the calculations, the data-handling instructions, and the logical decisions.

The following is an example of a program written in COBOL:

```
IDENTIFICATION DIVISION
PROGRAM-ID. REPORT 1.
*****************************************************
*THIS PROGRAM WILL PRINT A PAYROLL REPORT. THE      *
*  EMPLOYEE'S                                        *
*NUMBER, NAME, REGULAR PAY, AND OVERTIME PAY WILL BE *
*  TAKEN FROM                                        *
*A PAYROLL FILE. IN ADDITION TO THE ABOVE, A TOTAL PAY *
*  WILL BE                                           *
*CALCULATED AND ALSO PRINTED.                        *
*****************************************************
ENVIRONMENT DIVISION

CONFIGURATION SECTION
    SOURCE-COMPUTER. IBM-370
    OBJECT-COMPUTER. IBM-370
    SPECIAL-NAMES. CO1 IS TOP-OF-PAGE.

INPUT-OUTPUT SECTION
    FILE-CONTROL.
        SELECT IN-REC ASSIGN TO UR-3504-S-SYSIN
        SELECT PRINT ASSIGN TO UR-3504-S-SYSPRINT.
    DATA DIVISION.

    FILE SECTION
    FD IN-REC
        LABEL RECORDS ARE OMITTED
        DATA RECORD IS PAYROLL-CARD.
    01PAYROLL-CARD
    03FILLER            PIC X(8).
    03EMP-NO            PIC 9(5)
    03NAME              PIC X(20)
    03FILLER            PIC X(28)
    03REG-EARN          PIC 999v99
    03FILLER            PIC X
    03OVT-EARN          PIC 999V99
    03FILLER            PIC X(8)
FD PRINT
        LABEL RECORDS ARE OMITTED
        DATA RECORD IS OUTLINE
    01 OUTLINE          PIC X(133).
        WORKING-STORAGE SECTION.
1   77 EOF-MARK         PIC 90    VALUE 0.
2   01 LINE-KOUNTER PIC 99 VALUE 0.
```

```
    01 HEADER-LINE.
       03 TOP-HEADER.
3          05FILLER    PICX(40)  VALUE SPACES.
4          05FILLER    PICX(14)  VALUE'PAYROLLREPORT'
       03 TITLE LINE
5          05FILLER    PICX(8)   VALUE SPACES.
6          05FILLER    PICX(7)   VALUE'EMP NO'
7          05FILLER    PICX(17)  VALUE SPACES.
8          05FILLER    PICX(4)   VALUE 'NAME'
9          05FILLER    PICX(18)  VALUE SPACES.
10         05FILLER    PICX(7)   VALUE 'REGULAR'
11         05FILLER    PICX(4)   VALUE SPACES.
12         05FILLER    PICX(8)   VALUE 'OVERTIME'
13         05FILLER    PICX(7)   VALUE SPACES.
14         05FILLER    PICX(5)   VALUE 'TOTAL'
    01DETAIL-LINE.
15      03FILLER       PICX(9)   VALUE SPACES.
        03 EMP-NO-OUT     PIC99999.
16      03FILLER       PICX(10) VALUE SPACES.
        03NAME-OUT      PICX(30)
        03REG-EARN-OUT PICZZZ.99
17      03FILLER       PICX(6)  VALUE SPACES.
        03OVT-ERAN-OUT PICZZZ.999
18      03FILLER       PIC X(6) VALUE SPACES
        03TOTAL EARNINGS   PIC $$,$$$.99
19 PROCEDURE DIVISION


      MAIN-LOGIC
20      OPEN INPUT IN-REC,
        OUTPUT PRINT.
21    PERFORM HEARDER-ROUTINE.
22    READ IN-REC AT END MOVE 1 TO EDF-MSRK.
23    PERFORM SUB-LOGIC UNTIL EOF-MARK=1.
24    MOVE SPACES TO OUTLINE.
25    WRITE OUTLINE AFTER TOP-OF PAGE.
26    CLOSE IN-REC, PRINT.
27    STOP RUN.


      SUB-LOGIC


28    MOVE EMP-NO TO EMO-NO-OUT.
29    MOVE NAME TO NAME-OUT.
30    MOVE REG-EARN TO OVT-EARN-OUT.
31    MOVE OVT-EARN TO OVT-EARN-OUT.
32    ADD REG-EARN,OVT-EARN GIVING TOTAL-EARNINGS.
33    WRITE OUTLINE FROM DETAIL-LINE AFTER 1.
34    ADD 1 TO LINE-KOUNTER.
35    IF LINE-KOUNTER = 45
36      PERFORM HEADER-ROUTINE.
      ELSE
        NEXT SENTENCE.
37    READ IN-REC AT END MOVE 1 TO EOF-MARK.


    HEADER ROUTINE.
39    MOVE SPACES TO OUTLINE.
40    WRITE OUTLINE AFTER TOP-OF-PAGE.
41    WRITE OUTLINE FROM TOP-HEADER AFTER 2.
42    WRITE OUTLINE FROM TITLE-LINE AFTER 3.
43    MOVE SPACE TO OUTLINE.
44    WRITE OUTLINE AFTER 1.


********THERE ARE NOT STATEMENTS FLAGGED IN THIS
COMPILE.
```

RPG

Report Program Generator (RPG) is a very high-level language. In RPG the programmer tells the computer what to do and the computer figures out how to do it. RPGII is the latest version of RPG. It is a problem-oriented language, not a procedural language like COBOL or FORTRAN. Because of this difference, some programmers have difficulty learning RPGII. However, once learned, it is an excellent language and can be easily used even on small business computers. RPGII is designed so that programmers can feed certain information into one of five different specification sections that tell the computer what the programmer wants in return. From the information fed into the computer on the specifications sheet the computer generates its own program.

The five different specification sections, or sheets, used in RPG language are File Description, File Extension, Input, Calculation, and Output. They describe the size of the records in each file and define the input and output device used for storing each file. The File Description defines the characteristics of the input and output files. The File Extension is not used as frequently as the other types of specification sheets. This specification sheet is usually used to define tables within a program. Input specifications define in detail what is in each of the input files that were described in the File Description. The Calculation specification describes the calculation to be made within the program. On some machines the programmer can perform square root calculations, but on most machines may be limited to addition, subtraction, multiplication, and division. Finally, the Output sheet specifies in detail how each file is to be treated on the final report.

The following RPG program reads the number of seats register using three columns:

```
0001 01-020 FCARDIN IP F    80      READ05
0002 01-030 FOUTPUT O  F    132    OF  LPRINTER
0003 01-110 LOUTPUT 00660106012
0004S02-010 ICARDIN AA 01
0005 02-020 I                          1   30FLIGHTL1
0006 02-030 I                          4   8PLANE
0007 02-040 I                          9   110SEATS
0008 03-000 C   L1            SETON              OF40
0009 03-000 C        ROW      SUB ROW ROW 30
0010 03-005 C        COL1     SUB COL1 COL1 30
0011 03-010 C                 SETOF           102030
```

```
0012 03-300 C                    SETOF               1535
0013 03-000 C          SEATS     COMP1               3515
0014 03-000 C     15             SETON          30
0015 03-000 C     15
0016 03-000 COR 15             GOTO SKIP
0017 03-020 C          SEATS   DIV  3    ROW      30
0018 03-030 C                    MVR       ADJROW   10
0019 03-040 C          ADJROW  COMP 0             10
0020 03-050 C     N10  ROW     ADD 1     ROW
0021 03-060 C          LOOP     TAG
0022 03-070 C          COL1    ADD 1     COL1
0023 03-100 C          COL1    ADD ROW   COL2      30
0024 03-105 C     30             GOTO SKIP
0025 03-110 C          COL2    ADD ROW   COL3      30
0026 03-120 C          COL3    COMP SEATS          30
0027 03-130 C          SKIP     TAG
0028 03-140 C                    EXCPT
0029 03-145 C                    SETOF               L1
0030 03-150 C                    SETOF               OF40
0031 03-160 C                    SETON          40
0032 03-165 C          COL1    COMP ROW            20
0033 03-170 C                    GOTO LOOP
0034 04-010 O  OUTPUTH 201 OF
0035 04-030 O                    UDATE     Y    8
0036 04-040 O                              52 'PASSENGERL1'
0037 04-050 O                              56 '  ST'
0038 04-060 O                              86 'PAGE'
0039 04-070 O                    PAGE      91
0040 04-080 O      H   1 OF
0041 04-100 O                              14 'FLIGHT PLANE'
0042 04-110 O      H   2 OF
0043 04-130 O                              21 'NUMBER TYPE SEAT'
0044 04-140 O                              35 'PASSENGER'
0045 04-150 O                              63 'SEAT  PASSENGER'
0046 04-160 O                              91 'SEAT   PASSENGER'
0047 04-170 O      EF 2 01
0048 04-180 O                    L1  FLIGHTZ   4
0049 04-190 O                    L1  PLANE    14
0050 04-195 O                    OF  FLIGHTZ   4
0051 04-197 O                    OF  PLANE    14
0052 04-200 O     N15N35         COL1 2     21
0053S04-000 O          15              21 '1'
0054 04-210 O     N15N35         COL2 Z    49
0055 04-230 O     N15N35         COL3 Z    77
0056 04-240 O     35             42 '***ERROR-
                           NUMBER OF SE'
0057 04-250 O     35             66 'ATS FOUND WAS
                           ZERO OR NE'
0058 04-260 O     35             76 'GATIVE ***'

     E N D   O F   S O U R C E
```

BASIC

BASIC is the acronym for Beginner's All-purpose Symbolic Instruction Code. BASIC does not mean simple, although the instructions in this language are given to the computer in English-like commands. Of the computer languages described in this appendix, BASIC language is the closest to English in its use of vocabulary and sentence structure. Because of this similarity to English, BASIC is the most common high-level language in use today.

A BASIC program is a list of numbered lines of instructions that the computer carries out in numerical sequence. BASIC is an interpreted language and, therefore, tends to operate slowly. BASIC is now used in the most popular micro-computers, and the wide use of BASIC among different manufacturers' machines has caused the rise of "dialects" within the BASIC language. Many machines use a variation of Microsoft or MS-DOS BASIC. Microsoft is the BASIC dialect used by IBM microcomputers, and those machines using one of these variations are commonly referred to as IBM compatible. There are other dialects, such as Applesoft Basic, that are machine specific. The primary commands among these various dialects are identical. For the most part, it is the addresses and formatting of procedures that make up the main differences within these BASIC dialects.

The following is an example of a program written in BASIC. This program gives the monthly payments on a loan when the interest rate and the length of the loan period are known.

```
0       REM:REGULAR PAYMENT ON A LOAN
4    HOME
5    HTAB 6
7    HTAB 6
10   INVERSE:PRINT "REGULAR PAYMENT ON A LOAN"
15   NORMAL
16   PRINT:PRINT
20   INPUT" HOW MUCH DO YOU WANT TO BORROW?        $";P
25   PRINT
30   INPUT" HOW MANY YEARS DO YOU WANT TO PAY IT BACK? ";y
35   PRINT
40   INPUT" WHAT IS THE ANNUAL INTEREST RATE CHARGED? ";I
45   REM:CALCULATION BY FORMULA
50   R=((I/100*P/12)/(1-1/((I/100)/12+1)-(12*Y))
55   D-INT (R*100+.5)/100 : PRINT
56   REM:PRINTS RESULTS ON SCREEN
60   PRINT" WITH 12 PAYMENTS PER YEAR..."
65   PRINT" YOUR REGULAR PAYMENT WILL BE $";D
```

LOGO

LOGO is a beginning computer language designed for young people in 1967 by Seymour Papert and a group from Massachusetts Institute of Technology. It is a high-level interpreted language that allows the programmer to use simple commands to draw on the screen. Although LOGO was pilot tested on elementary school children in 1967, it was almost a decade before the microcomputer arrived on the scene and the general public learned about the wonders of LOGO.

It can be said that computer languages are taught for computer literacy, for self-perpetuation of computer technology, and to teach children to think. The name LOGO is derived from the Greek *logo*, meaning word or thought. It is not surprising, then, to learn that LOGO was created to teach creative thinking, or more correctly to teach children how to learn.

To enhance the LOGO learning process, the programmer is asked to direct a turtle. Children have a natural affinity for playing with animals and the turtle is seen as a friend. In LOGO this little friend can be envisioned as dragging a pen, and the pen draws a line each time the turtle is directed by a command to move. This is an easy concept for children to grasp and want to make happen on the screen.

The primary result of LOGO programming is graphic images, which further enhances its use in the educational field. Because of this predominance of simple graphics, many programmers consider LOGO to be a "toy" language that is not suitable for adults and should not be given serious consideration. This is far from the truth. The basic data components in LOGO are numbers, words, and lists, just like those of the "more powerful" languages. It also has the ability to be recursive; that is, it can call upon elements from within the same program. Other functions common among LOGO and other languages are the ability to do arithmetic expressions, contain variables, assign values, perform input and output operations, make simple selections like if–then–else, and test and contain loops within a program.

Two simple programs that may demonstrate the power and simplicity of LOGO follow. The first is a routine to draw a square on the screen.

```
FORWARD 15
RIGHT 90
FORWARD 15
```

```
RIGHT 90
FORWARD 15
RIGHT 90
FORWARD 15
END
```

The second program is a more complex application and results in a grade book.

```
TO ROSTER :CLASS
 PRINT FIRST FIRST :CLASS
END

TO GET :I :A
 IF :I=1 THEN OUTPUT FIRST :A
 OUTPUT GET (:I-1) BUTFIRST :A
END

TO GETNAME :NAME :CLASS
 ;Return the record of :NAME
 IF :CLASS=[ ]THEN PRINT [NOT FOUND] OUTPUT [ ]
   STOP
 IF :NAME=FIRST FIRST :CLASS THEN OUTPUT FIRST
   :CLASS
 OUTPUT GETNAME :NAME BUTFIRST :CLASS
END

TO GETSCORES :NAME :CLASS
 IF :CLASS=[ ]THEN PRINT [NOT FOUND]OUTPUT[
   ]STOP
 IF :NAME = FIRST FIRST :CLASS THE OUTPUT FIRST
   BUTFIRST FIRST :CLASS
 OUTPUT GETSCORES :NAME BUTFIRST :CLASS
END

TO GETTEST :I :RECORD
 ;Retrieve the test score from :RECORD
 IF :I=1 THEN OUTPUT FIRST :RECORD
 IF BUTFIRST :RECORD=[ ]PRINT [THERE AREN'T THAT
   MANY TESTS]OUTPUT[ ]STOP
 OUTPUT GETTEST (:I-1) BUTFIRST :RECORD
END
TO CLASSBOOK :CLASS
 PRINT FIRST :CLASS

  IF NOT BUTFIRST :CLASS-[ ]THEN CLASSBOOK
BUTFIRST :CLASS
END
```

The ease of programming with LOGO and its widespread use in the classroom have encouraged LOGO's growth and led most manufacturers to develop a version of LOGO for their computers. With the exception of the IBM and IBM compatibles, which use a common operating system, different versions of LOGO are required for LOGO computers made by different companies. Apple LOGO will not run on a Radio

Shack/Tandy computer, and vice versa, and neither will work on a Texas Instruments computer. This uniqueness is common to most computer languages.

Pascal

Pascal was published by Niklaus Wirth in 1971. Pascal is extremely popular and is probably, after BASIC, the high-level language most used on microcomputers. One of the principal reasons for the design of Pascal was to create a programming language that could be used to teach a careful, disciplined approach to programming and problem solving. Another intended purpose of Pascal was to provide a language that would be reliable, efficient, and able to handle complex data structures. One outstanding feature that has helped Pascal gain popularity is its ability to enable programmers to find coding errors quickly.

The following program written in Pascal can find the distance between two integer points on the same line:

```
PROGRAM DISTANCE(INPUT,OUTPUT)
VAR
 POINTX, POINTY, DISTANCE : INTEGER;

BEGIN
 WRITE ('Enter two whole number points on a
line . . .')
 READLN(POINTX,POINTY);
 IF (POINTX < 0) XOR (POINTY < 0)
  THEN
   DISTANT := ABS(POINTX) + ABS(POINTY)
  ELSE
   IF (POINTX < 0) AND (POINTY < 0)
    THEN BEGIN
     POINTX := ABS(POINTX)
     DISTANCE := POINTX + POINTY;
     DISTANCE := ABS(DISTANCE)
    END
   ELSE
    IF (POINTX > 0) AND POINTY > 0)
     THEN
      DISTANCE := ABS (POINTX-POINTY);
WRITELN('The distance between the points is
',DISTANCE :6)
END
```

C

C, a relatively new programming language, has the ability to deal directly with the codes in machine language and at the same time can ad-

dress the complex problems that are handled by high-level languages. Because of this unique ability, C is characterized as a medium-level language.

Programs written in C are not machine specific and are not dialectic, so they can be moved from machine to machine with a great deal of ease. Although C is not interactive in its use, as BASIC is, it is a highly extensible language that allows programmers to develop their own functions with minimal difficulty. The following is an example of a C program that converts kilometers to miles:

```
/ Convert Kilometers to miles
     for K = 0 to 50                 */
main ()
(
    int   start, end, kilo;
    float factor;
    start= 0;
    end =50;
    factor=1.609;
    for (kilo = start, kilo (= end, ++kilo)
     printf( "%3d %6.2fn", kilo, kilo*factor);
```

PL/I

PL/I was developed by IBM to be used as a synthesis of the best features of COBOL and FORTRAN. It was designed to combine the strengths of COBOL with the strengths of FORTRAN so that one language could be used for both business and technical applications. The version available for microcomputers (PL/M) was intended as a major general purpose language, but it is rather complicated to use and has not caught on even though PL/I is one of the most versatile of existing programming languages.

There are three reasons why PL/I makes writing programs very convenient. First, the programmer can write programs describing complicated computations in terms that are simple to understand. Second, the programmer can specify execution procedures in familiar terms. Third, PL/I is capable of operating with a minimal amount of specific information.

ADA

ADA is one of the newest languages available for microcomputers. Like COBOL, ADA was developed by the Department of Defense. It was modeled after Pascal and has been described as one of the most powerful programming languages available. Its power may be its drawback as well, because many programmers consider ADA too big for one program to handle. In the microcomputer field, only subsets of the complete ADA language are feasible to use.

FORTH

FORTH is a programming language that can be used to make languages. In FORTH many commands are redefined or deleted, making it almost impossible to use without changing it. Because of its flexibility, FORTH is very fast and very extensible.

Even though FORTH is criticized as being difficult to learn, impossible to read, and sometimes even bizarre, it still attracts users. Those who take the time to learn FORTH seldom use any other language to program.

PILOT

PILOT is the acronym for Programmed Inquiry, Learning, Or Teaching. SuperPILOT is the latest version of this language. PILOT is a highly specialized language that was developed to allow teachers to write their own instructional and tutorial programs. PILOT programs most often involve asking students questions, analyzing the answers, playing music, and showing pictures. PILOT is very easy to learn, and it is an attractive language for teachers who want to purchase prewritten programs as well as write their own programs.

JAVA

As the world got smaller through the Internet, the need grew for more powerful and more robust programs to run in a high-speed, often unstable environment. From this need came the Java Programming Language Environment, or more commonly called "Java."

Java emerged as part of a research project at Sun Microsystems to develop advanced software for a wide variety of devices connected together in a network or as part of another system. Java took advantage of the graphics capabilities—"a picture is worth a thousand words"—available in today's computer world.

In addition to being object oriented, Java is an interpreted language, which allows for faster program development cycles because the programmer can simply compile the program and run it without having to go through the loading, testing, and debugging steps of older program languages.

The growth of the Internet and World Wide Web has placed a great deal of emphasis on speed—not only the speed at which a computer communicates with others, but how fast the user can get something ready to send. This need for speed has driven Java with its simplicity, its ability to be used across multiple platforms (computer types and configurations), and its ability to manage the memory of a computer.

The following sample of a Java code enables a computer to average the numbers in an array:

```
float average (float numbers[])
{
double sum-0.0;
for(int i=0; i<numbers.length;i++)
 sum += numbers[i];
return sum/numbers.length;
}
```

HTML

The "hottest kid on the block" and the one educators are most likely to use, is Hypertext Markup Language (HTML). This is the language used when surfing the Net. When you are looking at all the sights and homepages in cyberspace and wondering how others did that and how you can do that, the answer is with HTML.

An HTML document is the list of instructions that tells a computer how and where to go on the Internet for information and how to display that information on the screen. HTML documents are plain-text (also known as ASCII) files that can be created using any text editor (e.g., Emacs on UNIX machines; BBEdit on a Macintosh;

Notepad on a Windows machine). Word processing software can be used by saving the HTML document as "text only with line breaks."

For this information to be of value, you need to have access to the Internet and World Wide Web. This will require you to have an online access provider (America Online, CompuServe, Microsoft Network, Mindspring, Prodigy, etc.). All of these access providers give you the required connection, usually for a monthly fee, to the Internet. Each of these will have a software program, called a Web browser, that uses the HTML documents that are already on the Internet and World Wide Web and those you would create to allow you and others to navigate your way along the myriad of pathways available.

In most cases the Web browser used has no impact upon the way HTML documents are accessed. The most common Web browsers used today are Netscape Navigator and Communicator and Microsoft Internet Explorer. Microsoft has long waged a war with Netscape to be *the* one Web browser; this battle continues to rage from your computer screen and into the courtrooms. From the user's viewpoint the screen displays have very little difference; however, some homepages (HTML documents) say, for example, "This document best viewed with Netscape Navigator" to identify which browser provides the best screen display. Even with this disclaimer, the homepage can be viewed satisfactorily with other Web browsers as long as the basic HTML protocol is used.

The extent to which you can go with HTML is limited only by your imagination. Uses for an HTML document and its contents are ever-changing and always growing. Three terms must be understood when discussing an HTML document, or program.

The first of these terms is *content.* As the name implies, it is whatever the programmer puts into the document: all the words, images, and links that Web surfers can use and interact with.

In the preceding paragraph I referred to a link. More correctly this is a *hyperlink,* which is the connection between one document and other documents or resources. When a link is included in an HTML document, it is usually highlighted

in some manner—it may be blue, underlined, or italic, depending upon the display. This tells viewers that double clicking on this text will take them to another site or page.

The third term, and most misunderstood, is the *Uniform Resource Locator,* or URL. This is the standard way of identifying the location and data type for a resource. URLs have a general form to their address. A common address starts "http://www," where the http stands for HyperText Transfer Protocol (the standard form used in transferring information along the internet) and the "www" is the World Wide Web. The remaining portion of the URL is like the street address of your home. Each portion of the address is separated, most commonly by a '.' (dot) (e.g., the online address for Microsoft is http://www.microsoft.com).

This is not intended to be a tutorial on how to develop an HTML document and, therefore, I will provide only a small example of what an HTML document looks like:

```
<HTML>
<HEAD>
<Computer Languages>
<!— Created 10/30/97 — >
</HEAD>
```

When run, this program would look like this: Computer Languages.

HTML is a growing language with new variations frequently. To learn more about this language, or how to build a Web page, check out your local library or bookstore, or do a search online for the latest information.

Resources

For more information on computer languages, check out the computer section of the local library. Another way to acquire the knowledge is to engage in in-depth reading and practice experiences. Excellent texts on computer languages that could be read include the following:

Baron, N. S. (1986). *Computer languages: A guide for the perplexed.* New York: Doubleday.

Bentley, J. L. (1982). *Writing efficient programs.* Englewood Cliffs, NJ: Prentice-Hall.

Berg, C. (1998). *Advanced Java development for enterprise applications*. Upper Saddle River, NJ: Prentice-Hall.

Christie, L., & Curry, J. W., (1983). *The ABC's of microcomputers: A computer literacy primer*. Englewood Cliffs, NJ: Prentice-Hall.

Covey, H. D., & McAlister, N. H. (1980). *Computer consciousness: Surviving the automated 80's*. Reading, MA: Addison-Wesley.

Curran, S., & Curnow, R. (1983). *Overcoming computer illiteracy—A friendly introduction to computers*. New York: Penguin.

Hollerbach, L. (1982). *A 60-minute guide to microcomputers: A quick course in personal buisness computing*. Englewood Cliffs, NJ: Prentice-Hall.

Lee, P. A., Philips, C., & Philips, C. (1996). *The apprentice C++: A touch of class*. Boston: PWS Publishing.

Meyer, E. A. (1997). *HTML: An Introduction*. Cleveland, OH: Case Western Reserve University.

Musciano, C., Kennedy, B., & Loukides, M. (Eds.). (1998). *Html: The definitive guide*. Sebastopol, CA: O'Reilly & Associates.

Peavy, W. E. (1983). *Microcomputers software selection guide*. Wellesley, MA: OED Information Sciences.

Perry, G. M. (1993). *The absolute beginner's guide to programming*. Indianapolis, IN: SAMS/Macmillan.

Ruan, P., & Hayman, J. (1984). *LOGO activities for the computer*. New York: Simon and Schuster.

Ruhl, J. (1989). *The programmer's survival guide*. Englewood Cliffs, NJ: Yourdon Press.

Spencer, D. D. (1981). *Data processing: An introduction* (2nd ed.). Columbus, OH: Merrill.

Spencer, D. D. (1985). *Principles of information processing*. Columbus, OH: Merrill.

Taylor, C. F., Jr. (1988). *Master handbook of microcomputer languages* (2nd ed.). Blue Ridge Summit, PA: Tab Books.

Appendix D

✣   ✣   ✣

Technology, Exceptional Individuals, and the Coming Millennium

Earl H. Cheek, Jr.
Louisiana State University,
Baton Rouge, Louisiana

R. Kenton Denny
Louisiana State University,
Baton Rouge, Louisiana

Gary E. Rice
University of Missouri–St. Louis

Typically, we as educators have been introduced to technology as a tool for education without carefully considering the implications of the term *tool*. Our thinking has been to consider technology as a tool for educators and students to use like any other writing device, such as a typewriter or a pencil; or as another piece of curriculum, such as a textbook; or as an appliance for learning, such as a microscope, centrifuge, or calculator. The person who uses the pencil reveals a particular belief, whether for the purpose of composing beautiful poems, highly political and agitating prose, or simply a few notes for a member of the household. All these acts of making meaning have represented in them certain artifacts of culture in a particular way. We easily view the most immediate tools in our educational surroundings as free from bias or as neutral. What we are suggesting is that inherent in any and all software programs is a particular way of thinking—a bias or an inherent ideology.

There are several reasons why this is important to understand. First, as we make mindful decisions about our use of technology with exceptional individuals, we need to understand not only the information that is evident on the surface of software programs, but also the implications of using particular images and text and the ways in which we may use particular features of these programs to manipulate images and text that represent a certain way of thinking and an approach to defining ourselves and our culture. We need to understand how our culture is repre-

sented within programs, how that culture is portrayed in particular ways, and how one culture is represented to the exclusion of others. This will enable educators to be aware of some of the problems inherent in software design and to assist students to develop critical thinking skills rather than to be passive users of technology. Computer programs are not neutral; that is, software in and of itself does not represent all the various dimensions of the real world. Instead, software represents what a particular programmer's view of the real world is or might be. This is an important point regarding the use of computer programs with exceptional individuals, especially considering how quickly software comes and goes in the educational marketplace. Teachers of exceptional individuals, as well as exceptional individuals themselves, need to develop a way of evaluating the software they choose to use to be certain that it is consistent not only with their pedagogical beliefs but also with their personal goals and the learning goals of their school and community.

The design of educational software programs, for example, reflects the programmer's particular way of thinking. The way in which the material is presented and the possibilities that students have available to them for processing or using that information is controlled within the program. This proclivity within programs is usually not a personal one on the programmer's part, but rather manifests itself as cultural. The cultural representations that are found in the educational software most generally represent the beliefs and values of the dominant culture, thus excluding rather than including exceptional individuals. The most recognizable software programs presenting a nonneutral stance on learning are found in simulation software. These types of programs have the students assume a particular role and then perform particular tasks that allow them to achieve a goal or outcome based on how the software is developed.

An example of a software program that projects a cultural bias is Sim City. In this software, children learn how the development of a city is accomplished. They "build" roads, utilities, factories, shopping centers, and parks, all with a limited budget determined by revenues generated from taxes. The role of mayor is assumed by the student player, and a scale determines the popularity of his or her civic decisions. For example, if there is an increase in pollution from the factories, the learner may decide to meet these needs, but only at the expense of depleting the operating budget. The program also shows when roads need to be repaired as "time" progresses and the roads become worn. This then requires an increase in taxes, which generally engenders unfavorable reaction from the "residents" of the city, which in turn makes it much more difficult to pass some sort of tax measure necessary for growth.

This program is interesting and complex in the ways that it balances growth and the consequences of it. As one thinks about how the program represents a particular approach to city planning and the consequences of growth, it is clear that a set of cultural beliefs is in operation. For example, the program uses a formula to determine if a park is needed or the benefits and costs of locating an airport in a residential area. The questions that need to be asked are these: Whose formula is this? How are the factors weighted for determining the negative (and positive) environmental and social consequences of parks or airports?

As educators, it is our responsibility to develop a thoughtful and mindful approach to the use of these and other types of programs. By developing a critical perspective, we can find ourselves in a much better position to make educational decisions and choices for our students.

As with any text used for educational purposes, software must be examined for fairness and equity in regard to the issues of race, gender, and exceptionalities. In recent years, much attention has been given to examining just how well computer programs used by students represent the diversity that make up the schools children attend, their communities, and the country. As educators, we have recognized the need for students to be able to connect with others (i.e., we have determined this to be a significant educational goal). Most of our accomplishments have been in the areas of management of educational environments and of inclusion of marginalized groups. Yet, there have been few accomplishments in changing school curriculum and teacher preparation so that these marginalized groups are recognized and appreciated.

Although some attempts have been made in traditional print media to address various cultures, computer software programmers have been slow to incorporate into their software features of language and behavior of diverse groups, such as individuals with exceptionalities. Few examples of software might be considered representative of equity for exceptional individuals. One could ask if such a goal is even attainable. The problem, therefore, is more one of moving toward equity within educational software than one of achieving a completely representative technological curriculum. With this in mind, let us focus on some of the ways we as educators may begin to recognize and at least in part address the shortcomings.

The first step in developing an understanding of how educational technology impacts students' awareness of diversity issues is to know that programs socialize students into a particular way of thinking and/or reinforce already learned cultural meanings and definitions acquired from home, school, or community. By recognizing that software programs are capable of "derailing" our best educational intentions without our knowing it, we must assume the same professional responsibility that we do with traditional paper-and-pencil presentations. We must recognize that the language used in educational software programs "controls" the ways in which students will construct meaning from the text they are presented.

For example, if we look at the popular educational software program Voyageur that is used to teach the history of the West, we find that the language used to describe the conditions of the territory and the role the student plays are opposed to the ways in which indigenous people of the area might portray it. As a part of its scaffolding, the program describes one area as "Northern Minnesota" (which is not what it was known as by the indigenous peoples), where at this time "fur trading was the main industry." The student's goal in this program is "to reach Rainy Lake with the most amount of furs in the least amount of time." In each of these statements, a particular bias can be detected that is contrary to the conditions that prevailed at that time. By examining records and logs of actual events and the lives of the fur traders, we discover that the traders' goals were not to amass the most furs in the least amount of time. Instead, fur traders were a much more complex group of individuals who in many cases had to work and live with the indigenous people and adopt many of their cultural beliefs. The programmers of the Voyageur program were much less adept at understanding and conveying the actual experiences of the people at that time than we may realize without a critical view of how the language is working.

As teachers, we may mediate this difficulty by recognizing whether the learners are being provided language and images consistent with the complexity that simulation programs intend to portray. The teacher's responsibility is to mediate the software's curriculum in such a way as to foster within students a critical reading and understanding of the programs they encounter.

As classrooms begin to use technology more, the nature of interactions within the classroom also changes in rather dramatic ways. When we think about the traditional classroom where the teacher is located in front of the room and children are seated at desks in rows, the interactions are primarily between teacher and student, and occasionally between student and student with the teacher moderating and carefully orchestrating and managing the discussion. In another type of classroom, the children are working cooperatively in circles with the teacher facilitating learning by moving from group to group, listening to the group members discuss and resolve issues that they have been directed to negotiate and resolve. In still another type of classroom, the students move from one learning station to another where various activities have been created by the teacher who now monitors, guides, directs, and answers questions that arise as students engage in the different learning situations. In each of these types of classrooms, learning is primarily the result of human-to-human interaction. The introduction of technology into the curriculum, however, changes these interactions.

When students begin using technology in the classroom, some interesting things begin to happen regarding their interactions with the teacher and with other students. Because the computer promotes more individualized rather than group interactions, teachers who use cooperative or collaborative learning models and techniques (which are more congruent with constructive learning) are presented with a problem. Because the nature of computers is such that only one person at a time can use the keyboard to input data and respond to the machine, the opportunity for group learning to take place is virtually nonexistent. While children are working in cooperative groups, only one child at a time can be assigned to input data, which means that at any given moment one child assumes responsibility for the entire group. What often occurs, then, is a *gatekeeper effect* where the other group members provide their responses to the individual working on the computer and he or she filters the group's information before or as it is being put onto the computer. When using the computer for reference information, one child must still be the gatekeeper and make the choices for, say, search terms when using an encyclopedia. While this is not unlike a note taker or secretarial role within groups, computer versus paper-and-pencil interactions are different. Because of the novelty of the computer and the necessary individual interaction with the software, more attention and involvement are required from the child typing the information into the computer than when he or she simply keeps notes of the group's progress.

The need for the teacher to be keenly aware that computers are primarily an individualized workstation is important for maintaining equitability within groups when the aim is to provide a cooperative or collaborative environment. Even when the teacher has provided plenty of structure regarding cooperation and group decision making, the social responsibilities of each group member must be carefully monitored. What this suggests is that socialization into the use of computers in educational settings demands carefully constructed roles and responsibilities for the students so that each member can participate as equally as possible.

As educators, we must recognize how technology changes our interactions and the social makeup of our classrooms, then develop an understanding of how these changes affect our pedagogy so that we can make adjustments to what and how we teach by reflecting upon these changes. Most affected by the introduction of technology into the classroom is the community. Our pedagogical stance affects how children think they should receive knowledge and how we think they should try to pass it on. We may think that knowledge is passed down in an authoritarian succession in our society, from one generation to the next. Consequently, we perceive that children learn the previous generation's values and beliefs. This ideology ignores the fact that knowledge is constructed with the help of others around us and is dependent upon unique situations that dictate purpose(s) and values(s) to be learned. This is to say that our curriculum and our pedagogy, especially as related to technology, is not neutral. If we believe that in our classrooms students' cooperating and working with others should occur in only informal ways, and that discussion about a learning experience occurs only aside from the actual production of knowledge using technology, then we are supporting the idea that we learn from an authority. Consequently, computers will be used alone, and meaning will be composed in isolation. Under these circumstances, we are ignoring the human need for social interaction as a means of verifying and receiving ideas.

As educators we are participating in building a new social consensus of inclusion for all students. The need for teachers to be mindful and reflective about how they organize their curriculum and teach is acutely demonstrated in the technology arena. As teachers of children and young adults, the need to recognize the inherent problems in the design of computers allows us to begin to make adjustments in what we teach and how we teach. We can use examples of bias exhibited by the hardware and software design to develop and advance our students' abilities to be reflective and knowledgeable about their world. We can use examples in our curriculum to demonstrate to students the images of individuals with exceptionalities and marginalized people that our culture maintains and perpetuates.

Entering the world of technology is a confusing exercise for most educators. The choices of configuring the hardware, organizing the classroom environment, and making decisions about appropriate software contribute to a mystifying experience. Educators may feel intimidated when confronted with these decisions. By developing an understanding of the issues discussed in this text, educators can begin to recognize the difficulties that await them or that confront them on a daily basis. By identifying the problem, questions can then be formed and action taken in terms of adapting instruction for individuals with exceptionalities. This will enable teachers to be in a position of reflection and action regarding what they teach and how they teach it. Students and educators will find that the educational community in which they are participants is more critical and instills in us the need to be thoughtful and unassuming about the culture of educational technology.

Appendix E

෴ ෴ ෴

Technology and Professional Competencies

Henry F. Thibodeaux, III
University of
Southern Mississippi,
Hattiesburg

Jana D. Bunkley
University of
Southern Mississippi,
Hattiesburg

John M. Avis
University of
Southern Mississippi,
Hattiesburg

The development of technology competencies for general and special needs professionals continues to be an ongoing concern. Niess (1990) indicated that professionals not only must have knowledge of technology, but also should use their knowledge of technology in the classroom. Developing technologically competent professionals requires that two issues be addressed: what technology competencies are required of professionals and what method to use to develop these competencies. Although the purpose of this appendix is to provide a listing of general competencies that special education professionals may need, this appendix may also be used to develop a self-check list for professionals.

Much attention is focused on the methods used to develop technological competencies in professionals (e.g., Balli & Diggs, 1996; Collier & LeBaron, 1995). Hoffman (1997) rank ordered several methods used by professionals to develop technological competencies. He proposed that self-study is the most effective method to teach professionals how to use new technology. Other researchers (e.g., Flake, 1990; Handler, 1993) made similar recommendations by emphasizing hands-on experience with technology. Therefore, if professionals are acquiring these skills through self-study, a tool to assist them in determining developmental needs is important. Professionals who are using self-study to develop their technological competencies can use the listed competencies to assess their technological strengths and weaknesses and to identify specific areas on which to focus their developmental activities. Figure E.1 provides a sample checklist that can be used by professionals.

The research of general education technologists and the explicit and implicit research and writings of various special needs professionals have fostered the special education computer competency initiative (e.g., Behrmann, 1984, 1988; Budoff & Hutton, 1982; Budoff, Thorman, & Gras, 1984; Hagen, 1984; Hofmeister, 1982; Lindsey, 1987, 1993; Roston & Sewell, 1984; Taber, 1981a, 1981b). Also, competencies for computer-using special needs professionals have evolved because of the efforts of national, state, and professional organizations (e.g., Closing the Gap, Council for Exceptional Children's Technology and Media Division, U.S. Office of Special Education Programs) and the publication of special education journals (e.g., *Journal of Special Education Technology*). However, it has been the work of Blackhurst and his associates (e.g., Kinney & Blackhurst, 1987) that has resulted in the delineation of specific technological competencies that professionals working with exceptional individuals should have. Blackhurst's continued activities are resulting in updated competencies for computer-using special needs professionals.

The focus of this appendix is a listing of general competencies professionals may need to effectively use technology with exceptional individuals. As in previous editions of this book, these competencies were derived by integrating the competencies reported by other authors (e.g., Kinney & Blackhurst, 1987; Niess, 1990) and discussed or alluded to by the authors in this book. The current edition of this list also incorporates Beigel's (1996) proposition regarding competencies required of special needs professionals beyond basic technological competencies.

Self-Check for Core Competencies

Instructions: *To assess individual technological competencies, complete the following self-check list. Assess your core competencies by marking that you meet the competency or need improvement in order to meet the competency. This self-check can assist in identifying specific areas of technological competence needing attention.*

Competency	Meets Competency	Needs Improvement
Operates and maintains multimedia systems and peripheral devices	☐	☐
Arranges physical setting to maximize use of technology	☐	☐
Executes basic computer operations (e.g., copying files)	☐	☐
Uses hardware and software to facilitate professional development	☐	☐
Integrates hardware and software into the curriculum	☐	☐
Collaborates with colleagues on computer-related activities	☐	☐
Uses electronic mail to communicate with other professionals	☐	☐
Uses Internet browsers and search engines to find resources	☐	☐
Uses technology for personal and instructional productivity	☐	☐
Complies with copyright laws and ethical computer issues	☐	☐
Ensures equal access to technology for all exceptional users	☐	☐
Assists others in seeing the benefits of computer technology	☐	☐
Supports the development of technology by education agencies	☐	☐
Maintains current knowledge of available technology	☐	☐

Figure E.1. Self-Check for Core Competencies.

These additional competencies focus on the unique needs of exceptional students. Also, the work of Collier and LeBaron (1995) and the International Society for Technology in Education's (1997) *Recommended Foundations in Technology for All Teachers* were used to expand the Internet and multimedia related competencies.

Two groups of technological competencies are listed (1) generic core competencies that may be required of all special needs professionals and (2) specific competencies listed by level, from infant to postsecondary. Rapid developments in technology and an increased understanding of the benefits of using this technology with and by exceptional individuals may result in the revision or elimination of some competencies. Also, as asserted by Kinney and Blackhurst (1987), care should be taken in using lists of competencies to ensure that they are valid for the context in which the user will need them.

Core Competencies for Special Needs Professionals

Special needs professionals should have certification or licenses and possess state and local computer literacy competencies. They should also maintain these competencies by using varied sources to acquire pertinent information to remain current on new technological advances. In addition to computer literacy competencies, special needs professionals should be aware of the impact and possible benefits that computers have on the ability to improve the daily lives of exceptional individuals. Special needs professionals should be able to do the following:

1. Perform basic functions to operate and maintain multimedia systems and peripheral devices (printers, scanners, video cameras, etc.).

2. Arrange the physical setting to maximize the use of technology.

3. Execute basic computer operations, such as using operating systems, installing programs on hard disks, running programs, formatting disks, copying files, and performing general troubleshooting activities (e.g., running diagnostic programs), to develop and implement lesson plans.

4. Use hardware and software to facilitate professional development.

5. Integrate hardware and software into the curriculum by identifying learning objectives and matching technology to reach the desired objectives.

6. Assist and collaborate with colleagues (technology teachers, physical therapist, occupational therapist, speech therapist, etc.) to identify, evaluate, select, and develop computer-related activities to meet teaching–learning objectives (e.g., multimedia, authoring systems, telecommunications) for exceptional students.

7. Use electronic mail to communicate with other special needs professionals to exchange information, ideas, and applications of technology in the classroom.

8. Use Internet browser software and Internet search engines to find resources for special needs professionals, curriculum information, and so forth.

9. Download and access Internet files containing information to use in the classroom to enhance learning.

10. Use technology for personal and instructional productivity (see Chapter 7) to model the benefits of technology for personal productivity.

11. Comply with copyright laws and address ethical computer issues.

12. Identify and address equality issues such as equal access for males and females, minorities, and all exceptional users to ensure equal access to technology.

13. Assist parents, colleagues, and students in seeing the benefits of using computer technology to increase motivation to develop technological competencies.

14. Support the development of appropriate technology-related concepts by state and local education agencies (e.g., inservices).

Age-Specific Competencies for Special Needs Professionals

Ages 0 to 5: Infant, Toddler, and Early Childhood

Special needs professionals working with infants, toddlers, and children in early childhood should be knowledgeable of infant, toddler, and early childhood special education computing topics and familiar with related educational materials in order to match learning needs with available technology. Early childhood special needs professionals should be able to do the following:

1. Determine the appropriate adaptive and augmentative communication-related technologies to enhance the learning environment and life of exceptional infants, toddlers, and early childhood individuals.

2. Use various procedures to teach exceptional infants, toddlers, and early childhood individuals the appropriate use of input devices (e.g., keyboarding, voice recognition, switches) and output devices (e.g., monitor, printer, speech synthesizer), robotics, and so forth.

Ages 6 to 11: Elementary School

Special needs professionals working with elementary school children should be knowledgeable of elementary school special education computing topics and familiar with related educational materials in order to match learning needs with available technology. Elementary school special needs professionals should be able to do the following:

1. Determine the appropriate adaptive and augmentative communication-related technologies to enhance the learning environment and life of exceptional elementary school individuals.

2. Use various procedures to teach exceptional elementary school individuals the appropriate use of input devices (e.g., disk drives, keyboarding, voice recognition, switches) and output devices (e.g., monitor, printer, speech synthesizer), applications software (e.g., word processing), authoring systems, multimedia, desktop publishing, telecommunications techniques, robotics, and so forth.

Ages 11 to 14: Middle School

Special needs professionals working with middle school children should be knowledgeable of middle school special education computing topics and familiar with related educational materials in order to match learning needs with available technology. Middle school special needs professionals should be able to do the following:

1. Use basic technology terminology to describe multimedia computer systems, peripherals, and software.

2. Determine the appropriate adaptive and augmentative communication-related technologies to enhance the learning environment and life of exceptional middle school individuals.

3. Use various procedures to teach exceptional middle school individuals the appropriate use of input devices (e.g., disk drives, keyboard-

ing, voice recognition, switches) and output devices (e.g., monitor, printer, speech synthesizer), applications software (e.g., word processing), authoring systems, multimedia, desktop publishing, telecommunications techniques, robotics, and so on.

4. Design computer-related teaching–learning activities to promote the development of moral, psychological, and sociological concepts.

Ages 15 to Adult: Secondary and Postsecondary Levels

Special needs professionals working with secondary or postsecondary students should be knowledgeable of secondary or postsecondary school special education computing topics and familiar with related educational materials in order to match learning needs with available technology. Secondary or postsecondary school special needs professionals should be able to do the following:

1. Use basic technology terminology to describe multimedia computer systems, peripherals, and software.

2. Determine the appropriate adaptive and augmentative communication-related technologies to enhance the learning environment and life of exceptional secondary or postsecondary individuals.

3. Use various procedures to teach exceptional secondary or postsecondary individuals the appropriate use of input devices (e.g., keyboarding, voice recognition, switches) and output devices (e.g., monitor, printer), applications software (e.g., word processing), authoring systems, multimedia, desktop publishing, telecommunications techniques, and so on.

4. Design computer-related teaching–learning activities to promote the development of moral, psychological, and sociological concepts.

5. Use hardware and software to develop exceptional individuals' career awareness and vocational abilities and competitiveness.

6. Develop transition plans to facilitate the students' moving from the academic world to the business world.

References

Balli, S. J., & Diggs, L. L. (1996). Learning to teach with technology: A pilot project with preservice teachers. *Educational Technology, 36*(1), 56–61.

Behrmann, M. M. (1984). *Handbook of microcomputers in special education.* Austin, TX: PRO-ED.

Behrmann, M. M. (1988). *Integrating computers into the curriculum.* Austin, TX: PRO-ED.

Beigel, A. R. (1996, March). Developing computer competencies among special needs educators. *Learning and Leading with Technology, 23*(6), 69–71.

Budoff, M., & Hutton, L. R. (1982). Microcomputers in special education: Promises and pitfalls. *Exceptional Children, 49*(2), 123–128.

Budoff, M., Thorman, J., & Gras, A. (1984). *Microcomputers in special education.* Cambridge, MA: Brookline Books.

Collier, C., & LeBaron, J. (1995). The impact of Internet access on designs for Internet training. *Journal of Information Technology for Teacher Education, 4*(3), 319–328.

Flake, J. L. (1990). Preparing teachers to integrate computers into mathematics instruction. *Journal of Computers in Mathematics and Science Teaching, 9*(4), 9–16.

Hagen, D. (1984). *Microcomputer resource book for special education.* Reston, VA: Reston.

Handler, M. G. (1993). Preparing new teachers to use computer technology: Perceptions and suggestions for teacher educators. *Computers and Education, 20,* 148–153.

Hoffman, B. (1997, January). Integrating technology into schools. *The Education Digest,* 51–55.

Hofmeister, A. M. (1982). Microcomputers in perspective. *Exceptional Children, 49,* 115–121.

International Society for Technology in Education. (1997). *Recommended foundations in technology for all teachers* [Online]. Available: http://www.iste.org

Kinney, T. G., & Blackhurst, A. E. (1987). Technology competencies for teachers of young children with severe handicaps. *Topics in Early Childhood Education, 7*(3), 105–115.

Lindsey, J. D. (Ed.). (1987). *Computers and exceptional individuals.* Columbus, OH: Merrill.

Lindsey, J. (Ed.). (1993). *Computers and exceptional individuals* (2nd ed.). Austin, TX: PRO-ED.

Niess, M. L. (1990). Preparing computer using educators in a new decade. *Computing Teacher, 18*(3), 10–15.

Roston, A., & Sewell, D. (1984). Microtechnology in special education. Baltimore: Johns Hopkins University Press.

Taber, F. M. (1981a). The microcomputer: Its application to special education. *Focus on Exceptional Children, 14*(2), 1–16.

Taber, F. M. (1981b). *Microcomputers in special education: Selection and decision-making process.* Reston, VA: Council for Exceptional Children.

Appendix F

かか かか かか

Software and Web Sites for Professionals and Exceptional Individuals

Henry Teller, Jr.
University of
Southern Mississippi,
Hattiesburg

Lee Terrio
University of
Southern Mississippi,
Hattiesburg

Stephen E. Oshrin
University of
Southern Mississippi,
Hattiesburg

Since the second edition of this text was published in 1993, a number of major developments have occurred in the use of technology for and by exceptional individuals. Five of the many developments are these: (1) more computers are available for students in special education; (2) most of these computers are located in the classrooms where students have ready access to them, rather than in computer laboratories outside the classrooms; (3) the computers are many times more powerful than those available when the second edition of this text was published; (4) schools are rapidly being wired for direct access to the Internet, and the World Wide Web, permitting the downloading of software from the Internet and Web; and (5) educational software is almost exclusively in the more powerful compact disc (CD) format (digital video or versatile disc titles are increasing) rather than the 3½-inch or 5¼-inch floppy disk formats in use when the previous edition of this book was published.

The following is a sampling of instructional programs which may be used by professionals working with exceptional individuals or by the exceptional individuals themselves. These products usually operate in both the IBM or compatible formats (DOS or Windows) and the Apple or Macintosh formats. A number of the programs cited are reviewed by organizations concerned with promoting quality educational software among parents and educators. Some Web sites useful to educators of exceptional individuals are also listed.

Early Childhood/Readiness

Title: JumpStart First Grade
Publisher: Knowledge Adventure
4100 West 190th Street
Torrance, CA 90504
800/542-4240
http://www.adventure.com
Level: Early Elementary
Content: JumpStart First Grade covers a full curriculum of music, math principles, money, vowel sounds, double-digit addition and subtraction, science, geography, and world cultures in one CD-ROM. Students can practice over 90 different skills which in 18 well-developed teaching modules. JumpStart First Grade is perfect for children who love learning and earning recognition by collecting milk caps while having fun (Velgos, 1997).

Reading

Title: Reader Rabbit's Interactive Reading Journey 2
Publisher: The Learning Company
6493 Kaiser Drive
Fremont, CA 94555
800/852-2255
Level: Kindergarten to Grade 3

Content: The student is guided through 30 storybooks and 15 learning activities. Corresponding hardcopy books are provided for additional reinforcement. Each story is presented by a narrator's introduction of the story theme and new vocabulary. A page is read by the narrator, and the user is encouraged to read the same passage aloud with the option of recording it on the computer. The user may then play back his or her reading and compare it to the narrator's reading of the same. This is a good program for children who are already familiar with the alphabet and the sounds associated with each letter (Superkids Educational Software Review, 1997).

Language Arts

Title: A to Zap
Publisher: Sunburst Communications, Inc.
101 Castleton Street
Pleasanton, NY 10570
800/321-7511
http://www.sunburstonline.com
Level: PreK to Early Elementary
Content: Through exploring the activities in A to Zap, children can learn to recognize and name the letters of the alphabet using picture referents and gain an understanding that letters combine to spell words. A to Zap provides practice in identifying words and their picture referents and helps the young computer user become familiar with some basic computer operations.

Mathematics

Title: Math Blaster 1: In Search of Spot
Publisher: Davidson and Associates
P.O. Box 2691

Torrance, CA 90509
800/545-7677
Level: Elementary
Content: Math Blaster has proven to be a high-interest program for students in the lower grades for a number of years. In this version Spot has been taken by the Trash Alien. To complete Spot's rescue, the student must solve math problems in order to collect and recycle space trash, follow the Trash Alien, and finally complete the rescue (SuperKids Educational Software Review, 1997).

Title: Math Rabbit Deluxe
Publisher: The Learning Company
6493 Kaiser Drive
Fremont, CA 94555
800/852-2255
Level: Kindergarten to Lower Elementary
Content: Math Rabbit teaches counting, number matching, and problem solving. Four levels of difficulty are within each game format. A ticket is issued when the student correctly answers all of the problems in a game set. The tickets may be applied to the purchase of a toy at the prize center.

The games are fun for young children, and exercise a variety of beginning math skills. In the Calliope Counting Game, the user makes music on a pipe organ by counting out notes, either an original tune or a tune that the rabbit leads. The Tightrope Show involves matching a number or equation to a given number. A number pattern must be uncovered in the Sea Lion Show to solve addition and subtraction problems. The Balloon Matching Game is a concentration game. Numbers are matched to the correct number of objects or equation solutions (SuperKids Educational Software Review, 1997).

Social Science

Title: Oregon Trail
Publisher: MECC
6160 Summit Drive North
Minneapolis, MN 55430-4004
800/685-MECC
http://www.mecc.com
Level: Grade 5 and up
Content: Oregon Trail is the descendant of the very popular earlier floppy version. Users are challenged to make a series of decisions to guide their party from Independence, Missouri, to Oregon's Willamette Valley, by covered wagon. These decisions include choosing a departure date, and daily decisions relating to pace, restocking, and direction. Users face an unending series of obstacles: fires, floods, injuries, no water, bad water, no grass, food spoilage, and so on (SuperKids Educational Software Review, 1997).

Title: Go West! The Homesteaders Challenge
Publisher: Sunburst/Edunetics
101 Castleton Street
Pleasanton, NY 10570
800/321-7511
http://www.sunburstonline.com
Level: Elementary to High School
Content: Go West is a realistic simulation of the homestead era. The student, taking the role of a Kansas pioneer, has to apply a variety of problem-solving strategies to establish a homestead on the prairie and "prove up" the land to satisfy the requirements of the Homestead Act of 1892. As the simulation progresses, the student faces bad weather, grasshoppers, plagues, prairie fires, changing interest rates on loans, and varying crop prices. Goals have to be set and decisions have to be made throughout. Go West! cuts across many curriculum areas.

Speech and Language

Title: Speech Viewer
Publisher: IBM
Department YEO56
4111 Northside Parkway
Atlanta, GA 30327
Level: PreK to 12
Content: Speech Viewer is Windows-based multimedia software for individuals with speech, language, or hearing impairments. Speech Viewer provides visual and auditory feedback through imaginative graphics to improve the effectiveness of speech–language therapy. Thirteen exercises allow individuals to work on any number of speech production behaviors. A demonstration version of Speech Viewer is available on the Internet at the following Web site: http://www.rs6000.ibm.com/sns/snsspv3.html.

Title: The Personal Communicator
Publisher: Instructional Media Center– Marketing Division
P.O. Box 710
Michigan State University
East Lansing, MI 48826-0710
517/353-9229
Content: The Personal Communicator is an award-winning tool designed to enable deaf students, to better communicate with their peers, teachers, and other associates, deaf or hearing. It has an ASL/English dictionary with over 3,000 videos of signs. Typing in a word gives the English definition, the ASL sign for that word, and synonyms for the signs. The Personal Communicator also has a speech/sign synthesizer and can serve as a medium for conversations between deaf and hearing peers. Field testing revealed that deaf students felt that it gave them more independence in their writing and allowed them to develop more

intimate relations with their hearing peers. It can be ordered for $49.95 plus shipping and handling.

Typing/Keyboarding

Title: Mavis Beacon Teaches Typing
Publisher: Mindscape, Inc.
88 Rowland Way
Novato, CA 94945
415/897-9900
http://www.Mindscape.com.80/
Level: Upper Elementary to Adult
Content: This is one of the best selling typing or keyboarding programs (5 million plus copies). It offers interactive typing instruction in a classroom setting with continuous user analysis and feedback in animated settings.

Career Awareness/Vocational Education

Title: Hotdog Stand: The Works!
Publisher: Sunburst Communications, Inc.
101 Castleton Street
Pleasanton, NY 10570
800/321-7511
http://www.sunburstonline.com
Level: Upper Elementary to High School
Content: This program presents students with the challenge of running their own small business. In the process students use and strengthen a variety of mathematics, problem-solving, and communication skills, including arithmetic operations, recognizing patterns, estimation, working backwards, data gathering, writing, data analysis, choosing appropriate tools, interpreting graphs, and translating information. The students take the role of food vendors at an arena. They begin with $500 in the bank and try to reach a given goal at the end of a number of events. They

must do the same things that professional vendors do before events in order to have adequate supplies on hand. They must check weather reports, get information about the events, check wholesale prices, order supplies, check inventories, and more.

Students then open the stand to see if their preparations pay off. After each event, the students return to the office to prepare for the next event. They can also replay an event to try to achieve a better outcome.

School and Class Management

Title: IEPplus for Windows Software
Publisher: Orion Systems Group, Inc.
3555 Veterans Memorial Highway
Suite F
Ronkonkoma, NY 11779
800/487-0041
info@orionsystems.com
http://www.orionsystems.com/company_info/co_prome.html
Level: Professional
Content: This Windows 95 or 98-compatible program is designed to track student data and automate paperwork and reports as mandated by state and federal regulations. Text from word processing programs may be copied and pasted into IEPplus. The program has an IEP Generator that tracks all information for the individual IEP on one screen. On-line help screens are available to guide the user through the process.

Useful Web Sites

Web site: Australian Educational Resources
Address: http://curriculum.qed.qld.gov.au/lisc/edsw/dossoft.htm
Content: A listing of MS-DOS software for different ages. Categories include astronomy, language and reading, mathe-

matics, and science and technology. Tutorial-based software is available in areas such as computer technology, food and cooking, health and fitness, and typing and keyboarding.

Web site: EOS: Educational Online Sources Home Page
Address: http://netspace.students.brown. edu/eos/main_image.html
Content: EOS is a clearinghouse for educational information. It is a consolidated collection of educational on-line sources that solicits broad participation and contributions from the educational community.

Web site: Forefront Curriculum Home Page
Address: http://www.4forefront.com/
Content: Educational Web site recommendations.

Web site: Handilinks
Address: http://www.ahandyguide.com/ index.htm
Content: Search the Web for any information by category and subject.

Web site: Inventory of Electronic Resources
Address: http://www.oltc.edu.au/ier/index.htm
Content: Listings in the arts, English, health and physical education, languages other than English, mathematics, science, society and the environment, and technology.

Web site: K–12 Resources
Address: http://www.lloydd.com/k12index.htm
Content: Links to National Aeronautics and Space Administration (NASA), National Science Foundation (NSF), public schools with an Internet homepage, United States Department of Education, United States Department of Health and Human Services, and United States Regional Educational Laboratories.

Web site: Kids' Web: ComputED Gazette
Address: http://www.primenet.com/~sburr/ comped.html
Content: Software reviews.

Web site: Low Incidence Support Centre: DOS Special Access Shareware
Address: http://curriculum.qed.qld.gov.au/lisc/ edsw/d-access.htm
Content: MSDOS Shareware Collection—Special access programs may be downloaded.

Web site: MSDOS Low Vision Shareware
Address: http://curriculum.qed.qld.gov.au/lisc. edsw.d-lowvis.htm
Content: Large-character, braille, and speech shareware programs may be downloaded.

Web site: Nerd's Heaven Software Directory
Address: http://boole.stanford.edu/ nerdsheaven. html
Content: A listing of general software links.

Web site: Nova Scotia Department of Education and Culture
Address: http://www.ednet.ns.ca/educ/ program/lrt/eval/listed.htm
Content: Educational Software reviews.

Web site: PEP (Parents, Educators, and Publishers)
Address: http://www.microweb.com/pepsite/
Content: Informational resource for parents, educators, and children's software publishers. The site includes ratings and reviews of children's software.

Web site: The REVIEW ZONE
Address: http://www.TheReviewZone.com
Content: In-depth, parent-friendly, independent reviews of today's best edutainment and educational software for kids and families.

Web site: Special Education Links for Teachers and Parents
Address: http://members.aol.com/LCantlin/ se_links.htm

Content: Site for special educators with links to virtually all areas of special education; federal, state, and local government; medicine and health; national and regional organizations; speech and language services; and universities and colleges.

Web site: Special Education Resources on the Internet (SERI)
Address: http://www.hood.edu/seri/serihome.htm
Content: SERI is a collection of Internet-accessible information resources for those involved in fields related to special education. This collection exists in order to make on-line Special Education resources more readily available in one location. The site continually modifies, updates, and adds additional informative links. Current site categories are as follows: General Disabilities Information; Disability Products and Commercial Sites; Legal & Law Resources; Special Education Discussion Groups; Mental Retardation; Physical and Health Disabilities; Learning Disabilities; Attention Deficit Disorders; Speech Disorders; Special Needs and Technology; Inclusion Resources; University Based Information; National Organizations; Parents & Educators' Resources; Medicine and Health; Hearing Impairments; Behavior Disorders; Vision Disabilities; Autism; Gifted and Talented; Psychology; and Transition Resources

Web site: SuperKids Educational Software Review
Address: http://www.superkids.com
Content: Guide for parents and teachers to review software and educational software.

Web site: Sunburst Online
Address: http://www.nysunburst.com
Content: On-line Demonstrations; Resources for Educators; Product Information; Free Publishing Opportunities.

Web site: Tudogs: Free Software
Address: http://tudogs.com/edu.html
Content: Reviews and grades free software, graphics, and other services.

Web site: WebEd: Curriculum Links
Address: http://badger.state.wi.us/agencies/dpi/www/WebEd.html
Content: Links to art, career planning, history, hobbies, libraries, math, multicultures, music, parents and parenting, science, search tools, sites for kids, sports, and writing.

Web site: The World Wide Web Virtual Library: Educational Technology
Address: http://tecfa.unige.ch/info-edu-comp.html
Content: Preparing courseware and distance learning packages.

Conclusion

This appendix lists only a tiny sampling of the available software and useful Web sites. The amount of relevant information on the Internet and Web and the quantity of commercial software tend to be overwhelming. Perhaps the best way to keep abreast is to use the Web sites that are attempting to keep current with new software as it is developed. Many software publishers also offer demonstration programs that may be downloaded from the Internet and used or reviewed free of charge. The computer user of today has a virtually infinite variety of useful learning experiences at the touch of the keyboard.

References

Lindsey, J. D. (Ed.). (1993). *Computers and exceptional individuals* (2nd ed.) Austin, TX: PRO-ED.

Review of Math Blaster 1: In Search of Spot. (1997). *SuperKids Educational Software Review* [On-line]. Available: http://www.superkids.com

Review of Math Rabbit Deluxe. (1997). *SuperKids Educational Software Review* [On-line]. Available: http://www.superkids.com

Review of Oregon Trail CD. (1997). *SuperKids Educational Software Review* [On-line]. Available: http://www.superkids.com

Review of Reader Rabbit's Interactive Reading Journey 2. (1997). *SuperKids Educational Software Review* [On-line]. Available: http://www.superkids.com

Velgos, T. (1997). Review of JumpStart First Grade. *The REVIEW ZONE* [On-line]. Available: http://www.The ReviewZone.com

Appendix G

✌ ✌ ✌

The SECTOR Courseware Evaluation Form

Robert C. Reid
Utah State University

Kim E. Allard
Utah State University

Alan M. Hofmeister
Utah State University

Introduction

This document has been prepared to assist computer users in evaluating instructional software using the SECTOR Courseware Evaluation Form. (The five pages of the form are shown at the end of this explanation.)

General Product Description and Summary

The first page of the evaluation form is reserved for general information including the program name, publisher, and price of the program. A grid had been established which includes (1) content, (2) instructional design, (3) record keeping/ management, and (4) ease of use as general areas of concern. At the completion of the evaluation, these areas may be rated on a 5-point scale from superior to poor. Package contents and hardware requirements are also documented on the front page of the evaluation form. Package contents include materials such as teacher's manual or guide, supplemental classroom activities, flash cards, black line masters, and backup diskettes.

Hardware requirements should include a description of the hardware necessary to operate the

The material in this appendix is reprinted with the permission of Systems Impact, Inc., 2084 North 1200 East, Logan, UT 84321.

program. This should include what types of micro-computer the program is used with, the number of disk drives which may be necessary to operate the program, and any extra peripheral devices that are needed. Peripherals include memory expansion boards, 80-column boards, cassette tape drives, speech synthesizers, and so on. Some programs do not require specific hardware but may recommend the optional use of paddles, joysticks, printers, or additional disk drives.

Content

Space has been provided under each section to make comments on that aspect of the program. Criteria for each section has been outlined in a checklist, and each is rated on a 4-point scale of *excellent, satisfactory, unsatisfactory,* or *not applicable*. Criteria are:

1. *Objectives are fully and clearly defined.* Specific instructional objectives should be provided. These objectives should indicate to the potential user the skills the pupils should demonstrate on successful completion of the program.

2. *Target audience is clearly defined.* As with other instructional materials, a target audience or population should be defined by the publisher. Generally, the target audience will be defined by grade level or special population (e.g., mildly mentally retarded) or by the prerequisite skills the pupil needs to participate successfully.

3. *Outside activities are appropriate and effective.* While some computer assisted instruction (CAI) materials do not provide outside activities, the ones that are provided should be appropriate and geared to the skills being worked on within the instructional program. Omission of activities or reference to activities that would help integrate the program into the classroom curriculum should be considered.

4. *Prerequisite skills are clearly defined.* CAI materials often require skills not required by other instructional materials. These generally include typing and hardware operation skills. These skills should be identified in the documentation accompanying the instructional program.

5. *Content is presented clearly and logically.* This is generally applicable in tutorial programs where a concept is being presented and built upon by the program. The appropriate sequencing of curriculum units will need to be considered.

6. *Content is transferable and generalizable.* Skills learned on the computer should be transferable to other environments. For example, a student may do well on math facts on the computer, but cannot answer the same questions on a worksheet. Skills which can only be used or applied on the computer may be of questionable value.

7. *Content is consistent with objectives.* Content of the instructional program should match the objectives defined for it. This is best done by examining the behavior that the program expects from the pupil.

8. *Vocabulary level is appropriate for subject area and learner level.* This criterion is particularly important in evaluating CAI materials because of the amount of reading usually required to use the programs. Appropriate vocabulary levels should not be restricted to the academic content, but should include the directions for use of the program as well as feedback on student progress. As the case with some basal texts, the vocabulary level for some CAI programs may be above that appropriate for the defined audience.

Instructional Design

Instructional design refers to the way which the formation is presented to the student. Criteria for instructional design are as follows:

1. *Learner controls rate and sequence of instruction.* The learner should generally be in charge of the rate and sequence of instruction. Students should be interacting with screens of text and graphics and cueing the program to continue after they are complete. Many programs accomplish this by having the student press the RETURN key when they are ready to continue. In many drill and practice programs, however, the student response rate is set by the teacher. In such cases, learner control may not be applicable.

2. *Program can be used independently.* While some programs are designed to be used with a teacher present, most CAI materials are designed to be used independently by the student. Options should be available for the student to receive help from the teacher if necessary.

3. *Learner interacts only with appropriate segments.* A program can be a powerful teaching tool by branching the student to appropriate instructional segments based on responses. Remedial segments or new concepts should be presented based on the progress the student is making. This is particularly important with tutorial programs where new concepts are being presented and students are being tested on those concepts. The student should not waste valuable time relearning concepts already mastered, but rather should use computer time productively to work on new skills.

4. *Program utilizes a variety of display and response modes.* There are a variety of ways in which the student can respond in a computer program. The most traditional is typing the answers at the keyboard. When responding via the keyboard, the program usually incorporates several response modes, including answering open questions, multiple choice, or true and false. Because of the difficulty involved with anticipating a variety of student responses, many programs will opt for a

straight multiple choice or true and false response mode. While this simplifies the programming process, it may also reduce the effectiveness of the program. Response models should be based on the learner's needs, not an ease of computer programming.

5. *Program minimizes necessary typing.* While some programs are designed to improve typing or spelling skills, typing errors or misspellings may be of secondary importance in other programs. Misspellings should be dealt with by the program and handled appropriately when encountered. Students should not be penalized for poor typing when engaging in a lesson which does not have improvement of typing skills as an objective.

6. *Program handles a wide range of student responses appropriately.* When presented with a question like, "Who was the first president?" a student may answer in a variety of ways. "Washington, George Washington, President Washington, and President George Washington" could all be correct answers to this question. The computer program should take into account a wide range of both correct and incorrect responses and provide appropriate feedback to the student. If appropriate, the program should have some method of handling unusual responses that may be correct. This may be done by branching to a multiple choice question to clarify the response.

7. *New material is presented in context and is related to previous material.* This criterion applies mainly to tutorial programs where concepts are being developed. Computer programs are not always as randomly accessible as textbooks. In a book, students can easily flip back a few pages to review a point they may have missed or misunderstood. Because microcomputer programs are not so easily manipulated, new material must be carefully presented in context and related to what the student has already learned.

8. *Summaries and reviews are provided, important concepts are restated.* Because of the way in which programs, especially tutorial programs are structured, each section should be reviewed, and important concepts restated and reviewed at appropriate times during the program.

9. *Programs can be adjusted by user for local needs.* CAI programs should be easily incorporated into the classroom formula. The classroom curriculum should not have to be adjusted to complement the CAI program. Programs should be adjustable by changing variables such as length of time the program is used by each student each day. In the case of drill and practice programs, the rate at which the drill is presented is a variable that should be changeable. In such cases, such as spelling programs, it may be desirable to allow the teacher to determine what content should be presented.

10. *Appropriate use of graphics/color/sound.* Graphics, color, and sound are used often is CAI programs. Sound can be very distracting to other students when used in a classroom situation. Many programs provide an option for the teacher to turn the sound off when desired. Graphics and color are sometimes used as integral parts of the instruction. More often, however, they are used as feedback. Graphics should enhance the instruction and motivational aspects of the program and not detract from the instructional process.

11. *Feedback is useful and appropriate.* Feedback in CAI varies from simple written "right" or "wrong" to fireworks going off, and happy or sad faces. Generally, feedback should let students know whether they are right or wrong and allow them to continue on to the next activity. Feedback may contain the correct answers or contain hints for the correct answers. Feedback should not be confusing to the student nor detract from the instructional message. Unnecessary extra feedback for correct answers is often boring and slows the progress of the student.

12. *Instruction is active rather than passive.* Many instructional programs, particularly those tutorials that are attempting to teach a concept, require the student to read excessively from the display screen. The student should interact with the program wherever appropriate by responding to questions which aid

understanding and application of the content. The microcomputer does not serve the student or teacher well when used as an expensive page turner.

14. *Program has consistent display rate.* Presenting information on the screen at a consistent rate results in students paying more attention to the material presented and devoting less time to distraction. Continual variations in computer presentation response handling time distracts students.

15. *Displays are clear, understandable, and effective.* Given the size limitation of most display screens, often too much material is included on one screen. Graphics should be clear and easily recognizable. Some programs do not have the appropriate levels of contrast for the quality of television monitors most commonly found in the classroom.

Record Keeping and Management

The computer gives the teacher a great deal of potential for storing and interpreting student data. Criteria to be considered include:

1. *Program keeps accurate records of student response.* Programs should keep accurate records of how the student is doing. Besides maintaining whether an answer is right or wrong, the program may also keep track of the length of the instructional session.

2. *Program keeps ongoing student records.* Comprehensive programs that students work on a daily basis should maintain student information from session to session. This places the burden of tracking daily progress on the computer not on the teacher or student.

3. *Program includes diagnostic/evaluative testing.* Comprehensive programs, that is programs which cover a variety of skills and levels, often have some method, usually a diagnostic test to appropriately place the student in the curriculum. Evaluative testing determines if the student has met the objectives of the program.

4. *Program generates further assignments.* Many newer programs can generate assignment sheets or additional practice based on student progress.

5. *Program graphically depicts student progress.* Programs can graphically depict either the progress of individual students or the entire class.

6. *Program provides statistical information on student progress.* Programs can calculate percentages, including error rates and correct responses.

7. *Program allows printout and screen display of student records.* Data collected on students should be easily accessible to the teacher both on the screen and in hard copy if a printer is available.

Ease of Use

The acceptability of any computer program is dependent on its practicality in the classroom. The ease of use criteria listed below apply to both the student and the teacher:

1. *Support materials provided are comprehensive and effective.* Support materials, such as teacher's manuals, worksheets, and flashcards, should enhance the use of the CAI program. Instruction on how to most effectively use the program should be clearly presented.

2. *Program is reliable in normal use.* Programs should obviously not fail while in use. In addition, programs should be foolproofed so that unexpected keyboard activity will not "crash" the program.

3. *"HELP" procedures are available.* Many programs allow the user to push a key such as the "?" to obtain help in working with the program.

4. *Program can be exited by student or automatically when appropriate.* When appropriate, students should be able to end their work session without teacher assistance and without destroying any progress data that may have been collected. Some programs allow the stu-

dents to decide at regular intervals whether to continue with or end their session.

Program Strengths and Weaknesses

This section of the coursework evaluation form allows the reviewer to describe the strengths and weaknesses of the program in relation to specific application.

Validation

CAI programs should have been field tested with the populations they were developed for. Field test data should be documented by the developers. Of particular interest will be the potential level of objectivity of the researchers. CAI has, unfortunately, a rather long history of obtaining results that could not be achieved by later independent researchers. By using a small group of high performing students for a short time, under novelty conditions, it is possible to make even the worst product look good. Some of our best students are "best students" because they learn in spite of poor instruction.

The credibility of field test data is considerably enhanced if it is known that the testers were not associated with the development of the product and that it was used with large numbers of representative students for long periods of time under normal classroom conditions.

SECTOR COURSEWARE EVALUATION FORM

Robert C. Reid, Kim E. Allard, and Alan M. Hofmeister
Utah State University

PROGRAM
NAME: _____

PUBLISHER: _____

PRICE: _____

	SUPERIOR	VERY GOOD	GOOD	FAIR	POOR
CONTENT					
INSTRUCTIONAL DESIGN					
RECORD KEEPING/MANAGEMENT					
EASE OF USE					

I. PACKAGE CONTENTS

II. HARDWARE REQUIREMENTS

Note: The SECTOR project is a state-funded special education computer technology resource located at the Exceptional Child Center, Utah State University, Logan. The SECTOR Courseware Evaluation Form is reprinted with the permission of Systems Impact, Inc., 2084 North 1200 East, Logan, UT 84321.

COURSEWARE EVALUATION FORM 　2

Content

	EXCELLENT	SATISFACTORY	UNSATISFACTORY	NOT APPLICABLE
Objectives are fully and clearly defined.				
Target audience is clearly defined.				
Outside activities are appropriate and effective.				
Prerequisite skills are clearly defined.				
Content is presented clearly and logically.				
Content is transferable and generalizable.				
Content is consistent with objectives.				
Vocabulary level is appropriate for subject area and learner level.				

COURSEWARE EVALUATION FORM   3

Instructional Design

	EXCELLENT	SATISFACTORY	UNSATISFACTORY	NOT APPLICABLE
Learner controls rate and sequence of instruction.				
Program can be used independently.				
Learner interacts only with appropriate segments.				
Program utilizes a variety of display and response modes.				
Program minimizes necessary typing.				
Program handles a wide range of student responses appropriately.				
New material is presented in context and is related to previous material.				
Summaries and reviews are provided, important concepts are restated.				
Program can be adjusted by user for local needs.				
Appropriate use of graphics/color/sound.				
Feedback is useful and appropriate.				
Instruction is active rather than passive.				
Learner expectancies are established.				
Program has consistent display rate.				
Displays are clear, understandable, and effective.				

COURSEWARE EVALUATION FORM $\boxed{4}$

Record Keeping & Management

	EXCELLENT	SATISFACTORY	UNSATISFACTORY	NOT APPLICABLE
Program keeps accurate records of student response.				
Program keeps ongoing student records.				
Program includes diagnostic/evaluative testing.				
Program generates further assignments.				
Program graphically depicts student progress.				
Program provides statistical information on student progress.				
Program allows printout and screen display of student records.				

Ease of Use

	EXCELLENT	SATISFACTORY	UNSATISFACTORY	NOT APPLICABLE
Support materials provided are comprehensive and effective.				
Program is reliable in normal use.				
"HELP" procedures are available.				
Program can be exited by student or automatically when appropriate.				

COURSEWARE EVALUATION FORM $\boxed{5}$

Program Strengths and Weaknesses _____
_____
_____
_____
_____
_____
_____
_____

Validation.

PROGRAM TESTED   From _____ To _____
_____ In house   _____ Independent
_____ Controled   _____ Uncontrolled

POPULATION(S) TESTED _____
_____

ASSESSMENT INSTRUMENT(S) _____
_____

EVALUATION SITE(S) _____
_____

RESULTS _____
_____

CONTACT PERSON _____
ADDITIONAL INFORMATION _____
_____
_____
_____

EVALUATED BY _____
Date _____

UConn Educational Software Evaluation Form

Judith P. Sweeney and Chauncy N. Rucker

Title: _____

Evaluated by: _____

Cost: _____   Stated Age/Grade Level: _____   Subject Area: _____

Computer Versions Available: ☐ Apple II Family ☐ Apple IIgs ☐ MS-DOS ☐ Macintosh   Min. required memory? _____

Evaluated on: ☐ Apple II Family ☐ Apple IIgs ☐ MS-DOS ☐ Macintosh   Memory of system evaluated on? _____

Contents of Package:	Required (R) Suggested (S) Peripherals	Publisher Policies	Documentation
___ # of original disks	___ Printer	☐ Preview Policy ___ days	☐ computer operation/use instructions
___ # of backup disks	___ Color Printer		☐ specific educational goals
___ pages of documentation	___ 1 disk drive	☐ Backup Policy ___ provided ___ available/mail at ___ cost.	☐ use for specific special populations
Other: List student worksheets, posters, books, workbooks, etc. This column should include every thing in the software package.	___ 2 disk drives		☐ sample program screens as examples
	___ color monitor		
	___ monochrome monitor	☐ Guarantee Policy ___ lifetime ___ days ___ only for defect ___ fee	☐ curriculum inclusion and scope
	___ speech synthesizer		☐ removable menu or direction cards
	___ mouse		☐ specially written student directions
	___ alternative keyboard		
___	___ Muppet Keyboard		
___	___ Power Pad		
___	___ Touch Window		
___	___ Other		

My Rating of Documentation/Contents/Policies: *(Circle one)*   1 ——— 1.5 ——— 2.0 ——— 2.5 ——— 3.0 ——— 3.5 ——— 4.0

Strengths and Weaknesses: *(Use back if necessary)*

Part 2: Learning Considerations

Category
- ☐ Tutorial
- ☐ Drill and Practice
- ☐ Simulation
- ☐ Demonstration
- ☐ Problem Solving
- ☐ Productivity
- ☐ Interactive Fiction
- ☐ Creativity
- ☐ Instructional Game
- ☐ Other _____

Learning Level Stressed
- ☐ Acquisition *Motor Skill*
- ☐ Acquisition *Facts*
- ☐ Acquisition *Concepts*
- ☐ Fluency *Motor Skill*
- ☐ Fluency *Verbal Skill*
- ☐ Fluency *Mathematics Skill*
- ☐ Application *Motor Skill*
- ☐ Application *Verbal Skill*
- ☐ Application *Mathematical Skill*
- ☐ Application *Conceptual*

Primary Intelligence Stressed *(Choose One)*
- ☐ Linguistic
- ☐ Logical/Mathematical
- ☐ Intrapersonal
- ☐ Interpersonal
- ☐ Spatial
- ☐ Musical
- ☐ Bodily/Kinesthetic

Response to Student Answers *(choose one)*
- ☐ Positive Rein.
- ☐ Negative Rein
- ☐ Punishment
- ☐ Correct response given after _____ attempts
- ☐ Correct response never given
- ☐ Lesson retaught after _____ incorrect answers
- ☐ Automatic branching in the program to higher or lower levels
- ☐ Correct concepts dependent on spelling

Presentation Mode
- ☐ Visual *verbal (text)*
- ☐ Visual *symbolic (pictures)*
- ☐ Auditory *verbal*
- ☐ Auditory *symbolic (sounds/music)*
- Paired Associate Learning
  - ☐ picture-word
  - ☐ picture-sound
  - ☐ word-sound
  - ☐ picture-word-sound

Reinforcement Mode
- ☐ Visual *verbal*
- ☐ Visual *symbolic (pictures)*
- ☐ Auditory *verbal*
- ☐ Auditory *symbolic (sounds/music)*
- ☐ Kinesthetic *reward game that requires motor input*
- ☐ Product Related Reinforcement *(print-outs)*

My Rating of Learning Considerations: *(Circle one)*   1 ——1.5——2.0——2.5——3.0——3.5——4.0

Strengths and Weaknesses: *(Use back if necessary)*

Part 3: Presentation and Instructional Quality

To successfully use this program, the student must:

Visual Considerations	Learning Considerations	Reading Level Considerations	Motor/Hand-Eye Considerations	Auditory Considerations	Response/Input Considerations
☐ read 20 column text	☐ spell responses correctly	☐ read directions	☐ respond within a time limit	☐ understand synthesized speech	☐ use multiple keystrokes
☐ read 40 column text	☐ use capital letters and/or punctuation correctly	☐ read menus	☐ use the keyboard	☐ remember auditory sequential directions	☐ use numerals
☐ read 80 column text	☐ remember menu commands	☐ read documentation	☐ use multiple keystrokes	☐ remember auditory directions	☐ use alpha keys
☐ have a color monitor	☐ remember a sequence of directions	☐ read information at indicated grade level	☐ use a mouse		☐ use symbol keys
☐ read upper and lower case	☐ move a cursor with arrows, letters or input device	☐ have adult help because of the reading level	☐ use a joystick		☐ use function keys
☐ differentiate colors			☐ use an alternative input device		☐ type with two hands
					☐ use a mouse

Modifications and Management Possible in This Software

Content Modifications	Criteria Modifications	Rate/Time Modifications	Sound Modifications	Adaptive Device Modifications	Student Record Keeping
☐ add to content	☐ adjust number of items	☐ adjust time allowed for response	☐ synthesized speech	☐ Unicorn Board	☐ auto save of student progress
☐ change content	☐ adjust number correct before lesson is completed	☐ change cursor movement speed	☐ digitized speech	☐ Touch Window	☐ print-out student records
☐ choose level or kinds of items	☐ adjust # of misses allowed	☐ change speed of presentation	☐ sound on/off	☐ Power Pad	maximum number of records: ___
☐ automatic branching			☐ requires a speech interface card	☐ Single Switch	
				☐ Muppet Keys	

My Rating of Presentation/Instructional Quality: *(Circle one)*   1 ——1.5——2.0——2.5——3.0——3.5——4.0

Strengths and Weaknesses: *(Use back if necessary)*

Part 4: Technical Quality

This program has the following technical capabilities:

	Good	Poor	N.A.
Reaction to illogical input	☐	☐	☐
Reaction to repeated incorrect responses	☐	☐	☐
Grammar and spelling on screen and in documentation	☐	☐	☐
Use with peripherals	☐	☐	☐
Way to exit an activity	☐	☐	☐
Lack of stereotypes	☐	☐	☐

	Good	Poor	N.A.
Changing disks	☐	☐	☐
Booting the program	☐	☐	☐
Private reinforcement	☐	☐	☐
Quality of speech synthesis	☐	☐	☐
Adjustable sound levels	☐	☐	☐
Graphics on a monochrome monitor	☐	☐	☐

	Good	Poor	N.A.
Help Screens	☐	☐	☐
WYSIWYG	☐	☐	☐
Disk access time	☐	☐	☐
Student motivation	☐	☐	☐
Graphic quality	☐	☐	☐
Cost effectiveness	☐	☐	☐
Other _____	☐	☐	☐

My Rating of Technical Quality: *(Circle one)*

1 ——— 1.5 ——— 2.0 ——— 2.5 ——— 3.0 ——— 3.5 ——— 4.0

Strengths and Weaknesses: *(Use back if necessary)*

Program Description

In 25 - 50 words, describe how the program works and its major goals and objectives.

Part 5: Summary Statements

**Based on the other 4 section ratings,
my overall rating of this program is:** *(Circle one)*

1 --------1.5 --------2.0 --------2.5 --------3.0 --------3.5 --------4.0

Strengths and Weaknesses: *(Be as specific as possible, attach print out copies if applicable)*

Appendix H

✌   ✌   ✌

Internet and World Wide Web Resources

Rodney W. Woods

de l'Epee Deaf Center, Gulfport, Mississippi

Before 1993 the Internet was more or less unknown to the general public. The Internet at that time was a general network for government workers and academics and was far too difficult for the average person to access and use. This all changed with the development and evolution of the World Wide Web and Netscape and other Web browsers that brought the Internet to the consumer in an easy to use format. In addition to providing commercial applications, the Internet and Web have become a valuable medium for teaching and learning. According to a recent survey (Recer, 1998), more than 320 million Web sites will be available on the Internet and accessible to the public by the year 2001.

The Internet, World Wide Web, and related resources (i.e., books, magazines, formal classes, and HELP sites on the Web) have the potential to assist professionals in growing professionally, engaging in research, developing instructional and clinical plans, implementing teaching and therapy activities, and supporting their home-related assignments. The sites and references listed in this book and appendix are only a few of the many thousands available, and it is important to realize that new sites are developed daily while "older" sites are removed from the Web regularly.

As a word of caution to professionals, Web sites and pages should be reviewed before use with and by school-aged exceptional individuals to ensure that information and materials provided and accessed by young people are appropriate. What follows is a listing of resources (e.g., books, magazines, and World Wide Web sites and pages) that professionals may want to use in addition to those presented in earlier chapters and appendixes to develop their understanding of the Internet and Web and their use of the "Super-Highway" for personal and instructional productivity purposes.

Books

Anderson, C., & Freeman, C. (1997). *The educators guide to the Internet: A handbook with resources and activities.* White Plains, NY: Longman/Addison-Wesley.

This book was written for professionals who want to use the Internet and are specifically looking for ways to use Telnet, Gopher, FTP, List servers, and the Web to improve the presentation of lessons. Topics include how to "surf" the Internet and how to find topics or subjects pertinent to the classroom.

Burgstahler, S. E. (1997). *Kids on the net: A tutorial for teachers, parents, and students.* Needham Heights, MA: Allyn & Bacon.

A hands-on book that guides readers through exercises that provide practice with the Internet tools used in educational settings. It covers topics including the Web, e-mail, downloading files, and searching the Net.

Cafolla, R., Kauffman, D., & Knee, R. H. (1997). *World Wide Web for teachers: An interactive guide.* Needham Heights, MA: Allyn & Bacon.

This is one of the few books that has been written exclusively about the relationship of the Web to education. It provides an overview to e-mail, the Web, the Netscape Browser, and a tutorial on accessing the Web for educational purposes.

Distefano, V. (Ed.). (1997). *Child safety on the Internet.* Englewood Cliffs, NJ: Prentice-Hall.

This book provides information to parents and professionals on how to teach children to use the Internet and Web sites appropriately. The book comes with a CD-ROM that provides a free copy of Netscape Navigator (a

Web browser) and directs the user to Hot Page links that provide up-to-date information on protecting children on-line.

Forsyth, I. (1996). *Teaching and learning materials on the Internet*. London: Kogan Page Limited.

This book presents information on managing and using the Internet and Web appropriately. The author also discusses ways that the Internet can change the roles of professionals and learners.

Gardner, P. (1997). *Internet for teachers and parents*. Needham Heights, MA: Teacher Created Materials.

This book is designed for professionals and parents and includes professional-tested methods for accessing and using material on the Internet. It also provides specifics for accessing and using appropriate Web sites and pages.

Hixon, S. (1998). *Beginner's handbook for developing Web pages for school and classroom*. Needham Heights, MA: Teacher Created Materials.

This book provides professionals with the information they need to develop Web pages and to assist their students/clients in developing Web pages.

Joseph, L. C., & Joseph, L. (1997). *World link: An Internet guide for educators, parents and students* (2nd ed.). Columbus, OH: Gryden Digital Press.

This book is a complete guide for professionals, parents, and students on how to use the Internet and World Wide Web via a single computer or a computer network.

Khan, B. (1997). *Web-based instruction*. Englewood Cliffs, NJ: Educational Technology.

The purpose of this book is to provide readers with information about the design, delivery, management, and evaluation of Web-based instruction. The book contains 59 chapters that are divided into five sections.

Leshin, C. (1996). *Internet adventures; Step-by-step guide for finding and using educational resources*. Needham Heights, MA: Allyn & Bacon.

This book is designed especially for professionals and includes everything the professional needs (i.e., student projects, guides to specific resources on the Internet, clear and nontechnical instructions for accessing the Internet and Web sites).

Offutt, E. R., & Offutt, C. (1996). *Internet without fear! Practical tips and activities for the elementary classroom*. Torrance, CA: Frank Schaffer Publications.

This book was written for general elementary classroom teachers but can also be used by special educators and other professionals. It gives practical ideas and tips to professionals so that they can access the Internet without panicking.

Porter, L. R. (1997). *Creating the virtual classroom: Distance learning with the Internet author*. New York: Wiley & Sons.

This book presents distance learning concepts for kindergarten through college settings and provides information on how to establish the different types of distance learn-

ing "vehicles," including Web sites, e-mail, and on-line conferencing.

Magazines

General Macintosh

MacWEEK
301 Howard Street
San Francisco, CA 94105
Voice: 415/243-3500
Web: http://zdnet.com.

MacWorld
P.O. Box 54529
Boulder, CO 80322
Voice: 303/665-8930
Web: http://www.macworld.zdnet.com
Note: MacUser is now a part of MacWorld.

General PC

Byte
29 Hartwell Avenue
Lexington, MA 02173
Voice: 800/323-BYTE
Web: http://www.byte.com

Computer Basics: PC Novice
120 West Harvest Drive
Lincoln, NE 68521
Voice: 800/733-3809
Web: http://www.smartcomputing.com

ComputerLife Magazine
60050 Townsend Street
San Franciso, CA 94103
Voice: 415/551-4500
Web: http://www.zdnet.com

FamilyPC
P.O. Box 55414
Boulder, CO 80328
Web: http://www.familypc.com

Laptop
P.O. Box 5020
Brentwood, TN 37024
Voice: 888/270-7652
Web: http://www.smartcomputing.com

PC Magazine
P.O. Box 54093
Boulder, CO 80322
Voice: 303/665-8930
Web: http://www.zdnet.com/pcmag

PC Novice: Guide to Netscape
120 West Harvest Drive
Lincoln, NE 68521
Voice: 800/733-3809
Web: http://www.smartcomputing.com

PC Novice: Guide to the Web
120 West Harvest Drive
Lincoln, NE 68521
Voice: 800/733-3809
Web: http://www.smartcomputing.com

PC Today
131 West Grand Drive
Lincoln, NE 68521
Voice: 800/544-1426
Web: http://www.pctoday.com

PC World
P.O. Box 55029
Boulder, CO 80322
Voice: 800/234-3498
Web: http://www.pcworld.com

Internet and Web

Broadwatch: Internet Service Providers
8500 Bowles Avenue
Littleton, CO 80123
Voice: 800/933-6038
Web: http://www.broadwatch.com

Internet Computing
P.O. Box 55485
Boulder, CO 80322
Voice: 800/825-4237

Web Guide Monthly
3400 Dundee Road Suite 245
Northbrook, IL 60062
Voice: 800/310-7047
Web: http://www.web-guide-mag.com

Web Techniques
P.O. Box 1246

Stokie, IL 60076
Voice: 800/677-2452
http://www.webtechniques.com

On-line

Internet Companion
http://www.obs-us.com/obs/english/books/ethnic

NC World Magazine
http://www.ncworldmag.com

YAHOO! Internet Life
http://www.zd.com

You can use a search directory (e.g., Yahoo) and a search engine (e.g., Alta Vista) and the search phrase "Computer (Magazine)" to identify and access other printed and on-line general computer and Internet/Web magazines

Web Sites or Pages

General

Computer Related Frequently Asked Questions
http://www.sparco.com/archive/cfaq.htm

Provides a list of frequently asked questions that can be a starting point for basic information about any subject. The site is connected to several hyperlinks that can help professionals find information about technology, the Internet, and the Web.

EFF's (Extended) Guide to the Internet
http://www.hep.net/documents/eegtti/eeg_toc.html

This is an extended guide to the Internet that takes you step by step through the process of connecting to the Internet and then finding your way around once you are on-line (i.e., logged on).

Internet Companion
http://www.obs-us.com/obs/english/books/ethnic

Internet Companion is a complete book published on the Internet in HTML format and can be used as a beginner's guide to global networking.

A Beginner's Guide to Effective E-Mail
http://www.webfoot.com/advice/email.top.html

This site provides the novice with valuable information on how to send and receive e-mail. It also explains how you can express yourself through gestures and intonations.

Students and Education

100 College and University Sites
http://www.101hot.com/college

This site lists 100 colleges with the number of hits per college ranked. Information at these sites may include admission requirements, faculty, financial assistance, and other topics about the colleges.

Kids ACE
http://www.ace.kids.com/bkround.html

This site is updated daily and includes Homework Helpers, K–12 Schools on the Web, and Kids on the Web.

Ask ERIC Virtual Library
http://ericir.syr.edu

This site is the national information center for ERIC. It is an excellent resource for professionals to identify and research topics of interest. This site includes a virtual library, lesson plans, and other resources.

Association for Experimental Education Home Page
http://www.princeton.edu/~rcurtis/aee.html

The Association for Experimental Education is a non-profit organization that provides information on the development, practice, and education of experimental learning.

Berit's Best Sites for Kids
http://db.cochran.com/db_HTML:theopage.db

This is a site compiled by Cochran Interactive as a guide to the best Web sites for children. This site is easy for children to use to find links to other sites with different activities, games, and sports.

B.J. Pinchbeck's Homework Helper
http://www.bjpinchbeck.com

This site has more than 200 hyperlinks to help children with homework. Titles found on the site include References, News and Current Events, Math, Science, History, and English.

Children's Pages at WombatNet
http://www.batnet.com/wombat/children.html

WombatNet provides sites for children that include information about animals, hobbies, and space. Other pages include High Schools, Museums, News, and publications.

Dr Internet
http://www.ipl.org/youth/Drintrnet

Dr. Internet is part of the University of Michigan's Internet Public Service, a News Library Project. It provides help with math and science homework.

George Lucas Education Foundation
http://glef.org

This site provides a newsletter featuring integration of technology with teaching and learning.

Home Schooling Zone
http://www.caro.net/~joespa

This zone provides information for families who want to teach their children through home schooling. It also provides links to other sites to provide educational resources to families.

Kids Safety on the Internet
http://www.uoknor.edu/oupd/kidssafe.htm

This site provides a text-based question-and-answer format that allows children and parents to sit together reading about the dangers of talking with strangers, approaching strange animals, and becoming lost (i.e., what a child should do).

Roget's Thesaurus of English Words and Phrases
http://www.thesaurus.com

This site provides information on how students can find the correct word. This site allows the student to click any letter and a list of indexed words will pop up.

Microsoft in K-12 Education
http://www.microsoft.com/education/K12

This site contains a vast collection of learning resources for professionals, parents, and students. Dozens of hyperlinks to different educational sites are also listed.

TestPrep.Cm
http://www.testprep.com

A Web-based Scholastic (SAT) preparation course for college-bound students. The course is free, but students must purchase *Scholastic Aptitude Test* (SAT) software, books, and materials.

Virtual School for the Gifted
http://www.vsg.edu.au

This is the home of the first school to operate on the Internet. The school is located in Australia and offers six pilot courses. Pertinent information (e.g., enrollment information and future courses) is regularly updated.

Homework Heaven
http://www.homeworkheaven.com

This is a well-organized Web site that has links to just about every subject of interest to elementary through college-level students.

Professionals and Education

The following sites offer information to support professionals in their development of teaching-learning lessons:

Encarta Online
http://encarta.msn.com/schoolhouse/

Encarta Online is a professional-friendly site providing professionals with lesson plans, professional materials, and worksheets. The site is updated monthly to provide new material for the professionals. Encarta also provides an archive of the monthly features so professionals can easily locate topics that fit into their current lesson plans.

The Busy Teacher's Web Site
http://www.ceismc.gatech.edu/BusyT/

This site makes it easy for the professional to find classroom activities, lesson plans, and resource materials in 19 different subject areas. Subject areas are catalogued and cross-referenced so there is need to backtrack to the home page, but the professional may use the provided quick links.

Connections+
http://www.mcrel.org./connect/plus

Internet Connections
http://www.mcrel.org/connect/

Both of these sites provide links to activities, lesson plans, and curriculum resources. The Internet connection has a database to other on-line services listed by state, activities, and general education.

Smithsonian Education
http://educate.si.edu/start.html

This site is designed especially for professionals, and its pages provide access to materials including all of Smithsonian's on-line exhibits. Lesson plans are developed for the professionals to help the professionals guide their students toward answering their own questions through exploring.

The following Web sites and pages are designed within specific curriculum areas and provide professionals with lesson plans as well as ideas to add to their own lesson plans:

The Art Teacher Connection
http://www.primet.com/~arted/
Th@anteroom
http://ecedWeb.arts.ufl.edu/art/rt_room/@rtroom_home.html

Economic Education EcEdweb Home
http://ecedWeb.unomaha.edu/

The History Channel
http://www.historychannel.com/

English and Library Lesson Plans
http://www3.sympatico.ca/ray.saitz/

PE Lesson Plans
http://www.geocities.com/Colosseum/333/2

Volcano Lesson Plans
http://www.volcano.und.nodak.edu/vwdocs/vwlessons/lesson.html

Social Studies Lesson Plans and Resources
http://www.csun.edu/~hcedu013

Web Sites and Related Links

The following sites provide various links to other sites or pages that can be used by professionals, students, and parents.

Web Site: http://www.hollywood-vine.com/educate.htm
   Links: CPSR Links for Educators
            Global Show-n-Tell
            Index to K–12 Resources from Yahoo's List
            InfoList for Teachers
            Instructional Technologies Resources
            K–12 Outpost
            Kids Safety on the Internet
            Teaching and Learning on the Web
            Clickable Map
            The Never-Ending Campus
            TENET Web
            Adventures in Education
            Educational Technology
            Computer Lab
            Library

Web Site: McGraw-Hill http://www.mhcollege.com/socialscience/education/websites.mhtml
   Links: INTERNET Resources for Educators
            Best Web Sites for K–12 Education
            Yahoo-Education

Web Site: http://www.aces.k12.ct.us/~crocker/ats/funding.html
   Links: Disability Resources
            Advocacy Tips
            Institute for Human Development
            Achieving Self-Support

A Final Word

Take a few minutes from your busy schedule in the coming week to catalogue some of the many printed and electronic Internet and World Wide Web resources available to you. These resources could have been listed in this book, given to you in other courses, or secured from your technology center. Also, expand your listing of resources by accessing information from the Internet and Web using a search directory (e.g., Yahoo) and search engine (e.g., HotBot) and the search phrases "Internet (Resources)" and then "World Wide Web (Resources)." Finally, collaborate with your peers to develop a listing of Internet and Web hardback books and magazines that can be found in your favorite Web bookstore, your school's bookstore and library, and the local education agency's technology resources.

References

Beaver, D. (1998). Education. *Your Guide to the Web, 2,* 46–49.

Cafolla, R., Kauffman, D., & Knee, R. H. (1997). *World-wide Internet for teachers: An interactive guide.* Needham Heights, MA: Allyn & Bacon.

Kobler, R. D. (Ed.). (1998). Computer Basics. *PC Novice—Learning Series, 3,* 71–76.

Kobler, R. D. (Ed.). (1998). Computers and the Internet. *PC Novice—Guide to the Web, 3,* 42–53.

Kobler, R. D. (Ed.). (1998). Education and children. *PC Novice—Guide to the Web, 3,* 70–83.

Kobler, R. D. (1998). Using Navigator. *PC Novice—Guide to NetScape, 4,* 30–53.

Recer, P. (1998, April 3). INTERNET spins a Web of 320 million pages. *The Sun Herald,* p. 1.

Appendix I

ঌ   ঌ   ঌ

Hardware and Software Resources

Compiled and Enhanced by David P. Fuller
Southeastern Louisiana University

Abbott Systems, Inc.
62 Mountain Road
Pleasantville, NY 10570
Voice: 800/552-9157
Fax: 914/747-9115
Web: http://www.abbottsys.com

AbleNet, Inc.
1081 Tenth Avenue SE
Minneapolis, MN 55414
Voice: 800/322-0956
Fax: 612/379-9143
Web: http://www.ablenetinc.com

Acer America Corporation
2641 Orchard Parkway
San Jose, CA 95134
Voice: 408/432-6200
Fax: 408/922-2933
http://www.acer.com

A.D.A.M. Software
1600 Riveredge Parkway, Suite 800
Atlanta, GA 30328
Voice: 770/980-0888
Fax: 770/955-3088
Web: http://www.adam.com

Adaptivation Incorporated
224 SE 16th Street, Suite 2
Ames, IA 50010
Voice: 800/723-2783 or 800/7-ADAPTED
Web: http://www.hometown.aol.com/adaptaac/
    index.htm

Adobe Systems, Inc.
345 Park Avenue
San Jose, CA 95110

Voice: 800/447-3577
Fax: 408/537-6000
Web: http://www.adobe.com

AI Squared
P.O. Box 669
Manchester Center, VT 05255
Voice: 802/362-3612
Fax: 802/362-1670
http://www.aisquared.com

Aldus Corp.
411 First Avenue South, Suite 200
Seattle, WA 98104-2871
Voice: 206/628-2372
Web: http://www.aldus.com

AlphaSmart by IPD, Inc.
20380 Town Center Lane, Suite 270
Cupertino, CA 95014
Voice: 405/252-9400
Web: http://www.alphasmart.com

America Online
8619 Westwood Center Drive
Vienna, VA 22180
Voice: 800/227-6364
Web: http://www.aol.com

American Foundation for the Blind
11 Penn Plaza, Suite 300
New York, NY 10011
Voice: 800/232-5463
Web: http://www.afb.org

American Phone Products, Inc.
5192 Bolsa Avenue #5
Huntington Beach, CA 92649

Apple Computer, Inc.
Apple Education Division MS 198-K12
2420 Ridgepoint Drive
Austin, TX 78754
Voice: 800/800-2775
Web: http://www.apple.com

Apple Computer, Inc.
1 Infinite Loop
Cupertino, CA 95014-2084
Voice: 408/996-1010
Web: http://www.education.apple.com

Arkenstone, Inc.
1390 Borregas Avenue
Sunnyvale, CA 94089
Voice: 800/444-4443
Fax: 650/603-8887
Web: http://www.arkenstone.org

ARS Nova
P.O. Box 637
Kirkland, WA 98083
Voice: 800/445-4866
Web: http://www.ars-nova.com

Articulate Systems, Inc.
600 West Cummings Park, Suite 4500
Woburn, MA 01801
Voice: 781/935-5656
Fax: 781/935-0490
Web: http://www.articulate.com

AST Research, Inc.
16225 Alton Parkway
Irvine, CA 92618
Voice: 949/727-4141
Web: http://www.ast.com

AT&T National Special Needs Center
2001 Route 46, Suite 310
Parsippany, NJ 07054
Voice: 800/233-1212
Web: http://www.att.com

Automated Voice Systems, Inc.
17059 El Cajon Avenue
Yorba Linda, CA 92686
Voice: 714/524-4488
Fax: 714/996-1127
Web: http://www.mastervoice.com

AverMedia
47923A Warm Springs Boulevard
Fremont, CA 94539
Voice: 800/863-2332
Web: http://web20.mindlink.net:80/aver

Berkeley Systems, Inc.
3095 Rose Street
Berkeley, CA 94709
Voice: 510/549-2300
Fax: 510/549-3978
Web: http://www.berksys.com

Biolink Computer Research and Development Ltd.
4770 Glenwood Avenue
North Vancouver, BC
V7R 4G8 Canada
Voice: 604/984-4099
Fax: 604/985-8493
Web: http://www.bctel.net/biolink

Brainstorm, distributed by Interplay
16815 Von Karman Avenue
Irvine, CA 92606
Voice: 714/553-6655
Web: http://www.interplay.com

Brøderbund Software, Inc.
500 Redwood Boulevard
Novato, CA 94948
Voice: 800/521-6263 or 415/382-4400
Fax: 415/382-4523
Web: http://www.broderbund.com

Bytes of Learning
150 Consumers Road, Suite 203
Willowdale, Ontario
M2J 1P9 Canada
Web: http://www.bytesoflearning.com

Caere Corporation
100 Cooper Court
Los Gatos, CA 95032
Voice: 408/395-7000
Fax: 408/354-2743
Web: http://www.caere.com

California State Library
Library Development Services
P.O. Box 942837
Sacramento, CA 94237-0001

Voice: 916/653-6822
Web: http://www.library.ca.gov

Casady and Greene
22734 Portola Drive
Salinas, CA 93908
Voice: 800/359-4920
Web: http://www.casadyg.com/C&G/Welcome.htm

Chancery Software Ltd.
4170 Still Creek Drive, Suite 450
Burnaby, BC
V5C 6C6 Canada
Voice: 800/999-9931
Fax: 604/294-2225
Web: http://www.chancery.com

Claris Corporation/File Maker, Inc.
5201 Patrick Henry Drive
Box 58168
Santa Clara, CA 95052
Voice: 408/987-7000
Web: http://www.claris.com

Classroom Connect
1866 Colonial Village Lane
P.O. Box 10488
Lancaster, PA 17605-0488
Voice: 888/CLASSROOM
Fax: 717/393-5752
Web: http//www.classroom.net

Closing the Gap
Box 68, 526 Main Street
Henderson, MN 56044
Voice: 507/248-3294
Fax: 507/248-3810
Web: http://www.closingthegap.com

Compaq
10251 North Freeway
Houston, TX 77037
Voice: 800/318-6919
Fax: 713/927-6798
Web: http://www.compaq.com

Connectix
2655 Campus Drive, Suite 100
San Mateo, CA 94403

Voice: 800/950-5880
Web: http://www.connectix.com

Corel
Corel Building
1600 Carling Avenue
Ottawa, Ontario
K1Z 8R7 Canada
Voice: 613/728-3733
Fax: 613/761-9176
Web: http://www.sellmorenow.com

CyberMax
133 North 5th Street
Allentown, PA 18102
Voice: 800/443-9868
Fax: 800/599-7576
Web: http://www.cybmax.com

Davidson & Associates
4100 West 190th Street
Torrance, CA 90504
Web: http://www.davd.com

Day Runner, Inc.
P.O. Box 57027
Irvine, CA 92619-7027
Voice: 800/232-9786
Web: http://www.dayrunner.com

Dell Computer Corporation
9505 Arboretum Boulevard
Austin, TX 78759
Voice: 800/426-5150
Fax: 800/727-8320
Web: http://www.dell.com

Diehl Graphsoft, Inc.
10270 Old Columbia Road
Columbia, MD 21046
Voice: 410/290-8050
Web: http://www.graphsoft.com

Digital
111 Powdermill Road
Maynard, MA 01754
Voice: 800/344-4825
Fax: 800/676-7517
Web: http://www.digital.com

Disney Interactive
500 South Buena Vista Street
Burbank, CA 91521
Voice: 800/965-5360
Fax: 518/745-0990
Web: http://www.disney.go.com/
disneyinteractive/index.html

DK Multimedia
95 Madison Avenue
New York, NY 10016
Voice: 212/213-4800
Web: http://www.dk.com

Don Johnston, Inc.
1000 North Rand Road, Building 115
P.O. Box 639
Wauconda, IL 60084-0639
Voice: 800/999-4660
Fax: 847/526-4177
Web: http://www.donjohnston.com

Dragon Systems
320 Nevada Street
Newton, MA 02160
Voice: 617/965-5200
Fax: 617/965-2374
Web: http://www.dragonsystems.com

Dunamis, Inc.
3620 Highway 317
Suwanee, GA 30174
Voice: 800/828-2443

Duxbury Systems, Inc.
435 King Street
P.O. Box 1504
Littleton, MA 01460
Voice: 978/692-3000
Fax: 978/692-7912
Web: http://www.duxburysystems.com

DynaVox Systems Technology, Inc.
2100 Wharton Street
Pittsburgh, PA 15203
Voice: 800/344-1778
Web: http://www.dynavoxsys.com

Echo Speech Corporation/Softseek
6460 Via Real
Carpinteria, CA 93013
Voice: 212/271-2542
Web: http://www.softseek.com

Edmark Corporation
P.O. Box 3218
Redmond, WA 98073-3218
Voice: 800/426-0856 or 206/861-8200
Fax: 206/861-8998
Web: http://www.edmark.com

Educational Resources
1550 Executive Drive
P.O. Box 1900
Elgin, IL 60121-1900
Voice: 800/624-2926
Fax: 847/888-8499 or 847/888-8689
Web: http://www.edresources.com

Elecede Technology
Fax: 408/441-6060
Web: http://www.e4.com

Emerging Technology Consultants, Inc.
2819 Hamline Avenue North
St. Paul, MN 55113
Voice: 800/395-3973
Fax: 651/639-0110
Web: http://www.emergingtechnology.com

Encyclopaedia Britannica, Inc.
310 South Michigan Avenue
Chicago, IL 60604
Voice: 800/621-3900 (USA), 800/465-9439
(Canada)
Web: http://www.eb.com

Epson America, Inc
20770 Madrona Avenue
Torrance, CA 90503
Voice: 310/782-0770
Fax: 310/782-5220
Web: http://epson.com

Fijitsu PC Corporation
598 Gibraltar Drive
Milpitas, CA 95035
Voice: 408/935-8800
Fax: 408/935-1501
Web: http://www.fujitsu-pc.com

File Maker, Inc.
5201 Patrick Henry Drive
Santa Clara, CA 95052
Voice: 800/325-2747
Web: http://www.claris.com

Fractal Design Corporation
P.O. Box 6959
Scotts Valley, CA 95067
Voice: 800/325-1270
Web: http://www.fractal.com

Franklin Learning Resources
One Franklin Plaza
Burlington, NJ 08016-4907
Voice: 800/266-5626
Web: http://www.franklin.com

Gateway 2000
610 Gateway Drive
North Sioux City, SD 57049
Voice: 800/846-2000 or 605/232-2000
Fax: 605/232-2023
Web: http://www.gateway.com

Grolier Interactive
90 Sherman Turnpike
Danbury, CT 06816
Voice: 800/285-4534
Web: http://www.grolier.com

Hartley
3451 Dunckel Road, Suite 200
Lansing, MI 48911
Voice: 800/247-1380

Hartley Courseware
9920 Pacific Heights, Suite 500
San Diego, CA 92121-4330
Voice: 800/247-1380

Harvard Associates
10 Holworthy Street
Cambridge, MA 02138
Voice: 617/492-0660
Web: http://www.harvassoc.com

Hewlett-Packard Company
3000 Hanover Street
Palo Alto, CA 94304
Voice: 800/322-4772
Web: http://www.hp.com

Hitachi PC Corporation
1565 Barber Lane
Milpitas, CA 95035
Voice: 408/546-8000
Web: http://www.hitachipc.com

Houghton Mifflin Interactive
120 Beacon Street
Somerville, MA 02143
Voice: 617/351-3333
Web: http://www.hminet.com

Hughes Electronics Corporation
P.O. Box 956
El Segundo, CA 90245
Voice: 310/364-6000
Web: http://www.hughes.com

IBM
1133 Westchester Avenue
White Plains, NY 10604
Voice: 800/IBM-CALL
Fax: 707/863-3030
Web: http://www.software.ibm.com

IBM Special Needs System
11400 Burnet Road
Austin, TX 78758
Voice: 800/426-4832
Web: http://www.ibm.com

IBM/Lotus Notes
Lotus Development Corp.
55 Cambridge Parkway
Cambridge, MA 02142
Voice: 617/577-8500
Web: http://www.lotus.com/programs/worktheweb.nsf

IBM Interactive Media
3200 Windy Hill Road, WF-02
Atlanta, GA 30339
Voice: 770/835-7750
Web: http://www.solutions.ibm.com/multimedia/
     media-home.html

IDG Books Worldwide, Inc.
2103 East Southlake Boulevard
Southlake, TX 76092
Voice: 800/434-2086
Web: http://www.idg.com

Impulse Development Company
3491-11 Thomasville Road, Suite 202
Tallahassee, FL 32308
Voice: 904/668-9865
Fax: 904/668-9866

Information Access Company
362 Lakeside Drive

Foster City, CA 94404
Voice: 800/227-8431
Web: http://www.iacnet.com

Ingeborg Huber Verlag
Postfach 46
87643 Schwangau
Voice: +49 (0) 8362 987073
Fax: +49 (0) 8362 987073
Web: http://aquad.com

Innocomp
26210 Emery Road, Suite 302
Warrensville Heights, OH 44128
Voice: 800/382-8622
Fax: 216/464-3638
Web: http://www.sayitall.com

Inspiration Software, Inc.
7412 SW Beaverton Hillsdale Highway, Suite 102
Portland, OR 97225-2167
Voice: 800/877-4292
Web: http://www.inspiration.com

IntelliTools, Inc.
55 Leveroni Court, Suite 9
Novato, CA 94949
Voice: 800/899-6687 (USA or Canada) or
    415/382-5959 (Worldwide)
Fax: 415/382-5950
Web: http://www.intellitools.com

Intuit, Inc.
63330 Nancy Ridge Drive, Suite 103
San Diego, CA 93121-3290
Voice: 800/446-8848
Web: http://www.intuit.com

Iomega Corporation
1821 West Iomega Way
Roy, UT 84067
Voice: 800/456-5522
Web: http://www.iomega.com

Jay Klein Productions
2930 Austin Bluffs Parkway, Suite 104
Colorado Springs, CO 80918
Voice: 719/599-8786
Fax: 719/599-8312
Web: http://www.gradebusters.com

JetForm Corp.
7600 Leesburg Pike

East Building, Suite 430
Falls Church, VA 22043
Voice: 800/224-4104
Web: http://www.jetform.com

Kay Elemetrics Corp.
2 Bridgewater Lane
Lincoln Park, NJ 07035-1488
Voice: 800/289-5297 (USA or Canada) or
    201/628-6200
Fax: 201/628-6363
Web: http://www.kayelemetrics.com

Kids Network
P.O. Box 98018
Washington, DC 20090-8018
Voice: 800/368-2728
Web: http://www.nationalgeographic.com

**Knowledge Adventure, distributed by CUC
    Software**
19840 Pioneer Avenue
Torrance, CA 90503
Voice: 310/793-0600
Web: http://www.adventure.com

Kurzweil Computer Products
52 Third Avenue
Burlington, MA 01803
Voice: 781/203-5000
Fax: 781/283-0986
Web: http://www.kurzweil.com

Language Analysis Lab
Waisman Center
1500 Highland Avenue
University of Wisconsin-Madison
Madison, WI 53705
Voice: 608/262-6966
Fax: 608/262-8848
Web: http://www.trace.wisc.edu

Laser Learning Technologies, Inc.
120 Lakeside Avenue, Suite 240
Seattle, WA 98122-6522
Voice: 800/722-3505

Laureate Learning Systems, Inc.
220 East Spring Street
Winooski, VT 05404
Voice: 800/562-6801
Fax: 802/655-4757
Web: http://www.laureatelearning.com

Lawrence Erlbaum Associates
10 Industrial Avenue
Mahwah, NJ 07430-2262
Voice: 800/9-BOOKS-9
Web: http://www.erlbaum.com

Lawrence Productions, Inc.
1800 South 35th Street
Galesburg, MI 49053
Voice: 616/665-7075
Fax: 616/665-7060
Web: http://st4.yahoo.com/lawrencesoftware.
  info.html

LCSI
P.O. Box 162
Highgate Springs, VT 05460
Voice: 800/321-5646
Web: http://www.lcsi.com

Learning Company
One Athenaeum Street
Cambridge, MA 02142
Voice: 617/494-1200
Fax: 617/494-1219
Web: http://www.learningco.com

Learning Technology Center
Peabody College
Vanderbilt University
Nashville, TN 37203
Voice: 615/322-8070

Little Planet Publishing
5045 Hillsboro Road
Nashville, TN 37215
Voice: 800/974-2248
Fax: 615/385-9496
Web: http://www.littleplanet.com

Lotus Development Corp.
55 Cambridge Parkway
Cambridge, MA 02142
Voice: 617/577-8500
Web: http://www.lotus.com

Macromedia
600 Townsend Street
San Francisco, CA 94103
Voice: 800/470-7211
Fax: 415/626-0554
Web: http://www.macromedia.com

Mastervoice (see Automated Voice Systems, Inc.)
10523 Humbolt Street
Los Alamitos, CA 70720
Voice: 800/735-MASTER

Mathsoft
101 Main Street
Cambridge, MA 02142
Voice: 800/628-4223
Web: http:///mathsoft.com

Mayer-Johnson Company
P.O. Box 1579
Solana Beach, CA 92075-1579
Voice: 619/550-0084
Fax: 619/550-0449
Web: http://www.mayer-johnson.com

MECC/The Learning Company
6160 Summit Drive North
Minneapolis, MN 55430-4003
Voice: 800/852-2255
Web: http://www.learningcompany.com

Meta Creations Corporation
P.O. Box 66959
Scotts Valley, CA 95067
Voice: 800/459-5188
Web: http://www.metatools.com

Micron Electronics
900 E. Karcher Road
Nampa, ID 83687
Voice: 800/347-3490 or 208/893-3434
Fax: 208/893-3424
Web: http://www.micron.com

Microsoft Corporation
One Microsoft Way
Redmond, WA 98052-6399
Voice: 800/426-9400 or 425/882-8080
Web: http://www.microsoft.com

Mindscape, Inc.
60 Leveroni Court
Novato, CA 94949
Voice: 415/883-9400
Web: http://www.mindscape.com

Mustek Systems, Inc.
No. 25 R&D Road II
Science-Based Industrial Park

Hsin-Chu
Taiwan, R.O.C.
Voice: 886-3-577-9373
Fax: 886-3-578-4139
Web: http://www.mustek.com

National Geographic Society
1145 17th Street NW
Washington, DC 20036
Voice: 202/857-7000
Web: http://www.nationalgeographic.com

National Technical Institute for the Deaf
Rochester Institute of Technology
52 Lomb Memorial Drive
Rochester, NY 14623
Voice: 716/475-6700 (also TTY)
Fax: 716/475-2696
Web: http://www.rit.edu/~418www

NEC Computer Systems
1 Packard Bell Way
Sacramento, CA 95828
Voice: 888/632-8701
Web: http://www.necnow.com

Netscape Communications Corp.
501 East Middlefield Road
Mountain View, CA 94043
Voice: 415/937-2555
Fax: 650/528-4124
Web: http://www.netscape.com

newAbilities System, Inc.
4070 San Antonio Road, Suite G
Palo Alto, CA 94306
Voice: 800/829-8889

Newsbank
58 Pine Street
New Canaan, CT 06840
Voice: 203/966-1100
Fax: 203/966-6254
Web: http://www.newsbank.com

Nordic Software, Inc.
P.O. Box 6007
Lincoln, NE 68506-0007
Web: http://www.nordicsoftware.com

Novell
Voice: 408/434-2300
Web: http://www.novell.com

NTS Computer Systems, Ltd.
11720 Stewart Crescent, Unit 10
Maple Ridge, British Columbia
V2X 9E7 Canada
Voice: 800/663-7173
Web: http://www.nts.dreamwriter.com

Opcode Systems, Inc.
3950 Fabian Way, Suite 100
Palo Alto, CA 94303
Voice: 415/856-3333
Web: http://www.opcode.com

Optical Data School Media
512 Means Street NW, Suite 100
Atlanta, GA 30318
Voice: 800/524-2481
Fax: 404/221-4520
Web: http://www.opticaldata.com

Optimum Resources, Inc.
5 Hiltech Lane
Hilton Head, SC 29926
Voice: 800/327-1473

Oracle Corporation
500 Oracle Parkway
Redmond Shores, CA 94065
Voice: 800/672-3531
Web: http://www.oracle.com

Orange Cherry
P.O. Box 505
Round Ridge, NY 10576
Voice: 914/764-4104
Fax: 914/764-0104
Web: http://byronpreiss.com

Packard Bell NEC, Inc.
One Packard Bell Way
Sacramento, CA 95828
Web: http://www.packardbell.com

Panasonic
2 Panasonic Way
Secaucus, NJ 07094
Voice: 800/742-8086
Web: http://www.panasonic.com

PEAL Software
P.O. Box 8188
Calabasas, CA 91372

Pelican, a division of Queue, Inc.
338 Commerce Drive
Fairfield, CT 06430
Voice: 800/232-2224

Perfect Solutions Software, Inc.
15950 Schweizer Court
West Palm Beach, FL 33414-7128
Voice: 800/726-7086
Web: http://www.perfectsolutions.com

Pierian Springs Software
5200 Southwest Macadam Avenue, Suite 570
Portland, OR 97201
Voice: 800/304-9236
Web: http://www.pierian.com

Playskool, Inc.
2050 North Stemmons Freeway
Dallas, TX 75258
Voice: 214/745-1620

Poor Richard's Publishing, Inc./LD Resources
P.O. Box 1075
Litchfield, CT 06759
Voice: 800/567-4307
Web: http://www.ldresources.com

Prentice-Hall, Inc. (Simon & Schuster Education Group)
P.O. Box 2649
Columbus, OH 43216
Voice: 800/848-9500
Web: http:///www.prenhall.com

Prentke Romich Company
1022 Heyl Road
Wooster, OH 44691
Voice: 800/262-1984
Web: http://www.prentrom.com

PRO-ED, Inc.
8700 Shoal Creek Boulevard
Austin, TX 78757-6897
Voice: 800/897-3202
Fax: 512/451-8542
Web: http://www.proedinc.com

ProGen Technology
15501 Red Hill Avenue
Tustin, CA 92680
Voice: 800/848-8777

Fax: 714/566-9267
Web: http://www.progen.com

Psion, Inc.
150 Baker Avenue
Concord, MA 01742
Voice: 800/99-PSION
Web: http://www.psioninc.com

Psychological Corporation
Harcourt Brace and Co.
555 Academic Court
San Antonio, TX 78204-2498
Voice: 800/228-0752
Fax: 800/232-1223
Web: http://www.harcourtbrace.com

QualComm, Inc.
6455 Lusk Boulevard
San Diego, CA 95610
Voice: 619/587-1121
Web: http://www.qualcomm.com

Quantex Microsystems
400B Pierce Street
Somerset, NJ 08873
Voice: 800/836-0566
Fax: 732/563-0407
Web: http://www.quantex.com

Quark, Inc.
1800 Grant Street
Denver, CO 80203
Voice: 800/476-4575
Web: http://www.quark.com

Que
201 West 103rd Street
Indianapolis, IN 46290
Web: http://www.mcp.com

Research Ware, Inc.
P.O. Box 1258
Randolph, MA 02368
Voice: 781/961-3909
Web: http://www.researchware.com

Roger Wagner Publishing
1050 Pioneer Way, Suite P
El Cajon, CA 92020
Voice: 800/524-2481 or 619/442-0522
Fax: 619/442-0525
Web: http://www.hyperstudio.com

SALT (Systematic Analysis of Language Transcription)
Jon F. Miller and Robin S. Chapman
Language Analysis Lab
Waisman Center
1500 Highland Avenue
University of Wisconsin–Madison
Madison, WI 53705

Sanctuary Woods Multimedia Corporation
1825 Grant Street, Suite 410
San Mateo, CA 94402
Voice: 415/286-6100

Scholastic, Inc.
555 Broadway
New York, NY 10012
Voice: 800/724-6527
Web: http://scholastic.com

Scientific Learning
1995 University Avenue, Suite 400
Berkeley, CA 94704-1074
Voice: 888/665-9707
Fax: 510/665-1717
Web: http://www.fastforward.com

Scolari, Sage Publications, Inc.
2455 Teller Road
Thousand Oaks, CA 91320
Voice: 805/499-0721
Web: http://sagepub.com

Sharp Electronics Corporation
Sharp Plaza
Mahwah, NJ 07430
Voice: 201/529-8200
Web: http://www.sharp-usa.com

Sierra On-Line, Inc.
3380 146th Place SE
Bellevue, WA 98007
Voice: 800/757-7707
Web: http://www.sierra.com

Simon and Schuster Interactive
1230 Avenue of the Americas
New York, NY 10020
Voice: 800/910-0099

SIRS, Inc.
P.O. Box 2348
Boca Raton, FL 33427-2348
Voice: 800/232-7477
Fax: 561/994-4704
Web: http://www.sirs.com

Skills Bank, Inc.
Parkview Center 1
7104 Ambassador Road
Baltimore, MD 21244
Voice: 800/222-3681
Web: http://www.skillsbank.com

Slipstream Software Systems, Inc.
122–15 Innovation Boulevard
Saskatoon, SK
S7N 2X8 Canada
Voice: 306/931-9732
E-mail: slipstream.soft@innovplace.saskatoon.sk.ca

SoftKey
6160 Summit Drive North
Minneapolis, MN 55430-4003
Voice: 800/685-6322
Web: http://www.softkey.com

Sony Corporation of America
3200 Zanker Road
San Jose, CA 95134
Voice: 888/970-7669
Web: http://www.sony.com

Speech Systems for the Blind
76 Wheaton Drive
Attleboro, MA 02703

Spinnaker/Software Solution
201 Washington Road
Rye, NH 03870
Voice: 800/484-7075
Web: http://www.spinnaker.org

Sun Microcomputers, Inc.
901 San Antonio Road
Palo Alto, CA 94303
Voice: 800/786-0404 or 415/960-1300
Fax: 415/969-9131
Web: http://www.sun.com

Sunburst Communications
101 Castleton Street
P.O. Box 40
Pleasantville, NY 10570-9807
Voice: 800/321-7511
Web: http://www.nysunburst.com

Symantec Corp
10201 Torre Avenue
Cupertino, CA 95014
Voice: 800/441-7234
Web: http://www.symantec.com

Syntha-Voice Computers Inc.
800 Queenston Road
Suite 304
Stoney Creek, Ontario
I8G 1A7 Canada

Systems Impact, Inc.
9302 Lee Highway, 12th Floor
Fairfax, VA 22031
Voice: 703/277-3147
Fax: 703/273-6098
Web: http://www.systemsimpact.com

Teacher Support Software, Inc.
3542 NW 97th Boulevard
Gainesville, FL 32606
Voice: 800/228-2871
Web: http://www.tssoftware.com

Technical Aids and Systems for the Handicapped, Inc.
Unit 1
91 Station Street
Ajax, Ontario
L1S 3H2 Canada

Telesensory Corporation
520 Almanor Avenue
Sunnyvale, CA 94086
Voice: 800/804-8004
Fax: 408/616-8720
Web: http://www.telesensory.com

Thinking Publications
424 Galloway Street
P.O. Box 163

Eau Claire, WI 54702-0163
Voice: 800/225-GROW
Fax: 800/828-8885
E-mail: ThinkPub@aol.com

3Com/US Robotics
7770 North Fronage Road
Skokia, IL 60077
Voice: 800/525-8771 or 408/326-5000
Fax: 847/262-0327
Web: http://www.3com.com

Thynx
619 Alexander Road
Princeton, NJ 08540
Voice: 609/514-1600
Web: http://www.thynx.com

Tom Snyder Productions
80 Coolidge Hill Road
Watertown, MA 02172-2817
Voice: 800/342-0236
Fax: 617/926-6222
Web: http://www.teachtsp.com

Toshiba America, Inc.
1251 Sixth Avenue, Suite 4100
New York, NY 10020
Voice: 212/596-0600
Web: http://www.toshiba.com

Trace Research and Development Center
University of Wisconsin–Madison
5901 Research Park Boulevard
Madison, WI 53719-1252
Voice: 608/262-6966
Fax: 608/262-8848
Web: http://www.trace.wisc.edu

Universal CD-ROM
520 Lawrence Expressway #307
Sunnyvale, CA 94086
Voice: 408/992-0543
Web: http://www.bigmall.com/subucr.html

Universal Learning Technology
39 Cross Street
Peabody, MA 01960

Voice: 888/858-9994
Web: http://www.universalearn.com

Visioneer
34800 Campus Drive
Fremont, CA 94555
Voice: 800/787-7007
Web: http://www.visioneer.com

Visualtek
1610 26th Street
Santa Monica, CA 90404

WACOM Technology Corporation
501 S.E. Columbia Shores Boulevard, Suite 300
Vancouver, WA 98661
Voice: 800/922-9348
Web: http://www.wacom.com

**Wayne County Regional Educational Services
    Agency (RESA)**
A.D.A.M. LAB Project
33500 Van Born Road
Wayne, MI 48184
Voice: 734/334-1610
Fax: 734/334-1432
Web: http://www.wcresa.k12.MI.US/adlab/index.htm

Word+, Inc.
40015 Sierra Highway, Building B-145
Palmdale, CA 93550

Voice: 805/266-8500
Fax: 805/266-8969
Web: http://www.words-plus.com

World Book Multimedia
525 West Monroe, 20th Floor
Chicago, IL 60661
Voice: 800/975-3250
Web: http://www.worldbook.com

Xerox Corporation
800 Long Ridge Road
P.O. Box 1600
Stamford, CT 06904
Voice: 800/334-6200
Web: http://www.xerox.com

Xerox Imaging Systems, Inc.
9 Centennial Drive
Peabody, MA 01960
Web: http://www.xerox.com

ZYGO Industries, Inc.
P.O. Box 1008
Portland, OR 97207-1008
Voice: 800/234-6006
Web: http://www.zygo.com

Author Index

Subject Index

❧   ❧   ❧